Springer Series on Rehabilitation

Myron G. Eisenberg, PhD, Series Editor
Veterans Affairs Medical Center, Hampton, VA
Thomas E. Backer, PhD, Consulting Editor
Human Interaction Research Institute, Los Angeles, CA

Fong Chan, PhD, is a professor in the Department of Rehabilitation Psychology and Special Education, University of Wisconsin-Madison. Dr. Chan is a licensed psychologist and a certified rehabilitation counselor. He is also a fellow in the American Psychological Association and a National Institute on Disability and Rehabilitation Research distinguished research fellow. He has published more than 100 refereed journal articles and book chapters. He is also the editor of a textbook, *Healthcare and Disability Case Management.* His awards include two Research Awards from the American Rehabilitation Counseling Association; a Research Award from the American Counseling Association; a James Garrett New Career Research Achievement Award from the American Psychological Association, Division of Rehabilitation Psychology; a James Garrett Distinguished Career in Rehabilitation Research Award from the American Rehabilitation Counseling Association; and an Educator of the Year Award from the National Council on Rehabilitation Education.

Norman L. Berven, PhD, is a professor and chair of the Rehabilitation Psychology Program, Department of Rehabilitation Psychology and Special Education, University of Wisconsin-Madison. He is licensed as a psychologist and as a professional counselor by the State of Wisconsin and also holds the certified rehabilitation counselor credential. He is a fellow in the American Psychological Association and is a member of several professional associations in counseling, rehabilitation counseling, assessment, and counselor education. Berven has published more than 65 papers in professional journals and textbooks on topics related to rehabilitation counseling, assessment, and counselor education and training. He has received the James Garrett Award for a Distinguished Career in Rehabilitation Research from the American Rehabilitation Counseling Association (ARCA), the ARCA Distinguished Professional Award, seven ARCA Research Awards, and the American Counseling Association (ACA) Research Award.

Kenneth R. Thomas, DEd, is currently Professor Emeritus at the University of Wisconsin-Madison. Thomas worked as a rehabilitation counselor for the Pennsylvania Bureau of Vocational Rehabilitation at the Pennsylvania Rehabilitation Center in Johnstown. Following a one-year academic appointment in the counselor education program at Penn State, he joined the faculty at the University of Wisconsin-Madison. At Wisconsin he held several administration positions, including chair of the Department of Rehabilitation Psychology and Special Education and director of the Educational and Psychological Training Center. Thomas has published two books and more than 100 refereed journal articles and book chapters in the areas of counseling, rehabilitation, and disability. He is a past-president of the American Rehabilitation Counseling Association, a fellow in three divisions of the American Psychological Association, and a recipient of the James Garrett Award for a Distinguished Career in Rehabilitation Research.

Counseling Theories
and Techniques for
Rehabilitation Health Professionals

Fong Chan, PhD
Norman L. Berven, PhD
Kenneth R. Thomas, DEd
Editors

 Springer Publishing Company

Springer Publishing Company, Inc.
536 Broadway
New York, NY 10012-3955

Acquisitions Editor: Sheri W. Sussman
Production Editor: Sally Ahearn
Cover design by Joanne Honigman

04 05 06 07 08 / 5 4 3 2 1

Library of Congress Cataloging-in-Publication Data

Counseling theories and techniques for rehabilitation health professionals /
    Fong Chan, Norman L. Berven, Kenneth R. Thomas, editors.
      p. cm.
    Includes bibliographical references and index.
    ISBN 0-8261-2384-8
    1. People with disabilities—Rehabilitation. 2. Rehabilitation counseling.
    I. Chan, Fong. II. Berven, Norman L. III. Thomas, Kenneth R.
  HV1568.C65 2004
  362.17'86—dc22   2003067304

Printed in the United States of America by Integrated Book Technology.

Contents

v

Section IV: Special Considerations

Section V: Professional Issues

Contributors

Richard Beck is a professor, Rehabilitation Institute, Southern Illinois University at Carbondale.

Malachy L. Bishop is an assistant professor, Department of Special Education and Rehabilitation Counseling, University of Kentucky.

Brian Bolton is a university professor emeritus, Department of Rehabilitation Education and Research, University of Arkansas at Fayetteville.

Marie Ciavarella is a psychologist, University of Chicago Center for Psychiatric Rehabilitation, Chicago, Illinois.

Daniel W. Cook is a professor, Department of Human Resources, and Communication Disorders, University of Arkansas at Fayetteville.

Patrick W. Corrigan is a professor, Department of Psychiatry and Executive Director, Center for Psychiatric Rehabilitation, University of Chicago.

Charles Degeneffe is an assistant professor, Rehabilitation Counseling Program, California State University-Fresno.

David DeVinney is a psychologist, Wisconsin Department of Corrections.

William I. Gardner is a professor emeritus, Department of Rehabilitation Psychology and Special Education, University of Wisconsin-Madison.

Gregory Garske is a professor, Division of Intervention Services, Bowling Green State University.

James T. Herbert is a professor, Department of Counselor Education, Counseling Psychology, and Rehabilitation Services, Pennsylvania State University.

John Hilburger is an assistant professor, Rehabilitation Psychology Programs, Institute of Psychology, Illinois Institute of Technology.

Jerome Holzbauer is a lecturer in the Rehabilitation Counseling Program, Department of Educational Psychology, University of Wisconsin-Milwaukee and in Special Education, Cardinal Stritch University.

Ruth Huebner is a professor, Department of Occupational Therapy, Eastern Kentucky University.

Brian Kamnetz is an assistant professor, Rehabilitation Counseling Program, New Mexico Highlands University.

Steven P. Kaplan is a rehabilitation psychologist in private practice in Appleton, Wisconsin, and a graduate lecturer at Lakeland College in Green Bay, Wisconsin.

Lynn C. Koch is an associate professor and coordinator, Rehabilitation Counseling Program, Department of Educational Foundations and Special Services, Kent State University.

John F. Kosciulek is an associate professor and coordinator, MA program in rehabilitation counseling, Office of Rehabilitation and Disability Studies, Michigan State University.

Chow S. Lam is a professor and director, Rehabilitation Psychology Programs, Institute of Psychology, Illinois Institute of Technology.

Hanoch Livneh is a professor and coordinator, Rehabilitation Counseling Program, Portland State University.

Connie McReynolds is an assistant professor, Rehabilitation Counseling Program, Department of Educational Foundations and Special Services, Kent State University

Nathalie Mizelle is an assistant professor, Rehabilitation Counseling Program, Department of Counseling, San Francisco State University.

Elias Mpofu is an associate professor and coordinator, Rehabilitation Counseling Program, Department of Counselor Education, Counseling Psychology, and Rehabilitation Services, Pennsylvania State University.

Kimberly M. L. Nania is a director, Bureau of Health Services Professions, State of Wisconsin Department of Regulation and Licensing.

Joseph N. Ososkie is a professor, Rehabilitation Counseling Program, Department of Human Services, University of Northern Colorado.

David B. Peterson is an associate professor, Rehabilitation Psychology Programs, Institute of Psychology, Illinois Institute of Technology.

Warren Rule is an emeritus professor, Department of Rehabilitation Counseling, Medical College of Virginia/Virginia Commonwealth University.

Phillip D. Rumrill is a professor, Rehabilitation Counseling Program, Department of Educational Foundations and Special Services, Kent State University.

John See is a professor emeritus, Department of Rehabilitation and Counseling, University of Wisconsin-Stout.

Linda R. Shaw is an associate professor and graduate coordinator, Department of Rehabilitation Counseling, University of Florida.

Jerome Siller is a professor emeritus, Department of Psychology, New York University.

Anne Helene Skinstead is an assistant professor, Department of Community and Behavioral Health, University of Iowa.

Jennifer L. Stoll is a clinical neuropsychologist, Mercy Health System, Jamesville, Wisconsin.

Elizabeth A. Swett is an assistant professor, Department of Rehabilitation Counseling, University of Florida.

Edna Mora Szymanski is dean, College of Education, University of Maryland at College Park.

Timothy Tansey is an assistant professor, Department of Special Education and Rehabilitation, Utah State University.

Ruth Torkelson Lynch is a professor, Department of Rehabilitation Psychology and Special Education, University of Wisconsin-Madison.

Robert W. Trobliger is a doctoral student in counseling psychology, Department of Applied Psychology, New York University.

Molly Tschopp is an assistant professor, Rehabilitation Counseling Program, Department of Counseling Psychology and Guidance Services, Ball State University.

Joseph Turpin is a professor and coordinator, Rehabilitation Counseling Program, California State University-San Bernardino.

Elizabeth Watson is a doctoral candidate, Department of Rehabilitation Psychology and Special Education, University of Wisconsin-Madison.

Stephen G. Weinrach is a professor, Department of Counselor Education, Villanova University.

Penny Willmering is an assistant professor, Rehabilitation Science Program, Arkansas Tech University.

Preface

The purpose of this book is to provide a state-of-the-art treatment of the dominant theories and techniques of counseling and psychotherapy from a rehabilitation perspective. In all cases, the chapters were contributed by rehabilitation professionals who have special, if not extraordinary, expertise and national visibility in the content areas addressed. The book is intended to be useful for practitioners, as well as for upper-level undergraduates and graduate students in rehabilitation counseling and psychology, and in other rehabilitation health care disciplines, such as nursing, occupational therapy, physical therapy, speech and language therapy, recreation, and social work. The chapters are written from a rehabilitation perspective, using rehabilitation examples when appropriate. Authors were asked to include a case example in each chapter to highlight the application of theories and techniques in working with rehabilitation-specific problems with people with disabilities.

It is not our philosophy that people with disabilities necessarily require different theories or interventions than nondisabled people. In fact, the opposite is true. People with disabilities or the agencies serving them may, however, present special needs or have special goals that require certain emphases and modifications in the application of particular theories and techniques. Although general textbooks on the theories and techniques of counseling and psychotherapy provide excellent discussions of those approaches, we feel they need to be supplemented with material that is specific to applications in rehabilitation settings. This book attempts to fulfill this need.

We are pleased to be part of this particular project for several reasons. First, it gave us an opportunity to work with rehabilitation professionals from around the United States who are clearly among the most esteemed leaders and academic scholars in our field. Many of these authors were once graduate students at the University of Wisconsin-Madison, and others have been professional associates of ours for many years. Some have worked with us in the past on scholarly projects, and we have known others through our work with professional associations. Still others we knew only initially through reputation, but we are now extremely pleased to have had an opportunity to work with them on this project.

Another reason for our pleasure in undertaking this project is our love of counseling. To us, counseling is the core of the rehabilitation process, and it is in all its various aspects the reason why most students and professionals are attracted to the field. The provision of vocational and psychosocial counseling is the unique contribution that rehabilitation professionals, generally, make to any multidisciplinary (or even interdisciplinary) effort to improve the lives of people with disabilities. We sincerely hope that the offerings in this book will not only excite and inform the reader about the counseling function and process, but ultimately will also benefit the thousands of clients with whom the readers will eventually have contact.

FC
NLB
KRT
Madison, Wisconsin

Introduction

Chapter 1

An Introduction to Counseling for Rehabilitation Health Professionals

Norman L. Berven, Kenneth R. Thomas, and Fong Chan

A s stated in the preface, the purpose of this book is to provide a state-of-the-art treatment of the dominant theories and techniques of counseling and psychotherapy from a rehabilitation perspective. This initial chapter presents several introductory topics, including definitions and terminology, the importance of counseling in professional practice, a historical context for understanding theories of counseling and psychotherapy, and the efficacy of counseling and psychotherapy. In addition, a brief overview of the remainder of the book is provided.

DEFINITIONS AND TERMINOLOGY

Counseling and Psychotherapy

Counseling and *psychotherapy* are commonly used terms, but they often mean different things to different people. Generally, counseling and psychotherapy are defined as encompassing a counseling relationship in which a professional interacts with one or more individuals who are seeking assistance in dealing with difficulties and making changes in their lives. In the context of rehabilitation settings, the individuals seeking assistance have disabilities or other special needs. The process may occur not only in a traditional office setting but also in a wide variety of community settings that provide opportunities for interaction between professionals and individuals who are seeking assistance.

According to the *Scope of Practice for Rehabilitation Counseling*, developed by the Commission on Rehabilitation Counselor Certification (CRCC, n.d.), counseling as a treatment intervention is defined as

> the application of cognitive, affective, behavioral, and systemic counseling strategies which include developmental, wellness, pathologic, and multicultural principles of human behavior. Such interventions are specifically implemented in the context of a professional counseling relationship and may include, but are not limited to: appraisal; individual, group, marriage, and family counseling and psychotherapy; the diagnostic description and treatment of persons with mental, emotional, and behavioral disorders or disabilities; guidance and consulting to facilitate normal growth and development, including educational and career development; the utilization of functional assessments and career counseling for persons requesting assistance in adjusting to a disability or handicapping condition; referrals; consulting; and research. (p. 2)

Counseling and psychotherapy share much in common with other human interactions that individuals may find helpful when they are struggling with problems, life decisions, or desired changes in their lives, whether the interactions occur with professionals, family members, or friends. A variety of rehabilitation health professionals other than those with the specific titles of *counselor* or *psychotherapist* attempt to understand the behavior and needs of others and to collaborate with them in devising strategies to accomplish change, including rehabilitation medicine specialists and other physicians, occupational therapists, physical therapists, speech and language therapists, audiologists, rehabilitation teachers, orientation and mobility specialists, and recreation therapists. The effectiveness of services provided by rehabilitation health professionals depends on their effectiveness in establishing a therapeutic working relationship with the individuals served; communicating with individuals in facilitative, helpful ways; obtaining information from individuals in a comprehensive and thorough manner; helping individuals to tell their stories and explain their problems and needs; understanding and conceptualizing behavior and problems in ways that will facilitate treatment and service planning; and facilitating follow-through on commitments and compliance with treatment and service plans that individuals have decided to pursue. All of these professional tasks may be conceptualized as components of counseling and related interactions, and professionals from a variety of rehabilitation health professions can thus benefit from an understanding of counseling theories and techniques.

Distinctions between the terms *counseling* and *psychotherapy* are ambiguous and have often been controversial. Some authors, such as Gelso and Fretz (1992), suggest that psychotherapy, in contrast to counseling, has greater depth and intensity, is of typically longer duration, and addresses personality reorganization and reconstruction, as opposed to the more reality-based problems addressed in counseling. Some (e.g., Tyler, 1958) would also suggest that psychotherapy is used to provide treatment or services to individuals with severe pathology, whereas counseling is applied to more "normal" problems of living, decision making, and personal growth. In addition, Sharf (2000) points out that terminology sometimes varies according to the setting in which practice occurs, with the term *psychotherapy* being more popular in medical settings and *counseling* more popular in educational and human service settings. However, many authors (e.g., Patterson, 1986) have long maintained that the definitions of psychotherapy and counseling overlap substantially and that the distinctions between the two are at best differences of degree, and at worst, arbitrary and meaningless. The views of Patterson and other authors will be followed here, and the terms *counseling*, *psychotherapy*, and *therapy* will be used interchangeably throughout the book.

Individuals Seeking Assistance from Rehabilitation Professionals

Different terms are also commonly used to refer to individuals engaged in treatment or service with rehabilitation health professionals, including *patient*, *client*, *consumer*, and *customer*. *Patient* has been traditionally used by physicians, nurses, other medical professionals, and practitioners in inpatient hospital treatment and mental health. In addition, practitioners who identify themselves as psychotherapists are more likely to use *patient* than those identifying themselves as counselors. *Client* has been commonly used in rehabilitation counseling and in community-based rehabilitation programs, with *consumer* emerging more recently and *customer* even more recently. There are different connotations associated with the various terms. For example, *patient* may imply a medical model to some professionals in conceptualizing needs, with a concomitant tendency on the part of people receiving services to defer to service providers in making treatment and service decisions. In contrast, the other alternative terms may be viewed as implying greater sharing of decision making or even complete control of decisions on the part of the individual served. Advances in the disability rights movement emphasizing consumerism and empowerment (e.g., see

Campbell, 1991; Holmes, 1993) have heightened sensitivity to terminology and its effects on people with disabilities, and the newer terms of *consumer* and *customer* have thus emerged. Terminology has become highly controversial. For example, Thomas (1993) has argued passionately that the term *client* is preferable, while Nosek (1993) has argued with similar passion that the term *consumer* should be used. Partly for historical reasons, including attempts to preserve some of the terminology used by theorists in their original work, the terms *client* and *consumer*, and sometimes *patient*, are used interchangeably, and it is hoped that no readers will be offended by any of the terminology used.

IMPORTANCE OF COUNSELING
AS A PROFESSIONAL FUNCTION

Rehabilitation counseling is one profession where considerable research has been devoted to empirically defining roles, functions, and knowledge and skill domains for professional practice, and counseling has repeatedly emerged as an essential function (e.g., Leahy, Shapson, & Wright, 1987; Leahy, Szymanski, & Linkowski, 1993; Muthard & Salomone, 1969; Rubin et al., 1984). In the seminal role and function study in rehabilitation counseling, Muthard and Salomone reported that state vocational rehabilitation counselors divide their time roughly into thirds: one third to counseling and guidance; one third to clerical work, planning, recording, and placement; and one third to professional growth, public relations, reporting, resource development, travel, and supervisory and administrative duties. In a recent study, Leahy, Chan, and Saunders (2003) surveyed certified rehabilitation counselors to examine the perceived importance of knowledge areas underlying credentialing in rehabilitation counseling, identifying six essential domains: Career Counseling, Assessment and Consultation; Counseling Theories, Techniques, and Applications; Rehabilitation Services and Resources; Case and Caseload Management; Healthcare and Disability Systems; and Medical, Functional and Environmental Implications of Disability. The first two represent knowledge domains in counseling and are related specifically to the content of this book.

The knowledge domains identified by Leahy, Chan, and Saunders (2003) reflect the current practice of rehabilitation counseling in private for-profit, private not-for-profit, and public rehabilitation settings. Regardless of practice settings, however, it is well documented that vocational adjustment is greatly affected by psychosocial issues and needs (O'Brien, Heppner, Flores, & Bikos, 1997). Not surprisingly, Rubin et al. (1984) found that affective counseling was one of the most important functions of rehabilitation counselors and that counselors spend considerable time focusing on the psychological counseling process aimed at changing the client's feelings and thoughts regarding self and others. Because of the generic professional counselor licensure movement in the United States, many rehabilitation counseling programs are changing from requiring 48 credit-hours for master's degrees to 60 credit-hours. This move is intended to ensure that master's degree graduates in rehabilitation counseling will have sufficient training in the foundations of human behavior and behavior change techniques. Also, many practitioners in the field are demanding that they be prepared as a professional counselor first and then practice rehabilitation counseling as a specialty within counseling. Currently, 47 states have passed legislation to regulate licensed professional counselors, and rehabilitation counselors are expected to have a solid grounding in theories and techniques for changing human behavior in a rehabilitation context. Similarly, many other rehabilitation health professionals, including rehabilitation nurses, occupational health nurses, social workers, and occupational, physical, speech and language, and recreation therapists, have become increasingly aware of the effects of psychosocial factors on rehabilitation outcomes and the importance of one-to-one and group interactions in professional practice. As a result, professional education programs in various rehabilitation health professions have begun to incorporate interviewing techniques, counseling interventions, and psychosocial adjustment content into their training curricula.

HISTORICAL CONTEXT FOR THEORIES OF COUNSELING AND PSYCHOTHERAPY

Psychological, sociocultural, and systemic theories typically guide the process of counseling and psychotherapy, facilitating the understanding of behavior and the formulation of intervention strategies that hold promise for accomplishing the desired changes. In fact, it is difficult to imagine a practitioner being able to function with any degree of effectiveness without the guidance of at least some basic theoretical direction. As stated by Prochaska and Norcross (1999):

> Without a guiding theory or system of psychotherapy, clinicians would be vulnerable, directionless creatures, bombarded with literally hundreds of impressions and pieces of information in a single session . . . theory describes the clinical phenomena, delimits the amount of relevant information, organizes that informa-

tion, and integrates it all into a coherent body of knowledge that prioritizes our conceptualization and directs our treatment. (p. 5)

Early Historical Roots

Arguably, the first psychotherapeutic treatment of a potential rehabilitation client took place outside Vienna between 1880 and 1882. The "counselor" was a Viennese physician named Joseph Breuer, and the patient was Bertha Peppenheim. Bertha, who is better known as Anna O, presented an array of symptoms, including paraphasia, a convergent squint, severe disturbances of vision, paralyses of her upper and lower extremities, eating and drinking disturbances, and a severe nervous cough (Breuer & Freud, 1893–1895/1966; Freud, 1910/1955). The treatment itself, which consisted primarily of hypnosis and catharsis, provided only temporary relief of Bertha's "conversion hysteria," and she experienced several relapses and hospitalizations after the premature termination of the treatment (Jones, 1953; Summers, 1999). However, the long-term ramifications of the treatment would eventually prove to exceed the wildest dreams of either Bertha or the physician. Breuer, who was a close friend, mentor, and early benefactor of Freud, was even credited by Freud, at least initially (e.g., see Freud, 1910/1955), for the creation of psychoanalysis. During the treatment, Bertha herself originated such famous terms as *the talking cure* and *chimney sweeping*, thus demonstrating remarkable insight into the dynamics of these early psychotherapeutic interventions and providing her own very substantial contribution to counseling and psychotherapy. Although the treatment itself was essentially a disaster, with Bertha having a hysterical pregnancy with Breuer as the alleged father and Breuer abandoning the treatment in fear of losing his professional reputation (Jones, 1953), the basis was laid for Freud's later, lifelong development of his theories and therapies of psychoanalysis.

One of Freud's dreams was that the benefits of psychoanalysis could eventually be spread to the general populace by using a cadre of trained, nonmedical therapists. It was, in fact, Freud's strong belief that psychoanalytically trained "laypersons" rather than physicians would make the best therapists (Freud, 1926/1959). Although this dream was never realized, especially in the United States, where a very restrictive medical community virtually prevented nonphysicians from receiving psychoanalytic training under the auspices of the American Psychoanalytic Association, Bertha's "talking cure" provided the basis for a variety of counseling and psychotherapeutic interventions, both psychoanalytic and otherwise.

From a rehabilitation standpoint, Bertha would have been, at least eventually, a remarkable success story. Despite her subsequent hospitalizations, she went on to have a distinguished career as a social worker, feminist, and writer and is, in fact, one of the most important individuals in the history of European social welfare. Although modern-day rehabilitation professionals use methods that are vastly different in scope and form from those used by Breuer, the goal of helping distressed individuals live more productive and happy lives is essentially the same.

More Recent Evolution of Theoretical Approaches

From the early roots of psychoanalysis, a variety of theoretical approaches to counseling and psychotherapy have developed. Garfield and Bergin (1994) reviewed the evolution of theoretical approaches, indicating that Freud's psychoanalytic theory, along with derivatives due to some of his followers, such as Alfred Adler, Carl Jung, Karen Horney, and Harry Stack Sullivan, were "from the end of the nineteenth century to about the 1960s, the dominant influence" (p. 3). The client-centered or person-centered theoretical approach, developed by Carl Rogers (1942), represented one of the major early departures from psychoanalytic theory, emphasizing the potential of people to self-actualize and the therapeutic qualities of empathy, unconditional positive regard, and genuineness that could nourish and release this positive growth potential toward constructive personality and behavior change. Behavior therapy, although beginning many years before, did not gain popularity until the 1950s, with the publication of Wolpe's (1958) book on reciprocal inhibition as an approach to psychotherapy. The community mental health movement in the 1960s brought a new focus on the mental health needs of low-income people, along with community-based treatment and crisis intervention. Long-term psychotherapy, particularly psychoanalytic approaches, were generally used by middle- and upper-income people, and briefer forms of counseling and psychotherapy became more popular leading to the rise of many different theoretical orientations.

A proliferation of approaches to counseling and psychotherapy has emerged over the years. Garfield (1982) identified 125 different approaches to psychotherapy in existence in the 1960s, and in the 1980s Herink (1980) identified more than 250 and Kazdin (1986) estimated more than 400, with most having received little or no systematic empirical evaluation. Adding to the variety of theoretical approaches in use is the popularity of eclecticism among practitioners, who draw from and integrate concepts and techniques from multiple theoretical approaches, rather than adhering to a single approach. Jensen, Bergin, and Greaves (1990) surveyed practitioners in psychiatry, clinical psychology, social work, and marriage and family therapy and found that 68% of respondents identified themselves as eclectics. Thus a wide variety of theoretical approaches to counseling and psychotherapy are in use by professional practitioners in rehabilitation and health settings, with many drawing from and attempting to integrate multiple approaches in their work.

Prochaska and Norcross (1999), compiling data from three different surveys (Norcross, Karg, & Prochaska, 1997; Norcross, Strausser, & Missar, 1988; Watkins, Lopez, Campbell, & Himmell, 1986), identified predominant theoretical orientations of practitioners in counseling and psychotherapy in the United States, including clinical psychologists, counseling psychologists, psychiatrists, social workers, and counselors. As was found in other studies, eclectic orientations were the most frequently indicated orientations among all of the respondent groups, varying from 27% of the clinical psychologists to 53% of the psychiatrists. Psychoanalytic/psychodynamic orientations were indicated by a large number of psychiatrists (35%) and social workers (33%) and also by a number of clinical psychologists (18%), counseling psychologists (12%), and counselors (11%). Cognitive-behavioral orientations tended to be most predominant among psychologists and counselors, with 27% of clinical psychologists indicating either cognitive or behavioral orientations, in addition to 19% of counseling psychologists and 16% of counselors. Humanistic orientations tended to be most predominant among counseling psychologists and counselors, with 21% of counselors indicating either Rogerian/person-centered or existential/humanistic orientations, in addition to 14% of counseling psychologists.

Since large numbers of practitioners in counseling and psychotherapy indicate that their orientations are eclectic, it should also be informative to ask eclectic practitioners about the theoretical orientations that they draw upon in forming their eclectic orientations. Jensen et al. (1990) asked this question of the 283 eclectic practitioners in their study, and they found a mean of 4.4 theories identified as influential, including dynamic (72%), cognitive (54%), behavioral (49%), and humanistic (42%), among those theories most frequently identified. On the basis of the available evidence, it would appear that a diverse array of theoretical orientations influence the practice of counseling and psychotherapy. In addition, it would appear that individuals who follow an eclectic orientation may often be influenced by diverse theoretical orientations themselves, suggesting the importance of understanding a variety of different theories of counseling and psychotherapy.

EFFICACY OF COUNSELING AND PSYCHOTHERAPY

Over the past several decades, psychotherapy researchers have devoted concerted efforts to examining the efficacy of counseling and psychotherapy. Recently, Wampold (2001) examined thousands of studies regarding the efficacy of psychotherapy using meta-analysis and concluded that at least 70% of psychotherapeutic effects are due to common factors, while only 8% are due to specific ingredients. The remaining 22%, which are unexplained, are due in part to client differences. Common factors are ingredients that all forms of counseling and psychotherapy share and exist across all forms and types as they are typically practiced. For Wampold (2001) the common factors include goal setting, empathic listening, and such considerations as the following:

- Allegiance (i.e., the degree to which the practitioner is committed to the belief that the therapy is beneficial to the client)
- The therapeutic alliance, defined pantheoretically by Wampold to include the following:

    a. The client's affective relationship with the therapist
    b. The client's motivation and ability to accomplish work collaboratively with the therapist
    c. The therapist's empathic response to and involvement with the client
    d. Client and therapist agreement about the goals and tasks of therapy

Conversely, specific ingredients, as distinguished from the common factors, include actions or techniques that are both essential and unique to a particular theory. Wampold (2001) has clearly demonstrated an important empirical link between common factors in the counseling relationship and outcomes. However, counselors must still formulate hypotheses about client problems and facilitate interactions with clients based on certain theoretical orientations. It can be argued that not every counselor will be comfortable with only one form or approach to counseling and psychotherapy. Conversely, the same is probably true for clients seeking assistance from professionals. In order to maximize the effects of the common factors, it might be critical to tailor counseling interventions to the individual differences and needs of rehabilitation clients. In a multimodal way, the method of treatment would depend, at the very least, on the needs, context, expectations, personality, and problems of the individual seeking help.

OVERVIEW OF SECTIONS AND CHAPTERS

In providing coverage of counseling theories and techniques for rehabilitation health professionals, the book is organized into sections, with each section comprising multiple chapters. After the present introductory section, the following sections are included: *Counseling Theories, Basic Techniques, Special Considerations*, and *Professional Issues*.

The *Counseling Theories* section provides reviews of 10 different theoretical approaches to counseling and psychotherapy, with an emphasis on their applications in rehabilitation settings. To the extent possible, each chapter is organized according to the following structure: History, Major Concepts, Theory of Personality, Description of the Counseling Process, Rehabilitation Applications, Case Example, Research Findings, and Prominent Strengths and Limitations. Thus, in addition to discussing the major components of each theoretical approach, each chapter emphasizes practical applications in rehabilitation health practice, including case examples to demonstrate applications. As previously discussed, there are literally hundreds of theoretical approaches to counseling and psychotherapy that have been developed, so the selection of theories to include was not an easy task. In general, an attempt was made to select the most prominent theoretical approaches, while also representing a broad spectrum of theories that have potential applicability in rehabilitation settings.

The *Counseling Theories* section is divided into three subsections, representing major categories of theoretical approaches. The first subsection is *Psychodynamic Approaches*, with two chapters covering psychodynamic therapy and Adlerian therapy. Psychodynamic approaches follow from Sigmund Freud's psychoanalysis and, as in the surveys previously cited, are popular among contemporary practitioners in counseling and psychotherapy, particularly among psychiatrists and social workers but also among those from other disciplines. In addition, as discussed by Corey (2001), the psychoanalytic model has been a

> major influence on all of the other formal systems of psychotherapy. Some
> are basically extensions of psychoanalysis, others are modifications of analytic
> concepts and procedures, and still others are positions that emerged as a reaction

against psychoanalysis. Many of the other theories of counseling and psychother-apy have borrowed and integrated principles and techniques from psychoanalytic approaches. (pp. 7–9)

The second subsection under the *Counseling Theories* is *Humanistic Approaches*, including three chapters that cover person-centered, Gestalt, and logotherapy approaches. In addition to being termed humanistic, these approaches could also have been categorized as experiential, existential, and relationship-oriented. Seligman (2001) categorized these three theories as "treatment systems emphasizing emotions and sensations," and Patterson and Watkins (1996) categorized person-centered and Gestalt approaches as "perceptual-phenomenological" and logotherapy separately as "existential psychotherapy." As indicated above, humanistic approaches would appear to be most widely used by counselors and counseling psychologists, among the various disciplines that practice counseling and psychotherapy. Because of their application in initiating counseling relationships and facilitating client exploration, including the exploration of emotions, some textbooks (e.g., James & Gilliland, 2003) place humanistic theories as the first theories covered. In addition, humanistic theories, particularly person-centered theories, emphasize the relationship between counselor and client, and this emphasis has been influential in the evolution of many other theoretical approaches.

The third subsection under *Counseling Theories* is *Cognitive and Behavioral Approaches*, comprising five chapters covering behavioral and cognitive-behavioral approaches, rational-emotive behavior therapy, reality therapy, and trait-factor theory. These five approaches are all systematic and action-oriented, and authors of textbooks on theories of counseling and psychotherapy have used terms such as *action* (Corey, 2001) and *action-oriented* (James & Gilliland, 2003) to refer to this category of approaches. As indicated in the surveys of practitioners discussed previously, cognitive and behavioral approaches are highly influential in the work of many practitioners in counseling and psychotherapy, particularly clinical psychologists, counseling psychologists, and counselors. Cognitive and behavioral approaches do not ignore emotions, but they tend to view emotions as a product of the ways that an "individual perceives, interprets, and assigns meaning" to events (Warwar & Greenberg (2000, p. 585), and interventions designed to influence emotions are primarily directed at thoughts and behaviors.

The *Basic Techniques* section begins with a chapter on communication and counseling techniques that are basic to both formal counseling interactions and to other interpersonal interactions between practitioners and clients. The next two chapters focus on group and family counseling, respectively, which are two types of counseling interactions that have a number of unique features relative to individual counseling. Finally, the section concludes with a chapter on career counseling, which represents an important specific component of counseling in rehabilitation settings.

The *Special Considerations* section discusses counseling and service considerations that are related to specific types of disabilities. As was true in selecting counseling theories, there were many potential choices as to the specific types of disability and client groups to include. The chapters in the section address four broad disability groups: substance abuse, physical disabilities, psychiatric disabilities, and mental retardation or cognitive disabilities. A fifth chapter in the section addresses multicultural considerations in counseling and psychotherapy, a particularly important and timely topic.

The *Professional Issues* section focuses on three general topics that are directly related to the practice of counseling in rehabilitation settings. The first chapter focuses on clinical supervision, a critical function in monitoring and improving the quality of service and treatment provided to clients; in addition, supervision is a critical function in facilitating the professional development of practitioners, as well as the learning and development of students preparing for professional practice careers. The second chapter in the section focuses on risk management in professional practice, including ethical issues, and the final chapter focuses on the conceptualization and measurement of rehabilitation outcomes.

In conclusion, the book provides an overview of prominent theoretical approaches to counseling and psychotherapy, along with some of the ways in which they can be applied in rehabilitation settings to assist people with disabilities. In addition, special considerations related to specific types of disabilities are presented, along with a discussion of selected professional issues related to professional practice. It is hoped that the content will help professional practitioners and students in rehabilitation health professions to better understand counseling and psychotherapy practice and the potential applications of theories and techniques in rehabilitation settings.

REFERENCES

Breuer, J., & Freud, S. (1966). Studies in hysteria. In J. Strachey (Ed. and Trans.), *The standard edition of the complete psychological works of Sigmund Freud* (Vol. 2). London: Hogarth Press. (Original work published 1893–1895)

Campbell, J. F. (1991). The consumer movement and implications for vocational rehabilitation services. *Journal of Vocational Rehabilitation, 1,* 67–75.

Commission on Rehabilitation Counselor Certification. (n.d.). *Scope of practice for rehabilitation counseling.* Rolling Meadows, IL: Author.

Corey, G. (2001). *Theory and practice of counseling and psychotherapy* (6th ed.). Belmont, CA: Brooks/Cole.

Freud, S. (1955). Five lectures on psycho-analysis. In J. Strachey (Ed. and Trans.), *The standard edition of the complete psychological works of Sigmund Freud* (Vol. 11). London: Hogarth Press. (Original work published 1910)

Freud, S. (1959). The question of lay analysis: Conversations with an impartial person. In J. Strachey (Ed. and Trans.), *The standard edition of the complete psychological works of Sigmund Freud* (Vol. 20; pp. 183–258). London: Hogarth Press. (Original work published 1926)

Garfield, S. L. (1982). Eclecticism and integration in psychotherapy. *Behavior Therapy, 13,* 610–623.

Garfield, S. L., & Bergin, A. E. (1994). Introduction and historical overview. In A. E. Bergin & S. L. Garfield (Eds.), *Handbook of psychotherapy and behavior change* (4th ed., pp. 3–18). New York: Wiley.

Gelso, C. J., & Fretz, B. R. (1992). *Counseling psychology.* Ft. Worth, TX: Harcourt Brace.

Herink, R. (Ed.). (1980). *The psychotherapy handbook: The A to Z guide to more than 250 different therapies in use today.* New York: Meridian/New American Library.

Holmes, G. E. (1993). The historical roots of the empowerment dilemma in vocational rehabilitation. *Journal of Disability Policy Studies, 4*(1), 1–19.

James, R. K., & Gilliland, B. E. (2003). *Theories and strategies in counseling and psychotherapy* (5th ed.). Boston: Allyn & Bacon.

Jensen, J. P., Bergin, A. E., & Greaves, D. W. (1990). The meaning of eclecticism: New survey and analysis of components. *Professional Psychology: Research and Practice, 21,* 124–130.

Jones, E. (1953). *The life and work of Sigmund Freud* (Vol. 1). New York: Basic Books.

Kazdin, A. E. (1986). Comparative outcome studies of psychotherapy: Methodological issues and strategies. *Journal of Consulting and Clinical Psychology, 54,* 95–105.

Leahy, M. J., Chan, F., & Saunders, J. L. (2003). Job functions and knowledge requirements of certified rehabilitation counselors in the 21st century. *Rehabilitation Counseling Bulletin, 46,* 66–81.

Leahy, M. J., Shapson, P. R., & Wright, G. N. (1987). Rehabilitation counselor competencies by role and setting. *Rehabilitation Counseling Bulletin, 31,* 94–106.

Leahy, M. J., Szymanski, E. M., & Linkowski, D. (1993). Knowledge importance in rehabilitation counseling. *Rehabilitation Counseling Bulletin, 37,* 130–145.

Muthard, J. E., & Salomone, P. R. (1969). The roles and functions of the rehabilitation counselor. *Rehabilitation Counseling Bulletin, 13,* 81–168.

Norcross, J. C., Karg, R. S., & Prochaska, J. O. (1997). Clinical psychologists and managed care: Some data from the Division 12 membership. *Clinical Psychologist, 50,* 4–8.

Norcross, J. C., Strausser, D. J., & Missar, C. D. (1988). The process and outcomes of psychotherapists' personal treatment experiences. *Psychotherapy, 25,* 36–43.

Nosek, M. A. (1993). A response to Kenneth R. Thomas' commentary: Some observa-
    tions on the use of the word "consumer." *Journal of Rehabilitation, 59*(2), 9–10.
O'Brien, K. M., Heppner, M. J., Flores, L. Y., & Bikos, L. H. (1997). The career
    counselling self-efficacy scale: Instrument development and training applications.
    Journal of Counseling Psychology, 44, 1–12.
Patterson, C. H. (1986). *Theories of counseling and psychotherapy* (4th ed.). New York:
    Harper & Row.
Patterson, C. H., & Watkins, C. E., Jr. (1996). *Theories of psychotherapy* (5th ed.).
    Boston: Allyn & Bacon.
Prochaska, J. O., & Norcross, J. C. (1999). *Systems of psychotherapy: A transtheoretical
    approach* (4th ed.). Pacific Grove, CA: Brooks/Cole.
Rogers, C. R. (1942). *Counseling and psychotherapy*. Boston: Houghton Mifflin.
Rubin, S. E., Matkin, R. E., Ashley, J., Beardsly, M. M., May, V. R., Onstott, K., et al.
    (1984). Roles and functions of certified rehabilitation counselors. *Rehabilitation
    Counseling Bulletin, 27*, 199–224.
Seligman, L. (2001). *Systems, strategies, and skills of counseling and psychotherapy*.
    Upper Saddle River, NJ: Merrill Prentice Hall.
Sharf, R. S. (2000). *Theories of psychotherapy and counseling: Concepts and cases* (2nd
    ed.). Belmont, CA: Brooks/Cole.
Summers, F. L. (1999). *Transcending the self: An object relations model of psychoanalytic
    therapy*. Hillsdale, NJ: Analytic Press.
Thomas, K. R. (1993). Commentary: Some observations on the use of the word "con-
    sumer." *Journal of Rehabilitation, 59*(2), 6–8.
Tyler, L. E. (1958). Theoretical principles underlying the counseling process. *Journal
    of Counseling Psychology, 5*, 3–10.
Wampold, B. E. (2001). *The great psychotherapy debate: Models, methods, and findings*.
    Mahwah, NJ: Erlbaum.
Warwar, S., & Greenberg, L. S. (2000). Advances in theories of change and counseling.
    In S. D. Brown & R. W. Lent (Eds.), *Handbook of counseling psychology* (3rd ed.).
    New York: Wiley.
Watkins, C. E., Lopez, F. G., Campbell, V. L., & Himmell, C. D. (1986). Contemporary
    counseling psychology: Results of a national survey. *Journal of Counseling Psychol-
    ogy, 33*, 301–309.
Wolpe, J. (1958). *Psychotherapy by reciprocal inhibition*. Stanford, CA: Stanford Univer-
    sity Press.

Counseling Theories

Psychodynamic Approaches

Chapter 2

Psychodynamic Therapy

Hanoch Livneh and Jerome Siller

Within counseling and psychotherapy, psychoanalytically and psychodynamically based interventions are distinguished by a focus on the importance of early experience and the role of unconscious mental functioning. In common with other approaches to counseling and psychotherapy, considerable attention is paid to family, social, vocational, and other aspects of life. It is the manner in which these nonpsychodynamic "realities" are viewed analytically that claims distinctiveness. Character change is usually the goal of psychodynamically oriented treatments, which strive to facilitate self-understanding. Alleviation of symptoms in effect is viewed as a by-product of characterological change. Psychoanalytic theories of personality development and structures serve as the basis for interventions to facilitate self-awareness, through which the consequences of developmental distortions, conflicts, and arrested development can be changed.

Within psychoanalysis and its various offshoots is much variation in theory and treatment procedures. Within rehabilitation, classical psychoanalytic treatment is not typically feasible, but a variety of psychodynamic procedures would appear to clearly have a place. Fundamental psychodynamic concepts deriving from psychoanalysis would appear to be invaluable for understanding the situations of people in general, including those with disabilities. Specific rehabilitation procedures can be informed by these concepts, including those that are not specifically psychodynamic (e.g., interventions involving mourning experiences). Sharp distinctions among various psychoanalytic "schools" or between psychoanalysis and psychotherapy in this context are not necessary. However, to convey the developing nature of psychoanalytic thought and treatment and its present status, a historical view of psychoanalysis follows. By focusing on the vicissitudes of mainstream psychoanalysis, we hope to represent the fundamental thrusts of psychodynamic thinking and applications to rehabilitation.

HISTORY

Pine (1988) suggested that clinical psychoanalysis has led to the development of four conceptually separate perspectives on the functioning of the human mind: psychologies of drive, ego, object relations, and self. The four perspectives overlap and add to an understanding of both theory and clinical treatment. In addition, expression of the four perspectives can be found in both psychodynamic and nonpsychodynamic approaches to counseling and psychotherapy.

In Freud's drive theory, mental life emerges from strong urges and wishes that are shaped by early bodily and family experiences and that power conscious and unconscious fantasies and behaviors. Many fantasies are experienced as dangerous and engender anxiety, guilt, shame, inhibition, symptom formation, and pathological character traits. Early bodily and family experiences are influential in determining personality, and, as pointed out by Siller (1976), early bodily experiences can be particularly important in the development of persons with physical disabilities or deformities. Fundamental concepts of drive theory include a presupposition of universal laws that govern all mental life, both normal and abnormal; psychic determinism; the human organism as an energy system; a personality structure with the constructs of id, ego, and superego; and a complex of other interrelated concepts, including an active unconscious with primary and secondary process modes of thought, repression, resistance, and transference. Among widely used terms originating in drive theory are the *id, psychosexuality, libido, fixation, repression, defense mechanisms, narcissism, the pleasure principle,* and *metapsychology.*

The catch phrase "where id was there ego shall be" (Freud, 1933/1964, p. 80) characterizes the therapeutic goal of treatment based on drive theory, with interpretation of the force of unconscious processes and the analysis of resistance and transference as the forces for change. Developments beyond pure instinct theory facilitated an oncoming ego psychology, and structural theory was also introduced (Freud, 1923/1961), along with a signal theory of anxiety (Freud, 1926/1959). Freud postulated, in place of conscious and unconscious systems in mental life, new structures of the id, ego, and superego, explicating their roles in intrapsychic conflict. According to Freud, anxiety is the fundamental phenomenon and focal problem of neurosis. He expanded the concept of anxiety from earlier conceptions where it was seen to result from the discharge of repressed somatic tensions (libido). Freud saw anxiety as a signal of danger to the ego and differentiated among three types: reality, neurotic, and moral. Defenses were then conceptualized as ego functions, and psychoanalytic treatment expanded from its initial somatic base. In addition to the translation of id forces into consciousness as a treatment goal, analysis of ego functions also came to be emphasized (Freud, 1926/1959).

Ego psychology emerged during the 1930s as the preeminence of the id began to be shared with that of the ego. The id had been seen as carrying all of the innate instinctual energy, with the ego emerging from the id and serving mainly to intervene with the environment to satisfy id-based wishes. Now the functions of the ego were emphasized in terms of capacities for adaptation, reality testing, and defense. A landmark in the development of ego psychology was Anna Freud's book on the relationship of the ego to the mechanisms of defense (A. Freud, 1936/1946). Leaders in pursuing psychoanalytic ego psychology were Heinz Hartmann, Melanie Klein, Ernst Kris, and Rudolf Lowenwstein.

Hartmann (1964) introduced a significant emphasis on adaptation to the average expectable environment, attempting to systematize and resolve contradictions in psychoanalytic theory. His conceptions included disagreements with major propositions of Freudian thinking in the development and functioning of the ego, the importance of ego structure in the totality of personality, and the relationship of the person to reality. Adding to the Freudian conception of the id existing at birth and the ego developing out of the id, Hartmann suggested that life begins with an undifferentiated phase during which both the ego and id form out of the totality of the individual's psychological inheritance. Ego development was viewed as an interactive function of biology and environment where heredity and maturation interact with the environmental forces of learning. Erik Erikson (1950,1968) also contributed substantially to conceptions regarding the ego and psychosocial development, and he was also identified as an ego psychologist. His contributions have been widely recognized; they widened the purview of psychoanalytic thinking by vividly demonstrating the role of the ego in relating to the environment and the continuing development of personality into adulthood and old age.

Ego psychology expanded psychoanalytic theory to encompass normal as well as abnormal phenomena. Psychoanalytic theory became more receptive to the idea of environmental forces serving as key influences in psychological development. Consciousness and cognitions came to have importance, and therapeutic interventions were then geared to all levels of personality, with the present and recent past being viewed as relevant, along with conscious awareness. Interpretations, while still symbolically based, tended to be less so, and current situations, needs, and explanations were given more attention. Object relations theory continued the movement of psychoanalytic thought from drive and instinct theory. Reactive to this movement, some psychoanalysts attempted to integrate object relations concepts with structural theory, while others strove to replace structural concepts with those derived from object relations. The origins of object relations theory can be found in the writings of Freud, Sandor Ferenczi, and Melanie Klein. Klein stimulated the writings of British analysts such as D. W. Winnicott, W. R. D. Fairbairn, and Harry Guntrip, whose work on object relations from the 1940s to the 1960s has had a profound influence in extending psychoanalytic theory and intervention. The psychology of object relations differs appreciably from the transactional or interpersonal theories of H. S. Sullivan, K. Horney, and E. Fromm, which stress the social and interactive nature of human relations and tend to downplay intrapsychic events. Object relations theory focuses on internalization of psychic events and intrapsychic processes. It is the representation and symbolization within the person of the other, rather than the actual transaction between them, that serves as the focus.

As characterized by Sandler and Rosenblatt (1962), through conscious and unconscious memories derived from early childhood, an internal drama occurs in which individuals enact one or more of the roles. New experiences are not experienced entirely as new, but are rather processed through internal images that are to varying degrees based upon childhood experience. Consistent with the psychoanalytic orientation, these internal dramas are dominated by experience with the primary objects of childhood. What the child experiences, however, is not a "true" representation of the relationship, since object relation consists of memories structured by feelings and wishes active at the time of the experience. As with ego psychology, object relations psychology readily fits within the psychoanalytic model and provides insights into such classical conceptions as transference and countertransference, early psychic development, and ongoing subjective states.

The fourth and most recent psychology identified by Pine is self-experience and is the source of much contemporary attention: "what I shall work with as the domain of psychology of self-experience is subjective experience specifically around feelings of self-definition in relation to the object" (Pine, 1988, p. 574). This domain involves seeing the individual in terms of the ongoing subjective state, particularly around issues of boundaries, continuity, and esteem, and reactions to imbalances in that subjective state (Sandler, 1960). Attention is also paid to such central features of the subjective state as degree of differentiation of self from other, separateness of boundaries, and loss or absence of boundaries.

Self-psychology, as developed by Heinz Kohut, has moved away from customary psychoanalytic thought. Kohut (1971, 1977, 1984) approached self-psychology in terms of narcissistic development. He conceptualized the emerging self as composed of the grandiose and idealizing lines of development. Phase-appropriate minor "failures" in empathy of "good-enough" parents can lead to healthy development. Disturbances in the self arise from severe, phase-inappropriate, and/or chronic frustration of the child's needs from mirroring of grandiosity and models worthy of idealizing.

The present writers hold with Pine (1988) that all four of the psychologies used as the organizing basis for this review are legitimately psychoanalytic and that they require just such a complex and multifaceted view of functioning that only psychoanalysis provides. The above considerations are not intended as "jurisdictional" quibbling but rather are meant to alert those not operating within the psychodynamic/psychoanalytic perspective to the vitality, flexibility, and growth within this framework that can be applied to the multinatured demands of rehabilitation.

MAJOR CONCEPTS

Psychoanalytic theory is all of the following: (a) a system of psychology and philosophy (metapsychology); (b) a theory developed by Freud and his followers to describe, explain, and analyze human emotional, cognitive, and behavioral processes; and (c) a therapeutic approach for the treatment of maladaptive feelings, thoughts, and behaviors (Cook, 1998; Fine, 1973). Psychodynamic theoretical systems, while varying in many ways from classical psychoanalysis and its later derivatives, draw considerably from the psychoanalytic theoretical base. Fundamental techniques and concepts of treatment from psychoanalysis are expanded, transformed, or dropped, depending upon the thrust of a particular psychodynamic orientation. In moving to psychodynamic, as contrasted with psychoanalytic, counseling and psychotherapy, certain constraints and procedures appropriate to the psychoanalytic process may be relieved and a wider assortment of interventions considered.

A core concept form early psychoanalysis that persists in psychodynamic theory is hedonism: striving for pleasure and avoiding pain. In Freud's instinct theory, Eros, the life drive, is based upon general biological energy (libido), which is guided by the pleasure principle and is expressed through self-love, love of others, and the uninhibited pursuit of pleasure. This drive is located in the unconscious and is represented by the id. The core of personality evolves out of a need to reach a compromise between the "pleasure principle" and the "reality principle," the latter embodying parental and societal demands, restrictions, and obligations in the act of seeking gratification. A second major drive proposed by Freud, Thanatos, the death drive, has never received general acceptance and will not be discussed here. Other basic concepts include the idea of a dynamic unconscious, the basic importance of early developmental history and experience, and the preeminent nature of repression. It has already been noted above that contemporary thinking has not been receptive to the energy theory of drives and other aspects of libido theory, including the well-known development of psychosexual stages. Thus libido theory and psychosexual stages are not fundamental concepts in psychodynamic theory, but the concepts of psychosexuality and character neurosis are important.

Primary perspectives in psychoanalysis include the following: (a) a physiological perspective emphasizing biological development; (b) a psychological perspective concerning inner psychological states of consciousness and unconsciousness; and (c) a sociocultural perspective including the importance of early, family-based experiences in shaping the life (psychological reality) of the individual, and the influence of sociocultural beliefs, values, demands, and expectations on families and child-rearing practices (Fine, 1973; Ford & Urban, 1998; Maddi, 2000). Modern psychodynamic models borrow from earlier psychoanalytic concepts but typically focus on a restricted range of personal and interpersonal domains, such as separation/autonomy versus merger/independence tendencies (e.g., the work of Angyal and Bakan); interpersonal transactions (e.g., the work of Kiesler); and in disability, work by Siller on attitude structure and Shontz on adjustment to disability.

THEORY OF PERSONALITY

As characterized by Dewald (1978), elements of personality emerge from inevitable conflicts experienced by the infant and young child in its interactions with important people in its environment and is elaborated in various intrapsychic functions and mental processes. Constitutional determinants are highly influential, and the process leads to the establishment of the "core" of personality and psychic function. The core psychic functions and organization are reasonably well established in most individuals with the passage through the Oedipal phase, and in ordinary psychic development these core psychological functions undergo repression with the onset of latency. As Dewald pointed out, following Rappaport (1960), " 'psychic structures' merely describes and defines specific individual psychological functions that, once established, tend to be stereotyped, automatic, unconscious, and tend to have a slow spontaneous rate of change. In other words, the core structures tend to be established early, and to remain relatively unchanged as the basic foundations of subsequent personality development" (p. 536).

Dewald (1978) emphatically rejected the idea that personality development ceases around the time of resolution of the Oedipus phase, or that there is a direct causal relationship between psychic functioning in the adult and the core psychic structures established during childhood (the genetic fallacy). Rappaport and Gill (1959), supplemented by others such as Arlow and Brenner (1964) and Fine (1973), identified the minimum number of assumptions upon which the system of psychoanalysis is based. The clinical implications of this conceptualization, as Greenson (1967, pp. 21–22) indicated, are "that in order to comprehend a psychic event thoroughly, it is necessary to analyze it from six different points of view— the topographic, dynamic, economic, genetic, structural, and adaptive."

- *Topographic*. Human consciousness includes a complex hierarchical layering from unconscious (perceived as the most significant determinant of behavior), to preconsciousness, to consciousness. Whereas unconscious activities are governed by primary thought processes, the remaining two are mostly influenced by secondary thought processes.
- *Genetic*. Human behavior follows a temporal process whereby present personality can be explained by earlier life experiences. Present behaviors, including personality traits and neurotic symptoms, are therefore determined by psychosexual phases of development from early childhood and cumulative experience. Biological-constitutional as well as experiential factors are stressed.
- *Dynamic*. Human behavior is determined by the interplay of dynamic impulses or drives. These desire are typically composed of libidinal (sexual) and aggressive drives. Hypotheses concerning instinctual drives, defenses, ego interests, and conflicts are based on this point of view. Examples of dynamics are ambivalence, overdetermination, and symptom formation.
- *Economic*. Human behavior requires energy. As such, it draws, disposes of, and is regulated by psychological energy. This energy feeds

psychic structures and process. The processes of binding and neutralizing energy are referred to as cathexes (to objects such as people).

- *Structural.* Human behavior relies upon the interaction among three main personality structures—the id, ego, and superego. These structures are persisting functional units. The id is the storehouse of all drives and instincts. The ego comprises a group of functions that coordinate and organize behavior, including the anxiety-minimizing defense mechanisms. The superego is the product of moral and social values. The primary function of the ego is to mediate conflicting demands from the id, superego, and external reality.
- *Adaptive.* Human behavior has to conform to the demands of the external reality, in particular, social reality.

Some additional points of view have been proposed, including the following:

- *Psychosocial.* Human behavior is strongly influenced by social forces, especially the early familial context.
- *Gestalt.* Human behavior is multiply determined and multifaceted. Despite its conceptual differentiation into perceptual, motor, cognitive, and affective aspects and the spatial and temporal contexts within which it occurs, it is ultimately integrated and indivisible.
- *Orgasmic.* Human behavior is not performed in isolation but rather is a reflection or component of the total personality. While full elaboration of the different assumptions involved is beyond the scope of this chapter, it seems important to point out the relevance of the theory for real persons in real-life contexts. This relevance is particularly apparent within the structural and functional framework of the total personality. Clinically, behavior performed in isolation from the context or the rest of the personality generally reflects pathology.

The enormous complexity and richness of the points of view or propositions (also referred to as metapsychological assumptions) should be juxtaposed with less ambitious conceptualizations. While full elaboration of the different assumptions involved rarely can be made, it does target an approach that attempts to appreciate real persons in real-life contexts. This complexity is particularly apparent in the area of diagnosis. Diagnostic evaluation from the psychodynamic point of view provides understanding of the psychological state of the person. Psychodynamic approaches deal with such psychological dimensions as growth, experience, family, society, self, relationships, intrapsychic phenomena, symbolization, subjectivity, spirituality, need, character, defenses, and behavior, among countless others. They also deal with constitution, temperament, and heredity and their roles in interaction with the foregoing dimensions. The whole person is always involved, and diagnosis focuses on such dimensions as ego strength, character style, and insight, with formal objective labels rapidly becoming irrelevant once the course of psychotherapy has been determined.

THE PROCESS OF PSYCHODYNAMIC COUNSELING

Psychodynamic counseling is not a lesser form of psychological intervention than psychoanalysis or any of its variants. It is intended for different purposes and often for different populations. In classical psychoanalysis there are rather stringent requirements for "suitability." For example, in an encyclopedic presentation of the psychoanalytic theory of neurosis of that time, Fenichel (1945) presented indications and contraindications for psychoanalytical treatment. In 1920 Freud divided neuroses into transference neuroses and narcissistic neuroses, which roughly correspond to neuroses and psychoses. The key criterion distinguishing the two is whether the person is able to establish transference (the warded-off impulses are striving for an expression in connection with a longing for objects). Persons with narcissistic neuroses, having regressed to a preestablished object relations phase, are unreliable in this regard because of a tendency to withdraw. Since the interpretation of transference is the main tool of psychoanalysis, transference neuroses are its indication, but in narcissistic neuroses it is inapplicable.

Specific contraindications for psychoanalytic treatment are elaborated upon by Fenichel (1945) and include advanced age, insufficient intelligence, unfavorable life situations, triviality of a neurosis, urgency of a neurotic symptom, severe disturbance of speech, lack of a reasonable and cooperative ego, certain secondary gains, and schizoid personalities. As psychoanalytic theory has developed, inroads have been made in a number of areas affecting some of these contraindications. For example, older persons in many instances have been found to be suitable for psychoanalysis. Modifications in psychoanalytic technique have opened analytic and analytically based approaches to those with borderline, schizoid, and even psychotic diagnoses. Considerable progress has been made in understanding pre-Oedipal psychic states, and hard-and-fast distinctions between transference and narcissistic neuroses continue to erode as a result.

Fundamental concepts of psychoanalytic therapy include free association, abreaction, transference, resistance, and interpretation (of symptoms, dreams, fantasies, defenses, and character style). Greenson's (1967, Chapter 1) review of the components of classical psychoanalytic technique serves as the basis for what follows.

Free association has priority over all other means of producing material in the analytic situation. It is the major method of producing material in psychoanalysis, but free association is used only selectively in psychoanalytically oriented psychotherapies.

Transference is defined by Greenson as "the experiencing of feelings, drives, attitudes, fantasies, and defenses toward a person in the present which are inappropriate to that person and are a repetition, a displacement of reactions originating in regard to significant persons of early childhood" (p. 33). Transference repetitions bring into the analysis material that otherwise is inaccessible. Freud also used the term *transference neurosis* to describe that constellation of transference reactions in which the analyst and the analysis have become the center of the patient's emotional life and the patient's neurotic conflicts are relived in the analytic situation (Freud, 1914/1958). As Greenson indicated,

> Psychoanalytic technique is so geared as to insure the maximal development of the transference neurosis. . . . The transference neurosis is an artifact of the analytic situation; it can be undone only by the analytic work. It serves as a transition from illness to health. . . . In the anti-analytic forms of psychotherapy the transference reactions are not analyzed but gratified and manipulated and are believed to lead to fleeting "cures" ("transference cures") and last only as long as the idealized transference to the therapist is untouched. (p. 35)

Resistance refers to all the forces within the patient that oppose the procedures and processes of psychoanalytic work. Resistance, regardless of its source, operates through the ego and operates both consciously and unconsciously. Resistance is seen through repetitions of all of the defense operations that the patient has used in his or her past life. A major task of psychoanalytic therapy is to thoroughly and systematically analyze resistance to uncover how the patient resists, what is being resisted, and why the resistance occurs. Ultimately, resistances are efforts to ward off a traumatic state.

In psychoanalysis, a wide variety of therapeutic procedures are used, all having the direct aim of furthering self-insight. Others do not add insight but strengthen those ego functions that are required for gaining insight. For example, Greenson used abreaction as an example of a nonanalytic procedure that may permit a sufficient discharge of instinctual tension to reduce feelings of endangerment and render the ego secure enough to work analytically. The most important analytic procedure is interpretation, with all others subordinated to it both theoretically and practically.

The crux of actually "analyzing" a psychic phenomenon usually involves four distinct procedures (Greenson, 1967). These include *confrontation*, *clarification*, *interpretation*, and *working through*.

- *Confrontation* is the first step in analyzing a psychic phenomenon. The phenomenon in question has to be made explicit to the patient's awareness. For example, failure to show up for a session by Mrs. K. was understood by the analyst as related to a general tendency to avoid unpleasantness. In the previous session, "controversial" material had been discussed that made her feel that the analyst was angry at her (supposed) misbehavior. "The specific fear, embedded in a general avoidance of possible unpleasantness, was then confronted in the next session." The analyst said, "You missed your last session not because you 'forgot' but you were frightened that I was going to be angry with you!"
- *Clarification* refers to those activities that aim at placing the psychic phenomenon being analyzed in sharp focus. Significant details have to be identified and separated from extraneous matter. The particular variety or pattern of the phenomenon in question has to be singled out and isolated. Mrs. K's characteristic avoidance of her anger by projecting it onto others was shown by invoking instances where she feared retaliation from her own "boldness" (hostility). The clarification demonstrated how she projected her anger onto others, and her subsequent fear of rejection.
- *Interpretation* is the "procedure which distinguishes psychoanalysis from all other psychotherapies because in psychoanalysis interpretation is the ultimate and decisive instrument. . . . To interpret means to make an unconscious phenomenon conscious. . . . To make conscious the unconscious meaning, source, history, mode, or cause of a given psychic event" (Greenson, 1967, p. 39). In the instance of Mrs. K., the interpretation offered was that she was transferring (repeating) toward the analyst complex feelings of ambivalence toward her father, based on both correct and distorted images of him. Specifically, she had the unconscious belief that opposition toward him would lead to rejection and even abandonment. Her family history and personal recollections suggested that while her father was somewhat authoritarian with the children, she greatly distorted the extent of his wrath. Typically, an indication of a correct and timely interpretation is the response of the person, such as the flow of associations.

- *Working through* is the final step of the analyzing process, "a complex set of procedures and processes which occur after an insight has been given. The analytic work, which makes it possible for an insight to lead to change, is the work of working through. It refers in the main to the repetitive, progressive, and elaborate explanations of the resistances which prevent an insight from leading to change" (Greenson, 1967, p. 42). Change actually occurs through the working through. For Mrs. K., one aspect of working through involved demonstrating the many situations wherein hostile feelings on her part were projected onto others, particularly parental figures. The expectation of retaliatory punishment and rejection could then be seen as her own childlike fear of abandonment for noncompliance and willfulness. Insight regarding her use of projection as a resistance against contacting her own hostile feelings was followed up as its many guises were revealed. Self-affirmation began to be distinguished from hostility and selfishness as fears of abandonment abated.

Termination of psychotherapy is arrived at by mutual and satisfactory agreement that the major goals of treatment have been attained by patient and analyst and that the transference has been resolved.

A final concept, the *working alliance*, completes this survey of major analytic concepts and processes. "The working alliance is the relatively nonneurotic, rational relationship between the patient and analyst which makes it possible for the patient to work purposefully in the analytic situation. . . . The working alliance along with the neurotic suffering provide the incentive for doing the analytic work; the bulk of the raw material is provided by the patient's neurotic transference reactions" (Greenson, 1967, pp. 46–47).

It is the focus on unconscious determinants and the role of transference that distinguishes psychodynamic psychotherapy (Patton & Meara, 1992). As with other counseling approaches, immediate imperatives regarding coping; dealing with affective responses; negotiating familial, functional, social, and vocational consequences; and combating stigmatization dominate encounters. Contents influenced by a psychodynamic orientation regarding loss, grief, self-image, shame, anger, and depression, while not exclusive to psychodynamic exploration, are given a particular slant because practical and socially directed interventions are not necessarily helpful. The role and need for mourning the loss of a function and/or body part and its status as an object loss can be missed in procedures directed toward functional restoration.

Typical rehabilitation situations do not justify the elaborate therapeutic activity of psychoanalysis. Thomas and Siller (1999) have noted that

> long-term characterological analysis in the overwhelming majority of rehabilita-
> tion situations is not feasible for practical reasons. Short-term, focused psychoana-
> lytic exploration at best inevitably will be the most available. . . . Apart from
> practical questions of short- term versus long-term, there is the theoretical issue
> of relative usefulness of intensive character as contrasted with a more focused
> exploration. First, relatively few persons in the general population meet the
> criteria or have the desire for intensive character analysis. For most persons
> newly disabled, the imperatives almost always are elsewhere such as for functional
> restoration and the medical situation. With this understanding persons newly
> disabled in most instances will be unsuitable for intensive characterological
> interventions. . . . Sufficient help can be obtained for both those newly disabled
> and those with longer lasting conditions through the use of more focused inter-
> ventions. Intensive character analysis is the choice when the presence of disability
> is secondary in importance to the general needs and character of the person.
> (pp. 193–194)

REHABILITATION APPLICATIONS

Psychodynamic and psychoanalytic applications to rehabilitation and disability studies may be conveniently categorized into four broad areas: (a)
the use of defense mechanisms by people with physical disabilities during
the process of psychosocial adaptation; (b) the effect of disability on the
person's body image and self-perception; (c) the study of reactions to loss,
trauma, and disability (e.g., mourning, depression, denial, anger); and (d)
the meaning and structure of attitudes toward people with disabilities.

Study of Defense Mechanisms Within the Context
of Coping With Physical Disability

A cardinal contribution of psychoanalysis and ego psychology to the understanding of how the onset of physical and sensory disabilities affect the
individual is the study of the ego defense mechanisms. Defense mechanisms
are viewed as unconscious processes that are mobilized when the ego is
unable to ward off anxiety and other disturbing emotions or unacceptable
impulses. To succeed in alleviating these noxious internal states, the ego
may resort to a number of psychological defense maneuvers:

1. *Repression.* Forcing out of conscious awareness those intrapsychic
    conflicts and painful experiences (e.g., the person with a visible,

congenital disability repressing feelings of shame triggered by early-life reactions of others).

2. *Projection.* Casting out or externalizing unconscious forbidden ideas, needs, and impulses and attributing them to others (e.g., the person with a recently acquired disability who attributes lack of progress in rehabilitation to medical staff incompetence rather than to own lack of efforts; the individual who blames environmental conditions for the onset of lung cancer rather than to heavy smoking).

3. *Rationalization.* Using after-the-fact, false reasons for engaging in unacceptable behaviors so that negative emotions or consequences can be prevented (e.g., the person who gradually loses hearing and attributes lack of participation in a conversation to boredom or fatigue).

4. *Sublimation.* Adopting useful and socially acceptable behaviors to express forbidden and socially unacceptable wishes and impulses (e.g., anger toward, and wishes to retaliate against, an uncaring society may be channeled into artistic endeavors).

5. *Reaction formation.* Substituting and expressing responses and feelings that are exact opposites of those that are forbidden (e.g., parents who demonstrate extreme manifestations of loving behaviors or overprotectiveness, rather than the initial feelings of aversion and rejection, toward their child who was born with a severe disfigurement).

6. *Regression.* The reverting to childlike behaviors first exhibited by the individual during an earlier developmental stage (e.g., a recently disabled person whose temper tantrums are activated when needs are not immediately gratified).

7. *Compensation.* Seeking to excel in functionally related (direct or primary compensation) or unrelated (indirect or secondary compensation) activities or behaviors to make up for disability-generated loss (e.g., the person who lost sight at an early age and has achieved success as a musician). Compensatory activities may or may not undercut the satisfaction achieved with success. That is, subjectively, one's gratification of mastery may become contaminated by a failure to achieve one's real goal (e.g., wholeness and nonstigmatization).

These and other defense mechanisms in the context of rehabilitation and disability studies are briefly discussed by Castelnuovo-Tedesco (1981), Cook (1998), Cubbage and Thomas (1989), Grzesiak and Hicok (1994), Kruger (1981–82), Livneh (1986), Neiderland (1965), and Siller (1960).

Finally, related concepts, although not traditionally regarded as defense mechanisms, are primary and secondary gain. Primary gain refers to those symptoms and behaviors directly linked to alleviation of the stress-inducing affect. Secondary gain, on the other hand, addresses some form of exploiting social (e.g., familial, occupational) sanctions, permitting the affected individual not to engage in previously performed roles and activities (e.g., the person with low back discomfort who refuses to discontinue receiving social security benefits or resume household chores, even after the condition has improved).

Disability Impact on Body Image and Self-Perception

Body image is the unconscious representation of one's own body (Schilder, 1950). Following the early contributions of Head (1920), who proposed that people create a set of reference models (schemata) of their own body structure, Schilder expanded those proposals to perceive body image as residing at the core of self-image, self-concept, and even personal identity and reflecting a three-dimensional image of symbolic and emotional significance including personal, interpersonal, environmental, and temporal dimensions (McDaniel, 1976; Shontz, 1975).

Chronic illnesses and disabilities are thought to alter, even to distort, the body image and therefore also the self-concept, because the imposed physical changes must be confronted by the person (Falvo, 1999). Furthermore, problems that stem from the new disability-associated reality (e.g., pain, disfigurement, sensory and mobility limitations, cognitive distortions) all threaten the stability of the body image and necessitate changes in its structure and dynamic operations (Bramble, 1995). Successful psychosocial adaptation to a disabling condition includes the integration of the imposed physical changes into a reconstructed body image and, therefore, personal identity. Unsuccessful adaptation, in contrast, is marked by physical experiences and psychiatric symptoms that often include psychogenic pain, chronic fatigue and energy depletion, feelings of anxiety, depression, and anger, social withdrawal, and attempts at denying loss or impaired functioning of the involved body part(s).

In the context of psychoanalytic theorizing, the onset of adventitious physical disability is tantamount to a profound narcissistic injury, since narcissism and body image progress in parallel routes during the course of normal human development (Grzesiak & Hicok, 1994). Moreover, since the body (or part of the body) is the initial object being cathected by the developing ego (Siller, 1988; Szasz, 1957), the body image acquires archaic and symbolic meanings. Injury to the body, therefore, particularly at early developmental stages, often results in identity confusion, impoverished self-esteem, and emotional distress (Greenacre, 1958).

In a similar vein, Neiderland (1965) and Castelnuovo-Tedesco (1981) contended that an early body defect leads to a narcissistic injury (at times referred to a narcissistic ego impairment) and, therefore, to an unresolved conflict because of its concreteness, permanency, and association with archaic forms of anxiety (e.g., body disintegration anxiety, castration anxiety). This unresolved narcissistic injury results in a disrupted body image and, consequently, may lead to an unrealistic self-concept that, although often distorted, may also give rise to heightened intellectual and artistic creativity. When the narcissistic injury expresses itself in a compensatory fashion, it may lead to increased aggressiveness, excessive vulnerability, impaired object relations, self-aggrandizement, and even delusional beliefs (Castelnuovo-Tedesco, 1978, 1981; Grzesiak & Hicok, 1994; Krystal & Petty, 1961; Neiderland, 1965).

Of utmost importance is the developmental stage during which the disability was acquired. Narcissistic injuries during the separation-individuation, Oedipal, and adolescent stages are thought to render the individual most vulnerable to body image distortion, self-representation instability, and self-concept traumatization (Castelnuovo-Tedesco, 1981; Earle, 1979). Loss or removal of body parts is fraught with potential psychological disturbances, and their gain or addition (e.g., organ transplantation) could be equally disturbing. The transplant situation triggers heightened life-death anxieties because the transplant organ is often obtained from a dead person or from a donor whose life may now be in greater jeopardy (e.g., kidney donors). Thoughts may then result of having robbed the donor of vital organs and the accompanying feelings of guilt, self-blame, and fears of punishment (Castelnuovo-Tedesco, 1978). Further discussion of the role of body image in the context of disability studies may be found in Block and Ventur (1963) and Lussier (1980).

Psychosocial Reactions to Loss and Disability

Numerous theoretical and clinical accounts of the nature, structure, and temporal sequencing of psychosocial reactions to the onset of chronic illnesses and physical disabilities have been provided in the literature. Tacit in all of the accounts is the assumption that a discernible order of reactions exists to account for the ways that the individual responds, copes with, or reacts to the newly acquired condition. Among psychoanalytically influenced writings are those of Bellak (1952), Blank (1961), Cubbage and Thomas (1989), Degan (1975), Engel (1962), Gunther (1971), Kruger (1981–82), Krystal and Petty (1961), Langer (1994), Neff and Weiss (1961), Nemiah (1964), Siller (1976), and Thomas and Siller (1999).

Most of the above writers view the process of psychosocial adaptation to the onset of a physically disabling condition as (a) reflecting a symbolic transition from possessing a "normal" or "whole" body ("former self") to that which is not complete or whole ("present self"); (b) having to accept a loss of previously attained physical, psychological, and social selves; (c) creating a need for a period of mourning (grieving) for the lost body part or function that, upon its successful resolution, leads to a reconstructed self-image as a person with a disability; (d) being determined by the symbolic meaning (both in its narcissistic connotations and functional impairment) of the disability and body parts involved, to the individual and society; and (e) following a complex series of psychic activities in which (i) cathexes are first withdrawn from the injured ego as well as from the outside world, and then after a period of denial (serving as a defensive role in minimizing the disability and its consequences), (ii) energies are gradually reinvested in a new body and self-images, alternative needs and gratification, and the reestablishment of contact with a newly perceived reality.

The following reactions of adaptation to the disability experience (often viewed as mostly internally determined psychosocial phases) are typically addressed in the psychoanalytically derived literature: (a) shock, disbelief, and chaotic disruption; (b) anxiety (injury, loss, and disability, such as blindness and amputation, are said to reawake archaic castration anxiety); (c) grief, mourning, and depression related to real object loss (and the necessitated changes in narcissistic investments, emotional cathexes, and self-image); (d) denial of illness or disability (denial of affect associated with the nature, functional implications, extent, or seriousness of the condition); (e) anger and aggression (turned inwardly and resulting in feelings of guilt and shame, or turned outwardly to trigger feelings of other-blame and need for revenge); and (f) adjustment and restitution (a successful resolution of the "work of mourning" and reformation of the self-image).

Attitudes Toward People with Disabilities

The origins, formation, and structure of attitudes toward people with disabilities have been addressed extensively from a psychodynamic perspective. Earlier psychoanalytic views posited that the often observed negative societal attitudes toward people with disabilities may be traced to (a) the belief that disability is an unjust punishment for sinful acts; (b) the projection of one's unacceptable impulses and wishes upon those with disabilities (those who were justly punished) since they are least likely to retaliate; (c) the perception that, if disability is an unjust punishment, then the person with disability is motivated to commit an evil act to counteract the injustice and is, therefore, dangerous and should be avoided; (d) unresolved conflicts over scopophilia and exhibitionism, during early psychosexual stages of development that trigger fascination/attraction versus repulsion/ avoidance conflict over seeing a person with a disability; (e) "guilt by association" that may render the nondisabled person as maladjusted, possibly resulting in social ostracism if interacting with people who are disabled; (f) guilt of being nondisabled when the other person has lost an important body part or function and is permanently affected by it (akin to the "survivor's guilt" phenomenon); (g) disability as a reminder of death, since loss and disability symbolize death and destruction, thereby rekindling archaic fears of annihilation and serving as reminders of mortality; and (h) disability as a threat to one's intact body image that reawakens earlier castration anxiety, along with fears of losing physical integrity (Barker, Wright, Meyerson, & Gonick, 1953; Blank, 1957; Degan, 1975; Livneh, 1982; Siller, 1976, 1984; Siller, Chipman, Ferguson, & Vann, 1967; Wright, 1983).

Siller and associates (Siller, 1970, 1984; Siller et al., 1967), in a multifaceted and extended series of studies, investigated the structure of attitudes toward persons with various disabilities. They concluded that attitudes toward persons with disabilities are, indeed, multidimensional in nature and typically reflect such components as interaction strain, rejection of intimacy, generalized rejection, authoritarian virtuousness, inferred emotional consequences, distressed identification, and imputed functional limitations, each of which may have different developmental and personological roots.

CASE EXAMPLE

Mr. J. B. was referred by his attorney to one of the authors (JS) for psychological counseling, in part to support a legal action for damages received while at work, and in part to provide psychological support for emotional distress in connection with his disability. The first session occurred approximately one year after an accident where Mr. J. B. was hit and pinned against a wall by a heavy weight that lurched forward because of a mechanical failure of a restraining part. His injuries included a crushed left leg that required an above-knee amputation and "minor" head injuries requiring stitches in the temporal area. A psychological report stated that his memory and other cognitive symptoms seemed to be "consistent with a post-concussion syndrome." About three months later, he was fitted for a prosthesis and began physical therapy and walking instructions that were continued at the time he was first seen in counseling.

Mr. J. B. was 49 years old at the time of the accident and had been working as the manager of the machine shop when injured. He was born and raised in Greece, and he moved to the United States about 10 years before the injury. His wife and two children lived in Greece, and long periods of separation from his family had been a way of life, although he was now considering returning to Greece. Since his injury he has lived with a brother and his family.

While profoundly distressed about his new status as a person with a disability, his presence in counseling was initiated by his attorney, primarily as a legal strategy. He appeared to be a pragmatic, sincere, and serious family and work-oriented person who was accustomed to working methodically, independently, and responsibly. The aftermath of his injuries was devastating, and he was trying to reconstitute himself functionally through applying himself to the prosthetic program. His emotional state was more problematic because he had no clear reference as to how to cope with strong feelings of stigmatization, shame, and diminished self-regard. He was seen for psychological counseling once per week for almost six months.

The first five sessions were focused mostly on information, limited mostly to the accident and present rehabilitation efforts, daily life, and background status. As focus shifted from the "external" situation to feelings about insecurities and fear of the future, a modified form of psychoanalytic psychotherapy was used. His report of dreams was encouraged, but interpretations were conservatively advanced and limited to issues germane to rehabilitation. A major stimulus for the shift to psychodynamic intervention was emotional distress created by the realization that prosthetic restoration had reached a plateau and was being terminated, far short of achieving his expectations.

Within the five sessions, the first three concentrated upon the themes of prosthetic restoration and his insecurity about his mobility, language, and memory. At the fourth session he began to speak of his sensitivity and awkwardness in being seen by people who knew him from before the accident, separation from his family, and feelings of "being less than a man." Transference occurred to the therapist as a rational authority; the therapist was viewed impersonally as a possible vehicle of benefit with expert status regarding disability. He experienced despair about his ultimate ability to use his prosthesis comfortably and effectively, although he was actively walking and exercising. Major resistances then appeared to be based in denial of the functional consequences of his amputation and concealment of the affect of shame. He was also concerned about his short-term memory. Neuropsychological testing revealed difficulty in attending and concentrating, slow but within normal range motor speed, no perceptual or auditory dysfunction, no evidence of aphasia, but significant impairment in linguistic skill, with an IQ in the average range and memory within normal limits. The cognitive difficulties, particularly in attention and concentration, appeared to be symptoms of postconcussion syndrome, possibly accounting for the self-reported memory difficulties.

The nature of counseling changed by the sixth session, since he was distraught about the failure of the prosthesis to return him to his original functional status. The therapist confronted him, indicating that he was underestimating the value of his prosthesis, because it was enabling him to move and travel quite well. Referring to a phrase he had already used, "I feel less of a man," an interpretation was offered: "You are feeling inadequate as a person physically and sexually, and in most respects your fantasy of being made whole by the prosthesis has been exploded." It was suggested that the main purpose of treatment was to restore his self-regard and appreciation of himself in a realistic context. His emotional distress enabled expansion of counseling from the prosthetic and functional focus to questions of self-regard, manhood, social worth, and more. His reticence about opening up emotionally to a stranger lessened and a new phase began.

The extended and only partially successful efforts at prosthetic restoration complicated body and self-image adaptation. Socket adjustments were frequently being made. Phantom sensations were present but did not seem to be a general concern. At the sixth session, when asked if anything was bothering him, he replied, "One of the worst times for me comes when retiring for the night. Taking off the prosthesis gives me the reality that I'm missing my leg." Talking about sleep and having to see his stump opened two lines of inquiry: the nature of his dreams and the process of mourning his lost part and status.

He generally did not have disturbing dreams, although there was a recurrent dream about a feeling of falling in space. He was not attuned to probing his dreams and was unable to pursue an associative path. He was asked whether he had such dreams before the injury and whether he felt that they were now connected with the injury. He did not remember having them before but stated that they might be connected to his balance and walking with a prosthesis. While agreeing that it was a likely connection, subsequent intervention was designed to go beyond the physical to more general insecurities. In effect, the therapeutic direction was to confront and to clarify the resistance through which he was trying to contain the unpleasantness of his self-feelings as a diminished man by focusing upon the functional/physical realm. Counseling returned to issues previously touched on at a more intellectualized level, such as stigmatization and fear of the future, with an extended perspective based upon transference and resistance.

In the next session, he was urged to further address feelings about seeing his stump. There appeared to be mixed feelings about his level of impairment, and the discussion was directed to the connection between his despair and his embarrassment at being seen by those who knew him from before. He observed that he was less uncomfortable at home with his brother's family, and for the first time the session was almost entirely directed toward emotional matters.

Prior adaptations to the expectations of his family and self now needed revision to restore value in his own eyes. Returning to an early theme of the need to mourn, the concept of mourning his loss of limb was discussed, along with impaired mobility and self-regard. As he was getting more comfortable with and less defensive about such considerations, the naturalness of mourning, placed in the context of all significant losses, became more acceptable and not a sign of weakness and unmanliness. During this period, there was an exacerbation of disturbing dreams involving potential danger (e.g., being on a ship in a hurricane, recurring thoughts of the accident). Work on interpreting dreams, along with discussions about his past and present relationships and feelings, helped to expand his sense of self and the disturbed dreams became less threatening. Near the end of counseling, he was much more active and insightful as to how much he determined his emotional state.

After some 20 sessions, Mr. J. B. left for a visit to family in Greece, and soon afterward a settlement was reached in his legal action, and he returned to Greece permanently. A telephone follow-up indicated that sensitivities, anxieties, and mood swings continued, but that he had a generally better feeling about his condition. Encountering former friends or coworkers had become easier. There were few disturbing dreams, and when they occurred, he thought of them along the lines that we had addressed. He also commented about more appreciative feelings toward his prosthesis.

The counseling experience was successful to the extent that a lessening of most of the complaints was achieved and the ability to appreciate the value of his prosthesis was enhanced by attention to the magical thinking surrounding it. Facilitating mourning by interpreting denial of affect and questions of "manhood" helped to make the prosthesis a support rather than a failure of fantasies about restoration. Technically, the major vehicle of change resided in a shift in transference. Rather than seeing the counselor as an objective and impersonal "disability expert," a more positive transference developed: seeing the counselor as a source of help with feelings and as someone who would not devalue him when he revealed his self-doubts and fears. Analytic tools of dream analysis, interpretation, confrontation, clarification, insight, working through, and analysis of resistance were used, but primarily in a modulated and selective way.

RESEARCH FINDINGS

Because of the scope and focus of this chapter, it is not reasonable to provide complete coverage of the extensive research findings generated by psychodynamic theory and therapy. Three broad research trends are evident in the extant literature: (a) the study of psychoanalytically derived concepts, such as defense mechanisms, the nature and function of dreams, and unconscious motivation; (b) the effectiveness of psychodynamic therapy; and (c) disability and rehabilitation applied research (e.g., the symbolic meaning of loss and disability, the structure of attitudes toward people with disability, body image and disability).

Research on Freudian Theory

Freud was quite skeptical of the value of empirical research on psychoanalytic concepts and procedures. For him, each session was an experiment in itself, and psychoanalysis needed no other support. For many years research on psychoanalytic theory and practice did nothing to disabuse this notion. More recent work is more reflective of the true character of the phenomena studied, and optimism is increasing regarding the possibility of subjecting psychoanalytic concepts to more adequate verification (e.g., Bornstein & Masling, 1998; Fisher & Greenberg, 1978, 1985). Significant problems, however, must be recognized. For example, Freudian theory, rather than being a unified coherent theory, is an amalgam of many theories. Further, as a psychology stressing unconscious phenomena, it deals with derivatives of the unconscious not directly reflected in behavioral acts. In addition, the complexity and abstractness of many psychoanalytic concepts render them very difficult to measure. The tautological nature of some of the constructs also may preclude direct refutation of their existence and operation. Yet, an enormous body of empirical research has been accumulated on psychoanalytic theory and practice. The results are equivocal, but as Kline (1981) concludes after a major critical review of empirical research on psychoanalytic theory: (a) much of the metapsychology is unscientific in that it cannot be subjected to any kind of empirical test and so be refuted (e.g., death instinct, pleasure principle); and (b) much of psychoanalytic theory consists of empirical propositions that can be tested, and many of the Freudian concepts most important to psychoanalytic theory have been supported (e.g., repression, the Oedipus complex). Kline concludes, "The status of psychoanalytic theory must now be clear. It must be retained not as a whole but only after rigorous objective research has revealed what parts are correct or false or in need of modification" (pp. 446–447). The reader may find additional sources on empirical studies in Bornstein and Masling (1998), Fisher and Greenberg (1978, 1985), and Maddi (2000).

Despite the equivocal empirical support, psychodynamic theory and research have enriched psychological testing immensely by introducing projective techniques into the mainstream of assessment. Projective tools include the Rorschach Inkblot Technique, the Thematic Apperception Test (TAT), the Draw-A-Person Test, the House-Tree-Person Test, the various word association procedures, the Blacky (Pictures) Test, and the more recent measures of defense mechanisms, including the Defense Mechanisms Inventory (DMI; Gleser & Ihilevich, 1969) and the Repression-Sensitization (R-S) Scale (Byrne, 1961).

Effectiveness of Psychoanalytically Derived Psychodynamic Therapy

It has been argued that adequate empirical studies to assess the effectiveness of psychoanalytically oriented therapy are scarce because of its complexity and the virtually impossible task of trying to control the many variables involved (Arlow, 2000). Moreover, Fisher and Greenberg (1985) speculated that comparisons of therapeutic efficacy between psychoanalytic therapy and other therapeutic approaches are doomed to failure because "the evidence indicates that there is no one conception of what psychoanalytic therapy is" (p. 41) and many analysts do not view change, especially behavioral change, as a primary therapeutic goal.

Earlier efforts by Fenichel (1930) and Knight (1941), as well as occasional studies by the American Psychoanalytic Association (Arlow, 2000;

Fisher & Greenberg, 1985), suggested that successful therapeutic outcomes typically ranged from a low of 25% (for patients diagnosed with psychoses) to a high of 65–75% (for patients diagnosed with neuroses). Meta-analytic studies in the 1980s and 1990s (Lipsey & Wilson, 1993; Prioleau, Murdock, & Brody, 1983; Shapiro & Shapiro, 1982; Smith, Glass, & Miller, 1980) found psychoanalytic and other psychodynamic therapies to be equal to slightly less effective than cognitive-behavioral therapies. In their review of controlled outcome research, Prochaska and Norcross (1999) concluded, "The measurable outcomes of psychoanalytic psychotherapy and short-term psychodynamic psychotherapy are superior to no treatment and slightly to considerably inferior to alternative psychotherapies" (p. 60).

The efficacy of psychotherapy is a complex and thorny issue. Psychodynamically based therapies do not foster a direct cause-and-effect link, and their effects are more diffuse and character-related. Goals and outcomes that focus on behavioral change only depict one isolated aspect of the complex nature of human experience. For other detailed reviews of the efficacy of psychoanalytic therapies, the reader is referred to Fisher and Greenberg (1985), Meltzoff and Kornreich (1970), Prochaska and Norcross (1999), and Roth and Fonagy (1996).

As methodological improvements occur and more appropriate evaluation and research studies are reported, increasing evidence will be forthcoming to substantiate the value of psychoanalytic psychotherapies. In 1997, Psychoanalytic Inquiry (Lazar, Ed.) published a supplement to their journal, with 12 articles supporting psychoanalytic therapies in various terms, including cost-effectiveness, clinical effectiveness, and public health. For example, Doidge (1997) reviewed the empirical evidence for psychoanalytic therapies and psychoanalysis and indicated that they are the most widely practiced of the more than 100 different types of psychotherapy. The results of studies consistently confirm the effectiveness of both psychoanalytic therapy and psychoanalysis when used with appropriate patient populations, with improvement rates of 60–90%.

Applied Research in Disability and Rehabilitation

Body Image and Adaptation to Disability

In a series of studies, Druss and associates (Druss, 1986; Druss, O'Connor, Prudden, & Stern, 1968; Druss, O'Connor, & Stern, 1969, 1972) explored changes in body image and psychosocial adaptation of patients who underwent colostomy and ileostomy following chronic ulcerative colitis and bowel cancer. The authors noted that, immediately after surgery, patients experienced shock and depressive reactions. Loss of a highly valued organ, the sense of mutilation, and heightened body awareness appeared evident. Furthermore, support was found for the notion of parallelism between surgery and feelings of castration and between the stoma and phallus. Research on disturbances of body image was also reported following spinal cord injury and brain injuries (Arnhoff & Mehl, 1963; Fink & Shontz, 1960; Mitchell, 1970; Nelson & Gruver, 1978; Shontz, 1956; Wachs & Zaks, 1960) and following limb amputation (Bhojak & Nathawat, 1988; Centers & Centers, 1963; Rybarczyk, Nyenhuis, Nicholas, Cash, & Kaiser, 1995).

Castration Anxiety, Death Anxiety, Object Representations, and Attitudes Toward People With Disabilities

The relationships between attitudes toward people with disabilities and several psychoanalytically derived personality constructs have been investigated. A number of empirical studies focused on the relationship between castration anxiety and intrapsychic perceptions (expressed as endorsed attitudes) of people with physical disabilities. The authors (Baracca, 1991; Fine, 1979; Follansbee, 1981; Gladstone, 1977; all cited in Thomas & Siller, 1999) investigated the effects of castration anxiety and level of object representation on attitudes toward persons with disabilities, using the Siller et al. (1967) Disability Factor Scales-General (DFS-G) measure. The findings suggested, albeit weakly, the following: (a) heightened castration anxiety is positively associated with more negative attitudes toward those with disabilities; (b) among preschool children, those who scored higher on castration anxiety (using the Blacky Test) also manifested more negative attitudes toward others with disabilities; (c) increased narcissistic vulnerability was found to be associated with more negative attitudes; and (d) those with more rigid defense mechanisms (using the Defense Mechanisms Inventory) were more rejecting of persons with physical disabilities (object relations theory views defenses as a central function of the ego in its efforts to ward off anxiety and stress, both triggered by a threat to one's own body integrity).

Finally, negative attitudes toward those with physical disabilities are posited by psychoanalytic theory to be linked to fears of insults to one's own body integrity (e.g., castration anxiety) and also to loss of one's life (i.e., death anxiety). Indeed, it was conjectured that archaic fears of physical deterioration and death are triggered when faced with situations that constitute symbolic reminders of death, such as the presence of a person with a visible disability. Empirical support for these notions was reported by Enders (1979), Fish (1981), and Livneh (1985).

Loss, Mourning, and Disability

Classical psychoanalytic theory regards the mourning process as a gradual decathexis of the mental representation of, and the affective investments in, the lost object (Frankiel, 1994). Disability-related conceptualizations equate the mourning process engendered by the death of significant others (interpersonal loss) with that triggered by loss of body parts or functions (personal loss). Research by Parkes (1972a, 1972b, 1975) comparing the psychosocial reactions of widows and people with amputation indicated that similar phases of grief and realization (e.g., shock, denial, depression, anger, acceptance), as well as defensive processes, were experienced by both groups.

PROMINENT STRENGTHS AND LIMITATIONS

General Strengths

- Psychoanalytically derived psychodynamic insights have been applied to therapy, dream interpretation, humor, child-rearing practices, educational and learning experiences, vocational development and occupational choice, history, religion and mythology, art, music, literature, political and social organizations, anthropology, psychological testing (projective techniques), and daily human experiences (slips of the tongue, gestures, symptomatic acts).
- Psychoanalytic theory provides the clinician with an extremely rich perspective on human emotions, cognitions, and behaviors. Its conceptual structure offers an unequaled opportunity to enjoin human functioning as a multileveled and multidetermined phenomenon.

Rehabilitation-Related Strengths

- Psychoanalytically derived psychodynamic concepts are well entrenched in rehabilitation practice (e.g., defense mechanisms, secondary gain, and body image).
- Adopting a psychodynamic perspective enables rehabilitation practitioners to focus on subjective and unique meanings of loss, grief,

and disability on the part of the affected individual and his or her family members.
- The psychodynamic approach affords the rehabilitation practitioner a dynamic and developmental perspective on the process of adaptation to disability across the lifespan (Cubbage & Thomas, 1989; Thurer, 1986).

General Limitations

- Problems of tautology, refutability, and controlled research make global assessment of the theory and its elements impossible. There is no global theory and, while various elements have received support, others have not, and many simply have not been adequately defined or tested (e.g., cathexis, id, libido).
- Clinical observations from case studies are often anecdotal in nature, uncontrolled for bias, and not representative of the general clinical population.
- Some classical psychoanalytic concepts, such as castration anxiety, penis envy, libido, and development of the woman's superego, have been strongly criticized as being gender- biased.
- Psychodynamic therapy focuses primarily on intrapsychic issues and conflicts and neglects broader social contexts (e.g., family dysfunction, social problems). This limitation, while operating in certain instances particularly in the past, seems archaic in the face of the reality of modern psychoanalysis. The role of the family and society was fundamental to psychoanalysis from the beginning, and nonlibidinal object relations, self theory, and adult relationships abound as prime factors in theory and clinical work.
- Assessment measures of clients' affective status and behavior have low validity and reliability (e.g., projective techniques), are highly subjective, and often lack standardization in administration, scoring, and interpretation (Ford & Urban, 1998; Liebert & Liebert, 1998; Maddi, 2000; Prochaska & Norcross, 1999).

Rehabilitation-Related Limitations

- Earlier, a rationale for short-term focused psychoanalytic exploration in the rehabilitation context was offered. Time constraints, lack of trained personnel, inability to meet the prerequisites of verbal capacity, diminished personal insight, and limitations induced by certain cognitive impairments (e.g., MR/DD clients, clients who sustained traumatic brain injury, clients with severe mental illness) are realities in rehabilitation. The practice of rehabilitation appropriately recognizes the importance of the "here and now" for the client.

- Psychoanalytically derived therapy emphasizes abstract, reflective, and insight-building processes, while rehabilitation focuses on concrete and pragmatic goals, emphasizing vocational and independent living pursuits.
- The goal of psychoanalytically driven therapy in rehabilitation is likely to focus on symptom alleviation and anxiety reduction rather than reconstructing personality, supporting defenses and dealing with self-feelings and projections into the future. As stated by Siller (1969), "The aim of [rehabilitation] is to assist the person toward reformulating a self that approves of continuing to be despite important discontinuities with its past identity. Specifically this means the promotion of a new self-image predicated on worth, rather than on deficiency and self-contempt" (p. 20, in Siller & Thomas, 1995). Rehabilitation requires a larger canvas within a team environment, merging medical attention, skill acquisition, education, and adaptation to disability. Psychoanalytic sensitivity to unconscious issues such as mourning and object loss can be invaluable for a newly disabled individual. The psychodynamic intervention, therefore, must occur within the larger rehabilitation context.

REFERENCES

Arlow, J. A. (2000). Psychoanalyis. In R. J. Corsini & D. Wedding (Eds.), *Current psychotherapies* (6th ed.). Itasca, IL: Peacock.

Arlow, J. A., & Brenner, C. (1964). *Psychoanalytic concepts and structural theory*. New York: International Universities Press.

Arnhoff, F. N., & Mehl, M. C. (1963). Body image deterioration in paraplegia. *Journal of Nervous and Mental Disease, 134,* 88–92.

Barker, R. G., Wright, B. A., Meyerson, L., & Gonick, M. R. (1953). *Adjustment to physical handicaps and illness: A survey of the social psychology of physique and disability* (rev. ed.). New York: Social Science Research Council.

Bellak, L. (1952). Introduction. In L. Bellak (Ed.), *Psychology of physical illness* (pp. 1–14). New York: Grune & Stratton.

Bhojak, M. M., & Nathawat, S. S. (1988). Body image, hopelessness, and personality dimensions in lower limb amputees. *Indian Journal of Psychiatry, 30,* 161–165.

Blank, H. R. (1957). Psychoanalysis and blindness. *Psychoanalytic Quarterly, 26,* 1–24.

Blank, H. R. (1961). The challenge of rehabilitation. *Israel Medical Journal, 20,* 127–142.

Block, W. E., & Ventur, P. A.(1963). A study of the psychoanalytic concept of castration anxiety in symbolically castrated amputees. *Psychiatric Quarterly, 37,* 518–526.

Bornstein, R. F., & Masling, J. M. (Eds.). (1998). *Empirical perspectives on the psychoanalytic unconscious.* Washington, DC: American Psychological Association.

Bramble, K. (1995). Body image. In I. M. Lubkin (Ed.), *Chronic illness: Impact and interventions* (3rd ed., pp. 285–299). Boston: Jones and Bartlett.

Byrne, D. (1961). The Repression-Sensitization Scale: Rationale, reliability, and validity. *Journal of Personality, 29,* 334–349.

Castelnuovo-Tedesco, P. (1978). Ego vicissitudes in response to replacement or loss of body parts: Certain analogies to events during psychoanalytic treatment. *Psychoanalytic Quarterly, 47,* 381–397.

Castelnuovo-Tedesco, P. (1981). Psychological consequences of physical defects: A psychoanalytic perspective. *International Review of Psycho-Analysis, 8,* 145–154.

Centers, L., & Centers, R. (1963). A comparison of the body images of amputee and non-amputee children as revealed in figure drawings. *Journal of Projective Techniques, 27,* 158–165.

Cook, D. (1998). Psychosocial impact of disability. In R. M. Parker & E. M. Szymanski (Eds.), *Rehabilitation counseling: Basics and beyond* (3rd ed., pp. 303–326). Austin, TX: Pro-Ed.

Cubbage, M. E., & Thomas, K. R. (1989). Freud and disability. *Rehabilitation Psychology, 34,* 161–173.

Degan, M. J. (1975). The symbolic passage from the living to the dead for the visibly injured. *International Journal of Symbology, 6,* 1–14.

Dewald, P. A. (1978). The process of change in psychoanalytic psychotherapy. *Archives of General Psychiatry, 35,* 535–542.

Doidge, N. (1997). Empirical evidence for the efficacy of psychoanalytic therapies and psychoanalysis. In S. G. Lazar (Ed.), *Extended dynamic therapy: Making the case in an age of managed care. Psychoanalytic Inquiry* (Suppl.), 102–150. Hillsdale, NJ: Analytic Press.

Druss, R. G. (1986). Psychotherapy of patients with serious intercurrent medical illness (cancer). *Journal of the American Academy of Psychoanalysis, 14,* 459–472.

Druss, R. G., O'Connor, J. F., Prudden, J. F, & Stern, L. O. (1968). Psychological response to colectomy. *Archives of General Psychiatry, 18,* 53–59.

Druss, R. G., O'Connor, J. F., & Stern, L. O. (1969). Psychologic response to colectomy: II. Adjustment to a permanent colostomy. *Archives of General Psychiatry, 20,* 419–427.

Druss, R. G., O'Connor, J. F., & Stern, L. O. (1972). Changes in body image following ileostomy. *Psychoanalytic Quarterly, 41,* 195–206.

Earle, E. (1979). The psychological effects of mutilating surgery in children and adolescents. *Psychoanalytic Study of the Child, 34,* 527–546.

Enders, J. E. (1979). Fear of death and attitudinal dispositions toward physical disability. *Dissertation Abstracts International, 39,* 7161A (University Microfilms No. 79-11825).

Engel, G. L. (1962). *Psychological development in health and disease.* Philadelphia: Saunders.

Erikson, E. (1950). *Childhood and society.* New York: Norton.

Erikson, E. (1968). *Identity: Youth and crisis*. New York: Norton.

Falvo, D. R. (1999). *Medical and psychosocial aspects of chronic illness and disability* (2nd ed.). Gaithersburg, MD: Aspen.

Fenichel, O. (1930). *Ten years of the Berlin Psychoanalytic Institute (1920–1930)*. Berlin: Author.

Fenichel, O. (1945). *The psychoanalytic theory of neurosis*. New York: Norton.

Fine, R. (1973). Psychoanalysis. In R. Corsini (Eds.), *Current psychotherapies* (pp. 1–33). Itasca, IL: Peacock.

Fink, S. L., & Shontz, F. C. (1960). Body-image disturbances in chronically ill individuals. *Journal of Nervous and Mental Diseases, 131,* 234–240.

Fish, D. E. (1981). Counselor effectiveness: Relationship to death anxiety and attitudes toward disabled persons. *Dissertation Abstracts International, 42,* 1488A (University Microfilms No. 81-21927).

Fisher, S., & Greenberg, R. P. (Eds.) (1978). *The scientific evaluation of Freud's theories and therapy: A book of readings*. New York: Basic Books.

Fisher, S., & Greenberg, A. P. (1985). *The scientific credibility of Freud's theories and therapy*. New York: Columbia University Press.

Ford, D. H., & Urban, H. B. (1998). *Contemporary models of psychotherapy: A comparative analysis* (2nd ed.). New York: Wiley.

Frankiel, R. V. (Ed.). (1994). *Essential papers on object loss*. New York: New York University Press.

Freud, A. (1946). *The ego and the mechanisms of defense*. New York: International Universities Press. (Original work published 1936)

Freud, S. (1958). Remembering, repeating, and working through. In J. Strachey (Ed. & Trans.), *The standard edition of the complete psychological works of Sigmund Freud* (Vol. 12, pp. 145–156). London: Hogarth Press. (Original work published 1914)

Freud, S. (1959). Inhibitions, symptoms, and anxiety. In J. Strachey (Ed. & Trans.), *The standard edition of the complete psychological works of Sigmund Freud* (Vol. 20, pp. 75–173). London: Hogarth Press. (Original work published 1926)

Freud, S. (1961). The ego and the id. In J. Strachey (Ed. & Trans.), *The standard edition of the complete psychological works of Sigmund Freud* (Vol. 19, pp. 3–66). London: Hogarth Press. (Original work published 1923)

Freud, S. (1964). New introductory lectures on psychoanalysis. In J. Strachey (Ed. & Trans.), *The standard edition of the complete psychological works of Sigmund Freud* (Vol. 22, pp. 3–182). London: Hogarth Press. (Original work published 1933)

Gleser, G. C., & Ihilevich, D. (1969). An objective instrument for measuring defense mechanisms. *Journal of Consulting and Clinical Psychology, 33,* 51–60.

Greenacre, P. (1958). Early physical determinants in the development of the sense of identity. *Journal of the American Psychoanalytic Association, 6,* 612–627.

Greenson, R. R. (1967). *The technique and practice of psychoanalysis*. New York: International Universities Press.

Grzesiak, R. C., & Hicok, D. A. (1994). A brief history of psychotherapy and physical disability. *American Journal of Psychotherapy, 48,* 240–250.

Gunther, M. S. (1971). Psychiatric consultation in a rehabilitation hospital: A regression hypothesis. *Comprehensive Psychiatry, 12,* 572–585.

Hartmann, H. (1964). *Essays on ego psychology: Selected problems in psychoanalytic theory*. New York: International Universities Press.

Head, H. (1920). *Studies in neurology, Vol. II*. London: Oxford University Press.

Kline, P. (1981). *Fact and fantasy in Freudian theory* (2nd ed.). London: Methuen.

Knight, R. P. (1941). Evaluation of the results of psychoanalytic therapy. *American Journal of Psychiatry, 98*, 434–446.

Kohut, H. (1971). *The analysis of the self*. New York: International Universities Press.

Kohut, H. (1977). *The restoration of the self*. New York: International Universities Press.

Kohut, H. (1984). *How does analysis cure?* Chicago: University of Chicago Press.

Kruger, D. W. (1981–82). Emotional rehabilitation of the physical rehabilitation patient. *International Journal of Psychiatry in Medicine, 11*, 183–191.

Krystal, H., & Petty, T. A. (1961). The psychological process of normal convalescence. *Psychosomatics, 2*, 366–372.

Langer, K. G. (1994). Depression and denial in psychotherapy of persons with disabilities. *American Journal of Psychotherapy, 48*, 181–194.

Lazar, S. G. (Ed.) (1997). Extended dynamic therapy: Making the case in an age of managed care. *Psychoanalytic Inquiry* (Suppl.). Hillsdale, NJ: Analytic Press.

Liebert, R. M., & Liebert, L. L. (1998). *Liebert and Spiegler's personality strategies and issues* (8th ed.). Pacific Grove, CA: Brooks/Cole.

Lipsey, M. W., & Wilson, D. B. (1993). The efficacy of psychological, educational, and behavioral treatment: Confirmation from meta-analysis. *American Psychologist, 48*, 1181–1209.

Livneh, H. (1982). On the origins of negative attitudes toward people with disabilities. *Rehabilitation Literature, 43*, 338–347.

Livneh, H. (1985). Death attitudes and their relationships to perceptions of physically disabled persons. *Journal of Rehabilitation, 51*, 38–41, 80.

Livneh, H. (1986). A unified approach to existing models of adaptation to disability: I. A model of adaptation. *Journal of Applied Rehabilitation Counseling, 17*(1), 5–16, 56.

Lussier, A. (1980). The physical handicap and the body ego. *International Journal of Psycho-Analysis, 61*, 179–185.

Maddi, S. R. (2000). *Personality theories: A comparative analysis* (6th ed.). Chicago: Dorsey.

McDaniel, J. (1976). *Physical disability and human behavior* (2nd ed.). New York: Pergamon.

Meltzoff, J., & Kornreich, M. (1970). *Research in psychotherapy*. Chicago: Aldine.

Mitchell, K. R. (1970). The body image barrier variable and level of adjustment to stress induced by severe physical disability. *Journal of Clinical Psychology, 26*, 49–52.

Neff, W. S., & Weiss, S. A. (1961). Psychological aspects of disability. In B. B. Wolman (Ed.), *Handbook of clinical psychology* (pp. 785–825). New York: McGraw-Hill.

Neiderland, W. G. (1965). Narcissistic ego impairment in patients with early physical malformation. *Psychoanalytic Study of the Child, 20*, 518–534.

Nelson, M., & Gruver, G. G. (1978). Self-esteem and body-image concept in paraplegics. *Rehabilitation Counseling Bulletin, 21*, 108–113.

Nemiah, J. C. (1964). Common emotional reactions of patients to injury. *Archives of Physical Medicine and Rehabilitation, 45*, 621–623.

Parkes, C. M. (1972a). *Bereavement: Studies of grief in adult life*. New York: International Universities Press.

Parkes, C. M. (1972b). Components of the reaction to loss of limb, spouse or home. *Journal of Psychosomatic Research, 16*, 343–349.

Parkes, C. M. (1975). Psycho-social transitions: Comparison between reactions to loss of limb and loss of spouse. *British Journal of Psychiatry, 127*, 204–210.

Patton, M. J., & Meara, N. M. (1992). *Psychoanaly counseling*. New York: Wiley.

Pine, F. (1988). The four psychologies of psychoanalysis and their place in clinical work. *Journal of the American Psychoanalytic Association, 36*, 571–596.

Prioleau, L., Murdock, M., & Brody, N. (1983). An analysis of psychotherapy versus placebo studies. *Behavioral and Brain Sciences, 6*, 275–310.

Prochaska, J. O., & Norcross, J. C. (1999). *Systems of psychotherapy: A transtheoretical analysis* (4th ed.). Pacific Grove, CA: Brooks/Cole.

Rappaport, D. (1960). The structure of psychoanalytic theory (Special issue). *Psychological Issues, 2*(6).

Rappaport, D., & Gill, M. M. (1959). The points of view and assumptions of metapsychology. *International Journal of Psychoanalysis, 40*, 153–162.

Roth, A., & Fonagy, P. (1996). *What works for whom? A critical review of psychotherapy research*. New York: Guilford.

Rybarczyk, B. D., Nyenhuis, D. L., Nicholas, J. J., Cash, S. M., & Kaiser, J. (1995). Body image, perceived social stigma, and the prediction of psychosocial adjustment to leg amputation. *Rehabilitation Psychology, 40*, 95–110.

Sandler, J. (1960). The background of safety. *International Journal of Psychoanalysis, 41*, 352–356.

Sandler, J., & Rosenblatt, B. (1962). The concept of the representational world. *Psychoanalytic Study of the Child, 17*, 128–145.

Schilder, P. (1950). *The image and appearance of the human body*. New York: International Universities Press.

Shapiro, D. A., & Shapiro, D. (1982). Meta-analysis of comparative therapy outcome studies: A replication and refinement. *Psychological Bulletin, 92*, 581–604.

Shontz, F. C. (1956). Body-concept disturbances of patients with hemiplegia. *Journal of Clinical Psychology, 12*, 293–295.

Shontz, F. C. (1975). *The psychological aspects of physical illness and disability*. New York: Macmillan.

Siller, J. (1960). Psychological concomitants of amputation in children. *Child Development, 31*, 109–120.

Siller, J. (1970). The generality of attitudes toward the disabled. *Proceedings of the 78th annual convention of the American Psychological Association, 5*, 697–698. Also in Siller & Thomas (1995).

Siller, J. (1976). Psychosocial aspects of disability. In J. Meislin (Ed.), *Rehabilitation medicine and psychiatry* (pp. 455–484). Springfield, IL: Thomas.

Siller, J. (1984). The role of personality in attitudes toward those with physical disabilities. In C. J. Golden (Ed.), *Current topics in rehabilitation psychology* (pp. 201–227). Orlando, FL: Grune & Stratton.

Siller, J. (1988). Intrapsychic aspects of attitudes toward persons with disabilities. In H. E. Yuker (Ed.), *Attitudes toward those with physical disabilities* (pp. 58–67). New York: Springer. Also in Siller & Thomas (1995).

Siller, J., Chipman, A., Ferguson, L. T., & Vann, D. H. (1967). *Attitudes of the nondisabled toward the physically disabled.* New York: New York University School of Education.

Siller, J., & Thomas, K. R. (Eds.). (1995). *Essays in research on disability.* Athens, GA: Elliott & Fitzpatrick.

Smith, M. L., Glass, G. V., & Miller, T. I. (1980). *The benefits of psychotherapy.* Baltimore, MD: Johns Hopkins University Press.

Szasz, T. S. (1957). *Pain and pleasure.* New York: Basic Books.

Thomas, K. R., & Siller, J. (1999). Object loss, mourning, and adjustment to disability. *Psychoanalytic Psychology, 16,* 179–197.

Thurer, S. (1986). A psychodynamic perspective. In T. F. Riggar, D. R. Maki, & A. W. Wolf (Eds.), *Applied rehabilitation counseling* (pp. 102–111). New York: Springer.

Wachs, H., & Zaks, M. S. (1960). Studies of body image in men with spinal cord injury. *Journal of Nervous and Mental Diseases, 131,* 121–125.

Wright, B. A. (1983). *Physical disability—A psychosocial approach* (2nd ed.). New York: Harper & Row.

Chapter 3

Adlerian Therapy

Warren R. Rule

In recent years, the contributions of Alfred Adler have received increasing attention. This rebirth is reflected by an increasing number of Adlerian practitioners, educational offerings, therapeutic centers, and publications. Despite this resurgence, not all of Adler's contributions have been acknowledged. Ellenberger (1970), in his monumental and comprehensive review of the history of psychotherapy and psychiatry, concluded that "it would not be easy to find another author from whom so much has been borrowed from all sides without acknowledgement than Alfred Adler" (p. 645).

Corey (2001), in his sixth edition of one of the most widely used textbooks on counseling and psychotherapy, underscored Adler's remarkable influence and contribution, concluding that Adler's ideas "have found their way to other psychological schools, such as family systems approaches, Gestalt therapy, learning theory, reality therapy, rational emotive behavior therapy, cognitive therapy, person-centered therapy, and existentialism" (p. 131). Also, specific to rehabilitation, an entire book was devoted to Adler's ideas as applied to counseling for adjustment to disability (Rule, 1984b). Thus Adler's approach, which he termed "individual psychology," with its pioneering emphasis on the social, phenomenological, holistic, and goal-directed nature of people, is maintaining and even increasing its application and popularity.

HISTORY

After practicing medicine for several years, Adler became associated with Sigmund Freud. However, Adler's developing ideas became increasingly dissimilar to Freud's, especially regarding Freud's conviction that sexual instinct was omnipotent, and they parted ways. His contributions have often been oversimplified or misrepresented, even in rehabilitation. Adler's earlier concepts (e.g., organ inferiority, compensation) tend to receive undue focus, probably because the terms sound as if they are directly related to disability and rehabilitation. However, his early emphasis on this limited organic perspective evolved over the subsequent quarter century into a sociopsychological explanation of behavior. This shift reflected an increased emphasis on the creativity of the individual and provided an even sharper emphasis on the personal attitude toward issues related to disability. Importantly, Adler believed that the attitude that a person adopted toward a disability was a function of the person's unique and fundamental mental pattern: the *lifestyle*. This term, which Adler coined and which has many different connotations today, has powerful implications for the rehabilitation practitioner and will be discussed more fully in the Theory of Personality section.

MAJOR CONCEPTS

Holistic Nature of People

A basic assumption that fits securely into the perspective of rehabilitation is Adler's belief in the wholeness of the individual. A person's wholeness or "holistic" nature is irreducible; to break up the personality or fragment it into parts is to destroy the wholeness and thereby undermine one's understanding of the individual. One cannot dissect a person without losing some understanding of the pattern or theme that runs through his or her life. Adler used an analogy from music, pointing out that music cannot be fully appreciated by studying each note itself; rather, one needs to have the context of the other notes to experience the melody.

The assumption that the unit (the individual) is indivisible is important, particularly for understanding the relationship of an individual to disability. The way in which individuals organize themselves as whole people influences their perceptions of themselves and others and has a large bearing on their goals and behavioral interactions with others. Adler was strongly convinced of the creative power of the individual, believing in "soft determinism" as opposed to "hard determinism" (Ansbacher & Ansbacher, 1956). He stated, "Do not forget the most important fact that not heredity and not environment are determining factors. Both are giving only the frame and the influences which are answered by the individual in regard to his styled creative power" (p. xxiv).

Social Context

Adler believed that people are social beings and that behavior can only be fully understood in a social context. Ansbacher and Ansbacher (1956) noted that Adler's approach could be properly referred to as a "context" psychology. He regarded personal problems basically as social or interpersonal problems. Related to this assumption about social nature is the desire to belong. Expressed in another way, each individual strives to have a place of significance in the eyes of others. The goal of obtaining a "place of somebodyness" is handled differently by different people. According to this view, a congenital or acquired disability would be handled differently by different lifestyles because both the perceived "place of somebodyness" and the social context or interpersonal world would vary from person to person.

Broadly speaking, the goals that one pursues and the behaviors one learns can be directly related to the innate desire to enhance oneself within a social context. Thus, in attempting to understand another person, a fundamental question would be: "How is this person seeking to be known by others?" The answer has obvious implications for rehabilitation.

Goal-Directedness

Adler believed that all behavior, including emotions, is goal-directed. Stated another way, all things that people do have a purpose and are a function of their ideas, both conscious and dimly conscious, about consequences to be obtained in the future. Behaviors that seemingly cannot be explained become more understood as the goal or purpose comes to light. So, even though people may be consciously aware of the purpose of thinking, feeling, or acting in a certain fashion, most of the time they are unaware of their goals, which operate at a dimly conscious level. People are not aware of how pervasively goals are at work in their daily lives—in the way they interact with others, in their choice of friends or consumer products, in their sense of accomplishment or vulnerability, or in the viewpoint taken toward the implications of disability.

Thus the individual seems to operate from a subjective mental framework and is not always fully conscious of his or her goals. In understanding someone, the focus must be on the person's subjective or internal frame of reference. This focus seems necessary because the individual's perceptions, including inner biases influencing his or her perceptions, determine his or her behavior more than "reality" does. Furthermore, the individual organizes his or her perceptions in a manner that influences personal goals. Thus the strong emphasis in Adler's approach is on a cognitive understanding of the individual.

Adler believed that the pattern of goals is organized around the subjectively determined concept of the ideal self, much of which the individual created during childhood years and continues to believe as long as it is useful. The person, in his or her private logic, continually moves through life with this self-ideal as a general reference point. Almost as if the individual is wearing blinders, the person strives, at a dimly conscious level, to become like the imagined social self. Subsequently, the person seems to treat himself or herself at a vague level of awareness as if he or she will only be truly OK or have a total sense of significance in the eyes of others and have a real feeling of security when he or she lives up to the ideal self. This self provides the main thrust that enables people to move, on a daily basis and throughout their lives, from a position of dimly felt inferiority or noncoping to a position of overcoming or coping. Adler believed that this pattern of goals is organized around a single "fictional final goal," and the pattern of complementing goals flows in this unified direction. Commensurate with the goal-directed nature of behavior, the individual is able, by his or her standards, to move from the felt minus state of non-enoughness to the felt plus state of enoughness. As the individual moves through life, it seems that he or she never quite gets "there" or is absolutely and totally satisfied.

Adler believed that early conclusions drawn before approximately age six or seven go a long way toward determining the dimly conscious goals that constitute this pattern. These conclusions appear to be drawn from experiences related to the person's first social group, the family. The approximate age of six or seven can be chosen as a general cutoff, primarily because the child is beginning to become enmeshed in a school setting at that time; that is, the individual has begun to broaden the range of influences received from his or her first social group, the family, to those of the next social group, the school.

The early conclusions that become goals of the person's pattern are drawn from a host of childhood impressions and experiences. Exceedingly important is the family constellation, including the development of siblings, age differences, ordering of genders, and alliance groups. Moreover, parental influences and expectations, family values and atmosphere, peers, and neighbors all contribute to the biased slice of life that is the *only* slice of life the child has available from which he or she can generalize. Considerable emphasis is placed, in attempting to understand a person, on the psychological "territory" that the individual chose to stake out as his or her own in an attempt to feel that "others take notice of me when I am like this." This sense of self-significance or belonging can be manifested in a variety of outlets (e.g., being the best, the worst, the charmer, or the tough one). Each sibling, Adlerians hypothesize, will move in a different overall direction in these areas or may even try to overtake a sibling in a chosen area. It is important to note that this pattern exists primarily on an unconscious level.

Individuals learn at an early age through trial and error what goals will be most apt to help them move toward a place of significance, and they begin to experiment with behaviors that are most useful in implementing the goals. Not surprisingly, individuals also learn behaviors, including emotions, consistent with the dimly conscious goals of the lifestyle that safeguard their vulnerabilities and sense of self-esteem. Generally speaking, then, the chosen pattern allows individuals to evaluate, to understand, to predict, and to control experience (Mosak, 2000).

THEORY OF PERSONALITY

The organizing structure for Adler's major concepts and theory of personality is the concept of *lifestyle*, a term that he originated. *Lifestyle* means something considerably more basic to the person than many contemporary uses of the word would suggest. A broad definition is "that unity in each individual, in his thinking, feeling, acting, in his so-called conscious and unconscious, in every expression of his personality" (Ansbacher & Ansbacher, 1956, p. 175). Expressed another way, lifestyle is seen as the individual's holistic pattern of beliefs and goals that he or she uses for interacting with others and for measuring self-worth.

Lifestyle, which is central to the Adlerian approach to individuals with or without disabilities, is pervasively at work in everyone's daily life. As highlighted previously, the lifestyle expresses itself broadly and often only dimly in the consciousness (e.g., in selection of friends, in work, in love relationships, in definition of success and failure, in spirituality, in self-regard, in automobiles purchased, and in views taken toward the limitations of a disability).

The overriding mental pattern is regarded by Adlerians as the unity that reflects the *key cognitive* dimensions on which a person takes a sensitive position. This mental pattern is useful to the individual because it works in terms of the person's subjective perspective. Just as blinders on a horse serve to focus, and to limit, perspective and to get the horse through heavy traffic, so do selective perceptions and goals get people through life. This overriding mental pattern, in turn, influences the individual's feelings and behaviors in reaction to life's challenges. Thus this unique pattern of thinking, the lifestyle, with its built-in blinders and tunnel vision, leads people to both their successes and failures, greatest strengths, and greatest weaknesses.

Because of the consistency of the cognitive nature of the lifestyle, it is often helpful to the individual to have an awareness of this unique lifestyle pattern when facing decisions or problems. The lifestyle, the time-tested pattern of basic attitudes and expectations, becomes most obvious when the person is experiencing stress. The lifestyle concept, as well as the appearance-under-stress phenomenon, has many helpful implications for rehabilitation practitioners.

DESCRIPTION OF THE COUNSELING PROCESS

Even though Adlerian therapy is regarded by some as the most eclectic of all systems, and despite the range of choices for adaptability that this approach provides, there are four broad stages in the counseling process that are generally regarded as characteristic: relationship, lifestyle investigation, lifestyle interpretation, and reorientation.

Relationship

The relationship is not technically a "phase" in the sense that the relationship ends distinctly at one point in the counseling process. The practitioner begins the helping process by building a relationship of trust, respect, genuineness, and empathy. These and other relationship factors continue to operate and provide the basis for the development of the subsequent phases. In addition to fostering those qualities upon which a solid counseling relationship is built, the relationship phase also serves other purposes: (1) the client has the opportunity to explore himself or herself in relationship to the disability; (2) the practitioner learns more about the client's internal frame of reference; and (3) the opportunity is provided for an exchange of specific information (e.g., medical, case history, procedural).

Lifestyle Investigation

Before conducting a formal lifestyle investigation, Adlerian practitioners often obtain from the client information that may have a significant bearing on the subsequent lifestyle discussion. The helper explores functioning with the client in the five areas of living, sometimes referred to as the five tasks of life. Adlerians believe that everyone takes a position, with varying degrees of success or failure, on these five areas of living: work (or school), love, friendship, spirituality, and getting along with self. If one of the tasks is evaded, difficulties may ultimately unfold in the other tasks as well, or the pattern that works well in one or two of the tasks may not do as well in the others. The Adlerian belief is that the individual's lifestyle, including its unique strengths, weaknesses, and blind spots, functions as a coping device in all areas of life. Therefore, an increased awareness of client functioning in the five areas provides a picture of the contributions of the chosen lifestyle to a client's problems or happiness. Generally, Adlerians believe that the lifestyle becomes most apparent when the individual is experiencing stress when what has proven most useful (i.e., the lifestyle) is relied on with greater intensity and frequency.

Another procedure that some practitioners use is asking "the question." This is simply asking the client what would be different if he or she were well or if the problem did not exist. Sometimes the answer to this question indicates the purpose for which individuals are experiencing unusual difficulties, against whom or what the symptoms are directed, or against what demands or threats they are defending themselves by having such a difficult adjustment.

The exploration of the five tasks of life and "the question" normally precedes the gathering of lifestyle information. The pre-lifestyle discussion might sometimes occur in the relationship phase, depending on appropriateness and the flow of the interaction. The demarcation points between the various stages, especially between relationship and lifestyle investigation, are not rigid; rather, one stage overlaps another until the later stage clearly emerges from the former.

Formal Assessment

There are a number of formal assessment forms or procedures that may be used (e.g., Dreikurs, 1967; Rule, 1984a, 1984c; Shulman & Mosak, 1988). The assessment, which takes an hour or two to complete (unless an abbreviated form is used), has traditionally been designed for adults and adolescents; however, adaptations have been developed for children as well (e.g., Statton & Wilbom, 1991; Stiles & Wilbom, 1992). The rationale for conducting the formal lifestyle assessment should be introduced to the client in a concise, respectful manner (see section on Case Example).

In the overwhelming majority of cases, clients are intrigued by the prospect of learning about the relationship that exists between early childhood and the present. This interest seems to hold for individuals who have experienced relatively unpleasant childhoods as well as for those who experienced pleasant ones. The counselor's introductory remarks, as well as the subsequent comments, should not depict the lifestyle exploration as a mystical, murky endeavor. Rather, the emphasis ought to reflect a sharing, educational process in which relationships between the early past and present are discussed. As previously noted, Adlerians rely on the selectivity of memory as providing information that is useful to the individual's chosen lifestyle.

Significance of Early Memory

Memory is believed to be selective. As Dreikurs (1967) contended, people operate on an economy principle by selectively using their memories in accordance with their individual purposes. Thus memories from early childhood serve as anchoring orientation points, reflecting the most important conclusions, expectations, and goals that crystallized during this formative period. Adlerians believe that these early impressions and memories reflect the ideas that are embedded in the individual's present outlook. So, in utilizing the selectivity-of-memory phenomenon, the helping practitioner is able to gather lifestyle information by asking the client significant questions and, as a result, is able tentatively to reconstruct important aspects of the client's early environment. Once this reconstruction is accomplished, the helper can look for themes in the remembered early environment that reflect the dimly conscious notions and goals the client is presently using.

Based on the client's memories (both real and even imagined) before approximately age six or seven, areas of lifestyle information include descriptions of self and siblings, sibling rankings on possible areas of competition (e.g., intelligence, pleasing, having one's own way, athletics, appearance, and temper), sibling interrelationships, parents and parental influence, family values and atmosphere, relationship to peers, and specific early recollections and dreams.

Family Constellation

Considerable emphasis is given to family constellation from a psychosocial perspective. Accordingly, attention is directed to sibling age differences, order of birth, genders, favoritism, uniqueness, alliance groups, development of patterns of siblings, and feeling of clients about their positions. Only-born children are often compared with playmates.

Shulman (1973) listed five basic positions: only, eldest, second, middle, and youngest child. Different variations and combinations for these basic positions exist. Each basic position has several very modest probabilities of stereotyped characteristics attached to it. The helper considers and refines the tentative hypotheses in line with the direction of movement reflected by the other lifestyle variables. For example, sometimes first-born children (both oldest and only-born) have taken a sensitive position in their early lives on mandates (e.g., "shoulds," "musts," and "ought tos," as well as the values of authority). The heightened sensitivity may have been the result of strong parental expectations, or it might have been influenced by the conclusion that one is only OK when one "achieves" in life (hence the usefulness of mandates as stimulators). A host of possible influences may have contributed to this sensitivity to "shoulds."

The practitioner can explore how the particular sensitivity is useful to the client in his or her own unique lifestyle as the person moves through life. Do clients use it to align themselves with authority or established values? Do they strive to be number one by setting lofty, perhaps unreasonable, "shoulds"? Do they passively-aggressively resist most of life's mandates? The emphasis for the practitioner would be on relating patterns of lifestyle movement, which are grounded in childhood conclusions, to difficulties that the client is presently experiencing. Expressed another way, the practitioner is interested in helping the client get in touch with how the lifestyle is contributing, however consciously, to one's problems.

Eliciting Specific Early Recollections

In completing the lifestyle assessment, great importance is given to the client's early specific recollections, memories, and dreams. Adlerians believe that there are no chance memories. That is, from the thousands of experiences to which an individual has been exposed in early childhood, only those recollections are remembered that coincide with one's present outlook on self, others, or life. Thus the person's early recollections reflect the same patterns; they are reminders that the individual carries around regarding personal limits and the meaning of circumstances (Ansbacher & Ansbacher, 1956).

Generally speaking, individuals can remember, when asked, at least six specific incidents that occurred during their early childhoods. Each early recollection, when considered in the context of the accompanying feelings about the remembered incident, reflects a current expectation. Adlerians focus on the manifest content of the early memory, not on hidden, symbolic meanings. Moreover, each recollection supplements and rounds out the outlook reflected by the other early recollections.

Adlerian practitioners generally believe that the individual is the product of both "individual laws" and "general laws." In other words, people are the result of individual laws that they created for themselves and the result of general laws that apply to all people or specified groups of individuals. In seeking to understand more fully another person, the practitioner focuses on both individual (ideographic) and general (nomothetic) understanding.

Other Sources of Lifestyle Information

Supplemental sources of information are usually available, some very broad and some very narrow. Lombardi (1973) discussed the importance of other case history data (knowing about clients), expressive behavior (observing clients), grouping (interacting with clients), and symptomatic behavior (clients' telltale signs). In addition to these frequent indications of lifestyle patterns, much can be learned from what the client avoids in life and what the client criticizes in others, and, as the great philosopher Goethe contended, nothing is more revealing about a person's character than what makes him or her laugh.

Lifestyle Interpretation

In searching for lifestyle "threads" or overriding goals, the helper relies on the client's awareness of modest probabilities of the relationship between lifestyle variables while, at the same time, trying to make deductions and identify logical patterns that will identify individual laws. While looking for tentative identification of the individual's network of goals, or the cognitive map, the practitioner is, in a sense, attempting to put together pieces of a jigsaw puzzle. The practitioner is wondering as he or she reviews the lifestyle material: "If this person has drawn these conclusions about self, others, and life, then what kind of overriding (future-oriented) goals would he or she have chosen to guide himself or herself in striving to be a coping, significant person?" In addition to seeking to identify broad, overriding goals, the counselor looks for specific convictions that relate to the client's present problem, such as issues related to disability.

Some examples of lifestyle themes are cited by Mosak (1971), who cautioned that predictions cannot be made as to what behavior will coincide with a given lifestyle. In addition, the uniqueness of the individual is violated by typologies, which should be viewed as strictly didactic contributions. Examples of these themes are controlling, getting, driving, always being right, pleasing, being the center or the best, being admired for moral superiority, being against, being the baby or a charmer, being victimized, being intellectually superior, being an excitement seeker, and being a martyr. If these examples appear to have a distinct self-serving flavor, several points might be kept in mind. First, individuals want to move from a position of dimly felt inferiority to a position of significance. The labels given to the themes reflect the powerful determination to enhance the self. Second, the lifestyle works to one's advantage as well as one's disadvantage. These themes can be channeled on the socially useful side of life and can truly enhance others as well as the self. Third, the creativity of the individual is ever present in choosing the subtle as well as the more obvious ways that the lifestyle is implemented.

There are a number of frameworks for presenting lifestyle interpretations. The perspective of "I am . . . ," "Others are . . . ," "Life is . . . " is one approach. Another is to emphasize the "shoulds" (e.g., "I am a person who should . . . ," "Others are people who ought to . . . ," "Life is a place that must . . . "). Often it is helpful to present the material in a goal-directed framework, which denotes a future orientation (e.g., "To . . . "). Mosak (2000) focuses on "basic mistakes" (e.g., overgeneralizations, false or impossible goals of "security," misperceptions of life and of life's demands, minimization or denial of one's worth, and faulty values). Rule (1982) utilizes the perspective of the individual's private logic within a social context; the technique involves reframing the practitioner's interpretation in a positive and socially acceptable manner and with the imaginary context of the client's ideal self as viewed by important others.

Reorientation

Reorientation emphasizes change and builds upon the practitioner's and the client's awareness of the client's lifestyle or cognitive map and its relationship to the presenting problem. Expressed another way, now that they both have insight into the client's daily implementation of the lifestyle, a springboard for agreed-upon change has been created. In addition to identifying the ultimately self-defeating features of the lifestyle and establishing goals and homework strategies for overcoming them, a broader educational perspective can often be utilized. This perspective might include exploring the interrelatedness between thinking, feeling, and doing, especially how thoughts are usually at the root of emotions that energize behavior; encouraging a belief in a significance of self that is not a function of comparisons with others or self-rankings; or fostering an increased other-directness (i.e., empathy or social interest toward other individuals).

Encouragement is a major Adlerian concept at this stage and should be a major component of strategies. As Dinkmeyer (1972) noted: "Encouragement on the part of the counselor is comprised of both verbal and nonverbal procedures that enable a counselee to experience and become aware of his own worth. The counselor expresses faith in and total acceptance of the counselee as he is, not as he could or should be" (p. 177).

Despite the conveyance of encouragement, however, the clinician places responsibility on the client for his or her own approach to a given situation. Moreover, the focus is kept on the (future-oriented) goals of a behavior or feeling, because this focus reduces the likelihood that the client will feel burdened by, or used to his or her "advantage," the "whys" or "causes" of behavior. The "whys" or "causes" reflect past, unchangeable reasons; "goals" indicate future-oriented, changeable targets. Because the helper creates an opportunity for an increased awareness of goals, the client is less likely to pursue the goals that ultimately work to his or her disadvantage. (Adler is said to have expressed this point in an unforgettable metaphor: once the therapist has spit into the client's soup, the client can continue to eat the soup, but it won't taste as good.)

The practitioner continually looks for opportunities to encourage the client to believe in a significance of self that is not a function of vertical rankings or comparisons with others. This awareness can be helpful to a client in learning to do a mental checkup when he or she experiences an unwanted negative emotion and then trying to discover how the lifestyle is dictating the message of inadequacy. This daily awareness of individual functioning can also be instrumental in avoiding future pitfalls.

The facilitative use of humor in conveying lifestyle awareness and in reminding the individual of lifestyle goals cannot be underestimated. Awareness may be accomplished by fables, parables, metaphors, cartoons, audiorecordings, photographs, and so on. Use of humor, as well as other Adlerian tactics and strategies, is handled in a spirit of true encouragement (not necessarily praise), conveying the worth, acceptance, and uniqueness of the client.

Mosak and Maniacci (1998) offered a large number of specific tactics in counseling and psychotherapy that are tailored to Adlerian applications. Compatible strategies and techniques from other approaches (e.g., rational-emotive-behavioral, Gestalt, behavioral and cognitive-behavioral, and family therapy) may be incorporated at this stage.

REHABILITATION APPLICATIONS

The most frequent misunderstandings of Adlerian therapy in rehabilitation appear to be the result of either an oversimplification or a misrepresentation of some of Adler's ideas. Most stem from an overemphasis on his earlier writings. Adler developed, early in his career, a theory of behavior based upon organ inferiority, which preceded the crystallization of his lifestyle concept. This theory, as well as related concepts (e.g., compensation, inferiority), has attracted particular attention in rehabilitation and, indeed, provides helpful concepts for the rehabilitation practitioner. However, often overlooked is the fact that in the subsequent quarter century Adler continued to change and refine his approach. A number of individuals attempting to apply Adler's ideas to rehabilitation have focused on the original, less developed concepts; because of their labels at the time, these appear to be the most related to rehabilitation. Unfortunately, generalizations were then made from the outdated, limited perspective to the overall current worth of the Adlerian lifestyle approach to rehabilitation.

In considering the utility of the Adlerian approach as a means to help a client with disability issues, it is important to remember that awareness is just as applicable to people with disabilities as to nondisabled people. Even the early and pioneering reviews of relevant investigations have concluded that few, if any, personality differences exist between these populations (e.g., Dunham & Dunham, 1978; English, 1974). Thus the lifestyle analysis would seem to have the same merit for understanding the "personality" of both groups. In addition, once a measure of lifestyle understanding is achieved between the practitioner and the client, exploration can be devoted to the extremely important issue of the relationship between the client's lifestyle and the disability.

It is important for the practitioner to remember that the rehabilitation client is creatively doing the best and most useful thing, within the blinders of his or her lifestyle, that the individual can do at the time. This realization results in a somewhat different meaning given to the "resistance" as compared to other conceptual frameworks. "Resistance" is essentially, as Dreikurs (1967) contended, a discrepancy between the goals of the client and the practitioner. Then, accepting the client's goals "as they are" has special meaning. Behind what may be labeled as "resistance" by the therapist may be rehabilitation client goals that are essentially self-protective devices against perceived dangers: being ridiculed, submitting to order, not getting necessary help, incurring disapproval, having to face responsibility, being taken advantage of, or having to face unpleasant consequences. Rule (2000) explored the internal dilemma of individuals experiencing resistance and change. Individual lifestyle information may shed light on the likelihood of whichever of these may be in operation. In addition, some considerations for dealing with what may be labeled as client "negativism" can be found in Rule (1977a) and Shulman (1973, 1977).

The creativity of the unique individual lifestyle is ever present, and the methods for struggling against symptoms in order to maintain face (Mosak, 1977; Shulman, 1973) vary from lifestyle to lifestyle. Illustrating how symptoms can be safeguards for self-esteem, Shulman (1973) cited possible purposes (secondary gains) for suffering: it can be used as justification ("I have a right to my own way . . . look how much I suffer when I don't get it"), as manipulation ("If you don't do what I want, I'll die and then you'll be sorry"), and as self-glorification ("The amount of my suffering proves my nobility").

Lifestyle understanding can often provide insight into the usefulness of substance abuse to the individual's "cognitive map" (i.e., the goals being met—or even the goal of avoiding having to meet another, more challenging goal—by being in a euphoric state of mind). Along another vein, maybe lifestyle barriers to acceptance or adjustment to disability need to be worked on, such as invidious comparisons related to vulnerabilities stemming from feelings of "near-normalcy," dependency, social consequences of loss of liberty, or inferiority feelings.

A sampling of Adlerian applications to specific disability issues would include Carlson's 1992 special issues in the most widely read Adlerian journal (now called the *Journal of Individual Psychology*) on the subject of aging and working with special adults, as well as the 1995 issue on counseling homosexuals and bisexuals. Mosak (1995) discussed an Adlerian approach to schizophrenia; Slavick, Sperry, and Carlson (1992) reviewed Adlerian treatment of schizoid personality; Maniacci (1996) discussed Adlerian brief therapy with personality disorders; Allers and Golson (1994) explored an Adlerian approach to multiple personality disorder; Axtell and Newton investigated the themes of bulimic women; Prinz (1993) and Keen and Wheeler (1994) discussed alcoholism and substance abuse; and Slavick, Carlson, and Sperry (1993, 1995) applied Adlerian concepts to histories of childhood sexual abuse.

CASE EXAMPLE

Sally J. was a 43-year-old female, having been married for the second time two years prior to her automobile accident in which her left leg was crushed. Despite a successful medical recovery, including a prosthesis, she was referred to therapy. Sally complained of feeling depressed and worthless. The two children by her former marriage were living away from home, and her husband was the only source of income for the household.

As the result of exploratory discussion, it seemed that the client blamed her accident for most of her unhappiness, feared that her relatively new husband would leave her because of her disfigurement, and found herself withdrawing socially as she continued to become increasingly depressed. The therapist gathered some lifestyle information, using an Abbreviated Lifestyle Form designed by Rule (1984a). The procedure was introduced in roughly the following manner:

> Sally, sometimes it is helpful to be in touch with some pretty broad attitudes and goals that are at work in major areas of a person's life. We are talking here about important beliefs that an individual has learned about herself, other people, and life that she probably is not completely aware of. One way that I have found very useful in trying to help someone identify them is by taking a look at what impressions from early childhood a person is choosing to continue to believe and that may be contributing to a person's difficulties. You and I could discuss for a while some of your early impressions and then talk about how these are operating right now, in your everyday life. Want to give it a try?

The client described herself in childhood as being the oldest of three, with a brother three years younger and a sister five years younger. She did not get along with her brother and saw him as bossy, deceitful, and her mother's favorite. She got along best with her sister, whom she viewed as cute, charming, and her father's favorite. She described herself as shy, with her feelings easily hurt, yet having a good sense of humor. She regarded her father as somewhat distant, intimidating, and having a drinking problem; he expected her to be perfect. Sally described her mother as attractive, easygoing, even submissive, and easy to please; she gave Sally no indication that she should have been different than she was. The family atmosphere was portrayed as tense and unpredictable. Sally's three early recollections were:

1. Age 3. I remember when my brother was born. That afternoon, Mom was holding him, looking at him and kissing his head. I was mostly watching from the kitchen.
   Feeling?: Sad, jealous.
   Most vivid part?: The look on her face.
2. Age 3¹/₂. I remember one time lying on the grass in my backyard. It was a clear, sunny day and the breeze was blowing gently. I was

looking at the different shapes of the clouds and how they were slowly moving.
Feeling?: Content, curious.
Most vivid part?: The soft look of the clouds.
3. Age 5. I was in kindergarten. The teacher, Miss Moore, went around the room looking at the crayon drawings we were doing at our desks. She lifted mine up, looked at it and said, "Nice work."
Feeling?: Proud, special.
Most vivid part?: Her looking at it.

As noted previously, the therapist relies on the selectivity of long-term memory as being an indicator of present expectations of self, others, and life. The lifestyle information seems to reveal that Sally is exceptionally sensitive to losing a place of importance, and that she regards herself as quiet and fragile, while wishing to be perfect. Her sensitivity to being unappreciated and to not measuring up is coupled with a desire to maintain a low profile. Gender guiding lines indicated that men can be powerful and challenging; women are expected to be accepting. Several areas were noted in the lifestyle patterns for possible therapeutic leverage: the client's achievement orientation, her distinct penchant for engaging life visually, and her capacity for humor.

Sally agreed with the therapist's interpretation of these issues, which touched a tender nerve. Based especially on her lifestyle sensitivities, the therapist made a special effort to emphasize to her, throughout the therapy process, the importance of speaking out if she felt that what she said was being taken lightly. (Rule [1984d] has addressed the key issue of therapist self-awareness and blind spots as an interactive factor with client vulnerability.) Considerable discussion was initially devoted to how these sensitivities were at work in her daily life, particularly how some of these notions converged to result in the irrational expectation that her husband would leave her and that others could not accept her because of her lost leg. These lifestyle beliefs included her sensitivity to losing a place of importance, seeking to measure up or be perfect, tending to expect males to challenge or to distance, and emphasizing—and thereby expecting others to emphasize—the visual aspects of life (her leg).

Becoming aware of and disputing these cognitive expectations were part of the initial strategy for change or reorientation. Mosak's (2000) push-button technique was utilized to teach Sally that thoughts largely control emotions. Ellis's (1994) A-B-C-D-E techniques, which are quite compatible with Adler's approach, were used to encourage her and to help her dispute her tendency to rate herself based on others', especially her husband's, total approval. The goal of increasing her unconditional self-acceptance was further strengthened by Ellis's (1994) shame-attacking exercises and rational-emotive imagery, which built upon her visual propensity; she was to imagine herself being self-accepting, regardless of her worst fear of others' disapproval of her or her amputated leg. On a daily basis, systematic exercises were later employed that capitalized on her ability to generate humor; these homework procedures were developed by Rule for increasing the internal locus of control using self-modeled humor by a visual method (Rule, 1979) and by an auditory self-imaging procedure (Rule, 1977).

After Sally achieved considerable progress with the cognitive strategies, the therapist used role playing with Sally to increase her assertiveness skills with others, particularly in communicating her concerns with her husband, who, although reluctant to participate in joint counseling, responded mostly favorably to her new-found approach to communication. To further build on the client's strengths and to increase her choices for attaining a place of lifestyle significance in keeping with the strengths of her self-ideal, the therapist explored her keen visual orientation. Standardized and informal testing revealed an aptitude for artistic pursuits, as well as a strong pattern of interests. After several courses in drawing and in painting at a community college, Sally achieved great satisfaction from volunteering to teach the joy of artistic expression to a small group of seniors at a nearby center.

In summary, the application of the lifestyle counseling process involves the realms of feeling, thinking, and behaving. A useful metaphor is that the interaction of relationship factors (feeling-oriented) is the key that opens the door to the dark room; the lifestyle self-understanding (thinking-oriented) creates light in the room; and the reorientation methods (action-oriented) rearrange the room and polish the furniture according to the wishes of the individual.

RESEARCH FINDINGS

The ongoing contributions of research include studies on clinical process and outcome, as well as validity and reliability studies of lifestyle variables. This research helps, in part, to prevent delusions about clinical observations. Coverage of the pioneering sources of Adlerian-related research may be found in publications such as Mosak (2000) and Kern, Matheny, and Patterson (1978). Approximately 1,000 studies have been conducted on variables related to birth order. A number of ground-breaking studies from an Adlerian perspective were completed on early recollections, and the bulk of these studies are discussed by Mosak (2000), Taylor (1975), and Olson (1979). A comprehensive bibliography by Mosak and Mosak (1975, 1985) is a helpful reference for many lifestyle-related studies, and Watkins (1982, 1983) has summarized many of the research activities. Research from 1976 to 1993 on birth order has been reviewed by Stewart and Stewart (1995), and Stewart and Campbell (1998) investigated the validity and reliability of a psychological birth order inventory; Wheeler, Kern, and Curlette (1991) contended that the lifestyle can be measured; and Wheeler and Acheson (1998) offer criterion-related validity of a lifestyle personality inventory. From a different perspective, Sperry and Maniacci (1992) integrated Adlerian case formations with the diagnostic psychiatric classifications.

Clinicians must be cautious, however, about worshiping empirical gods. Statistical research is capable of making a contribution in the study of nomothetic, or general, laws as related to the Adlerian lifestyle approach; however, the ideographic laws, or individual guidelines that the person created, often dimly consciously, for moving through life are considerably more difficult to study with statistical methods.

A sizable number of professionals in rehabilitation who apply psychological concepts tend to perceive helping people with disabilities as an art. Many years ago, Stubbins (1977) contended: "Partly as a consequence of self-understanding and partly through trained judgment, they practice the helping role as an art—something difficult to define but which most practitioners agree is important in applied psychology" (p. 295).

Very importantly, rehabilitation practitioners may be kidding themselves if they believe that objective measures can ever be the masters of subjective phenomena. This issue seems particularly complex when the interactive variable of therapist lifestyle is considered. A complete awareness on the therapist's part of all the empirical studies ever completed on all of helping will not prevent the clinician's own subjective lifestyle from slipping through the mask of objectivity into the interactive counseling process.

PROMINENT STRENGTHS AND LIMITATIONS

The resurgent interest in the Adlerian approach was briefly discussed in the introduction. Corey (2001), in evaluating its strengths, concluded that

> Adler was far ahead of his time, and most of the contemporary therapies have incorporated at least some of his ideas. Individual Psychology assumes that people are motivated by social factors; are responsible for their own thoughts, feelings, and actions; are the creators of their own lives, as opposed to helpless

victims; and are impelled by purposes and goals, looking more toward the future than the past. (p. 130)

These strengths seem to be compatible with the optimistic rehabilitation perspective of helping people with disabilities to live connected, self-directed lives. Other prominent strengths of Adler's are the emphases placed on subjectivity; on the cognitive nature of problems; on the importance of the family system; on the cooperative, egalitarian approach to therapy and to social living; on clients being psychologically discouraged by their lifestyle convictions rather than sick; and on a commonsense foundation as well as a viable, flexible potential for application. Corsini (1990) concluded that "the crowning advantage of Adler in therapy rests in the completeness and comprehensibility of Adlerian theory and the direct relationship between the theory and psychotherapeutic practice" (p. 47).

A chief criticism is the emphasis on general concepts that are hard to define and quantify (e.g., Ford and Urban, 1963). Some of Adler's concepts have been evaluated as being too simplistic and sounding like common sense (which is regarded as a strength by some clinicians). Adler has also been criticized for not providing enough specific procedures for lifestyle interpretation or for reorientation. Furthermore, Corey (2001) observed that, from a multicultural perspective, Adler's approach, which is characteristic of most Western models, "tends to focus on the self as the locus of change and responsibility" (p. 134); many cultures do not regard the individual self as being autonomous enough to be an agent of change. Yet within this culture and depending on one's clinical perspective on the purpose of rehabilitation practice, the strength or weakness of a particular approach to helping may be significantly related to its position on the locus of responsibility for change. Manaster (1982), for example, offered the insightful conclusion that

> Adlerian psychology has been too honest. The two most successful schools of psychology in this century have either damned man, and thereby provided an almost universal cop-out for people, or belittled man while holding out the promise that mechanical adjustments could improve his lot. Adlerian psychology has put the burden of proof, of success, of progress and fulfillment on the individual. It has said, in effect, life is not a bowl of cherries; you are not and won't be perfect but might be better—it is up to you. (p. 259)

REFERENCES

Allers, C. T., & Golson J. (1994). Multiple personality disorder: Treatment from an Adlerian perspective. *Individual Psychology: The Journal of Adlerian Theory, Research, and Practice, 50,* 262–270.

Ansbacher, H. L., & Ansbacher, R. W. (Eds.). (1956). *The individual psychology of Alfred Adler*. New York: Basic Books.

Axtell, A., & Newton, B. J. (1993). An analysis of Adlerian life themes of bulimic women. *Individual Psychology: The Journal of Adlerian Theory, Research, and Practice, 49*, 58–67.

Carlson, J. (Ed.). (1992). The process of aging and working with special adults [Special issue]. *Individual Psychology: The Journal of Adlerian Theory, Research, and Practice, 48*(4).

Carlson, J. (Ed.). (1995). Counseling homosexuals and bisexuals [Special issue]. *Individual Psychology: The Journal of Adlerian Theory, Research, and Practice, 51*(2).

Corey, G. (2001). *Theory and practice of counseling and psychotherapy* (6th ed.). Pacific Grove, CA: Brooks/Cole.

Corsini, R. (1990). Adlerian psychotherapy. In J. K. Zeig & W. M. Munion (Eds.), *What is psychotherapy?* (pp. 50–53). San Francisco: Jossey-Bass.

Dinkmeyer, D. (1972). Use of the encouragement process in Adlerian counseling. *Personnel and Guidance Journal, 51*, 177–181.

Dreikurs, R. (1967). *Psychodynamics, psychotherapy, and counseling*. Chicago: Alfred Adler Institute.

Dunham, J. R., & Dunham, C. S. (1978). Psychosocial aspects of disability. In R. Goldenson, J. Dunham, & C. Dunham (Eds.), *Disability and rehabilitation handbook*. New York: McGraw-Hill.

Ellenberger, H. (1970). *The discovery of the unconscious: The history and evolution of dynamic psychiatry*. New York: Basic Books.

Ellis, A. (1994). *Reason and emotion in psychotherapy revised*. New York: Carol Publishing.

English, R. W. (1974). The application of personality theory to explain psychological reactions to physical disability. In J. Cull & R. Hardy (Eds.), *Rehabilitation techniques in severe disability*. Springfield, IL: Charles C. Thomas.

Ford, D. H., & Urban, H. B. (1963). *Systems of psychotherapy*. New York: Wiley.

Keen, K. K., Jr., & Wheeler, M. S. (1994). Substance abuse in college freshmen and Adlerian lifestyle themes. *Individual Psychology: The Journal of Adlerian Theory, Research, and Practice, 50*, 97–10.

Kern, R. M., Matheny, K. B., & Patterson, D. (1978). *A case for Adlerian counseling: Theory, techniques, and research evidence*. Chicago: Alfred Adler Institute.

Lombardi, D. N. (1973). Eight avenues of lifestyle consistency. *Individual Psychologist, 10*(2), 5–9.

Manaster, G. J. (1982). Our personal views. In G. J. Manaster & R. J. Corsini (Eds.), *Individual psychology: Theory and practice* (pp. 257–259). Itasca, IL: Peacock.

Maniacci, M. P. (1996). An introduction to the brief therapy of the personality disorders. *Individual Psychology: The Journal of Adlerian Theory, Research, and Practice, 52*, 158–168.

Mosak, H. H. (1971). In A. Nikelly (Ed.), *Techniques for behavior change* (pp. 77–81). Springfield, IL: Charles C. Thomas.

Mosak, H. H. (1977). *On purpose*. Chicago: Alfred Adler Institute.

Mosak, H. H. (1995). Drugless therapy with schizophrenics. *Individual Psychology: The Journal of Adlerian Theory, Research, and Practice, 51*, 61–66.

Mosak, H. H. (2000). Adlerian psychotherapy. In R. J. Corsini & D. Wedding (Eds.), *Current psychotherapies* (6th ed.). Belmont, CA: Wadsworth.

Mosak, H. H., & Maniacci, M. P. (1998). *Tactics in counseling and psychotherapy*. Itasca, IL: Peacock.

Mosak, H. H., & Mosak, B. (1975). *A bibliography for Adlerian psychology* (Vol. 1). Washington, DC: Hemisphere.

Mosak, H. H., & Mosak, B. (1985). *A bibliography for Adlerian psychology* (Vol. 2). Washington, DC: Hemisphere.

Olson, G. (1979). *Early recollections: Their use in diagnosis and psychotherapy*. Springfield, IL: Charles C. Thomas.

Prinz, J. (1993). Alcoholics and their treatment: Current Adlerian thinking. *Individual Psychology: The Journal of Adlerian Theory, Research, and Practice, 49,* 94–105.

Rule, W. (1977). Increasing self-modeled humor. *Rational Living, 12,* 7–9.

Rule, W. (1979). Increased internal-control using humor with lifestyle awareness. *Individual Psychologist, 16,* 16–26.

Rule, W. (1982). Pursuing the horizon: Striving for elusive goals. *Personnel and Guidance Journal, 61,* 195–197.

Rule, W. (1984a). Abbreviated Lifestyle Form. In W. Rule (Ed.), *Lifestyle counseling for adjustment to disability* (pp. 343–346). Rockville, MD: Aspen.

Rule, W. (Ed.). (1984b). *Lifestyle counseling for adjustment to disability*. Rockville, MD: Aspen.

Rule, W. (1984c). Lifestyle Form. In W. Rule (Ed.), *Lifestyle counseling for adjustment to disability* (pp. 333–342). Rockville, MD: Aspen.

Rule, W. (1984d). Lifestyle self-awareness and the practitioner. In W. Rule (Ed.), *Lifestyle counseling* (pp. 319–330). Rockville, MD: Aspen.

Rule, W. (2000). Understanding and reframing resistance using angels and devils method. *Journal of Individual Psychology, 56,* 184–191.

Shulman, B. H. (1973). *Contributions to individual psychology*. Chicago: Alfred Adler Institute.

Shulman, B. H. (1977). Encouraging the pessimist: A confronting technique. *Individual Psychologist, 14,* 7–9.

Shulman, B. H., & Mosak, H. H. (1988). *LSI—Life Style Inventory*. Muncie, IN: Accelerated Development.

Slavick, S., Carlson, J., & Sperry, L. (1993). An Adlerian treatment of adults with a history of childhood sexual abuse. *Individual Psychology: The Journal of Adlerian Theory, Research, and Practice, 49,* 111–131.

Slavick, S., Carlson, J., & Sperry, L. (1995). Extreme life-styles of adults who have experienced sexual abuse. *Individual Psychology: The Journal of Adlerian Theory, Research, and Practice, 51,* 353–374.

Slavick, S., Sperry, L., & Carlson, J. (1992). The schizoid personality disorders: A review and Adlerian views of treatment. *Individual Psychology: The Journal of Adlerian Theory, Research, and Practice, 48,* 137–154.

Sperry, L., & Maniacci, M. P. (1992). An integration of DSM III-R diagnoses and Adlerian case formulations. *Individual Psychology: The Journal of Adlerian Theory, Research, and Practice, 48,* 175–181.

Statton, J. E., & Wilborn, B. (1991). Adlerian counseling and early recollections of children. *Individual Psychology: The Journal of Adlerian Theory, Research, and Practice, 47*, 338–347.

Stewart, A. E., & Campbell, L. F. (1998). Validity and reliability of the White-Campbell Psychological Birth Order Inventory. *Individual Psychology: The Journal of Adlerian Theory, Research, and Practice, 54*, 41–59.

Stewart, A. E., & Stewart, E. A. (1995). Trends in birth order research (1976–1993). *Individual Psychology: The Journal of Adlerian Theory, Research, and Practice, 51*, 21–36.

Stiles, K., & Wilborn, B. (1992). A lifestyle instrument for children. *Individual Psychology: The Journal of Adlerian Theory, Research, and Practice, 48*, 96–105.

Stubbins, J. (1977). Editorial introduction (Part III). In J. Stubbins (Ed.), *Social and psychological aspects of disability*. Baltimore: University Park Press.

Taylor, J. (1975). Early recollections as a projective technique. A review of some recent validation studies. *Journal of Individual Psychology, 31*, 213–218.

Watkins, C. E., Jr. (1982). A decade of research in support of Adlerian psychological theory. *Individual Psychology: The Journal of Adlerian Theory, Research, and Practice, 38*(1), 90–99.

Watkins, C. E., Jr. (1983). Some characteristics of research on Adlerian theory, 1970–1981. *Individual Psychology: The Journal of Adlerian Theory, Research, and Practice, 3*, 99–110.

Wheeler, M. S., & Acheson, S. K. (1998). Criterion-related validity of the Life-Style Personality Inventory. *Individual Psychology: The Journal of Adlerian Theory, Research, and Practice, 49*, 51–57.

Wheeler, M. S., Kern, R. M., & Curlette, W. L. (1991). Life-style can be measured. *Individual Psychology: The Journal of Adlerian Theory, Research, and Practice, 47*, 229–240.

Humanistic Approaches

Chapter 4

Person-Centered Counseling in Rehabilitation Professions

John See and Brian Kamnetz

> "It is as though he listened
> and such listening as his enfolds us in a silence
> in which at last we begin to hear
> what we are meant to be."
>
> Lao-tse, 500 B.C.

C arl Rogers was arguably the most influential psychologist in American history (Smith, 1982). The following are some of his major accomplishments (Kirschenbaum & Henderson, 1989):

- Founder of person-centered psychotherapy and counseling (a.k.a. client-centered or nondirective therapy).
- Pioneer in the development of humanistic psychology
- Pioneer in the development of the therapeutic encounter group
- Pioneer in extending principles of psychotherapy to the entire range of helping professions, such as social work, guidance and counseling, education, ministry, and child rearing
- Pioneer in the use of human relationship skills in international conflict resolution
- Pioneer in emphasizing the importance of scientific research in counseling and psychotherapy
- Author of 16 books and more than 200 papers and studies, with millions of copies printed in over 60 languages
- Ranked first among the 10 most influential psychotherapists, including Freud

- Ranked first as the psychologist whose writings have most stood the test of time

Rogers made many important contributions to the literature on counseling and psychotherapy, spanning five decades (e.g., Rogers, 1942, 1951, 1961, 1980). His first major theoretical contribution came in the early 1940s when, as a young psychologist, he audaciously advocated the belief that humans were basically good and could be trusted to direct their own lives (Rogers, 1942). This perspective was anathema to the then prevalent Freudian view of therapy as the process of helping people control their uncivilized impulses. In addition to this more optimistic view of human nature, he also formulated a totally new treatment approach based more on the personal characteristics of the therapist than on any techniques or formal training. He challenged the psychotherapy community by formally articulating the belief that the "facilitative conditions" of empathy, positive regard, and genuineness on the part of the therapist were the necessary and sufficient conditions for therapy (Rogers, 1957). Nothing more was needed; nothing less would do. This revolutionary idea meant that the medium as well as the essence of therapy was simply the *relationship* between the therapist and the client. These new humanistic formulations, so elegant and so powerful, would become the heart of the person-centered approach and the "quiet revolution" that Rogers was leading.

By the early 1970s Rogers had moved beyond his seminal work on individual psychotherapy and had turned to other person-centered applications in education, marriage therapy, and encounter groups. In the final decades of his life he took person-centered principles to the ultimate level of world peace. He and his colleagues conducted conflict resolution groups with warring factions, such as the Catholics and Protestants in Northern Ireland, blacks and whites in the Union of South Africa, and the antagonists in conflicts in El Salvador, Guatemala, and other Latin countries (Kirschenbaum & Henderson, 1989). His thoughts on international diplomacy might well be required reading for all leaders seeking rapprochement in a troubled world. He was nominated for the Nobel Peace Prize shortly before his death.

MAJOR CONCEPTS

According to Rogers' grand conception, humans have the inherent (almost magical) capacity to grow in a positive direction and to realize their full potential, if they are (lucky enough to be) nourished by the unconditional love and understanding of significant others. This pivotal idea, like the theme of a great symphony, would recur again and again in different variations throughout Rogers' life.

Of all of the major counseling theories, person-centered theory most epitomizes democratic and libertarian ideals. It is the ultimate statement about tolerance, acceptance, and willingness to allow others to live as they see fit. It most explicitly informs people that, if they want to help others to blossom, then they must love them but simultaneously stay out of their way.

Over the past half century this seemingly simple idea has grown into a far-reaching philosophical system with implications for virtually all areas of human interaction. Rogers (1980) was eventually to suggest a universal *formative* tendency that extended the idea of self-actualization to the entire universe. This formative tendency could be seen in rock crystals as well as living organisms, since they all seemed to grow in the direction of complexity, interrelatedness, and order. There are obvious philosophical and spiritual implications in the theory. Some have found ecclesiastical or deterministic overtones, while others have found almost the opposite, a total freedom from authority.

THEORY OF PERSONALITY

Rogers' theory of personality derives from his clinical practice, in which he saw people move naturally in the direction of wholeness and health. He also saw the negative emotions (e.g., anxiety, anger, jealousy, self-destruction), but these were viewed as secondary reactions to frustrations, while the overarching tendency was to heal or grow in a positive direction. The working principles to be discussed below are an adaptation of an earlier discussion by See (1986, pp. 138–139, adapted with permission).

Actualizing Tendency

According to Rogers, humans have an instinctive need to grow and develop in a positive direction. As the acorn follows its biological blueprint and develops into a mature tree, so do humans follow their blueprints. However, before this natural tendency can operate, it must be liberated by a loving and permissive environment. If the environment is nurturing, then the organism will reach its full potential. The growth process of self-actualization is characterized by increasing complexity, congruence, and autonomy.

Self-Concept

According to Rogers, the central personality construct is the picture that individuals have of themselves. It is the perceptual Gestalt and sum total of all of the thoughts, feelings, and values held and their relationships to things and people within the world. It is material consciously acknowledged about the self. It is more or less what individuals would say about themselves if they were to write a candid and exhaustive autobiography—in other words, who individuals think they are. The self-concept determines to a large extent how individuals behave.

Organismic Valuing Process

Infants evaluate experiences and behavior according to the feelings elicited. Behavior produces good feelings if it furthers the actualizing tendency of the organism. Infants do not need to be told what is right or wrong; they automatically sense it in an intuitive way. Both good and bad experiences become part of the self-concept and are accurately symbolized in awareness. Because adults lose much of this natural and wholesome reactivity to the world, the task of therapy is to help them relearn how to listen to these organismic messages from within. To the extent that adults can recapture the childlike ability to trust feelings, they become more autonomous, more alive, and more congruent.

Need for Positive Regard

During the early stages of development, a powerful secondary need emerges that can work for or against the organismic valuing process—the need for love, or positive regard, from others. When significant others provide unconditional love, infants are free to develop according to the actualizing tendency and will learn of their potential by directly experiencing the world. Because humans are instinctively good and act in ways that enhance the organism, this self-directed search for identity can be trusted to result in a well-developed and congruent personality. Certainly there will be many occasions when parental guidance or discipline is essential. For example, children cannot be given the option of deciding whether they will attend school, consume alcohol, or play with loaded guns. There are safety, health, and legal constraints that simply are not negotiable and where responsible parents must set standards. But there are also vast domains of childhood existence where it is safe and wholesome for them to choose for themselves what is best.

Things go badly for developing individuals when the love provided by significant others is dependent on how they behave. Conditional love cripples development because it requires that individuals listen to others rather than to themselves. When individuals conform in order to obtain love, they are living according to values introjected by others, or what Rogers calls the "conditions of worth." This emotional blackmail results in individuals who deny their own actualizing tendency and relinquish the right to discover their own uniqueness. In the extreme, they may become conforming, authoritarian types with rigid self-concepts.

Inner Conflict and Anxiety

Inner conflict results when individuals are torn between doing what comes naturally and what others expect. When individuals accept the values of others in order to gain positive regard, those values are internalized and become part of the personality. If the individual then behaves or thinks in ways that are inconsistent with those introjected values, the self-concept is violated and the person loses self-esteem and suffers anxiety. The mother who spanked a man 30 years ago for masturbatory activity has long been gone from this world, and yet the adult-child still gets nervous when he thinks of sex.

Individuals defend against anxiety and threats to self-esteem by developing a more rigid self-concept that will be less open to new and possibly disturbing experiences. They begin to distort reality through the use of defense mechanisms, such as denial, projection, and reaction formations. By putting tight reins on emotions, they can live out their lives in a stable but unfulfilled state. In order for therapy to be effective, there must be a weakening of these defenses to the point where the individual can sense the incongruity between the self-concept and the experiencing self. It is this identity crisis and the ensuing anxiety that may motivate the person to seek help and engage in the counseling process.

CLASSICAL PERSON-CENTERED THERAPY

In classical person-centered psychotherapy, treatment *is* the relationship between the counselor and the client. If that relationship is characterized by the following six "necessary and sufficient" conditions, then constructive personality change will take place (Rogers, 1957):

1. Two persons are in psychological contact.
2. The client is in a state of incongruence, being vulnerable or anxious.
3. The therapist is congruent or integrated in the relationship.
4. The therapist experiences unconditional positive regard for the client.

5. The therapist experiences an empathic understanding of the client's internal frame of reference and tries to communicate this experience back to the client.
6. The communication to the client of the therapist's empathic understanding and unconditional positive regard is to a minimal degree achieved.

To appreciate the above six points, it is necessary to become steeped in the material: to study, observe, and then experience it directly. The following quote from Rogers (1980, pp. 114–117) in *A Way of Being* gives an excellent subjective sense of the ways in which he saw the facilitative conditions working:

> What do I mean by a person-centered approach? It expresses the primary theme of my whole professional life, as that theme has become clarified through experience, interaction with others, and research. I smile as I think of the various labels I have given to this theme during the course of my career—non-directive counseling, client-centered therapy, student-centered teaching, group-centered leadership. Because the fields of application have grown in number and variety, the label "person-centered approach" seems the most descriptive.
>
> The central hypothesis of this approach can be briefly stated. (See Rogers, 1959, for a complete statement.) Individuals have within themselves vast resources for self-understanding and for altering their self-concepts, basic attitudes, and self-directed behavior; these resources can be tapped if a definable climate of facilitative psychological attitudes can be provided.
>
> There are three conditions that must be present in order for a climate to be growth-promoting. These conditions apply whether we are speaking of the relationship between therapist and client, parent and child, leader and group, teacher and student, or administrator and staff. The conditions apply, in fact, in any situation in which the development of the person is a goal. I have described these conditions in previous writings; I present here a brief summary from the point of view of psychotherapy, but the description applies to all of the foregoing relationships.
>
> The first element could be called *genuineness* [italics added], realness, or congruence. The more the therapist is himself or herself in the relationship, putting up no professional front or personal facade, the greater is the likelihood that the client will change and grow in a constructive manner. This means that the therapist is openly being the feelings and attitudes that are flowing within at the moment. The term "transparent" catches the flavor of this condition: the therapist makes himself or herself transparent to the client; the client can see right through what the therapist is in the relationship; the client experiences no holding back on the part of the therapist. As for the therapist, what he or she is experiencing is available to awareness, can be lived in the relationship, and can be communicated, if appropriate. Thus, there is a close matching, or congruence,

between what is being experienced at the gut level, what is present in awareness, and what is expressed to the client.

The second attitude of importance in creating a climate for change is acceptance, or caring, or prizing—what I have called *unconditional positive regard* [italics added]. When the therapist is experiencing a positive, acceptant attitude toward whatever the client is at that moment, therapeutic movement or change is more likely to occur. The therapist is willing for the client to be whatever immediate feeling is going on—confusion, resentment, fear, anger, courage, love, or pride. Such caring on the part of the therapist is nonpossessive. The therapist prizes the client in a total rather than a conditional way.

The third facilitative aspect of the relationship is *empathic understanding* [italics added]. This means that the therapist senses accurately the feelings and personal meanings that the client is experiencing and communicates this understanding to the client. When functioning best, the therapist is so much inside the private world of the other that he or she can clarify not only the meanings of which the client is aware but even those just below the level of awareness.

This kind of sensitive, active listening is exceedingly rare in our lives. We think we listen, but very rarely do we listen with real understanding, true empathy. Yet listening, of this very special kind, is one of the most potent forces for change that I know.

How does this climate which I have just described bring about change? Briefly, as persons are accepted and prized, they tend to develop a more caring attitude toward themselves. As persons are empathically heard, it becomes possible for them to listen more accurately to the flow of inner experiencings. But as a person understands and prizes self, the self becomes more congruent with the experiencings. The person thus becomes more real, more genuine. These tendencies, the reciprocal of the therapist's attitudes, enable the person to become a more effective growth-enhancer for himself or herself. There is a greater freedom to be the true, whole person.

Clearly, Rogers intended his theory to reach well beyond the boundaries of formal psychotherapy. It applies to any helping profession or situation where the intention is to promote the welfare or growth of another human being. It applies as much to the relationships between rehabilitation counselors and their clients as it does to relationships between parents and children or teachers and students. Whatever the situation, if the goal is self-actualization, then the means to that end is the therapeutic relationship as defined by the facilitative conditions.

CASE STUDY

The following excerpt from an interview carried out by Carl Rogers in 1983 illustrates some of the basic skills used in person-centered counseling (Raskin & Rogers, 1995, p. 144, reproduced with permission):

Therapist 1:   Ok, I think I'm ready. And you . . . ready?

Client 1:   Yes.

T-2:   I don't know what you might want to talk about, but I'm very ready to hear. We have half an hour, and I hope that in that half an hour we can get to know each other as deeply as possible, but we don't need to strive for anything. I guess that's my feeling. Do you want to tell me whatever is on your mind?

C-2:   I'm having a lot of problems dealing with my daughter. She's 20 years old; she's in college; I'm having a lot of trouble letting her go. . . . And I have a lot of guilt feelings about her; I have a real need to hang on to her.

T-3:   A need to hang on so you can kind of make up for the things you feel guilty about—is that part of it?

C-3:   There's a lot of that. . . . Also, she's been a real friend to me, and filled my life. . . . And it's very hard . . . a lot of empty places now that she's not with me.

T-4:   The old vacuum, sort of, when she's not there.

C-4:   Yes. Yes. I also would like to be the kind of mother that could be strong and say, you know, "Go and have a good life," and this is really hard for me to do that.

T-5:   It's very hard to give up something that's been so precious in your life, but also something that I guess has caused you pain when you mentioned guilt.

C-5:   Yeah, and I'm aware that I have some anger toward her that I don't always get what I want. I have needs that are not met. And, uh, I don't feel I have a right to those needs. You know. . . . She's a daughter; she's not my mother—though sometimes I feel as if I'd like her to be mother to me. It's very difficult for me to ask for that and have a right to it.

T-6:   So it may be unreasonable, but still, when she doesn't meet your needs, it makes you mad.

C-6:   Yeah, I get very angry, very angry with her.

PAUSE

T-7:   You're also feeling a little tension at this point, I guess.

C-7:   Yeah. Yeah. A lot of conflict . . .

T-8:   Umm-hmm . . .

C-8:   A lot of pain.

T-9:   A lot of pain. Can you say anything more what that's about?

C-9:	(sigh) I reach out for her, and she moves away from me. And she steps back and pulls back. . . . And then I feel like a really bad person. Like some kind of monster, that she doesn't want me to touch her and hold her like I did when she was a little girl. . . .
T-10:	It sounds like a very double feeling there. Part of it is, "Damn it, I want you close." The other part of it is, "Oh my God, what a monster I am to not let you go."
C-10:	Umm-hmm. Yeah. I should be stronger. I should be a grown woman and allow this to happen.

Raskin makes the following observation on this case study (Raskin & Rogers, 1995):

> The interview just quoted reveals many examples of the way in which change and growth are fostered in the person-centered approach. Rogers' straightforward statements in opening the interview (T-1 and T-2) allow the client to begin with a statement of the problem of concern to her and to initiate dialogue at a level comfortable for her. Just as he does not reassure, Rogers does not ask questions. In response to C-2, he does not ask the myriad questions that could construct a logical background and case history for dealing with the presenting problem. Rogers does not see himself as responsible for arriving at a solution to the problem as presented, or determining whether this is the problem that will be focused on in therapy, or changing the client's attitudes. The therapist sees the client as having these responsibilities and respects her capacity to fulfill them. (p. 148)

SUPPORTIVE RESEARCH

Historical Ebb and Flow of Research

Extensive empirical evidence has accumulated in support of person-centered therapy, dating back to the 1940s. In the 1950s and 1960s there was a virtual torrent of research inspired by Rogers and his colleagues that seemed to firmly establish the legitimacy of person-centered therapy (Carkhuff, 1969; Rogers, Gendlin, Kiesler, & Truax, 1967; Truax & Carkhuff, 1967). However, as pointed out by Corey (2001), little significant research on person-centered therapy has been produced in the past 20 years. In addition, as researchers examined issues more closely in the 1970s, they began to express reservations about the validity of the early findings. There was concern about the lack of rigor and quality of much of the research, and there were substantial difficulties in operationalizing the facilitative conditions (Corey, 2001; Hazler, 1999). For example, Gladstein and associates (1987) defined 18 types of empathy and eventually concluded that empathy was too complex to study. Another factor was the growing importance and influence of the behavioral therapies in the 1960s and, more recently, the cognitive and cognitive-behavioral therapies. There was also an element of benign neglect of empirical research that was shown by some humanists. Indeed, according to Cain (1993), there is a conservative influence within the person-centered school that is protective of the classical form of therapy and is unimpressed and unaffected by new findings in related fields, such as human development, clinical psychology, and psychiatry.

Possibly the greatest factor of all in the decline in popularity has been the historic migration of psychotherapy in general toward eclecticism. Sixty-eight percent of therapists have been found to claim that they were eclectic in orientation (Lambert & Bergin, 1994). In addition, there has been an ever-burgeoning number of minitheories, hybrids, and fads that have continued to emerge. Karasu (1986) estimated that there were more than 400 recognizable approaches to psychotherapy. Few of the theories have been carefully researched, and some of them can be considered dangerous, such as the regression techniques that produce false memories (Loftus, 1996). The evolution toward eclecticism, or what some have called integration, will likely continue into the future, with even less allegiance shown to discrete schools and theories, such as person-centered, behavioral, or psychoanalytical.

In spite of the historical decline in the popularity of classical person-centered therapy, substantial evidence has accumulated regarding the importance of the therapeutic relationship itself. The evidence strongly suggests that the facilitative conditions are necessary, as Rogers advocated, but they are not necessarily sufficient. In other words, empathy, positive regard, and genuineness should always be present, but there are times and situations where they will not be enough and will need to be augmented by more specialized techniques or procedures tailored to the client's needs. There is some evidence that cognitive and behavioral approaches may have advantages with particular individuals under certain circumstances, but even this conclusion is debatable and requires further documentation (Seligman, 1995).

The "Common Factors"

A timely vehicle for understanding the current status of person-centered therapy would seem to be the so-called common factors (Bergin & Garfield,

1994; Wampold, 2000, 2001). Briefly, there is considerable research evidence to support the effectiveness of psychotherapy in general, but very little support for the superiority of one type or approach over another. Thus, there probably are common factors, or nonspecific therapeutic ingredients, present in all types of therapies that account for client gain seen across different approaches.

The importance of the common factors, whatever they are, would appear to be substantial because they are known to be powerful healing agents, possibly accounting for up to 85% of the outcome variance in psychotherapy (Strupp, 1996). Research has not yet ferreted out exactly what these common factors are, but they could be something as fundamental as love, or human bonding, or the triggering of the placebo effect. Rogers' therapeutic relationship conditions are widely considered to be important components of the common factors. Lambert and Bergin (1994) had this observation:

> Among the common factors most frequently studied have been those identified by the client-centered school as "necessary and sufficient conditions" for patient personality change: accurate empathy, positive regard, nonpossessive warmth, and congruence or genuineness. Virtually all schools of therapy accept the notion that these or related therapist relationship variables are important for significant progress in psychotherapy and, in fact, fundamental in the formation of a working alliance. (p. 164)

Few contemporary scholars and researchers in counseling, even those who advocate the person-centered approach, believe that the therapeutic relationship conditions are necessary *and* sufficient for accomplishing change (Norcross & Beutler, 1997; Prochaska & Norcross, 1999). However, the belief that the conditions are necessary, although not sufficient, is commonly held, and the notion that the therapeutic relationship is a "common factor" represents a paradigm shift that could have major implications for counseling theories and the helping professions. If, for example, future research confirms that Rogers' therapeutic relationship conditions are indeed a key component of the "common factors," it would likely signal a revival of interest in person-centered therapy, and would also require other therapies to more deliberately incorporate the therapeutic relationship as a basic ingredient. The potential importance of this development was anticipated by Patterson (1986) in his *Theories of Counseling and Psychotherapy*:

> Considering the obstacles to research on the relationship between therapist variables and therapy outcomes and the factors that militate against achieving significant relationships, the magnitude of the evidence for the effectiveness of

empathic understanding, respect or warmth, and therapeutic genuineness is nothing short of astounding. The evidence for the necessity, if not the sufficiency, of these therapist qualities is incontrovertible. There is little or no evidence for the effectiveness of any other variables or techniques or for the effectiveness of other methods or approaches to psychotherapy in the absence of these conditions. (p. 562)

Although Patterson's tone might seem a bit strident, it is important to note that he is not making the claim that the conditions are sufficient, only that they are necessary. His final phrase, "in the absence of these conditions," suggests that, if the facilitative conditions were removed from the other therapies, then the techniques and procedures that remained would likely be a weak residue of questionable value. In other words, the therapeutic relationship is the platform or stage upon which more specialized techniques must operate. Other techniques cannot exist in isolation from the therapeutic relationship, and they are probably much less important.

Outcome Research

Greenberg, Elliot, and Lietaer (1994) conducted a meta-analysis of outcome studies on person-centered therapy, combined with other experiential therapies such as Gestalt, and compared them with nonexperiential therapies such as behavioral and cognitive approaches. This meta-analysis included 37 studies, involving 1,272 clients. They found that the average treated client moved from the 50th to the 90th percentile in relation to the pretreatment samples, which appeared to be a large treatment effect. When the different therapies were compared to each other, they all appeared to be equally effective, although the more directive forms seemed to have an advantage over the passive. This finding again confirmed the "Dodo bird" hypothesis from *Alice in Wonderland*: "The queen cried, 'You all win and you all get prizes!' "; in other words, all therapies work, and there does not seem to be a significant difference between them.

The following is a brief sample of outcomes of person-centered counseling that have been documented (Grummon, 1979):

- There is an improvement in psychological adjustment as shown on personality tests.
- There is less physiological tension and greater adaptive capacity in response to frustration.
- There is a decrease in psychological tension.

- There is a decrease in defensiveness.
- Friends tend to rate the client's behavior as more emotionally mature.
- There is an improvement in overall adjustment in the vocational training setting.
- Successful clients evidence strong gains in creativeness.

Some very impressive research on the person-centered approach comes, not from counseling, but from education. Aspy and Roebuck (1974) rated 550 elementary- and secondary-level teachers on the facilitative conditions (empathy, positive regard, and genuineness) and then correlated the ratings with a large number of student performance criteria. The findings seemed quite remarkable. The students of highly rated teachers showed greater gains in academic work as well as a number of nonacademic outcomes, such as creative problem-solving skills, more positive self-concept, fewer discipline problems, and lower absence rates.

In a nationwide study of practicing rehabilitation counselors, Bozarth and Rubin (1978) investigated the relationship of the facilitative conditions exhibited by counselors to rehabilitation gain exhibited by their clients. This five-year study of 160 rehabilitation counselors and 1,000 clients concluded, among other things, that "the counselors were at least as high on levels of empathy, respect, and genuineness dimensions as many other professional groups, including experienced psychotherapists in private practice" (p. 178). With reference to client gain, "the higher levels of the interpersonal skills, even though falling on the operational scale definition of minimally facilitative, tended to be related to higher vocational gain at closure, higher monthly earnings at follow-up, positive psychological change 10 months or more following intake, and greater job satisfaction at follow-up" (p. 178).

Although not an outcome study, Fier (1999) recently conducted a survey of 112 Wisconsin State Division of Vocational Rehabilitation counselors. The findings indicated that, when counselors referred their clients for psychotherapy, they sought the following theoretical orientations: eclectic or general (45 hits), behavioral (42 hits), client-centered (37 hits), reality (20 hits), and rational-emotive (11 hits); Gestalt, Freudian, trait-factor, transactional analysis, and holistic all received one or two hits. Clearly, the eclectic, behavioral, and client-centered approaches appeared to be the most popular for purchase by the counselors.

In conclusion, it is important to remember that, even though the classical person-centered approach has seen a decline in popularity, the empirical support for person-centered therapy appears to be strong and enduring.

The empirical support compares favorably with all of the other major theoretical approaches that have been examined over the years. It is possible that the growing awareness of the importance of the "common factors" could signal a renaissance of sorts for insight-oriented therapies such as the person-centered, existential, and psychodynamic approaches, where singular importance is attached to the therapeutic relationship.

PERSON-CENTERED PRINCIPLES IN REHABILITATION COUNSELING

Over the years numerous authorities in rehabilitation have recognized the critical role of the facilitative conditions in rehabilitation settings (e.g., Rubin & Roessler, 2001; See, 1986; Thomas, Thoreson, Parker, & Butler, 1998). Regarding the use of facilitative conditions in rehabilitation counseling settings, Rubin and Roessler (2001) stated:

> A quality relationship (i.e., one characterized by empathy, respect, genuineness, concreteness, and cultural sensitivity) facilitates client progress by providing a situation that the client will want to maintain, by enabling the client to verbalize real concerns, and by making the counselor a potent reinforcer in the client's life. Although a necessary element, a good relationship is not sufficient for ensuring positive rehabilitation outcomes. As Kanfer and Goldstein (1991) pointed out, a client should expect a counselor to be both "technically proficient" *and* empathic, respectful, and genuine. Rehabilitation counselor skills must be sufficiently comprehensive so that it is unnecessary for clients to make a choice between the two. (p. 265)

For those who wish to systematically incorporate person-centered principles into their rehabilitation practice, there are a few practical formulas to assist in the process. The rehabilitation service continuum can provide a framework, beginning with the client applying for services and moving through successive stages until eventual employment and successful case closure. The *first stage* is characterized by the diagnostic workup, along with the exploration of feelings and the engendering of hope. Rapport is established and the client comes to trust and value the counselor. Here the facilitative conditions are extremely important as the client struggles to find the words to symbolize the inner conflict and begins to develop an awareness of an emerging self with permission to move forward in the rehabilitation process.

After clients have made the existential determination that change is possible and desirable, they are ready to start thinking about options, goals, and strategies. This *second stage* is what might be called the thinking or planning stage, where clients and counselors together analyze and integrate the information that was collected during the initial diagnostic stage and try to develop a concrete vocational plan or goal. The Council on Rehabilitation Education (CORE, 2000) has specified that one of the educational outcomes for students of master's degree programs in rehabilitation counseling (Standard E.3.5) is the ability to "facilitate with the individual the development of a client-centered rehabilitation and/or independent living plan" (p. 25). In many ways this is the stage of common sense and logical deduction. If one needed a counseling theory for guidance at this stage, it would most likely follow from trait-and-factor or psychoeducational approaches. This stage is not as dependent on the facilitative conditions as the first stage, but, to the extent the client becomes anxious or worried, there will still be many opportunities to ventilate or "sort things out."

The *third stage* can be characterized as the action or implementation stage, in which the rehabilitation plan is implemented and the client actually begins a new job or training program. The counseling approaches that would have the most utility at this stage are action-oriented approaches, such as behavioral, rational-emotive, and reality therapy. Facilitative counseling remains part of the repertory, but it is used primarily to help the client deal with negative feelings that arise during the implementation of plans. For most clients this stage is uncharted territory and can be quite stressful and threatening. The anxiety that arises can jeopardize the rehabilitation program. The best preventative medicine at this stage is often a simple dose of the facilitative conditions in the form of "active listening" by the counselor.

A rule of thumb for incorporating a person-centered approach into rehabilitation might be stated as follows: The rehabilitation practitioner's function is to offer professional services as needed along a continuum from insight to action, remembering along the way to offer clients as much autonomy as they can handle, while still providing the support that they need. The facilitative conditions are absolutely essential during the initial self-exploration stages, but as the rehabilitation process evolves and the client's focus changes from subjective to objective realities, the counselor will increasingly need to provide services related to problem solving or skill development, consistent with behavioral and cognitive approaches. The facilitative conditions remain necessary throughout the rehabilitation process, but the sufficiency argument loses strength the further the process moves along the continuum toward engagement with the real world.

LIMITATIONS OF CLASSICAL PERSON-CENTERED COUNSELING IN REHABILITATION SETTINGS

The person-centered counseling perspective in its "classic" form possesses nearly insurmountable obstacles for rehabilitation practitioners. The term *classical* refers to in-depth therapy, guided by Rogers' formulations on personality development, that is totally nondirective. It relies exclusively on the necessity and sufficiency of the facilitative conditions. This classical approach is as distinctive for what it proscribes as for what it prescribes. The limitations listed below were identified in relation to state vocational rehabilitation practice by See (1986); however, with slight modification they can be applied to virtually any rehabilitation setting:

1. The classical model does not set goals, aside from self-actualization; yet the rehabilitation counselor is required by law to develop individualized service plans.
2. The classical model does not believe in diagnosing; yet the rehabilitation counselor is committed to using medical, psychological, and vocational evaluations.
3. The classical model does not give advice; yet one of the rehabilitation counselor's most distinctive assets is knowledge of occupational information and the world of work.
4. The classical model is relatively unconcerned with the external environment; yet the rehabilitation counselor is in constant interaction with the real world and spends considerable time coordinating community resources and delivering concrete services to the client.
5. The classical model is most effective with anxious and verbal clients; yet many rehabilitation clients do not fit this description.
6. The classical model is process oriented; yet rehabilitation counselors are accountable for end results.
7. The classical model calls for personality restructuring; yet the physically disabled are as psychologically sound as the nondisabled and do not necessarily need reorganization of the self-concept.
8. The classical model does not focus on client behavior; yet client skill development, education, and action are the lifeblood of rehabilitation. (p. 143)

In addition, there are other areas of difficulty faced by rehabilitation professionals who use person-centered principles.

Lack of Real-Life Experience

One of Rogers' basic assumptions is that "individuals have within themselves vast resources for self-understanding and for altering their self-
concepts, basic attitudes, and self-directed behavior . . . " (Rogers, 1980,
p. 114). This statement implies that clients have sufficient familiarity with
the outer world to weigh options and make choices based on reality testing.
In vocational rehabilitation the problem is complicated by the fact that
clients have often not experienced the world of work and so do not have
a basis for forming accurate self-concepts as workers. Persons without
disabilities spend a major part of their lives testing and adjusting the
self against real experiences in the environment, a lifelong developmental
process (Super, 1990). Unfortunately, persons with congenital disabilities
may have been deprived of these natural developmental experiences and
consequently can be vocationally immature as adults. Likewise, clients
who acquire a disability later in life can also face serious challenges. In
extreme cases (e.g., severe traumatic brain injury) the disability may largely
invalidate the prior experiences upon which vocational decisions were
made. For many such clients vocational rehabilitation becomes a crash
course in careers. They are expected to learn in months or years what
others have spent a lifetime absorbing, and they will likely need vocational
exploration and training more than psychotherapy. Their vocational uncertainty is often due to a lack of knowledge rather than deep inner conflicts.

Level on Needs Hierarchy

With many rehabilitation clients, it might be posited that they are more
in need of security than self-actualization. They are operating closer to the
bottom of Maslow's needs hierarchy than the top, and until they achieve
physical and psychological security, they will not have the energy or interest
to engage in self-exploration. Some years ago, an irreverent wag observed
that it's hard to think about self-actualization when you're "up to your ass
in alligators." About the only time that the facilitative conditions could
actually harm clients is when counselors are so ideologically driven that
they cannot see the alligators and insist on using insight-oriented therapy
when there are more fundamental needs, such as paying the rent or putting
food on the table. Security trumps autonomy most of the time for most
people.

Use of Confrontation

A common concern of rehabilitation professionals is the use of confrontation with clients who have inaccurate perceptions of their abilities in

relation to their vocational ambitions. For example, an egocentric client with poor people skills might decide that he wants to become a computer salesperson because of the large commissions. He is unaware that other people actively avoid talking to him. Most counselors and evaluators would agree that such a client must be confronted with the "reality" of his situation.

Many people mistakenly believe that person-centered principles are limited to techniques of attending and reflecting, seeing the therapist as supportive without being challenging (Corey, 2001). In fact, the use of confrontation is a special skill of person-centered therapists (Martin, 1983; Rogers, 1970 as cited in Graf, 1994). The essence of person-centered confrontation differs from conventional confrontation in that clients are not criticized or directed in any way; rather, they are simply shown the contradictions in their own thoughts and feelings. In the absence of external threat, they are often able to digest information and make appropriate behavior changes on their own. This type of confrontation requires considerable expertise, but it can be very effective.

Cross-Cultural Conflict

Although cross-cultural interactions have been a fertile ground for the application of person-centered principles, there have been concerns that person-centered values may conflict with the values of other cultures. For example, the person-centered emphasis on individualism, with the implied deemphasis on family, friends, and authorities, can run counter to the community-centered tenets of some cultures. Also seen as problematic is the person-centered emphasis on feelings and subjective experiences. This emphasis assumes an ability by the client to verbalize feelings and a willingness to share them in the moment with the therapist. Persons from some cultures may be reluctant or unable to participate adequately in these introspective techniques (Freeman, 1993; Usher, 1989).

CONCLUSION

Carl Rogers' contributions to the helping professions and society have been enormous. Rogers, Sigmund Freud, and B. F. Skinner are probably the three most influential behavioral scientists of the twentieth century. Each staked out a radically new way of viewing human nature. Freud, the pessimist, warned of the undercurrents, viewing people as possessed by demons and forces that need to be tamed. The role of psychotherapy and civilization is to create a veneer of sociability that will allow people to live in harmony with themselves and their neighbors. This theory was the origin and inspiration of the psychoanalytic movement and much of psychiatry. It was essentially a medical model to diagnose and treat mental illness.

B. F. Skinner, the disinterested scientist, had an entirely different view. He believed that human nature was neither good nor bad; it was simply a product of the environment. The organism, human or otherwise, learned according to the predictable principles of operant conditioning. The challenge to society is to engineer the environment so that individuals develop in directions that are socially desirable. Positive reinforcement is the *sine qua non* of the behavior therapies.

Carl Rogers, the optimist, saw the angels instead of the demons. He believed that people were innately good, with the capacity to self-actualize. This capacity, however, could only be unlocked by nurturing relationships with significant others. This perspective is the core of most humanistic and existential therapies. Some feel that Rogers' facilitative conditions (empathy, positive regard, and genuineness) come close to an operational definition of love. The person-centered approach is especially relevant for the rehabilitation professions because of its emphasis on growth and maximizing human potential.

Each of these remarkable thinkers contributed to an understanding of human nature. Their ideas have transcended psychotherapy and psychology and find expression in virtually all levels of modern discourse. In a very real sense they have taught people how to think about life. The well-informed helping professional will see these theories, and their many derivatives, as powerful tools for understanding and working with clients.

The past several decades have seen a general decline in the use of classical person-centered psychotherapy, as well as in the other long-term insight-oriented therapies. Paradoxically, however, there has been a growing conviction regarding the importance of the facilitative conditions as "common factors" that exert a positive influence in virtually all settings where humans interact. The necessity of the facilitative conditions in the helping professions is now so well established that it would seem to constitute an ethical violation to ignore or disregard them. On the other hand, taken alone, they would rarely be sufficient to promote the type of client gain that is associated with vocational and other rehabilitation programs. The sufficiency argument weakens the further the rehabilitation process moves along the continuum from insight to action therapy. Because rehabilitation is so firmly rooted in the real world, clients must be offered concrete and practical services along with the therapeutic relationship.

REFERENCES

Aspy, D. N., & Roebuck, F. N. (1974). From humane ideas to humane technology and back again many times. *Education, 95,* 163–171.

Bergin, A. E., & Garfield, S. L. (1994). Overview, trends, and future issues. In A. E. Bergin & S. L. Garfield (Eds.), *Handbook of psychotherapy and behavior change* (4th ed., pp. 821–829). New York: Wiley.

Bozarth, J. D., & Rubin, S. E. (1978). Empirical observations of rehabilitation counselor performance and outcome: Some implications. In B. Bolton & M. E. Jaques (Eds.), *Rehabilitation counseling: Theory and practice* (pp. 176–180). Baltimore: University Park Press.

Cain, D. J. (1993). The uncertain future of client-centered counseling. *Journal of Humanistic Education and Development, 31,* 133–139.

Carkhuff, R. R. (1969). *Helping and human relations* (Vols. 1–2). New York: Holt, Rinehart & Winston.

Corey, G. (2001). *Theory and practice of counseling and psychotherapy* (6th ed.). Belmont, CA: Brooks/Cole.

Council on Rehabilitation Education. (2000). *Accreditation manual for rehabilitation counselor education programs.* Rolling Meadows, IL: Author.

Fier, T. (1999). *Vocational rehabilitation counselors in the state of Wisconsin: Their theoretical orientation, the types of therapeutic intervention they purchase, and the usage and value of these techniques.* Unpublished master's thesis, University of Wisconsin-Stout, Menomonie, WI.

Freeman, S. C. (1993). Client-centered therapy with diverse populations: The universal within the specific. *Journal of Multicultural Counseling and Development, 21,* 248–254.

Gladstein, G. A., & associates (1987). *Empathy and counseling: Explorations in theory and research.* New York: Springer-Verlag.

Graf, C. (1994). On genuineness and the person-centered approach: A reply to Quinn. *Journal of Humanistic Psychology, 34,* 90–96.

Greenberg, L., Elliot, R., & Lietaer, G., (1994). Research on experiential psychotherapies. In A. E. Bergin & S. L. Garfield (Eds.), *Handbook of psychotherapy and behavior change* (4th ed., pp. 509–539). New York: Wiley.

Grummon, D. L. (1979). Client-centered theory. In H. M. Burks & B. Stefflre (Eds.), *Theories of counseling.* New York: McGraw-Hill.

Hazler, R. J. (1999). Person-centered theory. In D. Capuzzi & D. R. Gross (Eds.), *Counseling and psychotherapy: Theories and interventions* (pp. 179–201). Upper Saddle River, NJ: Merrill.

Karasu, T. B. (1986). The specificity versus nonspecificity dilemma: Toward identifying therapeutic change agents. *American Journal of Psychiatry, 14,* 687–695.

Kirschenbaum, H., & Henderson, V. L. (1989). *The Carl Rogers reader.* Boston: Houghton Mifflin.

Lambert, M. J., & Bergin, A. E. (1994). The effectiveness of psychotherapy. In A. E. Bergin & S. L. Garfield (Eds.), *Handbook of psychotherapy and behavior change* (4th ed., pp. 143–189). New York: Wiley.

Loftus, E. F. (1996). The myth of repressed memory and the realities of science. *Clinical Psychology: Science and Practice, 3,* 356–362.

Martin, D. G. (1983). *Counseling and therapy skills.* Monterey, CA: Brooks/Cole.

Norcross, J. C., & Beutler, L. E. (1997). Determining the therapeutic relationship of choice in brief therapy. In J. N. Butcher (Ed.), *Personality assessment in managed care: Using the MMPI-2 in treatment planning* (pp. 42–60). London: Oxford University Press.

Patterson, C. H. (1986). *Theories of counseling and psychotherapy* (4th ed., p. 562). New York: Harper & Row.

Prochaska, J. O., & Norcross, J. C. (1999). *Systems of psychotherapy: A transtheoretical analysis* (4th ed.). Pacific Grove, CA: Brooks/Cole.

Raskin, N. J., & Rogers, C. R. (1995). Person-centered therapy. In R. J. Corsini & D. Wedding (Eds.), *Current psychotherapies* (5th ed., pp. 144–149). Itasca, IL: Peacock.

Rogers, C. R. (1942). *Counseling and psychotherapy.* Boston: Houghton Mifflin.

Rogers, C. R. (1951). *Client-centered therapy.* Boston: Houghton Mifflin.

Rogers, C. R. (1957). The necessary and sufficient conditions of therapeutic personality change. *Journal of Consulting Psychology, 21,* 93–103.

Rogers, C. R. (1959). A theory of therapy, personality and interpersonal relationships. In S. Koch (Ed.), *Psychology: A study of science* (Vol. 3, pp. 184–256). New York: McGraw-Hill.

Rogers, C. R. (1961). *On becoming a person.* Boston: Houghton Mifflin.

Rogers, C. R. (1980). *A way of being.* Boston: Houghton Mifflin.

Rogers, C., Gendlin, E., Kiesler, D., & Truax, C. (1967). *The therapeutic relationship and its impact.* Westport, CT: Greenwood Press.

Rubin, S. E., & Roessler, R. T. (2001). *Foundations of the vocational rehabilitation process* (5th ed.). Austin, TX: Pro-Ed.

See, J. D. (1986). A person-centered perspective. In T. F. Riggar, D. R. Maki, & A. W. Wolf (Eds.), *Applied rehabilitation counseling* (pp. 135–147). New York: Springer.

Seligman, M. E. P. (1995). The effectiveness of psychotherapy: The Consumer Reports study. *American Psychologist, 50,* 965–974.

Smith, D. (1982). Trends in counseling and psychotherapy. *American Psychologist, 37,* 802–809.

Strupp, H. H. (1996). The tripartite model and the Consumer Reports study. *American Psychologist, 51,* 1017–1024.

Super, D. E. (1990). A life-span, life-space approach to career development. In D. Brown, L. Brooks, & associates, *Career choice and development: Applying contemporary theories to practice* (2nd ed., pp. 197–261). San Francisco: Jossey-Bass.

Thomas, K. R., Thoreson, R., Parker, R., & Butler, A. (1998). Theoretical foundations of the counseling function. In R. M. Parker & E. M. Szymanski (Eds.), *Rehabilitation counseling: Basics and beyond* (3rd ed., pp. 225–268). Austin, TX: Pro-Ed.

Truax, C. B., & Carkhuff, R. R. (1967). *Toward effective counseling and psychotherapy.* Chicago: Aldine.

Usher, C. H. (1989). Recognizing cultural bias in counseling theory and practice: The case of Rogers. *Journal of Multicultural Counseling and Development, 17,* 62–71.

Wampold, B. E. (2000). Outcomes of individual counseling and psychotherapy: Empirical evidence addressing two fundamental questions. In S. D. Brown & R. W. Lent (Eds.), *Handbook of counseling psychology* (3rd ed., pp. 711–739). New York: Wiley.
Wampold, B. E. (2001). *The great psychotherapy debate: Models, methods, and findings.* Mahwah, NJ: Erlbaum.

Chapter 5

Gestalt Therapy

Charles Edmund Degeneffe and Ruth Torkelson Lynch

The Gestalt therapeutic approach provides a theoretical model that has utility in providing rehabilitation interventions for people with disabilities. The central tenets include (a) a holistic view of self, (b) an understanding of the person and the environment (i.e., figure and ground), (c) a temporal emphasis on the here and now, (d) a horizontal relationship between client and counselor, and (e) an acknowledgement that awareness in the here and now leads to change (Cottone, 1992). These tenets are consistent with traditional values in rehabilitation.

HISTORICAL FOUNDATIONS

Fritz Perls is widely credited with the development of Gestalt therapy. Frederich (Fritz) Perls initially practiced as a neuropsychiatrist and was also influenced by the theater (as an actor in the Golden Twenties in Berlin), which resulted in his emphasis on nonverbal communication. Early in his career while training and practicing as a psychoanalyst, he was influenced by the work of Max Wertheimer, Wolfgang Kohler, and Kurt Koffka, all of whom believed that the psychological framework of humans was constructed from wholes, rather than collections of small and discrete units (Kogan, 1983; Passons, 1975). He was also influenced through his work with Kurt Goldstein, whose theory of holism and conceptualizations on figure-ground formulations, established major underpinnings in Gestalt theory and therapy (James & Gilliland, 2003). Gestalt therapy focuses on present experience and the cultivation of awareness of "how" clients arrive at their predicaments, in contrast to psychoanalysis, which is rooted in the unconscious, the past, and asks "why?" (Angermann, 1998).

In addition to these early teachers, Fritz Perls was influenced by his work with his wife Laura, whom he considered to be a cofounder of Gestalt therapy, and Paul Goodman, who coauthored a major Gestalt therapy text with Perls. Though they agreed on many aspects of Gestalt therapy, the two did appear to have differences in some of their therapeutic approaches. While Laura Perls promoted increased levels of permissiveness in the therapist-client relationship, Fritz Perls emphasized control. Though she worked closely with her husband on many aspects of the development of Gestalt theory as a psychotherapy, Laura Perls's contributions have largely been obscured (Kogan, 1983, pp. 244–245).

Fritz Perls lived in the United States from 1947 until his death in 1970 (Allen, 1986; Kogan, 1983). During that time, Gestalt therapy gained acceptance and recognition as a new psychotherapy, in part because of a human potential movement in the United States following World War II. During that time period, people began to seek a private understanding of meaning and values for their lives. Psychologists Abraham Maslow and Carl Rogers were important contributors in this movement. The themes of the human potential movement were consistent with the philosophical notions of understanding the nature of human personality as described by Fritz Perls in promoting Gestalt therapy. The growth of Gestalt therapy was also facilitated by the overall presence of psychotherapy as well as psychology as an academic discipline in the United States after World War II (Kogan, 1983).

In 1951, Fritz and Laura Perls founded the first Gestalt therapy institute in New York City. Therapists continue to be trained in Gestalt theory and therapy at institutes in San Francisco, New York, Los Angeles, Cleveland, and San Diego (Allen, 1986). The overall influences of Gestalt therapy have been widespread (Kogan, 1983). In addition to professionals who identify themselves as Gestalt therapists, many who practice psychotherapy from other theoretical orientations incorporate elements of Gestalt therapy into their work. Moreover, persons from various other professional disciplines (e.g., social workers, nurses, dentists, and college and high school counselors) utilize elements of the Gestalt approach.

MAJOR CONCEPTS

Theoretical Underpinnings

Gestalt therapy is based upon a set of assumptions of what it means to be human. It is distinguished from other forms of therapy by how its practitioners understand human personality. Gestalt theory postulates that humans are products of the dynamic interrelation of their mind, soul, sensations, thoughts, emotions, and perceptions, and not through discrete parts of the person (Livneh & Sherwood, 1991). Gestalt theorists do not subscribe to dichotomous concepts such as "mind" and "body," "real" and "emotional," and "unconscious" and "conscious." The focus on wholes explains the appellation *Gestalt*, which is a German word meaning the organization of a meaningful whole (Coven, 1979, p. 143). A central concept of this view of human nature is that the whole is greater than the sum of the parts. The organism functions as a whole. Therefore, difficulty in marriage will influence job performance, and failure in school is likely to affect interpersonal relationships (Patterson & Welfel, 2000). The concept of the whole also applies to interactions within the person, including the relationship between the physiological and psychological aspects of a person. As an example, emotion may be expressed through physical means, requiring a counselor to carefully observe both nonverbal and verbal behavior in order to fully understand a person (Patterson & Welfel, 2000). In fact, Perls's approach to learning about oneself does not focus much on words or thoughts, but rather on the feeling and awareness that are communicated through the body's nonverbal messages (Axelson, 1999).

Gestalt therapists stress that people have the ability to define their own reality and make their own choices (Coven, 1979), which is the basic force that shapes human life: "Every individual, every plant, every animal has only one inborn goal—to actualize itself as it is. A rose is a rose is a rose. A rose is not intent to actualize itself as a kangaroo. An elephant is not intent to actualize itself as a bird. In nature—except for the human being—constitution, and healthiness, potential growth, is all one unified something" (Perls, 1969, p. 31).

Gestalt therapy is based upon a collection of beliefs on what it means to be a human being. Passons (1975) summarized the beliefs as the following:

1. Man is a whole (rather than has) a body, emotions, thoughts, sensations, and perceptions, all of which function interrelatedly.
2. Man is part of his environment and cannot be understood outside of it.
3. Man is proactive rather than reactive. He determines his own responses to external and proprioceptive stimuli.
4. Man is capable of being aware of his sensations, thoughts, emotions, and perceptions.
5. Man, through self-awareness, is capable of choice and is thus responsible for covert and overt behavior.

6. Man possesses the wherewithal and resources to live effectively and to restore himself through this own assets.
7. Man can experience himself only in the present. The past and the future can be experienced only in the now through remembering and anticipating.
8. Man is neither intrinsically good nor bad. (p. 14)

Theory of Personality

When an individual makes choices in life that meet personal needs, homeostasis has been achieved. The natural inclination to move toward homeostasis is termed *organismic self-regulation*. Humans are seen as constantly striving for balance in their lives, and this balance is threatened by events outside oneself as well as by internal conflict (Patterson & Welfel, 2000). Needs are understood by the person through a fiqure-ground conceptualization. Figures are perceived by the person as an immediate need, as well as the strategies required to meet the need. Ground represents the physical and psychological environments having relation to the need and its fulfillment (Thomas, Thoreson, Parker, & Butler, 1998). When the figure is successfully achieved, it retreats to the background, permitting another figure to emerge to the foreground (Grossman, 1990).

People often find difficulty in reaching homeostasis because they do not know how to locate and engage with the figures in their environments that will assist them in meeting their needs. To fulfill needs, persons make contact with their environments; contact is achieved through the use of all of the senses, which include looking, listening, touching, talking, smelling, tasting, and moving (Polster & Polster, 1973). In addition, contact requires the support that comes from internal characteristics and collective experiences. According to Laura Perls (1976):

> Support is everything that facilitates the ongoing assimilation and integration for a person, a friendship, or a society: primary physiology (like breathing and digestion), upright posture and coordination, sensitivity and mobility, language, habits and customs, social manners and relationships, and everything else that we have learned and experienced during our lifetime. (p. 225)

Individuals may experience difficulties in successfully making contact because of limitations of internal, psychological growth. These limitations include introjection, projection, retroflection, deflection, and confluence (James & Gilliland, 2003; Polster & Polster, 1973). *Introjection* refers to the failure to assimilate facts, ethics, ideas, and norms from the surrounding environment. Rather than using assimilation, individuals "swallow" these concepts whole and are not able to integrate them into their personalities, resulting in feelings of phoniness, superficiality, and separation from others. Introjectors often fail to clarify preferences and expectations. *Projection* refers to placing responsibility for occurrences in life onto others. Common phrases in a projector's lexicon include *they, them, she, he,* and *you.* Projectors often feel powerless to effect change in their lives. *Retroflection* involves directing behavior toward the self that one would like to direct toward others. These behavioral impulses can be either antagonistic or loving. Retroflectors restrict interaction with their environments. *Deflectors* interact with their environments on a chance basis. They either do not spend energy or they place misguided focus on trying to make contact and, as a result, do not get from the environment what is required to have needs satisfied. With *confluence,* individuals lack a boundary between the self and the environment and with others. Confluence is often characterized by individuals who are afraid to recognize or value differences and distinctions from others.

Other problem areas that people experience in their attempts to meet life needs include unfinished business and fragmentation (Passons, 1975). *Unfinished business* refers to unfulfilled needs, unexpressed feelings, or other uncompleted important events in a person's life. The focus of the unfinished business often dominates the person's attention and awareness. Moreover, it encumbers the ability to attend to other life needs. Tobin (1983) provided an example of unfinished business in the following vignette of a worker's feeling toward his supervisor:

> A simple example would be the employee who feels angry toward his boss but, because he is frightened of being fired, decides not to express his feelings. Until he expresses his anger in some way, he is left with the physical tension that results from the impasse between the physical excitation of the anger and the inhibiting force that suppresses the emotion. He may try to deal with this unfinished situation in indirect ways, e.g., by having fantasies about telling his boss off or about the death of the boss in an accident, or by taking it out on his wife and children when he goes home that night. No matter what he does, he is tense and anxious and has a nagging feeling of not having done something he should have done. (pp. 373–374)

Fragmentation refers to denying or disowning essential needs of life (e.g., companionship) or to continuous dimensions of the self, such as thoughts, traits, values, and actions, becoming polarized (James & Gilliland, 2003). For example, an individual may identify with being only masculine or only feminine, failing to recognize dimensions of both characteristics within the self. Passons (1975) exemplified the limiting effects of dichotomization when he stated, "A person cannot feel the fullness of his strength unless he permits himself to experience enough of his weakness to be able to appreciate the contrast between the two" (p. 19).

Believing that instinct plays a part in motivating behavior, Fritz Perls emphasized a "hunger" instinct that motivates persons to take in elements of the environment. Although Gestalt theorists would view this instinct as driving the organism, behavior would not be seen as either "bad" or "good" but rather as "effective" or "ineffective" (Patterson & Welfel, 2000).

THE COUNSELING PROCESS

The purpose of counseling in the Gestalt system is to encourage personal growth. Simply put, Gestalt is an integrative approach to counseling, rooted in an existential orientation (Whitmore, 1991). Since client feelings are emphasized and the client is seen as responsible for his or her own coping behavior, Gestalt counseling is placed toward the affective and client-centered end of the continuum of counseling theories (Patterson & Welfel, 2000). Gestalt therapy is best used with individuals who seek self-growth and understanding. A basic premise of Gestalt therapy is that "individuals who are in touch with themselves, who are aware of the present, and who have a good clear sense of self and environment, when confronted by decision making are able to make decisions that are congruent with their needs and self-concepts" (Cottone, 1992, p. 142).

In the Gestalt approach, clients come for help because they are feeling that their lives are incomplete and their needs are unmet (Allen, 1986). People often develop a sense of hopelessness over the direction of their lives and are not aware of how they can help themselves (Passons, 1975). The focus of intervention involves assimilation of feelings, cognitions, beliefs, and perceptions and past, present, and future events to help in developing self-awareness and desired life needs. In the process of assimilating experience, addressing unfinished business, learning how to meet needs, and working toward becoming whole, the client works toward closure, otherwise known as "completing the unfinished Gestalt" (James & Gilliland, 2003).

A key assumption in Gestalt therapy is that clients must learn to accept responsibility for their behaviors and choices in life (Livneh & Sherwood, 1991). In his reference to Perls, Passons (1975) stressed that responsibility does not mean that clients try to meet others' expectations. Rather, taking responsibility refers to clients understanding their unique and individual abilities in achieving what they want out of life. As Perls stated (1969), "So what we are trying to do in therapy is step-by-step to re-own the disowned parts of the personality until the person becomes strong enough to facilitate his own growth, to learn to understand where are the holes, what are the symptoms of the holes. And the symptoms of the holes are always indicated by one word: avoidance" (p. 38).

Indicative of the emphasis on taking responsibility in Gestalt therapy, Allen (1986) noted that clients are continually asked to use personalizing pronouns, such as *I*, *me*, and *my*, rather than *it* or *you*, when describing their feelings and experiences. Allen suggested that nonpersonalizing pronouns allow clients to distance themselves from their situations. Allen also stressed that when clients are asked to make statements from their questions, they can re-own and take responsibility for their belief systems.

In addition to the emphasis on client responsibility, Gestalt therapy has a here-and-now orientation. There is a focus on the present behavior of the client and the meaning of the client's posture, breathing, mannerisms, gestures, voice, and facial expressions, referred to as *contact functions* (Polster & Polster, 1973). For example, clients who bow their heads or clench their fists are challenged by the therapist to recognize the associated feeling with the observed behavior (Thomas et al., 1998). Consistency between verbal statements and nonverbal behaviors is sought (e.g., "You say you were hurt and embarrassed but you are laughing"). Confrontation might also be used in response to discrepant components of verbal statements the client makes and to omissions—what the client is not saying—in order to move closer and closer to an authentic awareness and acceptance of experiences (Patterson & Welfel, 2000).

Attention to a client's senses is characteristic of the holistic orientation in Gestalt therapy, which involves the client cognitively, emotionally, sensorially, and physically (Coven, 1979). Indicative of this focus, Gestalt therapists believe that the present is the most important area of attention since the past is gone and the future has not yet arrived. In Gestalt therapy, the counselor attempts to have clients restate past and future events into present terms (Allen, 1986).

In Gestalt therapy, the relationship between the client and counselor is a dynamic, two-way encounter, referred to as the "I-thou" relationship (Yontef, 1983). Simkin (1976) suggested that in the I-thou relationship the counselor works on a horizontal level with the client. "For me, I see many therapists not sharing themselves nor encouraging the patient to invade the therapist's privacy. In the vertical relationship the 'I' remains private and hidden and deliberately or inadvertently fosters dependency and transference" (p. 79).

Gestalt counseling is not interpretive (i.e., the counselor does not interpret behavior), but the counselor needs sufficient diagnostic skills to recognize defensive attempts to hide rather than be authentic (i.e., to reflect his or her internal state accurately) (Patterson & Welfel, 2000). Gestalt therapists use an assessment method called *patterning* rather than traditional "diagnosis." This is a process of listening to the client and observing verbal and nonverbal gestures, and it requires a creative combination of therapeutic skills and theory with the therapist's awareness of her own past experiences and responses (Angermann, 1998). Such observation allows a picture or pattern to emerge about the client and his or her environment (e.g., family, relationships, peer groups).

Cottone (1992) reflected that there is no final determination or interpretation in Gestalt therapy; rather, the counselor enters into dialogue to facilitate growth of both the counselor's and the client's personality through interpersonal interactions. Although the counselor is active in the process of therapy, the interpretation of events, experiences, and even dreams is the client's responsibility. Change is allowed to unfold as clients become who they really are rather than expending energy on being someone they are not (Angermann, 1998).

STRATEGIES

Fritz Perls thought that the term *technique* sounded manipulative and controlling, but in reality he used several methods to engage and influence clients (Cottone, 1992). Angermann (1998) relates that "Gestaltists are not 'stuffy' people; they refer to their therapeutic techniques as rules and games" (p. 39). As part of achieving the goals of counseling in Gestalt therapy, the counselor attempts to engage the client in a multitude of experimental techniques by which, in the safety of the therapeutic relationship (James & Gilliland, 2003), the client is able to work through with the therapist the nature of what in the client's life is keeping him or her from fulfilling life needs. Moreover, experiments can help illustrate previously unrecognized skills and capabilities that clients already have that may be needed in achieving future goals (Polster & Polster, 1973). Gestalt techniques focus on enhancing active awareness. Commonly utilized experimental techniques include dream work, "focusing questions," role-playing via the empty chair technique, the exaggeration game, the "I take responsibility" game, and enactment.

Gestalt therapists view dreams as an existential message from one part of the self to another part (Appelbaum, 1983). Dreams can also be helpful in learning about the present relationship with the counselor as well as other group members during group therapy (Polster & Polster, 1973). In dream work, clients are asked to describe their dream as if the dream was presently occurring. Following this report, clients may then be requested to play out the various parts of the dream. This could occur by asking the client to engage in a conversation with parts of the self that were represented in the dream (James & Gilliland, 2003).

"Focusing questions" are designed to get the client to attend to certain experiences in the present, such as "How are you feeling now?" or "What are you thinking now?" (Cottone, 1992).

As implied by its name, the empty chair technique involves having the client speak to an empty chair. It is used to help clients reclaim what they have rejected (e.g., a physically abusive childhood) and teach them to use things perceived as painful and difficult (e.g., memories) to enhance their awareness and well-being (Zinker, 1977). The empty chair technique is a role-playing strategy applied to situations that require an integration of opposing parts of one's personality or a resolution of unfinished business. For example, the technique might be used to help a client communicate unexpressed feelings of anger toward a parent who died during the client's childhood. In such a scenario, the client would verbally express these feelings to the deceased parent, whom the client would imagine to be sitting in the empty chair. The client may then be asked to sit in the empty chair and assume the role of the parent, who will then communicate back to the child. The counselor functions as a "director" instructing the client to play various roles (Haney & Leibsohn, 1999).

In the exaggeration game, the client is asked to exaggerate a view that has been expressed and viewed by the counselor as defensive. The intention is for the client to see the inaccuracy of the view as the affect and content become exaggerated, so that the client may take back part of the original defensive statement (Patterson & Welfel, 2000).

The "I take responsibility" game works similarly to the exaggeration game, because the client is asked to repeat a questionable statement and follow it with the words "I take responsibility for what I have said." The client must alter the original statement if, in retrospect, he or she has doubts about it, or he or she will not feel able to take responsibility for the statement (Patterson & Welfel, 2000).

With enactment, clients are asked to act out in a dramatic manner an aspect of themselves (Polster & Polster, 1973). Enactment often addresses issues related to personal characteristics or to unfinished business, both from the distant and recent past. Through this exercise, clients often gain new insights into abilities, behaviors, and personal characteristics that had not been available to their conscious awareness. Polster and Polster (1973) presented an example of enactment as used during a group session:

> One example concerns Maeta, a young women who described herself as "being all tied up in knots." So, I asked her to tie herself up in knots and play out her own personal metaphor. This she did, twisting her arms, legs and body around in convoluted fashion, literally tying herself up. I asked her how she felt all tied up this way, and Maeta replied that she felt immobilized, tightly constricted and tense. What did she feel like doing? She felt like getting untied, and I directed her to do this gradually, untwisting one limb at a time and experiencing each of these loosenings separately. As she did this, she was surprised to realize that she was fearful of untying herself! No matter how painful and paralyzing being tied up in knots was, it was at least an identity of sorts, and if she got completely untied, she didn't know who or what she might become! (p. 276)

GESTALT APPLICATIONS TO REHABILITATION

Disability and rehabilitation have not been addressed directly in Gestalt therapy (Allen, 1986). However, it has been argued in the rehabilitation literature that Gestalt theory and therapy may have benefit in working with persons with disabilities (Allen, 1986; Coven, 1979; Grossman, 1990; Livneh & Sherwood, 1991; Thomas et al., 1998). Gestalt theory focuses on self-awareness, self-completion, self-integration, self-responsibility (Allen, 1986), and holism (Livneh & Sherwood, 1991), which is particularly relevant when working with persons with disabilities. Since one of the tasks of clients in counseling is to envision, conceptualize, and realize a new identity (e.g., after onset of a chronic illness or injury), the sustained work to "finish a gestalt" can be effective in rehabilitation. A goal of Gestalt therapy is "to aid the client to complete gestalts from the past, have richer experiences of self and others in the present, and to open a future full of new meanings that are always in formation" (Berger, 1999, p. 33). These attributes of Gestalt therapy have the potential to enhance rehabilitation practice.

Livneh and Antonak (1997, p. 3) noted that consumers of rehabilitation services, those with chronic illness and disability, face a potential array of psychological, emotional, and social stresses. Sources of these stresses include prognosis, performance of daily activities, impacts on family and friends, and fulfillment of life roles. Although a central aim of Gestalt theory is to help clients move away from an overreliance on the environment toward self-support, the theory does not ignore that fact that clients sometimes need healthy or nonmanipulative support from their environment (Bull, 1997). This balancing act between support that encourages autonomy and that which overwhelms the client is consistent with rehabilitation challenges. On a clinical level, Gestalt therapy may be helpful in helping rehabilitation clients adapt to these consequences of their impairments.

Gestalt therapy offers a number of experimental techniques for use in a rehabilitation counseling relationship. Many of these techniques may be helpful to rehabilitation clients in addressing anger (both internal and external), denial, depression, and other aspects of adapting and living with disability. Gestalt therapy interventions can be used to help clients become more aware of their feelings about living with disability, as well as ways in which they can achieve greater happiness and fulfillment in the future. Of particular utility in counseling with persons with disabilities is the focus on self-responsibility and personalizing pronouns, as well as the Gestalt experimental games of unfinished business, exaggeration, and dialogue (Livneh & Sherwood, 1991). As an example, Grossman (1990) noted that, through the empty chair technique, a client could engage in a dialogue with that part of the body (e.g., a lost limb, a prosthesis, or a phantom limb) that may have created an internal conflict between the able and disabled aspects of the client's personality.

Gestalt therapy interventions can be effective in helping persons with disabilities come to terms and bring closure to their feelings regarding what a disability has taken from their lives (Coven, 1979). Instead of only directing clients toward what their residual capabilities are, there is recognition of what has been lost. Counselors can prompt the client to discuss losses with phrases such as "what I now can't do is . . . " and "I'm frustrated by . . . " (p. 145).

In addition to its usefulness for addressing adjustment to disability issues, Gestalt therapy is also commonly used in other rehabilitation contexts, such as the treatment of alcoholism (Clemmens, 1997), group counseling (Feder & Ronall, 1980; Harman, 1996), and family counseling (Polster & Polster, 1973). Moreover, it has been used with other disability groups, including persons with mental retardation, emotional disturbances, generalized anxiety disorder, discomfort, psychosomatic disorders, and anomie; children and adolescents (Thomas et al., 1998); and persons with HIV/AIDS (Siemens, 2000) and eating disorders (Angermann, 1998).

Siemens (2000) noted the usefulness of the Gestalt approach for counseling persons with HIV/AIDS. Since a tremendous amount of shame toward the outside world remains in the lives of HIV-infected persons, Siemens noted that individuals may hide through retroflection to avoid exposure in the social community. However, there has also been a shift in perspective about HIV/AIDS, from viewing it as a terminal illness to viewing it as a chronic illness, with resulting changes in expectations for self-support. This leads to confusion for persons who are HIV-infected, many of whom have withdrawn from daily life events (including working and caring for a home). Gestalt therapy can address the retroflection process (i.e., aggression turned toward the self) and encourage the individual to realize a more accurate sense of self in the present.

There are several goals of counseling for individuals with eating disorders that Angermann (1998) asserts can be effectively addressed using Gestalt therapy: "(a) to bring awareness to internal physical and emotional states (somatic perception); (b) to understand how the client avoids contact and how boundary disturbances serve adaptive functions; (c) to integrate the self and self-image into a unified whole (address fragmentation); and (d) to examine unfinished business as it affects the present situation and blocks awareness and integration" (p. 38). For example, clients may be assisted in distinguishing between reality in their environment and the confabulations in their heads. For individuals with eating disorders, these dichotomies are present in the ways in which they see themselves and believe that others see them (e.g., physically), and in what they think of themselves (e.g., worthless, ugly) and what they assume others think of them (Angermann, 1998). The counselor might use the exaggeration technique to bring awareness to the amount of time that a person already gives to various obsessions in her or his inner world rather than facing the outer world. Another useful strategy might be the empty chair technique for the child-self and the adult-self when a client with eating disorders has assumed the role of caretaker in the family at an early age (e.g., alcoholic parents) and is trapped by a focus on the needs and expectations of others.

Coven (1979) suggested that the philosophies, theories, techniques, and rules associated with Gestalt therapy could be used in carrying out rehabilitation for individual clients and could be extended beyond a clinical level to a wider, service system domain. Yontef (1997) has suggested that Gestalt therapy has valuable applications for clinical supervision. On a clinical level, Gestalt perspectives could help clients in task completion and rehabilitation closure, help clients respond to feelings of vocational and personal inadequacy, and facilitate the process of achieving personal-vocational wholeness. For purposes of clinical supervision, a counselor could effectively help counselors in training to recognize, understand, contain, and appropriately express emotions with awareness and present-centeredness. On a broader service system level, Gestalt principles could be expressed so as to enhance client choice of services, increase the accessibility of rehabilitation professionals to their clients, and reduce the time required to go through the rehabilitation process. These types of system-level, Gestalt-based ideas appear to be consistent with many recent changes in the ways in which rehabilitation services are delivered to persons with disabilities. Especially relevant are the Gestalt ideas of humans defining their own realities and attention being given to the holistic needs of the individual. An emphasis on holism is present in disability movements, such as person-centered planning (Mount & Zwernik, 1988) and the emerging Participant-Directed Support funding models (Melda, 1997). For example, a goal established in the 1995–1997 Wisconsin Council on Developmental Disabilities state plan (Viehl & Wittenmyer, 1997) is reflective of several Gestalt-based values, including choice and recognition of personally defined needs:

> Individuals with developmental disabilities and their families have competencies, capabilities and personal goals that should be recognized, supported and encouraged. The goal for the State of Wisconsin is to support individuals and families as the primary decision makers regarding the supports and services they receive. Assistance to individuals and their families should be provided in a personalized manner, consistent with their unique strengths, resources, priorities, concerns, and capabilities. (p. 17)

It is hypothesized that rehabilitation professionals who are familiar with and identify with the philosophies and beliefs in the Gestalt approach may be more likely to support contemporary changes in the disability service system. These changes are consistent with the "I-thou" relationship between the counselor and client in which clients are the ones who determine what they want in life and who have a significant say in and personal responsibility for the ways in which they choose and utilize rehabilitation services.

CASE EXAMPLE

John is a 38-year-old man who six months ago experienced a spinal cord injury as the result of an automobile accident. He is paralyzed below the waist and lives alone in an apartment. At the insistence of his parents, John has agreed to participate in counseling. They have expressed to John their concerns that he is not adjusting well to his disability. John appears angry most of the time and has shut himself off from family and friends. When asked by others how he is feeling, John's usual response is to say things are fine and then to change the subject. The following excerpts are taken from a counseling session. In the session, John addresses his feelings about counseling and his current relationship with his parents.

Counselor:	What are your reasons for coming to counseling?
John:	My parents thought I needed it. They are concerned I haven't done well since my accident.
Counselor:	I see. How do you feel about being here today?
John:	It's all right I guess. It sounds like a good idea.
Counselor:	John, I want you to say that last sentence again. This time I want you to use "I" instead of "it" when telling me your feelings on being here.
John:	Why? What difference will that make?
Counselor:	Because you are making a statement about yourself. The way you phrased your statement doesn't sound like you are talking about your personal feelings toward counseling.
John:	Ok, here I go again. I think counseling is a good idea.
Counselor:	Do you hear the difference in the two statements?
John:	Yeah, I don't feel like I meant it the second time I told you.
Counselor:	So, how do you feel about your parents asking you to come to counseling?
John:	I understand why. They are just looking out for me. I guess it makes sense.
	(The counselor notices that John makes a fist with his right hand when he conveys his answer.)
Counselor:	Do you see what you did with your right hand when you told me that?
John:	It's in a fist.
Counselor:	What do you think that means?
John:	I'm not sure. I didn't even realize I did that.
Counselor:	John, I want you to put both of your hands in a fist for 10 seconds. When you do this, I want you to concentrate on how you feel.
Counselor:	(After 10 seconds) How do you feel now?
John:	I feel frustrated and upset.

The previous exchange illustrates the counselor's efforts to have John become self-aware of his feelings about counseling. By having John restate his original statement in terms of "I" and not "it" and having him focus on his nonverbal behavior, the counselor has facilitated the process of John owning and recognizing his true feelings. Later in the session, the counselor engages John in a discussion of his current relationship with his parents.

Counselor: How are things with your parents?
John: We get along ok. Sometimes though, they interfere too much in my life.
Counselor: How do they interfere?
John: They call every day. They come to my place and make sure I have enough food and that my personal care attendant is doing his job correctly.
Counselor: Have you told them how you feel about how much they are involved in your life?
John: No.
Counselor: Why not?
John: They are trying to help me. I couldn't say how I feel to their faces.
Counselor: John, I want you to try an experiment. I want you to talk to that empty chair next to us and pretend that you are actually talking to your parents about your feelings.
John: Ok, but this seems a bit strange. I've never done anything like this before.
Counselor: That's ok. Just give it a shot.
John: Mom and dad, I appreciate what you try to do for me. But I want to live my own life. I'm 38 years old and I can do things for myself.
Counselor: Are you angry with them?
John: Yeah, but I understand why they interfere.
Counselor: I don't want you to focus on their feelings. I want you to focus on how you feel and I want you to express your anger.
John: Mom and dad, you embarrass me when you come over and check my cabinets for food. You make me angry when you interrogate my attendant on how he does things. (John's face becomes flushed and he begins to raise his voice.) Live your own life and let me live mine! I can't worry about making sure you're satisfied on what goes on with my life! Let me worry about that.

With the empty chair technique, John gets the experience of actually saying out loud what he has been feeling about his relationship with his parents. He begins to allow himself to consciously feel what he has tried to suppress and, for the first time, has an experience related to what he might actually say in the future to his parents. Later in the session, the counselor asked John to pretend that he was his own parent who was speaking to him about why they are so involved in his life. The use of the empty chair may be part of a foundation on which John will develop a better relationship with his parents, especially on issues related to autonomy, choice, and independence. He can learn to recognize his feelings prior to an actual interaction, to acknowledge those feelings, and to rehearse an approach that will convey his feelings without necessarily being hurtful (which would end up being counterproductive).

RESEARCH FINDINGS

Research on the processes and outcomes of Gestalt therapy has been limited (Allen, 1986; Fagan & Shepherd, 1970; Simkin, 1976) because of both methodological factors (Fagan & Shepherd, 1970; Thomas et al., 1998) and philosophical considerations (Allen, 1986; Livneh & Sherwood, 1991). As previously mentioned, Gestalt therapy is an existential approach, and therefore the measurement of therapeutic outcomes poses several difficulties (May & Yalom, 1995), since goals often focus on deep layers of client self-perception and a search for life meaning. This type of focus is difficult, if not impossible, to quantify. As Fagan and Shepherd (1970) stressed:

> Most often, hard data are difficult to obtain: the important variables resist quantification; the complexity and multiplicity of variables in therapist, patient, and the interactional processes are almost impossible to unravel; and the crudeness and restrictiveness of the measuring devices available cannot adequately reflect the subtlety of the process. (p. 241)

Beyond these methodological considerations, Gestalt therapists have traditionally been philosophically resistant to formal measurement of the outcomes of their interventions. In his reference to Simkin, Allen (1986) noted that Gestalt therapists often do not see the benefits of research methodology or formal psychodiagnostic evaluation. Moreover, Gestalt therapists often subscribe to the belief that the most efficacious tool for evaluating client outcomes is clinical judgment. They commonly believe that therapeutic outcome can be evaluated by subjective indicators, such as client change in outlook, adequate self-expression, the ability to extend awareness to the verbal level, and assumption of responsibility (Livneh & Sherwood, 1991, p. 531).

There have been recent efforts in psychology to expand the extent to which components of Gestalt therapy are evaluated and are based on established methods. Thomas et al. (1998) noted that there have been recent efforts to integrate a variety of theoretical and empirical outcomes from mainstream psychology into the ways in which Gestalt therapy is conducted. Indicative of the growing emphasis on quantitative evaluation, Greenberg, Elliott, and Lietaer (1994) conducted a review of previous research on Gestalt therapy outcome, process, and specific therapeutic task interventions. Regarding outcome, Greenberg and colleagues cited research indicating that Gestalt therapy was equal in effectiveness to nondirective-plus bibliotherapy in the treatment of depression. Moreover, Gestalt therapy was found to be equally effective with behavioral therapy on client outcomes, using measures of target complaints, personal orientation, and adjustment. They also noted that psychotherapy process research has identified the common counseling strategies used in Gestalt therapy, including in-session advisement, reflections, interpretations, disclosure, questions, and information. Research on psychotherapy process variables has also indicated that Gestalt therapists most often focus on issues related to the here and now, to experiences, and to feelings, and a majority of the time they use action verbs in their responses to clients.

Finally, Greenberg et al. (1994) reviewed research on two Gestalt therapy interventions, the two-chair and empty chair dialogue techniques. Based on several studies comparing two-chair dialogue with non-Gestalt interventions, two-chair dialogue was found to be a superior strategy in working with clients who are experiencing splits or conflicts between two aspects of self. Two-chair dialogue was effective in helping clients achieve enhanced depth of experiencing, focusing ability, and decision-making skills. Regarding empty chair dialogue, research has indicated it to be an effective method for addressing unfinished business.

STRENGTHS AND SHORTCOMINGS OF THE GESTALT APPROACH

A review of the strengths of Gestalt therapy is somewhat limited to anecdotal sources of support since there has only been limited research on therapeutic outcomes. However, its effectiveness is demonstrated by the fact that it is a well-developed, often used approach for many different types of clients with a variety of types of need.

Gestalt therapy has made a number of contributions to counseling and psychotherapy in general (James & Gilliland, 2003). It has identified the importance of not only attending to the client's verbal statements and cognitive processing, but also to the client's existential understanding of what is happening in therapy and in the client's life. In contrast to therapies that stress technique rather than process, it has brought a creative approach to therapy, since Gestalt therapists approach each encounter with clients as a unique existential experience. They attempt to respond to clients in ways that are uniquely focused on the needs and personality of each individual. In addition to its applicability to disability issues, Gestalt therapy works well for many different types of counseling needs, including gender issues, crisis, and poverty, as well as with interaction groups. Finally, Gestalt therapy has emphasized the idea that significant therapeutic meaning can come from a client's nonverbal behavior and language.

Gestalt therapy works best for people whose enjoyment of life seems to be minimal and who appear to be internally restrictive and overly socialized, restrained, and constricted, those often referred to as neurotic, phobic, perfectionistic, ineffective, and depressed (Shepherd, 1970). Gestalt therapy also works best for clients who are cerebral, referred to by Simkin (1976, p. 35) as being "up in their head." Clients who experience Gestalt therapy should be willing to change and take responsibility for their emotional, cognitive, and physical behavior (Passons, 1975). Gestalt therapy does not work as well for clients who are less organized, more severely disturbed, or psychotic (Shepherd, 1970), and, because of these limitations, it may be ruled out as a counseling approach of choice for some rehabilitation clients.

Another limitation of Gestalt therapy is the extensive training required of its practitioners, which includes receiving Gestalt therapy as a counselee as a part of training; this may limit its use by rehabilitation counselors (Thomas et al., 1998). Because clients may have a wide range of reactions to the dynamic and experimental nature of Gestalt therapy, practitioners need extensive training and must have a solid understanding of what exactly will work for each individual client (Passons, 1975).

Despite its limitations, practitioners in rehabilitation can use many of the techniques, philosophies, and emphases of Gestalt therapy in working with and understanding their clients. The theory offers a client-focused, process-oriented, existential approach for understanding people with disabilities who are participating in rehabilitation and for facilitating their growth and awareness. Gestalt philosophy and theory are generally consistent with values that have long been held in rehabilitation and can provide important elements and techniques for use in counseling.

REFERENCES

Allen, H. A. (1986). A Gestalt perspective. In T. F. Riggar, D. R. Maki, & A. W. Wolf (Eds.), *Applied rehabilitation counseling* (pp. 148–157). New York: Springer.

Angermann, K. (1998). Gestalt therapy for eating disorders: An illustration. *Gestalt Journal*, 21(1), 19–47.

Appelbaum, S. A. (1983). A psychoanalyst looks at Gestalt therapy. In C. Hatcher & J. Aronson (Eds.), *The handbook of Gestalt therapy* (3rd ed., pp. 753–778). New York: Jason Aronson.

Axelson, J. A. (1999). *Counseling and development in a multicultural society.* Pacific Grove, CA: Brooks/Cole.

Berger, G. (1999). Why we call it Gestalt Therapy. *Gestalt Journal*, 22(1), 21–35.

Bull, A. (1997). Models of counselling in organizations. In M. Carroll & M. Walton (Eds.), *Handbook of counseling in organizations* (pp. 29–41). Thousand Oaks, CA: Sage.

Clemmens, M. C. (1997). *Getting beyond sobriety: Clinical approaches to long-term recovery.* San Francisco: Jossey-Bass.

Cottone, R. (1992). *Theories and paradigms of counseling and psychotherapy.* Boston: Allyn & Bacon.

Coven, A. B. (1979). The Gestalt approach to rehabilitation of the whole person. *Journal of Applied Rehabilitation Counseling, 9,* 144–147.

Fagan, J., & Shepherd, I. L. (1970). *Gestalt therapy now: Theory, techniques, applications.* New York: Harper & Row.

Feder, B., & Ronall, R. (1980). *Beyond the hot seat: Gestalt approaches to group.* New York: Brunner/Mazel.

Greenberg, L. S., & Elliott, R. K. (1994). Research on experimental psychotherapies. In A. E. Bergin & S. L. Garfield (Eds.), *Handbook of psychotherapy and behavior change* (pp. 509–539). New York: Wiley.

Grossman, E. F. (1990). The Gestalt approach to people with amputations. *Journal of Applied Rehabilitation Counseling, 21*(1), 16–21.

Haney, H., & Leibsohn, J. (1999). *Basic counseling responses: A multimedia learning system for the helping professions.* Pacific Grove, CA: Brooks/Cole.

Harman, R. L. (1996). *Gestalt therapy techniques: Working with groups, couples, and sexually dysfunctional men.* Northvale, NJ: Jason Aronson.

James, R. K., & Gilliland, B. E. (2003). *Theories and strategies in counseling and psychotherapy* (5th ed). Boston: Allyn & Bacon.

Kogan, J. (1983). The genesis of Gestalt therapy. In C. Hatcher & J. Aronson (Eds.), *The handbook of Gestalt therapy* (3rd ed., pp. 235–258). New York: Jason Aronson.

Livneh, H., & Antonak, R. F. (1997). *Psychological adaptation to chronic illness and disability.* Gaithersburg, MD: Aspen.

Livneh, H., & Sherwood, A. (1991). Application of personality theories and counseling strategies to clients with physical disabilities. *Journal of Counseling and Development, 69,* 525–538.

May, R., & Yalom, I. (1995). Existential psychotherapy. In R. J. Corsini & D. Wedding (Eds.), *Current psychotherapies* (5th ed., pp. 262–292). Itasca, IL: Peacock.

Melda, K. (1997). *Participant-directed managed supports: Breaking new disabilities services*. Salem, OR: Human Services Research Institute.

Mount, B., & Zwernik, K. (1988). *It's never too early, it's never too late: A booklet about personal futures planning*. St. Paul, MN: Metropolitan Council.

Passons, W. R. (1975). *Gestalt approaches in counseling*. New York: Holt, Rinehart & Winston.

Patterson, L. E., & Welfel, E. R. (2000). *The counseling process* (5th ed.). Belmont, CA: Wadsworth/Thomson Learning.

Perls, F. S. (1969). *Gestalt therapy verbatim*. Lafayette, CA: Real People Press.

Perls, L. (1976). Comments on the new directions. In E. W. L. Smith (Ed.), *The growing edge of Gestalt therapy* (pp. 221–226). New York: Brunner/Mazel.

Polster, E., & Polster, M. (1973). *Gestalt therapy integrated* (3rd ed.). New York: Brunner/Mazel.

Shepherd, I. L. (1970). Limitations and cautions in the Gestalt approach. In J. Fagan & I. L. Shepherd (Eds.), *Gestalt therapy now: Theory, techniques, applications* (pp. 234–238). Palo Alto, CA: Science & Behavior Books.

Siemens, H. (2000). The Gestalt approach: Balancing hope and despair in persons with HIV/AIDS. *Gestalt Journal, 23*(2), 73–79.

Simkin, J. S. (1976). *Gestalt therapy mini-lectures*. Millbrae, CA: Celestial Arts.

Thomas, K. R., Thoreson, R. W., Parker, R. M., & Butler, A. J. (1998). Theoretical foundations of the counseling function. In R. M. Parker & E. M. Szymanski (Eds.), *Rehabilitation counseling: Basics and beyond* (3rd ed., pp. 225–268). Austin, TX: Pro-Ed.

Tobin, S. A. (1983). Saying goodbye in Gestalt therapy. In C. Hatcher & J. Aronson (Eds.), *The handbook of Gestalt therapy* (3rd ed., pp. 371-385). New York: Jason Aronson.

Viehl, W., & Wittenmyer, J. (1997). *Self-determination and full citizenship throughout one's lifespan: Proposed three year plan for supporting people with developmental disabilities 1998–2000*. Madison, WI: Wisconsin Council on Developmental Disabilities.

Whitmore, D. (1991). *Psychosynthesis counselling in action*. Newbury Park, CA: Sage.

Yontef, G. M. (1983). The theory of Gestalt therapy. In C. Hatcher & J. Aronson (Eds.), *The handbook of Gestalt therapy* (3rd ed., pp. 213–222). New York: Jason Aronson.

Yontef, G. (1997). Supervision from a Gestalt Therapy perspective. In C. E. Watkins, Jr. (Ed.), *Handbook of psychotherapy supervision* (pp. 147–163). New York: Wiley.

Zinker, J. (1977). *Creative process in Gestalt therapy*. New York: Brunner/Mazel.

Chapter 6

Logotherapy

Joseph N. Ososkie and
Jerome J. Holzbauer

Viktor Frankl's logotherapy is an existential counseling approach, or "existential psychiatry" (Frankl, 1986), that is primarily focused upon an individual's search for meaning in life (Frankl, 1984). In fact, logotherapy has been described by Gould (1993) as meaning analysis. It would also qualify as a form of existential psychodynamics (May & Yalom, 2000); however, inner conflict does not involve psychosexual urges or conscious and unconscious drives. Rather, this conflict is "between the individual and the 'givens' of existence" (p. 273). Logotherapy is concerned with assisting clients in their effort to find meaning in life in relation to prominent existential concerns of death, freedom, responsibility, isolation, and meaninglessness (Corey, 2001; May & Yalom, 2000; Patterson & Watkins, 1996). Additionally, Frankl's logotherapy has been referred to as the third Viennese school of psychotherapy (Barnes, 1995), following Freud's psychoanalysis and Adler's individual psychology. The three theories differ in their motivational conceptualizations. Freud argued for the pleasure principle, and Adler acknowledged the importance of striving for superiority (Corey, 2001). Frankl described these two concepts as the will to pleasure and the will to power, respectively, with his motivational concept being the will to meaning (Frankl, 1988).

Gould (1993) indicates that logotherapy is utilized effectively as a supplementary therapy: "Counselors trained in meaning analysis are often able to help persons who have to deal with the deterioration of or injuries to the body and enable them to recognize, appreciate, and build on the parts of the self that are still healthy and intact" (p. 151). Logotherapy can be an effective counseling approach in assisting clients in their search for a meaningful life with a disability. Individuals who have disabilities may not control fate, but they are able to decide what their attitudes regarding their fate will be. According to Frankl (1984), individuals can find meaning in unavoidable suffering, which he termed "tragic optimism."

HISTORY AND DEVELOPMENT

The theories of Victor Frankl were exemplified in the sufferings in his life. "His life was an illustration of his theory, for he lived what his theory espouses" (Corey, 2001, p. 141). No more compelling example of transcending tragedy can be found than the account of Frankl's experiences in Nazi death camps, detailed in his acclaimed, internationally received, and powerful book *Man's Search for Meaning* (Frankl, 1984). He began writing this book prior to imprisonment, had the notes taken from him upon capture, and lived the philosophy of the book while facing the horrible suffering in the concentration camps of Auschwitz and Dachau. His parents, brother, and pregnant wife were killed in the camps (American Counseling Association, 1997). He lost everything but "the last of human freedoms—to choose one's attitude in any given set of circumstances, to choose one's own way" (Frankl, 1984, p. 104).

Frankl's book, *Man's Search for Meaning*, effectively conveyed the message of logotherapy. The book has been translated into over 20 languages (Corey, 2001) and has been reprinted numerous times, selling more than 10 million copies. Currently, there is a European Logotherapy Institute and the Viktor Frankl Institute of Logotherapy in the United States. A World Congress of Logotherapy is convened every other year, and logotherapy training and credentialing are offered through the Viktor Frankl Institute of Logotherapy. *The International Forum for Logotherapy* is the English-language professional journal that publishes articles and research dealing with applications and theses regarding logotherapy.

According to Patterson and Watkins (1996), Frankl began his professional career in psychiatry with a psychoanalytic orientation. Frankl never denied the existence of the unconscious process in human personality. However, he repudiated the thesis that it is a purely instinctive sphere of psychic activity. He rejected the deterministic notions of Freud. To Frankl, more important than the unconscious psychic drives was the spiritual unconscious, because spirituality was viewed as the source of conscience and love (Tweedie, 1961).

Frankl first used the term *logotherapy* in his writings in 1938. The Greek word, *logos*, was taken to have a twofold sense of "meaning" and "spirit."

On the one hand, it refers to the necessity of meaningfulness in human experience beyond the level of the merely psychological. On the other hand, *logotherapy* also refers to the spiritual factor, which is the cornerstone on which the structure of Frankl's theory stands (Tweedie, 1961). *Logos* is meaning and *therapie* is healing. Therefore, logotherapy signifies healing through meaning (Gould, 1993). Gould relates that Frankl preferred the term *existential analysis* but that Ludwig Binswanger had already introduced that term. In fact, Gould himself prefers to refer to logotherapy as *meaning analysis*. He indicates that "it is difficult for any group—including the followers of Frankl—to agree on a common title for his philosophy and method" (p. xii).

Frankl was influenced by the writings of existential philosophers, including Kierkegaard, Nietzsche, Heidegger, and Jaspers. He developed his own existential philosophy and psychology after studying these authors. His subsequent theory, logotherapy, does not appear rooted in any of the modern existential philosophical systems. Instead of overemphasizing self-conscious, subjective states of experience like the other existential philosophers, Frankl emphasized that true existence is a decisive commitment away from self to the objective world of meaning and value (Tweedie, 1961). Existence is predicated on the attitudes that one holds in terms of the meanings attached to experiences within one's world and in interaction with others within one's world.

Gould (1993) compares Frankl with Greek and German philosophers, Eastern philosophers, and Native American shamans. He suggests that Frankl, "while aware of the Greek contribution, represents a philosophical viewpoint that is a mixture of secularized Judaism, Renaissance thinking, German Enlightenment, existentialism, phenomenology, and Humanistic psychology" (p. 159). Some of these philosophical viewpoints may at times seem to be contradictory, but Frankl employs what he has grasped from these writings to weave a holistic philosophical and psychological theory. These collective influences on Frankl may account for his widespread impact on people from various cultures and on individuals and professionals adhering to differing spiritual as well as psychological beliefs.

THEORETICAL CONCEPTS

Probably the most critical and central theoretical concept of logotherapy is the will to meaning (Frankl, 1988). The following affirmations are thematic and philosophical directives of logotherapy: (a) life has meaning; (b) we are motivated by our will to meaning; (c) we have freedom to find meaning; and (d) the dimensions of the self are mind, body, and spirit (Gould, 1993). People are soma, psyche, and noetic. The noetic dimension is what differentiates logotherapy from most all other psychological theories. It is this dimension of the self that defines the individual as truly human. Logotherapy can be characterized as unequivocally rejecting nihilism, reductionism, and pandeterminism (Frankl, 1984). It is existential, humanistic, and phenomenological. Choice, freedom, responsibility, and meaningfulness define logotherapy.

Meaning in Life

A logotherapeutic assumption is that life has meaning in all circumstances and that people are free to choose meaning in life. Along with the freedom to choose comes the responsibility to exercise choice and to search for personal meaning (Frankl, 1984). People are in fact motivated by a will to meaning (Frankl, 1988). Accordingly, they are not living responsibly if they are not seeking it. This search for meaning does not have to be a search for the ultimate meaning in life. "What matters, therefore, is not the meaning of life in general but rather the specific meaning of a person's life at a given moment" (Frankl, 1984, p. 131). Such a here-and-now perspective highlights the importance of living in the moment, of finding purpose in the present moment.

Frankl (1984) explains that there is meaning in love, work, suffering, the finiteness of life, and supermeaning. What is evident is that meaning comes from involvement in one's world. Meaning is found experientially. He indicates that perhaps life questions individuals rather than individuals questioning life. People are challenged by life, according to Frankl, and they act responsibly when life's challenges, including life's transitoriness, are accepted. "Instead of possibilities, I have realities in my past, not only the reality of work done and of love loved, but of suffering bravely suffered" (p. 144). Lukas (1983) relays that life connects people to the world. Meaning does not result from withdrawal and isolation.

Meaning is discovered by way of creative values, experiential values, and attitudinal values (Frankl, 1984). Creative values are realized by achieving tasks. Experiential values are realized by experiencing what is beautiful in the world. Experiencing the uniqueness of another, or loving another, is an experiential value. Attitudinal values are realized by the attitude taken toward fate or suffering. Frankl (1984, 1986, 1988) clearly reports that people may not be able to control what life presents, but they are able to choose their attitude toward these situations.

Because there is meaning in life, Frankl (1984) reasoned that there is meaning in suffering, since suffering and death are ineradicable aspects of life. Of course, "to suffer unnecessarily is masochistic rather than heroic" (p. 136). But not finding meaning in suffering, according to Frankl, can result in despair and self-destruction. It would appear that he is direct in his assertion that to live responsibly, people must search for what meaning can be found in suffering, and if they do not, there is little reason to carry on. "Once an individual's search for meaning is successful, it not only renders him happy but also gives him the capability to cope with suffering" (Frankl, 1984, p. 163).

A chronic existential vacuum, or meaninglessness, which Frankl called noogenic neurosis, can be the result of the pursuit of happiness or the frustration of the will to meaning (Frankl, 1988). Meaning must ensue and cannot be pursued. An outside focus or perspective is important. May and Yalom (2000) suggest that the solution to meaninglessness is in fact engagement. One must be able to look beyond oneself to combat the existential vacuum. The pursuit of happiness is elusive, but the pursuit of meaning is within reach. Upon finding meaning, one will find happiness.

Self-Transcendence

Happiness was perceived by Frankl (1984) not as a goal, but as an automatic by-product of a meaningful life, in which one finds satisfaction in forgetting oneself. He speaks of how humans are capable of self-detachment or self-transcendence (Frankl, 1986). Frankl insists that people are directed "toward something or someone other than oneself, namely, toward meanings to fulfill, or toward other human beings to encounter lovingly" (p. 294).

Barnes (1995) recognized that individuals may find meaning through self-discovery, choice, uniqueness, responsibility, and self-transcendence. The last-mentioned, self-transcendence, allows the individual to find meaning by reaching out to others. Helping others in this case may result in personal satisfaction. "Inner directedness, isolation, and self-absorption do not equate with sufficient mental health according to logotherapeutic perspectives" (Ososkie, 1998, p. 219). The capacity for self-transcendence may reduce psychological stress if meaning in the outside environment is perceived (Lukas, 1983).

Will to Meaning

Frankl (1988) contended that humans have a motivation toward meaning fulfillment, or a will to meaning. The will to meaning contrasts with the will to pleasure and the will to power. Freud's pleasure principle and Adler's striving for superiority, respectively, differ in that both theoretical, motivational constructs apply at less mature levels of personality development. Pleasure may have more applicability at the child level of development, and power may have more applicability at the adolescent level of development. In other words, pleasure guides the child and power guides the adolescent (Frankl, 1988). Also, pleasure may result from meaning fulfillment and not directly by pursuing happiness.

Frankl (1988) contends that the pursuit of meaning in life is accomplished at a truly human level of the self. Power and pleasure satisfaction do not bring individuals to a level that is solely a human level. What makes a person truly human is exercising a higher dimension of the self, the spiritual or noetic dimension.

In existential terms, anxiety or some sense of tension is part of being human, or existing (Corey, 2001; May & Yalom, 2000). A search for meaning may result in a degree of tension, which "is inherent in being human and is indispensable for mental well-being" (Frankl, 1988, p. 48). The responsibility to choose is also part of finding meaning. According to Frankl, "meaning fulfillment always implies decision-making" (p. 43).

Dimensional Ontology

Humans are composed of three dimensions: somatic, or physical; psychic, or psychological; and noetic, or spiritual (Frankl, 1986). The dimensions of the self are a unity and are interdependent. The spiritual dimension, the noetic, is the truly human dimension of the self. The physical and psychological dimensions include inherited factors (Patterson & Watkins, 1996) and can be seen as comprising drives, but spirituality is viewed as the characteristic distinguishing people from animals. Frankl (1957; cited in Tweedie, 1961) promoted the importance of the spiritual unconscious. "In other words, we know and acknowledge, not only an instinctive unconscious, but rather also a *spiritual unconscious*, and in it we see the supporting ground of all conscious spirituality. The ego is not *governed* by the id, but the spirit is *borne by the unconscious* (p. 57). The noetic dimension is the primary and guiding aspect of the individual.

Freedom is the second characteristic of human existence. Individuals have freedom in regards to instincts, inheritance, and environment (Patterson & Watkins, 1996). Humans are free to choose values and attitudes in relation to circumstances and conditions of life. "Thus human beings do not simply exist; they decide what their existence will be" (p. 433). Deciding on what one's existence will be is being future-directed.

Responsibility is the third characteristic of human existence (Patterson & Watkins, 1996). Individuals do not only have freedom *from* something, they have freedom *to* something, and these are the individual's responsibilities, according to Frankl (1984). Here again, engagement and personal involvement are critical in terms of freedom and responsibility. Responsibility is always in relation to something or someone, and one becomes part of a community (Patterson & Watkins, 1996).

LOGOTHERAPEUTIC PROCESS

Logotherapy as a psychotherapeutic approach includes the techniques and constructs of paradoxical intention, dereflection, hyperreflection, self-distancing, attitude modulation, Socratic dialogues, and self-transcendence (Gould, 1993; Lucas & Hirsch, 2002). It is an existential psychotherapy that relies on a phenomenological perspective. It is humanistic and didactic and requires clients to consider their attitudes toward circumstances in their lives (Frankl, 1986). It helps people deal with somatogenic, psychogenic, and sociogenic problems (Gould, 1993).

Gould (1993) outlines the process of meaning analysis as (a) symptom distancing by means of dereflection, (b) attitude modulation, (c) openness to change, and (d) finding purpose and meaning. Dereflection is intended to counteract hyperreflection, or excessive attending to one's symptomatology. This fosters movement toward the positive aspects of one's life. The counselor facilitates movement away from symptoms by focusing on what clients are able to change and their attitudes toward that which they cannot change. However, counselors should be cautioned against symptom denial and realize that effective symptom distancing can only come after acknowledgment of the problem. Attitude modulation is within the grasp of the client. Individuals are able to detach from their problems and to decide what their attitudes will be about their situations (Frankl, 1986). Openness to change is possible when symptoms and cognitions about these symptoms do not dominate the individual's thinking.

Finding meaning and purpose in life is the essence of logotherapy. It stresses uniqueness, dignity, and a holistic self (Gould, 1993). Tension exists within the individual in the exploration of meaning. Homeostasis of spirit and psyche is not encouraged; if one does not search for meaning, stagnation, frustration, and neurosis will be the result. A key component in meaning exploration is self-awareness. Life is an individual journey in relationship with others. "This self-awareness increases both inward knowledge of our drives, our needs, and our aspirations and an outward

understanding of what it means to live our lives in relation to others"
(Gould, 1993, p. 145).

Lukas (1980) discusses a three-step process: (a) gaining distance from
the symptoms that cause distress and despair, (b) modifying of unhealthy
attitudes, and (c) searching for new meanings. Lukas has noted:

> Identification with their symptoms locks them into self-centeredness. Excessive
> attention to negative factors blocks their view beyond themselves. Only when
> they have broken through the shells of their self-centeredness and the barriers
> of the negative factors are they able to see the positive factors in new meaningful
> activities and experience beyond themselves, and thus the way is open to a
> healing process. (p. 34)

The logotherapeutic process allows individuals to move beyond their symptoms and illnesses and to take a stand regarding them. Clients are in a
position to distance themselves and to, in effect, self-transcend. Meanings
are established in outward activities and involvements.

Therapist Role and Responsibilities

Guttman (1996) indicated that the neglect of the helping professional's
own spiritual dimension is a recognized problem. Whether one believes
in God is a personal matter and a private value. However, logotherapists
need to formulate a worldview, a basic perception of the world that gives
them a sense of security. Without a sense of spiritual security, logotherapists
can find themselves in a conflict over personal and professional values.

The logotherapist must not impose personal values upon clients. Clients
must be free to decide. In the same manner, logotherapists should not
decide what new meanings will be for clients. Assisting clients in attitude
modulation and the search for new meanings requires the therapist to
foster client choice, freedom, and responsibility. It may be necessary to
help clients discover alternatives and to consider various perspectives.
Decision making, however, is the responsibility of the client.

Logotherapists may employ a variety of therapeutic techniques to assist
clients in their search for new meanings (Frankl, 1986). The logotherapist
does utilize dialogue techniques and questions client motivations. Didactic
methods may also be used to help clients grasp the ideas inherent in
attitude modulation, self-detachment, and self-transcendence. It may be
beneficial to recognize that clients may have difficulty determining what
meaning in life applies from suffering. Finding meaning in suffering may
elude individuals initially devastated by disaster, chronic illness, or injury.

Logotherapists must be cautioned not to rush the therapeutic process and rescue clients from their pain and struggles.

Paradoxical Intention

The capability of individuals to self-transcend and to self-detach are qualities of human existence that Frankl (1988) relies upon in the logotherapy techniques of dereflection and paradoxical intention. Dereflection combats hyperreflection or excessive attention on oneself or on a characteristic of oneself. Constant or excessive attending to oneself will result in a limiting and stressful relationship with others. Since the logotherapy concept of will to meaning is actually directed outward, the hyperreflective individual is not effectively open to fulfilling meanings in relation to others. Attitude modulation (Gould, 1993) is hindered by hyperreflection. Dereflection gives an individual the chance to contemplate existence with the understanding that existence does not occur in isolation. Hyperreflection hampers the experiential nature of human existence.

By means of the logotherapeutic technique of paradoxical intention, Frankl (1986) used short-term or brief therapy to treat obsessive-compulsive disorders and phobias (Frankl, 1988). "Paradoxical intention means that the patient is encouraged to do, or wish to happen, the very things he fears" (p. 102). The wish of the symptom is the paradox, and the fear of the event happening again is broken by the wish that it will happen. Paradoxical intention rests on an individual's ability to self-detach, to look at oneself from a distance. Frankl (1988) indicated that a degree of humor should accompany the paradoxical directive of the therapist. He felt that the human quality of humor facilitates the technique of paradoxical intention because it "allows man to create perspective, to put distance between himself and whatever may confront him" (p. 108). Paradoxical intention interferes with what Frankl (1988) referred to as "anticipatory anxiety." Experiencing anxiety out of fear that a symptom may recur is reinforcing of the symptom. A cycle is established that can be broken by paradoxical intention.

LOGOTHERAPEUTIC REHABILITATION COUNSELING

Ososkie (1998) introduced the term *logotherapeutic rehabilitation counseling* to address the utility of logotherapy in rehabilitation counseling applications. "The positive and optimizing nature of logotherapy fits well into the similar rehabilitation philosophy" (p. 219). Logotherapy could be used by rehabilitation counselors in the process of disability adjustment. For persons with chronic illness or physical disability in hospitals or rehabilitation settings, the opportunity for rehabilitation practitioners to deal with spirituality and meaning in life is significant. The effective rehabilitation counselor must make a conscious effort to enter the client's value system and to use it in a responsible manner to assist clients with spiritual concerns (Guttman, 1996).

Adjustment to Disability

Whether a disability is chronic or progressive or whether it has an early or late onset, life with a disability presents individuals with issues of freedom, isolation, anxiety, meaning, and possibly death. Facing death or escaping early death, for example, places that existential issue at the forefront of a person's life. The search for meaning in life in relation to the prospect of death may include spiritual factors. Facing stigma (Goffman, 1963) because of the attitudes of the populace toward disability may mean that isolation and aloneness must be confronted.

Theories of adjustment to disability explain a process and typically include a chance for movement beyond the apparent limits of a disability. Psychological and even spiritual change may become accessible for persons as a result of being presented with a disability. The fact of the disease, illness, or injury precipitates contemplation of its place within the psyche of the individual.

Value and attitude changes on the part of a person with a disability are incorporated into disability adjustment. In Wright's (1983) somatopsychology, value changes focus on containing disability effects, subordinating physique, enlarging the scope of values, and moving from comparative to asset values. Modification of values and attitudes is a critical step in the process of logotherapy (Gould, 1993; Lukas, 1980). Alteration of how one views oneself with a disability can be seen as a step in the process of finding meaning in life with a disability.

Vash's (1981) transcendence of disability theorizes personal movement from acknowledging the facts of a disability to rising above them. Levers and Maki (1995) consider transcendence upon confronting adversity in their investigation of African healing practices. "The person transcends the adversity by undergoing the process of becoming a healer and healing others—a process that has a spiritual link to its larger cultural context" (p. 138). Self-transcendence in logotherapy is movement beyond oneself by reaching out to others within one's family or community in order to attach meaning to life. Lukas (1983) showed that the capacity for self-transcendence enables people with disabilities to be independent of psychological stress if a meaning in the outside world is perceived. "The major activity of all human beings is to extract meaning from their encounters with the world" (Vash, 1994, p. 209). Psychospiritual growth may ensue when one experiences adversity and transcends it, according to Vash. Even suffering in life affords the sufferer the opportunity to find meaning in the suffering and thus meaning in life (Frankl, 1984).

Logotherapy and Rehabilitation Counseling

Logotherapy may be employed by rehabilitation counselors to facilitate meaning exploration. Dereflection is a helpful technique by which clients focus attention away from their disabilities and toward their intact capabilities. A value change regarding the disability would be a goal to successfully gain distance from the disability or symptoms of the disability. A change in perception is possible despite an inability to change the actual disability. The rehabilitation counselor is in a position to help clients see what it is that they can control.

Another basic tenet of logotherapy, self-transcendence, allows the person to understand, bear, tolerate, and accept pain and suffering because of knowing why (Guttman, 1996). Rehabilitation counselors may help clients tap into their self-transcendent capacities so that they may move beyond the limits imposed by their disabilities to find satisfactory meaning in life with a disability.

Rehabilitation counselors are called upon to facilitate personal interaction and community involvement and to help clients combat personal isolation. They help clients decide to return to families and careers and to see that alternatives are open to them. Perhaps the component of rehabilitation that needs to be added is a concentration on efforts that promote awareness of meaning that can be uncovered in everyday life with a disability. Purpose in life exists for clients with disabilities. The disability must be secondary to the person who has the disability, and this must be understood by the rehabilitation counselor. The rehabilitation counselor must be capable of seeing beyond the disability, or in effect transcending the disability.

Rehabilitation counselors should not assume that all persons with disabilities are suffering, or have necessarily suffered. However, an issue that may be related to suffering for people with physical disabilities is boredom, which is a reminder of inactivity. Frankl (1986) related that boredom is there to help one flee from inactivity so that meanings may be pursued. For persons with physical disabilities who are unable to work in competitive employment, it is still possible to engage in various other activities, to use time constructively, and to take an attitude toward life that is affirming.

Finding meaning in life with a disability, disease, or illness may dictate the direction of rehabilitation counseling. The process of logotherapy, or meaning analysis (Gould, 1993), which includes dereflection, attitude modulation, and search for new meanings, is a valuable tool to be incorporated into the repertoire of the rehabilitation counselor.

CASE EXAMPLE

The following logotherapy case study demonstrates the use of attitudinal values to dereflect attention from a disability and determine action that circumvents personal limitations and magnifies remaining assets. It is slightly adapted from a case presented by Crumbaugh and Henrion (1994, pp. 4 and 5).

After 16 years in the navy, Mike sustained a brain injury and skeletal fractures in an automobile accident at the age of 30. Prior to his accident, Mike had considered himself to be "on target" for success, and he had twice traveled around the world. After recovering consciousness two weeks after the injury, he was afraid that his naval career was over. He experienced the first stages of the grieving process: disbelief, shock, and denial.

In brain injury rehabilitation, Mike learned how to read and write again, to adapt to his short-term memory deficit, and to manage basic skills of daily living. During this time his wife divorced him. A female companion remained with him for a brief period and then left. However, his immediate family provided emotional support.

Mike was referred to a logotherapy program at the Veterans Affairs outpatient clinic for the treatment of depression. He presented himself as a suffering person with feelings of hopelessness, confusion, and lack of future direction. He was evaluated as a good candidate for dereflection within the logotherapy process, and during therapy his achievement in adapting to his physical disability and his potential accomplishments were emphasized. Ego strength, self-esteem, and socialization soon increased. His attitude became more positive.

Mike completed the program and was evaluated for a volunteer position through vocational rehabilitation. He became interested in finding a meaningful relationship, getting married, and having children. At that point, he was able to sense his capacity to use his unique experience in a new way—to find meaning and achieve goals, in spite of challenges, that had become possible only because he had sustained that fateful head injury.

EVALUATION

The optimizing nature of logotherapy does fit well with the maximizing nature of rehabilitation philosophy, with emphasis placed on remaining capacities. Attention in logotherapy is focused on that which is under the control of the person. Fate is not under such control, but one's attitude toward one's fate is. Accordingly, life would have meaning despite suffering and desperate human conditions. The positive and controllable aspects of life are the focus of logotherapy.

Logotherapy is an existential approach and, as such, seeks to help clients find meaning in suffering, work, love, aloneness, and death. This focus of logotherapy is important in psychotherapy and rehabilitation counseling. Rehabilitation counseling clients may have experienced an injury that has resulted in a severe disability. A client may question, "Why is life worth living with this disability?" and "Why did this happen to me?" These ontological probes are within the purview of the rehabilitation practitioner. Logotherapy assists the counselor in addressing these philosophical questions. Finding meaning in life with a disability should be a clinical concern for rehabilitation counselors.

Patterson and Watkins (1996) report that attitudinal values are a major theoretical contribution from logotherapy. He adds that meaning and values have often been ignored in psychology. Addressing this neglected area of the person is the primary theoretical concept of logotherapy. It deals with meaning in life and one's attitude toward uncontrollable fate.

The spiritual or noetic dimension of the individual is also an important strength of logotherapy. This truly human dimension is where Frankl rests his faith in the capacity of the individual. Here he is both existential and humanistic. The capacity of individuals to self-detach and to self-transcend are affirming of what a person can accomplish. In fact, people are only responsible if they exercise choice, and the affirming nature of logotherapy is invaluable in rehabilitation.

A focus on the spiritual aspect of an individual's life may be very important for a client. Whereas other psychotherapies may not attend to this aspect of the person, logotherapy has as its core the spiritual dimension (Byrd, 1997; Levers & Maki, 1995; Vash, 1994).

Rehabilitation counselors should always be reminded that attitude modulation (Gould, 1993) doe not mean imposition of values. The logotherapist must assist clients in finding new meanings and must not tell clients what their new meanings will be. Counselors should not impose values. Imposing values is contrary to Frankl's existential view regarding the responsibility of the individual to exercise personal choice.

A related caution is that Frankl (1986) did not intend to equate *spiritual* with *religious*. A counselor's understanding of the ultimate meaning in life should not be forced onto clients. Psychotherapy is not the place for religious conversion. It has been suggested that the term *philosophical* may be substituted for *spiritual* in logotherapy theory (Patterson & Watkins, 1996). The important contribution of the spiritual dimension should not be diminished by these cautions, however. Attention to a spiritual dimension and meaning-in-life considerations are noteworthy contributions that Frankl has made to psychotherapy and to psychotherapy theory.

LOGOTHERAPY RESEARCH

Applied research in logotherapy addresses the logotherapeutic approach or some theoretical concepts in clinical applications. Key concepts such as purpose in life, meaning, values, attitudes, and self-transcendence have been examined. These concepts do lend themselves to measurement. Examples of empirical research studies that utilize logotherapy concepts and approaches with clinical populations include the following: self-transcendence in a breast cancer support group (Coward, 1997); psychological adjustment in adults with cancer (Heidrich, Forsthoff, & Ward, 1994); purpose in life among gay men with HIV disease (Bechtel, 1994); meaning and purpose in the lives of persons with AIDS (Coward, 1994); coping with life-threatening illness using a logotherapeutic approach (Kass, 1996); meaning levels and drug abuse therapy (De La Flor, 1997); depression, meaninglessness, and substance abuse (Kinneir, Metha, Keim, et al., 1994); and adolescent substance abuse and psychological health (Kinneir, Metha, Okey, & Keim, 1994),

The above-referenced studies provide a sampling of the types of applied clinical research utilizing logotherapeutic concepts. The effectiveness of logotherapy in treatment samples has shown promise. However, research has been criticized as being minimal, primarily descriptive in nature, and lacking in rigor (Lukas & Hirsch, 2002). Additional research would further the development of the various applications of the approach. Continued emphasis in the research literature to highlight key concepts would strengthen its theoretical uniqueness. Some further attention to samples of individuals who have disabilities would support the effectiveness of logotherapy in rehabilitation counseling, supplementing previous research that has been conducted with people with disabilities.

SUMMARY

Viktor Frankl's logotherapy is an existential psychotherapy that incorporates a spiritual aspect in its dimensional ontology of soma, psyche, and noos. Logotherapy is focused primarily on meaning in life and the alteration of attitudinal values. The therapeutic process includes dereflection, attitude modulation, and the search for new meanings. Finding meaning in life is possible, and attempting to change fate is futile. Finding meaning in unavoidable suffering is also possible (Frankl, 1984). In fact, individuals are responsible when they exercise their freedom to choose and decide.

Logotherapy has existential, spiritual, and humanistic characteristics. It is a psychotherapy that does not have many techniques other than paradoxical intention. Frankl (1984, 1986, 1988) indicated that the individual is capable of self-detachment, and he capitalizes on this human quality in paradoxical intention and dereflection. Self-transcendence allows the individual to move beyond personal limits by reaching outside of himself or herself. Logotherapy would then be described as experiential. Being part of the community and family is what creates mental health.

Self-transcendence is found in theories of adjustment to disability (Vash, 1981). Moving beyond the limits of the disability is similar to Frankl's conception of self-transcendence. Logotherapy is considered a supplement to the therapeutic approaches employed by rehabilitation counselors in assisting clients with adjustment to disability issues. Inclusion of the spiritual dimension as described by Frankl makes sense in counseling clients with disabilities, who may have confronted various existential situations, including death, aloneness, isolation, and choice. Empirical research supports the effectiveness of logotherapy with a variety of clinical populations, some of them clients with disabilities. Frankl's genius appears to be evident in his attention to the spiritual or philosophical dimension of the individual.

REFERENCES

American Counseling Association. (1997, October). Viktor Frankl dies at age 92. *Counseling Today, 14.*

Barnes, R. C. (1995). *Viktor Frankl's logotherapy.* Unpublished manuscript, Viktor Frankl Institute of Logotherapy.

Bechtel, G. (1994). Purpose in life among gay men with HIV disease. *Nursing Connections, 7*(4), 5–11.

Byrd, E. K. (1997). Concepts related to inclusion of the spiritual component in services to persons with disability and chronic illness. *Journal of Applied Rehabilitation Counseling, 28*(4), 26–29.

Corey, G. (2001). *Theory and practice of counseling and psychotherapy* (5th ed.). Belmont, CA: Brooks/Cole.

Coward, D. (1994). Meaning and purpose in the lives of persons with AIDS. *Public Health Nursing, 11*, 331–336.

Coward, D. (1997, June 26). *Facilitation of self-transcendence in a breast cancer support group.* Paper presented at the Eleventh World Congress on Logotherapy, Dallas, TX.

Crumbaugh, J. C., & Henrion, R. (1994). The *ECCE HOMO* technique: A special case of dereflection. *International Forum for Logotherapy, 17*, 1–7.

De La Flor, M. A. N. (1997). Meaning levels and drug-abuse therapy: An empirical study. *International Forum for Logotherapy, 20*(1), 46–52.

Frankl, V. E. (1984). *Man's search for meaning.* New York: Washington Square Press.

Frankl, V. E. (1986). *The doctor and the soul: From psychotherapy to logotherapy* (3rd expanded ed.). New York: Vintage Books.

Frankl, V. E. (1988). *The will to meaning: Foundations and applications of logotherapy* (expanded ed.). New York: Meridan.

Goffman, E. (1963). *Stigma: Notes on the management of spoiled identity.* New York: Simon & Schuster.

Gould, W. B. (1993). *Viktor E. Frankl: Life with meaning.* Pacific Grove, CA: Brooks/Cole.

Guttman, D. (1996). *Logotherapy for the helping professional: Meaningful social work.* New York: Springer.

Heidrich, S., Forsthoff, C., & Ward, S. (1994). Psychological adjustment in adults with cancer: The self as mediator. *Health Psychology, 13*, 346–353.

Kass, J. (1996). Coping with life-threatening illness using a logotherapeutic approach: Stage II. Clinical mental health counseling. *International Forum for Logotherapy, 19*(2), 113–118.

Kinneir, R., Metha, A., Keim, J., Okey, J., Adler-Tabia, R., Berry, M., & Mulvenon, S. (1994). Depression, meaninglessness, and substance abuse in "normal" and hospitalized adolescents. *Journal of Alcohol and Drug Education, 39*, 101–111.

Kinneir, R., Metha, A., Okey, J., & Keim, J. (1994). Adolescent substance abuse and psychological health. *Journal of Alcohol and Drug Education, 40*, 51–56.

Levers, L. L., & Maki, D. R. (1995). African indigenous healing and cosmology: Toward a philosophy of ethnorehabilitation. *Rehabilitation Education, 9*, 127–145.

Lukas, E. (1980). Modification of attitudes. *International Forum for Logotherapy, 3*, 25–34.

Lukas, E. (1983). Love and work in Viktor Frankl's view of human nature. *International Forum for Logotherapy, 6*, 103–104.

Lukas, E., & Hirsch, B. Z. (2002). Logotherapy. In F. W. Kaslow, R. F. Massey, & S. D. Massey (Eds.), *Comprehensive handbook of psychotherapy, Volume 3. Interpersonal/ humanistic, existential* (pp. 333–356). New York: Wiley.

May, R., & Yalom, I. (2000). Existential psychotherapy. In R. J. Corsini & D. Wedding (Eds.), *Current psychotherapies* (6th ed.). Belmont, CA: Wadsworth.

Ososkie, J. N. (1998). Existential perspectives in rehabilitation counseling. *Rehabilitation Education, 12*, 217–222.

Patterson, C. H., & Watkins, C. E., Jr. (1996). *Theories of psychotherapy* (5th ed.). Boston: Allyn & Bacon.

Tweedie, D. F. (1961). *Logotherapy and the Christian faith: An evaluation of Frankl's existential approach to psychotherapy*. Grand Rapids, MI: Baker Book House.

Vash, C. L. (1981). *The psychology of disability*. New York: Springer.

Vash, C. L. (1994). *Personality and adversity: Psychospiritual aspects of rehabilitation*. New York: Springer.

Wright, B. A. (1983). *Physical disability: A psychosocial approach* (2nd ed.). New York: Harper & Row.

Cognitive and Behavioral Approaches

Chapter 7

Behavior Therapy

Jennifer L. Stoll

MAJOR CONCEPTS

Common Characteristics of Behavior Therapy

Behavior therapy is a collection of approaches and techniques that is used to decrease maladaptive behaviors and increase adaptive ones. Although behavioral techniques may differ in the manner through which they achieve behavior change, they share three common characteristics. First, behavioral approaches emphasize the importance of current behavior rather than focusing on past behavior (Corey, 2001; Wilson, 2000). Thus behavior theorists treat the behavior itself rather than underlying hypothesized causes of behavior; this represents a marked contrast to more traditional models of psychotherapy (e.g., psychoanalysis), which focus on the past or historical events that contribute to the development and manifestation of maladaptive behavior. Second, behavior therapies employ the scientific approach to evaluate the effectiveness of behavioral techniques through clearly defined, objective, measurable goals (Corey, 2001). The third common characteristic that all behavioral therapies share is their use of multiple assessments that are conducted throughout the treatment process (Corrigan & Liberman, 1994).

Assumptions of Behavior Therapy

In addition to the three central commonalities identified above, Rotgers (1996) identified seven assumptions of behavior therapy: (1) human behavior is largely learned rather than determined by genetics; (2) the same learning processes that create maladaptive behaviors can be used to change or eliminate them; (3) behavior is predominantly determined by contextual and environmental mediators; (4) covert behaviors, such as thoughts and feelings, are subject to change through the implementation of learning processes; (5) actual performance of new behaviors in the contexts in which they are to be performed is a critical aspect of behavior change; (6) each client is unique and requires an individualized assessment of inappropriate behavior; and (7) the cornerstone of successful treatment is a thorough behavioral assessment.

Approaches to Behavioral Treatment

Behavior therapy encompasses three distinct approaches to accomplishing the same ultimate goals of reducing inappropriate behaviors and increasing appropriate behaviors. The three approaches include classical conditioning, operant conditioning, and cognitive-behavioral approaches (Craighead, Craighead, Kazdin, & Mahoney, 1994). Both classical and operant conditioning will be discussed in this chapter. Cognitive-behavioral approaches are discussed in another chapter in this volume.

The purpose of the present chapter is to provide an overview of behavior therapy when implemented within a rehabilitation context. For the sake of clarity, classical conditioning and operant conditioning will be discussed separately in regard to the following: history of the approach; central tenets; factors influencing effectiveness of the approach; and treatment techniques based on the approach.

Classical Conditioning

Classical conditioning originated with the Russian physiologist Ivan Pavlov (Kazdin, 2000). Pavlov had been investigating digestive processes in dogs when he learned that the animals would salivate not only to the taste, sight, or smell of meat powder, but also when no meat powder was present, beginning to salivate upon entering the room where experiments were being conducted. His experiments usually involved the pairing of a neutral stimulus that did not produce salivation with the presentation of meat powder that naturally induces salivation. After multiple pairings, Pavlov found that the neutral stimulus came to produce salivation on its own.

Conditioning Process

To describe the conditioning process, Pavlov introduced a set of terms. He called the stimulus that naturally elicits the desired response the unconditioned stimulus (UCS), and the naturally occurring response was called the unconditioned response (UR) (Craighead et al., 1994). The neutral stimulus was referred to as the conditioned stimulus (CS), because it is that stimulus that becomes "conditioned" to produce the target response (Craighead et al., 1994). Finally, the conditioned response (CR) is the response that is elicited subsequent to the presentation of the CS (Craighead et al., 1994). It should be noted that the CR and the UR are the same response, with the only difference being the way in which the response is achieved.

Extinction of Classically Conditioned Responses

Once the relationship between the CS and CR is established, the association will disappear if the CS is repeatedly presented without the US. This process is referred to as classical extinction (Schloss & Smith, 1994). Maintenance of a classically conditioned response often requires "booster" sessions in which both the US and CS are again paired (Mueser, 1993). If classical extinction does occur, relearning the association between the CS and US often occurs more rapidly than was necessary to learn the task initially (Schloss & Smith, 1994). Extinction generally does not occur all at once. Rather, if the CS and US are paired following extinction, spontaneous recovery may occur, defined as exhibiting a CR in response to the CS after the target behavior was regarded as extinguished (Schloss & Smith, 1994).

Stimulus Generalization and Discrimination

After a conditioned response has been established, the organism may demonstrate either stimulus generalization or stimulus discrimination in response to the CS. If stimulus generalization is demonstrated, the conditioned behavior will be performed in the presence of the CS as well as other similar stimuli (Schloss & Smith, 1994). For example, suppose a client who recently underwent a hip replacement participates in physical therapy. The therapist informs the client to remain seated until he is able to adjust the therapy equipment to the appropriate tension; however, contrary to the therapist's request, the client attempts to stand, loses her balance, and falls, with the physical therapist unable to reach her in time to prevent the fall. Subsequently, the client develops symptoms of anxiety (e.g., difficulty breathing, rapid heart rate, and perspiration) whenever she has a physical therapy session. If the client's symptoms of anxiety occur only when she works with the therapist who was near her when she fell, the client would be demonstrating stimulus discrimination. On the other hand, if the woman experiences anxiety whenever she has a physical therapy session, regardless of the therapist providing treatment, stimulus generalization would be occurring.

Factors Influencing the Effectiveness of Classical Conditioning

The effectiveness of classical conditioning is influenced by a variety of factors. First, the CS-US sequence is important because, in order for classical conditioning to occur, the CS must precede the US. The second important factor that influences the effectiveness of classical conditioning is the delay between presentation of the CS and US (Kiernan, 1975). The number of trials also influences the effectiveness of classical conditioning. Generally, the intensity and persistence of the CR is related to the number of conditioning trials, with a greater number of trials associated with greater intensity. Finally, specific characteristics of the US and CS may facilitate or hinder the effectiveness of the conditioning process. Generally, a CR is easier to establish when the US is strong and produces a rapid response (Kiernan, 1975). Subsequent to the conditioning process, the strength of the CR is determined through assessing its strength or frequency of response, the length of time between the presentation of the CS and occurrence of the CR, and the persistence of the CR (i.e., the length of time that the CR is elicited by the CS in the absence of the US).

Treatment Techniques Derived from Classical Conditioning Principles

Because classical conditioning does not entail learning a new response, but rather developing an association between an existing response and a new stimulus (Craighead et al., 1994), techniques based upon this approach are directed toward helping clients to "unlearn" connections between specific stimuli and inappropriate behaviors, or conversely, to learn a connection between specific stimuli and appropriate behaviors (Papajohn, 1982).

One of the techniques based upon classical conditioning is systematic desensitization, which requires the client and therapist to construct a hierarchy of anxiety-producing scenes surrounding one particular fear. Therapy requires clients to remain relaxed as they imagine each scene in the hierarchy until they reach the most anxiety-provoking scene and are able to remain relaxed (Emmelkamp, 1994).

Flooding is another example of a therapeutic technique derived from classical conditioning (Emmelkamp, 1994). It involves exposing clients to a feared stimulus while making escape or avoidance impossible. Implosive therapy is similar to flooding except that clients imagine being placed in the fear-eliciting situation without opportunity for escape (Papajohn, 1982).

Finally, aversive therapy is also based upon principles of classical conditioning and attempts to eliminate inappropriate behavior by pairing it with a stimulus that naturally produces an unpleasant response. For example, in treating intravenous drug use, clients may be injected with a substance that induces nausea subsequent to the intravenous drug use. Consequently, they may come to associate intravenous drug use with nausea and thereby cease to continue the behavior.

Operant Conditioning

The two primary founders of operant conditioning are E. L. Thorndike and B. F. Skinner (Wilson, 2000). Through his studies with animals, Thorndike developed several laws of learning, the most important being the law of effect, which states that behaviors that lead to satisfaction will be reinforced, whereas behaviors that do not lead to satisfaction will not be reinforced. Like Thorndike, Skinner also believed that complex behaviors resulted from the ways that the organism interacted with or "operated" on the environment because of behavioral consequences (Corey, 2001).

Reinforcement and Punishment

The key components of operant conditioning are reinforcement and punishment. Reinforcement is anything that increases the frequency of a behavior, whereas punishment is anything that decreases the frequency of the behavior (Craighead et al., 1994). Reinforcers and punishers can be either positive or negative (Kiernan, 1975). Positive reinforcement involves the administration of a positive reward for good behavior (Craighead et al., 1994). In contrast, negative reinforcement occurs when the frequency of a behavior increases through the elimination of an aversive stimulus (Papajohn, 1982). Punishers may also be positive or negative. Positive punishment occurs when an undesired behavior decreases following administration of a particular stimulus (e.g., placing a client in physical restraints subsequent to assaulting another client) (Craighead et al., 1994). In contrast, negative punishment occurs when a positive stimulus is removed following an undesired behavior (e.g., when a client involved in a residential substance abuse program loses his privilege to go out on pass because he has become verbally aggressive toward staff) (Kiernan, 1975).

Schedules of Reinforcement

Reinforcers can be delivered through a variety of reinforcement schedules; however, behaviors are usually acquired more efficiently when reinforcement is delivered on a continuous schedule (i.e., the client is reinforced after each occurrence of the desired behavior) (Walker, Greenwood, & Terry, 1994). A fixed interval schedule provides reinforcement to the client after a consistent time interval regardless of how many times the desired behavior occurred within that time interval (e.g., a client in supported employment receives a paycheck every two weeks). Similarly, a fixed ratio schedule is provided when a client is reinforced after he or she makes a specified number of the desired responses (e.g., a client is allowed to take a five-minute break after boxing ten packages of batteries).

Once a behavior has been acquired, however, it is best maintained through a schedule of partial or intermittent reinforcement (i.e., behavior is not reinforced after every occurrence) (James & Gilliland, 2003). A variable interval schedule of reinforcement involves providing reinforcement after an unpredictable period of time (e.g., incarcerated juveniles are informed that they will have six random room checks during the year but are not informed of the dates when the checks will occur). Finally, a variable ratio schedule of reinforcement entails the provision of reinforcement after a client demonstrates a variable number of desired responses. This type of reinforcement schedule produces the highest rates of responding, because the relationship between the response and administration of the reinforcer is unpredictable (e.g., clients participating in a residential substance abuse treatment program may earn reinforcers after submitting urine samples that are negative for drugs, but the number of negative test results varies from 2 to 6 before a client may earn a reinforcer).

Extinction of Conditioned Responses

Like classical conditioning, operant conditioning can also undergo extinction. In operant conditioning, this process occurs when reinforcement is withheld from a previously reinforced behavior to decrease or eliminate the undesired behavior (Wilson, 2000). Operant extinction generally does not occur all at once. Rather, abrupt removal of reinforcement will often produce a temporary increase in the frequency of the maladaptive behavior before the frequency decreases or is eliminated (Corrigan & Liberman, 1994). This temporary increase is referred to as an extinction burst.

Stimulus Generalization and Discrimination

Sometimes a behavior only occurs under certain specific conditions in the environment. The environmental factors that must be present for the behavior to occur are referred to as positive discriminative stimuli (Kiernan,

1975). In contrast, the desired behavior will not occur in the presence of negative discriminative stimuli. Whenever the manifestation of a behavior occurs under discriminative stimuli, the behavior is said to occur under stimulus control (Kazdin, 2000). Stimulus discrimination is demonstrated when an individual with a head injury is taught how to cook successfully on a stove within a rehabilitation facility but is unable to even turn on the stove once the client returns home.

In contrast to stimulus control where a behavior occurs only under specific environmental conditions (Schloss & Smith, 1994), sometimes similar stimuli are capable of eliciting the same behavioral response. This phenomenon is referred to as stimulus generalization (Craighead et al., 1994). An example of stimulus generalization occurs when an individual with mental retardation mistakenly identifies all four-legged animals as "dog."

Factors Influencing the Effectiveness of Operant Conditioning

In order for operant conditioning to be effective, the reinforcers must be meaningful for a client (Mueser, 1993). There are two types of reinforcers. Primary reinforcers are inherently reinforcing (Craighead et al., 1994; James & Gilliland, 2003), whereas secondary reinforcers derive their reinforcing properties through learning and experience (e.g., tokens earned in a token economy that can be exchanged for desired rewards) (Craighead et al., 1994).

An array of factors may affect the potency of positive reinforcement (Walker et al., 1994): (1) whether there is a contingent relationship between manifestation of the target behavior and provision of the reinforcer; (2) the immediacy of the reinforcer subsequent to demonstration of the desired behavior; (3) the magnitude or strength of the reinforcer; (4) the schedule of reinforcement; (5) the inclusion of verbal and/or physical prompting to enhance the likelihood of behavioral demonstration; and (6) the likelihood of generalizability or ease of transfer of training of the target behavior.

Treatment Techniques Derived from Operant Conditioning Principles

There are multiple operant techniques to increase the frequency of behavior using positive reinforcement; they include shaping, differential reinforcement (Walker et al., 1994), behavioral contracts, token economies (Allyon & Azrin, 1968), and social skills training (SST) (Emmelkamp, 1994). Shaping involves reinforcing closer and closer approximations of the desired target behavior until the target behavior is demonstrated. This technique is most helpful in situations where the target behavior never or rarely occurs in the natural environment (Craighead et al., 1994).

Differential reinforcement occurs when all behaviors except the target behavior are positively reinforced. Because this technique also involves withholding reinforcement following a response, differential reinforcement is essentially a combination of both positive reinforcement and extinction. For example, suppose a client with a brain injury consistently chooses to eat all foods with her fingers during mealtimes. In this situation, the client is provided with positive reinforcement (e.g., verbal praise) for using the proper utensils during mealtimes, but is ignored or asked to sit at a table alone when she eats with her fingers. Depending on the goal of behavior change, differential reinforcement may be implemented in a variety of ways. The above example demonstrates differential reinforcement of incompatible behavior (DRI) because, if the client is using eating utensils (i.e., the reinforced behavior), eating with her fingers is incompatible with the desired behavior. Other variations of this technique include differential reinforcement of low rates of responding (DRL), differential reinforcement of alternative behaviors (DRA), and differential reinforcement of other behaviors (DRO) (for a more detailed discussion of these techniques, refer to Craighead et al., 1994; Kazdin, 2000; and Walker et al., 1994).

Behavior can also be modified through contingency or behavioral contracts, which are essentially agreements made between the behavior therapist and the client (Kazdin, 2000). The contract is a statement that identifies behaviors that are to be changed and the reinforcers and punishers that will be instrumental in the behavior change. Although effectiveness of the behavioral contract is enhanced by client participation during contract development, effective contracts contain five additional elements: (1) identification of reinforcers; (2) identification of target behaviors; (3) a process for making alterations to the contract if attempts at behavioral change are unsuccessful; (4) identification of extra reinforcers for consistent compliance with the terms outlined in the contract; and (5) provision of frequent feedback regarding the client's progress toward behavior change (Kazdin, 2000).

Behavior can also be modified through a token economy (Ayllon & Azrin, 1968). Token economies are generally implemented in a structured environment in which desirable behaviors are reinforced with tokens, which can then be exchanged for other desired reinforcers (Corrigan & Liberman, 1994). All effective token economies have the following characteristics: (1) clearly identified and defined target behaviors; (2) reinforcers provided following presentation of the desired behavior; (3) implementation of a system of constant monitoring and evaluation of the effectiveness of the token economy; and (4) a plan implemented to assist the individual in maintaining appropriate behavior in the absence of a token economy upon reintegration into the community (James & Gilliland, 2003). Consequences for inappropriate behavior may vary from one token system to another and may involve loss of tokens for undesirable behavior (i.e., response cost) or prevention of earning additional tokens for a specified amount of time.

Finally, behavior can also be modified through social skills training (SST) (Emmelkamp, 1994; Marzillier, Lambert, & Kellett, 1976), which is often implemented to enhance communication, assertiveness, problem solving, and other desired social skills (Corrigan & Liberman, 1994; Mueser, 1993). Unlike other behavioral techniques discussed previously, SST is unique in that it derives its effectiveness from a combination of operant conditioning, classical conditioning, and social learning theory. For this reason, a variety of techniques may be implemented during SST, including modeling, coaching, behavior rehearsal, feedback, reinforcement, and homework.

Numerous other techniques have been derived from operant principles to decrease behavior through punishment. Some of these techniques include verbal reprimands, overcorrection (i.e., overcorrecting negative behavior while also practicing positive behavior), response cost (i.e., loss of a reinforcer following undesired behavior), and time out from reinforcement (Craighead et al., 1994; Walker et al., 1994).

THEORY OF PERSONALITY

Maladaptive behaviors are learned and can also be unlearned through either classical conditioning or operant conditioning. From a behavioral perspective, when maladaptive behavior was originally learned, a specific function was fulfilled, and the behavior was maintained through either positive reinforcement (e.g., continuing to use heroin to experience the "high" without regard for negative physical and social consequences) or negative reinforcement (e.g., drinking in the morning to prevent withdrawal symptoms).

The presence of aversive stimuli plays a major role in both the initial development of maladaptive behavior and the maintenance of the behavior. Through avoidance of or escape from an aversive situation, the behavior is strengthened. Nevertheless, if there is a significant quantity of aversive stimuli present during the conditioning history, persistent avoidance of these stimuli will lead to either withdrawal into a fantasy world free from aversive stimuli (e.g., a client who develops disassociative personality disorder in response to contact with an environment with extreme abuse and aversive situations), or emotional problems such as fear, guilt, anger, depression, and anxiety (James & Gilliland, 2003). For example, suppose a male child is inconsistently subjected to severe physical punishment from his father for trivial reasons (e.g., failing to make his bed in the morning); however, when the punishment is inflicted, the boy is unable to escape the situation because his father locks him in a closet following the beating. After the boy's father lets him out of the closet, the child is left feeling confused about why the punishment occurred, angry that he had no control over the situation and the resulting punishment, and fearful that the punishment may occur again. If the punishment does continue to occur, the boy may begin to develop maladaptive behaviors, including anger, depression, guilt, and anxiety. Conversely, the boy may retreat into a fantasy world in which punishment and aversive consequences are either not present or avoided.

DESCRIPTION OF THE COUNSELING PROCESS

From a behavioral perspective, a thorough discussion of the counseling process includes the following elements: the therapeutic process, the therapist's role in behavior therapy, the therapeutic relationship, and length of treatment.

The Therapeutic Process

The focus of behavior therapy is corrective learning, which encompasses the acquisition of new coping skills, enhancement of communication, and the overcoming of maladaptive emotional conflicts (Wilson, 2000). When implementing behavior therapy, all learning occurs within a structured environment. Nevertheless, to the greatest extent possible, behavior therapists emphasize that clients should take an active role in effecting change during their activities in the real world between therapy sessions (Wilson, 2000).

Kuehnel and Liberman (1986) describe behavior therapy as a six-stage process. First, a behavioral assessment is conducted, which helps to identify maladaptive behaviors. Second, a client's assets and strengths are noted to help identify strategies and approaches that may serve as templates for effective treatment interventions. The third step in the therapeutic process is relating the identified or target behaviors to the context in which they occur. Possible behavioral antecedents and consequences are specified. The fourth step entails developing a process to measure the problematic behavior(s). This is accomplished by assessing the frequency of a target behavior during a baseline period (i.e., prior to the initiation of treatment). The baseline becomes the reference point for determining treatment effectiveness. The fifth step in the process requires identification of reinforcers. These may include activities, people, or things that will provide motivation for treatment, as well as the maintenance of the desired behavior after treatment has ended. The final step in the counseling process is the development of treatment goals, which are developed jointly between the counselor and client. Generally the client determines the behaviors that will be changed, whereas the therapist determines how the changes will best be made (Wilson, 2000).

The process of developing treatment goals has been delineated by Cormier and Nurius (2003) and involves the following steps. First, the behavior therapist explains the purpose of goals to the client. The client then identifies desired outcomes as a result of counseling. The client and therapist then jointly discuss whether the desired outcomes are outcomes that the client is committed to achieving and whether the treatment goals are realistic. This is followed by a discussion between both parties of the advantages and disadvantages of the treatment goals. Finally, the therapist and client collaboratively define the treatment goals through identifying the behaviors involved, the methods of change, and the degrees of change desired.

The Therapist's Role in Behavior Therapy

As indicated above, all aspects of behavior therapy are conducted jointly between the therapist and the client. It is thought that through actively participating during development of the treatment plan, the client will be more invested in behavioral change and more likely to work toward goal attainment (Corey, 2001). While developing treatment goals and implementing the treatment plan, the behavior therapist focuses on current behavior rather than underlying causes for the behavior (Corey, 2001). Any investigation of the client's past is considered important only as it relates to the present.

The Therapeutic Relationship

Behavior therapists are active and direct in their interactions with clients and typically function as consultants and problem solvers (Wilson, 2000).

Historically, behavior therapists have been viewed as behavioral experts; however, more contemporary views of the behavior therapist's role emphasize the collaborative relationship between client and counselor. Furthermore, behavior therapists were often previously stereotyped as indifferent, mechanical, and manipulative technicians, but today they are often described as understanding, friendly, caring, and personal (James & Gilliland, 2003).

Although behavior therapy utilizes a systematic and structured approach to treatment, the therapeutic relationship is important and contributes to the process of behavioral change (Wilson, 2000). Clients are more invested in treatment if the therapeutic relationship is characterized by the client's belief in the therapist's competence and regards him or her as honest and trustworthy (Wilson, 2000). Nevertheless, Corey (2001) contends that the core conditions (i.e., congruence, acceptance, and empathy) are necessary but not sufficient for behavioral change to occur.

Length of Treatment

Wilson (2000) views behavior therapy as a short-term therapy. Treatment is often comprised of 25–30 sessions; however, although many clients require more than 30 sessions, more than 100 sessions is extremely rare. Guidelines for establishing the length of treatment are quite general and consist of three processes (Wilson, 2000). First, an assessment of maladaptive behavior is conducted and target behaviors are identified. Second, treatment interventions are implemented as soon as possible. Finally, progress in treatment is continually assessed against clearly defined, objective, measurable therapeutic goals. Because all clients have different therapeutic goals and life circumstances, the length of treatment, the number of sessions required, and the time spent in treatment will vary from one client to another. Thus, treatment length is determined by the rate at which clients demonstrate progress toward treatment goals (Wilson, 2000).

REHABILITATION APPLICATIONS

Behavioral techniques have been implemented to treat maladaptive behaviors long before the procedures were identified as a cohesive theory of counseling. Within the past few decades, these techniques have been implemented to treat multiple maladaptive behaviors of people with a wide variety of disabilities, including substance abuse (Rotgers, 1996), traumatic brain injury (Giles, Ridley, Dill, & Frye, 1997; Horton & Barrett, 1988), developmental disabilities (Griffiths, Feldman, & Tough, 1997; Madle &

Neisworth, 1990), mental illness (Corrigan & Liberman, 1994), schizophrenia (Mueser, 1993), depression (Gloaguen, Cottraux, Cucherat, &
Blackburn, 1998), and chronic pain (McCracken, 1997; Slater, Doctor,
Pruitt, & Atkinson, 1997). For the sake of brevity, the following portion
of this chapter will address the application of behavior therapy to substance
abuse, traumatic brain injury, and developmental disabilities.

Substance Abuse

Behavioral approaches had been used to treat substance abuse for many
years prior to the establishment of behavior therapy as a major theoretical
orientation. Substance abuse treatment has employed behavioral techniques
derived from both classical and operant conditioning perspectives. Commonly employed classical techniques include cue exposure and covert
sensitization, whereas frequently used operant techniques include community reinforcement and psychological modeling. Because substance abuse
is multidimensional in nature, treatment techniques often encompass other
behavioral techniques as well.

Cue Exposure

Classical conditioning has been regarded as the primary process through
which environmental cues elicit urges to use drugs or alcohol (Rotgers,
1996). Treatment techniques attempt to break the association between the
environment and the urges that are assumed to form the motivation for
an individual's continuous search for and use of substances (Emmelkamp, 1994).

Covert Sensitization

Covert sensitization involves the induction of verbally produced nausea
subsequent to imagining a situation where alcohol is consumed. After the
client has imagined consuming alcohol, the therapist describes scenes in
which the individual experiences nausea and vomiting and eventually runs
from the drinking setting. Research findings on covert sensitization appear
inconclusive, with some individuals benefiting from the technique and
others continuing to experience substance abuse difficulties (Ellkins, 1980;
Hedberg & Campbbell, 1982).

Community Reinforcement

From an operant perspective, substance abuse treatment focuses on re-
arranging an individual's environment so that reinforcement for engaging

in activities other than substance abuse becomes more attractive than the reinforcement experienced through substance use (e.g., prevention of withdrawal symptoms). The community reinforcement approach takes advantage of natural supports in the community and employs them as reinforcers (Hunt & Azrin, 1973). Specifically, the technique rearranges the life of the individual who engages in substance abuse so that time out from important reinforcers, such as family, friends, and employment, occurs if and when the individual begins to drink. If he or she refrains from drinking, positive reinforcement is provided through social interactions with family and friends. Research investigating the effectiveness of the technique has revealed that clients who received community reinforcement have been more sober, have spent greater percentages of time gainfully employed, have earned almost twice as much, and have spent more time with their families and in the community when compared to a control group (Hunt & Azrin, 1973).

Psychological Modeling

Psychological modeling has been regarded as the most effective and most rapid strategy for achieving behavioral change (Rotgers, 1996). The technique is particularly valuable in that it can be used to teach abstinence or alternative activities to substance abuse, as well as social skills and intrapersonal skills such as relaxation, coping self-statements, and anger management (Rotgers, 1996).

Traumatic Brain Injury

Maladaptive behavior commonly occurs after onset of traumatic brain injury (TBI) (Horton & Barrett, 1988). Fortunately, the behavioral approach to treatment is particularly appropriate for TBI rehabilitation (Eames & Wood, 1985; Giles et al., 1997). A variety of behavioral approaches have been employed to increase behavioral deficits or reduce behavioral excesses among persons with TBI; they include positive reinforcement, time out, and overcorrection.

Positive Reinforcement

Positive reinforcement involves provision of a desired reinforcer subsequent to exhibition of a desired target behavior and has been regarded as the cornerstone of behavior management techniques (Lewis & Bitter, 1991). To enhance the effectiveness of positive reinforcement among persons with

TBI, Lewis and Bitter (1991) identified six guidelines: (1) reinforcers should be provided immediately after the client demonstrates the desired response; (2) the client should be made aware of which specific behaviors will be reinforced and which will not; (3) when identifying reinforcers and behaviors to clients, speech should be slow to enhance the ability of the individual with TBI to process the information; (4) instructions should be broken down and presented in small steps; (5) a variety of reinforcers should be offered to prevent the client from satiating on one particular reinforcer; and (6) throughout the treatment process, reinforcers should be provided on a continuous schedule because of the length of time that is often required for persons with TBI to learn the association between the behavior and subsequent reinforcement. Once the association is learned, intermittent reinforcement will more effectively maintain the desired behavior.

Time Out

Time out from reinforcement involves removing the individual from all sources of reinforcement subsequent to demonstration of maladaptive behavior. Marr (1982) proposed guidelines to enhance the effectiveness of time out when implemented with a person with TBI. First, the individual should receive a time out immediately after the inappropriate behavior occurs. Next, the individual must be informed of the specific behavior that resulted in the time out. Third, the duration of time the individual remains in time out should be brief, limited to five to ten minutes. Because many individuals with TBI experience memory difficulties, if the time spent in time out becomes too long, the individual may have minimal or no recollection of the reasons that he or she has been placed in time out. Furthermore, impaired memory, in turn, may potentially result in escalation of the individual's behavior because of frustration over the reasons that he or she has been removed from positive reinforcement.

Overcorrection Positive Practice

Overcorrection positive practice requires the individual to repeatedly perform an appropriate response or behavior that is incompatible with behavior that is targeted for reduction or elimination (Madle & Neisworth, 1990). This procedure is particularly applicable to individuals with TBI who possess impairments in memory and planning ability, because it provides them with opportunities to rehearse a desired behavior over multiple trials while simultaneously reducing the frequency of performing the maladaptive behavior.

Developmental Disabilities

Within the past 30 years, behavior therapy has had a strong influence in treatment of maladaptive behaviors of persons with developmental disabilities and mental retardation. Behavioral techniques have been used to treat a variety of behaviors successfully, including toileting (Azrin & Foxx, 1971; Madle & Neisworth, 1990), pica (Paisey & Whitney, 1989), and impulsivity and self-control (Schwietzer & Sulzer-Azaroff, 1988).

Toileting

Toileting was one of the first targeted behaviors that received significant research attention from a behavioral perspective; however, Azrin and Foxx (1971) were the first to report the implementation of multiple procedures simultaneously to accomplish toilet training. Some of the techniques employed included modeling, shaping, positive reinforcement, and punishment (i.e., verbal reprimands, time out). Over the past 25 years, additional research has been conducted on toilet training and has indicated that, while other toilet training programs exist besides those proposed by Azrin and Foxx (1971), specific behavioral techniques, including reinforcement, chaining, shaping, prompting, and punishment are required for successful results (Madle & Neisworth, 1990).

Pica

Pica is defined as the ingestion of inedible substances (Piazza et al., 1998). This behavior occurs with as many as 25% of persons with mental retardation (Danford & Huber, 1982) and, unfortunately, it is often resistant to treatment (Piazza et al., 1998). Nevertheless, pica has been treated successfully through the use of various reinforcers and punishers (Paisey & Whitney, 1989), as well as through other behavioral techniques. Fisher et al. (1994) employed behavioral assessment results to identify reinforcers and punishers from empirically derived consequences and were effective in reducing the pica behavior of three children to near-zero levels. In another study, Piazza et al. (1998) conducted functional analyses on three participants with pica. Results revealed that the pica of one participant was maintained by automatic reinforcement (e.g., oral stimulation), whereas the pica of the other two participants was maintained by a combination of both social and automatic reinforcement. The researchers then provided the participants with stimuli that either matched or did not match the function of their pica behavior. When the participants were given stimulation that did not match the sensory components of pica, the behavior was maintained. In contrast, when the individuals were given matched stimuli, pica was reduced.

Impulsivity and Self-Control

Behavioral techniques have also been implemented to teach self-control and reduce impulsivity among persons with mental retardation. Self-control has been defined as "behavior that results in access to a larger reinforcer after a longer delay, rather than impulsive behavior that results in a small reinforcer after a shorter or no delay" (Schwietzer & Sulzer-Azaroff, 1988). Dixon et al. (1998) conducted a study to examine the effects of concurrent fixed-duration and progressive-duration reinforcement schedules as a means of teaching self-control and increasing the targeted behaviors of three individuals with developmental disabilities. Results demonstrated that, by establishing a reinforcement history in which participants are gradually exposed to increasingly longer delays prior to access to a larger reinforcer and are required to demonstrate a target behavior during the delay, greater self-control and reduced impulsivity may both occur with greater frequency. These results are consistent with those of Schwietzer and Sulzer-Azaroff (1988), which argued that gradually increasing the delay to access of a desired reinforcer might increase self-control.

Other Behaviors

A variety of applications of behavior therapy to persons with mental retardation have been discussed; however, behavioral techniques have also been applied successfully to many other behaviors commonly exhibited. These treatment interventions have focused on the following: (1) activities of daily living (i.e., feeding and dressing) (Madle & Neisworth, 1990); (2) speech, language, and communication (Hagopian, Fisher, Sullivan, Acquisto, & LeBlanc, 1998; Lancioni, Van Houten, & Ten Hoopen, 1997); (3) community preparation (Bourbeau, Sowers, & Close, 1986; Williams & Cuvo, 1986); (4) aggressive and disruptive behavior (Lennox, Miltenberger, Sprengler, & Erfanian, 1988); (5) sleep disturbances (Didden, Curfs, Sikkema, & de Moor, 1998); and (6) reduction of cigarette smoking (Peine, Darvish, Blakelock, Osborne, & Jenson, 1998).

CASE EXAMPLE

The following case example attempts to demonstrate the application of behavioral techniques discussed in this chapter, including positive and negative reinforcement, punishment, shaping, time out, token economies, self-control and impulsivity, and the collaborative client-therapist relationship.

Annie is an 18-year-old Caucasian female who was born with mental retardation. She has an IQ score of 55 to 60. She lived at home with her parents and two sisters until the age of nine. At that age, because of significant behavioral problems, Annie went to live in an eight-bed group home two miles from her home. Although Annie could be charming and very social, her inappropriate and aggressive behaviors were the primary reason that she left home.

Annie's family frequently allowed her to have her own way and did not realize that they were actually reinforcing each other by continuing to do so. Annie had learned through previous instances that if she became verbally or physically aggressive, she would get what she wanted. Annie's family also learned that if they conceded to Annie's demands, Annie's verbal and physical aggression would either stop or be prevented altogether (i.e., negative reinforcement). Nevertheless, Annie continued to make demands, and her family continued to give in.

As Annie grew older, her demands continued. Her family was getting frustrated with her increasingly aggressive behavior and realized that, over the years, Annie's behavior had become uncontrollable. They sought an alternative residence for her and ultimately decided that Annie would best be served in a group home. Annie stayed overnight at the group home for a "trial" visit so that she would have the opportunity to meet the staff and other residents, and staff would have the opportunity to observe her behaviors. Group home staff felt that Annie's behaviors could be addressed and treated successfully, and Annie moved in a few days later.

On her first day living at the group home, Annie was told that the home had one rule: respect others. Knowing Annie's behavioral history, staff provided Annie with numerous examples of respectful behavior (e.g., not causing emotional or physical harm to another; completing assigned chores; not taking others' possessions without permission). Annie was told that for each day she demonstrated respectful behavior for the entire day, she would be able to choose a reward for herself at the end of the day (e.g., a phone call home or an ice cream sundae). Annie was given a wall calendar, and for each day that she earned a reward, she was to draw a star to remind her that she showed appropriate behavior all day. As a means of encouraging consistent behavior over a longer time duration, Annie was told that every time she earned five stars consecutively, she could choose a larger reward (e.g., going out to eat or shopping). Finally, Annie was told that if she demonstrated disrespectful behavior toward any other resident or staff, she would be told to go to the "quiet room" for ten minutes to think about what she had done (i.e., time out).

Annie's first few months at the group home consisted of behavioral ups and downs. Her calendar revealed that she would go for a few days with appropriate behavior, followed by a few days of disrespectful and aggressive behavior toward others. Yet, over time, group home staff noticed a trend in Annie's behavior. It appeared that Annie was able to demonstrate respectful behavior for a greater length of time if she chose to make a phone call to her family as her daily reward. Group home staff approached the family with this observation and asked them if they would be willing to have Annie return home for a weekend visit if she was able to demonstrate two consecutive weeks of respectful behavior; however, the family had to agree to implement the same behavioral strategies at home that were implemented at the group home (e.g., positive reinforcement and time out). Annie's family agreed that this would be an appropriate goal for which Annie should strive, in hopes that it would increase her self-control and decrease her impulsive tendencies. The idea was discussed with Annie, who became very excited when she heard that she could go home for the entire weekend. Annie had indeed demonstrated an improvement in her maladaptive behaviors since coming to live in the group home, and staff decided to implement the idea for a weekend home visit. Initially, it took Annie almost two months to achieve two consecutive weeks of respectful behavior; however, as Annie's time living at the group home continued to increase, the frequency of her inappropriate behaviors continued to decrease. Eventually, she was able to earn weekend visits home almost always twice per month.

RESEARCH

Although behavior therapy has only been established as a major form of psychotherapy within the past 40 years (Wilson, 2000), behavioral techniques have been applied to a wide variety of individuals with disabilities and have addressed a broad range of psychological disorders. Furthermore, behavior therapy has been regarded as the treatment of choice for specific psychological disorders, including phobia, obsessive-compulsive disorder, sexual disorders, and childhood disorders (Wilson, 2000). Successful implementation of behavioral techniques has been noted in a variety of settings, including education, medicine, and rehabilitation. With regard to rehabilitation, in the present chapter applications to substance abuse, traumatic brain injury, and developmental disabilities have been discussed;

however, behavior therapy has also been successfully implemented with people with many other types of disabilities, including mental illness (Corrigan & Liberman, 1994), schizophrenia (Mueser, 1993), depression (Gloaguen et al., 1998), and chronic pain (McCracken, 1997; Slater et al., 1997).

In contrast to traditional approaches to psychotherapy (e.g., psychoanalysis, Adlerian therapy), the behavioral approach typically requires less time for psychological change to occur because of its focus on current symptoms and behaviors rather than identification and treatment of underlying causes of inappropriate behavior. For this reason, it appears that the behavioral approach is consistent with the medical movement toward managed care and the provision of time-limited services.

With regard to the future of mental health treatment, Norcross, Alford, and De Michele (1992) conducted a survey of 75 psychotherapists of various theoretical orientations to solicit their predictions regarding the future of mental health treatment. The therapists predicted that future approaches would primarily be composed of directive, solution-focused brief treatments in order to contain costs. Consistent with this approach to mental health treatment, the treatment interventions predicted to increase in frequency the most included homework assignments, real-life exposure, and cognitive-behavioral interventions. These predictions appear to suggest that behavioral approaches will indeed play a larger role in the treatment of psychological disorders in the future as continued increases in costs move mental health services in the direction of managed care and away from long-term treatment.

REFERENCES

Ayllon, T., & Azrin, N. H. (1968). *The token economy.* New York: Appleton-Century-Crofts.

Azrin, N. H., & Foxx, R. (1971). A rapid method of toilet training the institutionalized retarded. *Journal of Applied Behavior Analysis, 4,* 89–99.

Bourbeau, P. E., Sowers, J. A., & Close, D. W. (1986). An experimental analysis of generalization of banking skills from classroom to bank settings in the community. *Education and Training of the Mentally Retarded, 21,* 98–107.

Corey, G. (2001). *Theory and practice of counseling and psychotherapy* (4th ed.). Pacific Grove, CA: Brooks/Cole.

Cormier, S., & Nurius, P. S. (2003). *Interviewing and change strategies for helpers: Fundamental skills and cognitive behavioral interventions* (5th ed.). Pacific Grove, CA: Brooks/Cole.

Corrigan, P. W., & Liberman, R. P. (1994). Overview of behavior therapy in psychiatric hospitals. In P. W. Corrigan & R. P. Liberman (Eds.), *Behavior therapy in psychiatric hospitals* (pp. 1–38). New York: Springer.

Craighead, L. W., Craighead, W. E., Kazdin, A. E., & Mahoney, M. J. (1994). *Cognitive and behavioral interventions: An empirical approach to mental health problems*. Needham Heights, MA: Allyn & Bacon.

Danford, D. E., & Huber, A. M. (1982). Pica among mentally retarded adults. *American Journal on Mental Deficiency, 87,* 141–146.

Didden, R., Curfs, L. M. G., Sikkema, S. P. E., & de Moor, J. (1998). Functional assessment and treatment of sleeping problems with developmentally disabled children: Six case studies. *Journal of Behavior Therapy and Experimental Psychiatry, 29,* 85–97.

Dixon, M. R., Hayes, L. J., Binder, L. M., Manthey, S., Sigman, C., & Zdanowski, D. M. (1998). Using a self-control training procedure to increase appropriate behavior. *Journal of Applied Behavior Analysis, 31,* 203–210.

Eames, P., & Wood, R. (1985). Rehabilitation after severe brain injury: A follow-up study of a behavior modification approach. *Journal of Neurology, Neurosurgery, and Psychiatry, 48,* 613–619.

Elkins, R. L. (1980). Covert sensitization treatment of alcoholism: Contributions of successful conditioning to subsequent abstinence maintenance. *Addictive Behavior, 5,* 67–89.

Emmelkamp, P. M. (1994). Behavior therapy with adults. In A. E. Bergin & S. L. Garfield (Eds.), *Handbook of psychotherapy and behavior change* (4th ed., pp. 379–427). New York: Wiley.

Fisher, W. W., Piazza, C. C., Bowman, L. G., Kurtz, P. F., Sherer, M. R., & Lachman, S. R. (1994). A preliminary evaluation of empirically derived consequences for the treatment of pica. *Journal of Applied Behavior Analysis, 26,* 23–36.

Giles, G. M., Ridley, J. E., Dill, A., & Frye, S. (1997). A consecutive series of adults with brain injury treated with a washing and dressing retraining program. *American Journal of Occupational Therapy, 51,* 256–266.

Gloaguen, V., Cottraux, J., Cucherat, M., & Blackburn, I. (1998). A meta-analysis of the effect of cognitive therapy in depressed patients. *Journal of Affective Disorders, 49,* 59–72.

Griffiths, D., Feldman, M. A., & Tough, S. (1997). Programming generalization of social skills in adults with developmental disabilities: Effects on generalization and social validity. *Behavior Therapy, 28,* 253–269.

Hagopian, L. P., Fisher, W. W., Sullivan, M. T., Acquisto, J., & LeBlanc, L. A. (1998). Effectiveness of functional communication training with and without extinction and punishment: A summary of 21 inpatient cases. *Journal of Applied Behavior Analysis, 31,* 211–235.

Hedberg, A. G., & Campbell, L. (1982). A comparison of four behavioral treatments of alcoholism. In E. M. Pattison (Ed.), *Selection of treatment for alcoholics* (pp. 218–226). New Brunswick, NJ: Rutgers Center on Alcohol Studies.

Horton, A. M., & Barrett, D. (1988). Neuropsychological assessment and behavior therapy: New directions in head trauma rehabilitation. *Journal of Head Trauma Rehabilitation, 3,* 57–64.

Hunt, G. M., & Azrin, N. H. (1973). A community-reinforcement approach to alcoholism. *Behaviour Research and Therapy, 11,* 91–104.

James, R. K., & Gilliland, B. E. (2003). *Theories and strategies in counseling and psychotherapy* (5th ed.). Boston: Allyn & Bacon.

Kazdin, A. E. (2000). *Behavior modification in applied settings* (6th ed.). Belmont, CA: Wadsworth.

Kiernan, C. (1975). Behaviour modification. In D. Bannister (Ed.), *Issues and approaches in the psychological therapies* (pp. 241–260). New York: Wiley.

Kuehnel, J. M., & Liberman, R. P. (1986). Behavior modification. In I. L. Kutash & A. Wolf (Eds.), *Psychotherapist's casebook* (pp. 240–262). San Francisco: Jossey-Bass.

Lancioni, G. E., Van Houten, K., & Ten Hoopen, G. (1997). Reducing excessive vocal loudness in persons with mental retardation through the use of a portable auditory feedback device. *Journal of Behavior Therapy and Experimental Psychiatry, 28,* 123–128.

Lennox, D. B., Miltenberger, R. G., Sprengler, P., & Erfanian, N. (1988). Decelerative treatment practices with persons who have mental retardation: A review of five years of the literature. *American Journal on Mental Retardation, 92,* 492–501.

Lewis, F. D., & Bitter, C. J. (1991). Applied behavior analysis and work adjustment training. In B. T. McMahon (Ed.), *Work worth doing: Advances in brain injury* (pp. 137–165). Boca Raton, FL: CRC Press-St. Lucie Press.

Madle, R. A., & Neisworth, J. T. (1990). Mental retardation. In A. S. Bellack & M. Hersen (Eds.), *International handbook of behavior modification and therapy* (2nd ed., pp. 731–762). New York: Plenum.

Marr, J. N. (1982). Behavioral analysis of work problems. In B. Bolton (Ed.), *Vocational adjustment of disabled persons* (pp. 127–147). Baltimore: University Park Press.

Marzillier, J. S., Lambert, C., & Kellett, J. (1976). A controlled evaluation of systematic desensitization and social skills training for socially inadequate psychiatric patients. *Behavior Research and Therapy, 14,* 225–228.

McCracken, L. M. (1997). "Attention" to pain in persons with chronic pain: A behavioral approach. *Behavior Therapy, 28,* 271–284.

Mueser, K. T. (1993). Schizophrenia. In A. S. Bellack & M. Hersen (Eds.), *Handbook of behavior therapy in the psychiatric setting* (pp. 269–292). New York: Plenum.

Norcross, J. C., Alford, B. A., & De Michele, J. T. (1992). The future of psychotherapy: Delphi data and concluding observations. *Psychotherapy, 29,* 150–158.

Paisey, T. J. H., & Whitney, R. B. (1989). A long-term case study of analysis, response suppression, and treatment maintenance involving life-threatening pica. *Behavioral Residential Treatment, 4,* 191–211.

Papajohn, J. C. (1982). *Intensive behavior therapy: The behavioral treatment of complex emotional disorders.* New York: Pergamon.

Peine, H. A., Darvish, R., Blakelock, H., Osborne, J. G., & Jenson, W. R. (1998). Nonaversive reduction of cigarette smoking in two adult men in a residential setting. *Journal of Behavior Therapy and Experimental Psychiatry, 29,* 55–65.

Piazza, C. C., Fisher, W. W., Hanley, G. P., LeBlanc, L. A., Worsdell, A. S., Lindauer, S. E., & Keeney, K. M. (1998). Treatment of pica through multiple analyses of its reinforcing functions. *Journal of Applied Behavior Analysis, 31,* 165–189.

Rotgers, F. (1996). Behavioral therapy of substance abuse treatment: Bringing science to bear on practice. In F. Rogers, D. S. Keller, & J. Morgenstern (Eds.), *Treating substance abuse: Theory and technique* (pp. 174–201). New York: Guilford.

Schloss, P. J., & Smith, M. A. (1994). *Applied behavior analysis in the classroom*. Boston: Allyn & Bacon.

Schwietzer, J. B., & Sulzer-Azaroff, B. (1988). Self-control: Teaching tolerance for delay in impulsive children. *Journal of the Experimental Analysis of Behavior, 50*, 173–186.

Slater, M. A., Doctor, J. N., Pruitt, S. D., & Atkinson, J. H. (1997). The clinical significance of behavioral treatment for chronic low back pain: An evaluation of effectiveness. *Pain, 71*, 257–263.

Walker, D., Greenwood, C. R., & Terry, B. (1994). Management of classroom disruptive behavior and academic performance problems. In L. W. Craighead, W. E. Craighead, A. E. Kazdin, & M. J. Mahoney (Eds.), *Cognitive and behavioral interventions: An empirical approach to mental health problems* (pp. 215–234). Boston: Allyn & Bacon.

Williams, G. E., & Cuvo, A. J. (1986). Training apartment upkeep skills to rehabilitation clients: A comparison of task analytic strategies. *Journal of Applied Behavior Analysis, 19*, 39–51.

Wilson, G. T. (2000). Behavior therapy. In R. J. Corsini & D. Wedding (Eds.), *Current psychotherapies* (6th ed.). Itasca, IL: Peacock.

Chapter 8

Cognitive-Behavioral Therapy

Elizabeth A. Swett and Steven P. Kaplan

Cognitive-behavioral therapy (CBT) as a therapeutic system holds that how one thinks largely determines how one feels and behaves (Beck & Weishaar, 2000). This basic assertion differentiates CBT from systems emphasizing affect (Tomkins, 1984), unconscious conflicts (Freud, 1923/1961), behavioral antecedents (Wolpe, 1958), or other determinants as being primarily responsible for thought, emotion, and behavior. CBT approaches have been identified as growing in popularity and are among the most heavily researched of all approaches to counseling and psychotherapy (Cormier & Nurius, 2003; Prochaska & Norcross, 1999).

CBT uses an amalgam of therapeutic techniques from behavior therapy, rational-emotive behavior therapy (REBT; Ellis, 1962, 2000), and generic counseling (i.e., rapport building), as well as some techniques that stem directly from its cognitive base. CBT is conceptualized as a collaborative investigation undertaken by the therapist and the client; it explores thinking patterns and beliefs that an individual holds that may lead to maladaptive behaviors, erroneous beliefs about oneself and others, and debilitating relationships with the world.

CBT, like all therapeutic systems, seeks to improve an individual's emotional health and strengthen his or her repertoire of adaptive behaviors. It focuses on the empirical investigation of a person's thinking patterns and cognitive assumptions, which, the theory holds, drive maladaptive, erroneous thoughts and behaviors.

THEORETICAL FOUNDATIONS

CBT asserts that psychological disorders can be traced to both inappropriate learning and to maladaptive thinking. Cognition (from the Latin *cognito,* to know or to learn) is itself subserved by information-processing functions that lead to various conclusions about one's situation, which in turn control affect and behavior. At a basic level, CBT views the adaptive processing of information as being crucial to an organism's survival (Beck & Weishaar, 1989). The theory gives credence to the importance of learning and environmental influences on personality development, while emphasizing information processing and cognitive mediation in the development and treatment of psychological disorders (James & Gilliland, 2003). Based on these emphases, CBT purports to produce change by influencing an individual's thinking patterns and subsequent affect and behaviors. How a person interprets events, what something means to someone, plays a crucial role in how that person responds to the world.

Emphasizing an individual's perception of events or information as the driver of emotional health has deep roots in Western culture. The Christian New Testament invokes the logic that "believing is seeing" indicating the belief that the ways in which individuals interpret events influence their personal reality. The Greek Stoics also viewed self-perception and beliefs as primary motivations for behavior. In addition, Shakespeare's Hamlet stated "there's nothing good nor bad, but thinking makes it so." Finally, Kant emphasized the German idealist's school of philosophy in which psychological growth is obtained through personal meaning and idiosyncratic construct development. Kant and others held that the ways in which individuals view the self influence the ways in which they grow and relate to the world. Lyons (1998) offers a detailed outline of several philosophical approaches that address the relationship of cognition and emotion.

CBT, in our view, places little emphasis on the development or exegesis of individual personality characteristics. Personality, per se, is seen as an enduring set of consistent behavioral and emotional responses to stimuli that results in idiosyncratic ways of relating to the world. CBT holds that individuals have innate dispositions that interact with the environment to shape their responses and worldviews (Beck & Weishaar, 2000). The development of psychological disorders, and conversely, the development of positive emotional responses and coping behaviors, are assumed to rely on one's evaluations of environmental stimuli interacting with personal, innate dispositions. Modifying an individual's cognitive processing, which is the primary goal of therapy, is thought to change the way a person evaluates and interacts with the world, and, as such, constitutes a method of personality change.

CBT has some overlap with several other psychotherapy systems, sharing techniques and/or philosophical preferences with REBT (Ellis, 1962), behavior therapy (Wolpe, 1958), and social learning systems (Bandura, 1977). CBT derives some of its viewpoints from Kelly's (1955) personal constructs, and it acknowledges Sullivan's (1953) interpersonal therapy as informing its philosophical base. Constructivists also share some techniques and points of view with CBT (Ramsay, 1998; Winter & Watson, 1999). While CBT does use a wide range of counseling techniques, many of which were developed from the above theoretical orientations, it is not merely an "eclectic" approach. The techniques chosen by a cognitive-behavioral therapist are used for specific purposes based on the therapist's cognitive conceptualization of the client and his or her treatment plan (Freeman, Pretzer, Fleming, & Simon, 1990).

THERAPEUTIC TECHNIQUES

CBT utilizes a collaborative relationship between the client and therapist to explore and modify the client's dysfunctional interpretations of stimuli (Beck & Weishaar, 1989). The therapist operating under the CBT modality strives to develop an individualized intervention plan for each client, based on an understanding of the person gained from this relationship (Freeman et al., 1990). A typical primary CBT strategy, collaborative empiricism, views the client as a practical scientist who lives by interpreting stimuli, but who has been temporarily inhibited by problems with information gathering and integrating mechanisms. A second general strategy, guided discovery, is directed toward identifying similarities that pervade the client's present misperceptions and beliefs, and connecting those to similar past experiences (Beck & Weishaar, 1989).

CBT uses a variety of procedures and techniques to assist clients in changing negative cognitions into realistic appraisals (Cormier & Nurius, 2003; James & Gilliland, 2003; O'Kearney, 1998). Cognitive techniques focus on an individual's misinterpretations of stimuli and provide mechanisms for testing them, investigating their logical (or illogical) basis, and revising them if they fail an empirical or logical test (Shafran & Somers, 1998). Craighead, Craighead, Kazdin, and Mahoney (1994) described five widely used cognitive procedures in CBT: (a) identification of dysfunctional and distorted cognitions, and the subsequent realization that they lead to negative feelings and maladaptive behaviors; (b) self-monitoring of negative thoughts, or "self-talk"; (c) identification of the relationships between thoughts, underlying beliefs, and feelings; (d) identification of alternative (i.e., functional and nondistorted) thinking patterns; and (e) personal hypothesis testing regarding the validity of basic assumptions about self, world, and future.

Craighead et al. (1994) also identified several methods for modifying negative cognitions: (a) distancing, (b) decentering, (c) reattribution, and (d) decatastrophizing. Distancing involves evaluating ingrained beliefs and judgments by making them more explicit and then testing their validity. Decentering encourages an understanding that one is not the focus of all events. Reattribution focuses on positive changes in perceptions and beliefs about the cause of particular events. Decatastrophizing centers on increasing the amount of information and length of time that is used in making evaluative decisions.

A wide variety of procedures and techniques fall under the umbrella of CBT. Most practitioners of CBT use an amalgam of cognitive and behavioral strategies (Spiegler & Guevremont, 1993; Tarrier et al., 1999). Some common techniques include (a) thought stopping, (b) meditation, (c) relaxation, (d) systematic desensitization, (e) mental and emotive imagery, (f) cognitive modeling, (g) cognitive restructuring, (h) reframing (Freeman et al., 1990; James & Gilliland, 2003), and (i) stress inoculation (Meichenbaum, 1993).

Thought stopping is used to help clients control unproductive, debilitating, and self-defeating thoughts and images through both sudden and progressively systematic elimination of maladaptive thoughts and emotions. The process involves teaching the client how to interrupt the stream of thoughts with a sudden stimulus, and then switching to other thoughts before the dysfunctional thoughts resurface. The stimulus can either be imagined or real (Freeman et al., 1990).

Meditation and *relaxation* can be useful tools for helping clients obtain a sense of control over anxiety and minimize anxiety level (Freeman et al., 1990). Meditation helps clients concentrate on some internal or external stimulus, which serves to focus attention away from aversive stimuli. It is designed to help clients consciously concentrate on positive, self-enhancing thoughts, as opposed to dwelling on negative, self-defeating thoughts and ruminations. Relaxation is predicated on the notion that it is impossible to be completely physically relaxed and emotionally anxious simultaneously. The reverse is also held to be true: one cannot be totally relaxed mentally and at the same time experience physical tension. To reach a state of deep relaxation, the client learns to (a) relax all muscle groups, thereby placing the whole body in a state of complete physical relaxation; (b) relax mentally (i.e., cognitively); (c) reduce anxiety while being totally relaxed; (d) omit extraneous background cognitions while dealing with the anxiety or problem at hand; and (e) use relaxation to control not only the problem under study but other debilitating stressors as well (James & Gilliland, 2003).

Systematic desensitization (SD), promulgated by Wolpe and Lazarus (James & Gilliland, 2003; Rimm & Masters, 1974), uses internal mental processes to help individuals control their responses to aversive stimuli and thereby inhibit undesirable behaviors (James & Gilliland, 2003). SD follows standard learning procedures to substitute one type of response for another and specifically targets the alleviation of maladaptive anxiety. It typically pairs deep relaxation with imagined scenes depicting personally anxiety-provoking situations (Rimm & Masters, 1974). In practicing SD, the client progresses through a hierarchy of envisioned scenes, beginning with a situation that brings out only a mild level of anxiety. The client then imagines the scene over and over, coupled with relaxation techniques, until he or she is at ease while envisioning the situation. The client then continues in a stepwise fashion until he or she is calm while envisioning the scenes that initially would have been the most anxiety-producing (Freeman et al., 1990).

Mental imagery is a process of focusing on vivid mental pictures of experiences or events—past, present, and future; it has utility for both problem identification and the therapeutic process. *Emotive imagery* involves imagining, in a covert but vivid way, the emotion involved in an actual situation or behavior. A mental image becomes emotive when one imagines an emotional or feeling state paired with a specific image. The person focuses on safe, positive, and pleasant images as a strategy for blocking out and/or coping with actual anxiety-provoking situations (James & Gilliland, 2003). One technique often used is to combine the systematic desensitization with mental imagery by having the client envision an anxiety-provoking situation, imagine that the problems that he or she fears will occur, and then visualize coping effectively with the stress and anxiety (Freeman et al., 1990).

Cognitive modeling combines covert and overt modeling strategies to assist clients in learning appropriate self-talk in order to avoid self-defeating thoughts and behaviors, while simultaneously performing adaptive tasks. Initially, the therapist serves as a model by performing the desired task. The client is then told to perform the task, as modeled by the therapist, while the therapist instructs the client aloud. As the therapy progresses, the client is asked to perform the same task while engaging in overt self-instruction, which becomes increasingly covert over time. The client eventually performs the task while self-instructing in a wholly covert manner (James & Gilliland, 2003).

Cognitive restructuring teaches people to replace negative, debilitating cognitions with positive, self-enhancing thoughts and actions. It assumes that self-defeating behaviors flow from either the development of defective cognitions or from irrational thinking and/or self-defeating statements. The technique also assumes that modifying personal cognitions can alter a person's defective thinking or self-defeating statements (James & Gilliland, 2003). Cognitive restructuring can assist the client in learning to take the needed time to look analytically at the thoughts and feelings produced in various situations, thereby reducing the inclination to routinely jump to conclusions (Freeman et al., 1990). The recommended six steps in cognitive restructuring are (a) defining a verbal set, which includes the rationale of the procedure; (b) identifying client thoughts during problem situations; (c) introducing and practicing positive coping thoughts; (d) shifting away from self-defeating thoughts; (e) introducing and practicing positive or reinforcing self-statements; and (f) completing homework and following up. The therapist acts as a consultant, facilitator, mentor, and coach. The therapy typically involves several cognitive and behavioral techniques, such as relaxation, imagery, modeling, reframing, rehearsal, stress inoculation, and thought stopping (James & Gilliland, 2003).

Reframing, also known as reformulating, relabeling, or refocusing, seeks to modify or restructure one's perceptions of problems or behaviors at hand. It is valuable in cases where reframing the problem situation, the behaviors or motives of others, or the attitudes of the client changes his or her perspective by rendering the issue more understandable, acceptable, or solvable (James & Gilliland, 2003). One way to use this technique is to have the client completely occupy his or her mind with neutral or pleasant thoughts, thereby blocking dysfunctional thoughts for a short period of time. Although this technique diminishes dysfunctional thoughts for only a short time, it can be useful in permitting the client to generate some control over his or her thinking and to have a short "vacation" from the dysfunctional thoughts (Freeman et al., 1990).

Stress inoculation is a process of teaching clients both cognitive and physical skills for autonomously coping with future stressful situations. Stress inoculation is predicated on the notion that exposing clients to milder forms of stress attenuates or diffuses responses to major life stressors (Meichenbaum, 1993), and it seeks to improve a person's skill set for dealing with future problems. Meichenbaum (1993) suggested an overlapping three-phase intervention approach consisting of (a) conceptualizing the nature of the stressor and its effects on the individual's emotions and behavior, (b) learning coping skills through acquisition and rehearsal strategies, and (c) inoculation, which provides opportunities for the individual to apply new coping measures across increasing levels or intensities of stressors. The major difference between cognitive restructuring and stress inoculation is the latter's emphasis on remaining proactive and future-oriented (James & Gilliland, 2003).

In summary, CBT practitioners have a wide range of strategies and techniques at their disposal. Predictably, several subsystems of CBT have been promulgated, each with varying degrees of cohesiveness to cognitive and behavioral theories. Examples include Beck (1983), Ellis (1979), Meichenbaum (1995), and Nezu (1987), with each theorist setting forth his particular version of CBT. Beck emphasizes positive changes in negative cognitive content, Ellis focuses on irrational belief systems, Meichenbaum combines cognitive change with specific behavioral interventions, and Nezu approaches CBT through problem solving rather than a focus on specific cognitive content.

While CBT obviously offers a myriad of therapeutic options, the nature of their differences also detracts from the theory's overall cohesion. CBT is possibly most efficacious within rehabilitation contexts when it is seen more as an amalgam of intervention strategies to be used in consort with other rehabilitation means, and less as a theoretical orientation to which the practitioner must strictly adhere. Examples of using CBT in combination with other theoretical approaches may be found in King, Scahill, Findley, and Cohen (1999), Leggett, Hurn, and Goodman (1997), and Smith (1993).

CBT IN THE CONTEXT OF REHABILITATION

As a general concept, the term *rehabilitation* can be used as both verb and noun. It refers to, or describes, both the process and philosophy behind aiding individuals in some restorative activity. The general concept of rehabilitation is applicable whether those activities are focused on regaining physical function after injury, restoring emotional equilibrium after a devastating loss, training for a new vocation after job loss due to disability, regaining a sense of personal control after cessation of dysfunctional substance use, or finding meaning in life after disability onset. In actual practice, most individuals who undergo some type of rehabilitation process will experience multiple, mutually exacerbating problems (physical and/or emotional) that are mediated by self-appraisal, belief structures about personal worth, and problem-solving proclivities, and CBT may be applied to such problems.

CBT is utilized in a variety of rehabilitation contexts. For example, individuals with schizophrenia have shown improved community functioning and have reported decreased positive symptoms when CBT is used as an adjunct to pharmacotherapy (Bustillo, Lauriello, & Keith, 1999; Chadwick & Lowe, 1990). Svensson and Hansson (1998) found that the use of CBT in inpatient treatment with people with schizophrenia was related to positive outcomes.

CBT has been employed in the treatment of obsessive-compulsive disorder (Salkovskis, Forrester, & Richards, 1998; Salkovskis, Richards, & Forrester, 1995), a syndrome that can be extremely debilitating to employability. It has also shown efficacy for people experiencing severe anxiety (Bruce, Spiegel, & Hegel, 1999; Heimberg et al., 1998; Hofmann & Spiegel, 1999), and in the treatment of posttraumatic stress disorder (PTSD; Meadows & Foa, 1999). Both anxiety and one of its extreme manifestations, PTSD, are fairly common sequelae of disability. In fact, Anderson and Grunert (1997) found PTSD to be a common consequence of injuries sustained in the workplace. Anderson and Grant used CBT as part of a return-to-work treatment program for employees with traumatic injuries in several industries, and found that behaviorally oriented interventions had the greatest correlation with successful workplace readjustment. Primarily cognitive interventions also had some recognized positive effects, but they were less compelling than behavioral intervention outcomes.

People with specific learning disabilities (SLD) often have difficulties with self-appraisal of competency. Lloyd, Hallahan, Kauffman, and Keller (1998) addressed these issues with a student group using CBT, as did Weller, Watteyne, Herbert, and Crelly (1994). Rossiter, Hunnisett, and Pulsford (1998) outlined an anger management program for students with SLD that used CBT techniques, while Trapani and Gettinger (1996) outlined a variety of treatment strategies based on CBT, also for students with SLD. Lindsay (1999) cites strong evidence that people with SLD are prone to serious emotional and behavioral disorders, including depression, anger, and anxiety, and refers to 50 clinical cases evincing positive effects of CBT treatment on long-lasting behavior change with clients with SLD. However, Kroese (1998) cautioned that CBT is only useful for people with SLD under certain conditions. It should be considered as a therapeutic option only when clients have sufficient self-regulation and abstract thinking capabilities, along with the capacity to render accurate self-reports, attributes that may often be compromised with SLD.

Problems with alcohol and other drug abuse (AODA) may be found with a number of people with disabilities (Corbitt, Luyegu, & Moore, 1999; Ingraham, Kaplan, & Chan, 1992), and significant inverse relationships have been found between ongoing substance use and successful rehabilitation outcome (Corbitt et al., 1999). AODA is a known risk factor for incurring disabilities, including spinal cord injury (SCI; Heinemann, Doll, & Schnoll, 1989), and continued postinjury substance abuse increases the risk of suicidality in people with SCI (Kewman & Tate, 1998). AODA also increases the possibility of incurring traumatic brain injuries (Wesolowski & Zencius, 1994) and serious orthopedic injuries (Falvo, 1999). Long-term alcohol abuse alone increases a person's risk for debilitating problems, such as peripheral neuropathy, cerebral atrophy, end organ dysfunction, and negative metabolic changes (Lezak, 1995).

CBT approaches have shown some efficacy in AODA treatment. Bell, Montoya, Richard, and Dayton (1998) found higher levels of problem awareness and openness to treatment among people who abuse substances when a CBT paradigm was employed. Smokowski and Wodarski (1998) advocate CBT for persons with drug addictions, and Wanberg and Milkman (1998) recommend CBT for individuals who have AODA problems together with histories of criminal conduct. However, a National Institutes of Health (NIH, 1998) study found CBT to be only marginally successful in promoting and maintaining alcohol cessation, and Sandahl, Herlitz, Ahlin, and Roennberg (1998) found other therapeutic approaches to have superior outcomes than CBT for maintaining abstinence behaviors. Overall, CBT interventions with people with AODA problems have only modest and mixed empirical support (Hollon & Beck, 1994).

CBT lends itself well to some problems associated with traumatic brain injury (TBI) and related neurological problems. Corrigan and Yudofsky (1996) stated that cognitive therapy aims at symptom reduction and at controlling dysfunctional behaviors in people with neurological conditions. However, the cautions noted by Kroese (1998) for individuals with SLD would also apply to TBI, since some individuals with brain injuries may have limited capacity for insight, abstract concept formation, or learning, reducing the effectiveness of standard CBT interventions.

Depression and related mood disorders are often found in people with disabilities as both primary diagnoses or as secondary disability sequelae. Depression is quite common in neuropathological conditions such as stroke (Lezak, 1995), TBI (Dixon & Layton, 1999), and multiple sclerosis (Rao, 1990). Mood disorders are also found in higher concentrations among individuals with SCI (Elliott & Frank, 1996), chronic pain (Alexy, Webb, Crismore, & Mark, 1996), and psychosis (Bustillo et al., 1999). Devins and Binik (1996) found dysphoria to be common in a mixed population of individuals with disabilities or chronic illnesses.

People with disabilities do not, as a matter of course, always become depressed, and it is well known that a one-to-one correspondence does not exist between severity of disability and mood status (Hopkins, 1971; Kaplan & Questad, 1980). We believe that an individual's appraisal of his or her situation after disability onset is a major moderating variable in mood and adjustment status. CBT can be effective in clarifying, challenging, and modifying negative self-appraisal and should, theoretically, lead to reduced frequency and severity of depression after disability onset.

Since the introduction of CBT, mood disorders have constituted its major clinical and research foci (Beck, 1963). CBT has shown some efficacy in treating unipolar depression and in reducing the risk of recurrence (Blackburn, Eunson, & Bishop, 1986; Miranda, Gross, Persons, & Hahn, 1998; Segal, Gemar, & Williams, 1999). Some researchers have claimed that CBT is more effective in treating mood disturbance than either pharmacotherapy or other psychotherapeutic systems (e.g., Bowers, 1990; Dobson, 1989). However, well-controlled research has not fully supported these assertions (Hollon & Beck, 1994), and a recent NIH study found no outcome differences between CBT and interpersonal therapies (Ablon & Jones, 1999). However, CBT would appear to be useful in treating people who have disabilities and who are experiencing a mood disorder.

ADJUSTMENT ISSUES
IN REHABILITATION AND DISABILITY

Psychological factors in adjustment to disability have always been a major focus of philosophy and practice in rehabilitation. The seminal works of Dembo, Leviton, and Wright (1956) and Wright (1983) highlighted value change, stigma management, and self-evaluation as critical components of coping with acquired disability. A veritable cornucopia of theory and research has evolved focusing on ways to help people make the best possible adjustment to disability and loss, as well as facilitating understanding of the reasons that some individuals adjust better than others. Authors have emphasized various psychological and social factors in adjustment to disability, such as meeting the social needs of self and others (Vash, 1981), obtaining social support to overcome shame and manage the stigma of disability (Jones et al., 1984; Kaplan, 1994), and redefining oneself through phased adjustment (Livneh & Antonak, 1991). Interested readers can consult a myriad of scholarly work on adjustment to disability, including Vash (1981), Wright (1983), Marinelli and Dell'Orto (1999), and Smart (2001).

CBT approaches adjustment as a collaborative task between a counselor and client that focuses on identifying and changing negative cognitions associated with disability. Incurring a disability can place individuals at a higher risk for depression because of globalized negative self-statements ("I'm worthless because I can't work"), which affect self-regard, mood, and behavior. CBT procedures should not seek to change negative perceptions into positive ones or attempt to rid people of their disabilities (Beck & Weishaar, 2000). Rather, in order to cope with a disability, CBT interventions should remain reality-based and directed toward minimizing negative biases, increasing positive risk taking, and facilitating realism in client self-appraisals.

Despite the apparent logical rationale for using CBT with people with disabilities, few studies have been reported that test this approach on people with disabilities (Mpofu, Thomas, & Chan, 1996). Most of the research identified by Mpofu et al. concentrates on chronic pain (Flor & Birbaumer, 1993; James, Thorn, & Williams, 1993; Spence, 1989). Mpofu et al. identified one paper that describes CBT treatment for individuals with multiple sclerosis (Larcombe & Wilson, 1984).

The paucity of research literature is explained in part by the difficulty of applying CBT to several types of disability sequelae. For example, individuals with central nervous system processing disorders, as found in some types of traumatic brain injury, mental retardation, learning disabilities, a variety of diseases resulting in dementia (e.g., Huntington's, Alzheimer's, Wilson's), cerebral vascular accidents, alcoholism, several subtypes of psychosis, and other problems may not have the capacity to accurately self-assess, provide valid self-reports, or process abstract concepts (Kroese, 1998). If these capabilities are absent or significantly compromised, a client may not be a good candidate for CBT intervention. Disability categories that increase the risk of cognitive processing problems represent the majority of persons with severe disabilities in the United States (United States Census Bureau, 1997); CBT may therefore not have the widest ranging applicability of the several therapeutic options available to rehabilitation counseling professionals.

Some conceptual work has been set forth that promotes the use of CBT in rehabilitation counseling. Mpofu et al. (1996) recommend CBT for use with individuals who have incurred a physical disability, and they then go on to illustrate the CBT counseling process, using a case example of work with an individual who sustained severe burns. Mpofu et al. balance their opinions by underscoring that CBT may not be the optimal counseling approach for all persons with disabilities. Stewart (1996) conceptually tied CBT to Livneh's (1986) model of adaptation to disability. Stewart emphasized how various CBT techniques can be employed at different stages in the adaptation to disability process, and also offered case examples to illustrate his concepts.

In summary, there is a well-developed conceptual framework for CBT applications in rehabilitation, and a poorly developed research base to support its utilization. Clearly, research is needed to begin to address basic questions about when, how, and with whom CBT should be employed.

CASE EXAMPLE

The client (called LP for our purposes) is a 45-year-old divorced female with a high school education and no recent history of employment. She presented for adjustment counseling at the advice of her vocational rehabilitation counselor because of ongoing emotional turmoil related to her disabilities. LP had been diagnosed with systemic lupus erythematosus (SLE or lupus), rheumatoid arthritis (RA), and a benign optic nerve tumor. She was judged as unemployable, and as a result, began receiving Social Security Disability Insurance benefits.

Initially, LP complained of feeling "worthless," "of no value," and "totally damaged." She presented with anxiety and depressed mood and affect, and she had persistent death wishes with no suicidal intent or push.

LP had a very small, dense social support network consisting of a few friends. She had little contact with her family of origin and continually acrimonious relationships with her ex-husband and one of her two children.

During the first interview, the therapist (SK) found that LP responded well to cognitive interpretations. Clinical testing revealed no difficulties with LP's verbal abstraction, short-term memory, information-processing speed, or intellect.

Initial CBT interventions centered on identifying LP's distorted cognitions and relating them to her subsequent negative feelings and maladaptive behaviors. LP stated that she was "taught to be a good girl and not make waves" by her punitive, depressed mother. LP was able to see how these messages were at least partially responsible for her feelings of anxiety ("I will be punished for not working") and depression ("I'm no good because I don't contribute; in fact, I take money from the government, which makes me even worse"). These messages, which formed the basis for much of her self-talk, also influenced her lack of assertiveness toward a male friend with whom she was interested in developing a romantic relationship ("good girls don't ask men for dates, and who could care about me?").

LP was asked to consciously monitor her thoughts and note examples of negative self-talk and globalized self-demeaning statements. When she recognized such an internal event, LP was instructed to replace the thought with a neutral or positive self-statement, thereby encouraging her to lessen the pernicious impact of constant self-destructive ideation.

As therapy progressed, LP was able to acknowledge feelings of anger and resentment that she had repressed or incorrectly attributed to her own inadequacies. A variety of imagery techniques were utilized in which she imagined confronting people, events, and even her own physical problems. She was able to decenter on herself as "the source of all wrong" and reattribute several negative life events into a more rational, reality-based focus.

Imagery was also utilized to increase LP's assertiveness. She imagined herself being able to "reach out and grab some life" despite her serious physical limitations. Emotional risk taking was also overtly rehearsed by asking her male acquaintance for a date.

LP was able to utilize the skills that she learned in therapy in the context of her everyday life. She began to think of herself as "a worthwhile human" who was not "consigned to life's junk pile" as a result of her disabilities. She was able to act more freely and directly in her own best interest when she successfully challenged her dysfunctional cognitions and replaced them with self-affirming, reality-based thoughts. She felt better able to defend against her ex-husband's derisive comments and to set stronger boundaries with her son.

LP continues to experience negative physical effects from her disabilities, but they no longer fully dictate her mood or her self-perception. Although she is often ill or fatigued, she can now separate these experiences from her self-evaluations and, as a result, is far less angry, anxious, and depressed. She is also enjoying her relationship with her significant other, and he was thrilled when she asked him for that date.

CONCLUSION

CBT clearly has a place in rehabilitation practice. Some research and a variety of anecdotal accounts clearly speak to its efficacy in helping people adjust to disability. However, the possible shortcomings of CBT must be acknowledged relative to its use with people with disabilities. Having been originally promulgated for purposes of aiding people who were depressed but were neurologically intact, its methods may not be useful for a large segment of rehabilitation consumers. The available research literature shows mixed findings on the utility of CBT across rehabilitation settings, and scant data are available concerning its use in vocational rehabilitation settings. Additional research findings on CBT are needed to garner a lucid picture of when, where, with whom, and under which circumstances CBT techniques might be effectively used in rehabilitation settings.

REFERENCES

Ablon, J. S., & Jones, E. E. (1999). Psychotherapy process in the National Institute of Mental Health Treatment of Depression Collaborative Research Program. *Journal of Consulting and Clinical Psychology, 67,* 64–75.

Alexy, W., Webb, P., Crismore, L., & Mark, D. (1996). Utilizing psychological assessment in rehabilitating patients with occupational musculoskeletal injuries. *Journal of Back and Musculoskeletal Rehabilitation, 7,* 41–51.

Anderson, R., & Grunert, B. (1997). A cognitive behavioral approach to the treatment of post-traumatic stress disorder after work related trauma. *American Society of Safety Engineers, ASSE Technical Forum, 42,* 39–42.

Bandura, A. (1977). *Social learning theory.* Englewood Cliffs, NJ: Prentice-Hall.

Beck, A. T. (1963). Thinking and depression: I. Idiosyncratic content and cognitive distortions. *Archives of General Psychiatry, 9,* 324–333.

Beck, A. (1983). Cognitive therapy of depression: New perspectives. In P. Clayton (Ed.), *Treatment of depression: Old controversies and new perspectives* (pp. 191–233). New York: Raven.

Beck, A. T., & Weishaar, M. E. (1989). Cognitive therapy. In A. Freeman, K. Simon, L. Beutler, & H. Arkowitz (Eds.), *Comprehensive handbook of cognitive therapy* (pp. 21–36). New York: Plenum.

Beck, A. T., & Weishaar, M. E. (2000). Cognitive therapy. In R. J. Corsini & D. Wedding (Eds.), *Current psychotherapies* (6th ed., pp. 241–272). Itasca, IL: Peacock.

Bell, D. C., Montoya, I. D., Richard, A. J., & Dayton, C. A. (1998). The motivation for drug abuse treatment: Testing cognitive and 12-step theories. *American Journal of Drug and Alcohol Abuse, 24,* 551–571.

Blackburn, I. M., Eunson, K. M., & Bishop, S. (1986). A two-year naturalistic follow-up of depressed patients treated with cognitive therapy, pharmacotherapy and a combination of both. *Journal of Affective Disorders, 10,* 67–75.

Bowers, W. (1990). Treatment of depressed in-patients: Cognitive therapy plus medication, relaxation plus medication, and medication alone. *British Journal of Psychiatry, 156,* 73–78.

Bruce, T., Spiegel, D., & Hegel, M. (1999). Cognitive-behavioral therapy helps prevent relapse and recurrence of panic disorder following alprazolam discontinuation: A long-term follow-up of the Peoria and Dartmouth studies. *Journal of Consulting and Clinical Psychology, 67,* 151–156.

Bustillo, J. R., Lauriello, J., & Keith, S. J. (1999). Schizophrenia: Improving outcome. *Harvard Review of Psychiatry, 6,* 229–240.

Chadwick, P. D., & Lowe, C. F. (1990). Measurement and modification of delusional beliefs. *Journal of Consulting and Clinical Psychology, 58,* 225–232.

Corbitt, E., Luyegu, A., & Moore, D. (1999). *Substance use among vocational rehabilitation consumers with a mental illness.* Paper presented at the American Psychological Association annual conference.

Cormier, S., & Nurius, P. S. (2003). *Interviewing and change strategies for helpers: Fundamental skills and cognitive behavioral interventions* (5th ed.). Pacific Grove, CA: Brooks/Cole.

Corrigan, P. W., & Yudofsky, S. C. (1996). What is cognitive rehabilitation? In P. W. Corrigan & S. C. Yudofsky (Eds.), *Cognitive rehabilitation for neuropsychiatric disorders* (pp. 53–69). Needham Heights, MA: Allyn & Bacon.

Craighead, L. W., Craighead, W. E., Kazdin, A. E., & Mahoney, M. J. (1994). *Cognitive and behavioral interventions: An empirical approach to mental health problems.* Needham Heights, MA: Allyn & Bacon.

Dembo, T., Leviton, G. L., & Wright, B. A. (1956). Adjustment to misfortune: A problem of social-psychological rehabilitation. *Artificial Limbs, 3*(2), 4–62.

Devins, G. M., & Binik, Y. M. (1996). Facilitating coping with chronic physical illness. In M. Zeidner & N. S. Endler (Eds.), *Handbook of coping: Theory, research, applications* (pp. 640–696). New York: Wiley.

Dixon, T. M., & Layton, B. S. (1999). Traumatic brain injury. In M. G. Eisenberg, R. L. Glueckauf, & H. H. Zaretsky (Eds.), *Medical aspects of disability: A handbook for the rehabilitation professional* (2nd ed., pp. 98–120). New York: Springer.

Dobson, K. S. (1989). A meta-analysis of the efficacy of cognitive therapy for depression. *Journal of Consulting and Clinical Psychology, 57,* 414–419.

Elliott, T., & Frank, R. (1996). Depression following spinal cord injury. *Archives of Physical Medicine and Rehabilitation, 77,* 816–823.

Ellis, A. (1962). *Reason and emotion in psychotherapy.* New York: Stuart.

Ellis, A. (1979). The practice of rational-emotive therapy. In A. Ellis & J. M. Whitely (Eds.), *Theoretical and empirical foundations of rational-emotive therapy* (pp. 61–100). Monterey, CA: Brooks/Cole.

Ellis, A. (2000). Rational emotive behavior therapy. In R. J. Corsini & D. Wedding (Eds.), *Current psychotherapies* (6th ed.). Itasca, IL: Peacock.

Falvo, D. (1999). *Medical and psychosocial aspects of chronic illness and disability* (2nd ed.). Gaithersburg, MD: Aspen.

Flor, H., & Birbaumer, N. (1993). Comparison of the efficacy of electromyographic biofeedback, cognitive-behavioral therapy, and conservative medical interventions in the treatment of chronic musculoskeletal pain. *Journal of Consulting and Clinical Psychology, 61,* 653–658.

Freeman, A., Pretzer, J., Fleming, B., & Simon, K. (1990). *Clinical applications of cognitive therapy.* New York: Plenum.

Freud, S. (1961). *The standard edition of the complete psychological works of Sigmund Freud. Vol. XIX: The ego and the id and other works* (J. Strachey, Trans.). London: Hogarth. (Original work published 1923)

Heimberg, R. G., Liebowitz, M. R., Hope, D. A., Schneier, F. R., Holt, C. S., Welkowitz, L. A., et al. (1998). Cognitive behavioral group therapy vs. phenelzine therapy for social phobia: 12-week outcome. *Archives of General Psychiatry, 55,* 1133–1141.

Heinemann, A. W., Doll, M., & Schnoll, S. (1989). Treatment of alcohol abuse in persons with recent spinal cord injuries. *Alcohol, Health and Research World, 13,* 110–117.

Hofmann, S. G., & Spiegel, D. A. (1999). Panic control treatment and its applications. *Journal of Psychotherapy Practice and Research, 8,* 3–11.

Hollon, S. D., & Beck, A. T. (1994). Cognitive and cognitive-behavioral therapies. In A. E. Bergin & S. L. Garfield (Eds.), *Handbook of psychotherapy and behavior change* (4th ed., pp. 428–466). New York: Wiley.

Hopkins, M. T. (1971). Patterns of self-destruction among the orthopedically disabled. *Rehabilitation Research and Practice Review, 3*(1), 5–16.

Ingraham, K., Kaplan, S., & Chan, F. (1992). Rehabilitation counselors' awareness of client alcohol abuse patterns. *Journal of Applied Rehabilitation Counseling, 23*(3), 18–22.

James, L. D., Thorn, B. E., & Williams, D. A. (1993). Goal specification in cognitive-behavioral therapy for chronic headache pain. *Behavior Therapy, 24,* 305–320.

James, R. K., & Gilliland, B. E. (2003). *Theories and strategies in counseling and psychotherapy* (5th ed.). Boston: Allyn & Bacon.

Jones, E. E., Farina, A., Hastorf, A. H., Markus, H., Miller, D. T., & Scott, R. A. (1984). *Social stigma: The psychology of marked relationships.* New York: Freeman.

Kaplan, S. (1994). Metaphor, shame, and people with disabilities. *Journal of Applied Rehabilitation Counseling, 25*(2), 15–18.

Kaplan, S., & Questad, K. (1980). Client characteristics in rehabilitation studies: A literature review. *Journal of Applied Rehabilitation Counseling, 11,* 165–168.

Kelly, G. (1955). *The psychology of personal constructs.* New York: Norton.

Kewman, D. G., & Tate, D. G. (1998). Suicide in SCI: A psychological autopsy. *Rehabilitation Psychology, 43,* 143–151.

King, R. A., Scahill, L., Findley, D., & Cohen, D. J. (1999). Psychosocial and behavioral treatments. In J. F. Leckman & D. J. Cohen (Eds.), *Tourette's syndrome—Tics, obsessions, compulsions: Developmental psychopathology and clinical care* (pp. 338–359). New York: Wiley & Sons.

Kroese, B. S. (1998). Cognitive-behavioral therapy for people with learning disabilities. *Behavioural and Cognitive Psychotherapy, 26,* 315–322.

Larcombe, N. A., & Wilson, P. H. (1984). An evaluation of cognitive-behaviour therapy for depression in patients with multiple sclerosis. *British Journal of Psychiatry, 145,* 366–371.

Leggett, J., Hurn, C., & Goodman, W. (1997). Teaching psychological strategies for managing auditory hallucinations. *British Journal of Learning Disabilities, 25,* 158–162.

Lezak, M. D. (1995). *Neuropsychological assessment* (3rd ed.). New York: Oxford University.

Lindsay, W. R. (1999). Cognitive therapy. *Psychologist, 12,* 238–241.

Livneh, H. (1986). A unified approach to existing models of adaptation to disability: I. A model adaptation. *Journal of Applied Rehabilitation Counseling, 17*(1), 5–16, 56.

Livneh, H., & Antonak, R. F. (1991). Temporal structure of adaptation to disability. *Rehabilitation Counseling Bulletin, 34,* 298–319.

Lloyd, J. W., Hallahan, D. P., Kauffman, J. M., & Keller, C. E. (1998). Academic problems. In R. J. Morris & T. R. Kratochwill (Eds.), *The practice of child therapy* (3rd ed., pp. 167–198). Needham Heights, MA: Allyn & Bacon.

Lyons, W. (1998). Philosophy, the emotions, and psychopathology. In W. F. Flack, Jr., & J. D. Laird (Eds.), *Emotions in psychopathology: Theory and research* (pp. 3–19). New York: Oxford University.

Marinelli, R. P., & Dell'Orto, A. E. (Eds.). (1999). *The psychological and social impact of disability* (4th ed.). New York: Springer.

Meadows, E. A., & Foa, E. B. (1999). Cognitive-behavioral treatment of traumatized adults. In P. A. Saigh & J. D. Bremner (Eds.), *Posttraumatic stress disorder: A comprehensive text* (pp. 376–390). Needham Heights, MA: Allyn & Bacon.

Meichenbaum, D. (1993). Stress inoculation training: A 20-year update. In P. M. Lehrer & R. L. Woolfolk (Eds.), *Principles and practice of stress management* (2nd ed., pp. 373–406). New York: Guilford.

Meichenbaum, D. H. (1995). Cognitive-behavioral therapy in historical perspective. In B. M. Bongar & L. E. Beutler (Eds.), *Comprehensive textbook of psychotherapy: Theory and practice* (pp. 140–158). New York: Oxford University Press.

Miranda, J., Gross, J. J., Persons, J. B., & Hahn, J. (1998). Mood matters: Negative mood induction activates dysfunctional attitudes in women vulnerable to depression. *Cognitive Therapy and Research, 22*, 363–376.

Mpofu, E., Thomas, K., & Chan, F. (1996). Cognitive-behavioural therapies: Research and applications in counselling people with physical disabilities. *Australian Journal of Rehabilitation Counseling, 2*, 99–114.

National Institutes of Health-NIAAA. (1998). Matching alcoholism treatments to client heterogeneity: Treatment main effects and matching effects on drinking during treatment. *Journal of Studies on Alcohol, 59*, 631–639.

Nezu, A. M. (1987). A problem-solving formulation of depression: A literature review and proposal of a pluralistic model. *Clinical Psychology Review, 7*, 121–144.

O'Kearney, R. (1998). Responsibility appraisals and obsessive-compulsive disorder: A critique of Salkovskis's cognitive theory. *Australian Journal of Psychology, 50*, 43–47.

Prochaska, J. O., & Norcross, J. C. (1999). *Systems of psychotherapy: A transtheoretical analysis* (4th ed.). Pacific Grove, CA: Brooks/Cole.

Ramsay, J. R. (1998). Postmodern cognitive therapy: Cognitions, narratives, and personal meaning-making. *Journal of Cognitive Psychotherapy, 12*, 39–55.

Rao, S. M. (1990). Multiple sclerosis. In J. L. Cummings (Ed.), *Subcortical dementia* (pp. 164–180). New York: Oxford University Press.

Rimm, D. C., & Masters, J. C. (1974). *Behavior therapy: Techniques and empirical findings.* New York: Academic.

Rossiter, R., Hunnisett, E., & Pulsford, M. (1998). Anger management training and people with moderate to severe learning disabilities. *British Journal of Learning Disabilities, 26*, 67–74.

Salkovskis, P. M., Forrester, E., & Richards, C. (1998). Cognitive-behavioural approach to understanding obsessional thinking. *British Journal of Psychiatry, 173* (Suppl 35), 53–63.

Salkovskis, P. M., Richards, H. C., & Forrester, E. (1995). The relationship between obsessional problems and intrusive thoughts. *Behavioural and Cognitive Psychotherapy, 23*, 281–299.

Sandahl, C., Herlitz, K., Ahlin, G., & Roennberg, S. (1998). Time-limited group psychotherapy for moderately alcohol dependent patients: A randomized controlled clinical trial. *Psychotherapy Research, 8*, 361–378.

Segal, Z. V., Gemar, M., & Williams, S. (1999). Differential cognitive response to a mood challenge following successful cognitive therapy or pharmacotherapy for unipolar depression. *Journal of Abnormal Psychology, 108*, 3–10.

Shafran, R., & Somers, J. (1998). Treating adolescent obsessive-compulsive disorder: Applications of the cognitive theory. *Behaviour Research and Therapy, 36,* 93–97.

Smart, J. (2001). *Disability, society, and the individual.* Gaithersburg, MD: Aspen.

Smith, J. (1993). Working close to the edge: The use of dual paradigms in psychotherapy with an adolescent girl. *Australian Journal of Psychotherapy, 12,* 152–165.

Smokowski, P. R., & Wodarski, J. S. (1998). Cognitive-behavioral treatment for cocaine addiction: Clinical effectiveness and practice guidelines. *Journal of Applied Social Sciences, 23*(1), 23–32.

Spence, S. H. (1989). Cognitive-behavior therapy in the management of chronic, occupational pain of the upper limbs. *Behaviour Research and Therapy, 27,* 435–446.

Spiegler, M. D., & Guevremont, D. C. (1993). *Contemporary behavior therapy* (2nd ed.). Pacific Grove, CA: Brooks/Cole.

Stewart, J. R. (1996). Applying Beck's cognitive therapy to Livneh's model of adaptation to disability. *Journal of Applied Rehabilitation Counseling, 27*(2), 40–45.

Sullivan, H. S. (1953). *The interpersonal theory of psychiatry* (H. S. Perry & M. L. Gawel, Eds.). New York: Norton.

Svensson, B., & Hansson, L. (1998). Perceived curative factors and their relationship to outcome: A study of schizophrenic patients in a comprehensive treatment program based on cognitive therapy. *European Psychiatry, 13,* 365–371.

Tarrier, N., Pilgrim, H., Sommerfield, C., Faragher, B., Reynolds, M., Graham, E., et al. (1999). A randomized trial of cognitive therapy and imaginal exposure in the treatment of chronic posttraumatic stress disorder. *Journal of Consulting and Clinical Psychology, 67,* 13–18.

Tomkins, S. (1984). Affect theory. In K. R. Scherer & P. Ekman (Eds.), *Approaches to emotion* (pp. 163–195). Hillsdale, NJ: Erlbaum.

Trapani, C., & Gettinger, M. (1996). Treatment of students with learning disabilities: Case conceptualization and program design. In M. A. Reinecke, F. M. Dattilio, & A. Freeman (Eds.), *Cognitive therapy with children and adolescents: A casebook for clinical practice* (pp. 251–277). New York: Guilford.

United States Census Bureau. (1997). *Selected characteristics of individuals 25 years old and over by disability status: 1997.* Retrieved April 9, 2002, from http://www.census.gov/hhes/www/disable/sipp/disab97/ds97t3.html

Vash, C. L. (1981). *The psychology of disability.* New York: Springer.

Wanberg, K. W., & Milkman, H. B. (1998). *Criminal conduct and substance abuse treatment: Strategies for self-improvement and change: The provider's guide.* Thousand Oaks, CA: Sage.

Weller, C., Watteyne, L., Herbert, M., & Crelly, C. (1994). Adaptive behavior of adults and young adults with learning disabilities. *Learning Disabilities Quarterly, 17,* 282–295.

Wesolowski, M. D., & Zencius, A. H. (1994). *A practical guide to head injury rehabilitation: A focus on postacute residential treatment.* New York: Plenum.

Winter, D. A., & Watson, S. (1999). Personal construct psychotherapy and the cognitive therapies: Different in theory but can they be differentiated in practice? *Journal of Constructivist Psychology, 12,* 1–22.

Wolpe, J. (1958). *Psychotherapy by reciprocal inhibition.* Stanford, CA: Stanford University Press.

Wright, B. (1983). *Physical disability: A psychosocial approach* (2nd ed.). New York: Harper Collins.

Chapter 9

Rational-Emotive Behavior Therapy

Gregory G. Garske and Malachy L. Bishop

Rational-emotive behavior therapy (REBT) is considered to be an active-directive and multimodal therapy that employs cognitive, emotive, and behavioral techniques. REBT posits that rather than events themselves, it is irrational beliefs, dogmatic musts, and imperative demands about events that cause the resulting self-defeating feelings and dysfunctional behaviors that hinder goal attainment. REBT tenets suggest that if a person can take primary responsibility for his or her emotional problems and work in a determined fashion to combat the irrational thinking that underpins them, the result will be a minimizing of self-defeating upsets and an enhanced chance for happiness and satisfaction (Yankura & Dryden, 1994).

HISTORY

Albert Ellis developed rational-emotive behavior therapy (REBT) and remains the chief proponent of this therapeutic approach. In early stages of his career, Ellis practiced classical analysis and psychoanalytically oriented therapy, but he became increasingly disillusioned with what he considered to be the passivity, inefficiency, and ineffectiveness of psychoanalysis. By 1953 he almost completely rejected the psychoanalytic approach (Yankura & Dryden, 1994). He "intensively studied hundreds of other methods" for two years and, as a result of this research and his clinical experiences, developed rational therapy (RT) in 1955, which became rational-emotive therapy (RET) in 1961 and rational-emotive behavior therapy (REBT) in 1993 (Ellis, 1996, p. 5). The changes in the name of the therapy reflected a clarification and inclusion of elements that have always been present in the theory, rather than basic philosophical or practical changes in the theory or practice of REBT (Ellis, 1995a).

Ellis has cited a number of influences in the development of REBT, including stoic philosophy and the "philosophy of human happiness" (Ellis, 1996, p. 5), behavior theory and therapy, Karen Horney's "tyranny of the shoulds" (Horney, 1965), and the theory and therapy of Alfred Adler (Ellis, 1973). He was particularly influenced by the stoic philosophies of Epictetus, Seneca, and Marcus Aurelius, which maintained happiness or misery results not from events but from perceptions and thinking about those events. Ellis credits Adler with the realization that behavior stems from ideas and calls Adler "the modern psychotherapist who was the main precursor of REBT" (Ellis, 1995b, p. 167). From the behavioral therapies Ellis chose and developed a number of counseling and therapeutic interventions (Ellis, 1989; Livneh & Wright, 1995).

MAJOR CONCEPTS

Since introducing REBT, Ellis has refined and embellished his early conceptualization (Bernard, 1995). However, the basic concepts have remained essentially unchanged.

Duality of Human Nature

The fundamental REBT principle is that people are born with the potential for rational (healthy, logical, and constructive), as well as irrational (harmful, absolutist, and defeatist), thoughts, feelings, and behaviors. Ellis agrees with Adler that people are goal-oriented and with such humanistic theorists as Maslow and Rogers that people have innate tendencies for self-preservation, happiness, communion with others, and self-actualization. However, he also recognizes that humans have an inborn and primarily biologic tendency toward self-destruction, perfectionism, thought avoidance, procrastination, and growth avoidance (Corey, 2001; Ellis, 1979). Although REBT recognizes that these tendencies toward irrationality and emotional disturbance can be exacerbated by familial and societal influences, it emphasizes their biological origin (Dryden, 1990; Ellis, 1993).

Holism

Ellis proposes that the basic human processes of thinking, emoting (feeling), and behaving are interrelated and generally simultaneous. According to Ellis (1996), thinking, feeling, and behaving are not separate, but integrated, conjoined, and holistic. For example:

> When you think negatively ("I'm an inadequate person when I fail to win John's [or Joan's] approval!"), you tend to *feel* badly (e.g., anxious) and act dysfunctionally (e.g., beg for approval or avoid John [or Joan]). When you *feel* anxious, you tend to *think* negative thoughts and to *act* compulsively or avoidantly. When you act compulsively, you tend to *think* and *feel* negatively. (Ellis, 1996, p. 14)

Following this line of reasoning, the most effective and "elegant" method of therapy will engage the client on all three levels. *Elegant* is an REBT term referring to a deep or fundamental change in one's philosophical framework, as opposed to "mere symptom removal" (Weinrach, 1980, p. 156).

The ABC Model

Ellis conceptualizes the mechanics of emotional disturbance and dysfunctional behavior by means of the ABC model (Ellis, 1977). Through this model people are seen as goal-directed. Ellis (1991) identified fundamental goals (FGs) and subgoals, as well as primary goals (PGs). The fundamental goals are "to survive, to be relatively free from pain, and to be reasonably satisfied or content" (p. 142). The primary goals include (a) being happy when alone; (b) being happy with others in both intimate relationships and wider social relationships; and (c) being happy with educational, vocational, economic, and recreational activities (Ellis, 1991).

In the course of pursuing these goals, people often experience adversity or events that thwart them in their attempts. In the most simplified form of the ABC model, A stands for the activating event, or adversity that acts to block goal attainment; B represents the beliefs or attitudes, both rational and irrational, that the individual holds regarding the activating event; and C connotes the emotional and behavioral consequence or reaction of the individual to A as a result of holding particular beliefs at B (Ellis, 1991; 1996; Yankura & Dryden, 1994).

This theory of disturbance disputes the generally and tacitly held, but commonly uninvestigated, belief that A, the event that acts to impede goal attainment, is the direct cause of C, the resulting reaction or consequence. Rather, it is B, the individual's beliefs and attitudes about A that cause the resulting emotional and behavioral reactions. These beliefs are evaluative cognitions or views of the world that are either flexible or rigid. If the beliefs are rational beliefs (rBs), they are flexible. They are expressed as preferences, hopes, and wishes. For example, when an adverse event occurs, such as the loss of a job, a person might respond with a self-statement such as "I wish I had not lost my job, but I did. It is unfortunate but I can certainly continue with my life and find happiness in another position." Alternately, people may respond with irrational beliefs (iBs), which are characterized by inflexibility, overgeneralizations, and absolutist musts, shoulds, and oughts. The self-statements may sound more like this: "I should never have lost my job. It is awful that I lost my job, and my being let go proves that I am a worthless person" (Dryden, 1990; Ellis, 1996). Beliefs are not facts but can rather be considered hypotheses. Unlike facts, which are based on observables, hypotheses are testable and challengeable (Ellis, McInerney, DiGiuseppe, & Yeager, 1988).

The explicating and teaching of the theory behind the ABC model can be a therapeutic counseling technique in itself. The understanding that (a) people choose to disturb and upset themselves by holding and actively maintaining irrational beliefs about the events in their lives and that (b) they are therefore capable of changing these beliefs can be both encouraging and empowering. For both counselors and indoctrinated clients, the model can also be used to identify and understand the origin of the upsets and disturbances (Yankura & Dryden, 1994).

Since its original presentation, Ellis has continually modified and expanded the ABC model (Ellis, 1991, 1996). In more recent writings he has acknowledged the interactive nature of activating events, cognitions, and consequences. "In essence, Ellis is no longer as absolutistic about beliefs being the sole cause of emotional disturbance. Events (As) and consequences (Cs) contribute" (Weinrach, 1986, p. 646). Ellis also added the D and E components to the model, with D representing the active disputing of irrational beliefs, and E representing the effective new philosophy, emotion, and behavior. Originally the disputing of irrational beliefs was conceived as primarily a cognitive exercise. It has since evolved into a more comprehensive and multimodal component, and, as will be seen below, REBT counseling and psychotherapy involve cognitive, emotive, and behavioral techniques.

Irrational Beliefs

Since presenting REBT, Ellis has examined and written extensively about commonly held and basic irrational beliefs. In his earlier writings Ellis (1962, pp. 60–88) proposed a set of 11 specific irrational beliefs that were most frequently the causes of emotional upset:

1. The idea that it is a dire necessity for an adult human being to be loved or approved by virtually every significant person in his community
2. The idea that one should be thoroughly competent, adequate, and achieving in all possible respects if one is to consider oneself worthwhile
3. The idea that certain people are bad, wicked, or villainous and that they should be severely blamed and punished for their villainy
4. The idea that it is awful and catastrophic when things are not the way one would very much like them to be
5. The idea that human unhappiness is externally caused and that people have little or no ability to control their sorrows and disturbance
6. The idea that, if something is or may be dangerous or fearsome, one should be terribly concerned about it and should keep dwelling on the possibility of its occurring
7. The idea that it is easier to avoid than to face certain life difficulties and self-responsibilities
8. The idea that one should be dependent on others and should need someone stronger than oneself on whom to rely
9. The idea that one's past history is an all-important determiner of one's present behavior and that because something once affected one's life, it should indefinitely have a similar effect
10. The idea that one should become quite upset over other people's problems and disturbances
11. The idea that there is invariably a right, precise, and perfect solution to human problems and that it is catastrophic if this solution is not found

More recently, Ellis reduced the list of irrational beliefs and attitudes to three main "musts" or demands (Dryden, 1990; Ellis, 1996; Livneh & Wright, 1995):

1. *Demands about the self:* "I absolutely must, at practically all times, be successful and demonstrate competency in my endeavors and win the approval of virtually all the significant people in my life." Such beliefs often lead to feelings of anxiety, depression, shame, and guilt and such behaviors as avoidance, withdrawal, and addiction.

2. *Demands about others:* "Other people must, practically always, treat me considerately, kindly, fairly, and lovingly. If they don't then it is awful and they are no good and deserve no joy in their lives." These beliefs often lead to feelings of anger, rage, passive-aggressiveness, and resentment and behaviors such as fighting and violence.

3. *Demands about the world/living conditions:* "I need and must have the things I want. Conditions under which I live must be comfortable, pleasurable, and rewarding. If they are not I can't stand it, and it is terrible." Feelings that result from such beliefs include rage, self-pity, and low frustration tolerance. Actions that may result include withdrawal, procrastination, and addiction.

THEORY OF PERSONALITY

REBT is primarily a theory of personality change, rather than a theory of personality (Ellis, 1995b). A developmental theory of personality has emerged over time, however, almost retrogressively to Ellis's original presentations and early formulations. Livneh and Wright (1995) stated as a limitation of the theory that little systematic theory building has been offered on the process of abnormal and normal personality development.

While holding that people have strong self-actualizing capacities toward growth and health, and that these propensities are inborn, Ellis concurrently asserts that there are tendencies toward self-defeat and self-sabotage. Both of these opposing tendencies are seen as arising from a combination of biological or physiological, social, and psychological influences.

Biological Aspects

While recognizing that external factors play a role in the development of personality, REBT emphasizes the biological and innate aspects of human personality (Ellis, 1995b; Yankura & Dryden, 1994). Ellis has offered a number of arguments supporting his hypothesis that there is a biologically based tendency toward irrationality, including the following (Ellis, 1976): (a) virtually all people demonstrate self-defeating tendencies and irrationalities, regardless of family background, culture, or ethnicity; (b) many of the irrational beliefs go counter to the teachings of parents, teachers, and other social influences; and (c) even bright and competent individuals who give up a set of irrational beliefs tend to adopt a new set, and individuals who tend to think rationally will sometimes revert to irrational beliefs.

REBT is not, however, a deterministic theory. Rather, it is humanistic, seeing people as capable, growth-oriented, and having inherent worth (Dryden, 1990). They are recognized as having the unique ability to think about their own thinking. Because of this ability, they are also capable of learning and understanding that for the most part they are choosing their upsetting and disturbing beliefs and behaviors, and so are capable of changing these behaviors. Habits only stay habits when they are left alone. Hence, self-defeating ideas remain self-defeating when they are accepted without question (Young, 1974).

Social Aspects

Humans are social animals, reared in, and for the most part remaining in, social and familial units. Included among the primary goals of humans are to be happy and successful socially (Ellis, 1991). A person's sense of self is to a great extent influenced by the complex social interactions that he or she experiences. Ellis describes a healthy individual as one who "finds it enjoyable to love and be loved by significant others and to relate to almost everyone he or she encounters" (Ellis, 1995b, p. 170). When one develops an irrational and exaggerated importance of the acceptance and caring of others, emotional disturbance occurs. Cases of such troublesome and unhealthy beliefs occur when people base their own worth and self-regard almost entirely on the whims of others. Alternately, a pathological disregard for the value of others may be seen.

Psychological Aspects

The REBT view of psychological health, versus a lack thereof, rests on the fundamental tenet that emotional upsets and disturbances largely stem from irrational beliefs about events that occur in one's life, as expressed in the ABC model. Persons who develop healthy personalities evidence logical and flexible thinking, foster self-enhancing beliefs, have a sense of mastery and control over their destiny, and are aware that they are capable of changing their thoughts (Ellis, 1989; Livneh & Wright, 1995). Conversely, people who exhibit and experience emotional upset and disturbance hold various absolutist and illogical beliefs and expectations about themselves, others, and the world. Not only do such people hold those beliefs, but they indoctrinate themselves with them repeatedly, and hence the beliefs are reinforced. Because there is no sense, no awareness, that one can change the beliefs, people experiencing such disturbances feel powerless over the events that "cause" them such misery. The ABC model of emotional disturbance presented earlier clearly portrays these mechanisms of disturbance and, as mentioned, provides counselors a way of teaching the theory.

DESCRIPTION OF THE COUNSELING PROCESS

The process of REBT counseling is essentially one of educating the client in the skill of identifying and effectively disputing irrational beliefs. Once irrational and self-defeating beliefs have been identified, the REBT counselor can, through a number of techniques, teach the client to dispute and change a belief into one that is more functional. More importantly, the counselor teaches the client to dispute irrational beliefs on his or her own. The client also learns that the process of deep and fundamental change is a long-term, in fact, lifelong process, requiring vigilance and persistence.

REBT is an active-directive and problem-focused therapy, and counselors will often utilize time-saving and efficient tools such as questionnaires, self-help forms, and homework such as the reading of or listening to psychoeducational materials. There are also certain procedures and techniques, viewed as inefficient and indirect, that are not likely to be seen in an REBT counseling session. For example, Ellis himself avoids the use of standard diagnostic tests, particularly projective tests such as the Thematic Apperception Test (TAT), believing that the way the client reacts to the first few sessions is more telling than any amount of objective or projective testing (Yankura & Dryden, 1994). In addition, an REBT counselor is not likely to spend a great deal of time, if any at all, discussing the client's problem history. Such "obsessing" is seen as having "little or nothing to do with the client's present disturbances. Therefore, REBT therapists encourage their clients to narrate their Activating Experiences in a relatively brief and non-obsessive manner" (Ellis, 1979, p. 95).

Clients are viewed as often entering counseling with beliefs and values that will act to prevent any therapeutic change, and these beliefs must therefore be addressed immediately in the counseling process. Such beliefs place the cause and responsibility on external and often uncontrollable factors. Examples are the blaming of current attitudes and conditions on poor parenting, critical friends, or a stress-filled work environment (Yankura & Dryden, 1994). A similar, externally based hindrance to therapeutic growth and change is the expectation that the therapist, or the simple experience of being in counseling, will somehow magically produce results. Before counseling can be effective and produce gains, the counselor must convey three main insights of REBT to the client (Yankura & Dryden, 1994, p. 48):

1. You largely choose to disturb yourself about the unpleasant events in your life, even though you may be influenced to do so by external factors. You mainly feel the way you think.
2. Regardless of how or when you acquired your present self-disturbing and self-defeating beliefs, you are choosing to maintain them in the present, and that is why you are disturbed now. Your past history and your present life conditions affect you, but they don't disturb you.
3. There is no magical way for you to change your personality and your tendencies to upset yourself. This change will require work and practice.

The overriding goal of REBT is to help clients acquire a more realistic, rational, and tolerant philosophy of life (Ellis, 1995b). "REBT is designed to induce people to examine and change some of their most basic values that keep them disturbed. For example, if a client's fear is of failing in her marriage, the aim is not merely to reduce that specific fear but to work with her exaggerated fears of failing in general" (Corey, 2001, p. 302). In attaining this broad goal of "elegant" change, REBT allows for considerable flexibility on the part of the practitioner in terms of techniques and procedures (George & Christiani, 1995). As mentioned above, REBT is a multimodal therapy in which practitioners employ cognitive, emotive, and behavioral techniques, and a summary of those types of techniques follows (Corey, 2001; Dryden, 1990; Ellis, 1973; James & Gilliland, 2003; Livneh & Wright, 1995; Mpofu, Thomas, & Chan, 1996).

Cognitive Techniques

The most common cognitive technique, particularly early on, is the active disputation of the client's irrational beliefs, attitudes, and self-talk. Four disputing strategies have been suggested as being particularly effective and helpful (Beal, Kopec, & DiGiuseppe, 1996):

1. Logical disputes, which aim to weaken the client's affinity for an iB by pointing out the faulty logic of it. Common leads in this type of disputing would be "Does it follow that . . . ?" "Does that seem consistent to you?" "Does that follow logically from . . . ?"
2. Empirical disputes, which invite the client to provide evidence for the iB, trying to show that the iB is inconsistent with empirical

reality. For example, the counselor may say "Where is the evidence for your belief that (you are worthless)?"

3. Functional disputes, which aim to show the client that it is not pragmatic to continue to hold the iB and that there are emotional and behavioral consequences for continuing to do so. Common leads here are: "Does your holding this belief get you what you want in life?" "Can you tell me what feelings you are experiencing as a result of that belief?"

4. Rational alternative disputes, which attempt to restructure or modify maladaptive beliefs; it is necessary to keep in mind that one is not likely to change a belief, despite overwhelming evidence to the contrary, unless an alternative belief of equal or superior value is offered. In other words, the counselor must offer an alternative, replacement belief that is more logical, more empirically sound, with fewer emotional and behavioral consequences. Examples are "It would be very disappointing if I didn't get (X), but it would not be terrible, awful, or the end of the world." or "If they don't like me, that is perhaps unfortunate, but it does not mean that I am a bad or worthless person."

Other cognitive techniques include:

- Semantic precision, which is utilized to help the client to become aware of language use that serves to perpetuate irrational beliefs. As an example, a client might be asked to restate the phrase "I can't do that" as "I have not done that yet."
- Rational coping self-statements, which involve having the client repeatedly remind himself or herself of rational beliefs in the form of short coping self-statements.
- Reframing, through which the client is taught to redefine a situation in a more positive light.
- Referenting, through which the client is encouraged to identify both the positive and negative referents of a particular concept and so to develop a more holistic view. For example, if the client is focusing on the positive aspects of a particular self-defeating behavior, he or she may come to acknowledge the negative results as well, increasing motivation to change.
- Humor, which can show the client that part of the problem may be taking things too seriously. Ellis often uses humorous songs in his sessions, and other techniques such as dramatic exaggerations, irony, and feigned incredulity.

Behavioral Techniques

- Homework, which is a particularly important component and may include completion of self-help forms that the counselor provides, teaching REBT to others, or psychoeducational methods, such as reading or listening to REBT books and tapes.
- Skill training techniques to teach and help clients acquire and utilize social skills, assertiveness skills, and relaxation techniques.
- Systematic desensitization, which entails the use of imagery to overcome fear, anxiety, shyness, and other irrationally based behaviors and emotions.
- Penalties and rewards, which are used to encourage clients to undertake uncomfortable assignments in pursuit of long-range goals.

Emotive Techniques

REBT counselors will not spend much time, if any, exploring with clients the emotions experienced in relation to the presenting problem. However, because of the interactive nature of cognition, behavior, and emotion, selective emotive exercises and techniques are employed to help clients become aware of and change dysfunctional and hindering emotional responses. Some of these techniques are:

- Rational-emotive imagery, which encourages clients to mentally practice thinking, feeling, and acting the way that they would like to behave in real life. Clients can also imagine the worst thing that could happen related to a given situation, imagine the experience of inappropriate emotions, and then mentally see themselves changing the emotions to more productive or appropriate ones.
- Role playing, which may be used to dramatically show clients the interpersonal and emotional effects of their irrational beliefs. Clients can also use this format to rehearse new and more effective behaviors and to experience the resulting positive emotions.
- Shame-attacking exercises, which can demonstrate the irrational nature of the fear of embarrassment or shame that prevents certain actions or behaviors, with clients given assignments directly related to their particular fears. For example, a client may be assigned the task of approaching strangers and initiating conversations, asking a silly question at a lecture, or singing out loud. In completing these assignments, clients learn that they can train themselves to not be controlled by the responses or potential responses of others.

Counselor-Client Relationship

The counselor-client relationship has been well defined in the REBT model. The counselor's role is primarily that of an educator, and the client's that of student. Ellis (1973, 1980) has characterized the REBT counselor as active-directive with most clients, as a risk taker, as intelligent and knowledgeable, as vigorous in detecting and disputing irrational ideas, and as persistent and empathic. REBT counselors confront clients directly with their problems so as not to waste unnecessary time, and they appeal to clients' reasoning powers rather than their emotions. Although REBT counselors, and Ellis in particular, believe that a counseling relationship characterized by warmth, affection, or love toward the client is not necessary, effective, or efficient, good rapport and full, unconditional acceptance of the client are important (Livneh & Wright, 1995). The counselor's acceptance of the client may be communicated verbally, and the counselor's self-acceptance is modeled by his or her behavior in the counseling sessions (e.g., not seeking the client's approval).

REHABILITATION APPLICATIONS

Elements of REBT make it inherently well suited for, while also inherently problematic, in some potential applications to rehabilitation counseling. REBT's strengths in this respect include the counselor's full and unconditional acceptance of the client: valuing the client for himself or herself; listening to the client's worldviews without judging, and then allowing the client to collect evidence to provide support for these views; reinforcing reality without judging the client; helping the client give up absolutist expectations about the world; and helping the client to focus on learning new skills (Balter, 1997a). With the awareness of certain potential problems and considerations, which are discussed below, the REBT counseling process can be effectively and productively applied to the realm of rehabilitation counseling.

Because it is a focused, active-directive, and "intrinsically brief" form of therapy (Ellis, 1996, p. 6), REBT is well suited to rehabilitation facilities and agencies, such as the State-Federal Vocational Rehabilitation system, where counseling is short-term and goal-oriented. In the REBT framework, people with disabilities are viewed "no differently from people who experience any other life misfortune (e.g., loss of job, loss of home, loss of loved one)" (Livneh & Sherwood, 1991, p. 32). When the focus of the counseling is the disability itself, the disability is perceived as an activating event, and counseling focuses, as usual, on self-acceptance, while also identifying and attacking irrational beliefs and attitudes that surround the event. "The counselor interrupts, confronts, and disputes any self-defeating verbalizations and illogical beliefs, and demonstrates to the client how these ideas are exaggerated and globalized" (Livneh & Sherwood, 1991, p. 532). REBT counselors can further help clients by teaching them how to break down problems perceived as insurmountable into smaller and more manageable units (Livneh & Sherwood, 1991).

A number of REBT writers have asserted that REBT is appropriate and helpful with clients from diverse cultures, educational backgrounds, intelligence levels, and types of disabilities, including mental illness (Balter, 1997a; Ellis, 1973, 1994; Gandy, 1995; Olevitch, 1995). At the same time, however, REBT is probably inappropriate and is unlikely to benefit persons who are not in touch with reality, are seriously brain-injured, are highly manic, have autism, or have moderate to severe mental retardation (Ellis & Harper, 1979; Ostby, 1986).

A potential problem with using REBT in rehabilitation settings arises when considering the adjustment to disability process. The hallmark REBT assumption is that clients are basically irrational in their beliefs, but it may also be important to realize that situational factors related to severe disability could result in a "genuinely awful experience" (Mpofu et al., 1996, p. 104). Further, when applying REBT in the early stages of the adjustment process, REBT counselors may seek to attack and negate a client's reactions, such as denial, which are often a natural part of the adjustment process and temporarily necessary to support psychological well-being. For this reason, Calabro (1990) pointed out that there are times, early in the adjustment process, when more supportive techniques are indicated. Active-directive and confrontational REBT methods can be well suited to later stages in the adjustment process, however, particularly when working with clients experiencing depression (Calabro, 1990; Livneh & Sherwood, 1991).

The REBT focus on unconditional acceptance and its assertion that a person has worth and value apart from the role that he or she plays in life, makes it both highly appropriate and empowering in the process of counseling people with disabilities (Balter, 1997b). The counselor's extension of this unconditional acceptance to the client is particularly helpful, for example, if the client engages in negative self-rating in relation to the disability or has experienced negative evaluations by significant others (Balter, 1997a).

CASE EXAMPLE

Samantha G. was a 37-year-old woman who was experiencing adjustment difficulties due to an occupational injury. Samantha worked as a critical care nurse in a local hospital until she experienced a severe back injury while attempting to lift a patient. Samantha recovered from back surgery, but she was informed that she would not be able to return to work as a critical care nurse or in any other type of nursing duties that required strenuous physical demands.

Samantha agreed to begin seeing a rehabilitation counselor on an outpatient basis. The counselor quickly learned that Samantha was depressed and lacking in self-worth. Working from an REBT framework, the counselor attempted to focus on the client's primary goals. In this case, regaining vocational satisfaction and self-worth were major concerns. The therapeutic approach consisted of weekly counseling sessions and homework assignments.

In the counseling sessions, the counselor challenged any self-defeating verbalizations and illogical beliefs. The ABC model was used in a rapid-fire, active-directive-persuasive-philosophic methodology. According to Ellis (1995), REBT practitioners challenge clients to try to defend their ideas; show them that they contain illogical premises; analyze these ideas and actively dispute them; and show how these ideas can be replaced with more rational philosophies. In addition, the client is taught how to minimize future problems by employing more logical thinking with subsequent irrational ideas and illogical deductions that may lead to self-defeating feelings and behaviors.

In Samantha's case, discussion focused on thoughts about her occupational future.

Cl: I am so disgusted with myself. My life will be so awful if I can't return to my job.

Co: Why is it so awful that you can't return to critical nursing?

Cl: Critical nursing allowed me to make a real difference. Sometimes I helped save lives.

Co: Do you mean to tell me that critical nursing is the only way that you can make a difference?

The intent is to challenge or dispute the client's rigid and absolute thinking about her life situation. The counselor pursues questioning that illicits alternative, and hopefully more rational, thinking. Irrational ideas are not always given up easily. The counselor will have to be persistent. In this case, the counselor posed other questions:

Co: Surely there are other ways of serving as a nurse or health care practitioner?

Co: Have you ever dealt with other life changes?
Co: How have you handled these changes?

The counselor was attempting to demonstrate that the client is capable of successful life change. Other client successes are used to demonstrate client capabilities. For example, the client noted that her role as a mother changed since her children were older now and more independent. Samantha's acceptance of her changing parental role was emphasized to show that she is capable of dealing with life change.

Besides the ongoing counseling sessions, homework assignments were used to fortify the client's logical thinking. In this case, the client was asked to read recommended REBT books, practice REBT reasoning when dealing with her family, and talk with nurses who work in other types of nursing.

Over a period of weeks, it was obvious that Samantha was becoming more flexible and rational in her thinking, emotions, and behaviors. The weekly REBT sessions and homework assignments proved to be helpful to a client who was once convinced that her life would be unfulfilling if she could not return to critical care nursing. Through persistence and hard work, the client's thinking became less illogical and sabotaging. Samantha returned to work in health care and was successfully adjusting to this new phase in her career and life.

RESEARCH FINDINGS

Historically, empirical support for the fundamental hypotheses of REBT has been underscored with limitations and problems. Among the main cognitive-behavioral approaches, REBT remains the least adequately tested, and the majority of the supportive studies have been based on nonclinical populations and case studies (Hollon & Beck, 1994; Livneh & Wright, 1995). Indeed, many of the main proponents of the theory have acknowledged this limitation, and there is currently an effort to rectify and strengthen the base of empirical support (Hollon & Beck, 1994; Bernard, 1995). Hollon and Beck (1994) pointed out that a lack of adequate evaluation should not be confused with lack of efficacy, and that REBT has generally performed well in studies in which it was adequately operationalized.

In terms of its scientific reputation, REBT has been hampered by ambiguities in the theory (e.g., nature of irrational beliefs), deficiencies in the experimental design of many REBT studies and the absence of studies involving large clinical groups, and deficiencies in formulating the REBT hypotheses in terms of researchable questions (Bernard, 1995). Further, the eclectic nature of the therapy and the flexibility allowed REBT counselors do not lend themselves to operationalization and controlled research (Corey, 2001).

In spite of these problems, there have been a number of large-scale reviews of outcome studies supportive of the efficacy and clinical effectiveness of REBT. McGovern and Silverman (1984) reviewed 47 studies from 1977 to 1982 and found that 31 reported significant findings in favor of the efficacy of REBT. Another review of 89 outcome studies by Silverman, McCarthy, and McGovern (1992) yielded similarly positive results. Lyons and Woods (1991) conducted a meta-analysis of 70 REBT outcome studies. A total of 236 comparisons of REBT to baseline, control groups, cognitive behavior modification (CBM), behavior therapy, and other psychotherapies were examined. The results indicated that participants receiving REBT demonstrated significant improvement over baseline measures and control groups, while the comparisons between REBT, CBM, and behavior therapy produced nonsignificant differences.

PROMINENT STRENGTHS AND LIMITATIONS

Some of the limitations that are unique to REBT have already been mentioned, including potential limitations in counseling for adjustment to disability, and research limitations. Another commonly noted limitation is that REBT may oversimplify and neglect aspects of the human experience when attempting to fit experiences into the ABC model (Livneh & Wright, 1995). Livneh and Wright also suggest that REBT may undermine therapeutic progress by underemphasizing the importance of the counselor-client relationship and ignoring the establishment of rapport. There is potential for those counselors who use REBT in their practice, because of the emphasis on persuasion, suggestion, and repetition, to impart their own values and expectations on clients (George & Christiani, 1995). Finally, Weinrach (1996) suggested that REBT has not adequately addressed issues relating to diversity-sensitivity.

On the other hand, REBT has made a number of important contributions to the field of counseling and psychotherapy, the most prominent of which is its emphasis on and clarification of the relationship between cognition and emotion (James & Gilliland, 2003). Ellis's initial and ongoing challenge to the psychological status quo revolutionized and eventually led to ongoing questioning, research, and development in the areas of cognitive-behavioral interventions, the client-counselor relationship, and the emerging power and responsibility of the client in the therapeutic relationship. Particular to REBT, the eclectic combination of cognitive, behavioral, and emotive techniques; the deemphasis of the importance of the past in light of present problems; the educational, preventive, and accepting nature of treatment; and the development of the role of the active-directive counselor have all been important contributions to the mental health professions (James & Gilliland, 2003).

REFERENCES

Balter, R. (1997a). Using REBT with clients with disabilities. In J. Yankura & W. Dryden (Eds.), *Special applications of REBT: A therapist's casebook* (pp. 69–100). New York: Springer.

Balter, R. (1997b). Introduction to the special issue [Special issue]. *Journal of Rational-Emotive and Cognitive-Behavior Therapy, 15*, 191–192.

Beal, D., Kopec, A. M., & DiGiuseppe, R. (1996). Disputing clients' irrational beliefs. *Journal of Rational-Emotive and Cognitive-Behavior Therapy, 14*, 215–229.

Bernard, M. E. (1995). It's prime time for rational emotive behavior therapy: Current theory and practice, research recommendations, and predictions. *Journal of Rational-Emotive and Cognitive-Behavior Therapy, 13*, 9–27.

Calabro, L. E. (1990). Adjustment to disability: A cognitive-behavioral model for analysis and clinical management. *Journal of Rational-Emotive and Cognitive-Behavior Therapy, 8*, 79–102.

Corey, G. (2001). *Theory and practice of counseling and psychotherapy* (6th ed.). Pacific Grove, CA: Brooks/Cole.

Dryden, W. (1990). *Rational-emotive counselling in action.* London: Sage.

Ellis, A. (1962). *Reason and emotion in psychotherapy.* Seacaucus, NJ: Lyle Stuart.

Ellis, A. (1973). *Humanistic psychotherapy: The rational-emotive approach.* New York: Julien.

Ellis, A. (1976). The biological basis of human irrationality. *Journal of Individual Psychology, 32*, 143–168.

Ellis, A. (1977). The basic clinical theory of rational-emotive therapy. In A. Ellis & R. E. Grieger (Eds.), *Handbook of rational-emotive therapy* (pp. 3–34). New York: Springer.

Ellis, A. (1979). The practice of rational-emotive therapy. In A. Ellis & J. M. Whitely (Eds.), *Theoretical and empirical foundations of rational-emotive therapy* (pp. 61–100). Monterey, CA: Brooks/Cole.

Ellis, A. (1980). Rational-emotive therapy and cognitive behavior therapy: Similarities and differences. *Cognitive Therapy and Research, 4*, 325–340.

Ellis, A. (1989). Rational-emotive therapy. In R. J. Corsini & D. Wedding (Eds.), *Current psychotherapies* (4th ed., pp. 197–238). Itasca, IL: Peacock.

Ellis, A. (1991). The revised ABC's of rational-emotive therapy (RET). *Journal of Rational-Emotive and Cognitive-Behavior Therapy, 9*, 139–172.

Ellis, A. (1993). Fundamentals of rational-emotive therapy for the 1990s. In W. Dryden & L. K. Hill (Eds.), *Innovations in rational-emotive therapy* (pp. 1–32). Newbury Park, CA: Sage.

Ellis, A. (1994). The treatment of borderline personalities with rational emotive behavior therapy. *Journal of Rational-Emotive and Cognitive-Behavior Therapy, 12,* 101–119.

Ellis, A. (1995a). Changing rational-emotive therapy (RET) to rational emotive behavior therapy (REBT). *Journal of Rational-Emotive and Cognitive-Behavior Therapy, 13,* 85–89.

Ellis, A. (1995b). Rational emotive behavior therapy. In R. J. Corsini & D. Wedding (Eds.), *Current psychotherapies.* Itasca, IL: Peacock.

Ellis, A. (1996). *Better, deeper, and more enduring brief therapy: The rational emotive behavior therapy approach.* New York: Brunner/Mazel.

Ellis, A., & Harper, R. (1979). *A new guide to rational living.* N. Hollywood, CA: Wilshire.

Ellis, A., McInerney, D. F., DiGiuseppe, R., & Yeager, R. J. (1988). *Rational-emotive therapy with alcoholic and substance abusers.* New York: Pergamon.

Gandy, G. L. (1995). *Mental health rehabilitation: Disputing irrational beliefs.* Springfield, IL: Charles C. Thomas.

George, R. L., & Christiani, T. S. (1995). *Counseling: Theory and practice* (4th ed.). Needham Heights, MA: Allyn & Bacon.

Hollon, S. D., & Beck, A. T. (1994). Cognitive and cognitive-behavioral therapies. In A. E. Bergin & S. L. Garfield (Eds.), *Handbook of psychotherapy and behavior change* (pp. 428–466). New York: Wiley.

Horney, K. (1965). *Collected works.* New York: Norton.

James, R. K., & Gilliland, B. E. (2003). *Theories and strategies in counseling and psychotherapy* (5th ed.). Boston: Allyn & Bacon.

Livneh, H., & Sherwood S. (1991). Application of personality theories and counseling strategies to clients with physical disabilities. *Journal of Counseling and Development, 69,* 525–538.

Livneh, H., & Wright, P. E. (1995). Rational-emotive therapy. In D. Capuzzi & D. R. Gross (Eds.), *Counseling and psychotherapy: Theories and interventions* (pp. 325–352). Englewood Cliffs, NJ: Prentice Hall.

Lyons, L. C., & Woods, P. J. (1991). The efficacy of rational emotive therapy: A quantitative review of the outcome research. *Clinical Psychology Review, 11,* 357–369.

McGovern, T. E., & Silverman, M. S. (1984). A review of outcome studies of rational-emotive therapy from 1977 to 1982. *Journal of Rational-Emotive Therapy, 2,* 7–18.

Mpofu, E., Thomas, K. R., & Chan, F. (1996). Cognitive-behavioural therapies: Research and applications in counselling people with physical disabilities. *Australian Journal of Rehabilitation Counselling, 2,* 99–114.

Olevitch, B. A. (1995). *Using cognitive approaches with the seriously mentally ill: Dialogue across the border.* Wesport, CT: Praeger.

Ostby, S. (1986). A rational-emotive perspective. In T. F. Riggar, D. R. Maki, & A. W. Wolf (Eds.), *Applied rehabilitation counseling* (pp. 135–147). New York: Springer.

Silverman, M. S., McCarthy, M., & McGovern, T. E. (1992). A review of outcome studies of rational-emotive therapy from 1982–1989. *Journal of Rational-Emotive and Cognitive Behavior Therapy, 10,* 111–175.

Weinrach, S. G. (1980). Unconventional therapist: Albert Ellis. *Personnel and Guidance Journal, 59*, 152–160.

Weinrach, S. G. (1986). Ellis and Gloria: Positive or negative model? *Psychotherapy, 23*, 642–647.

Weinrach, S. G. (1996). Reducing REBT's "wince factor": An insider's perspective. *Journal of Rational-Emotive and Cognitive-Behavior Therapy, 14*, 63–78.

Yankura, J., & Dryden, W. (1994). *Albert Ellis.* Thousand Oaks, CA: Sage.

Young, H. S. (1974). *A rational counseling primer.* New York: Institute for Rational-Emotive Therapy.

Chapter 10

Reality Therapy

Joseph Turpin and Joseph N. Ososkie

T he rehabilitation counselor who has an effective grasp of the intervention tools available in reality therapy can help the client focus on those behaviors that will shape the client's future and result in both adjustment and goal direction. William Glasser's reality therapy is presented to help the counselor recognize the utilitarian value of the process when working with a rehabilitation client in developing independence, sense of a positive self, and personal responsibility.

HISTORY

Reality therapy presents a process that helps clients achieve goals and thereby gain an increased level of self-accomplishment. Reality therapy is a commonsense approach to making changes in behavior. It is about emphasizing reality and responsibility. Dr. William Glasser, whose works have spanned almost 50 years, developed his theory in reaction to the many Freudian techniques that were present in the 1950s. Reality therapy stresses the responsibility that individuals should take for their behavior. Glasser's work continues to evolve from his early efforts in rehabilitation, juvenile corrections, and public schools. His early works were formulated in mental health practice, and his later work concentrated more on personal improvement in lives, systems, and relationships. Currently, his emphasis has turned more toward choice theory, which stresses the importance of self-evaluation and improvement (Corey, 2001; James & Gilliland, 2003; Seligman, 2001; Sharf, 2000).

Glasser's career began in the mental health system. He worked with individuals with severe psychiatric disorders, and in this setting many of the concepts of reality therapy were formulated. He later became concerned with developing a classroom environment that would lead students to establish values and to become goal-oriented, with acceptance of personal responsibility (Glasser, 1969). His work during this period centered on the development of choices that individuals had in controlling their futures. More recently, Glasser's interest has centered around the choices that create a directionality to one's goals. Choice theory evolved from this thinking and is now the framework in which reality therapy resides (Glasser, 1984).

With the refinements that Glasser has made in his theory, the use of reality therapy for the rehabilitation counselor remains fundamentally unchanged. The work that the individual must accomplish in reality therapy is to develop a success identity, to understand and possess personal values, and to accept and initiate responsibility based on a clear grasp of the reality of the world.

THEORY OF PERSONALITY

Early in Glasser's career he described this concept about the world: "We are often given the illusion that we can change our surroundings when in fact either they change in their own inconsistent pattern and/or we change our position relative to the world" (Glasser, 1960, p. 8). Glasser emphasized the concepts of (1) individual responsibility and (2) the inability to change other people to make them fulfill one's own personal needs. Glasser noted that the alternative to facing reality and acting in a responsible fashion was to change one's environment by leaving the area and moving to a different location. However, many needs continue to exist regardless of where an individual happens to be geographically located. Personal responsibilities center around general living and work. Because humans have little power to change other people, Glasser stated that individuals must face reality and accept control over their lives, learn how to meet their needs in appropriate ways, and act responsibly with regard to their understanding of reality. Reality therapy recognizes individuals as having a natural desire for a successful self-image and responsibility through an involvement with other people. To develop a positive self-image, individuals must be actively involved with others, meeting individual needs and taking responsible actions.

According to Glasser (1984, 2000), individuals have the following needs: (a) the need to survive and reproduce; (b) the need to belong; (c) the need for power; (d) the need for freedom, and (e) the need for fun. Total behavior (doing, thinking, feeling, and physiology) is determined by how need fulfillment is perceived on the part of the individual. Individual perception, or control, is the internal motivator that guides purposeful behavior (Corey, 2001).

Control theory focuses on the perceptions of individuals about their worlds and how they make choices to be successful in these worlds. Glasser (1984) contended that individuals even choose misery so that they can (a) keep control of their anger, (b) control themselves or others, (c) ask for help indirectly, and (d) use misery as an excuse for not doing something that is more effective. In fact, personal responsibility is explicit in the choice of behaviors like "depressing, anxieting, and headaching," which Glasser believes are used to control others and to avoid pain. These total behaviors are attempts to block realization of the ineffectiveness of cognitions that do not meet reality. An alteration of perception is hampered by efforts to change what cannot be changed instead of changing what can be changed.

MAJOR CONCEPTS

The concept of identity is basic to reality therapy (James & Gilliland, 2003). Glasser indicates that people may have either success or failure identities, which are developed through the feedback of interacting with others. Individuals also gain their identity through personal experience with other individuals and objects in the environment. Through these situations they gain a concept of themselves that may or may not be the same as that perceived by others, a process that is highly personal.

Glasser and Zunin (1973) indicated that identity forms near the age of five years. Those individuals with a success identity tend to associate with others who also see themselves as successes, while individuals who hold failure identities tend to associate with others who have failure identities. Thus it would appear that success matches success and failure breeds failure. Individuals with success identities possess two specific traits. First, they know that there is at least one other person that loves them and that they love that person in return. Second, they appear to possess the knowledge that they are worthwhile individuals and that at a minimum one other person also believes this to be true. Reality therapy recognizes that those individuals with failure identities share the common experience of loneliness and deal with this discomfort through the use of denial or ignoring reality. Thus the view of the world in reality therapy is directly related to the individual's view regarding self-image, or success identity. The self-image aspect of an individual's life is revealed by whether he or she behaves responsibly or irresponsibly.

A second major concept is responsibility. It has been defined as "the ability to fulfill one's needs, and to do so in a way that does not deprive others of the ability to fulfill their need" (Glasser, 1975, p. 15). Glasser further stated that behaving responsibly promotes a positive self-image by demonstrating self-worth and value to others. In reality therapy, responsibility is learned through a shared, caring relationship. The individual's self-worth improves as the individual demonstrates the ability to handle limited responsibility and is then challenged to handle greater responsibility. This process leads to successes that continue to demonstrate the individual's positive self-image.

A third concept that is emphasized in reality therapy is involvement. Involvement is seen as the process whereby people naturally fulfill needs and enhance their self-image as successes. Involvement in reality therapy is also related to the genuine, caring counselor-client relationship. The counselor-client involvement should not be misconstrued as the same as transference. Rather, involvement is the process through which the therapeutic gains made through counseling will be maintained following termination of treatment. Reality therapy sees involvement as "the primary intrinsic driving force governing all behavior" (Glasser & Zunin, 1973, p. 296).

The principles outlined in reality therapy suggest a view of people as being intrinsically self-determined. Given an individual's assets and limitations relating to both biological and psychological inheritance and the environment in which the individual lives, exists, and functions, people determine what they will become. People are what they do, and individuals have a vast array of behaviors from which to choose their actions. The way in which an individual behaves "depends upon decisions rather than conditions" (Glasser & Zunin, 1973, p. 306). In reality therapy each individual is viewed as having a "health or growth force, implying that each individual has a natural inclination to strive in the direction of successes, responsible behaviors, and meaningful relationships with others" (Glasser & Zunin, 1973, p. 297).

DESCRIPTION OF COUNSELING PROCESS

Reality therapy is best described as a philosophy of treatment and a process of therapy rather than as a collection of techniques. A variety of accepted techniques are used, but only as they fit into the basic philosophy of individual responsibility for behavior and caring. Further, reality therapy does not engage in diagnostic labeling of individuals. Diagnostic labels are viewed as counterproductive. Rather, individuals with psychosocial disorders are viewed as irresponsible in their acknowledgement of reality. This irresponsibility leads to the unhappiness that is experienced through either denial or ignoring of reality. The result is an inability to meet one's personal needs.

The philosophy of reality therapy encourages individual responsibility for behavior and promotes involvement with others to learn and maintain responsible behavior. Techniques such as role playing, contracting, and homework assignments are employed, but these are used only as they fit with the basic philosophic intent. There is an effort to challenge the client to be responsible, to find and acknowledge personal values, to make commitments, and to achieve. The reality therapist believes that the key event that changes behavior is the acknowledgement of personal values.

Reality therapy attempts to challenge the client to become responsible and make commitments and, consequently, to achieve more. The concepts of reality therapy are all designed to achieve these goals, with the anticipated result that individuals who once viewed themselves as failures will increasingly accept responsibility, accumulate accomplishments, and begin to feel successful. Individuals with all diagnoses are treated with essentially the same basic process. The individual is helped to "fulfill his needs in the real world so that he will have no inclination in the future to deny its existence" (Glasser, 1960, p. 7). Thus the counselor teaches responsibility to the individual who did not learn it early in life.

The practice of reality therapy is incorporated into a WDEP system of techniques and skills employed by counselors to help clients take effective control of their lives (Corey, 2001; Glasser & Wubbolding, 1995; Seligman, 2001). The WDEP system is carried out through questioning in the four areas of client functioning. *Ask clients what they want (W)*. Wants are related to client needs and include their perceptions. Wants are related to needs of belonging, survival, power, fun, and freedom. *Ask clients what they are doing and what their direction (D) is*. This includes the choices that clients are making and how those choices affect the directions the clients want in their lives or, in other words, the goals that they have for themselves. *Ask clients to self-evaluate (E)*. Evaluation is important if wants are to be realistic and beneficial. Other areas of evaluation are behavior, actions, and perception. *Ask clients to make plans (P) to effectively meet their needs*. Plans help clients take control of their lives, and they become successful when accomplishing these plans. The client plan should be simple, attainable, measurable, immediate, and committed.

Questioning is an important tool utilized by reality therapists in the process of counseling and psychotherapy. The intent of counseling is to help clients understand their wants and needs and recognize that they are personally responsible to make choices regarding the elements of life that are under their control.

PRINCIPLES OF COUNSELING

Glasser and Zunin (1973) described the therapy process as based upon eight principles.

Personal Involvement

First, the counselor is involved and cares; thus the counseling is personal. Involvement takes place as the counselor relates to the client as a caring, genuine, and real individual. The counselor acts to demonstrate responsibility and insists that the client act responsibly, while maintaining the caring relationship. This therapeutic stance is subtle and often requires a delicate balance. The counselor is willing to share personal experiences and is open to having his or her values and standards challenged.

Focus on Behavior, *Not* Feelings

The focus of counseling is behavior, not feelings. Reality therapists have found that it is easier to intervene in a cycle of negative events by doing something different than by first feeling something different. Behavior is believed to be easier for an individual to control than feelings.

Focus on the Present

Counseling deals mainly with the present. The past cannot be changed, and too much time is typically spent dwelling on past failures. In dealing with the present and the future, discussion and planning can turn to the more positive direction of what people are doing or can do to improve their situations.

Value Judgment

Reality therapy counselors deal with value judgments. They expect clients to identify goals, values, and standards for behavior and to measure their own behavior against those criteria.

Planning

Once the client identifies general directions and ways to change behavior, the counselor has the client make plans to specify the change in terms of when, where, and with whom.

Commitment

Early in the counseling process the client is encouraged by the counselor to follow through with actions "for the counselor" and later "for himself or herself." In both cases the commitment to an action is required.

No Excuses

No excuses are acceptable. The counselor realizes that plans do fail at times, but the concern is only for specifying when the plan or an alternative will be tried again. The counselor does not focus on the reasons for failure.

Eliminate Punishment

The final principle is eliminating punishment. Punishment is not viewed as an effective way to help people with poor self-images change and view themselves as more responsible and successful.

STAGES OF COUNSELING

In addition to the eight principles, five stages of counseling are identified to guide clients in the process of clarifying values, goals, and standards for behavior; identifying behaviors that interfere with their accomplishments; and generating alternative behaviors (Bassin, Bratter, & Rachin, 1976).

Problem-Solving

First, the problem-solving process is initiated by asking "What are you doing?" and probing for details such as "What happened? Where? When? How?" but not "Why?"

Involvement

In the second stage, the counselor asks if the client's past actions accomplished anything good. This question is commonly met with resistance.

Thus the counselor must be involved with the client if the client is to respond honestly to this crucial question. If the client maintains that he or she acted properly and would continue to behave in the same way, the counselor leaves the issue until the client expresses a desire to alter the behavior. The counselor remains available to help at any time that the client wishes to work further. Ideally, the trust nurtured through involvement, coupled with the client's natural urge to grow, will lead to change. Self-evaluation of behavior is essential, since individual responsibility is the core of the counseling process. If a client admits that a behavior is negative, counseling continues.

Relearning

The third stage begins the process of relearning, as the counselor asks what the client's plan is for changing behavior. The plan of action is "pinned down" at this point. This process may include looking at alternatives through brainstorming and role playing. The process also considers future strategies, times, places, and backup plans, which are then specified in detail.

Contract and Follow-up

In the fourth and fifth stages, a contract stating details of the plan for behavior, such as time, place, and so on, is signed by the client and a follow-up session is scheduled for the client to report how the plan progressed or to revise the plan if necessary. Counseling may involve a lively verbal exchange, with the emphasis always on the client's positive points and potentials. The counselor's role is more like that of a teacher than a traditional counselor, and, as such, the counselor is willing to be a real person, revealing personal information, values, and opinions (Bassin, Bratter, & Rachin, 1976; Glasser, 1975; Glasser & Zunin, 1973). Conversational content during counseling will likely range over a wide array of daily events as the counselor and the client identify problems of social interaction and seek alternate ways for the client to become meaningfully involved with others. As Glasser (1960) stated, "When values, standards, and responsibility are in the background, all discussion is relevant to therapy. Continually stressing responsibility is artificial" (p. 38). The pivotal issue on which behavior change hinges is identifying the client's values.

If standards and values are stressed, therapy will only lead individuals to become more comfortable in their irresponsibility. Because effort is always directed toward helping clients fulfill their needs, counselors insist on their striving to reach the highest possible standards.

It is clear that reality therapy involves a strong element of challenge to help the client live up to self-professed standards. The client maintains control of the pace of counseling by deciding whether or not to acknowledge irresponsible behavior.

REHABILITATION APPLICATIONS

The application of reality therapy to work with persons with alcoholism and other disabilities has been demonstrated (N. Glasser, 1980). Glasser (1984) discussed its utility with psychological problems and addictions. Using reality therapy to facilitate adaptation to disability has been considered by Livneh and Sherwood (1991), and Corey (2001) discusses its applicability in rehabilitation. Reality therapy can be used by rehabilitation counselors to help clients with disabilities understand what is under their control and what is not. The implication is that needs may be fulfilled and choice can be exercised in order to live life responsibly. The question of what individuals are doing reveals both responsibility and behavior. Asked to evaluate their total array of feelings, thoughts, behaviors, and physiology in relation to living life with a disability impresses clients with the reality of how much is under their control. Deciding to meet belonging needs by interacting with others demonstrates what clients must do to satisfy needs. Choosing "depressing" because life was not supposed to include a disability may be challenged by rehabilitation counselors when helping clients to evaluate wants and direction in life. Helping clients see that using alcohol may only serve to anesthetize feelings of pain and failure, and thus mask reality, is another function of reality therapy. It is emphasized that choice, freedom, and belonging are still within reach, despite a disability. Reality therapists who do not accept excuses and who help clients see what they can do promote the optimizing aspects of reality therapy.

The process of reality therapy is focused on a success identity and personal responsibility. Rehabilitation counselors are in a position to help clients in these efforts. A success identity means that clients with disabilities will not choose giving up, negative symptoms, and negative addictions, but will rather choose change and growth, positive symptoms, and positive addictions (Glasser & Wubbolding, 1995). The rehabilitation counselor should encourage clients with disabilities to become involved in their community and with their families. Needs are better fulfilled in relation to others or in involvements with others. Giving up because of a disability is an issue that must be confronted by rehabilitation counselors who deal with such clients.

The stages of reality therapy and the WDEP system are effective tools for rehabilitation counselors. Helping clients evaluate their needs, wants, and behaviors in relation to life with a disability places choice, and thus a sense of power, within their control. Changing the disability may not be under their control, but what they do about their lives with a disability is under their control.

CASE EXAMPLE

Fred, age 30, is a college graduate working in an engineering position with a large corporation. He was divorced from his wife nearly one year ago and indicates that she left him because of his drinking. He reports that he is not involved in any serious relationship at this time. Fred works many hours each week, brings work home, and watches television during his free time. He has two older brothers, and his parents live a distance from him. His siblings are married with children, and his parents have been married for over 40 years. Fred's brothers are attorneys. Although he has always been employed in his field since graduating from a large state university, Fred has never felt that he has lived up to his family's career expectations for him. He is considering obtaining a master's degree in business so that he will be able to take an administrative position with his company.

Fred was seen on an outpatient basis for alcohol dependence. This after-work program lasted three months. He indicated that he had felt depressed for the past four months. Specifically, he reported not eating well and losing interest in his work. He saw a family physician one month previously for a prescription for antidepressants. Fred is seeking assistance from the corporate psychologist, who is a reality therapist.

While establishing a fair working relationship with Fred, the reality therapist explored the nature of his problem. This process involved determining what Fred was doing and assessing his total behavior. Fred explained his depression, and the therapist focused her questions on what he was doing. Fred spoke about watching more television, eating less, and thinking about how bad things were for him. The reality therapist showed Fred that he was not depressed, but rather that he was depressing. Her attention on what he was doing was her attempt to keep Fred focused on behavior. Thus he was able to understand that he did have control over what he did. Fred was not sick; he was choosing his misery and could choose to act differently. He was encouraged to do something rather than sit and watch television.

Fred discussed his past failures with the therapist. She helped him stay centered on the present by looking at what he could do and what he was doing successfully. As he repeatedly spoke about his failed marriage, the rehabilitation counselor worked to have him consider her question, which focused on direction: *what are you doing*, and *is it getting you what you want?*

The reality therapist asked Fred questions focused on his Wants, Directions, Evaluation, and Plans. By employing the WDEP system, the therapist was able to help Fred explore his desires or mental pictures of a perfect marriage and a successful career like his brothers had, in terms of his needs for belonging and power. Fred did not think that he was a success in his career because he was not an attorney as were his brothers. His need for belonging in regards to his family was not being met. He wanted to be accepted by them as successful, and he thought he failed them because he decided to be an engineer and not a lawyer.

Fred's marriage ended in divorce. Thus his need for belonging was not being met through a marital relationship. His perception of the perfect marriage was explored. His direction in terms of relationships was discussed. He spoke about being to blame because of his drinking and excessive working behaviors. His therapist helped him to look at the past only as it related to the present. He wanted to have a relationship with a woman, but he was acting quite the opposite. He was working constantly and watching television excessively. He was not drinking excessively like before, but he was choosing behaviors that interfered with his personal involvement with others in his life. He was picking depressing and working to mask the pain that he felt in not meeting his need for belonging.

The reality therapist worked with Fred to focus attention on what he was able to accomplish in his life. She attempted to facilitate his switch to a success identity by helping him choose what worked to meet his needs.

An evaluation of his wants revealed that his perception of marriage was not realistic. He perceived that he needed to provide for his wife financially. He did not see the need to do anything else. His relationship suffered because he did not do anything else for his wife. He wanted her to understand his neglect because he was making money so that they would have a nice house and automobile. He expected her to understand, as did his brothers' wives. His therapist helped him look at how that perception of a relationship could be problematic with other women as well.

Fred stayed in therapy, stopped taking medication, and made plans to become less isolated and to do things to get him involved in his community.

He agreed to try to spend less time watching television, complete work assignments in a timely fashion so that he could socialize more, and continue to examine his wants, perceptions, and goals. He learned that he is a success by seeing that he completed college, has a good job, and that he stopped his excessive drinking. He feels more in control of his life because he makes choices and is living responsibly.

RESEARCH FINDINGS

Reality therapy has relied primarily upon qualitative research to assess the changes that counseling has produced. A limited number of quantitative studies have also been conducted. Banmen (1982) reviewed studies working with African Americans and with disturbed populations in educational environments and found more positive results in studies relating to behavioral change than to change in self-image.

More recent studies are very limited in providing a quantitative analysis of reality therapy. Within rehabilitation, studies have concentrated mainly within corrections. Williams (1976), for example, found that inmates viewed reality therapy (1) as better than previous therapies, (2) as very helpful, and (3) as very much enjoyed. Williams attributed these findings to the fact that reality therapy provided a support by emphasizing the way life is, rather than fantasy. Another plus was placing importance on goals that are attainable, rather than on past difficulties. Drummond (1982) investigated correctional workers who saw reality therapy as a methodology in working with adolescents. Drummond reported that years of formal education and the inclination of correctional workers to not accept excuses were significantly related to acceptance of reality therapy as a positive technique. Yarish (1986) studied the use of reality therapy with young male offenders to determine whether the counseling method would produce positive changes in the participants' perceptions of their relationships to events. The study concluded that, based upon the use of the Nowicki-Strickland Locus of Control Scale for Children, reality therapy caused the treatment group to perceive events in their lives as more contingent on their own behavior and actions.

Parish, Martin, and Khramtsova (1992) examined the effectiveness of reality therapy on increasing congruence between perceived and ideal self-image. Findings indicated that reality therapy significantly reduced the distance between perceived and ideal self-concept and interactions with others.

Dolly and Page (1981) reported on the use of reality therapy with 20 individuals with dual diagnosis (severe retardation and emotional disturbance) using reality therapy supplemented with behavior modification. The study found significant positive gains in behavior. Rachor (1995) investigated the value of a reality therapy–based educational intervention program for domestic violence that would treat domestic violence as a human problem and not as a gender issue, recognizing and teaching that both the abused and the abuser choose their behaviors to meet their needs. Follow-up with participants revealed that the female graduates of the program reported that they had experienced no threats of violence or actual violence by partners. Over 80% of the male graduates reported that they had experienced (1) increased self-control, (2) major changes in their lives, or (3) improvement in their relationships with others.

PROMINENT STRENGTHS AND LIMITATIONS
Strengths

Reality therapy is a useful counseling approach because it focuses on what the individual wishes to accomplish and the value judgments related to the behaviors that will help accomplish that goal. When working with individuals, reality therapists quickly convey to their clients that they themselves are an avenue to their own success. Reality therapy becomes an action-oriented therapy, allowing the client an opportunity to plan and commit to action. Within the therapy session the individual can also be involved in role playing, and, as part of the therapy, the client may actively participate in self-determined homework between sessions. Reality therapy encourages the client to participate in therapy by examining the present and looking at ways to adjust for success in the future. It is a therapy that builds on past success and how those successes can be used in the future. Through the use of reality therapy, individuals are encouraged to see value judgments and to link those judgments to their choices of goals and standards of behavior. When individuals are not successful, the therapy does not spend therapeutic time on excuses or societal judgment of failure, but turns its attention to new ways to generate successful accomplishment of the desired goal. Reality therapy considers the effect of ethnic, gender, religious, or sexual orientation bias within the environment as a barrier to a plan for reaching goals. Such factors are not valued positively or negatively, as reality to be considered in reaching one's goals.

Limitations

Reality therapy is criticized for denying the existence of painful emotional disturbances and for overemphasizing individual responsibility when environmental factors may be more to blame. For example, individuals with disabilities who acquired their disabilities as a result of a significant traumatic experience are asked to focus on a goal rather than dealing with painful experiences. Other limitations include a lack of clearly associated techniques; that is, the techniques that are used by reality therapy are also utilized by other counseling theories. The lack of definitive and quantitative research also has been seen as a limitation. The quantitative studies that have been reported in the literature have been equivocal in their results. The theory has also been criticized for its sole reliance on verbal therapy.

REFERENCES

Banmen, J. (1982). Reality therapy research review. *Journal of Reality Therapy, 2,* 28–32.

Bassin, A., Bratter, T. E., & Rachin, R. L. (Eds.). (1976). *The reality therapy reader: A survey of the work of William Glasser, M.D.* New York: Harper & Row.

Corey, G. (2001). *Theory and practice of counseling and psychotherapy* (6th ed.). Pacific Grove, CA: Brooks/Cole.

Dolly, J. P., & Page, D. P. (1981). The effects of a program of behavior modification and reality therapy on the behavior of emotionally disturbed institutionalized adolescents. *Exceptional Child, 28,* 191–198.

Drummond, R. J. (1982). Determinants of attitudes toward reality therapy. *Journal of Reality Therapy, 1,* 22–25.

Glasser, N. (Ed.). (1980). *What are you doing? How people are helped through reality therapy.* New York: Harper & Row.

Glasser, W. (1960). *Mental health or mental illness? Psychiatry for practical action.* New York: Harper & Row.

Glasser, W. (1969). *Schools without failure.* New York: Harper & Row.

Glasser, W. (1975). *Reality therapy: A new approach to psychiatry.* New York: Harper & Row.

Glasser, W. (1984). *Take effective control of your life.* New York: Harper & Row.

Glasser, W. (2000). *Reality therapy in action.* New York: HarperCollins.

Glasser, W., & Wubbolding, R. E. (1995). Reality therapy. In R. Corsini & D. Wedding (Eds.), *Current psychotherapies* (5th ed., pp. 293–321). Itasca, IL: Peacock.

Glasser, W., & Zunin, L. M. (1973). Reality therapy. In R. Corsini (Ed.), *Current psychotherapies.* Itasca, IL: Peacock.

James, R. K., & Gilliland, B. E. (2003). *Theories and strategies in counseling and psychotherapy* (5th ed.). Boston: Allyn & Bacon.

Livneh, H., & Sherwood, A. (1991). Application of personality theories and counseling strategies to clients with physical disabilities. *Journal of Counseling and Development, 69,* 525–538.

Parish, T. S., Martin, P., & Khramtsova, I. (1992). Enhancing convergence between our real and ideal selves. *Journal of Reality Therapy, 11,* 37–40.

Rachor, R. E. (1995). An evaluation of the First Step PASSAGES domestic violence program. *Journal of Reality Therapy, 14,* 29–36.

Seligman, L. (2001). *Systems, strategies, and skills of counseling and psychotherapy.* Upper Saddle River, NJ: Merrill Prentice Hall.

Sharf, R. S. (2000). *Theories of psychotherapy and counseling: Concepts and cases* (2nd ed.). Belmont, CA: Brooks/Cole.

Williams, E. W. (1976). Reality therapy in a correctional institution. *Corrective and Social Psychiatry and Journal of Behavior Technology, Methods and Therapy, 22,* 6–11.

Yarish, P. (1986). Reality therapy and the locus of control of juvenile offenders. *Journal of Reality Therapy, 6,* 3–10.

Chapter 11

The Trait-Factor Approach

John F. Kosciulek and David J. DeVinney

The trait-factor counseling approach rests on the assumptions that people have different traits, that occupations require a particular combination of worker characteristics, and that effective vocational counseling matches a person's traits with job requirements (Parsons, 1909). Because trait-factor counseling has proven effective in assisting people with disabilities to secure employment (Dawis & Lofquist, 1984; Szymanski & Hershenson, 1998), it has been widely used in rehabilitation counseling (Kosciulek, 1993; Lynch & Maki, 1981; Schmitt & Growick, 1985; Thomas, Thoreson, Parker, & Butler, 1998). This chapter will illustrate how the trait-factor counseling approach, and more specifically, the current person-environment fit perspective, remains useful in rehabilitation and may be applied to individuals with disabilities.

HISTORY

The origins of the trait-factor approach can be traced to Parsons' (1909) proposition that vocational choice involves the individual, the work environment, and an understanding of the relationship between the two. Parsons based the first major theory of vocational counseling on the assumptions that people have different traits, that occupations require a particular combination of worker characteristics, and that effective vocational guidance matches a person's traits with job requirements. The objective of vocational guidance, according to Parsons, was to match a person's traits with a particular combination of worker characteristics. He advocated that individuals should gain a full understanding of their personal attributes, including both strengths and weaknesses, along with a thorough understanding of the conditions of success in given occupations. Parsons developed his approach in response to the dramatic social, political, and economic upheavals that were occurring in the United States in the early 20th century. Trait-factor counseling offered a pragmatic approach to the resultant problems of occupational choice and adjustment, particularly among young adults (Swanson, 1996). Parsons' ideas provided the impetus for research and continued development of the trait-factor approach, which evolved into newer decision-making and problem-solving models (Ivey, D'Andrea, Ivey, & Simek-Morgan, 2002; Ivey & Ivey, 2003; Kosciulek, 1993).

Through the efforts of researchers affiliated with the Minnesota Employment Stability Research Institute at the University of Minnesota, Parsons' ideas were expanded after his death. Drawing from differential psychology, the Minnesota group developed tests and other psychometric instruments that provided career counselors and clients with tools to conduct the personal analysis necessary for effective vocational decision making. Early applications of the instruments developed by the Minnesota group included assessing the vocational abilities of unemployed people during the Great Depression and classifying and assigning military personnel during World War II. Many of the vocational tests and occupational information systems used in career counseling today (e.g., Minnesota Importance Questionnaire) are direct results of the Minnesota research (Chartrand, 1991). One of the members of the Minnesota group, E. G. Williamson, emerged as the major spokesperson for the *Minnesota point of view*, a term often used synonymously with *trait-factor counseling*.

The trait-factor approach was the sole method of career counseling until the emergence of client-centered therapy in the 1950s. Associated with the introduction of Carl Rogers' 1942 publication, *Counseling and Psychotherapy*, the emergence of client-centered therapy corresponded not only with a decline in trait-factor counseling specifically, but also with an overall decline in career counseling in general (Crites, 1981). According to Chartrand (1991), the maturation and ensuing sophistication of developmental and social learning approaches also had the effect of displacing trait-factor counseling as the unique approach to career counseling.

When client-centered therapy became the preferred mode of counseling, a concomitant value was placed on the role of the client-counselor relationship as the means for therapeutic change. The role of the counselor was accordingly deemphasized, and so was the role of the counselor as the expert in the counseling relationship. Thus trait-factor counseling was perceived and criticized as being overly directive (Swanson, 1996). In addition, the trait-factor approach was criticized as oversimplifying the complexities of counseling people with a wide range of career problems and causing counselors to underserve the needs of clients (Krumboltz, 1994). Further, Crites (1981) stated that trait-factor counseling ignored the psychological realities of decision making that lead to indecision and limited realism in career choice. His often-referenced characterization of trait-factor counseling was "three interviews and a cloud of dust" (Crites, 1981).

According to Rounds and Tracey (1990), however, after about 20 years, reports of the death of trait-factor counseling were greatly exaggerated. In revisiting the original works of Williamson (1965, 1972), it was noted that influential reviewers had misinterpreted the writings and had made assumptions without corresponding documentation. Brown (1990) argued that counselors who applied a simplistic formulation of Williamson's model did not fully understand the approach. Brown further observed that in the ensuing years no other career counseling approach or theory had satisfactorily replaced "trait-oriented" thinking. Rounds and Tracey (1990) also reported that Holland's (1973, 1985) research and conceptualizations had expanded and clarified the original Parsonian assumptions of matching people and occupations, leading to current trait-factor practices that were more flexible, efficient, and effective. In addition, vocational assessment practice is linked historically to trait-factor conceptions of vocational counseling, and current assessment processes continue to be influenced by the original Parsonian assumptions (Rounds & Tracey, 1990).

Zytowski and Borgen (1983) described how trait-factor counseling has evolved from Parsons' developmental model to a congruence model. The congruence model focuses on matching and choice processes. Primary assumptions of the model are that (a) well-adapted individuals within an occupation share certain psychological characteristics; (b) measurable and practical differences exist in people and occupations; (c) outcome is a function of individual-environmental fit; and (d) person and job characteristics demonstrate sufficient time and situation consistency to justify prediction of outcome over the long term.

MAJOR CONCEPTS

Parsons believed that choosing a vocation was more important than securing work, and he postulated that there were three broad factors involved in the wise choice of a vocation. The first factor was knowledge of self, aptitudes, interests, ambitions, resources, and limitations. The second was knowledge of the requirements and conditions of success, advantages and disadvantages of specific jobs, compensation, opportunities, and prospects in different lines of work. The third factor was accurate reasoning on the relation of these two groups of facts (Parsons, 1909).

Traits offered a definition of human behavior in terms of constructs such as aptitudes and interests that could be integrated into constellations of individual characteristics called *factors*. Traits, and assessment instruments that measure the traits, make up one major set of ingredients in trait-factor theory. The second set of ingredients comprises job factors or requirements, which are often gleaned from job analyses. Individual traits are then compared to job factors to determine potential matches. In trait-factor counseling, traits and factors are first defined and operationalized. A problem-solving matching method is then applied that leads to predictable outcomes across varied individuals and work environments (Gilliland & James, 1998).

Underlying Assumptions

As discussed by Kosciulek (1993), the trait-factor counseling approach rests on the assumption that people have different traits and that occupations require a particular combination of worker characteristics. In the trait-factor approach, vocational guidance matches the person's traits with job requirements. In the development of his model, however, Parsons (1909) was more concerned with career choice than job placement, and it was not until later formulations of trait-factor theory (e.g., Williamson, 1972) that environmental factors were stressed.

Key assumptions of the trait-factor counseling approach include the following: (1) each person is keyed to a few correct occupations; (2) clients need vocational guidance to avoid wasting time and risking the selection of an inappropriate occupation; (3) correct occupations influence other personal decisions over time; (4) occupational decisions remain constant; (5) trait-factor counseling provides information about many relevant aspects of life; (6) life is generally predictable; and (7) the trait-factor approach provides a basis for action, as well as a number of useful comparisons of individual traits to job tasks. Another key assumption is that clients will generally have personal problems solved or already under control (Schmitt & Growick, 1985). However, it is also accepted that vocational adjustment has much to do with life adjustment in general, and, for many individuals, career factors spill over into other aspects of their lives (Gilliland & James, 1998).

As described above, numerous researchers (e.g., Crites, 1981; Klein & Weiner, 1977) have reviewed the general assumptions of trait-factor counseling. In addition, Brown (1990) and Kosciulek (1993) have summarized current thinking on the underlying assumptions and propositions of trait-factor theory as follows:

1. Each individual has a unique set of traits that can be measured reliably and validly.
2. Occupations require that workers possess certain very specific traits for success, although a worker with a rather wide range of characteristics can still be successful in a given job.
3. The choice of an occupation is a rather straightforward process, and matching is possible.
4. The closer the match between personal characteristics and job requirements, the greater the likelihood of success (productivity and satisfaction).

THE COUNSELING PROCESS

Williamson (1965, 1972) articulated an empirically oriented counseling process guided by Parsons' concept of matching people and work environments. He emphasized the importance of reliably and accurately assessing career problems and individual characteristics. He viewed counseling as facilitating self-understanding, realistic planning, and decision-making skills (Chartrand, 1991).

Williamson (1972) described a six-step counseling process that included analysis, synthesis, diagnosis, prognosis, counseling, and follow-up. The first three steps involve gathering demographic and clinical information, synthesizing that information to determine client strengths and limitations, and then drawing inferences based on those strengths and developmental needs. A diagnosis is based on both the nature and cause of the career development or vocational decision-making problem (Brown, 1990).

The counselor next makes a prognosis by estimating the probability of client adjustment under different conditions or choice options. The prognosis is then followed by a rational, problem-solving approach to counseling that includes follow-up after the client makes a career decision. In the trait-factor counseling process, the counselor assumes a tutorial or advisor role with the client. Typical trait-factor counseling activities include assisting the client in obtaining data about self or jobs, presenting and discussing alternative options and actions, and attempting to help the client reach the best choice or decision (Rounds & Tracey, 1990).

APPLICATIONS TO REHABILITATION COUNSELING

Several authors have shown the utility of trait-factor approaches for rehabilitation counseling practice. Szymanski and Hershenson (1998) pointed out that trait-factor theory underlies much of rehabilitation counseling practice in both public and private sectors, including job matching systems, analysis of transferable skills, and ecological assessment processes used in supported employment, which are "obvious manifestations of trait-factor theory" (p. 336). Further, Lynch and Maki (1981) presented a structure for vocational rehabilitation services based on a trait-factor approach that viewed the rehabilitation counselor as a problem solver, with the goal of assisting clients in achieving optimal functional independence.

In the trait-factor approach, vocational difficulties are viewed as resulting from a lack of information and the inability to make effective decisions. Hence, consistent with the philosophies of empowerment and consumer choice (Kosciulek, 1999), the trait-factor approach to rehabilitation counseling attempts to improve client problem-solving and decision-making skills, and thus promoting self-determination. Vocational and personality traits are considered to be measurable and stable but not rigid. Lynch and Maki (1981) considered the assessment of client interests, aptitudes, and skills to be the core of trait-factor rehabilitation counseling.

Schmitt and Growick (1985) also examined the trait-factor approach from a rehabilitation perspective. These authors viewed trait-factor counseling as most useful when little or no prospect for independent client change appears possible. They suggested that rehabilitation counselors might successfully apply trait-factor methods with persons with mental, physical, or emotional impairments, who find job selection difficult and confusing. They viewed the rehabilitation counselor as a mediator in facilitating the placement and adjustment process.

According to Thomas et al. (1998), trait-factor counseling closely parallels the practice of most rehabilitation counselors, particularly in state vocational rehabilitation agencies. Goals of trait-factor counseling are generally congruent with the broader goals of rehabilitation. Thomas et al. reported that trait-factor counseling techniques are usually well within the repertoire of skills of many rehabilitation counselors and are deemed appropriate in most rehabilitation settings. The existing literature thus strongly suggests that the trait-factor counseling approach is useful for rehabilitation counseling in meeting the needs of persons with disabilities.

Support for the use of trait-factor counseling in rehabilitation has been provided through research on the validity of the Minnesota Theory of Work Adjustment (MTWA; Dawis & Lofquist, 1984). Because the MTWA was developed specifically to address the needs of persons with disabilities, it has provided rehabilitation counselors with a systematic and reliable model for applying trait-factor counseling methods. Consistent with the general trait-factor approach, the MTWA focuses on matching an individual with a work environment. Lofquist and Dawis (1969), originators of the theory, defined work adjustment as the "continuous and dynamic process by which the individual seeks to achieve and maintain correspondence with the work environment" (p. 46). In the MTWA, the work adjustment process involves matching the person's abilities and work-related needs, respectively, with the ability requirements and reinforcer system of the work environment. The match between a person's abilities and the ability requirements of a work environment determines satisfactoriness (i.e., the extent to which the person is able to perform the job). The match between the person's needs and the reinforcer systems of the work environment determine the satisfaction with the job. Tenure, the length of time that the person stays on the job, is a function of both satisfaction and satisfactoriness, and there is considerable empirical support to document this relationship (Swanson & Gore, 2000).

While providing a theoretical framework for rehabilitation programs serving persons with disabilities, the MTWA also offers a way to conceptualize disability, identify necessary vocational assessment information, suggest counseling procedures, and evaluate the effectiveness of rehabilitation counseling (Dawis & Lofquist, 1984). However, because it is based on a trait-factor approach, the MTWA is susceptible to the same criticisms as general trait-factor theory.

LIMITATIONS OF THE TRAIT-FACTOR APPROACH FOR REHABILITATION COUNSELING

Numerous authors have addressed the limitations of trait-factor counseling. Szymanski and Hershenson (1998) pointed out that trait-factor approaches do little to compensate for the limited early experiences of persons with congenital disabilities or to suggest supportive interventions that can permit persons with disabilities to enter, function, and sustain themselves in work environments. They further indicated that the focus of the theory on current individual traits ignores the potential of people with significant disabilities to perform jobs with appropriate assistive devices and job modifications.

Gilliland and James (1998) refuted the trait-factor counseling assumption that clients can "see the light" if the facts and consequences of behavior are presented. Weinrach (1979) interpreted Williamson's (1972) supposition that people are rational beings as an overly cognitive view that fails to consider affective processes. He also characterized trait-factor counselors as overly directive and authoritarian. The rehabilitation counselor who is controlling and who avoids the emotional impact of work may fail to assist individuals with disabilities with successful adjustment to the work environment (Kosciulek, 1993).

Crites (1981) criticized trait-factor approaches on the grounds that they are atheoretical, analytic, and atomistic in their orientation. The rehabilitation counselor who falls into what Crites described as "test and tell" counseling, which unfolds as "three interviews and a cloud of dust," is most likely not providing individualized or comprehensive services (Kosciulek, 1993). Szymanski and Hershenson (1998) questioned how trait-factor counseling approaches could describe the human personality in all its dimensions when client motivation is not considered in the counseling process. Finally, Kosciulek (1993) concluded that trait-factor counseling may be prone to ignoring interactions of a familial, social, economic, or political nature, variables critical to successful employment and independent living among persons with disabilities. In sum, a lack of comprehensiveness in trait-factor counseling is a consistent point of attack by critics.

As described in the following section, however, recent advances in trait-factor counseling theory provide rehabilitation counselors with a model for overcoming these limitations. The person × environment (P × E) fit approach (Chartrand, 1991; Kosciulek, 1993; Rounds & Tracey, 1990), an updated perspective on trait-factor counseling, extends beyond the assessment of individual abilities and work factors and captures the dynamic nature of person-environment interactions. Hence, many of the previous criticisms of trait-factor counseling are no longer fully warranted.

CONTEMPORARY TRAIT-FACTOR COUNSELING: THE PERSON × ENVIRONMENT (P × E) FIT APPROACH

During the 1990s, a general conceptual shift from a trait-oriented to a P × E perspective has occurred in the rehabilitation, counseling, and psychology literature. The focus of trait-factor theory has moved from a static matching view to a more dynamic interpretation of persons selecting and shaping environments (Hershenson, 1996; Pervin, 1987). From a P × E perspective, the guiding questions in rehabilitation counseling have become

(a) What kinds of personal and environmental factors are salient in predicting vocational choice and adjustment? and (b) How is the process of person and environment interaction best characterized? (Kosciulek, 1993).

Chartrand (1991) described three basic assumptions that have been transmitted from original trait-factor vocational counseling to the P × E fit approach. First, people are viewed as capable of making rational decisions. Affective processes are not ignored; rather, a cognitive orientation guides the search for intervention tactics. Rehabilitation counseling is embodied as a cognitive approach that emphasizes learning processes (Kosciulek, 1993).

Second, people and work environments differ in reliable, meaningful, and consistent ways. This assumption does not mean that a person with a disability prefers and best performs a specific job. Rather, it implies that important work behaviors, skill patterns, and working conditions can be identified to organize both people and work environments. The third assumption states that the better the congruence between personal characteristics and job requirements, the greater the likelihood of success. This means that knowledge of person and environment patterns can be used to inform people about the probability of satisfaction and adjustment to different work settings (Kosciulek, 1993). The P × E fit approach moves beyond the assumption of congruence to include the notion of dynamic reciprocity (Rounds & Tracey, 1990). That is, P × E is a reciprocal process, with individuals shaping the environment and the environment influencing individuals.

The counselor in P × E counseling generally uses a supportive, teaching approach with the types of treatment and intervention recommended as a function of the level of the client's information-processing abilities. A teaching approach is well suited for clients who are motivated and willing but lack the skills, understanding, ability, or confidence to effect change (Chartrand, 1991). Many individuals with disabilities fit such a client profile.

In the P × E fit approach, clients are considered capable of rational decision making. It is also assumed that reliable and meaningful individual differences can be assessed and that psychometric instruments may be utilized to predict relevant personal and occupational criteria (Chartrand, 1991). Given the pressures of time constraints in many rehabilitation counseling environments, a trait-factor/P × E approach may be the appropriate choice, since it is usually conducted within a brief counseling framework. In further consideration of time and money economy, P × E principles are well suited for group counseling (Lunneborg, 1983). A specific example of a rehabilitation-related, P × E group counseling approach is the Job

Club (Azrin & Besalel, 1980), which is used in the provision of job development and placement services.

As the Job Club example illustrates, trait-factor counseling in rehabilitation has generally been considered in terms of career counseling and job placement. However, Rounds and Tracey (1990) proposed that the P × E approach has a broader range of applications than just vocational problems. These authors stated that a P × E problem-solving framework that integrates components of decision making and information processing could be applied to diverse clients with varying needs and goals. Support for this concept can be drawn from Blustein and Spengler (1995), who found that a P × E career counseling approach resulted in significant and positive noncareer outcomes, including improved self-concept (self-esteem and interpersonal competence), more positive personal attitudes, an increased internal locus of control, and decreased anxiety. This extended application of the P × E approach lends support to the expanded MTWA conceptual framework proposed by Lofquist and Dawis (1991), which includes the interrelationship between personal, interpersonal, and environmental factors.

The current P × E interaction model expands the original formulations of trait-factor counseling. It differs from earlier trait-factor theory in that the P × E approach considers the joint contribution of two variables, person and environment, in the prediction of behavior. Trait-factor formulations were generally focused on the contributions of person-centered traits (Chartrand, Strong, & Weitzman, 1995). The P × E model generates information that is pragmatically useful in understanding the world of work and how people fit into it. Therefore, the contemporary P × E counseling approach serves as a useful model for the provision of vocational counseling in a variety of settings, including rehabilitation counseling with persons with disabilities.

CONCLUSION

Persons with disabilities often seek rehabilitation services to enhance the match between themselves and their work, home, or community environments. The trait-factor counseling approach has proven effective for assisting people with disabilities in securing and maintaining employment (Dawis & Lofquist, 1984; Szymanski & Hershenson, 1998). It has been widely used in rehabilitation counseling (Lynch & Maki, 1981; Schmitt & Growick, 1985; Thomas et al., 1998). However, numerous criticisms and limitations of trait-factor counseling have been cited in the career counseling and rehabilitation literature (e.g., Gilliland & James, 1998; Kosciulek, 1993). In this chapter, an updated perspective on trait-factor counseling, the P × E fit approach, was introduced as a potentially useful model for counseling persons with disabilities in rehabilitation settings. This approach compensates for previous criticisms of trait-factor counseling by considering the reciprocal and dynamic relationship between the individual and the environment. Through ecological, P × E rehabilitation counseling, persons with disabilities can be empowered to maximize the quality of their interpersonal and vocational life activities.

REFERENCES

Azrin, N. H., & Besalel, V. A. (1980). *Job club counselor's manual: A behavioral approach to vocational counseling.* Austin, TX: Pro-Ed.

Blustein, D. L., & Spengler, P. M. (1995). Personal adjustment: Career counseling and psychotherapy. In W. B. Walsh & S. H. Osipow (Eds.), *Handbook of vocational psychology: Theory, research, and practice* (2nd ed., pp. 295–329). Hillsdale, NJ: Erlbaum.

Brown, D. (1990). Trait and factor theory. In D. Brown, L. Brooks, & Associates (Eds.), *Career choice and development* (pp. 13–36). San Francisco: Jossey-Bass.

Chartrand, J. M. (1991). The evolution of trait-and-factor career counseling: A person × environment fit approach. *Journal of Counseling and Development, 69,* 518–524.

Chartrand, J. M., Strong, S. R., & Weitzman, L. M. (1995). The interactional perspective in vocational psychology: Paradigms, theories, and research practices. In W. B. Walsh & S. H. Osipow (Eds.), *Handbook of vocational psychology: Theory, research, and practice* (2nd ed., pp. 35–65). Hillsdale, NJ: Erlbaum.

Crites, J. O. (1981). *Career counseling: Models, methods, and materials.* New York: McGraw-Hill.

Dawis, R. V., & Lofquist, L. H. (1984). *A psychological theory of work adjustment.* Minneapolis, MN: University of Minnesota Press.

Gilliland, B. E., & James, R. K. (1998). *Theories and strategies in counseling and psychotherapy* (4th ed.). Boston: Allyn & Bacon.

Hershenson, D. B. (1996). Work adjustment: A neglected area in career counseling. *Journal of Counseling & Development, 74,* 442–446.

Holland, J. L. (1973). *Making vocational choices: A theory of careers.* Englewood Cliffs, NJ: Prentice-Hall.

Holland, J. L. (1985). *Making vocational choices: A theory of vocational personalities and work environments* (2nd ed.). Englewood Cliffs, NJ: Prentice-Hall.

Ivey, A. E., D'Andrea, M., Ivey, M. B., & Simek-Morgan, L. (2002). *Theories of counseling and psychotherapy: A multicultural perspective* (5th ed.). Boston: Allyn & Bacon.

Ivey, A. E., & Ivey, M. B. (2003). *Intentional interviewing and counseling: Facilitating client development in a multicultural society* (5th ed.). Pacific Grove, CA: Brooks/Cole.

Klein, K. L., & Weiner, Y. (1977). Interest congruency as a moderator of the relationship between job tenure and job satisfaction and mental health. *Journal of Vocational Behavior, 10,* 91–98.

Kosciulek, J. F. (1993). Advances in trait-and-factor theory: A person × environment fit approach to rehabilitation counseling. *Journal of Applied Rehabilitation Counseling, 24*(2), 11–14.

Kosciulek, J. F. (1999). Consumer direction in disability policy formulation and rehabilitation service delivery. *Journal of Rehabilitation, 65*(2), 4–9.

Krumboltz, J. D. (1994). Improving career development theory from a social learning perspective. In M. L. Savickas & R. W. Lent (Eds.), *Convergence in career development theories: Implications for science and practice* (pp. 9–31). Palo Alto, CA: CPP Books.

Lofquist, L. H., & Dawis, R. V. (1969). *Adjustment to work: A psychological view of man's problems in a work-oriented society.* New York: Appleton-Century-Crofts.

Lofquist, L. H., & Dawis, R. V. (1991). *Essentials of person-environment correspondence counseling.* Minneapolis, MN: University of Minneapolis Press.

Lunneborg, P. W. (1983). Career counseling techniques. In W. B. Walsh & S. H. Osipow (Eds.), *Handbook of vocational psychology: Applications* (Vol. 2). Hillsdale, NJ: Erlbaum.

Lynch, R. K., & Maki, D. R. (1981). Searching for structure: A trait-factor approach to vocational rehabilitation. *Vocational Guidance Quarterly, 30,* 61–68.

Parsons, F. (1909). *Choosing a vocation.* Boston: Houghton-Mifflin.

Pervin, L. A. (1987). Person-environment congruence in light of the person-situation controversy. *Journal of Vocational Behavior, 31,* 222–230.

Rogers, C. R. (1942). *Counseling and psychotherapy: Newer concepts in practice.* Boston: Houghton-Mifflin.

Rounds, J. B., & Tracey, T. J. (1990). From trait-and-factor to person-environment fit counseling: Theory and process. In W. B. Walsh & S. H. Osipow (Eds.), *Career counseling: Contemporary topics in vocational psychology* (pp. 1–44). Hillsdale, NJ: Erlbaum.

Schmitt, P., & Growick, B. (1985). Trait-factor approach to counseling: Revisited and reapplied. *Journal of Applied Rehabilitation Counseling, 16,* 100–106.

Swanson, J. L. (1996). The theory is the practice: Trait-and-factor/person environment fit counseling. In M. L. Savickas & W. B. Walsh (Eds.), *Handbook of career counseling theory and practice* (pp. 93–108). Palo Alto, CA: Davies-Black.

Swanson, J. L., & Gore, P. A., Jr. (2000). Advances in vocational psychology theory and research. In S. D. Brown & R. W. Lent (Eds.), *Handbook of counseling psychology* (3rd ed., pp. 233–269). New York: Wiley.

Szymanski, E. M., & Hershenson, D. B. (1998). Career development of people with disabilities: An ecological model. In R. M. Parker & E. M. Szymanski (Eds.), *Rehabilitation counseling: Basics and beyond* (3rd ed., pp. 327–378). Austin, TX: Pro-Ed.

Thomas, K. R., Thoreson, R. W., Parker, R. M., & Butler, A. J. (1998). Theoretical foundations of the counseling function. In R. M. Parker & E. M. Szymanski (Eds.), *Rehabilitation counseling: Basics and beyond* (3rd ed., pp. 225–268). Austin, TX: Pro-Ed.

Weinrach, S. G. (1979). Trait-and-factor counseling: Yesterday and today. In S. G. Weinrach (Ed.), *Career counseling: Theoretical and practical perspectives* (pp. 59–69). New York: McGraw-Hill.

Williamson, E. G. (1965). *Vocational counseling*. New York: McGraw-Hill.

Williamson, E. G. (1972). Trait-factor theory and individual differences. In B. Stefflre & W. H. Grant (Eds.), *Theories of counseling* (pp. 136–176). New York: McGraw-Hill.

Zytowski, D. G., & Borgen, F. H. (1983). Assessment. In W. B. Walsh & S. H. Osipow (Eds.), *Handbook of vocational psychology* (Vol. 2). Hillsdale, NJ: Erlbaum.

Section **III**

Basic Techniques

Chapter 12

Basic Counseling Skills

Lynn C. Koch, Connie McReynolds, and Phillip D. Rumrill

ehabilitation professionals must form effective working relationships with clients, their family members, and other rehabilitation team members if quality services are to be provided and successful outcomes are to occur. Given the current emphasis in managed disability and health care on efficiency, cost-effectiveness, and time-limited programming, establishing effective working relationships can prove to be a challenging task.

The purpose of this chapter is to introduce basic counseling skills that can be used by rehabilitation professionals in the modern era of managed care, cross-referrals, and professional specialization to (a) facilitate cooperative interactions among rehabilitation team members, and (b) address a wide range of client needs in a comprehensive, cost-conscious manner. Recognizing that rehabilitation professionals (e.g., nurses, rehabilitation counselors, physical therapists, occupational therapists, speech therapists) have varying levels of training in counseling skills, interpersonal communication strategies are discussed that can be used by service providers from all rehabilitation and allied health disciplines.

The chapter begins with a discussion of the working alliance as a framework for establishing cohesive, goal-oriented rehabilitation partnerships. Then, the core conditions of counseling (empathy, warmth, genuineness) are reviewed in terms of their applicability to rehabilitation settings and clientele. The remainder of the chapter focuses on specific counseling skills (attending, listening, questioning, information gathering, goal setting, problem solving, rehabilitation planning, conflict resolution, management of resistance) that facilitate the development of effective working relationships and promote positive client outcomes.

THE WORKING ALLIANCE: A FRAMEWORK FOR ESTABLISHING REHABILITATION PARTNERSHIPS

The coordination of client-centered rehabilitation services requires the active participation of clients, rehabilitation professionals, and other team members in all phases of rehabilitation planning. This collaborative effort is similar to the Bordin (1979) concept of the "working alliance," composed of bonds, goals, and tasks. For the alliance to be maximally effective, mutual agreement between partners regarding the importance of each component must be reached. The *equality* of partners must also be recognized, and *shared responsibility* for planning and outcomes must be maintained (McAlees & Menz, 1992).

The effectiveness of rehabilitation professionals is determined, in large measure, by their ability to "connect with" clients and other members of the rehabilitation team. Bonds are the positive, personal attachments that develop among members of the working alliance. Bonds comprise mutual trust, respect, and acceptance as manifested by a sense of shared commitment to the goals and tasks of an activity (Bordin, 1994). Goals are the targets of intervention, such as a return to employment, increased independence, or improvement in physical, cognitive, or emotional functioning. Tasks are the specific activities that the partnership engages in to facilitate change, comprising the essence of the rehabilitation process. If the working alliance is to operate smoothly, its members must perceive the tasks as pertinent to achieving desired rehabilitation outcomes (Horvath & Greenberg, 1989).

THE CORE CONDITIONS OF COUNSELING: EMPATHY, WARMTH, AND GENUINENESS

Three facilitative conditions have been identified as critical to the establishment of working alliances: *empathy, warmth,* and *genuineness*; these are derived from person-centered therapy and have been described as "necessary and sufficient" factors for therapeutic gain (Raskin & Rogers, 1989; Rogers, 1957). It is unlikely that bonds will be established or that the goals of rehabilitation will be achieved in the absence of these conditions.

Empathy

Empathy is the act of "coming to know a person from his (or her) internal frame of reference, gaining some flavor of his (or her) moment-by-moment experience" (Truax & Carkhuff, 1967, p. 42). As a core element of effective rehabilitation, the importance of empathy cannot be overstated. Rehabilitation professionals who effectively demonstrate empathy are able to establish rapport, convey support and acceptance, and demonstrate respect and civility to clients (Thomas & Parker, 1986).

Professional empathy (Rumrill, 1996) is also critical in the modern era of managed care, increased professional specialization, and cross-referrals. Never before has it been more important to understand the personal, political, practical, and ethical realities of the situations of each rehabilitation team member. Professional empathy is conveyed by (a) concentrating with intensity on the person's expressions (both verbal and nonverbal), (b) formulating responses in language that is attuned to the person, (c) responding in a feeling tone similar to that communicated by the person, (d) moving toward clarifying and expanding the person's experiences, and (e) employing the person's behavior as the best indicator of the effectiveness of the rehabilitation professional's communications (Carkhuff; 1969; Rumrill & Scheff, 1996).

Warmth

The rehabilitation professional who demonstrates warmth to clients and other rehabilitation team members facilitates a working alliance marked by reciprocal positive regard and acceptance. The communication of respect is the key ingredient in warmth (Hackney & Cormier, 2000; Pietrofesa, Hoffman, Splete, & Pinto, 1978). Methods of engendering respect include (a) responding to others' messages with nonjudgmental verbal and nonverbal reactions, (b) praising individual team members for their efforts and accomplishments, (c) expressing appreciation to the entire team at the beginning and end of meetings, and (d) paying deference to the expertise and perspective of each team member (including the client).

Genuineness

Being real, honest, and authentic is a quality that enables rehabilitation professionals to quickly establish bonds with members of the working alliance. In the words of Gazda (1973), "The genuine counselor employs no facades. Defenses are reduced, and he or she is open to, and integrated into, the human experience" (p. 58).

Genuineness is communicated to clients and other members of the alliance when rehabilitation professionals use appropriate humor and take responsibility for their mistakes. Self-disclosure (sharing one's own experi-

ences, feelings, or perceptions) can also be used to demonstrate genuineness
(Hackney & Cormier, 2000). However, self-disclosure can be detrimental
to the working alliance if it detracts attention from the client concerns,
and professionals must carefully consider their intents and the desired
effects before using this particular technique.

Another important element of genuineness is communicating at a language level that is understandable to clients and other members of the
working alliance. Professional jargon and acronyms should be kept to a
minimum, and the reactions of others to the statements of rehabilitation
professionals should be regarded as a vehicle for corrective change (Roessler & Rubin, 1992). In other words, the genuineness of one's presentation
is best reflected in the expressions of others.

ATTENDING AND LISTENING SKILLS

Basic attending and listening skills are essential tools for promoting open
and honest communication among members of the working alliance. These
skills are not peculiar to rehabilitation and other helping professionals;
rather, they are often used in everyday communications and, through
training, are adapted to the rehabilitation process (Thomas & Parker,
1986).

Nonverbal Skills

The manner in which rehabilitation professionals physically orient themselves serves to communicate to others whether they are being actively
listened to and understood. Simple behaviors such as posturing the body
in an open, nondefensive manner indicate interest in what the other person
is saying. Leaning slightly forward with relaxed arms and both feet on the
floor communicates availability (Egan, 2001; Ivey & Ivey, 2003).

Maintaining appropriate eye contact is another way to communicate
availability and interest. In the dominant North American culture, appropriate eye contact consists of a fairly steady gaze without staring. However,
other cultures have different norms regarding what is considered appropriate eye contact, and a steady gaze may be considered disrespectful.
Therefore, it is important for rehabilitation professionals to acknowledge
and respect individual differences and cultural norms regarding eye contact
(Ivey & Ivey, 2003).

Supportive silence also communicates empathy, warmth, and genuineness. Silence provides the opportunity for the other person to organize his

or her thoughts when attempting to communicate painful feelings or difficult ideas. It may seem unnatural to remain silent at these times, and rehabilitation professionals may feel the need to say something to alleviate the other person's discomfort. However, when someone is experiencing emotional turmoil, the best support is sometimes to simply *be* with that person, without talking.

In addition to adopting a posture that communicates involvement and interest in the interaction, rehabilitation professionals must closely observe the nonverbal communications of other members of the working alliance. In so doing, they must pay attention to whether their verbal and nonverbal cues are consistent. Sometimes facial expressions, bodily movements, and voice quality can communicate more than mere words. For example, a client may verbally state that he or she is relaxed, but nonverbal cues such as fidgeting, a knitted brow, and a hesitancy in speech may suggest otherwise. The rehabilitation professional then gently informs the client that inconsistencies between his or her verbal and nonverbal behaviors are noted and explores with the client what this means.

Verbal Skills

A very effective verbal strategy that communicates active listening is to restate or paraphrase, in one's own words, what the other person says. This response gives rehabilitation professionals an opportunity to verify that what was intended to be communicated is what was actually heard. It also gives the other person a chance to correct misinterpretations. Phrases such as "What I hear you saying is . . . In other words . . . It sounds to me like . . . Let me see if I understand correctly . . . " are effective lead-ins for paraphrasing.

Summarizing can be used to demonstrate careful listening and to give the other person an opportunity to add to or modify what was said. At the end of each meeting, for example, rehabilitation professionals can summarize what transpired and what the next steps to be taken will be. This strategy, again, provides opportunities to clarify miscommunications and ensures that all members of the working alliance leave the interaction with the same understanding of what occurred.

INTERVIEWING SKILLS

Interviewing is a method used by rehabilitation and other helping professionals to gather information about an individual to describe the individual and make predictions (Berven, 2001; Groth-Marnat, 1997). The manner in which interviews are conducted has major implications for establishing the working alliance and laying the groundwork for positive client outcomes.

Although the purpose of the interview varies somewhat by rehabilitation setting, interviews are generally conducted to (a) establish rapport; (b) provide clients with information about the role and functions of the agency or program, available services, and client responsibilities; (c) identify the client expectations about the rehabilitation process and outcomes; (d) facilitate the self-understanding of client strengths, weaknesses, personality traits, and aptitudes; (e) ease potential anxiety about the rehabilitation process; and (f) provide the client, rehabilitation professional, and other rehabilitation team members with preliminary planning information (Koch & Rumrill, 1998; Power, 2000).

Approaches to interviewing range from highly unstructured to highly structured (Berven, 2001; Groth-Marnat, 1997). Unstructured interviews do not follow any specific format or guidelines. The interviewer determines what questions to ask, and interviewees have freedom to drift from one topic to the next. Structured interviews, on the other hand, are directive and usually follow a format that determines the specific questions to be asked and the order in which they are to be presented. The unstructured interview has the advantages of being flexible and conducive to establishing rapport. However, unstructured interviews have been criticized for their relative subjectivity. Structured interviews have stronger psychometric qualities (e.g., reliability and validity) but may be viewed as more impersonal (Berven, 2001; Groth-Marnat, 1997).

Interviews conducted in rehabilitation settings tend to be semistructured. Although the interviewer determines the information to seek, intake forms are often used to supplement interview data with basic client information (e.g., name, address, phone number, birth date, referral source, diagnosis). Checklists may also be used to guide the rehabilitation professional in identifying client issues of concern.

The information that is gathered through interviewing falls within the broad categories of (a) nature of the problem or reason for referral, (b) personal history, (c) family background, (d) medical history, (e) educational or vocational background, and (f) client expectations. Interviews are typically centered around specific themes (e.g., independent living, vocational planning, medical issues) relevant to the professional role of the interviewer and the functions of the rehabilitation setting that he or she represents.

Effective interviewing occurs when specific issues pertinent to rehabilitation planning are adequately addressed. To identify these issues, rehabilitation professionals must be skillful listeners who pose questions that get beyond vague generalities and communicate a desire to know and understand the other person from his or her frame of reference. The three types of questions useful for gathering client information are open-ended questions, closed-ended questions, and clarifying questions (Hackney & Cormier, 2000).

Open-Ended Questions and General Leads

Questions that encourage others to talk are called *open-ended* questions. They are questions that require more than a few words to answer. Open-ended questions typically begin with *what, how, where, when,* or *who* (e.g., "What brings you here today?", "How do you feel about that?"). *What* questions are used to obtain facts and information. *How* questions are used to gain information about the other person's emotions or elicit information about a sequence of events. *Where* and *when* questions elicit information about time and place, and *who* questions solicit information about people (Ivey & Simek-Downing, 1980). General leads (e.g., "Tell me about . . . ") can also be used to convey active listening and to encourage others to talk.

Open-ended questions and general leads are broad in nature and require the other person to express views, thoughts, opinions, and feelings (Evans, Hearn, Uhlemann, & Ivey, 2004; Ivey & Ivey, 2003). They are used to begin the interview or session, help the client feel at ease, and facilitate exploration of topics. Open-ended questions and general leads can also be used when rehabilitation professionals need to *probe* for additional information (e.g., "When do you feel anxious?", "Tell me more about . . . "; Hackney & Cormier, 2000). These responses help to deepen the interpersonal relationship, promoting development of rapport.

It is noteworthy to mention that questions beginning with the word *why* may often put clients on the defensive (Brammer & MacDonald, 2003; Meier & Davis, 1997). *Why* questions are perceived as requiring explanations and cause a distancing in the client-professional relationship (e.g., "Why did you do that?", "Why are you feeling like that?").

Closed-Ended Questions

Questions that focus the interaction and elicit specific information are referred to as *closed-ended* questions. They can typically be answered with a minimum of words. Closed-ended questions generally begin with words like *are, do, is* (e.g., "Do you need help with transportation?", "Are you living at home?").

Rehabilitation professionals should attempt to avoid a series of closed-ended questions when they are seeking to facilitate client self-exploration (Meier & Davis, 1997). If specific types of information are required, rehabilitation professionals should stagger closed-ended questions with open-ended questions to keep clients engaged in the interaction. A series of closed-ended questions generally has the unwanted effect of causing the client to *shut down* instead of *opening up*, and the burden of the conversation remains on the rehabilitation professional. This approach to questioning also puts the rehabilitation professional in the directive expert role. In general, use closed-ended questions as minimally as possible and only to obtain information pertinent to the progress of the session.

Closed-ended questions can also cause difficulty when used inappropriately (e.g., asking questions that limit the client's responses or asking too many questions). Clients may feel *closed off* and unable to respond in an open manner. By asking questions in this manner (e.g., "You don't seem to like this situation, do you?"), the client is not given the opportunity to express his or her own feelings and thoughts to the referenced incident. Rather, the rehabilitation professional is interpreting the client's feelings and then asking a closed-ended question that suggests the client go along with the professional's interpretation.

Clarifying Questions

Frequently rehabilitation professionals need to gain a deeper understanding or clearer idea of what the client is trying to express. To accomplish this objective, professionals use clarifying questions to gain more information or bring vague material into clearer focus (e.g., "I'm not sure I understand; would you tell me that again?")

General guidelines for clarifying questions include admitting confusion about the client's meaning and asking the client to clarify by repeating the information or providing an example (Brammer & MacDonald, 2003). When rehabilitation professionals *own* their confusion, the client is given the opportunity to provide more clarification. It is *possible*, for example, that the professional's confusion is the result of inattention. Although he or she may have a strong desire to guess or make assumptions about the client's meaning, such speculation is discouraged in favor of eliciting additional material from the client. Furthermore, the opportunity to discuss the material again may lead to greater insight on the part of the client.

Finally, rehabilitation professionals must remain aware of the potential pitfalls of questions. Questions can be overused and underused. When overused, they can distract clients from the topic, interfere with client thoughts, cause the client to avoid sensitive issues, and place the control of the session with the professional (Thomas & Parker, 1986). Likewise, too many questions can cause the client to feel *bombarded, put on the spot,* or *grilled.* When underused, the rehabilitation professional may have difficulty understanding the client's position and risk inaccurate conclusions (Hackney & Cormier, 1999). Therefore, the goal when using questions is to elicit enough information to assist clients while refraining from distancing them.

GOAL-SETTING, PROBLEM-SOLVING, AND PLANNING SKILLS

After the rehabilitation professional, client, and other members of the working alliance have identified the issues to be addressed in the rehabilitation process, the next step is to establish short-term, intermediate, and long-term goals. Although each member of the rehabilitation team brings his or her own priorities to the goal-setting process, the working alliance exists primarily to serve the client. Hence, the needs of others (e.g., vendor's needs to make a profit, sponsor's needs to control costs, and rehabilitation counselor's needs to close cases) must be viewed as factors that help to clarify and, in some cases, modify the client's goals, not as outcomes in and of themselves.

Short-term client goals are best reflected in a clear description of the purpose of each meeting of the working alliance. Rehabilitation professionals who organize the alliance should develop a specific agenda for each meeting and make every effort to adhere to the list of topics and time frames. To carry the sense of purpose forward in every interaction, rehabilitation professionals must ensure that the client (and each team member) knows why he or she is there and what his or her role will be. Providing this structure is especially important when new or replacement members are added to the team.

In setting intermediate and long-term goals, rehabilitation professionals are reminded that clients are their own "best experts" and most eloquent advocates (Roessler & Rumrill, 1995; Rumrill, 1996). Accordingly, clients play superordinate roles in asserting the outcomes expected from the working alliance. The foremost role of rehabilitation professionals is to find ways to actualize those expectations. If and when client expectations exceed the ability of the alliance to help, rehabilitation professionals must (a) help clients to formulate more realistic goals or (b) add members to the team whose services and resources are compatible with client expectations.

Facilitating the goal-setting process can be viewed from a problem-solving perspective (D'Zurilla, 1999). In this context, the problem is considered an opportunity for change or a need for services. The goal is the desired outcome of the working alliance, as stated in the client's terms. The tasks that each team member performs to assist clients in attaining goals constitute solutions.

The first step in the goal-setting process is to understand the clients' perception of their need for services. In acquiring this understanding, rehabilitation professionals must also determine whether the client perceptions coincide with the assessments of referral sources and other rehabilitation team members.

In the second step, rehabilitation professionals consider the circumstances that have led clients to seek help from rehabilitation professionals. Ask the client why he or she was referred for services. Find out whether the client is receiving services voluntarily or conditionally.

The third step is to assess client appraisal of the opportunities that are available to them. Assess the clients' understanding of the resources that are available to address their needs. Determine client level of commitment to making positive changes with the help of the working alliance.

In the fourth step, rehabilitation professionals gauge client level of personal control. What steps did he or she take to enroll in services? What is the client's historical pattern of adjustment or coping? How motivated is he or she to participate in the working alliance?

The fifth step requires a commitment of time and effort to meeting the client needs. It must be specified how much time, effort, and expense the rehabilitation provider and other professional team members are able to invest in this effort. Of equal importance, how much time, effort, and expense is the client willing and able to invest?

In the sixth step, factual information is gathered regarding the resources within and outside the working alliance that exist to meet the client needs. In gathering this information, it is also important to identify the constraints that are present within the service delivery structure and how others in similar situations to those of the client have fared within that structure.

In the final step, the rehabilitation professional, client, and other team members set a realistic goal. To identify this goal, the following questions must be answered: What does the client see as the most desirable outcome of the working alliance? How does each team member assess the appropriateness of that goal? Does the goal need to be modified to fit the parameters of the working alliance, or do the working alliance's parameters need to be expanded? How will the client know when his or her goal has been attained? What are the client's timelines for attainment? Are the goal attainment criteria and timelines compatible with the ability of the working alliance to help? Do they need to be modified?

Once clients have assessed their need for services, considered their expectations of the working alliance, and formulated specific goals, the working alliance shifts to the planning or *solution* phase of the rehabilitation process. Specifically, the focus is placed on what each team member will do, when he or she will do it, and how it will be monitored for progress toward client goals. Adopted from D'Zurilla's (1999) problem-solving model, task formation and goal attainment activities include (a) reappraising a goal's appropriateness and modifying it (if necessary); (b) generating solution-oriented tasks to be assigned to each member of the alliance; (c) developing a contingency plan to identify alternatives if a task is not completed, to adapt the assignment of tasks if team members are added or replaced, or to address potential client changes in motivation or ability to participate; (d) anticipating positive outcomes when client goals will be met, future needs for follow-along services, and other referrals that may be necessary; (e) reinforcing task performance by extending appreciation for the individual and collective efforts of team members; (f) troubleshooting and recycling (if necessary); and (g) recognizing goal attainment while taking steps toward closure and planning for follow-up services (if needed).

DEALING WITH RESISTANCE AND CONFLICT

Even when rehabilitation professionals successfully implement the counseling skills described above, they may still encounter client resistance and conflict in the working alliance. As in any type of interpersonal relationship, the potential exists for misunderstandings caused by differences in interpretations and perceptions. Ultimately the effectiveness of rehabilitation professionals is not determined by their ability to avoid or suppress resistance and conflict, but rather by the ability to diminish resistance, negotiate fair agreements, and resolve differences in a proactive and forthright manner.

Client Resistance

Unless properly understood, client resistance can create a substantial block to effective rehabilitation. Resistance is often perceived by rehabilitation professionals as unwillingness, lack of motivation, reluctance to follow through on assigned activities, or, at times, obstinance, on the part of the client. The perception of resistance can interfere with service delivery, impede effective communication between clients and rehabilitation professionals, and circumvent positive rehabilitation outcomes. Therefore, it is necessary that rehabilitation professionals redefine and more fully understand the actual meaning of resistance.

Miller and Rollnick (2002) reframed the nature of resistance in a manner that may be useful to rehabilitation professionals. They suggested that by reconstructing resistance as a natural part of the client's process toward change, an enhanced understanding of the client's situation is developed. As rehabilitation professionals change their perception of resistance from a negative viewpoint to a more accepting one, clients naturally become less defensive. Miller and Rollnick suggest consideration of the following: (a) therapeutic counseling styles make a significant difference in managing resistance and change; (b) ambivalence is normal, and it is therefore important to attempt to understand client feelings of ambivalence toward proposed changes; (c) it is important to avoid argumentation and aggressive confrontation; and (d) it is important to become familiar with the critical conditions necessary to achieve lasting change.

The manner in which rehabilitation professionals interact with clients can either heighten or diminish client resistance. A great deal of research has been conducted regarding the most effective strategies, techniques, skills, and approaches that rehabilitation professionals can employ to facilitate change in clients. Evidence indicates that the single most effective tool available to rehabilitation professionals is the therapeutic style employed (Hackney & Cormier, 2000). More specifically, rehabilitation professionals who are able to convey empathy, warmth, and genuineness are more effective at alleviating client resistance and promoting successful outcomes than those who do not convey these core conditions of therapeutic change.

Rehabilitation professionals who encounter client ambivalence sometimes view it as resistance, but ambivalence is a normal part of the process of change. Ambivalence occurs when a person has mixed feelings about a situation, event, person, activity, or belief. In considering ambivalence from this perspective, rehabilitation professionals can reframe their thinking, realizing that clients are having normal reactions to the proposed changes. Clients are not trying to be difficult but, rather, are grappling with an internal sense of conflict: "I want to change, but I don't want to change." Providing clients with a safe environment in which to fully explore contradictory feelings helps clear the way for further change.

By neither engaging clients in argument nor trying to persuade them to endorse a change, rehabilitation professionals actually facilitate change and reduce resistance. Argumentation only serves to further client resistance, diminish rapport, and close down the lines of communication. Perception of a lack of client motivation may be more productively viewed as a therapeutic challenge rather than a fault of clients for which they should be blamed (Miller & Rollnick, 2002). When rehabilitation professionals are overly directive and confrontational, higher levels of resistance in clients tend to result. The more general interpretation of therapeutic confrontation is one in which clients can see reality and accept it as such (Miller & Rollnick, 2002). As a goal, this type of confrontation is consistent with the core conditions (empathy, warmth, genuineness) discussed above. According to Miller and Rollnick, a first step toward change is to see a situation clearly.

Prochaska and DiClemente (1982) developed a model of the process of change. The "wheel of change" consists of six stages: precontemplation, contemplation, determination, action, maintenance, and relapse (see Miller and Rollnick, 2002, for a more in-depth discussion). Resistance and ambivalence can occur in any of these six stages. With skillful and purposeful therapeutic interventions, clients can be assisted in negotiating the "rough waters" of change. This model has been used effectively in assisting individuals to overcome their addictions. Likewise, it offers promise for rehabilitation professionals in further understanding resistance and in developing effective therapeutic skills to enhance successful outcomes.

Conflict

Conflicts can arise when rehabilitation professionals and clients experience discrepancies between their expectations and their perceptions. Conflicts can be related to expectations regarding their respective roles and responsibilities, the manner in which services are delivered, and/or the types and amounts of services provided. Conflicts may surround issues of client eligibility, timeliness of services, rehabilitation professional error, program policies, and/or case closure (Holmes, Hall, & Karst, 1989). Addressing conflicts at the working alliance level demonstrates to clients that they are valued members of the rehabilitation team, will be treated fairly, and will receive quality services.

The same approaches to resolving conflicts at industrial and international levels can be applied at the working alliance level. Conflict occurs when an individual's actions or goals are *perceived* as incompatible with the actions or goals of another person (Fisher & Brown, 1988; Fisher, Ury, & Patton, 1991). However, in many conflict situations, it is not the actual goals or actions of the parties that are incompatible; rather, conflict arises from the *misperceptions* of incompatibility.

One approach to conflict resolution (Fisher & Brown, 1988; Fisher et al., 1991) is applied to the rehabilitation planning process in the following sections. This approach involves (a) dispelling myths about "good" working relationships, (b) defining and understanding the conflict from the perspectives of each partner in the working alliance, (c) clarifying misperceptions, (d) generating options for resolving differences, and (e) implementing solutions.

Dispelling Myths About "Good" Working Relationships

Three of the most common myths about relationships are the following: (a) the best partnership is one in which *no* discrepancies are present; (b) partners in effective working relationships have shared values and perceptions; and (c) the goal of such relationships is to avoid disagreements and conflict. Effective working alliance relationships are best described as those in which the parties deal effectively with conflicts; seek to understand each other's values and perceptions, even if they differ; and agree to work through disagreements in a manner benefiting everyone.

Defining the Conflict

The process of conflict resolution begins with accurately defining the conflict. The aim of effective communication is to develop an acceptance of each other's interests, values, perceptions, and notions of fairness, even if these differ. Conflict can be reframed as a difference in interests and goals rather than a contest of wills. It also promotes a "we" attitude or an interdependency of partners who are striving toward the mutual goal of maximizing the effectiveness of the working alliance.

Clarifying Misperceptions

After the nature of the conflict has been accurately defined and understood by each member of the working alliance, the next step is to clarify misperceptions. Often, misperceptions are the real problem rather than true discrepancies. Clarifying what has been said as well as how one's statements are interpreted can prevent miscommunications.

Generating Options

This step in the conflict resolution process involves the mutual sharing of ideas toward the development of a set of shared expectations. Reconciling interests needs to be the goal, as opposed to compromising one's position. The guidelines and boundaries within which the rehabilitation or treatment team works must be clearly communicated and understood by all parties.

Implementing and Evaluating Resolutions

The final step comprises the actual implementation and evaluation of resolutions. Members of the working alliance should reach agreement on what each person's roles and responsibilities will be. Co-developing a written agreement outlining specific roles and responsibilities, revisiting the agreement at various points during the relationship, and revising the agreement as needed will minimize the risk of future discrepancies (Curl & Sheldon, 1992).

SUMMARY

Facilitating cooperative interactions among all participants in the rehabilitation process can be a daunting task. Basic counseling skills can be utilized by rehabilitation professionals to establish cohesive, goal-oriented rehabilitation partnerships with clients, their family members, and interdisciplinary rehabilitation team members. The working alliance provides a framework for interdisciplinary service delivery, along with the core conditions of effective counseling (empathy, warmth, genuineness). Finally, specific counseling skills (attending, listening, questioning, information gathering, goal setting, problem solving, rehabilitation planning, management of resistance, and conflict resolution) can facilitate the development of effective working relationships and the promotion of positive client outcomes.

REFERENCES

Berven, N. L. (2001). Assessment interviewing. In B. F. Bolton (Ed.), *Handbook of measurement and evaluation in rehabilitation* (pp. 197–213). Gaithersburg, MD: Aspen.

Bordin, E. S. (1979). The generalizability of the psychoanalytic concept of the working alliance. *Psychotherapy: Theory, Research, and Practice, 16,* 252–260.

Bordin, E. S. (1994). Theory and research on the therapeutic working alliance: New directions. In A. O. Horvath & L. S. Greenberg (Eds.), *The working alliance: Theory, research, and practice* (pp. 13–37). New York: Wiley.

Brammer, L. M., & MacDonald, G. (2003). *The helping relationship: Process and skills* (8th ed.). Boston: Allyn & Bacon.

Carkhuff, R. R. (1969). *Helping and human relations.* New York: Holt, Rinehart, & Winston.

Curl, R. M., & Sheldon, J. B. (1992). Achieving reasonable choices: Balancing the rights and responsibilities of consumers with those of rehabilitation counselors. *Rehabilitation Education, 6,* 195–205.

D'Zurilla, T. J. (1999). *Problem solving therapy: A social competence approach to clinical intervention* (2nd ed.). New York: Springer.

Egan, G. (2001). *The skilled helper: A problem-management and opportunity-development approach to helping* (7th ed.). Belmont, CA: Brooks/Cole.

Evans, D. R., Hearn, M. T., Uhlemann, M. R., & Ivey, A. E. (2004). *Essential interviewing: A programmed approach to effective communication* (6th ed.). Belmont, CA: Brooks/Cole.

Fisher, R., & Brown, S. (1988). *Getting together: Building a relationship that gets to yes.* Boston: Houghton Mifflin.

Fisher, R., Ury, W., & Patton, B. (1991). *Getting to yes: Negotiating agreement without giving in.* Boston: Houghton Mifflin.

Gazda, G. M. (1973). *Human relations development.* Boston: Allyn & Bacon.

Groth-Marnat, G. (1997). *Handbook of psychological assessment* (3rd ed.). New York: Wiley.

Hackney, H. L., & Cormier, L. S. (1999). *Counseling strategies and interventions* (5th ed.). Boston: Allyn & Bacon.

Hackney, H. L., & Cormier, L. S. (2000). *The professional counselor: A process guide to helping* (4th ed.). Boston: Allyn & Bacon.

Holmes, G. E., Hall, L., & Karst, R. H. (1989). Litigation avoidance through conflict resolution: Issues for state rehabilitation agencies. *American Rehabilitation, 15*(3), 12–15.

Horvath, A. O., & Greenberg, L. S. (1989). Development and validation of the Working Alliance Inventory. *Journal of Counseling Psychology, 36,* 223–233.

Ivey, A. E., & Ivey (2003). *Intentional interviewing and counseling: Facilitating client development in a multicultural society* (5th ed.). Pacific Grove, CA: Brooks/Cole.

Ivey, A. E., & Simek-Downing, L. (1980). *Counseling and psychotherapy: Skills, theories, and practice.* Englewood Cliffs, NJ: Prentice Hall.

Koch, L. C., & Rumrill, P. D., Jr. (1998). The working alliance: An interdisciplinary case management strategy for health professionals. *Work: A Journal of Prevention, Assessment, and Rehabilitation, 10,* 55–62.

McAlees, D., & Menz, F. (1992). Consumerism and vocational evaluation. *Rehabilitation Education, 6,* 213–220.

Meier, S. T., & Davis, S. R. (1997). *The elements of counseling* (3rd ed.). Pacific Grove, CA: Brooks/Cole.

Miller, W. R., & Rollnick, S. (2002). *Motivational interviewing: Preparing people for change.* New York: Guilford.

Pietrofesa, J., Hoffman, A., Splete, H., & Pinto, D. (1978). *Counseling: Theory, research, and practice.* Chicago: Rand McNally.

Power, P. W. (2000). *A guide to vocational assessment* (3rd ed.). Austin, TX: Pro-Ed.

Prochaska, J. O., & DiClemente, C. C. (1982). Transtheoretical therapy: Toward a more integrative model of change. *Psychotherapy: Theory, Research, and Practice, 19*, 276–288.

Raskin, N. J., & Rogers, C. R. (1989). Person-centered therapy. In R. J. Corsini & D. Wedding (Eds.), *Current psychotherapies* (4th ed., pp. 155–194). Itasca, IL: Peacock.

Roessler, R. T., & Rubin, S. E. (1992). *Case management for rehabilitation counselors.* Austin, TX: Pro-Ed.

Roessler, R. T., & Rumrill, P. D., Jr. (1995). Promoting reasonable accommodations: An essential postemployment service. *Journal of Applied Rehabilitation Counseling, 26*(4), 3–7.

Rogers, C. R. (1957). The necessary and sufficient conditions of therapeutic personality change. *Journal of Consulting Psychology, 21*, 95–103.

Rumrill, P. D., Jr. (1996). *Multiple sclerosis and the world of work.* New York: Demos.

Rumrill, P. D., Jr., & Scheff, C. M. (1996). Enhance productivity and reduce turnover with worksite safety and disability management. *Journal of Long-Term Care Administration, 24*(3), 32–35.

Thomas, K., & Parker, R. (1986). Counseling interventions. In T. F. Riggar, D. R. Maki, & A. W. Wolf (Eds.), *Applied rehabilitation counseling.* New York: Springer.

Truax, C. B., & Carkhuff, R. R. (1967). *Toward effective counseling and psychotherapy.* Chicago: Aldine.

Chapter 13

Group Procedures

Ruth A. Huebner

HISTORY AND MAJOR CONCEPTS

Humans have always been social beings, seeking the comfort of others in times of loss, the safety of others in times of threat, the wisdom of others in times of change, and the joy of others in times of celebration. Group counseling arose from the universal roots of social interaction and has evolved over time. From 1932 to the 1960s, for example, group counseling was applied to a wider variety of individuals, spurred by necessity after World War II; more recently it has become a means of facilitating personal growth and providing support (Shapiro, 1978). An emerging body of research demonstrates that group methods are effective, that the benefits are maintained over time, and that best practices in group procedures are associated with improved outcomes (Bednar & Kaul, 1994).

Definition of the Group

The composition of groups for group counseling and psychotherapy ranges from couples to families to large groups of anonymous individuals. Across this range of compositions, common goals include self-understanding, personal growth, and building upon inner resources (Corey & Corey, 2001). Within the continuum from couples counseling to large-group counseling is a smaller group of individuals who come together and form a social system with norms and expectations, who interact with each other as well as with the leader, who share needs and experiences, who assume both the role of helper and helpee, and who form an identity as members of the group. Counseling with such smaller groups is the focus of this chapter.

In group counseling, the group context and the group process constitute the treatment intervention. The therapeutic effects originate within the group context and are based on the fundamental assumption that the presence of others provides a unique opportunity for self-exploration and learning that is not present in individual approaches. The group process and interaction are the mechanisms that produce the therapeutic effects. The general therapeutic effects are described in both the classic and the current literature on group procedures (Corey & Corey, 2001; Posthuma, 1998; Yalom, 1995) and are associated with group process regardless of the theoretical approach.

General Therapeutic Effects

Groups may *instill a sense of hope* to members of the group. Seeing and hearing others cope with the same concerns diminishes the myth that change is impossible or requires rare characteristics. Group members provide multiple models of coping and may be at different points in their adjustment to disability or in their rehabilitation programs. Newer group members are exposed to the adjustment that has been achieved by more seasoned group members, who in turn may be socially reinforced as a role model. In rehabilitation, the need for a sense of hope may be particularly salient for individuals who have experienced a traumatic onset of disability, such as spinal cord injury, a chronic illness such as bipolar mood disorder, or attempts to pursue a return to work after chronic unemployment. Participating in a group may intensify a sense of *universality*; group members may come to understand that their problems or concerns are not unique, diminishing the myth that they are alone with their problems. The universality effect may promote an acceptance of feelings as normal responses, thus reducing catastrophizing or shame associated with a disability.

A spirit of *altruism* with unique implications for rehabilitation may develop as group members help each other. In short-term illnesses, people temporarily relinquish social roles and become more dependent on others. Long-term dependency, however, is associated with psychological distress (Newsom & Shulz, 1998); adjustment to chronic illness requires cultivation of a sense of health despite disability (Ben-Yishay & Daniels-Zide, 2000). Altruistic behavior may signal a paradigm shift from dependency to the norm of reciprocal support and personal empowerment (Zimmerman & Warschausky, 1998) by building a sense of personal control and participatory power. Altruism may be particularly therapeutic in rehabilitation, where reciprocally supportive relationships are associated with increased social support and higher occupational functioning (Rintala, Young, Hart, & Fuhrer, 1994).

Social or vicarious learning occurs by watching other group members learn or work through their own problems and emotional responses. Wright (1983) suggested that groups generate novel solutions to problems, changes in values, or changes in fundamental expectations. Therapeutic *catharsis* from expressing emotions and then experiencing acceptance by peers may be perceived as more genuine than the support of paid professionals operating within their professional expectations. Within the peer group, a *sense of cohesiveness* is similar to the therapeutic bond or rapport between client and counselor, but on a larger scale. When group cohesiveness is optimal, there is an anticipation of being with the group members, a feeling of unity, contemplation of the events in the group between sessions, and a general caring for each group member (Posthuma, 1998). Group cohesiveness may be reflected in attendance, sharing between group members, self-disclosure of feelings, and risk taking within the group.

Theory-Related Therapeutic Factors

Additional therapeutic effects are conceptualized in particular theoretical approaches. In psychodynamic approaches, the group process is conceptualized as recapitulating the social experiences of a family or other groups. This therapeutic effect has been termed *family reenactment* (Posthuma, 1998) or a *social microcosm* (Marshak & Seligman, 1993). Extending the metaphor of a family, the group theoretically provides a *corrective emotional experience* to reshape and reframe the early experiences of an individual. In both psychodynamic and experiential approaches, group processes stimulate a range of possible transference experiences. An understanding of transference may elucidate distortions in interaction and provide opportunities to work through interpersonal conflicts and to develop new skills and healthier expectations in relationships. Both psychodynamic and experiential approaches emphasize procedures to elicit *catharsis* and thus stimulate emotional release.

In the cognitive-behavioral approach, the group is conceptualized as affording an opportunity to examine one's own behavior and distortions in thinking, and to develop new skills. Therapeutic effects may be associated with *social learning*, *skill development*, and *social reinforcement*. Similarly, in the psychoeducational approach, therapeutic effects are conceptualized as due in part to *shared learning* and *imitative behavior* in which participants gain information and models of coping.

APPLICATION OF THEORIES TO GROUP PROCEDURES

Multiple theoretical approaches, derived in large part from methods and theories applied to individual counseling (Bednar & Kaul, 1994), have also been applied to group counseling. Four broad categories of theories are conceptualized here to elucidate the fundamental differences between theoretical approaches. Intervention strategies and application to rehabilitation are also discussed for each theory to assist the rehabilitation professional in matching the needs of the group, the professional's skills, and the theoretical approach.

Psychodynamic Approaches

Concepts from psychoanalysis, object relations, and interpersonal theory may be grouped together under the psychodynamic approach. The goal of intervention is to provide a climate in which clients may reexperience relationships with family members or close peers. The group process may elicit transference and defense mechanisms in any group member. For example, one group member may remind another member of a mother, a father, a close friend, or an authority figure. The transference then elicits an interaction pattern that may be dysfunctional in the current context. If analyzed and interpreted by the group, the interaction pattern provides an opportunity to develop insights into the origins of faulty psychological development, expectations in relationships that may be self-defeating or self-fulfilling, personal strengths and weaknesses, and new ways of interacting. Dysfunctional patterns of interaction are not unique to individuals with disabilities (Marshak & Seligman, 1993), but interpersonal experiences may be complicated by experiences associated with disability (Huebner & Thomas, 1995).

Transference may at times challenge the whole group. For example, a member may expect abandonment or rejection from the group, just as the family or peer group did. As a consequence of this expectation, the group member may interact in a way that elicits rejection and abandonment (Teyber, 1992). If the group leader and group members discern the interpersonal expectation, then the interaction pattern provides an opportunity for developing insight and encouraging the member to articulate his or her experience, while the group supports the member through this cathartic insight. According to Teyber, developing insight into the origins of dysfunctional patterns of interaction reduces the shame associated with recognizing weaknesses, because weaknesses are understood as logical adaptive responses to experiences. Effective psychodynamic therapy requires time to build trust in the relationships between group members and with the group leader.

For persons with disabilities, the psychodynamic approach may not be appropriate during the initial adjustment to disability, because ego strength and some emotional stability are required to withstand the introspection inherent in this approach. However, persons with disabilities are just as likely as all people to experience life issues pertinent to relationships, emotional distress, culture, abuse, and more (Patterson, McKenzie, & Jenkins, 1995). Optimal function with a disability may also require enhanced social skills and social competence in order to put others at ease, present oneself to others, and interact with care providers. Experiences with disability may elicit stereotypical responses, including inaccurate perceptions of abilities, the spread of disability to all aspects of life, lowered expectations for adaptation, and distancing from others (Marshak & Seligman, 1993). Effective group leaders recognize that these expectations and stereotypical responses may be enacted in the group, providing opportunities to practice alternative responses to develop social competence.

The psychodynamic group process may emerge from an unstructured approach with clients sharing thoughts, experiences, and emotions and exploring their roots with the group. The group process may also be more structured for persons with limited cognitive abilities, for those who have more difficulty sharing and articulating their feelings, or at early stages of group development. For example, sharing memories of early life and one's early experience with disability, sharing photographs of oneself interacting with others, making a collage of different stages of life, drawing a timeline of one's life, or doing art or imaging exercises may be used to activate self-awareness and group experiences. The sharing and processing of these experiences among group members to enhance insight is a critical component of the psychodynamic approach.

Experiential Approaches

Concepts from Gestalt therapy, reality therapy, existential therapy, and person-centered therapy are grouped here under experiential approaches. The goal of experiential approaches is to develop a realistic and a present-centered understanding of self and to empower group members to change and take responsibility for their lives. The group provides a safe climate where members can explore the full range of emotions while experiencing acceptance by the group. The focus of group work is on present feelings and responses. Nonverbal behaviors are attended to as clues to masked feelings. For example, the client may say that life is fine, but the downturned eyes and wringing hands may suggest otherwise. In response, the group may point out the inconsistency and help the person express more of his or her present emotional experience. The focus on the "here and now" experience is intended to increase awareness of emotions, provide catharsis, and develop congruence between actions and feelings.

Experiential groups in rehabilitation settings may help individuals experience mourning or anger related to their disabilities or other people. Because people with disabilities are expected to be cheerful and to inspire others, individuals may deny emotions incongruent with societal demands. In the experiential approaches, these here-and-now emotions are identified, experienced, expressed, explored, and ultimately accepted as legitimate aspects of self.

Unstructured intervention may be used with clients sharing life events and exploring nonverbal behaviors, emotions, and thoughts as they emerge. Role playing, empty chair techniques, empathic group responses, reflection, modeling, and a variety of active exercises are used to elicit and experience feelings. Specific role-playing activities might be introduced, such as role-playing requests for help in the bathroom or for facing an unsupportive employer. The feelings elicited during role play would then be explored. Use of an empty chair technique may encourage a group member to mourn a disability, say goodbye to a former self, express an emotion to a specific person, or accept a disowned part of the self. For groups needing more structure, members could be asked to write down a feeling toward another group member and then express it, engage in tug of war, or pair up to interview another person; the here-and-now aspects of the emotional experience are then explored. Keeping a journal of emotions and thoughts between sessions might be useful for group members who are slower in responding during group meetings. Group members are encouraged to confront denial, entitlement, and anger and then to acknowledge, own, and accept responsibility for their emotions and actions.

Cognitive-Behavioral Approaches

Concepts from behavior therapy, rational-emotive therapy, cognitive therapy, stress inoculation, and solution-focused therapy are grouped together here. The goal of cognitive-behavioral approaches is to replace maladaptive behavior and thinking with adaptive behavior and rational cognition. The group members and leader reinforce adaptive behavior and thoughts, seek to extinguish maladaptive responses, and promote direct and vicarious learning.

The cognitive-behavioral focus is attractive in rehabilitation because it facilitates collaboration, focuses on presenting problems, is structured, and can be documented for reimbursement (Bowers, 1988). Numerous examples of the application of this approach are found in the literature. Group role plays and structured experiences may be used, for instance, to teach the social skills of asking for help, training care providers, demonstrating equipment, or interviewing for a job using a structured approach (Liberman, DeRisi, & Mueser, 1989). Using inoculation (Meichenbaum, 1985), group members dissect an overwhelming problem to more manageable segments, practice coping skills, and reward positive coping strategies (e.g., de Voogd, Knipping, Blecourt, & van Rijswijk, 1993). Specific cognitive distortions identified with disability, such as "I can't live with this disability," "Because I am disabled, I am entitled to more tolerance of my inappropriate behavior," or "Because of my disability, I am useless" (Calabro, 1990), may be reframed by a group into more adaptive responses associated with improved adjustment to disability (Sweetland, 1990). A group may differentiate the problems that are related to disability from those that are not and identify environmental constraints and solutions to overcome problems (Marshak & Seligman, 1993). Using a solution-focused approach (Talmon, 1993), any effective strategy used by the client is highlighted and reinforced while problems are downplayed. For example, coming to the group is a positive coping strategy; the question posed by the group might be "How did you do it?" The group then assists the members in identifying and expanding adaptive strategies and strengths.

Intervention strategies used in the cognitive-behavioral approach tend to be more structured, often with specific behavioral objectives (Burns & Beck, 1999). Workbooks and readings (e.g., Burns, 1990; McKay, Davis, & Fanning, 1998) can be assigned between group sessions, using workbooks that are sensitive to disability issues. Role playing, systematic desensitization, relaxation, meditation, assertiveness, time management training, and many other techniques are often used. Members may establish weekly goals, share these goals with the group, devise methods to achieve them, and return to share their progress and the strategies they found effective. The group could be organized around a common goal, such as preparing a meal, planning an outing, or completing a community service project. Tangible reinforcement like tokens or stickers may be used to visualize progress. White and Epston (1990) send a brief note between sessions to help reframe a client's life story into a more adaptive narrative.

Psychoeducational Approaches

Educational groups, support groups, and self-help groups are included here under psychoeducational approaches. The goals are to impart and acquire knowledge, to develop pragmatic coping strategies, and to exchange social support with others who have similar experiences. At times, support groups evolve into political action groups around a particular issue. The group leader may be very active in planning and running a support group, leadership may rotate among members, or there may not be a formal group leader. Group membership may be stable or change virtually every session. The level of self-disclosure and cohesiveness may vary from nearly anonymous to highly cohesive. Group members function as a support and knowledge base for one another and as a source of practical solutions to problems and action.

There are numerous support groups for problems related to almost any concern, and information on any topic is usually available through the World Wide Web. In rehabilitation, there are psychoeducational groups within inpatient, outpatient, and vocational programs. Groups can be organized to impart information about an illness or disability and to teach management skills; they are often organized around a particular issue such as heart conditions, arthritis, and brain injury. Job clubs may support those with chronic unemployment through a structured and intensive job search and training process (Salomone, 1996). Groups in industry may be set up to learn injury prevention, biomechanics, or exercise to minimize work injury symptoms. Specific job skills for the transition to work may be taught using a group format (McWhirter & McWhirter, 1996). The interventions used in the psychoeducational approaches are the most structured of any group approach and often include educational techniques such as lectures, videotapes, an established curriculum, reading materials, and guided group exercises.

GROUP PROCEDURES AND PROCESSES

Formation of Groups

The theoretical approach utilized and the specific methods employed in a group will be dictated in part by the constraints of the environment and the needs of the individual in the group. For example, cost containment initiatives in hospitals have resulted in group therapy being the only form of therapy available to most patients in psychiatric units (Yalom, 1995). These inpatient groups may be marked by rapid changes in group composition and leadership, acute psychopathology, and heterogeneous patient populations. In these instances, groups may be divided on the basis of level of functioning or on the basis of acute versus chronic conditions. In acute rehabilitation similar cost containment constraints may dictate that groups are composed of members with a wide age and interest span and multiple disabilities. Structured interventions are more appropriate when group cohesiveness is likely to be minimal.

Multiple opportunities for group intervention exist in outpatient, extended care, residential care, schools, vocational rehabilitation, work, or occupational conditioning programs. In these settings, groups could be developed based on a match between the needs of individuals and a theoretical approach. For example, people who desire major changes in their interaction patterns may benefit from the psychodynamic or experiential approaches. Those who desire skill development may benefit from cognitive-behavioral approaches, and knowledge gained through a psychoeducational group may be most helpful in acute-care settings. Alternatively, groups could be based on homogeneous characteristics such as anxiety, pain management, neurological injury, or unemployment.

Regardless of what type of group is formed, fundamental guidelines for group formation are commonly described in the literature (Corey & Corey, 2001; Marshak & Seligman, 1993; Yalom, 1995). Groups should not be smaller than 4 to 5 people or larger than 12 people. Ideally, a group of 6 to 8 people allows all parties time to participate as well as time to process and observe the group activities. The meeting space should allow all group members to see each other. A circular arrangement is the most common but may vary for role playing or other experiential techniques. Meeting times for people without physical disabilities are usually 90 minutes but may be as long as three hours. There are few guidelines in the literature regarding the frequency of group meetings. Group membership may be open, with new members joining and other members leaving; open membership promotes learning for the novice from the more seasoned member, but it diminishes group cohesiveness. Closed group membership encourages members to bond over time; however, the group size may gradually diminish and the group may ultimately disband as members leave.

Participants and Their Rights and Responsibilities

Participants in a group must be able to engage in the group task, at least minimally, without significantly disrupting the group. In most settings, groups are voluntary and participants have the right to receive some help and self-disclose at a comfortable pace. Each member of the group should be informed of group processes, techniques, fees, and risks. Group members are usually individually oriented to the group and procedures by the group leader before the first meeting. Members have the right to confidentiality from all other group members. An informed consent procedure that outlines the specifics of the group and the risks of group membership, as well as a contract for group attendance and adherence to group rules, is important to consider. Each group member then indicates his or her understanding of and commitment to confidentiality and the group's rules by signing a form that is often witnessed, with members retaining one copy.

The risks involved in group membership may be substantial, including group pressure, scapegoating, threats to confidentiality, and the precipitation of emotional crisis (Corey & Corey, 2001). Participants might feel pressure to disclose more than is comfortable. Certain group techniques are powerfully confrontive and may lead to psychological decompensation. The behavior of other group members cannot be controlled outside of the group; thus, a potential exists for invasion of privacy and breach of confidentiality. These risks can be minimized through careful screening and orientation of group members, contracts, ongoing group dialogue, and the leader's skills.

Leader Characteristics and Skills

Skills in listening and individual counseling are required in both individual and group counseling. Group procedures also demand that the leader be aware of all of the members in the group, focus on the group dynamics, and possess group leadership skills. Early in the group formation, the leader facilitates interactions between group members rather than solely with the leader. The leader might provide more structure as needed, guide each member to explore his or her own feelings, explore the individual responses to the group process, and teach members interaction skills. The leader might model, for example, reflection of feelings and empathic responses and encourage members to practice these skills. As the group progresses, the leader may identify group processes such as cohesiveness, scapegoating, or moralizing by group members and assist the group to process this feedback to facilitate change.

Regardless of the theoretical orientation of the group, the leader must help members return to the present context of the group and use the group to validate or clarify a member's experience. In order to share group leadership among all members, the leader must relinquish control at times, trust in the capacity of others to guide their own lives, and empower others. This more submissive response of relinquishing control to the group may be difficult for professionals in rehabilitation (Huebner & Thomas, 1996). Coleading of a group may be effective if the leaders agree on procedures or model conflict resolution (Posthuma, 1998).

Self-disclosure by the leader has been the focus of many studies (see Bednar & Kaul, 1994). The goal of effective self-disclosure is to model this behavior and to convey to the group a sense of personal humanness. Self-disclosure about the leader's feelings in response to the group process may be a particularly useful technique to involve the leader in the group, model self-disclosure, and facilitate the group experience (Posthuma, 1998).

The leader must be sensitive to the key blocks to therapeutic change that are described in the literature (e.g., Posthuma, 1998; Yalom, 1995). Blocks include scapegoating a group member as the one to blame for personal or group problems. A single group member may monopolize the group discussion, push others to disclose, seek to control the group, or avoid group participation. Excessive questioning, moralizing, or intellectualizing by group members may block more therapeutic reflection and clarification. Subgroups may form within the larger group and undermine the whole group process. A skilled leader will recognize that any block to the group process provides an opportunity to help group members change. The leader may help all members focus on their feelings and power to influence the situation, and then assist the group in responding to these blocks. If the group leader fundamentally believes that each group member has the potential to learn to deal with problems, then he or she has the ability to empower the group members to solve the problem using their own inner resources.

Group Stages

Although different stages of group process are defined in the literature, all authors agree that the character of a group evolves in a somewhat predictable developmental process. Tuckman's (1965) classic work on group processes is recognized as contributing to an understanding of four phases of group development: forming (orientation), storming (dissatisfaction), norming (resolution), and performing (production) stages. Corey and Corey (2001) described the stage of coming together and getting to know each other superficially (forming); this stage as marked by dependence on the leader (Posthuma, 1998). As this phase ends, a period of hostility among members and toward the leader may emerge. The first genuine feelings expressed in a group may be negative feelings (storming). As this stage wanes, a period of negotiation ensues to define how the group will work, who will share the leadership, and how the responsibility for the work of the group will be shared (norming). Ideally, a period of group cohesion then emerges marked by shared leadership and group responsibility, group stability, and engagement in group work (performing). As groups disband, the group is likely to experience a period of adjournment, including grieving the loss. Although these stages are frequently cited as existing in groups, the stages of group process may differ for people with disabilities (Marshak & Seligman, 1993). For example, the process of grieving a loss of function may interact with the group stages to produce more anger or dependency than might be typical.

Disability Variables and Their Potential Influence

Much of the classic information on group procedures has been based on groups with mild to moderate emotional or adjustment disturbances (Stein, 1996; Yalom, 1995). In rehabilitation, however, group membership may be highly heterogeneous, with challenging degrees of cognitive, psychosocial, or physical disabilities that require adaptation of group procedures (Patterson et al., 1995; Stein, 1996). Disability-related problems and requisite accommodations gleaned from the literature or practice are displayed in Table 13.1 with the hope that future research will investigate the usefulness of these accommodations.

Heterogeneity of the group is likely with disorders such as brain injury, developmental disabilities, and dual diagnoses, along with groups in inpatient rehabilitation settings or vocational agencies. A buddy system between clients with complementary skills or collaborative subgroups may encourage higher-functioning group members to assist lower-functioning members. Initially the group leader may need to teach collaborative skills and define group members' roles within the buddy system. Collaborative modifications to group procedures promote experiences of teaching and altruism among higher-functioning individuals and provide the individualized attention needed among lower-functioning individuals. Within heterogeneous groups, individuals might work toward their own individualized goals in the group. For example, an educational activity designed to increase an understanding of brain injury may help one client understand that he or she has a brain that was injured and another client to understand the functions of specific brain sites.

Groups with members who have limited cognitive abilities will also require more structure from the group leader. Nonetheless, a group leader must strive to relinquish control to the group members with the belief that all people have some, perhaps untapped, ability to manage themselves and their lives. Increasing the predictability of the group may empower

TABLE 13.1   Challenges Associated with Disabilities and Accommodations in Group Procedures

Challenge	Accommodation
Heterogeneity of the group	Buddy system
	Collaborative learning
	Leader provides training in collaboration
	Individual goals within group goals
Cognitive limitations	Predictable activities at start and end
	Consistent structure and agenda
	Visual cues about the group agenda
	Specific training in group tasks to share leadership
	Frequent summarization of the conversation
	Videotaped feedback
	Simple consistent group norm or group goal
	Request and give concrete examples
	Use sensory or motor activities
Communication limitations	Use of verbal and nonverbal activities
	Augmentative communication devices
	Attention to nonverbal communication
	Model acceptance of all differences
Behavioral difficulties	Varied passive and active activities
	Short but more frequent group sessions
	Teach skills to cope with strong emotions
	Engage members in planning and running the group
Mobility and sensory limitations	Careful attention to seating arrangements
	Summarize group processes
	Verbal or visual cuing
	Assistive technology

members. Each meeting, for instance, could be started and ended with a particular activity such as a specific motor or musical activity to provide variety in group activities and a novel signal to alert group members to group work. The schedule of each group meeting might remain the same, but the specific activities of the group may change. Visual cues might help group members anticipate and prepare for the events of the group. For example, the schedule could be displayed in pictures attached with velcro; as each agenda item is concluded, the picture could be taken down. Key leadership roles within the group might be identified and members taught how to lead the group through tasks such as a brief exercise session, a calendar review, a job list, or the structured start/end activity. A group leader may need to stop the group often to help members restate and rephrase the events of the group and to ensure that all members are following the group process and activities. Videotapes and audiotapes may provide additional feedback on behavior or discussion and reinforce group structure and learning between sessions.

Because the focus of groups is often verbal, communication disorders can be particularly difficult to manage. A variety of verbal and nonverbal tasks may allow all parties an opportunity to participate. Augmentative communication devices may give some individuals an opportunity to express ideas. Individuals can be encouraged to communicate nonverbally through sign language, body gestures, drawing, and writing. Paying particular attention to nonverbal cues may help the leader recognize critical moments that signal a need to validate or explore feelings with group members who have communication disorders. All group members may benefit from learning to wait for slower communication by a member and from observing and responding to nonverbal communication among all members (Marshak & Seligman, 1993). A group leader is one who models this patience and respect for individual differences in any group.

Behavioral difficulties, such as a short attention span, may dictate that group activities are frequently varied between active and passive tasks; short but more frequent groups may be more beneficial than fewer longer groups. Participants may express strong emotions of grieving or anger toward care providers; recognizing this as a grieving process may increase group members' support of each other and provide models for their own grieving process (Marshak & Seligman, 1993). Group members who exhibit uncooperative or avoidant behavior might be invited to take over a portion of a group task, such as planning the agenda.

Mobility and sensory disabilities may also challenge the group. Group members within rehabilitation settings may attend a group with traction devices, wheelchairs, or oxygen tanks, for example. These devices must be accommodated in a manner that allows all members of the group to see each other and interact. Marshak and Seligman (1993) suggest that a forced seating arrangement to accommodate these devices may diminish group interaction and an individual's sense of control; they recommend that group members be given choices about group seating arrangements. Hearing impairments may be accommodated by looking directly at the group member with a hearing loss while speaking, summarizing the group process that may have been missed, and including a scribe or interpreter in the group. People with visual impairments may miss the nonverbal communication of members and be uncertain when they have a turn to speak. Assistive technologies exist to enlarge written materials or enhance hearing and should be incorporated into the group. All disability variables provide an opportunity to develop solutions to accommodate group members' differences.

REHABILITATION APPLICATIONS AND CASE EXAMPLES

Adolescents in a Psychodynamic Approach

In this section, specific examples found in the literature are presented to illustrate the integration of many of the concepts already presented. Mishna (1996) utilized an interpersonal psychodynamic approach for 17 weeks with a group of adolescents with learning disabilities. To accommodate for the learning disabilities, the leaders actively and specifically clarified verbal and nonverbal messages and monitored discussions to ensure that all group members followed the conversation. Group members displayed limited social skills and behaviors such as spinning in circles. Rather than confront the behavior, the leaders supported the group in understanding and interpreting this behavior and in expressing their emotions and needs. Through this "holding" environment, the author reasoned that the adolescents' progress resulted from an improved self-regulation of emotional state. The group members attributed the positive therapeutic effects that they experienced to a sense of mutual recognition among the group, meaning that they saw themselves in others while realizing that others saw themselves in the participant. This mutual recognition was characterized by feelings of safety and trust, cohesiveness, catharsis, identification, universality, altruism, and hope. Participants also credited their progress to reciprocal learning and feedback, development of social skills, and the expression of both positive and negative feelings.

Job Club Approach in Rehabilitation

The job club or job-finding club is a strategy combining psychoeducational and cognitive-behavioral approaches that is frequently applied in rehabilitation (Salomone, 1996) and social services (Sterrett, 1998). Initially developed by Azrin, Flores, and Kaplan (1975), the job club is a highly structured and standardized group intervention. Job club lessons and protocols are designed to assist participants to develop readiness for work, identify job interests, locate job leads, contact employers, complete job applications, develop job interview skills, and find jobs. The group process promotes self-efficacy and empowerment through team building, clear goals, training in skills, a buddy system, and group practice. Because obtaining a job is defined as a full-time activity, the job club may meet daily. The goal of a job club is to find employment, and participants make contacts with potential employers, complete applications, identify their strengths, and engage in a variety of structured exercises. The resources of the sponsoring agency, such as the telephone, fax machine, and computer access, are available to participants.

The research literature on the outcomes of job clubs is encouraging. Sterrett (1998) found, for example, that 8 of 11 welfare recipients obtained employment during or after completing 10 job club sessions (3 hours/day, 2 days/week). Participants demonstrated improved self-efficacy that the author attributed to mastery of tasks, vicarious learning in the group, verbal persuasion by group members, and adjuncts to control anxiety such as relaxation. Corrigan, Reedy, Thadani, and Ganet (1995) found that 30% of 45 clients with mental illness completed the three-month program and were more often employed at six-month follow-up. The earliest reports of job club outcomes (Azrin & Philip, 1979) found that 95% of job club members with disabilities obtained jobs. Although Salomone (1996) criticized the rigor and conclusions of this study, he recognized that the high intensity of the job club is likely to improve outcomes.

Persons with Severe Disabilities

Rose (1996) used cognitive-behavioral treatment for persons with severe mental retardation and aggressive behaviors to teach anger management during 16 weekly sessions. To accommodate for cognitive limitations, each group member was accompanied by a staff member, and a consistent group schedule was maintained. Structured activities such as pictures, videotapes, and individual work with a staff member were used to guide the self-exploration of feelings and antecedents of anger. Role playing was used to practice alternative behaviors, and cognitive strategies, such as self-statements to moderate anger and thought-stopping techniques, were taught. A reduction in aggressive behavior in all group members was found that persisted for at least three months after the conclusion of the group.

Stein (1996) provided group psychotherapy for persons having neurological injury with affective changes, behavioral disorders, impaired abstract reasoning, distractibility, and communication disorders. To adapt to these demands, Stein reinforced an explicit group norm of mutual assistance at every session, arranged for shorter but more frequent sessions, regularly summarized the discussion, wrote on a chalkboard to highlight the problem-solving process, and made frequent requests for concrete examples. Educational materials were introduced to help individuals develop insight into the nature of their brain injuries with a here-and-now focus.

Ross (1997) described a structured five-stage group model that utilized sensory stimulation within the group to reduce aggression or agitation among adults with regression or very low functioning. Group sessions ranged from 30 to 50 minutes. In the orientation phase, simple greeting activities were introduced such as shaking hands, writing a first name, or passing a simple musical toy. The second stage included movement games and activities such as simple Tai Chi motions. Visual perceptual games were introduced in the third stage, including matching dominoes, puzzles, or drawing. Memory games, photographs, or blackboard tasks were introduced next to stimulate cognition. And in the fifth stage, a closing activity was introduced, such as a small snack or holding hands in a circle.

RESEARCH FINDINGS

Bednar and Kaul (1994) noted that little research has been conducted to isolate group treatment variables and explain the source of treatment effects. They advocate research that measures and describes group process and group outcomes specifically, rather than simply borrowing measures from research with individuals. Although group therapy is sometimes described as the treatment, descriptions of specific treatment processes are often omitted from research, limiting the understanding of group psychotherapy. Nonetheless, there is compelling evidence that group therapy produces positive benefits for a wide range of clients in a wide variety of settings, and that these benefits persist at follow-up in about half the outcome studies. Group treatment is generally found to be as effective as individual therapy in about 75% of studies that included a comparison group; however, group members prefer individual therapy to group therapy (Budman et al., 1988).

Best practices supported by outcomes literature (Bednar & Kaul, 1994) include an orientation of clients to the group that is associated with improved attendance, clearer expectations of the group, and more desirable group behavior. Positive feedback during the group is associated with increased group interaction, increased self-disclosure, and greater cohesiveness and caring among group members. Participants prefer to receive and give positive feedback and are concerned about confidentiality, fear of self-disclosure, and uncertainty about group norms, concerns that were barriers to participation. Self-disclosure by group members or by group leaders was not associated with any clear trends in outcomes.

In rehabilitation, Subramanian (1991) found that an eight-week structured group treatment consisting of cognitive-behavioral strategies, cognitive restructuring, and social skills training was effective in improving both physical and psychological functioning among adults with chronic pain. These positive outcomes were maintained at six months despite the fact that participants did not report a decrease in subjective pain. Older adults did as well as or better than younger adults in learning to cope and function with chronic pain.

PROMINENT STRENGTHS AND WEAKNESSES

The prominent strengths and weakness of group procedures in rehabilitation are summarized in the following section.

Strengths:

- Possible cost-containment with unique benefits to clients
- Therapeutic factors of universality and hope
- Altruism and empowerment of the client
- Social learning through direct and vicarious learning
- Generation of novel solutions to problems
- Amenable to use with multiple theoretical approaches

Weaknesses:

- Limited research on group processes and group outcome
- Limited research on group procedures in rehabilitation
- Few guidelines on problems that are more amenable to group vs. individual counseling
- Difficult logistics of finding a common group meeting time and place
- Persistent desire for individual attention
- Limited methods available that are unique to group counseling
- Description and study of adaptations of group procedures for rehabilitation needed

REFERENCES

Azrin, N. H., Flores, R., & Kaplan, S. J. (1975). Job-finding club: A group-assessed program for obtaining employment. *Behavior Research and Therapy, 13,* 17–27.

Azrin, N. H., & Philip, R. A. (1979). Job club method for the handicapped: A comparative outcome study. *Rehabilitation Counseling Bulleting, 23,* 144–155.

Bednar, R. L., & Kaul, T. (1994). Experiential group research: Can the cannon fire? In A. E. Bergin & S. L. Garfield (Eds.), *Handbook of psychotherapy and behavior change* (4th ed., pp. 631–663). New York: Wiley.

Ben-Yishay, Y., & Daniels-Zide, E. (2000). Examined lives: Outcomes after holistic rehabilitation. *Rehabilitation Psychology, 45,* 112–129.

Bowers, W. A. (1988). Beck's cognitive therapy: An overview for rehabilitation counselors. *Journal of Applied Rehabilitation Counseling, 19,* 43–46.

Budman, S. H., Demby, A., Redondo, J. P., Hannan, M., Feldstein, M., Ring, J., & Springer, T. (1988). Comparative outcome in time-limited and group psychotherapy. *International Journal of Group Psychotherapy, 38,* 63–85.

Burns, D. D. (1990). *Feeling good handbook.* New York: Plume.

Burns, D. D., & Beck, A. T. (1999). *The new mood therapy.* New York: Harper.

Calabro, L. E. (1990). Adjustment to disability: A cognitive-behavioral model for analysis and clinical management. *Journal of Rational-Emotive and Cognitive-Behavior Therapy, 8,* 79–103.

Corey, M. S., & Corey, G. (2001). *Groups: Process and practice* (6th ed.). Pacific Grove, CA: Brooks/Cole.

Corrigan, P. W., Reedy, P., Thadani, D., & Ganet, M. (1995). Correlates of participation and completion in a job club for clients with psychiatric disability. *Rehabilitation Counseling Bulletin, 39,* 42–53.

de Voogd, J. N., Knipping, A. A., Blecourt, A. C. E., & van Rijswijk, M. H. (1993). Treatment of fibromyalgia syndrome with psychomotor therapy and marital counseling. *Musculoskeletal Pain, Myofascial Pain Syndrome, and Fibromyalgia, 1,* 273–281.

Huebner, R. A., & Thomas, K. R. (1995). The relationship between attachment, psychopathology, and childhood disability. *Rehabilitation Psychology, 40,* 111–124.

Huebner, R. A., & Thomas, K. R. (1996). A comparison of the interpersonal characteristics of rehabilitation counseling of students and college students with and without disabilities. *Rehabilitation Counseling Bulletin, 40,* 45–61.

Liberman, R. P., DeRisi, W. J., & Mueser, K. T. (1989). *Social skills training for psychiatric patients.* Boston: Allyn & Bacon.

Marshak, L. E., & Seligman, M. (1993). *Counseling for persons with physical disabilities.* Austin, TX: Pro-Ed.

McKay, M., Davis, M., & Fanning, P. (1998). *Thoughts and feelings: Taking control of your moods and your life.* Oakland, CA: New Harbinger.

McWhirter, P. T., & McWhirter, J. J. (1996). Transition-to-work group: University students with learning disabilities. *Journal for Specialists in Group Work, 21,* 144–148.

Meichenbaum, D. (1985). *Stress inoculation training.* New York: Pergamon.

Mishna, F. (1996). Finding their voice: Group therapy for adolescents with learning disabilities. *Learning Disability Research and Practice, 11,* 249–258.

Newsom, J. T., & Shulz, R. (1998). Caregiving from the recipient's perspective: Negative reactions to being helped. *Health Psychology, 17,* 172–181.

Patterson, J. B., McKenzie, B., & Jenkins, J. (1995). Creating accessible groups for individuals with disabilities. *Journal for Specialists in Group Work, 20,* 76–82.

Posthuma, B. W. (1998). *Small groups in counseling and therapy: Process and leadership* (3rd ed.). Boston: Allyn & Bacon.

Rintala, D. H., Young, M. E., Hart, K. A., & Fuhrer, M. J. (1994). The relationship between the extent of reciprocity with social supporters and measures of depressive symptomatology, impairment, disability, and handicap in persons with spinal cord injuries. *Rehabilitation Psychology, 39,* 15–27.

Rose, J. (1996). Anger management: A group treatment program for people with mental retardation. *Journal of Developmental and Physical Disabilities, 8,* 133–149.

Ross, M. (1997). *Integrative group therapy: Mobilizing coping abilities with the five-stage group.* Bethesda, MD: American Occupational Therapy Association.

Salomone, P. R. (1996). Career counseling and job placement: Theory and practice. In E. M. Szymanski & R. M. Parker (Eds.), *Work and disability* (pp. 365–420). Austin, TX: Pro-Ed.

Shapiro, J. L. (1978). *Methods of group psychotherapy: A tradition of innovation.* Itasca, IL: Peacock.

Stein, S. M. (1996). Group psychotherapy and patients with cognitive impairment. *Journal of Developmental and Physical Disabilities, 8,* 263–273.

Sterrett, E. A. (1998). Use of a job club to increase self-efficacy: A case study of return to work. *Journal of Employment Counseling, 35,* 69–78.

Subramanian, K. (1991). Structured group work for the management of chronic pain: An experimental investigation. *Research on Social Work Practice, 1,* 32–45.

Sweetland, J. D. (1990). Cognitive-behavior therapy and physical disability. *Journal of Rational-Emotive Therapy and Cognitive-Behavior Therapy, 8,* 71–78.

Talmon, T. (1993). *Single session solutions: A guide to practical, effective, and affordable therapy.* Reading, MA: Addison-Wesley.

Teyber, E. (1992). *Interpersonal processes in psychotherapy: A guide for clinical training* (2nd ed.). Pacific Grove, CA: Brooks/Cole.

Tuckman, B. W. (1965). Developmental sequence in small groups. *Psychological Bulletin, 63,* 384–399.

White, M., & Epston, D. (1990). *Narrative means to therapeutic ends.* New York: Norton.

Wright, B. A. (1983). *Physical disability: A psychosocial approach.* New York: HarperCollins.

Yalom, I. D. (1995). *Theory and practice of group psychotherapy* (4th ed.). New York: Basic Books.

Zimmerman, M. A., & Warschausky, S. (1998). Empowerment theory for rehabilitation research: Conceptual and methodological issues. *Rehabilitation Psychology, 43,* 3–16.

Chapter 14

Family Counseling

John F. Kosciulek

D isability affects not only the person who is born with or acquires a disability, but also his or her entire family system. In fact, Brooks (1991) and Kosciulek (1995) have suggested that the impact of disability is at least as great for families as for the affected person, and family members are often more distressed than the person with the disability. Thus, coping with the impact of disability is one of the most difficult tasks that can confront a family (Power, 1995). Ongoing challenges that families of individuals with disabilities may encounter include (a) emotional, personality, behavioral, and physical changes in the family member with the disability; (b) lack of information and appropriate services; (c) financial burden as a result of disability-related medical, rehabilitation, education, and independent living needs; and (d) emotional strain from prolonged caregiving. Functional consequences of such difficulties for families include marital discord, psychological distress, substance abuse, depletion of family finances, and social isolation (Berry & Hardman, 1998; Williams, 1991).

In most programs that deal with individuals with disabilities, families are perceived as resources in facilitating rehabilitation. However, family members themselves are a high-risk group for physical, emotional, and social difficulties. Families require help in their own right and not only as a by-product of the counseling or rehabilitation process with the family member with the disability.

In consideration of the ongoing family life challenges that families of persons with disabilities may experience, the number of families who may seek and benefit from the services of counselors is substantial. Counselors working with families in a variety of settings, including medical facilities, vocational rehabilitation agencies, community mental health centers, family clinics, and private practice, can expect to serve families of persons with disabilities. Thus, an increased awareness of the impact of disability on families will enable counselors to meet the needs of individual family members and entire family systems.

The purpose of this chapter is to present a model that assists counselors in understanding the family adaptation process following disability onset. The Resiliency Model of Family Stress, Adjustment, and Adaptation (Kosciulek, McCubbin, & McCubbin, 1993) is offered as a clinical and theoretical family stress and coping framework that suggests effective assessment and intervention approaches with families of individuals with disabilities. Following presentation of the Resiliency Model framework, specific strategies for counseling families of persons with disabilities are provided.

RESILIENCY MODEL OF FAMILY STRESS, ADJUSTMENT, AND ADAPTATION

The Resiliency Model of Family Stress, Adjustment, and Adaptation (Kosciulek et al., 1993), a stress and coping framework based on a family systems approach, is a clinical and conceptual framework that is particularly useful for describing a family's response to disability. The Resiliency Model has as its origin the seminal family stress and coping work of Reuben Hill (1958), the Double ABCX Model of Family Adjustment and Adaptation (McCubbin & Patterson, 1983), and the more recent Typology Model of Family Adjustment and Adaptation (McCubbin & McCubbin, 1989). These original efforts focus upon the following factors: (a) illness and disability as potential family stressors, (b) family resistance resources (e.g., economic, psychological), (c) the family's appraisal of a disability, and (d) family coping patterns designed to protect the family from breakdown and facilitate adjustment to disability. The Resiliency Model represents a contemporary updating, reframing, and expansion of the earlier theory-building efforts and underscores the importance of family adaptation, rather than adjustment, to disability (Kosciulek et al., 1993).

Adjustment Phase of the Resiliency Model

The Resiliency Model is composed of two major phases: adjustment and adaptation. During the adjustment phase, families attempt to maintain patterns of interaction, roles, and rules that have been established to guide day-to-day family activity. The adjustment phase is characterized by a series of interacting components that shape the family process and outcomes. These components include (a) residual problems in the member with the disability as a family stressor, (b) family vulnerability to stress, and (c) family functioning patterns or types. In addition, family capabilities such as resources, coping, and appraisal serve as buffers to the stress imposed on families by disability.

Outcomes of family adjustment efforts may vary along a continuum from the more positive outcome of bonadjustment to the other extreme of maladjustment (McCubbin & McCubbin, 1991). Bonadjustment is characterized by the maintenance of established family functioning patterns and a sense of family control over environmental influence, while maladjustment is characterized by the deterioration of individual family member development and family ability to accomplish life tasks (Patterson, 1988).

In some instances, unfortunately, the most common consequences of disability for the family may be negative (Brooks, 1991). Existing family capabilities may be inadequate to meet the emotional, social, and financial demands placed on the family as a result of having a member with a disability. Families dealing with the chronic hardships of disability are not likely to achieve stability without making substantial changes in family roles, priorities, goals, and rules. In these situations involving the disruption of established family patterns, the family in all likelihood will experience maladjustment and a resulting state of crisis (Kosciulek et al., 1993).

Family Crisis

Family crisis has been conceptualized as a continuous condition denoting the amount of disruptiveness, disorganization, or incapacitation in the family social system (Burr, 1973). Crisis is a state of tension brought about by demand-capability imbalance in the family. Families in crisis after disability onset have a situational inability to restore stability, are often trapped in a cyclical trial-and-error struggle to reduce tensions that tends to make matters worse rather than better, and tries to make small changes in the family structure and patterns of interaction when newly instituted patterns of family functioning are required. It is important to note that, in the Resiliency Model, a family "in crisis" does not carry the stigmatizing judgment that somehow the family unit has failed or is dysfunctional (McCubbin & McCubbin, 1991). Rather, family crisis denotes family disorganization and a demand for basic changes in the family patterns of functioning in order to restore stability, order, and a sense of coherence. This movement to initiate changes in the family system's pattern of functioning marks the beginning of the adaptation phase of the Resiliency Model.

Adaptation Phase of the Resiliency Model

Family adaptation is the central concept in understanding the focus of the family's struggle to manage the situation of having a member with a disability over time. It is used to describe the outcome of family efforts to bring a new level of balance, harmony, coherence, and a satisfactory level of functioning to a family following disability onset (Kosciulek et al., 1993). The adaptation phase of the Resiliency Model, as shown in Figure 14.1, may be described as follows:

> The level of family adaptation in response to a crisis situation (e.g., disability onset) is determined by the pile-up of demands on or in the family system created by the crisis situation, life cycle changes, and unresolved strains; interacting with the family's level of regenerativity determined in part by the concurrent pile-up of stressors, transitions, and strains; interacting with the family's typology (e.g., rhythmic); interacting with the family's strengths; interacting with the family's appraisal of the situation (i.e., meaning attached to the situation) and the family's schema (i.e., worldview); interacting with the support from friends and the community (i.e., social support); interacting with the family's problem-solving and coping responses to the total family situation.

Figure 14.1 illustrates how family adaptation, similar to family adjustment, occurs along a continuum of outcomes that reflect family efforts to achieve a balance in functioning. The positive end of the continuum, called bonadaptation, is characterized by (a) positive physical and mental health of individual family members, (b) continued facilitation and promotion of individual member development, (c) optimal role functioning of individual members, (d) the maintenance of a family unit that can accomplish its life-cycle tasks, and (e) the maintenance of family integrity and sense of control over environmental influence. Family maladaptation, at the negative end of the continuum, is characterized by a continued imbalance at one of two family functioning levels: (a) individual-to-family, or (b) family-to-community. Maladaptation may also occur when achievement of a balance at both levels is accomplished, but at a price in terms of (a) deterioration of individual member health and/or development, or (b) deterioration of family unit integrity, autonomy, or the ability to accomplish life-cycle tasks. An important distinction about family adaptation in contrast to adjustment is that adaptation usually evolves over a longer period of time and has long-term consequences (Kosciulek et al., 1993; McCubbin & McCubbin, 1989).

Counselors must be aware that the process of family adaptation to disability continues for many years following initial medical and rehabilita-

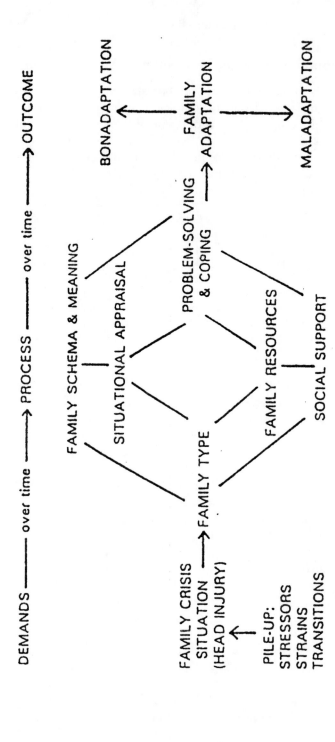

FIGURE 14.1   Adaptation phase of the resiliency model of family stress, adjustment, and adaption.

Note: From J. F. Kosciulek, M. A. McCubbin, & H. I. McCubbin, A theoretical framework for family adaptation to head injury, *Journal of Rehabilitation*, 59(3), p. 42

tion services (Kurylo, Elliott, & Shewchuk, 2001). The demands placed on the family by disability, as well as family functioning over time, determine the level of family adaptation (Kosciulek et al., 1993). As shown in Figure 14.1, the Resiliency Model contains multiple interacting components that describe the family adaptation process. Each component will be discussed as it relates to family adaptation to disability; also, ways to develop effective clinical plans for family assessment and intervention will be suggested.

Family Demands: Pile-Up

Because family crises after the onset of a congenital or acquired disability evolve and are resolved over a period of time, families are seldom dealing with disability in isolation. A pile-up of demands following disability onset is commonplace and a critical factor that should be taken into account as part of clinical family assessment. Six broad categories of stresses and strains contribute to a pile-up of demands on the family system.

The Disability and Related Hardships Over Time

When a family member experiences a disability, specific hardships associated with the disability may increase or intensify the difficulties that families face. Hardships associated with disability can include the ambiguity surrounding the disability, such as in the case of psychiatric disabilities, the course of long-term outcome, increased marital or sibling relationship strains, parent-child conflicts, and increased emotional or financial hardships (Brooks, 1991; Williams, 1991).

Normative Transitions

Families are not static social units. They go through a predictable and expected series of transitions as the result of (a) the normal development of young members (e.g., the need for nurturing), (b) the career development of adult members, (c) changes in the extended family system such as the death of a grandparent, and (d) predictable family changes (e.g., children entering school, retirement). Therefore, in addition to the issues surrounding the disability, family assessment procedures conducted by counselors must consider what other family life-cycle issues might be pertinent for a particular family (DePompei & Zarski, 1991).

Prior Strains Accumulated Over Time

Family systems carry with them some residual of strain that may be the result of unresolved hardships from earlier stressors, transitions, or illness. Prior strains may be exacerbated in the face of disability and consequently contribute to the pile-up of family difficulties. For example, Livingston (1987) found that the preinjury psychological and physical health of family members was related to family burden after a member sustained a traumatic brain injury. Therefore, upon intake, counselors should gather information concerning predisability family functioning (e.g., relationship dynamics). Such information may provide important clues for planning appropriate family intervention strategies.

Situational Demands and Contextual Difficulties

Often, in cases where families struggle with a member's disability, the medical and rehabilitation systems that families are required to work with may create additional demands that may undermine, if not curtail, family system functioning. For example, the continuum of brain injury rehabilitation services spans from trauma units, to rehabilitation centers, to vocational rehabilitation agencies. The requirements of a family during inpatient medical rehabilitation vary dramatically from community-based vocational rehabilitation. Anecdotal reports document family frustration with the transition to these varying agencies (Brooks, 1991; Williams & Kay, 1991). Thus, counselors must be aware that transitions from one service system to another create additional family burden (e.g., time commitment, financial expense).

Consequences of Family Efforts to Cope

The fifth source of pile-up includes stresses and strains that emerge from specific behaviors or strategies that a family may have used in the adjustment phase, such as increased rigidity or suppression of anger (McCubbin & McCubbin, 1991). For example, Willer, Allen, Durnan, and Ferry (1990) listed suppression of feelings and frustrations as a coping strategy used by siblings of persons with disabilities. Such coping efforts, while initially perceived as a good strategy, may produce unanticipated burdens on the family. Acting-out behavior by siblings over time due to suppression of feelings may cause more family stress than addressing individual member needs early following disability onset.

Intrafamily and Social Ambiguity

Because the family is altering its structure, roles, and responsibilities, adaptation after disability onset has a certain amount of ambiguity and uncertainty. Boss (1980) has suggested that boundary ambiguity within the family system is a major stressor since a family needs to be sure of its components, that is, who is inside and outside family boundaries, both physically and psychologically. Disruption and ambiguity in family structure may follow disability onset because the member with the disability can no longer assume the same role (e.g., primary breadwinner). In addition, it is probable that families will face the strain of social ambiguity. For example, the ways in which families should best manage a member who has sustained severe physical and cognitive limitations due to brain injury are not clearly prescribed. The lack of long-term care guidelines and appropriate support services results in additional burden on the family that has a member with a significant disability (Kosciulek, 1995; Kurylo et al., 2001).

FAMILY TYPES AND NEWLY INSTITUTED PATTERNS OF FUNCTIONING

The next component of the Resiliency Model, family typology, is a set of basic family patterns of behavior that explain how the family system typically operates. Research on families faced with an illness-induced crisis has introduced two family system types that are critical for positive family adaptation to disability. The first type, regenerative families, is characterized by coherence and hardiness (i.e., internal strengths and locus of control). Rhythmic families, the second type, focus on family time together and routines as the family's way of maintaining family life in the face of a chronic stressor (McCubbin, Thompson, Pirner, & McCubbin, 1988).

Because a disability calls for changes in a family's established patterns of functioning, a family's typology is often dramatically and permanently altered. Such instances call for family patterns aimed at establishing a new typology. Counseling interventions focused on developing effective family types, such as regenerative and rhythmic, will enable families to achieve the optimum level of adaptation possible following the onset of a disability.

Family Strengths, Resources, and Capabilities

In the Resiliency Model, capability is defined as the potential of the family for meeting its demands. Two major sets of capabilities are emphasized:

(a) resources, which are what the family has; and (b) coping behaviors and strategies, which are what individual members and the family as a unit do to deal with demands (Kosciulek et al., 1993). Three potential resources available to the family after disability onset include individual members, the family working as a unit, and the community, which includes counselors and the disability service system.

Personal Resources

Some of the important personal resources that may be used by the family in adaptation to disability include (a) the innate intelligence of family members; (b) personality traits (e.g., sense of humor); (c) physical and emotional health; (d) a sense of mastery, which is the belief that one has some control over the circumstances of one's life; and (e) self-esteem. The importance of accurately assessing the personal resources of individual members cannot be overstated. For example, counselors may overestimate the basic knowledge of biological matters and the emotional and cognitive abilities of family members to process new medical and disability-related information that may be highly emotionally threatening (Brooks, 1991). Such errors in clinical judgment may lead to ineffective family intervention and inappropriate long-term planning.

Family System Resources

Two prominent family system resources critical for successful adaptation to disability are cohesion and adaptability. Cohesion is the unity running through the family, and adaptability is the family's capacity to meet obstacles and shift course (Olson, Sprenkle, & Russell, 1979). Another resource, family organization, includes agreement, clarity, and consistency in the family role and rule structure. Since it is often disrupted after disability, counselors would do well to assist families with reestablishing an organizational structure immediately following the onset of a disability. Other family resources that were previously mentioned, family time together and family routines, are critically important and relatively reliable indices of family integration. Families that make an effort to maintain basic family routines that create family continuity and stability may have a higher probability of enduring than those families that fail to maintain routines.

Community Resources and Supports

Community resources and supports include all those social, rehabilitation, friendship, and community-based activities outside the family that the family unit, faced with a disability, may call upon, access, and use to cope with the situation and to bring demands under control. The services of institutions, such as schools, churches, and employers, are also resources for the family. At the broad social level, local, state, and federal disability policies that enhance and support persons with disabilities and their families may also be viewed as community resources (Kosciulek, 1999).

The community resource that is perhaps most influential in facilitating positive family adaptation to disability is social support. Social support is viewed as one of the primary buffers between stress and health breakdown (Cobb, 1976). A study by Kozloff (1987) marked an important step in understanding the importance of social support in family adaptation to disability. Kozloff found that over time the social networks of individuals with disabilities decreased in size and increased in density. Thus, as family members served more and more functions to meet their member's needs, they became more socially isolated and the quality of family social support decreased markedly. The findings in Kozloff's study indicate that counselors must be keenly aware that a key ingredient in successful family adaptation to disability is meaningful social support.

Family Situational Appraisal

The next component of the Resiliency Model is the family's appraisal of the disability situation. Families assess the degree of controllability of the disability, the amount of change expected of the family system, and whether or not the family is capable of responding effectively to the situation. Given the often ambiguous nature of disability, family appraisal is crucial in shaping positive adaptation. For instance, Florian, Katz, and Lahav (1989) found that a family's positive or negative perception of a member's emotional and behavioral functioning following brain injury influenced the family's overall response to the brain injury. Viewing a disability as a manageable family challenge rather than as a catastrophe will affect how a family adapts over time.

Family Schema and Meaning

Sachs (1991) addressed the importance of family themes, identity, and relationships with the outside world following disability onset. This global view of the family system is the family's schema. In the face of disability, the family is called upon to appraise its past and future in an attempt to give meaning to the disability and the resulting changes in the family system needed to facilitate adaptation. Families who reveal a strong schema emphasize the family unit, shared values and goals, and investment in the collective "we" rather than "I," all guided by a relativistic view of life circumstances and willingness to accept less than perfect solutions to their demands (McCubbin & McCubbin, 1991). The family schema is considered a relatively stable reference against which situational appraisals are contrasted and shaped.

Family adaptation is likely to require changes in the family schema, particularly the family's values, goals, expectations, rules, and priorities (Kosciulek et al., 1993). Developing a shared sense of family meaning to changes created by disability is a difficult process, achieved only through perseverance, negotiation, and a shared commitment to the family. What meanings families give to the newly reshaped family unit are important to counselors seeking to foster positive family adaptation to disability.

Adaptive Coping and Management

The process of acquiring, allocating, and using resources for meeting demands is a critical aspect of family adaptation to disability. The family system can be characterized as a resource exchange network. Coping is viewed as the action for this exchange. In the Resiliency Model, coping behavior is a specific effort (covert or overt) by which an individual family member or the family unit functioning as a whole attempts to reduce or manage a demand on the family (Kosciulek et al., 1993). Coping patterns are generalized, rather than stressor-specific, responses to different kinds of stressful situations. Four categories characterize the ways in which coping facilitates family adaptation to disability:

1. Coping can involve direct action to eliminate or reduce the number and/or intensity of demands created by the disability.
2. Coping can involve direct action to acquire additional resources not already available to the family unit faced with a member with a disability.
3. Managing tension associated with ongoing strains resulting from a disability (e.g., emotional, financial) is another function of coping.
4. Coping can also involve family-level appraisal to create, shape, and evaluate meanings that families may give to a disability to make it more constructive, manageable, and acceptable.

These coping strategies, which operate simultaneously in the situation of a disability-induced family crisis, serve as a guide for understanding the process of family adaptation to disability.

Summary of the Process of Family Adaptation to Disability

Family adaptation is a process in which families engage in direct response to excessive demands, depleted resources, and the realization that systematic changes are needed to restore functional stability and improve family satisfaction in the face of a disability. Once changes have been instituted as new family patterns, family adaptation is enhanced by efforts to encourage family members to value, accept, and affirm these changes over time (Kosciulek et al., 1993). Coping strategies play a critical role in adaptation. They facilitate the family's ability to work together as a unit to achieve a lifestyle not normally attained by the efforts of only one member, but which is achieved by family interdependence and mutuality.

Family adaptation is not confined strictly to internal changes. It is not sufficient for families to merely restructure internally. They must also maintain a level of rapport and interaction with the community at large. A quality social support system and long-term community support services (e.g., respite, support groups) are critical ingredients for positive family adaptation to disability (Kosciulek, 1995). Following disability onset, counseling assessment and intervention efforts should be aimed at current issues affecting family life, the pile-up of demands, effects of family coping efforts, and family capabilities and social support. By understanding these dynamic family properties, counselors will be in a position to guide families toward successful adaptation to having a member with a disability.

FAMILY COUNSELING STRATEGIES

Marshak and Seligman (1993) presented a guide that seems particularly useful for conceptualizing the intensity of counselor interface with the family needs and preferences, noting that the intervention of counselors with families who have a member with a disability could occur at any of the following five levels:

- Level 1—Focus on the individual client (emphasis on the needs of the client, especially his or her problems; no direct involvement with the client's family)
- Level 2—Provide information for the family (minimum involvement with the client's family, restricted to "fact" or "information" communication)
- Level 3—Provide emotional support for the family (encourage family members to disclose their feelings; seek to show sympathy and emotional support to family members)

- Level 4—Provide structured assessment and intervention (provide well-planned support in reducing family stress and tension; empower the family by changing the family patterns associated with the disability)
- Level 5—Provide family therapy (professional intervention for families that become dysfunctional due to disability)

Many counselors are able to provide high-quality intervention with families at Levels 1 through 3 with relative ease. However, according to Roessler, Chung, and Rubin (1998), in order for effective family counseling to occur at Levels 4 and 5, counselors must possess both structural and relationship skills. Structural skills refer to the counselor's ability to identify problems or needs, define outcomes and alternatives, and confront family members' resistance. Relationship skills include the capacities to build rapport with and express empathic understanding to families.

Dell Orto and Power (1994) provided an additional perspective on counseling families of persons with disabilities by differentiating between the counselor's intervention at the acute and extended phases of adjustment to disability. During the acute phase, the individual with the disability and his or her family encounter and cope with the onset of the impact of disability. During this initial phase, the family may be experiencing fear, shock, and distress. The role of the counselor at this stage is congruent with crisis intervention, with an emphasis on listening, understanding, observing, supporting, and encouraging. Dell Orto and Power (1994) report that counseling objectives during the acute phase include:

1. establishing a trusting relationship with the family,
2. learning early in family intervention the meaning of the disability to the family members, their expectations for the client and for each other, and family goals,
3. attempting to build self-esteem among the family member, and
4. observing the communication patterns among the family members.

During the extended phase of counseling, the client and his or her family members are in the process of gradually adapting to the disability. The counselor is then to be an advocate and resource person, emphasizing a proactive intervention approach (Dell Orto & Power, 1994). Counseling objectives in the extended phase include (a) providing information, (b) identifying and prioritizing presenting problems, (c) improving family interaction, and (d) developing and implementing treatment plans.

Muir, Rosenthal, and Diehl (1990) also have provided useful clinical guidelines for structuring the counseling process. They stated that counseling should help families deal with the anxiety, guilt, and other emotional reactions to disability and should reinforce their feelings of adequacy, self-worth, and competence. According to Muir et al., counselors should assist individual family members with learning how to draw on their own strengths while using the family unit as a source of support. Further, counselors must encourage families to explore their concerns regarding changing roles, sibling relationships, marital issues, and community reactions to disability onset within a family. Counseling should also help families adjust to the daily disruptions caused by disability, work to restore relationships, and approximate a normal family lifestyle. To achieve these objectives, counseling must be designed to meet such long-term family needs as maintaining a social support network, respite, obtaining services for the member with the disability, and managing legal and financial matters.

Given the potential complexity of the disability and its deleterious effect on families, a team approach, in which one cofacilitator specializes in family issues and the other specializes in disability sequelae (e.g., impact of psychiatric disability on a family), may be a very effective intervention format (Kosciulek, 1995). Another issue facing the counselor is whether to include the person with the disability in family counseling sessions. Muir et al. (1990) indicated that counselors must exercise caution when considering whether to involve the family member with the disability, particularly in the situation of a cognitive or emotional disability, since the individual must be able to participate in a meaningful way. DePompei and Zarski (1991), however, believe that the severity of the disability is not a reason to exclude the person with the disability from counseling sessions. These authors state that if the therapist has reasons to believe that the person with the disability can learn and profit from the experience, family counseling can be a meaningful intervention for the entire family.

In situations in which family members feel uncomfortable or unable to express their feelings and concerns in the presence of the family member with the disability, counseling with individual members or family subgroups may be necessary. Spouses, parents, and siblings may express, or otherwise demonstrate, the need for individual counseling sessions. Muir et al. (1990) pointed out that this may occur for a variety of reasons, such as greater acceptance of professional counseling help by one individual than by the rest of the family, the need to express feelings that would be too uncomfortable to express in the presence of other family members, or simply greater comfort with individual counseling than with the group process.

The Resiliency Model and family and disability literature suggest several additional counseling approaches that may be particularly effective with families of persons with disabilities. One approach involves emphasizing the mutuality of responsibility for family problems and shifting the burden of causality from the member with the disability to the dysfunctional areas of the family system. A second approach focuses on strengthening the positive aspects of the family system (e.g., coping styles and communication patterns). Another potentially effective counseling approach may involve exploring dysfunctional interaction patterns by reenacting family conflicts and assisting family members in substituting conflict resolution strategies that are acceptable within their family system. Finally, prescribing homework assignments for the family to practice outside counseling sessions may foster generalization of behavior change.

Facilitating Family Social Support

As previously stated, a key ingredient in successful family adaptation to disability is meaningful social support. Thus, in addition to direct counseling, counselors may effect positive family adaptation to having a member with a disability by assisting families with developing support networks. Strong social supports may alleviate family difficulties related to social isolation and the constant care of a member with a significant disability (Kurylo et al., 2001). Primary resources for developing long-term family supports are the various national and state organizations that provide information and supports for individuals with disabilities and their families. Examples of such organizations include the National Brain Injury Association and the National Alliance for the Mentally Ill. Families can contact such organizations at the national, state, or local level and receive information and guidance about resources in their geographic area related to their specific needs, such as information on educational and rehabilitation programs, support groups for the member with the disability and family unit, federal, state, and local financial assistance programs, and related community-based services (Berry & Hardman, 1998; Roessler et al., 1998).

The family's participation in support groups and contact with other families in similar disability-related situations are important supplements to professional counseling. The education and emotional support provided by support groups complement the support provided by the counselor. There are some things that families may appreciate or understand only after communicating with other families who have had similar experiences. For example, decisions about treatment alternatives and difficult stages in rehabilitation processes may be made more readily by the family if they have discussed the issues with families who have made similar decisions (Sachs, 1991). Many counselors in the rehabilitation field view this family-to-family support as a crucial element in helping families work through the adaptation process (Kosciulek, 1995). More importantly, family members themselves find this type of mutual support and information exchange extremely valuable (Muir et al., 1990).

In addition to encouraging family participation, counselors may benefit from actual participation in family support groups. Listening and interacting with families in a support group environment will give the counselor a larger view of the family's experience. With this experience, the counselor can be more sensitive and effective in his or her work with the family.

CONCLUDING REMARKS

Coping with the impact of disability is one of the most difficult tasks that can confront a family (Power, 1995). Effective counseling with families of persons with disabilities thus can be instrumental for facilitating positive family adaptation to disability. As presented in this chapter, the Resiliency Model of Family Stress, Adjustment, and Adaptation (Kosciulek et al., 1993) may assist counselors in understanding the family adaptation process following disability onset and suggests effective assessment and intervention approaches with families of individuals with disabilities. Further, the specific counseling strategies provided in this chapter should help counselors expand their counseling repertoire to include those skills and techniques necessary to effectively serve families of persons with disabilities.

REFERENCES

Berry, J. O., & Hardman, M. L. (1998). *Lifespan perspectives on the family and disability*. Boston: Allyn & Bacon.

Boss, P. (1980). Normative family stress: Family boundary changes across the lifespan. *Family Relations, 29*, 445–450.

Brooks, D. N. (1991). The head-injured family. *Journal of Clinical and Experimental Neuropsychology, 13*, 155–188.

Burr, W. F. (1973). *Theory construction and the sociology of the family*. New York: Wiley.

Cobb, S. (1976). Social support as a moderator of life stress. *Psychosomatic Medicine, 38*, 300–314.

Dell Orto, A. E., & Power, P. W. (1994). *Head injury and the family: A life and living perspective.* Winter Park, FL: PMD Publishers Group.

DePompei, R., & Zarski, J. J. (1991). Assessment of the family. In J. M. Williams & T. Kay (Eds.), *Head injury: A family matter* (pp. 101–120). Baltimore: Paul H. Brookes.

Florian, V., Katz, S., & Lahav, V. (1989). Impact of traumatic brain damage on family dynamics and functioning: A review. *Brain Injury, 3,* 219–233.

Hill, R. (1958). Generic features of families under stress. *Social Casework, 49,* 139–150.

Kosciulek, J. F. (1995). Impact of head injury on families: An introduction for family counselors. *Family Journal: Counseling and Therapy for Couples and Families, 3,* 116–125.

Kosciulek, J. F. (1999). Implications of consumer direction for disability policy development and rehabilitation service delivery. *Journal of Disability Policy Development, 11,* 82–94.

Kosciulek, J. F., McCubbin, M. A., & McCubbin, H. I. (1993). A theoretical framework for family adaptation to head injury. *Journal of Rehabilitation, 59*(3), 40–45.

Kozloff, R. (1987). Networks of social support and the outcome from severe head injury. *Journal of Head Trauma Rehabilitation, 2,* 14–23.

Kurylo, M. F., Elliott, T. R., & Shewchuk, R. M. (2001). Focus on the family caregiver: A problem-solving training intervention. *Journal of Counseling and Development, 79,* 275–281.

Livingston, M. G. (1987). Head injury: The relative's response. *Brain Injury, 1,* 33–39.

Marshak, L. E., & Seligman, M. (1993). *Counseling persons with physical disabilities: Theoretical and clinical perspectives.* Austin, TX: Pro-Ed.

McCubbin, M. A., & McCubbin, H. I. (1989). Theoretical orientations to family stress and coping. In C. R. Figley (Ed.), *Treating stress in families* (pp. 3–43). New York: Brunner-Mazel.

McCubbin, M. A., & McCubbin, H. I. (1991). Family stress theory and assessment: The Resiliency Model of family stress, adjustment, and adaptation. In H. I. McCubbin & A. I. Thompson (Eds.), *Family assessment inventories for research and practice* (pp. 3–32). Madison: University of Wisconsin-Madison.

McCubbin, H. I., & Patterson, J. M. (1983). The family stress process: The Double ABCX Model of adjustment and adaptation. In H. I. McCubbin, M. B. Sussman, & J. M. Patterson (Eds.), *Social stress and the family: Advances and developments in family stress theory and research* (pp. 7–37). New York: Haworth Press.

McCubbin, H. I., Thompson, A. I., Pirner, P., & McCubbin, M. A. (1988). *Family types and family strengths: A life cycle and ecological perspective.* Edina, MN: Burgess.

Muir, C., Rosenthal, M., & Diehl, L. N. (1990). Methods of family intervention. In M. Rosenthal, E. R. Griffith, M. R. Bond, & J. D. Miller (Eds.), *Rehabilitation of the adult and child with traumatic brain injury* (2nd ed., pp. 433–448). Philadelphia: Davis.

Olson, D., Sprenkle, D., & Russell, C. (1979). Circumplex model of marital and family systems. *Family Process, 18,* 3–28.

Patterson, J. M. (1988). Families experiencing stress. *Family Systems Medicine, 6,* 202–237.

Power, P. W. (1995). Family. In A. E. Dell Orto & R. P. Marinelli (Eds.), *Encyclopedia of disability and rehabilitation* (pp. 321–326). New York: MacMillan.

Roessler, R. T., Chung, W., & Rubin, S. E. (1998). Family-centered rehabilitation case management. In R. T. Roessler & S. E. Rubin, *Case management and rehabilitation counseling: Procedures and techniques* (3rd ed., pp. 231–254). Austin, TX: Pro-Ed.

Sachs, P. R. (1991). *Treating families of brain-injury survivors*. New York: Springer.

Willer, B., Allen, K., Durnan, M. C., & Ferry, A. (1990). Problems and coping strategies of mothers, siblings and young adult males with traumatic brain injury. *Canadian Journal of Rehabilitation, 3*, 167–173.

Williams, J. M. (1991). Family reaction to head injury. In J. M. Williams & T. Kay (Eds.), *Head injury: A family matter* (pp. 81–99). Baltimore: Paul H. Brookes.

Williams, J. M., & Kay, T. (Eds.). (1991). *Head injury: A family matter*. Baltimore: Paul H. Brookes.

Chapter 15

Career Counseling

Edna Mora Szymanski, Penny Willmering, Molly Tschopp, Timothy Tansey, and Nathalie Mizelle

Career counseling (Hershenson & Liesener, 2003) is a central element of the services offered by rehabilitation counselors to people with disabilities. This importance derives from two facts. First, work is a central element in human life that is connected with both economic and psychological well-being (Quick, Murphy, Hurrell, & Orman, 1992; Szymanski, Ryan, Merz, Treviño, & Johnston-Rodriguez, 1996). Second, people with disabilities have significantly higher rates of unemployment and underemployment than the general population (Louis Harris & Associates, 1994).

The theoretical foundation of career counseling is threefold. First, career counseling is clearly counseling (Gysbers, Heppner, & Johnston, 1998) and, thus, is informed by counseling theories and research (see other chapters in this volume). Second, career counseling is concerned with vocational behavior and is thus informed by theories of career development, occupational choice, and vocational behavior (Gysbers et al.; Savickas & Walsh, 1996). Third, because of the complexity of the connection between career theories and practice (see, e.g., Savickas & Walsh, 1996), there is a separate body of literature relating to the practice of career counseling.

THEORIES OF VOCATIONAL BEHAVIOR

Theories from a variety of disciplines (e.g., counseling, business, vocational psychology, sociology) inform vocational behavior. "Each academic discipline happily develops its own concepts but does not feel obligated to connect them to the concepts that flow from other disciplines" (Schein, 1986, pp. 315–316). Recently, however, there have been efforts to examine the convergence of some career theories (Savickas & Lent, 1994a). Although some convergence has occurred over time, the multiple theories remain important lenses from which to interpret research and understand behavior (Savickas & Lent, 1994b). "In short, all theories are incomplete formulations that will never be adept at answering everyone's questions" (Holland, 1996, p. 6).

Theories, Constructs, Processes, and the Ecological Model

A theory is "a set of interrelated constructs (concepts), definitions, and propositions that present a systematic view of phenomena by specifying relations among variables, with the purpose of explaining and predicting phenomena" (Kerlinger & Lee, 2000, p. 11). Theories of vocational behavior explain how people choose careers, develop in their career and work lives, and negotiate the world of work (Szymanski, 2001). They also form the basis for assessment instruments that are used to predict behavior and assist individuals in decision making, computer-assisted career guidance systems, and career interventions (Savickas & Walsh, 1996). Readers are referred to Brown, Brooks, and Associates (1996) for an overview of most of the theories, and to Szymanski and Hershenson (1998) and Szymanski, Enright, Hershenson, & Ettinger (2003) for a discussion of the theories and their application to people with disabilities.

Szymanski and colleagues (Szymanski et al., 2003; Szymanski, Hershenson, Enright, & Ettinger, 1996; Szymanski & Hershenson, 1998) have reduced the theories to an underlying group of constructs and processes that constitute the ecological model of vocational behavior. Figure 15.1 shows the constructs and processes, their definitions, and their interrelation. Table 15.1 shows the relationship of each construct and process to the theories of vocational behavior. The ecological model can be used for assessment and planning of interventions in vocational rehabilitation (Szymanski & Hershenson, 1998) and rehabilitation psychology (Szymanski, 2001) and has been used to interpret research results (see Conyers, Koch, & Szymanski, 1998).

Applicability of Theories

Applicability to the Changing World of Work

The workplace is changing (see, e.g., Gowing, Kraft, & Quick, 1998). This means that theories must evolve in order to more adequately represent the

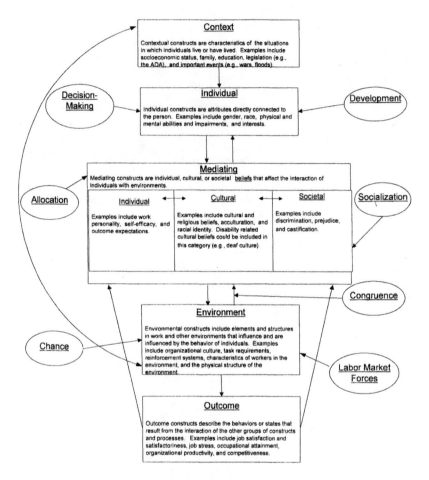

FIGURE 15.1 Vocational behavior of people with disabilities: an ecological model. *Congruence* is the process of relative match or mismatch between individuals and their environments. *Development* describes the process that produces systematic changes over time, which are interwoven with characteristics and perceptions of individuals and reciprocally influenced by the environment. *Decision-making* is the process by which individuals consider career related alternatives and formulate decisions. *Socialization* is the process by which people learn work and life roles. *Allocation* is the process by which societal gatekeepers use external criteria to channel individuals into or exclude them from specific directions. *Chance* is the occurrence of unforeseen events or encounters. *Labor market forces* are the economic and business forces that affect individual and organizational opportunities.

TABLE 15.1 Relationship of the Ecological Model to the Constructs and Processes of Career Development Theories

Model Elements	Super's Theory	Holland's Typology	Trait-Factor	LTCC[a]	MWA[b]	HWAT[c]	SCCT[d]	DC[e]	S&E[f]	Org.[g]
Constructs										
Individual	X	X	X	X	X	X	X	X	X	X
Contextual	X			X			X	X	X	
Mediating	X			X		X	X	X	X	
Environment	X	X	X	X	X	X	X	X	X	X
Outcome	X	X	X	X	X	X	X	X	X	X
Processes										
Development	X			X						
Decision-Making				X		X	X	X	X	X
Congruence	X	X	X		X					
Socialization	X			X		X	X	X	X	
Allocation								X	X	
Chance				X		X	X	X		
Labor Market Forces	X			X		X	X	X	X	X

Source: From "Career Development Theories, Constructs, and Research: Implications for People with Disabilities," by E. M. Szymanski, M. S. Enright, D. B. Hershenson, and J. M. Ettinger, in press in E. M. Szymanski and R. M. Parker (Eds.), *Work and Disability* (2nd ed.). Austin, TX: PrO-Ed. Copyright by Pro-Ed. Reprinted with permission.

[a] LTCC = Krumboltz's Learning Theory of Career Counseling; [b] MWA = Minnesota Theory of Work Adjustment; [c] HWAT = Hershenson's Work Adjustment Theory; [d] SCCT = Social Cognitive Career Theory; [e] DC = Developmental Contextualism; [f] S&E = Sociological and Economic Theories; [g] Org. = Organizational Theories.

current reality (Herr, 1996). Factors that must be addressed include, but are not limited to, the following:

> [a] the globalization of the workforce; . . . [b] a growing global labor surplus; . . . [c] organizational transformations in the workplace; . . . [d] the rise of a contingent workforce in the United States and around the world; . . . [e] the rising importance of the knowledge worker and of literacy, numeracy, communication, and computer literacy skills as prerequisites for employability and lifelong learning in many of the emerging occupations and in the primary labor market; . . . [f] the growing awareness of linkages between positive and negative career experiences and mental health, self-esteem, purposefulness, physical well-being, the ability to support and maintain a family, and the perception that one has life options and can practice an internal locus of control; . . . [g] the recent appearance of new government policy and legislation on the school-to-work transition and work-based learning that address the problems of work-bound youth; and [h] the demographic trends related to new entrants to the workforce between now and 2005 or beyond: particularly women, people of color, and immigrants. (Herr, 1996, pp. 13–15)

Applicability to Minorities

Most career development theories are based on the assumption that people have the opportunity for choice, the background to promote informed choice, and the freedom to choose (Osipow & Littlejohn, 1995). Some individuals from racial and ethnic minority groups live in poverty and lack the educational opportunities that enable career choice (Kozol, 1991). Thus, the theories may have limited applicability for those individuals (Arbona, 1995). Other minority individuals may practice more collectivist approaches to career decision making (Bowman, 1995). Thus, assumptions regarding freedom of choice may not fully apply.

In discussing the applicability of theories to individuals from diverse racial and ethnic backgrounds, it is important to consider the constructs of acculturation (LaFromboise, Coleman, & Gerton, 1993) and racial identity (Bowman, 1995). These constructs address the degree to which individuals identify with their culture of origin or with the majority society. Knowledge of individual racial or ethnic background is not sufficient to judge theory applicability (Szymanski, Treviño, & Fernandez, 1996).

Applicability to People With Disabilities

Over the years, there has been some discussion about the application of career development theories to people with disabilities (see e.g., Conte, 1983; Curnow, 1989; Rojewski, 1994; Hershenson & Szymanski, 1992).

The heterogeneity of people with disabilities and racial and ethnic minorities means that there can be no simple application or non-applicability of any theory . . . the predictive utility of theories depends, at least to some extent, on the degree to which the individuals comprising the populations of interest are relatively homogeneous with normal population distributions on the phenomena of interest. . . . (Szymanski, Hershenson, Enright, & Ettinger, 1996, p. 104)

In summary, disability (Rojewski, 1994) and minority status (Leong, 1995) are risk factors for career development. Similarly, the changing workplace limits the applicability of some theories (Herr, 1996). Nonetheless, the theories do provide constructs and processes that can be judiciously applied with cognizance of disability, minority status, social class, and workplace conditions.

The Relationship of Theory to Practice

The relationship of career development theory to career counseling practice has been the subject of considerable controversy. In fact, a recent edited book has been devoted to this relationship (see Savickas & Walsh, 1996), which is intertwined with the earlier discussion of theory convergence (see Savickas & Lent, 1994a).

The different purposes of theories and practice help to explain the controversy. "In essence, career theory primarily elaborates the targets for intervention rather than provides a theory of intervention itself" (Herr, 1996, p. 17). On the other hand, a model for practice "is a descriptive guide, often for change, and is judged by pragmatic outcomes" (Chartrand, 1996, p. 121). This distinction means that theories of vocational behavior remain important as tools to help counselors understand consumers and plan interventions. In addition, the theories inform models of practice that specifically guide interventions.

CAREER COUNSELING PRACTICE

Career counselors face unique challenges in working with individuals with disabilities. As with all counseling clients, people with disabilities are people first. To that end, traditional career counseling processes should prove beneficial. However, special considerations must be addressed depending on the specific type of disability and its impact on the individual (Hershenson, 1996). A highly individualized approach "can be instrumental in empowering the life choices, inclusion, and independence of people with disabilities" (Kosciulek, 1998, p.115). To facilitate application, we present the following topics: (a) Gysbers, Heppner, and Johnston's (1998) two-phase model, (b) Salomone's (1996) five-stage model, and (c) selected research.

Gysbers, Heppner, and Johnston's (1998) Two-Phase Model

Gysbers, Heppner, and Johnston (1998) have proposed a two-phase process to career counseling. Phase 1, Client Goal or Problem Identification, Clarification, and Specification, begins with the opening and formation of the working alliance, and proceeds through gathering client information and understanding and hypothesizing client behavior. Phase 2, Client Goal and Problem Resolution, involves taking action, developing career goals and plans of action, and evaluating the results and closing the relationship.

Salomone's (1996) Five-Stage Model

Salomone (1996) built on Parson's 1909 model to develop a five-stage process of client-centered career counseling designed to be applicable to people with and without disabilities. The model is built on the premise of developing client independence and responsibility. Counselors should "*do very little for* people but, instead, should *help them to do for themselves*" (p. 373). The stages of Salomone's model are (1) helping the client to understand self, (2) helping the client to understand the environment, (3) helping the client to understand decision making, (4) implementing career and educational decisions, and (5) adjustment, adaptation, and advancement. Salomone points out that although the stages represent a step-by-step process, rarely is counseling a linear venture.

Selected Research

General Meta-Analyses

Research has shown that career counseling works. A series of meta-analyses has examined the overall effectiveness of a variety of counseling interventions. These studies involved general populations, often college or high school students, and did not focus on people with disabilities. Nonetheless, their results are important in understanding career counseling, and we will discuss briefly the two more recent studies.

Oliver and Spokane (1988) reviewed 58 studies that examined the effectiveness of interventions ranging from individual counseling through group counseling, individual test interpretation, career workshops and classes, and computer programs. They found that the interventions were generally effective, with individual counseling being the most effective per session in producing client gain. Intensity or length of treatment was generally positively related with client gain.

Whiston, Sexton, and Lasoff (1998) replicated Oliver and Spokane's study, examining 47 studies, and found that individual counseling was again the most effective and efficient approach. Interestingly, computer interventions were the most cost-effective. In contrast to Oliver and Spokane (1988), Whiston et al. did not find a relationship between treatment intensity and the amount of client gain.

Specific Research on People with Disabilities

A number of studies have examined various interventions with people with disabilities, and a number of examples will be reviewed here. Bolton and Akridge (1995) conducted a meta-analysis of 15 studies of 10 Arkansas skill-training interventions that centered around a common model and were generally found to be effective. The model included the following emphases: "active participation by trainees, focus on specific behaviors, mastery and maintenance of these target behaviors, reliance on established learning principles, emphasis on both didactic and experimental activities, establishment of clear goals, and careful monitoring of individual progress" (p. 263).

Shorter workshop programs have also been found to be effective. For example, Ericson and Riordan (1993) found a series of four weekend workshops effective with young adults with end stage renal disease. Merz and Szymanski (1997) found a six-session, 18-hour workshop to be effective for vocational rehabilitation clients with low levels of career commitment or vocational identity. Conyers and Szymanski (1998) found that a 10-hour, four-session workshop was effective with college students with and without disabilities.

Outcome measures for most of the first and second group of studies included measures of various aspects of the career development process. Examples included career maturity, vocational identity, and career indecision.

CAREER DECISION MAKING

Decision making is an integral part of career counseling. It has been described as a complex continuous process (Brown, 1990). Career decision making was originally characterized by Parsons in 1909 as comprising three components: (1) clear self-understanding, (2) knowledge of occupations, and (3) an ability to draw a relationship between self and occupational knowledge (cited in Phillips & Pazienza, 1988). With the advent of the consumer movement and attention to factors that contribute to decision making, the process has evolved into a partnership between the counselor and the individual seeking guidance in the career choice process. Attention has been increasingly focused on individual needs and values (Brown, 1996).

Descriptive and Prescriptive Models

Descriptive models attempt to answer the question of how decisions are made (Phillips & Paziena, 1988). Descriptive vocational decision-making models "purport to represent the ways people generally make vocational decisions, i.e., the 'natural' phenomena" (Jepsen & Dilley, 1974, p. 333). Examples of descriptive models are Tiedeman, Tiedeman and O'Hara, Hilton, Vroom, Fletcher, and Harren.

While descriptive models address how are decisions made, "prescriptive models represent attempts to help people make better decisions—rules people should use—to reduce errors" (Jepsen & Dilley, 1974, p. 333). Implicit in these models is the assumption that individuals are capable of rational thought in problem solving and decision making. Phillips and Pazienza (1988) note that "these models tend to portray the ideal decision maker as a scientist, seeking out information and using it to arrive at a choice that maximizes the chance for successful implementation" (p. 15). Examples of prescriptive models include Gelatt's 1962 model, the Katz paradigm of 1963, and Kaldor and Zytowski's 1969 work.

Phillips and Pazienza (1988) suggested that some theoretical paradigms are, in reality, descriptive models with prescriptive implications. Examples of this combined model are Krumboltz and Hamel's DECIDES model, Janis and Mann's Vigilant Information Processing model, and Heppner's problem solving paradigm.

Two Recent Approaches

The Cognitive Information Processing (CIP) Model described by Peterson, Sampson, Reardon, and Lenz (1996), is another example of the descriptive/prescriptive approach. The CIP is concerned with thought and memory processes in solving career problems and arriving at decisions. Individuals move along a continuum of indecision to decision. In the indecision end of the spectrum, persons may experience confusion, anxiety, depression, external locus of control, compulsions, and physiological stress reactions. In the decision end of the spectrum, individuals will likely contribute feelings of integration, planfulness, hope, self-confidence, internal locus of control, and general well-being. The sequence that facilitates movement from the indecisive to decisive end of the spectrum is composed of the following: (1) defining the problem, (2) understanding the etiology of the problem, (3) formulating alternatives, (4) prioritizing alternatives and arriving at a first choice, (5) implementing solutions, and (6) evaluating outcomes.

Another relative newcomer to the models of career decision making is that proposed by Brown (1996). In this model the question "How do people decide what [career] outcomes are more important than others?" is answered by investigating an individual's value system. Based on previous work by Rokeach, Super, and Beck (as cited in Brown), values are conceptualized as the foundation of personality; they function as guides for socially acceptable behavior and provide standards for judging one's own behavior and that of other people. In Brown's model values are the "basis of goal-setting" (p. 340). The model is based on the following assumptions: (1) Each person develops a relatively small number of values that are prioritized in a values system, and work values constitute a subset of life values; (2) highly prioritized values are the most important determinant of life role choices; (3) values are acquired as a result of values-laden information from the environment interacting with the inherited characteristics of the individual; (4) life satisfaction will be dependent upon fulfilling an array of life roles that satisfy all essential values; (5) the salience of a role is related to the degree to which it is expected to be a source of satisfaction of essential values; and (6) success in any life depends upon a combination of factors. In the values-based approach to career counseling designed to facilitate career decision making, the counselor attends to the individual needs, moods, and values of each client or consumer. Attempts are made to provide the client with career information and to assist the individual in assessing his or her own skills and values.

Special Considerations for People with Disabilities

Although this support is a vital part of the process for all persons engaged in the process of making career decisions, it appears particularly important that counselors possess the knowledge to facilitate the process for individuals with disabilities. Szymanski and Hershenson (1998) note that "decision making processes and career goals are of particular concern in career planning" for people with disabilities (p. 360). Consumer choice, self-determination, and cultural preferences are important considerations in facilitating the decision-making process. Also, many persons with disabilities may not have had as many educational, life, and job experiences as others (Szymanski, Hershenson, Ettinger, & Enright, 1996; Szymanski & Hershenson, 1998).

CAREER COUNSELING TOOLS

Rehabilitation counselors providing career counseling have a variety of available tools. Szymanski, Fernandez, Koch, and Merz (1995) recommended that counselors assemble tool kits with various tools and procedures so that they can pick the right tools to meet individual client needs. Tools may or may not involve technology and may involve one or more parts of the career counseling process. Two books are recommended as sources of worksheets and processes that can be used in various parts of the process. They are Bolles (1999), *What Color Is Your Parachute 2002*; and Hecklinger and Black (1997), *Training for Life: A Practical Guide to Career and Life Planning*.

Tools for Self-Understanding

A full range of qualitative and quantitative assessment tools are available to assist clients in better understanding themselves in the career counseling process. These include interest and aptitude tests (Kapes, Mastie, & Whitfield, 1994) and a range of specific interview techniques (Gysbers, Heppner, & Johnston, 1998).

Tools for Understanding Educational and Work Options

Tools in this category include a wide range of occupational and related information, such as vocational information on occupations, trends and outlooks, job training, and employment opportunities, and educational information on status and trends, schools and colleges, and financial aid (Patterson, 2003). The occupational classification systems that define codes, such as the Dictionary of Occupational Titles (DOT), Roe's occupational classification system, Holland's classification systems, and the Minnesota Occupational Classification system, quantify careers according to a series of numbers or letters (Osipow & Fitzgerald, 1996). The classification depicts either the nature of the work or the average characteristics or personalities of persons working in that field (Boyd & Cramer, 1995). Occupational coding, although allowing for greater efficiency in matching person to career, does have its drawbacks. There is growing concern that personality-oriented coding systems do not take into account issues of economic survival and cultural background (Osipow & Fitzgerald, 1996).

A technique that is particularly useful with people with disabilities is the informational interview. It provides a low-stakes way for clients to learn more about the requirements of different positions of interest (Hecklinger & Black, 1997). In addition to providing information, it has the added benefit of helping clients develop interview skills and take more responsibility in career exploration. It can be useful in helping to choose a college major as well as in exploring different potential job opportunities before, after, or in the absence of specialized training.

Tools for Career Decision Making

Many of the career decision-making models presented earlier in this chapter are tools in and of themselves. Some have balance sheets that can be used to help clients list and weigh various alternatives according to individually determined criteria. Some individuals may prefer more people-oriented approaches to decision making. Hecklinger and Black's (1997) suggestion of enlisting family and friends as a personal board of directors may be particularly helpful.

The Portfolio as a Total Process Tool

Portfolios are gaining increasing popularity as tools for career counseling, and they may be particularly useful in career counseling with people with disabilities (Koch & Johnston-Rodriguez, 1997). Portfolios help clients organize information about themselves, including their interests and desires, along with information about vocational or educational options, and they are aids to decision making. The process of gathering and organizing such information can serve as an aid to group and individual career counseling processes.

The career resilience portfolio involves assembling information relating to a series of questions grouped in the following four sections: (1) current knowledge and skills; (2) future goals and required knowledge, skills, and experience; (3) plan for acquiring necessary knowledge, skills, and experience; and (4) stress analysis and strain prevention (Szymanski, 1999).

The goal is independent functioning and empowerment of the consumer. The counselor's tasks in the portfolio process include (a) introducing the consumer to the portfolio process; (b) assessing the consumer's level of independence in using the portfolio process; (c) providing support or scaffolding to assist the consumer with the process while at the same time working towards an independent, consumer-controlled portfolio process; and (d) serving as a consultant to the consumer as needed (Szymanski, 1999, p. 286).

Internet and Computer-Assisted Tools

With the development of the Internet and computer systems, the practice of career counseling has begun to change (Noll & Graves, 1996). Counselors are able to use computer-assisted career guidance systems and Internet information to assist clients in the career counseling process. In addition, job matching is facilitated because various Internet sites now allow employers and job seekers to post their needs and skills.

There are several different types of computer-assisted career guidance systems that rely on varying kinds of information. These systems match either personality traits or skills with either worker characteristics or job requirements (Boyd & Cramer, 1995; McCormac, 1988). Examples include SIGI Plus, DISCOVER, CHOICES CT, and OASYS.

There are, however, drawbacks to any of these systems. For instance, many systems will rank-order professions according to the degree to which the person matches their worker characteristics or requirements. There is a risk that this approach limits an individual's desire to explore further and expand his or her experience base so that he or she can make an "informed" decision (Gati, 1996). In addition, many systems may limit the scope of the databases from which they provide career options. With the increased usage of CD-ROM databases that can be accessed by a variety of programs, this limiting effect is starting to diminish (Imel, 1996). Programs are now able to access a greater range of occupational roles, allowing for more exploration toward a suitable career.

Computer systems have come a long way since their first use. Now in their fifth generation of development (Carson & Cartwright, 1997), they take in more information and make better comparisons and matches. The computer systems and the Internet, although useful tools for exploration and guidance, do not work with the individual on how to enter a career field and why, but rather focus on what career to choose. Having the people to help guide individuals in their career decision making is imperative to the process (Stevens & Lundberg, 1998).

In summary, a variety of tools are available to assist the career counseling process. Tools must be individually chosen according to the client needs and counselor abilities and styles.

SUMMARY AND CONCLUSION

We have described theories of vocational behavior, career counseling processes, career decision making, and career counseling tools. We provided an overview to introduce the topics and their connections. More study of the various topics in this chapter is recommended for rehabilitation counselors who are providing career-related services. There is no real distinction between career and personal counseling. Rather, career counseling is counseling with a focus on work. It addresses "client problems dealing with work and career issues that require theoretical conceptions and interventions originating from career development theory, research, and practice" (Gysbers et al., 1998, p. 3).

REFERENCES

Arbona, C. (1995). Theory and research on racial and ethnic minorities: Hispanic Americans. In F. T. L. Leong (Ed.), *Career development and vocational behavior of racial and ethnic minorities* (pp. 37–66). Mahwah, NJ: Erlbaum.

Bolles, R. N. (1999). *What color is your parachute 2000?* Berkeley, CA: Ten Speed.

Bolton, B., & Akridge, R. L. (1995). A meta-analysis of skills training programs for rehabilitation clients. *Rehabilitation Counseling Bulletin, 38,* 262–273.

Bowman, S. L. (1995). Career intervention strategies and assessment issues for African Americans. In F. T. L. Leong (Ed.), *Career development and vocational behavior of racial and ethnic minorities* (pp. 137–164). Mahwah, NJ: Erlbaum.

Boyd, C. J., & Cramer, S. H. (1995). Relationship between Holland high-point code and client preferences for selected vocational counseling strategies. *Journal of Career Development, 21,* 213–221.

Brown, D. (1990). Models of career decision making. In D. Brown, L. Brooks, & Associates (Eds.), *Career choice and development* (pp. 395–421). San Francisco: Jossey-Bass.

Brown, D. (1996). Brown's values-based, holistic model of career and life-role choices and satisfaction. In D. Brown, L. Brooks, & Associates, *Career choice and development* (3rd ed., pp. 337–372). San Francisco: Jossey-Bass.

Brown, D., Brooks, L., & Associates. (1996). *Career choice and development* (3rd ed.). San Francisco: Jossey-Bass.

Carson, A. D., & Cartwright, G. F. (1997). Fifth generation computer-assisted career guidance systems. *Career Planning and Adult Development Journal, 13,* 19–40.

Chartrand, J. M. (1996). Linking theory with practice: A sociocognitive interactional model for career counseling. In M. L. Savickas & W. B. Walsh (Eds.), *Handbook of career counseling theory and practice* (pp. 121–134). Palo Alto, CA: Davies-Black.

Conte, L. (1983). Vocational development theories and the disabled person: Oversight or deliberate omission. *Rehabilitation Counseling Bulletin, 26,* 316–328.

Conyers, L. M., Koch, L., & Szymanski, E. M. (1998). Lifespan perspectives on disability and work: A qualitative study. *Rehabilitation Counseling Bulletin, 42,* 51–75.

Conyers, L., & Szymanski, E. M. (1998). The effectiveness of an integrated career intervention on college students with and without disabilities. *Journal of Postsecondary Education and Disability, 13*(1), 23–34.

Curnow, T. C. (1989). Vocational development of persons with disability. *Vocational Guidance Quarterly, 37,* 269–278.

Ericson, G. D., & Riordan, R. J. (1993). Effects of a psychosocial and vocational intervention on the rehabilitation potential of young adults with end-stage renal disease. *Rehabilitation Counseling Bulletin, 37,* 146–162.

Gati, I. (1996). Computer-assisted career counseling: Challenges and prospects. In M. L. Savicks & W. B. Walsh (Eds.), *Handbook of career counseling theory and practice* (pp. 169–190). Palo Alto, CA: Davies-Black.

Gowing, M. K., Kraft, J. D., & Quick, J. C. (Eds.). (1998). *The new organizational reality: Downsizing, restructuring, and revitalization.* Washington, DC: American Psychological Association.

Gysbers, N. C., Heppner, M. J., & Johnston, J. A. (1998). *Career counseling: Process, issues, and techniques.* Boston: Allyn & Bacon.

Hecklinger, F. J., & Black, B. M. (1997). *Training for life: A practical guide to career and life planning* (5th ed.). Dubuque, IA: Kendall/Hunt.

Herr, E. L. (1996). Toward the convergence of career theory and practice: Mythology, issues, and possibilities. In M. L. Savickas & W. B. Walsh (Eds.), *Handbook of career counseling theory and practice* (pp. 13–35). Palo Alto, CA: Davies-Black.

Hershenson, D. B. (1996). Career counseling. In A. E. Dell Orto & R. P. Marinelli (Eds.), *Encyclopedia of disability and rehabilitation* (pp. 140–146). New York: Simon & Schuster.

Hershenson, D. B., & Liesener, J. J. (2003). Career counseling with diverse populations: Models, interventions, and applications. In E. M. Szymanski & R. M. Parker (Eds.), *Work and disability* (2nd ed., pp. 281–316). Austin, TX: Pro-Ed.

Hershenson, D., & Szymanski, E. M. (1992). Career development of people with disabilities. In R. M. Parker & E. M. Szymanski (Eds.), *Rehabilitation counseling: Basics and beyond* (2nd ed., pp. 273–303). Austin, TX: Pro-Ed.

Holland, J. L. (1996). Integrating career theory and practice: The current situation and some potential remedies. In M. L. Savickas & W. B. Walsh (Eds.), *Handbook of career counseling theory and practice* (pp. 1–11). Palo Alto, CA: Davies-Black.

Imel, S. (1996). Computer-based career information systems. ERIC Digest. Columbus, Ohio: Eric Clearinghouse on Adult, Career, and Vocational Education.

Jepsen, D. A., & Dilley, J. S. (1974). Vocational decision-making models: A review and comparative analysis. *Review of Educational Research, 44,* 331–350.

Kapes, J. T., Mastie, M. M., & Whitfield, E. A. (Eds.). (1994). *A counselor's guide to career assessment instruments* (3rd ed.). Alexandria, VA: National Career Development Association.

Kerlinger, F. N., & Lee, H. B. (2000). *Foundations of behavioral research* (4th ed.). Belmolnt, CA: Wadsworth.

Koch, L., & Johnston-Rodriguez, S. (1997). The career portfolio: A vocational rehabilitation tool for assessment, planning, and placement. *Journal of Job Placement, 13*, 19–22.

Kosciulek, J. (1998). Empowering the life choices of people with disabilities through career counseling. In N. C. Gysbers, M. J. Heppner, & J. A. Johnston, *Career counseling: Process, issues, and techniques* (pp. 109–122). Boston: Allyn & Bacon.

Kozol, J. (1991). *Savage inequalities: Children in America's schools.* New York: Crown.

LaFromboise, T., Coleman, H. L. K., & Gerton, J. (1993). Psychological impact of biculturalism: Evidence and theory. *Psychological Bulletin, 114*, 395–412.

Leong, F. T. L. (Ed.). (1995). *Career development and vocational behavior of racial and ethnic minorities.* Mahwah, NJ: Erlbaum.

Louis Harris & Associates, Inc. (1994). *N.O.D./Harris Survey of Americans with Disabilities.* Washington, DC: National Organization on Disability.

McCormac, M. E. (1988). The use of career information delivery systems in the states. *Journal of Career Development, 14*, 196–204.

Merz, M. A., & Szymanski, E. M. (1997). The effects of a vocational rehabilitation based career workshop on commitment to career choice. *Rehabilitation Counseling Bulletin, 41*, 88–104.

Noll, C. L., & Graves, P. R. (1996). The impact of technology on career center practices. *Journal of Career Planning and Employment, 56*, 41–46.

Oliver, L. W., & Spokane, A. R. (1988). Career-intervention outcome: What contributes to client gain? *Journal of Counseling Psychology, 35*, 447–462.

Osipow, S. H., & Fitzgerald, L. F. (1996). *Theories of career development* (4th ed.). Needham Heights: Allyn & Bacon.

Osipow, S. H., & Littlejohn, E. M. (1995). Toward a multicultural theory of career development: Prospects and dilemmas. In F. T. L. Leong (Ed.), *Career development and vocational behavior of racial and ethnic minorities* (pp. 251–261). Mahwah, NJ: Erlbaum.

Patterson, J. B. (2003). Occupational and labor market information: Resources and applications. In E. M. Szymanski & R. M. Parker (Eds.), *Work and disability: Issues and strategies in career development and job placement* (pp. 247–279). Austin, TX: Pro-Ed.

Peterson, G. W., Sampson, J. P., Reardon, R. C., & Lenz, J. G. (1996). A cognitive information processing approach to career problem solving and decision making. In D. Brown, L. Brooks, & Associates, *Career choice and development* (pp. 423–476). San Francisco: Jossey-Bass.

Phillips, S. D., & Pazienza, N. J. (1988). History and theory of the assessment of career development and decision making. In W. B. Walsh & S. H. Osipow (Eds.), *Career decision making* (pp. 1–32). Hillsdale, NJ: Erlbaum.

Rojewski, J. W. (1994). Applying theories of career behavior to special populations: Implications for secondary vocational transition programming. *Issues in Special Education and Rehabilitation, 9*(1), 7–26.

Quick, J. C., Murphy, L. R., Hurrell, J. J. Jr., & Orman, D. (1992). The value of work, the risk of distress, and the power of prevention. In J. C. Quick, L. R. Murphy, & J. J. Hurrell, Jr. (Eds.), *Stress and well-being at work: Assessments and interventions for occupational mental health* (pp. 3–13). Washington, DC: American Psychological Association.

Salomone, P. R. (1996). Career counseling and job placement: Theory and practice. In E. M. Szymanski & R. M. Parker (Eds.), *Work and disability: Issues and strategies in career development and job placement* (pp. 365–420). Austin, TX: Pro-Ed.

Savickas, M. L., & Lent, R. W. (Eds.). (1994a). *Convergence in career development theories: Implications for science and practice.* Palo Alto, CA: CPP.

Savickas, M. L., & Lent, R. W. (1994b). Introduction: A convergence project for career psychology. In M. L. Savickas & R. W. Lent (Eds.), *Convergence in career development theories: Implications for science and practice* (pp. 1–6). Palo Alto, CA: CPP.

Savickas, M. L., & Walsh, W. B. (Eds.). (1996). *Handbook of career counseling theory and practice.* Palo Alto, CA: Davies-Black.

Schein, E. H. (1986). A critical look at current career development theory and research. In D. T. Hall & Associates, *Career development in organizations* (pp. 310–331). San Francisco: Jossey-Bass.

Stevens, D. T., & Lundberg, D. J. (1998). The emergence of the Internet: Enhancing career counseling education and services. *Journal of Career Development, 24,* 195–208.

Szymanski, E. M. (1999). Disability, job stress, the changing nature of careers, and the career resilience portfolio. *Rehabilitation Counseling Bulletin, 42,* 279–289.

Szymanski, E. M. (2001). Disability and vocational behavior. In R. Frank & T. R. Elliot (Eds.), *Handbook of rehabilitation psychology* (pp. 499–517). Washington, DC: American Psychological Association.

Szymanski, E. M., Enright, M., Hershenson, D. B., & Ettinger, J. (2003). Career development theories, constructs, and research: Implications for people with disabilities. In E. M. Szymanski & R. M. Parker (Eds.), *Work and disability: Issues and strategies in career development and job placement* (2nd ed., pp. 91–153). Austin, TX: Pro-Ed.

Szymanski, E. M., Fernandez, D., Koch, L., & Merz, M. A. (1995). *Career planning: Preparing for placement. Training Materials.* Madison, WI: University of Wisconsin-Madison, Rehabilitation Research and Training Center on Career Development and Advancement.

Szymanski, E. M., & Hershenson, D. B. (1998). Career development of people with disabilities: An ecological model. In R. M. Parker & E. M. Szymanski (Eds.), *Rehabilitation counseling: Basics and beyond* (3rd ed., pp. 327–378). Austin, TX: Pro-Ed.

Szymanski, E. M., Hershenson, D. B., Enright, M. S., & Ettinger, J. (1996). Career development theories, constructs, and research: Implications for people with disabilities. In E. M. Szymanski & R. M. Parker (Eds.), *Work and disability: Issues and strategies in career development and job placement* (pp. 79–126). Austin, TX: Pro-Ed.

Szymanski, E. M., Hershenson, D. B., Ettinger, J. M., & Enright, M. S. (1996). Career development interventions for people with disabilities. In E. M. Szymanski & R. M. Parker (Eds.), *Work and disability* (pp. 255–271). Austin, TX: Pro-Ed.

Szymanski, E. M., Ryan, C., Merz, M. A., Treviño, B., & Johnston-Rodriguez, S. (1996). Psychosocial and economic aspects of work: Implications for people with disabilities. In E. M. Szymanski & R. M. Parker (Eds.), *Work and disability: Issues and strategies in career development and job placement* (pp. 9–38). Austin, TX: Pro-Ed.

Szymanski, E. M., Treviño, B., & Fernandez, D. (1996). Rehabilitation career planning with minorities. *Journal of Applied Rehabilitation Counseling, 27*(4), 45–49.

Whiston, S. C., Sexton, T. L., & Lasoff, D. L. (1998). Career-intervention outcome: A replication and extension of Oliver and Spokane (1988). *Journal of Counseling Psychology, 45,* 150–165.

Section IV

Special Considerations

Chapter 16

Substance Abuse Counseling

David B. Peterson, Anne Helene Skinstead, Robert W. Trobliger

Substance abuse is a significant problem in the United States and most of the Western world (Benshoff & Janikowski, 2000; Cardoso et al., 1999; Doweiko, 1999; Substance Abuse and Mental Health Services Administration, 2002). The consequences of substance abuse are far-reaching, as discussed by Heinemann (1993) and others, and rehabilitation professionals will inevitably encounter substance-related issues in professional practice regardless of setting. Thus, all rehabilitation professionals should become familiar with substance abuse counseling literature, including theory, research, and techniques that show promise in effecting therapeutic change.

MODELS OF ADDICTION

During the first half of the 20th century, professionals generally viewed addiction as a moral dilemma or the consequence of poor character. More recently, medicine has likened addiction to other disease processes, a paradigm that remains strong today. In contrast, more recently developed models of addiction describe patterns of behavior that are learned, resulting in maladaptive consequences. Progressive views of addiction support multiple etiologies (Benshoff & Janikowski, 2000; Cardoso et al., 1999; Siegal et al., 1995), including environmental and contextual factors that result in a biopsychosocial approach (Donovan & Marlatt, 1988).

Addiction as Sin or Immoral Behavior

The view of addiction as sin is not exclusively associated with the era of prohibition, and some treatment programs continue to embrace the view that substance abuse is freely chosen and is a consequence of widespread moral decay (Thombs, 1994). Treatment typically tends to be punitive (punishment or application of sanctions), with a goal of abstinence and a return to more traditional family values. History suggests that this approach to treatment often fails to effect change, since the complexities of the etiology of addiction may not be adequately considered (see Cardoso et al., 1999). A challenge to the immorality or free-choice paradigm is evidence suggesting that social and environmental contexts have a strong influence on conduct and should therefore be considered in treatment (see Thombs, 1994).

Addiction as a Disease

Etiology

Disease-oriented perspectives in addictions suggest a mechanistic nature to behavior, with possible genetic behavioral influences (Azar, 1999). The addicted person is a victim of an illness that results in a loss of control, perhaps triggered by a genetic predisposition to addiction. Contrary to the addiction-as-sin paradigm, the disease model refutes punishment as an intervention and encourages clients to process addiction issues without guilt.

During the 1970s, the founders of Alcoholics Anonymous (AA) likened alcohol dependence to a "disease of the spirit" that required intervention from a higher power (AA, 1976). AA embraced a form of the religious need for "redemption" from addictive forces but defined the source of that redemption more broadly than religious organizations, which viewed addiction as sinful. AA's 12-step program is based on the disease model of alcoholism and is often influenced by spiritual constructs familiar to moral models of addiction. For example, step 1 of AA's "12 steps" is an admission of powerlessness over alcohol (AA, 1981). In addition to physicians and alcohol treatment programs, the disease model of treatment may also use formerly addicted persons as counselors, "sponsors," or social support systems (see also Johnson, 1980; Milam & Ketcham, 1983; Nowinski, 1996; Vaillant, 1990; Wallace, 1996). The Project MATCH Research Group (1993) suggested that successful treatment of addiction rests in the appropriate match between client and program. Researchers found that a well-controlled, outpatient 12-step treatment program was as effective as cognitive-behavioral therapy or brief motivational enhancement therapy.

Disease Process

Several theorists have posited that addiction follows a disease progression (see Johnson, 1980; Milam & Ketcham, 1983; Talbott, 1989). Some disease model theorists embrace a chronic disease perspective which suggests, for example, "once an alcoholic, always an alcoholic," necessitating sustained abstinence with social support to successfully avoid substance use. In contrast, the National Institute on Alcohol Abuse and Alcoholism (1990) has suggested that the empirical evidence does not support a predictable progression for addiction.

Central to the disease model of addiction is the concept of denial. Denial as a basic defense mechanism allows continued use of a substance in spite of negative consequences (George, 1990). The concept of denial has driven some disease and moral model treatment approaches to be coercive with users (e.g., family confrontations), which could perhaps strengthen a healthy denial response (Saunders, Wilkinson, & Towers, 1996). One might actually garner the opposite effect; the healthy denial response associated with refuting or denying imposing values may subsequently strengthen one's rationale to keep using.

Addiction as a Learned/Maladaptive Behavior

Behavior-oriented theorists suggest that addiction is brought about by destructive learning conditions. The rewards of substance use may drive the compulsion to use (operant conditioning), while certain contexts may be associated with triggering the desire to use (classical conditioning). Treatment focuses on learning principles and skill development that prevent relapse (learning new skills, unlearning old habits). The client is considered a victim with some degree of control over his or her substance abuse. A review of the learning theory literature suggests that multiple factors may influence addiction (Beck, Wright, Newman, & Liese, 1993; Heath, Jardine, & Martin, 1989; McGue, Pickens, & Svikis, 1992).

Contrary to the disease model orientation, which posits loss of control, Fingarette (1991) noted that the amount of substance abused is a function of perceived costs and benefits by the user. Addiction is related, in part, to the lack of positive reinforcement of alternative behaviors, the lack of punishment or negative reinforcement for experimenting with drugs or alcohol, and the reinforcing mood alteration that accompanies substance use. The latter factor, because of its unchanging nature, remains a regular threat to maintaining abstinence. Social reinforcers may also encourage addictive behavior. Additionally, cessation of substance use may be avoided because of the punishing effects of withdrawal (see also Rotgers, 1996).

Tension Reduction Hypothesis

Jellinek (1945) suggested that tension reduction was not the only reason for drinking, but an important motivation. Conger (1956) established the "tension reduction hypothesis" (TRH) through animal studies, suggesting that alcohol mitigates aversive states such as fear or tension. In their review of research, Langenbucher and Nathan (1990) suggest that there is much support for the validity of TRH, but Cappell and Greeley's (1987) review cautions that high quantities of alcohol may actually exacerbate responses to stress, arguing for consideration of individual differences. In addition, the impact of social stressors upon stress responses in real-life situations is much less consistent than in controlled experiments, suggesting more complex relationships between alcohol use and stress reduction.

Social Learning Theory (SLT)

Vicarious learning is an integral component of SLT and may describe the development of addictive behavior. Bandura (1977) observed three effects associated with model emulation. First, observational learning effects may occur as someone observes a peer (model) using a given drug, introducing substance use. Second, further observation (e.g., a model describes the euphoria experienced from smoking crack) may result in disinhibitory effects that increase substance use, or, in contrast, inhibitory effects that decrease substance use through the demonstration of negative consequences to behavior, such as withdrawal or incarceration. Third, response facilitation effects are associated with established behaviors. For example, at a given social event where others partake in smoking crack, the observed behavior may elicit similar behavior from others who have used crack. Another example of response facilitation might be the rate of alcohol consumption at a college party.

In contrast to the disease model, which suggests a loss of control, SLT suggests that addictive behavior is self-regulated and goal directed, the goal being to acquire the effects of a preferred substance. Self-medication for dealing with stress (e.g., drinking alcohol after a very stressful day) may reflect an effort to self-regulate. SLT suggests that humans regulate their behavior by way of internal standards and self-evaluation. Self-regulation, rather than environmental control, would appear to be suggested by the amount of effort that chemically dependent people devote to substance acquisition despite the negative consequences (e.g., litigation, expense, and social stigma).

ASSESSMENT IN SUBSTANCE ABUSE COUNSELING

Contemporary assessment practices acknowledge the need for using multi-dimensional functional assessment (see Cardoso et al., 1999). Clinical observations, medical examinations, diagnostic interviews, and psychometric evaluations are the tools used to complete the functional assessment. The American Society of Addiction Medicine (ASAM) has developed the Patient Placement Criteria (ASAM, 1996), which attempts to match substance-abusing clients to four levels of care: (a) outpatient treatment, (b) intensive outpatient/partial hospitalization treatment, (c) residential inpatient treatment, and (d) medically managed intensive inpatient treatment. Placement decisions are based on signs and symptoms in the clients across six dimensions: (a) acute intoxication and/or withdrawal, (b) biomedical conditions and complications, (c) emotional-behavioral complications, (d) treatment acceptance/resistance, (e) relapse potential, and (f) recovery/living environment. Currently, clinicians use these criteria for placement in specific treatments; however, these criteria have little research support (Finney & Moos, 1998). Thus, the following are recommended: (a) outpatient treatment for clients with sufficient social support and resources and no medical or psychiatric impairment; (b) less costly intensive outpatient treatment for clients who have failed in brief treatment and may need more intensive treatment, without the structure of residential treatment; and (c) residential treatment for clients with few social resources, and/or with home environments providing relapse risks. A more thorough treatment of substance abuse assessment can be found elsewhere (see Center for Substance Abuse Treatment, 1995; Donovan & Marlatt, 1988; Doweiko, 1999; National Institute on Alcohol Abuse and Addiction, 2000).

CONTEMPORARY TREATMENT APPROACHES

Psychodynamic

Early psychodynamically oriented professionals working in substance abuse counseling associated substance abuse with the death instinct (thanatos, or an unconscious death-wish) or with the self-destructive tendencies of the id. Khantzian (1980) equated substance abuse with slow suicide. Those ascribing to psychosexual stages of development hypothesized an oral fixation associated with dependency conflicts (Leeds & Morgenstern,

1996). Other psychodynamic adherents suggest that addiction is evidence of a deficient ego (Wurmser, 1980), whereby the abuse itself becomes a dysfunctional defense mechanism. Theoretically, a weak ego makes an addicted person dependent upon external supports (substance abuse) for satisfaction, and the same weak ego has difficulty with self-monitoring the negative impact of substance abuse. The weakened ego's drug of choice is related to the addicted person's psychic experience; if a person is very anxious, the ego may cope through self-medication with some type of anxiolytic or a substance that serves as a depressant (e.g., alcohol).

Contemporary psychodynamic treatment focuses first on abstinence as a confound to successful therapy, since the individual needs to recognize the addiction in order to get at its roots. Attention is then given to transference and countertransference in the therapeutic process (Thombs, 1994). Psychodynamic approaches emphasize early childhood and parent relationships as possible origins of addictive behavior. Counselors are encouraged to avoid the sterile couch approach and to emphasize a warm and caring relationship, minimizing interpretation (Yalisove, 1989). Brief models of psychotherapy have emerged by necessity, largely due to managed care (Tarvydas & Peterson, 1999). A recently developed model of psychodynamically oriented brief psychotherapy integrates development, attachment, self-efficacy, and problem solving (see Basch, 1995; Khantzian, Halliday, & McAuliffe, 1990).

Psychodynamic approaches have historically been difficult to validate, resulting in a paucity of research. Some have suggested that psychodynamic therapy be considered an adjunct only to more contemporary substance abuse treatments that lead to an extended period of abstinence, after which character issues can be addressed with greater clarity (Leeds & Morgenstern, 1996; Keller, 1996).

Behavioral Approaches

Behavioral approaches to substance abuse counseling generally begin with identifying problem behaviors, environmental reinforcers, and plans to manipulate the environment to alter behavior in the desired fashion (e.g., increasing disincentives and avoiding incentives for the behavior to be changed or extinguished). Prevention in the behavioral realm may best be implemented before alcohol tolerance is high, arguing for early intervention. Goals may incorporate controlled drinking, modeling recovery behaviors, decreasing drug use, and other approaches described below.

Controlled Drinking

In the early 1970s, Mark and Linda Sobell compared a controlled drinking approach to treatment to an abstinence approach, reporting that controlled drinking was superior to abstinence across several outcome measures. In fact, follow-up studies at 19 to 24 months suggested that the controlled drinking group faired better than the abstinence group in using little or no alcohol (Sobell & Sobell, 1976). The controlled drinking approach has been controversial. The recovery movement (disease model adherents such as AA, medical treatment programs, and some mental health professionals) adamantly oppose the controlled drinking approach. A common point of contention within the disease model is whether one can be addicted and later return to "controlled drinking," since any use is believed to quickly lead to a loss of control. Many biopsychosocial factors rule out the use of the controlled drinking approach for some people, especially those who have developed physical dependence (Lewis, Dana, & Belvins, 1988), but this may not hold true for those who abuse but are not dependent.

It has been difficult to recruit clients for research on controlled drinking, limiting research on the approach (Thombs, 1994). Some evidence suggests that individuals who use alcohol chronically can drink in a controlled manner in a laboratory setting (Pattison, Sobell, & Sobell, 1977), but a laboratory lacks the dynamics of sociocultural environments. Furthermore, later research has shown that controlled drinking is not effective with clients with chronic alcohol problems but may be effective with early-stage problem drinkers (Nathan & Skinstead, 1987).

Blood Alcohol Discrimination

Blood alcohol discrimination is the ability to sense when one's blood alcohol level implies moderate, nonproblematic consumption of alcohol in comparison to inebriation. Studies exploring blood alcohol discrimination suggest that persons with high tolerance for alcohol do not have the ability to discriminate in comparison to nonaddicted persons (Brick, 1990; Nathan & Lipscomb, 1979). Thus, problem drinkers may need to rely on external, rather than internal, cues to control their drinking.

Contingency Contracting

Contingency contracting employs the establishment of goals, with successful goal attainment rewarded and failure punished. Thombs (1994) suggested nine behavioral goals that promote abstinence (the first three are components of the spiritual/disease paradigms as well): (1) attending AA/NA meetings; (2) calling one's sponsor; (3) reading self-help literature (e.g., the AA "Big Book"); (4) getting to work on time; (5) avoiding "slipping places"; (6) taking Antabuse as prescribed; (7) socializing with fellow recovering addicted people (or nonusing friends); (8) practicing relaxation exercises or other coping skills; and (9) attending to family responsibilities. For example, if one succeeds in fulfilling weekly family responsibilities, a reward might be private time away with friends. Punishment could be a charitable donation to an organization that one disdains. Two factors appear to have been most influential with this approach: temporal proximity of the reinforcer or punisher to the target behavior and the potency of the contingency (Miller, 1980). Rewards and punishments must be meaningful to the individual and must occur in close approximation to the target behavior.

Token Economies

Residential substance abuse treatment settings have employed token economies to shape behaviors that are associated with recovery (Mehr, 1988). Initially, recovery behaviors can be identified as markers for a course of treatment, and a reward system can be established reflecting progression from beginning to more advanced stages of treatment. The reinforcers are tokens that are redeemable for material goods or privileges, and a system of fines may also be employed, discouraging behaviors that are inconsistent with recovery (see Pickens & Thompson, 1986).

Higgins et al. (1991) suggested several important challenges to popularly held notions about substance abuse treatment: (1) reinforcers (e.g., money) can compete with powerfully addictive drugs; (2) polysubstance abusers do not need to stop use of all drugs at the same time, but may rather focus on eliminating drug use one substance at a time; and (3) incentives and anticipated benefits of contingencies are critical in maintaining abstinence, especially early in treatment.

There are limitations in the use of behaviorally oriented techniques. It can be difficult to monitor or control contingencies, particularly in outpatient treatment, and many clients lack the motivation to employ such a system. In addition, behavioral approaches have been criticized for being superficial and failing to address underlying causes of substance abuse. However, with the increasing pressures of managed care to provide accountability through outcome-based monitoring of mental health services, behaviorally oriented treatments warrant consideration (see also Morgan, 1996).

Cognitive/Behavioral Approaches

Since Bandura's presentation of cognitive social learning theory (1969, 1977, 1986), a variety of approaches have evolved based on cognitive models of addiction (Marlatt & Gordon, 1985). However, pure cognitive approaches appear to have given way to cognitive-behavioral substance abuse counseling (Beck, Wright, Newman, & Liese, 1993; Rotgers, Keller, & Moregenstern, 1996).

Self-Efficacy

In their review of social learning theory approaches to alcoholism treatment, Abrams and Niaura (1987) define self-efficacy as "a perception or judgment of one's capability to execute a particular course of action required to deal effectively with an impending situation" (p. 134). Research has suggested that an auspicious goal of substance abuse counseling is the enhancement of a person's sense of self-efficacy (Marlatt & Gordon, 1985; Wilson, 1988), which is particularly important for relapse prevention. Bandura (1977) suggested four sources of information that can impact self-efficacy. Past successes and failures (performance accomplishments) appear to be most influential. Vicarious experiences (learning from other's successes and failures) are influential as well. Verbal persuasion, while a frequently used intervention, tends to have little lasting value without corroborative personal experience. Finally, emotional arousal can mediate perceived self-efficacy (Annis & Davis, 1988). For example, high levels of anxiety and fear can undermine a person's confidence. Paradoxically, appropriate levels of anxiety may enhance the desire to achieve.

Specific treatment approaches to enhance self-efficacy might include the provision of opportunities for simple goals that are achievable followed by increasingly more challenging but achievable tasks (Basch, 1995). Exposure to successfully recovering people dealing with addiction may provide tips for dealing with difficult emotional states and encouragement that success is possible. Finally, the treatment paradigm encourages counselors to note the minimal impact of verbal persuasion in the absence of interventions that enhance self-efficacy.

Relapse Prevention

According to SLT, relapse is associated with an inability to cope with life stressors. Social and interpersonal situations that are associated with negative emotional states may precipitate relapse behavior. Cummings,

Gordon, and Marlatt (1980) explored situations associated with relapse and found that high-risk situations tended to encompass emotional (negative emotional states), social (social pressures), and psychological (interpersonal conflicts) factors. The substance abuse counselor's awareness of the individual's needs may inform the development of counseling strategies that teach specific coping strategies, which may help minimize the negative response to emotional states. In the event that relapse occurs (the literature suggests that the probability is quite high), SLT suggests framing the relapse as an opportunity for learning. Interpreting the event as a failure or a violation may lead to more profound relapses (Abrams & Niaura, 1987; Buelow & Buelow, 1998; Marlatt & Gordon, 1985).

Motivational Approaches

Miller and Rollnick (2002) suggest that many people struggling with substance abuse are ambivalent about changing, rather than being resistant, weak-willed, or poor in character. They define motivation to overcome ambivalence as a state of readiness, which may change from one time and situation to another. Building upon Bandura's (1977) notions of self-efficacy, Miller and Rollnick suggest avoiding attempts at persuading clients to change, which may bring increased resistance to therapy. Instead, their person-centered yet directive approach focuses on developing client internal motivation to change.

Prochaska, DiClemente, and Norcross (1992) addressed motivation through a five-stage model describing motivation to change. At first individuals are described as least concerned about overcoming problems with substance abuse and least motivated to make any change in behavior (*precontemplation stage*). When individuals are willing to consider issues related to substance use and the implications of change, but without constructive action, they are considered to be in the *contemplation stage*. Willingness to seek out help describes the *preparation stage*, which is followed by the *action stage*, involving a commitment to change through action and behavior modification and considered the most stressful of the stages. The *maintenance stage* is most closely associated with relapse prevention, which attempts to continue the processes begun in the contemplation and action stages.

Prochaska and DiClemente (1986) suggested that the motivational process is complex and nonlinear, and may include multiple cycles through the five stages before accomplishing the long-term goal, while some may get stuck in early stages. The counselor's awareness of the client's current status or stage may facilitate the selection of the intervention that is appropriate for the client's current motivational status. For example, counselors should use more directive interventions for clients with low motivation (e.g., drug courts) and use less directive therapies for highly motivated clients, maximizing potential for the best outcome (see also Bell & Rollnick, 1996; Project Match Research Group, 1997; Saunders, Wilkinson, & Towers, 1996).

Psychosocial Treatments

Finney and Moos (1998) reported that community reinforcement approaches and social skills training seemed to be most consistently effective for treatment of people with alcohol use disorders. Community reinforcement approaches consist of working with families, assisting the client with job-related difficulties and legal problems, and having clients join social, non-alcohol-using groups as alternatives to socializing with alcohol. Social skills training focuses on development of assertiveness and communication skills, using therapeutic techniques such as role play, feedback, and modeling of other people's behaviors in a group setting. The core focus in the community reinforcement approach has shifted away from medication to family issues, job-related problems, and client drinking behaviors.

Family approaches to substance abuse treatment have grown over the past 60 years from their psychodynamic origins into sociological stress models, family systems models, behavioral models, and family disease models, and the latter three dominate current family-centered approaches (McCrady & Epstein, 1996). These models seek to describe the etiology and maintenance of addictive behaviors through family-centered constructs and are supported by a rich body of empirical literature (see McCrady & Epstein, 1996; McKay, 1996). Behavioral marital therapy in particular has demonstrated some success (O'Farrell, Choquette, Cutter, Brown, & McCourt, 1993). This approach seeks to improve a couple's relationship and communication style, to resolve their marital conflicts, and to increase positive interactions (e.g., showing more affection and engaging in more recreational activities together). The focus on drinking behavior attempts to help the client establish drinking and Antabuse contracts.

In a small-sample study, contingency contracting that focused on the individual, combined with community reinforcement, resulted in more positive outcomes than a traditional 12-step program (Higgins et al., 1991). The vocational, recreational, social, and familial spheres of life can serve as effective domains of reinforcement in psychosocial substance abuse counseling interventions.

Biopsychosocial Approach

A biopsychosocial approach was first introduced in the substance abuse counseling literature by Donovan and Marlatt (1988). Babor (1993) described such a model of substance abuse treatment as integrating biological, psychological, and sociological factors into treatment. Babor focused upon two risk components: vulnerability, based upon physiological, psychological, and social traits; and exposure to substances in different sociological contexts. Contemporary substance abuse treatments acknowledge the roles of environmental factors, genetic predisposition, and psychological mechanisms that impact addiction (Edwards, Marshall, & Cook, 1997).

Treatments employed from a biopsychosocial approach include medical treatment, cognitive remediation (positive self-statements, enhancing self-efficacy, coping imagery, self-talk, and distraction), skill building (role playing, self-monitoring, refusal skills, and relapse rehearsal), social change (changing nonfacilitative cohort, avoiding relapse-evoking contexts), and lifestyle modification (exercise, relaxation techniques, and effective time management) (Donovan & Marlatt, 1988). Similar techniques are employed throughout the previously reviewed approaches, but not necessarily in this integrated fashion.

Drug Courts

In response to the revolving door in the criminal justice system with respect to drug offenders, more and more communities are establishing special drug courts (Bart, 1999a). These courts provide supervised rehabilitation programs for nonviolent offenders whose primary affiliation with the court system is drug-related. The programs consist of multiphased outpatient treatment; weekly and/or daily meetings with a substance abuse counselor; drug testing; judicial review hearings; and other support services (e.g., vocational, educational, family, and medical).

A drug court is administered by a judge, and participation is voluntary in principle. Most programs last from 12 to 18 months and require considerable effort from the offender. Drug courts have shown promise in curbing substance abuse by using frequent drug testing to ensure that clients who are in litigation remain abstinent. Sanctions are given for noncompliance, and rewards are given for success. Continued noncompliance (e.g., three strikes rule) with drug court mandates may result in expulsion from the program and incarceration, but great effort is taken along the way to facilitate success in the program. Bart (1999a) reported that drug courts were operating in 39 states, the District of Columbia, and Puerto Rico.

Columbia University's National Center on Addiction and Substance Abuse (CASA) found that drug courts substantially limit drug use and criminal behavior while the offender is enrolled, and they also reduce recidivism after treatment. According to the U.S. Department of Justice, 70% of the 100,000 offenders assigned to drug courts to date remain successfully enrolled or have completed treatment (Bart, 1999a). According to a survey conducted by the Drug Court Clearinghouse in Washington, D.C., recidivism among all drug court participants has ranged between 5 and 28%, with graduates experiencing less than 4% recidivism. Drug courts serve as a buffer between court and incarceration, giving the offender time to contemplate and commit to recovery (see Buelow & Buelow, 1998; Prochaska, DiClemente, & Norcross, 1992). Ironically, drug courts also save money; average costs per drug court participant range from $1,200 to $3,000, with concomitant savings in jail bed days of $5,000 per defendant (Bart, 1999a).

Case Management Approaches

Substantial efforts to contain the costs of substance abuse treatment have occurred because of the rise of health maintenance organizations (HMOs). According to Anderson and Berlant (1995), specialized managed substance abuse care is rooted in four key principles of clinical treatment: (a) alternatives to psychiatric hospitalization; (b) alternatives to restrictive treatment; (c) goal-directed therapy; and (d) crisis intervention.

Lightfoot et al. (1982) described a five-point approach to alcohol abuse treatment: (a) securing support of the alcohol abuser's family, employer, and significant others; (b) being alert to changing needs, providing reassessment during ongoing treatment; (c) following-up on persons who leave treatment prematurely; (d) providing ongoing support of the individual in his or her community; and (e) providing early intervention for prevention of relapse (see also Timney & Graham, 1989).

One approach to case management is the strengths perspective (Siegal et al., 1995). The medical model of addiction has been criticized for being overly simplistic in addressing the complexity of substance abuse or chemical dependency. In contrast, the strengths perspective seeks to "encourage patients to become more deeply involved in their own treatment while simultaneously assisting them in learning how to acquire and retain those resources that will support their recovery" (Siegal et al., 1995, p. 69). The strengths perspective is based upon five principles whereby the case manager (a) facilitates the client's identification of his or her strengths, abilities, and assets; (b) assists the client in focusing goals, identifying alternatives, and locating resources by encouraging the client to identify his or her own needs; (c) serves as primary advocate for the client, and coordinates all relevant services; (d) encourages positive and proactive identification of resources in the client's environment, including community agencies and social supports (e.g., friends, families, and neighbors); and (e) works with the client in the community to maximize the fidelity of the provider's perceptions and the client's experiences.

Pacione and Jaskula (1994) used an approach that matched client needs to level of care and individualized treatment protocols (see also Project MATCH Research Group, 1997). Three clinical guidelines facilitated this process: (a) using the least restrictive level of care most likely to initiate abstinence; (b) assessing the likelihood of treatment failure at the level of care chosen and the risks to the client if treatment fails; and (c) identifying treatment failure quickly and moving the client to a more intensive level of care if significant risks are present. This perspective has been proposed as a good model for treating women who have substance abuse issues through "client empowerment, which reflects the ability of an individual to act on their own behalf and ultimately gain a measure of control over their lives" (Sullivan, 1994, p. 160).

Comparing research results across case management–oriented programs is difficult. Precisely operationalizing the case management construct has been elusive (Timney & Graham, 1989), and substantial variation between programs makes comparisons difficult (Teague, Drake, & Ackerson, 1995). Early research suggested improved treatment outcomes but was inconclusive (Lightfoot et al., 1982). Studies conducted by the National Institute on Alcohol Abuse and Alcoholism (NIAAA) had design confounds and inconclusive results (Ridgely, 1994).

Addiction research has shown generally that client retention in treatment alone is associated with better outcomes, suggesting that the approach used may be less important than the contact involved in treatment or just being "treated" (Institute of Medicine, 1990). More study is needed regarding the degree to which the type of program influences retention. Generally speaking, case management approaches to substance abuse treatment are promising for the improvement of treatment outcomes (Sullivan, Hartmann, Dillon, & Wolk, 1994; Sullivan, Wolk, & Hartmann, 1992). Client, therapist, process, and outcome variables associated with case management approaches need further exploration (Anderson & Berlant, 1995; Ridgely, 1994; Teague et al., 1995; Timney & Graham, 1989).

Dual Diagnosis and Substance Abuse Treatment

Mental Illness and Substance Abuse

Between 25% and 58% of clients with a psychiatric disorder have a co-occurring substance abuse disorder (Brems & Johnson, 1997; Miller, 1995; Mueser, Bellack, & Blanchard, 1992). Substance abuse frequently complicates mental illness, resulting in adjustment difficulties and negative outcomes (e.g., medication and treatment noncompliance, recidivism, suicide, homelessness, violent behavior, incarceration, HIV infection, and early mortality) (Drake & Noordsy, 1994).

Evidence continues to accumulate suggesting that intensive case management team approaches to treatment of dually diagnosed persons have been relatively successful. Abstinence rates as high as 60% at four years after treatment have been reported for case management techniques that use integrated treatments and engagement in community-based services (Drake, McHugo, & Noordsy, 1993; Kofoed, Kania, Walsh, & Atkinson, 1986; Mercer-McFadden & Drake, 1994; Ridgely, 1994; Schizophrenia Patient Outcomes Research Team, 1994).

Programs have been composed of multidisciplinary teams with backgrounds in psychiatry, nursing, case management, substance abuse, and rehabilitation (Drake & Noordsy, 1994). Assertive outreach and community-based programming are implemented, and motivational approaches are used to counter the premotivational state of many clients. Long-term approaches are supported, as opposed to short-term approaches, and substance abuse treatment is provided in the context of the comprehensive services of a community support system model (Stroul, 1989).

Seven mental health agencies in New Hampshire that treated co-occurring severe mental disorders and substance abuse disorders using continuous treatment teams were evaluated by Teague et al., (1995). The programs incorporated features of the Program of Assertive Community Treatment (PACT), which is characterized by small, shared caseloads, frequent team meetings, and comprehensive, direct services delivered over time. The PACT model includes the following nine elements: (a) continuity of staffing, where the treatment team maintains the same staff over time; (b) provision and monitoring of services in the community (in vivo); (c) assertive engagement of clients, with intensive outreach, visits to community settings, and legal mechanisms; (d) use of a multidisciplinary team of psychiatrist, nurse, and substance abuse expert; (e) continuous 24-hour responsibility of the treatment team for a discrete group of clients; (f) small caseloads, with a ratio of 10:1; (g) a high level of service intensity; (h) a team approach with all clients; and (i) and teamwork with client support systems such as employers, landlords, and family members (Teague et al., 1995).

The continuous treatment team approach has also incorporated four substance abuse specific criteria: (a) individualized substance abuse treatment by the staff who provide mental health services; (b) utilization of a dual disorders model providing nonconfrontational, behaviorally oriented treatment in the context of an abstinence-oriented stage model (Osher & Kofoed, 1989); (c) dual disorder groups during the stages of persuasion or active treatment; and (d) a team focus on clients with dual disorders. The program combination was compared to standard case management, where clinicians had caseloads of moderate size and provided some direct service but primarily referred clients to prescribed services outside of the local mental health agency. The results of the comparison study indicated that the continuous treatment team model was ultimately more effective in implementing substance abuse treatment than the case management control. Because of the high rate of comorbidity in mental illness and substance abuse, the four-criteria enhancement to the nine general elements of the PACT model was recommended (see Teague et al., 1995).

Other Disabilities and Substance Abuse

According to the Substance Abuse and Mental Health Services Administration (SAMHSA) and the Center for Substance Abuse Treatment (CSAT), people with cognitive as well as physical disabilities have a higher probability of substance abuse than nondisabled persons (Bart, 1999b). The Center for Substance Abuse Treatment (1998b) recently disseminated the 29th in a series of Treatment Improvement Protocols (TIPs) that addressed substance use disorder treatment for people with physical and cognitive disabilities. Other TIPs are scheduled to be published that address substance abuse and rehabilitation issues.

A rehabilitation model of substance abuse counseling has recently been developed and expounded upon by Benshoff and Janikowski (2000). The model embraces the philosophies, theories, and constructs emanating from rehabilitation counseling. Rehabilitation counseling philosophy embraces holistic, individual, functional, and vocationally oriented approaches to working with clients. The model itself argues for consideration of substance abuse as a disability that is best treated with a functional assessment approach.

Psychopharmacological Treatments

Alcohol

Psychopharmacological treatments of alcohol use disorders have focused mainly on the effectiveness of the use of disulfiram (Antabuse). The purpose of taking Antabuse is to produce an unpleasant feeling when alcohol is consumed (i.e., nausea or increased heart rate), which discourages further drinking (Fuller, 1995). It is administered orally or as a subdermal implant. It may reduce drinking in older clients who have relapsed but are motivated to stop drinking, and in those who have moderate social stability. Without social support and volition, the use of disulfiram is no more effective than a placebo in reducing drinking (O'Brian & McKay, 1998). It may be more effective in preventing relapse when it is monitored by another person and combined with other treatment interventions (O'Farrell, Cutter, & Floyd, 1985).

Naltrexone, another antagonist medication, reduces the craving for alcohol and has shown promise in preventing full-blown relapses (O'Malley et al., 1996). The effect of Naltrexone extends beyond the period that the drug is taken. It appears to be especially effective in preventing relapse in individuals who are treatment compliant and who have many somatic complaints, poor learning abilities, and a high level of craving at the outset of treatment (O'Brien & McKay, 1998).

Opiates

The relapse rate for opiate dependence is very high (O'Brian & McKay, 1998). In the 1960s, methadone, a long-lasting opioid (non-opium-derived synthetic narcotic), was introduced as a maintenance treatment for opiate dependence. The opiate-dependent person was administered methadone orally once a day (compared to the intravenous user, who needs three to four injections of heroin daily to avoid the craving and intense withdrawal). This treatment has been controversial (Institute of Medicine, 1998), but methadone treatment has proven to enhance day-to-day functioning and to drastically reduce opiate abuse, without being a cure for the substance use disorder. Other interventions (e.g., counseling) are necessary to enhance treatment outcome (O'Brian & McKay, 1998).

Matching Treatment to the Individual

The Project MATCH (Project MATCH Research Group, 1993) compared the effectiveness of three treatment approaches to alcohol abuse and dependence: cognitive-behavioral treatment, motivational enhancement treatment, and 12-step facilitation treatment. Nine hundred clients received outpatient treatment and follow-up, and results suggested that the three approaches showed comparable success, and none was superior to the others (Project MATCH Research Group, 1997; see also Mattson et al., 1994). However, in a naturalistic, multisite evaluation within the Department of Veterans Affairs, 3,000 inpatients received either 12-step facilitation treatment, cognitive-behavioral treatment, or both. Results indicated that clients receiving the 12-step facilitative treatment were more likely to stay sober at follow-up than those who did not (Ouimette, Finney, & Moos, 1997). These two large-scale studies indicated that the clients with low psychiatric severity who received treatment based on the 12-step facilitative approach seemed to do slightly better at follow-up than clients who received cognitive-behavioral treatment (Finney & Moos, 1998).

Duration of Treatment

Brief treatment of alcohol abuse seems to be more effective than no intervention and often as effective as interventions of a longer duration (Bien, Miller, & Tonigan, 1993). Further, length of stay in inpatient treatment does not seem to have an impact on outcome (Mattick & Jarvis, 1994), with the exception of more severely impaired clients with little social support, who may profit from longer inpatient treatment (Finney & Moos, 1998). Outpatient or aftercare treatment is intended to continue the support from residential treatment. Aftercare has been linked to positive treatment outcomes (O'Farrell et al., 1993), and aftercare seems to be beneficial for clients discharged from their first treatment experience (Ito & Donovan, 1986).

CONCLUSION

Ray and Ksir (1993) suggested that federal funds used for drug interdiction should be re-appropriated to addiction treatment and research. Thombs (1994) suggested that the competency expectations for addictions counselors should be raised to better prepare them to consume research and contribute toward new research. The National Curriculum Development committee within the Addiction Technology Transfer Centers has developed standards for professional substance abuse practice, published in the 21st Technical Assistance Publication Series (TAP 21; Center for Substance Abuse Treatment, 1998a), that outline the knowledge, skills, and attitudes necessary for competent substance abuse counseling practice. In the future this document may serve as the basis for certification of substance abuse counselors. In addition, optimal practice guidelines for substance abuse counselors should be developed, based upon empirical research.

REFERENCES

Abrams, D. B., & Niaura, R. S. (1987). Social learning theory. In H. T. Blane & K. E. Leonard (Eds.), *Psychological theories of drinking and alcoholism.* (pp. 131–172). New York: Guilford.

Alcoholics Anonymous (AA). (1976). *The story of how many thousands of men and women have recovered from alcoholism* [the "Big Book"]. New York: AA World Services.

Alcoholics Anonymous (AA). (1981). *Twelve steps and twelve traditions.* New York: AA World Services.

American Society of Addictive Medicine (1996). *Patient placement criteria for treatment of substance-related disorders (2nd. edition): ASAM PPC-2.* Chevy Chase, MD: American Society of Addictive Medicine.

Anderson, D. F., & Berlant, J. L. (1995). Managed mental health and substance abuse services. In P. R. Kongstvedt (Ed.), *Essentials of managed health care* (pp. 150–162). Gaithersburg, MD: Aspen.

Annis, H. M., & Davis, C. S. (1988). Assessment of expectancies. In D. M. Donovan & G. A. Marlatt (Eds.), *Assessment of addictive behaviors* (pp. 84–111). New York: Guilford.

Azar, B. (1999). New pieces filling in addiction puzzle. *APA Monitor*, January.

Babor, T. (1993). Substance use and persons with physical disabilities: Nature, diagnosis, and clinical subtypes. In A. W. Heinemann (Ed.), *Substance abuse and physical disability* (pp. 43–56). New York: Hawthorn.

Bandura, A. (1969). *Principles of behavior modification.* New York: Holt, Rinehart & Winston.

Bandura, A. (1977). *Social learning theory.* Englewood Cliffs, NJ: Prentice Hall.

Bandura, A. (1986). *Social foundations of thought and action: A social cognitive theory.* Englewood Cliffs, NJ: Prentice-Hall.

Bart, M. (1999a). Drug courts found effective in curbing substance abuse, crime. *Counseling Today*, January.

Bart, M. (1999b). Substance abuse in people with disabilities. *Counseling Today*, March.

Basch, M. F. (1995). *Doing brief psychotherapy.* New York: Basic Books.

Beck, A. T., Wright, F. D., Newman, C. F., & Liese, B. S. (1993). *Cognitive therapy of substance abuse.* New York: Guilford.

Bell, A., & Rollnick, S. (1996). In F. Rotgers, D. S. Keller, & J. Morgenstern (Eds.), *Treating substance abuse: Theory and technique* (pp. 266–285). New York: Guilford.

Benshoff, J. J., & Janikowski, T. P. (2000). *The rehabilitation model of substance abuse counseling.* Belmont, CA: Brooks/Cole.

Bien, T. H., Miller, W. R., & Tonigan, J. S. (1993). Brief interventions for alcohol problems: A review. *Addictions, 88*, 315–336.

Brems, C., & Johnson, M. E. (1997). Clinical implications of the co-occurrence of substance use and other psychiatric disorders. *Professional Psychology: Research and Practice, 28,* 437–447.

Brick, J. (1990). Learning and motivational factors in alcohol consumption. In W. M. Cox (Ed.), *Why people drink: Parameters of alcohol as a reinforcer.* New York: Gardner.

Buelow, G. D., & Buelow, S. A. (1998). *Psychotherapy in chemical dependence treatment: A practical and integrative approach.* Pacific Grove, CA: Brooks/Cole.

Cappell, H., & Greeley, J. (1987). Alcohol and tension reduction: An update on research and theory. In H. T. Blane & K. E. Leonard (Eds.), *Psychological theories of drinking and alcoholism.* (pp. 15–54). New York: Guilford.

Cardoso, E., Chan, F., Thomas, K. R., Peterson, D. B., Mpofu, E., & Leahy, M. (1999). Substance abuse, disability, and case management. In F. Chan & M. Leahy, *Disability and health care: Case manager's desk reference.* (pp. 663–703). Lake Zurich, IL: Vocational Consultants Press.

Center for Substance Abuse Treatment (1995). *Assessment and treatment of patients with coexisting mental illness and alcohol and other drug abuse. Treatment Improvement Protocol (TIP) series # 9.* Rockville, MD: U.S. Department of Health and Human Services. DHHS Publication No. (SMA) 95-3061.

Center for Substance Abuse Treatment (1998a). *Addiction counseling competencies: The knowledge, skills, and attitudes of professional practice. Technical Assistance Publication (TAP) series #21.* Rockville, MD. U.S. Department of Health and Human Services. DHHS Publication. No. (SMA) 98-3171.

Center for Substance Abuse Treatment (1998b). *Substance use disorder treatment for people with physical and cognitive disabilities. Treatment Improvement Protocol (TIP) series # 29.* Rockville, MD: U.S. Department of Health and Human Services. DHHS Publication No. (SMA) 98-3249.

Conger, J. J. (1956). Alcoholism: Theory, problem, and challenge: II. Reinforcement theory and the dynamics of alcoholism. *Quarterly Journal of Studies on Alcohol, 13,* 296–305.

Cummings, C., Gordon, J. R., & Marlatt, G. A. (1980). Relapse: Strategies of prevention and prediction. In W. R. Miller (Ed.), *The addict behaviors* (pp. 231–321). Elmsford, NY: Pergamon.

Donovan, D. M., & Marlatt, G. A. (Eds.). (1988). *Assessment of addictive behaviors.* New York: Guilford.

Doweiko, H. E. (1999). *Concepts of chemical dependency* (4th ed.). Pacific Grove. CA: Brooks/Cole.

Drake, R. E., McHugo, G. J., & Noordsy, D. L. (1993). A pilot study of outpatient treatment of alcoholism in schizophrenia: Four-year outcomes. *American Journal of Psychiatry, 150,* 328–329.

Drake, R. E., & Noordsy, D. L. (1994). Case management for people with coexisting severe mental disorder and substance use disorder. *Psychiatric Annals, 24,* 427–431.

Edwards, G., Marshall, E. J., & Cook, C. C. H. (1997). *The treatment of drinking problems: A guide for the helping professions* (3rd ed.). New York: Cambridge University Press.

Fingarette, H. (1991). Alcoholism: The mythical disease. In D. J. Pittman & H. R. White (Eds.), *Society, culture, and drinking patterns reexamined. Alcohol, culture, and social control monograph series* (pp. 417–438). New Brunswick, NJ: Rutgers Center of Alcohol Studies.

Finney, J. W., & Moos, R. H. (1998). Psychosocial treatments for alcohol use disorder. In P. E. Nathan & J. M. Gorman (Eds.), *A guide to treatment that works* (pp. 156–166). New York: Oxford University Press.

Fuller, R. K. (1995). Antidipsotropic medications. In R. K. Hester & W. R. Miller (Eds.), *Handbook of alcoholism treatment approaches: Effective alternatives* (2nd ed., pp. 123–133). Needham Heights, MA: Allyn & Bacon.

George, R. L. (1990). *Counseling the chemically dependent: Theory and practice.* Englewood Cliffs, NJ: Prentice-Hall.

Heath, A. C., Jardine, R., & Martin, N. G. (1989). Interactive effects of genotype and social environment of alcohol consumption in female twins. *Journal of Studies in Alcohol, 50*(1), 38–48.

Heinemann, A. W. (1993). *Substance abuse and physical disability.* New York: Hawthorn.

Higgins, S. T., Delaney, D. D., Budney, A. J., Bickel, W. K., Hughes, J. R., Foerg, F., & Fenwick, J. W. (1991). A behavioral approach to achieving initial cocaine abstinence. *American Journal of Psychiatry, 148*, 1218–1224.

Institute of Medicine (1990). The effectiveness of treatment. In D. R. Gerstein & H. J. Harwood (Eds.), *Treating drug problems* (pp. 132–199). Washington, DC: National Academy Press.

Institute of Medicine (1998). *Bridging the gap between practice and research: Forging partnership with community-based drug and alcohol treatment.* Washington, DC: National Academic Press.

Ito, J., & Donovan, D. M. (1986). Aftercare in alcoholism treatment: A review. In W. R. Miller & N. Heather (Eds.), *Treating addictive behaviors: Process of change* (pp. 435–452). New York: Plenum.

Jellinek, E. M. (1945). The problem of alcohol. In Yale Studies on Alcohol (Ed.), *Alcohol, science, and society* (pp. 13–30). Westport, CT: Greenwood Press.

Johnson, V. E. (1980). *I'll quit tomorrow.* San Francisco: Harper & Row.

Keller, D. S. (1996). Exploration in the service of relapse prevention: A psychoanalytic contribution to substance abuse treatment. In F. Rotgers, D. S. Keller, & J. Morgenstern (Eds.), *Treating substance abuse: Theory and technique.* (pp. 84–116). New York: Guilford.

Khantzian, E. J. (1980). An ego/self theory of substance dependence: A contemporary psychoanalytic perspective. In D. J. Lettieri, M. Sayers, & H. W. Pearson (Eds.), *Theories on drug abuse: Selected contemporary perspectives* (DHHS Publication No. ADM 84-967). Washington, DC: U.S. Government Printing Office.

Khantzian, E. J., Halliday, K. S., & McAuliffe, W. E. (1990). *Addiction and the vulnerable self: Modified dynamic group therapy for substance abusers.* New York: Guilford.

Kofoed, L. L., Kania, J., Walsh, T., & Atkinson, R. M. (1986). Outpatient treatment of patients with substance abuse and coexisting psychiatric disorders. *American Journal of Psychiatry, 143*, 867–872.

Langenbucher, J. W., & Nathan, P. E. (1990). The tension-reduction hypothesis: A reanalysis of some early crucial data. In W. M. Cox (Ed.), *Why people drink: Parameters of alcohol as a reinforcer.* New York: Gardner.

Leeds, J., & Morgenstern, J. (1996). Psychoanalytic theories of substance abuse. In F. Rotgers, D. S. Keller, & J. Morgenstern (Eds.), *Treating substance abuse: Theory and technique* (pp. 68–83). New York: Guilford.

Lewis, J. A., Dana, R. Q., & Blevins, G. A. (1988). *Substance abuse counseling: An individualized approach.* Pacific Grove, CA: Brooks/Cole.

Lightfoot, L., Rosenbaum, P., Ogurzsoff, S., Laverty, G., Kusiar, S., Barry, K., & Reynolds, W. (1982). *Final report of the Kingston Treatment Development Research Project.* (Submitted to Health Promotion Directorate, Health and Welfare Canada). Toronto, Ontario: Addiction Research Foundation.

Marlatt, G. A., & Gordon, J. R. (Eds.). (1985). *Relapse prevention.* New York: Guilford.

Mattick, R. P., & Jarvis, T. (1994). In-patient setting and long duration for the treatment of alcohol dependence? Out-patient care is good. *Drug and Alcohol Review, 13,* 127–135.

Mattson, M. E., Allen, J. P., Longabaugh, R., Nickless, C. J., Connors, G. J., & Kadden, R. M. (1994). A chronological review of empirical studies of matching alcohol dependent clients to treatment. *Journal of Studies on Alcohol (Suppl. 12),* 16–29.

McCrady, B. S., & Epstein, E. E. (1996). Theoretical bases of family approaches to substance abuse treatment. In F. Rotgers, D. S. Keller, & J. Morgenstern (Eds.), *Treating substance abuse: Theory and technique* (pp. 117–142). New York: Guilford.

McGue, M., Pickens, R. W., & Svikis, D. S. (1992). Sex and age effects on the inheritance of alcohol problems: A twin study. *Journal of Abnormal Psychology, 101,* 3–17.

McKay, J. R. (1996). Family therapy techniques. In F. Rotgers, D. S. Keller, & J. Morgenstern (Eds.), *Treating substance abuse: Theory and technique* (pp. 143–173). New York: Guilford.

Mehr, J. (1988). *Human services: Concepts and intervention strategies.* Boston: Allyn & Bacon.

Mercer-McFadden, C., & Drake, R. E. (1994). *A review of demonstration programs for young adults with co-occurring substance use disorder and severe mental illness.* Rockville, MD: Substance Abuse and Mental Health Services Administration.

Milam, J. R., & Ketcham, K. (1983). *Under the influence.* New York: Bantam.

Miller, L. K. (1980). *Principles of everyday behavior analysis.* Monterey, CA: Books/Cole.

Miller, N. S. (1995). *Addiction psychiatry: Current diagnosis and treatment.* New York: Wiley-Liss.

Miller, W. R., & Rollnick, S. (2002). *Motivational interviewing: Preparing people for change* (2nd ed.). New York: Guilford.

Morgan, T. J. (1996). Behavioral treatment techniques for psychoactive substance use disorders. In F. Rotgers, D. S. Keller, & J. Morgenstern (Eds.), *Treating substance abuse: Theory and technique* (pp. 202–240). New York: Guilford.

Mueser, K., Bellack, A., & Blanchard, J. (1992). Co-morbidity of schizophrenia and substance abuse: Implications for treatment. *Journal of Consulting and Clinical Psychology, 60,* 845–856.

Nathan, P. E., & Lipscomb, T. R. (1979). Studies in blood alcohol level discrimination: Etiologic cues to alcoholism. In N. A. Krasnegor (Ed.), *Behavioral analysis and treatment of substance abuse* (pp. 178–190). Washington, DC: NIDA.

Nathan, P. E., & Skinstead, A. H. (1987). Alcoholism treatment outcomes: Current methods, problems, and results. *Journal of Consulting and Clinical Psychology, 55,* 332–340.

National Institute on Alcohol Abuse and Alcoholism (1990). *Alcohol and health: Seventh special report to the U.S. Congress* (DHHS Publication No. ADM 90-1656). Washington, DC: U.S. Government Printing Office.

National Institute on Alcohol Abuse and Alcoholism. (2000). Research refines alcoholism treatment options. *Alcohol Research and Health, 24,* 53–61.

Nowinski, J. (1996). Facilitating 12-step recovery from substance abuse and addiction. In F. Rotgers, D. S. Keller, & J. Morgenstern (Eds.), *Treating substance abuse: Theory and technique* (pp. 37–67). New York: Guilford.

O'Brian, C. P., & McKay, J. R. (1998). Psychopharmacological treatments of substance use disorders. In P. E. Nathan & J. M. Gorman (Eds.), *A guide to treatments that work* (pp. 127–155). New York: Oxford University Press.

O'Farrell, T. J., Choquette, K. A., Cutter, H. S. G., Brown, E. D., & McCourt, W. F. (1993). Behavioral marital therapy with and without additional couples relapse prevention sessions for alcoholics and their wives. *Journal of Studies on Alcohol, 54,* 652–666.

O'Farrell, J. J., Cutter, H. S., & Floyd, F. J. (1985). Evaluating family marital therapy for male alcoholics: Effects on marital adjustment and communication from before to after therapy. *Behavioral Therapy, 16,* 47–167.

O'Malley, S. S., Jaffe, A. J., Chang, G., Rode, S., Schottenfeld, R. S., Meyer, R. E., & Rounsaville, B. J. (1996). Six month follow-up of Naltrexone and psychotherapy for alcohol dependence. *Archives of General Psychiatry, 49,* 881–887.

Osher, F. C., & Kofoed, L. L. (1989). Treatment of patients with psychiatric and psychoactive substance abuse disorders. *Hospital Community Psychiatry, 40,* 1025–1030.

Ouimette, P. C., Finney, J. W., & Moos, R. H. (1997). Twelve-step and cognitive-behavioral treatment for substance abuse: A comparison of treatment effectiveness. *Journal of Consulting and Clinical Psychology, 65,* 230–240.

Pacione, T., & Jaskula, D. (1994). Quality chemical dependency treatment in an era of cost containment: Clinical guidelines for practitioners. *Health & Social Work, 19*(1), 55–61.

Pattison, E. M., Sobell, M. B., & Sobell, L. C. (1977). *Emerging concepts of alcohol dependence.* New York: Springer.

Pickens, R. W., & Thompson, T. (1986). Behavioral treatment of drug dependence. In J. Grabowski, M. L. Stitzer, & J. E. Henningfield (Eds.), *Behavioral intervention techniques in drug abuse treatment* (DHHS Publication No. ADM 86-1281). Washington, DC: U. S. Government Printing Office.

Prochaska, J. O., & DiClemente, C. C. (1986). Toward a comprehensive model of change. In W. R. Miller & N. Heather (Eds.), *Treating addictive behaviors: Processes of change* (pp. 3–27). New York: Plenum.

Prochaska, J. O., DiClemente, C. C., & Norcross, J.C. (1992). In search of how people change: Applications to addictive behaviors. *American Psychologist, 47,* 1102–1114.

Project MATCH Research Group (1993). Project MATCH: Rationale and methods for multisite clinical trial matching alcoholic patients to treatment. *Alcoholism: Clinical and Experimental Research, 17,* 1130–1145.

Project MATCH Research Group (1997). Matching alcoholism treatment to client heterogeneity: Project MATCH post-treatment drinking outcomes. *Journal of Studies on Alcohol, 58,* 7–29.

Ray, O., & Ksir, C. (1993). *Drugs, society, and human behavior.* St. Louis: Mosby.

Ridgely, M. S. (1994). Practical issues in the application of case management to substance abuse treatment. *Journal of Case Management, 3,* 132–138.

Rotgers, F. (1996). Behavioral theory of substance abuse treatment: Bringing science to bear on practice. In F. Rotgers, D. S. Keller, & J. Morgenstern (Eds.), *Treating substance abuse: Theory and technique* (pp. 174–201). New York: Guilford.

Rotgers, F., Keller, D. S., & Morgenstern, J. (Eds.) (1996). *Treating substance abuse: Theory and technique.* New York: Guilford.

Saunders, B., Wilkinson, C., & Towers, T. (1996). Motivational and addictive behaviors: Theoretical perspectives. In F. Rotgers, D. S. Keller, & J. Morgenstern (Eds.), *Treating substance abuse: Theory and technique* (pp. 241–265). New York: Guilford.

Schizophrenia Patient Outcomes Research Team (PORT). (1994). *Phase IA literature review: Treatment approaches for schizophrenia.* Baltimore: University of Maryland, Center for Mental Health Services Research.

Siegal, H. A., Rapp, R. C., Kelliher, C. W., Fisher, J. H., Wagner, J. H., & Cole, P. A. (1995). The strengths perspective of case management: A promising inpatient substance abuse treatment enhancement. *Journal of Psychoactive Drugs, 27*(1), 67–72.

Sobell, M. B., & Sobell, L. C. (1976). Second year treatment outcome of alcoholics treated by individualized behaviour therapy: Results. *Behaviour Research and Therapy, 14,* 195–215.

Stroul, B. A. (1989). Community support systems for persons with long-term mental illness: A conceptual framework. *Psychosocial Rehabilitation Journal, 12,* 9–26.

Substance Abuse and Mental Health Services Administration. (1998). *Substance use disorder treatment for people with physical and cognitive disabilities.* Rockville, MD: U.S. Department of Health and Human Services.

Substance Abuse and Mental Health Services Administration. (2002). *Results from the 2001 National Household Survey on Drug Abuse* (NHSDA Series H-17 DHHS Publication No. SMA 02-3758). Rockville, MD: U.S. Department of Health & Human Services.

Sullivan, W. P. (1994). Case management and community-based treatment of women with substance abuse problems. *Journal of Case Management, 3*(4), 58–161.

Sullivan, W. P., Hartmann, D. J., Dillon, D., & Wolk, J. L. (1994). Implementing case management in alcohol and drug treatment. *Families in Society: The Journal of Contemporary Human Services, 75,* 67–73.

Sullivan, W. P., Wolk, J. L., & Hartmann, D. J. (1992). Case management in alcohol and drug treatment: Improving client outcomes. *Families in Society, 73,* 195–203.

Talbott, G. D. (1989). Alcoholism should be treated as a disease. In B. Leone (Ed.), *Chemical dependency: Opposing viewpoints.* San Diego: Greenhaven.

Tarvydas, V. M., & Peterson, D. B. (1999). Clinical decision-making and ethical issues in case management. In F. Chan & M. Leahy, *Disability and health care: Case manager's desk reference.* (pp. 317–356). Lake Zurich, IL: Vocational Consultants Press.

Teague, G. B., Drake, R. E., & Ackerson, T. H. (1995). Evaluating use of continuous treatment teams for persons with mental illness and substance abuse. *Psychiatric Services, 46,* 689–695.

Thombs, D. L. (1994). *Introduction to addictive behaviors.* New York: Guilford.

Timney, C. B., & Graham, K. (1989). A survey of case management practices in addiction programs. *Alcoholism Treatment Quarterly, 6*(3/4), 103–127.

Vaillant, G. E. (1990). We should retain the disease concept of alcoholism. *Harvard Medical School Mental Health Letter, 6*(9), 4–6.

Wallace, J. (1996). Theory of 12-step-oriented treatment. In F. Rotgers, D. S. Keller, & J. Morgenstern (Eds.), *Treating substance abuse: Theory and technique* (pp. 13–36). New York: Guilford.

Wilson, G. T. (1988). Alcohol use and abuse: A social learning theory analysis. In C. D. Chaudron & D. A. Wilkinson (Eds.), *Theories on alcoholism.* Toronto: Addiction Research Foundation.

Wurmser, L. (1980). Drug use as a protective system. In D. J. Lettieri, M. Sayers, & H. W. Pearsons (Eds.), *Theories on drug abuse: Selected contemporary perspectives* (DHHS Publication No. ADM 84-967). Washington, DC: U.S. Government Printing Office.

Yalisove, D. L. (1989). Psychoanalytic approaches to alcoholism and addiction: Treatment and research. *Psychology of Addictive Behaviors, 3,* 107–113.

Chapter 17

Counseling People With Physical Disabilities

Daniel W. Cook

D
efining the term *physical disability* is not as straightforward as might be supposed. In order to deal with counseling issues related to physical disability (e.g., adjustment issues related to disability as a crisis situation), it is important to put *physical disability* in context. Nagi (1976) suggested the context of disease-pathology, illness, and impairment. According to Nagi (1976, 1991), disease-pathology is a factor or combination of factors that results in the deterioration of biologic health. Disease-pathology is an active state in which the organism seeks to restore itself to a healthy state, and it may stem from infection, degenerative processes, trauma, or other etiology, sometimes resulting in illness or impairment.

Illness exists on a continuum of acute to chronic and is generally thought to reflect temporary biologic malfunctioning; however, as a chronic state, it can result in impairment. An impairment is the residual effect of disease-pathology or illness, and its defining characteristic is some resulting functional limitation or restriction or loss in ability to perform some duty of daily living. Impairments can usually be medically specified and can result in functional limitations in emotional performance (as in schizophrenia), sensory performance (deafness or blindness), intellectual performance (mental retardation), or physical performance (amputation).

Nagi (1976) suggested that, when a person has a *permanent* or long-lasting impairment, such that the person is unable to perform *key* life functions, the person is said to be disabled. Disability thus is a relational term in that the impairment is considered in terms of the degree of functional limitation imposed. In the United States, disability has traditionally been defined in economic terms. For example, eligibility for Social Security

Disability Insurance (SSDI) depends on the extent to which the impairment limits a person's ability to work. With passage of federal legislation, specifically section 504 of the 1974 Rehabilitation Act and the Americans with Disabilities Act of 1990, disability has a broader definition reflecting the inability to perform major life tasks, such as self-care. Therefore *disability* can be defined as "any restriction or lack of ability to perform an activity within what is considered normal for a human being" (Liss & Kewman, 1996, p. 7). *Handicap*, a term once used as synonymous to *disability*, now reflects the disadvantages that result from environmental barriers. Nagi's emphasis on human functioning in defining disability has been incorporated in the World Health Organization's International Classification of Impairments, Disabilities, and Handicaps (DeAngelis, 2001). Physical disability, as differentiated from emotional, sensory, and intellectual disabilities, is most frequently associated with body extremity impairments, such as amputation or spinal cord injury. However, many also include chronic illness or disease (e.g., cancer, diabetes) as physical disabilities (e.g., Livneh & Antonak, 1997; Marshak & Seligman, 1993).

Physical disability and counseling concerns may be viewed from the perspective of visibility and onset of the disability. Hidden disabilities such as diabetes mellitus may not carry the same stigma as visible physical disabilities, such as spinal cord injuries. Also, the sudden onset of disability may result in different counseling-related issues than more insidious onset or congenital disabilities. Concerns related to counseling people with physical disabilities include client motivation, emotional concomitants associated with the disability, and the sequence of challenges involved in adjusting to or learning to cope with the disability.

MOTIVATION AND PHYSICAL DISABILITY

Why do some people seem driven to perform? Why are some people unwilling to attempt a task, even when they have a good chance to successfully complete it? Answering these types of questions is of critical importance to counselors who work with people with physical disabilities. Research on the perceptions of rehabilitation counselors (Thomas, Thoreson, Parker, & Butler, 1998; Zandy & James, 1979) has suggested the primacy of client motivation. Indeed, Thoreson, Smits, Butler, and Wright (1968) found that nearly half (44%) of a sample of rehabilitation counselors rated "lack of client motivation" as the central problem in counseling clients with physical disabilities. Thoreson et al., suggested five areas of counseling concern: (a) the client feels hopeless and depressed because of the disability; (b) the client assumes a passive role in counseling; (c) the client has unrealistic goals; (d) the client is receiving financial aid that acts as a disincentive to rehabilitation; and (e) there is a lack of jobs available to the client (p. 19).

In her now classic book, Safilios-Rothschhild (1970) reached similar conclusions in suggesting that motivation appeared to be a central construct in the rehabilitation of people with physical disabilities. In her view, a client is likely to be labeled as "unmotivated," which she defined as an unwillingness by the client to mobilize the physical and psychological resources to cope with the disability, when the client (a) refuses to follow prescribed tasks; (b) tries a task but gives up quickly; (c) keeps trying but fails to learn; and (d) is not insightful and does not accept professional definitions and solutions.

Following the analysis of Thoreson et al. (1968) and Safilios-Rothschild (1970), it seems clear that motivation covers both internal and external determinants of behavior, and it is thus important for counselors to attend to client needs and desires as well as to possible external disincentives such as SSDI payments. In any case it is of practical concern for the counselor to learn how to assist clients to do what is needed for client goal attainment to occur.

In understanding and incorporating motivational concepts into counseling, a thorough grounding in motivational theory is important. Implicit in all counseling is a motivational component (see Section II, chapters 2 through 11), or a rationale to explain why people behave as they do. Vinacke (1962) has described motivation as "the condition responsible for variation in intensity, direction, and persistence of ongoing behavior" (p. 3). From that definition flows the framework for attending to the various facets of motivation; that is, what is it that governs and enhances the intensity of behavior, goal choice or the direction of behavior, and the persistence or maintenance of behavior?

Different counseling theories use different concepts to explain client motivation. Most if not all motivation approaches can be placed into one of four categories.

1. *Tension reduction approaches*, including psychoanalytic theories and drive and need reduction theories. The basic premise is that people are pushed by some internal force to meet a need or reduce a drive. The emphasis is on reaching and/or maintaining psychic homeostasis (see chapters 2, 3).
2. *Progressive movement approaches*. The person is thought to be proactive and forward moving. The person is pulled toward a goal and need fulfillment (see chapter 4).

3. *Motivation as extrinsic to the person.* Behavior is controlled by reinforcement contingencies. There is no such thing as "internal motivation" (see chapter 7).
4. *Motivation as cognitive expectations.* Internal needs interact with environment incentive conditions. Emphasis is placed on goal striving and expectations concerning situational determinants (see chapters 8, 9, and 10).

Two motivational models, McDaniel's (1976) decision-making approach and the Minnesota Work Adjustment Model (Dawes, Lofquist, & Weiss, 1968) are particularly appropriate for counselors working with persons with physical disabilities. McDaniel's approach (see also Roessler, 1989) focuses on work motivation and is based on the cognitive-expectancy model of Vroom (1964). According to Vroom, people attach positive or negative value to objects and outcomes that they encounter. Certain outcomes, such as earning money, generally have positive value, although not always, as when earning too much money may disqualify one for valued services. Other actions, such as requesting a job accommodation, can have a negative value. In addition, people hold expectations that by acting they will in fact achieve the desired outcomes. McDaniel elaborated Vroom's model by developing a motivational equation specific to counseling people with physical disabilities. According to McDaniel, whether or not a person will engage in a task, such as participating in physical therapy or seeking a job interview, will depend on three things: (a) the person's cognitive appraisal of the cost or effort involved, (b) the personal value of completing the task, and (c) the estimated chance of actually completing the task. The three factors identified by McDaniel are subjective estimates of the cost, value, and likelihood of success made by the person before engaging in the task at hand. By putting these estimates into a formula whereby motivation equals estimated task utility or value multiplied by estimated probability of a favorable outcome, divided by the estimated personal "cost" of engaging in the task, the counselor has a powerful tool to make concrete the abstract concept of client motivation. This approach is particularly valuable in assisting clients to make comparisons, weigh difficult choices, and deal with "unrealistic" vocational goals.

The Minnesota Theory of Work Adjustment (MTWA) is a rarity, a substantial model of work motivation developed specifically for vocational rehabilitation counseling. According to the model (Dawes, 1976), work adjustment problems are likely to develop when workers either are not able to satisfy their work-related needs or when employers find worker ability to perform job tasks unsatisfactory. Basically, the MTWA approach considers the use of specially developed instruments designed to measure the work-related motivation (needs) of persons with physical disabilities and the specific need-satisfying reinforcers found in different jobs. Other instruments measure the abilities of the person and the ability requirements of the job. Job success is defined by length of tenure on the job and is predicted by the match between the job-related needs and abilities of the individual and the ability requirements and need-satisfying conditions inherent in the job. In the MTWA model, motivation is defined as the presence of need-satisfying conditions in the job and is a key component in predicting job success.

Motivation is a key construct in working with people with physical disabilities. From the counselor's perspective, learning how to help clients do what is needed for successful rehabilitation to occur is of central concern. It is equally important to consider the client's perspective. Being reluctant to pursue a task or choose a goal does not mean that one is "unmotivated"; it is more accurate to say that one's goals do not completely agree with the counselor's goals. There is no such thing as an unmotivated client. People work to achieve goals, which vary by time and place.

PSYCHOLOGICAL ADJUSTMENT AND PHYSICAL DISABILITY

An understanding of psychological reactions associated with physical disability is of prime importance to counselors. According to early clinical wisdom, the severity of the physical disability was a key predictor of psychological adjustment; that is, the more severe the disability, the more likely that psychological problems would occur. It was also thought that certain personality traits would be associated with certain disabilities; for example, people who are deaf were thought likely to exhibit characteristics of paranoia. Classic in-depth reviews of the research evidence by Shontz (1971) and Wright (1960) concluded that there is virtually no support for such assertions. However, that does not mean there are no psychological concomitants associated with severe physical disability. Rather, the relationship between psychological adjustment and physical disability is complex, multidimensional, and moderated by other variables, such as gender, socioeconomic status, and availability of social supports. Current research has focused on the underlying process that people may experience in dealing with a physical disability and the specific emotional reactions experienced with the onset of a physical disability.

One of the most popular approaches in studying adaptation or coping with physical disability is based on stage theories, which are based almost entirely on clinical observation that uses the framework of a developmental sequence. Most of the more than twenty models suggesting an adjustment sequence or "stages" of adjustment were developed through the study of spinal cord injury (e.g., Dunn, 1975; Hohmann, 1975) because, by any definition, spinal cord injury presents a crisis situation and people who experience a spinal cord injury go from a state of independence to dependence, while remaining cognitively intact.

Stage theories, or the hypothesized sequenced steps or stages that people go through in adjusting to the psychological effects of a severe disability, can and do serve as a guide to counseling interventions (Livneh & Antonak, 1997). For example, Dunn (1975) suggested five stages in the adjustment process to a spinal cord injury.

1. *Acute or shock stage*, which occurs soon after injury. The prevalent psychological reactions are anxiety, confusion, and disorientation. Counselors are encouraged to supply information and nonjudgmental support, while avoiding ambiguity.
2. *Mourning*, when awareness of the consequences of the injury occurs. The emotional response is similar to mourning the death of a loved one, and withdrawal may take place. Counselors should not support the person's attempt to withdraw, and social interaction should be encouraged.
3. *Denial*, when active avoidance of the consequences of the injury takes place. The person sets unrealistic personal expectations and may exhibit hostility in counseling. Counselors should use a realistic matter-of-fact attitude and should encourage the person to set goals.
4. *Depression*, when rehabilitation begins to bring to awareness the full range of disability-related deprivations. Rehabilitation-related frustrations lead to discouragement, sadness, and loss of purpose. Reactions are similar to mourning, but the person is less withdrawn. Counselors should deal with self-esteem issues at this stage.
5. *Adaptation*. Adjustment is not the end stage; rather the person adapts disability-appropriate responses in different life domains (e.g., vocational, social, and physical functioning).

Dunn (1975) believes that emotional reactions may alternate between stages and that a person may recycle through earlier stages before reaching the adaptation stage.

Livneh (1986) has integrated some 20 different stage theories into what he calls a unified model of adaptation to physical disability that specifies

five stages: initial impact, defense mobilization, initial realization, retaliation, and reintegration. Livneh describes each stage in detail, including
defense mechanisms specific to that stage and affective, behavioral, and
cognitive correlates. For example, the defense mobilization stage is viewed
as consisting of two substages, expectancy of recovery and denial (see
Dunn's stage 3). The operative defense mechanism is denial, along with
such other ego defenses as suppression and intellectualization. Affective
correlates include both cheerfulness (optimistic expectations) and anger.
Cognitive correlates include distortion of factual events and rejection of
counseling efforts.

While the process of adjustment or adaptation to physical disability is
almost certainly developmental in nature, stage theory remains controversial. One criticism of stage theory is methodological; that is, the models
were developed almost entirely on the basis of clinical anecdotes, and
there is almost no empirical evidence supporting the approach. Also, stage
theories often lack clear theoretical attributes, with clear and explicit constructs. For example, theorists often specify separate stages of mourning
and depression without drawing clear distinctions between the constructs.
Stage theories tend to be popular with practitioners because they provide
guidelines for practice. However, counselors need to be aware of the dangers
in uncritical acceptance of stage theories, such as setting unwarranted
counselor expectations (e.g., that depression is a "normal" course of events
in the psychological adjustment process and is, in fact, expected to occur).
For an in-depth review of stage theories and related constructs, see Caplan
and Shechter (1987), Livneh and Antonak (1997), and Marshak and Seligman (1993).

Whether or not people with physical disabilities follow a well-defined
sequence of adjustment stages, specific emotional reactions are of vital
interest to counselors, especially of those who are newly disabled. For
example, McDaniel (1976) suggests that treatment environments themselves may contribute to observed emotional reactions because they can
foster anxiety and arousal. As McDaniel has pointed out, it is not surprising
that common reactions to the stress of a severe physical disability often
include increased somatic preoccupation, depressive symptoms, and hypo-
chondriasis or increased attention to somatic sensations. Perhaps the most
studied emotion in the context of counseling people with physical disabilities is depression.

DEPRESSION AND PHYSICAL DISABILITY

There is some evidence (e.g., Turner & McLean, 1989) to suggest that
people with physical disabilities, as a group, are more likely to experience

major depression than nondisabled people, and that people with certain physical disabilities, such as multiple sclerosis (Schubert & Foliart, 1993), may be at higher risk for depression. While depression among people with physical disabilities is not universal, Turner and McLean found that people with physical disabilities were four times as likely as nondisabled bodied people to experience major depression, and counselors should thus be alert to the possibility.

Berven, Habeck, and Malec (1985), in a well-conceived study representative of the research on disability and physical disability, examined the psychological characteristics of a sample of rehabilitation medical inpatients. Based on scores obtained from the MMPI-168, a short form of the Minnesota Multiphasic Personality Inventory (MMPI), they were able to identify four distinct patient subgroups. The largest subgroup (50% of the sample) showed no clinical elevations on any of the MMPI scales but did have an average score profile suggesting somatic concerns, not a surprising finding given the study setting. People in this subgroup were seen as successfully coping. The second largest subgroup (20% of the sample) exhibited higher clinical scale elevations, indicating "severe personality disorganization, accompanied by depression, anxious worrying and disorganized thinking" (p. 215). People in this subgroup exhibited the most severe personality problems and appeared to be in need of immediate psychological intervention. The third subgroup (17% of the sample) had MMPI scale profiles suggesting depression, anxious worrying, and social isolation as significant problems. The fourth subgroup (13% of the sample) was marked by distress and affective disturbances concerning "somatic focusing." It seems important to note that nearly half of the sample of people with physical disabilities undergoing medical treatment were in fact "coping" with their disabilities and did not exhibit any severe psychological problems. On the other hand, about one fifth of the sample were experiencing substantial psychological problems and were in need of counseling interventions, although there was no evidence that the disability was the *cause* of the problems.

Research findings on the nature and scope of psychological distress, especially the incidence and prevalence of depression, is anything but clear (Livneh & Antonak, 1997; Marshak & Seligman, 1993). However, it is reasonable to expect that in samples of people with physical disabilities, a substantial proportion, perhaps as large as 40%, are at risk for major depression, and about 20% may in fact be experiencing extreme personality disorganization (Berven et al., 1985; Cook, 1980). Much of the research on psychological adjustment and physical disability is cross-sectional in nature and seeks to identify the incidence of psychological problems at one point in time. Unfortunately, such research does not address the prevalence of psychological problems across the lifespan.

COUNSELING INTERVENTIONS FOR PEOPLE WITH PHYSICAL DISABILITIES

There is little reason to doubt that most, if not all, counseling theories and techniques are applicable to people with physical disabilities. However, in two instances theories have been modified to address specific concerns of counselors working with people with physical disabilities. In one instance rehabilitation psychologists have illustrated how behavior modification techniques, especially B. F. Skinner's (1987) conceptualization of operant conditioning, can be applied as an intervention in counseling people with physical disabilities. In the other instance, the seminal work of Kurt Lewin (1935, 1936) has been adapted in a model called somatopsychology, which attends to important variables in counseling people with physical disabilities.

In rehabilitation there is a long history of applying behavior modification or behavioral analysis techniques to helping people with physical disabilities regain lost physical and social functioning (Bednar & Zelhart, 1968; Marr & Means, 1980; Walls, 1969). Wilbert Fordyce (1971, 1976) was an early spokesman for the application of operant conditioning in rehabilitation. Basically, an operant is any freely emitted response that is observable and quantifiable. Such responses are controlled by reinforcement contingencies, where reinforcement is anything that will increase the probability that a response will reoccur, and contingencies refer to the rate at which the behavior or operant must occur before reinforcement results. Application of this technology to rehabilitation requires a careful analysis of the specific behavior to be addressed, noting where, when, and under what specific conditions the behavior does or does not occur (see Marr & Means, 1980, for specific procedures on how to conduct this analysis). Generally, the idea is to isolate the target behavior and focus on either increasing the frequency of the behavior (when there is a behavioral deficit), decreasing the frequency of the behavior (when there is a behavioral excess), teaching the behavior (when the behavior is not in the person's behavioral repertoire), or maintaining the behavior at its current level.

According to Fordyce (1976), there are three core types of behavioral problems that counselors are likely to see in working with people with physical disabilities: dealing with crisis management, extinguishing disability-inappropriate behavior, and teaching and maintaining new disability-appropriate behavior. With the onset of a physical disability the person is often faced with immobilization and sensory deprivation. In this crisis situation the person can lose those things found to be previously reinforcing, while experiencing the aversive effects associated with the disability. These adverse aspects often function as negative reinforcers; that is, they strengthen those behaviors that lead to escape or avoidance of rehabilitation-appropriate behaviors. Fordyce suggested that it would not be unusual for counselors to observe people in these circumstances using fantasy and withdrawal as mechanisms to avoid such potentially painful rehabilitation tasks as physical therapy.

The primary behavioral intervention when a person is in the crisis phase is to decrease the aversive nature of rehabilitation (rehabilitation functioning as punishment) by decreasing the reinforcing aspects of avoidance or escape behavior. Similarly, counselors might focus on decreasing such disability-inappropriate behavior as fantasizing about those now inaccessible social and vocational activities the person engaged in prior to the onset of the disability, while working with the person to increase disability-appropriate behaviors, such as meeting environmental demands.

Somatopsychology or "body psychology" (Barker, Wright, Meyerson, & Gonick, 1953; Wright, 1960, 1983) is based on Lewin's (1935) field theory as applied to understanding the psychological adjustment process of people with physical disabilities. Barker et al. defined somatopsychology as "those variations in physique that affect the psychological situation of [the person's] body as a tool for action or by serving as stimulus . . . to others" (p. 1). As such, somatopsychology makes use of such Lewian concepts as the life space, environmental barriers to life goals, and expectations concerning life goal attainment, while also making use of Lewin's popular dictum that behavior is a function of the interaction of the person with the environment.

In planning counseling interventions, the somatopsychological model places emphasis on values held by both the counselor and the client. For example, Dembo (1964) urged counselors to consider the perspective of people with disabilities, whom she called "insiders," as well as the perspective of nondisabled people, whom she viewed as "outsiders," when considering adjustment to disability. Outsiders sometimes imply that people with disabilities are suffering psychological misfortune, when that is not the case. Similarly, Wright (1960) suggested the phenomenon of the "requirement of mourning," whereby nondisabled observers assume that people with physical disabilities, especially those who are newly disabled, "mourn" over lost function resulting from the disability, when in reality they may not mourn.

As an intervention technique, somatopsychology stresses analysis of the person-by-situation interaction. Counselors are urged to attend to both the importance of the person's values and personal self-perception of disability *and* the situation of the person with the disability. This is especially important because somatopsychologists believe that disability can act as a stimulus to others in the person's life space.

Wright (1960, 1975, 1983) has written extensively on applying somatopsychological principles to analyzing and understanding the psychological framework underlying the process of adjustment when people experience physical disability. She suggested that a main goal when counseling a person with a physical disability is facilitation of the coping process. According to Wright, the main problem often facing counselors when working with persons with physical disabilities, especially those who are newly disabled, is succumbing to the effects of the disability. Succumbing rather than coping is likely when the person with a disability is placed in a situation where:

1. The emphasis is on what the person cannot do.
2. Little weight is given to areas of life in which the person can participate.
3. The person is seen as passive, as a victim of misfortune.
4. Prevention and cure are the only solutions.
5. The person is pitied and devalued (Wright, 1975, p. 219).

Succumbing to the effects of a disability is also likely when the person assumes an inferior status position. According to Wright (1983), people who have assumed an inferior status position:

1. Hold dual identifications by identifying with the disability group they are a part of, as well as with the larger nondisabled population.
2. Engage in "as if" behavior by acting "as if" they are not disabled.
3. Engage in the idolization of normal standards and try to reach unattainable standards of "normal performance."
4. Attend to what they cannot do rather than what they can do.

Through the counseling relationship, counselors can facilitate the adjustment process by helping persons with physical disabilities to learn to view the disability as merely another personal characteristic. That is, the person does not devalue himself or herself as a disabled person, but as a person *with* a disability. Wright (1983) views that the optimum adjustment or coping process will occur when a person:

1. Enlarges the scope of his or her values by dealing with other than disability-related values.
2. Subordinates physique by limiting the importance of physical appearance and ability.
3. Contains the spread of disability by limiting disability to the actual impact of the impairment.
4. Places emphasis on asset values rather than comparative values.

In the context of the counseling relationship, the somatopsychological model provides the framework for understanding the key elements of succumbing or coping when adjusting to the effects of a physical disability.

REFERENCES

Barker, R. G., Wright, B. A., Meyerson, L., & Gonick, M. R. (1953). *Adjustment to physical handicap: A survey of the social psychology of physique and disability* (2nd ed.). New York: Social Science Research Council.

Bednar, R. L., & Zelhart, P. F. (1968). An introduction to behavior therapy for rehabilitation workers. *Rehabilitation Research and Practice Review, 1*(1), 39–47.

Berven, N. L., Habeck, R. V., & Malec, J. (1985). Predominant MMPI-168 profile clusters in a rehabilitation medicine sample. *Rehabilitation Psychology, 30,* 209–219.

Caplan, B., & Shechter, J. (1987). Denial and depression in disabling illness. In B. Caplan (Ed.), *Rehabilitation psychology desk reference* (pp. 133–170). Rockville, MD: Aspen.

Cook, D. W. (1980). Psychological adjustment to spinal cord injury: Incidence of denial, depression, and anxiety. *Rehabilitation Psychology, 26,* 97–104.

Dawes, R. V. (1976). The Minnesota theory of work adjustment. In B. Bolton (Ed.), *Handbook of measurement and evaluation in rehabilitation* (2nd ed., pp. 203–218). Baltimore, MD: University Park Press.

Dawes, R. V., Lofquist, L. H., & Weiss, D. J. (1968). A theory of work adjustment. *Minnesota Studies in Vocational Rehabilitation, Vol. XXIII.* Minneapolis: University of Minnesota.

DeAngelis, T. (2001). APA has lead role in devising classification system. *Monitor on Psychology,* February, 54–56.

Dembo, T. (1964). Sensitivity of one person to another. *Rehabilitation Literature, 25,* 231–235.

Dunn, M. K. (1975). Psychological intervention in a spinal cord injury center: An introduction. *Rehabilitation Psychology, 22,* 165–178.

Fordyce, W. (1971). Behavioral methods in rehabilitation. In W. S. Neff (Ed.), *Rehabilitation psychology* (pp. 74–108). Washington, DC: American Psychological Association.

Fordyce, W. (1976). A behavioral perspective on rehabilitation. In G. L. Albrecht (Ed.), *The sociology of physical disability and rehabilitation* (pp. 73–96). Pittsburgh: University of Pittsburgh Press.

Hohmann, G. (1975). Psychological aspects of treatment and rehabilitation of the spinal cord injured person. *Clinical Orthopedics, 112,* 81–88.

Lewin, K. (1935). *A dynamic theory of personality.* New York: McGraw-Hill.

Lewin, K. (1936). *Principles of topological psychology.* New York: McGraw-Hill.

Liss, M., & Kewman, D. G. (1996). Implications for rehabilitation psychology of the World Health Organizations' international classification of impairments disabilities and handicaps (1980): A brief overview. *Division 22 Newsletter, 23*(2), 7–8.

Livneh, H. (1986). A unified approach to existing models of adaptation to disability: Part I. A model of adaptation. *Journal of Applied Rehabilitation Counseling, 17,* 5–16.

Livneh, H., & Antonak, R. F. (1997). *Psychological adaptation to chronic illness and disability.* Rockville, MD: Aspen.

Marr, J. N., & Means, B. L. (1980). *Behavior management manual: Procedures for psychological problems in rehabilitation.* Fayetteville, AR: Arkansas Rehabilitation Research and Training Center.

Marshak, L. E., & Seligman, M. (1993). *Counseling people with physical disabilities.* Austin, TX: Pro-Ed.

McDaniel, J. W. (1976). *Physical disability and human behavior* (2nd ed.). New York: Pergamon.

Nagi, S. D. (1976). An epidemiology of disability among adults in the United States. *Milbank Memorial Fund Quarterly: Health and Society, 54,* 439–467.

Nagi, S. D. (1991). Disability concepts revisited: Implications for prevention. In A. M. Pope & A. R. Tralov (Eds.), *Disability in America: Toward a national agenda for prevention.* Washington, DC: National Academy Press.

Roessler, R. T. (1989). Motivational factors influencing return to work. *Journal of Applied Rehabilitation Counseling, 20,* 14–17.

Safilios-Rothschild, C. (1970). *The sociology and social psychology of disability and rehabilitation.* New York: Random House.

Schubert, D. S,. & Foliart, R. H. (1993). Increased depression in multiple sclerosis patients. *Psychosomatics, 34,* 124–130.

Shontz, F. C. (1971). Physical disability and personality. In W. S. Neff (Ed.), *Rehabilitation psychology.* Washington, DC: American Psychological Association.

Skinner, B. F. (1987). What ever happened to psychology as the science of behavior? *American Psychologist, 42,* 780–786.

Thomas, K. R., Thoreson, R. W., Parker, R. M., & Butler, A. J. (1998). Theoretical foundations of the counseling function. In R.M. Parker & E.M. Szymanski (Eds.), *Rehabilitation counseling: Basics and beyond* (pp. 235–268). Austin, TX: Pro-Ed.

Thoreson, R. W., Smits, S. J., Butler, A. J., & Wright, B. A. (1968). Counselor problems associated with client characteristics. In G. N. Wright (Ed.), *Wisconsin studies in vocational rehabilitation* (Vol. 3, pp. 1–32). Madison: University of Wisconsin Regional Rehabilitation Research Institute.

Turner, R. J., & McLean, P. D. (1989). Physical disability and psychological distress. *Rehabilitation Psychology, 34,* 225–242.

Vinacke, E. (1962). Motivation as a complex problem. *Nebraska Symposium on Motivation 10,* 1–45.

Vroom, V. (1964). *Work and motivation.* New York: Wiley.

Walls, R. T. (1969). Behavior modification and rehabilitation. *Rehabilitation Counseling Bulletin, 13,* 173–183.

Wright, B. A. (1960). *Physical disability: A psychological approach.* New York: Harper & Row.

Wright, B. A. (1975). Social-psychological leads to enhance rehabilitation effectiveness. *Rehabilitation Counseling Bulletin, 18,* 214–223.

Wright, B. A. (1983). *Physical disability: A psychosocial approach* (2nd ed.). New York: Harper & Row.

Zandy, J. J., & James, L. F. (1979). The problem with placement. *Rehabilitation Counseling Bulletin, 22,* 439–442.

Chapter 18

Counseling Intervention and Skills Training for People With Psychiatric Disabilities

Marie Ciavarella, Patrick W. Corrigan, John Hilburger, Chow S. Lam, and Fong Chan

Traditionally, rehabilitation counselors have had a strong emphasis on serving people with physical disabilities, but this trend has been gradually changing. For example, Ingraham, Rahimi, Tsang, Chan, and Oulvey (2001) reported that the number of mental illness cases served by some state rehabilitation agencies has now surpassed the number of physical disability cases. In a recent study, Chan et al. (2003) reported that knowledge of mental health and substance abuse issues has been identified by practicing rehabilitation counselors as an important training need.

The rehabilitation counseling profession has a history of serving people with serious psychiatric disabilities. The Vocational Rehabilitation Amendments of 1943 (PL 78-113), the Barden-LaFollette Act, extended state vocational rehabilitation services from serving only people with primarily physical disabilities to serving persons with mental retardation and mental illness. The 1979 community mental center legislation (PL 94-63) also recognized the importance of rehabilitation services and mandated that these services be included as a part of the essential components of a community mental health center (Anthony, 1980). In 1979, the Rehabilitation Services Administration (RSA) provided funding to Boston University to establish the country's first rehabilitation research and training center in mental illness. In addition, the first university program to offer a master's degree in rehabilitation counseling with an emphasis on psychiatric rehabilitation was established in 1971 in the Department of Rehabilitation Counseling at Boston University (Farkas, O'Brien, & Nemec, 1988).

In the late 1970s, the Community Support System (CSS) initiative was established as the result of the disastrous consequences of the rapid deinstitutionalization of people with serious mental illness (Anthony, 1996). The Community Support Program (CSP) of the National Institute of Mental Health (now the Center for Mental Health Services) provided federal guidelines and resources necessary to further the CSS initiative. The CSP defined the range of services (e.g., case management, rehabilitation, family and peer support, housing, and crisis response) needed for a CSS to effectively serve people with serious mental illness. Although these CSS services received little attention in traditional mental health systems during the time of deinstitutionalization, they have always been the central focus of federal-state vocational rehabilitation agencies. Not surprisingly, the development of psychiatric rehabilitation integrates the philosophy and principles of vocational rehabilitation with various psychotherapeutic techniques (Farkas et al., 1988).

Anthony (1996) enumerated the underlying principles of psychiatric rehabilitation as "(a) equipping clients with skills; (b) client self-determination; (c) using the resources of the environments; (d) social change; (e) differential assessment and care; (f) emphasis on employment; (g) emphasis on the here and now; and (h) early intervention" (p. 27). Underlying these principles are the values emphasized by psychiatric rehabilitation (i.e., treating the individual with dignity and respect in a caring and compassionate way).

Persons with severe mental illness struggle with a variety of disabilities. They may have deficits in cognition, social skills, hygiene and personal management, coping skills, interpersonal support, symptom management, and motivation. Comprehensive psychiatric rehabilitation programs, combined with appropriate medication management, help individuals meet the variety of needs and challenges imposed by their psychiatric disabilities. According to Corrigan, Rao, and Lam (1999), the goal of a psychiatric rehabilitation program is to help people with psychiatric disabilities achieve the following goals:

- *Inclusion.* People with psychiatric disabilities want to be included in the activities and experience of everyday life.
- *Opportunities.* People with psychiatric disabilities need opportunities to achieve the range of life activities and experiences in their community.

- *Independence*. People with psychiatric disabilities want to achieve the goals of inclusion and opportunities, without requiring undue dependence on rehabilitation programs or their staff.
- *Recovery*. Recovery means helping persons with psychiatric disabilities control the symptoms and overcome the deficits that result from mental illness.
- *Quality*. People with psychiatric disabilities want to have a good quality of life.

To help people with psychiatric disabilities achieve these rehabilitation goals, rehabilitation programs are designed to help individuals diminish their psychiatric symptoms, learn and use interpersonal skills, learn and use coping skills, avail themselves of community resources, and avail themselves of community supports. Counseling and community-based interventions for people with severe and persistent mental illness are necessary for achieving these goals, which varied considerably from the in-office therapeutic approaches.

PRACTICAL AND THEORETICAL CONSIDERATIONS IN COUNSELING PEOPLE WITH MENTAL ILLNESS

Building Rapport and Establishing Trust

People with severe and persistent mental illness generally have a difficult time establishing relationships. After multiple hospitalizations, many experiences with mental health professionals for short periods of time, and many "failures" in their lives (Horowitz, Farrell, Forman, & Dincin, 1995), they are not likely to quickly establish a relationship with a new counselor, case manager, worker, or other mental health professional who comes into their life. They may be having realistic life issues, such as food, shelter, and health problems, and may be experiencing frightening and debilitating symptoms.

The first meeting needn't be long. The counselor helps the client establish immediate priorities (e.g., does the client need a place to live, need food or clothing, have access to transportation, have medical problems needing immediate attention?). A good way to begin establishing a relationship is to do something for the person. People with mental illness must often negotiate a complex system of service providers in order to achieve goals, and the system is often overwhelming because their mental illnesses may cause them to be extremely disorganized. Helping the person negotiate the system (e.g., SSI, SSDI, State VR, Mental Health, Medicaid, Medicare) can demonstrate concern and desire to help in concrete and tangible ways.

Establishing trust is difficult, because people with mental illness may be seen for short periods of time and then "handed off "to the next professional in the next stop in the continuum of care. Although it may not be possible to slowly develop a relationship over an extended time, it is important to use the listening skills of encouraging, paraphrasing, and summarizing (Ivey & Ivey, 2003) that are taught in counselor training. Since time with a consumer may be limited, it is important to establish the necessary conditions (e.g., empathic understanding, respect and uncon-ditional positive regard, genuineness, concreteness) relatively quickly. Showing interest in this way helps consumers feel that there is a reason to invest their trust in a practitioner who will support them in their efforts to accomplish change and who seems sincerely interested in helping them find ways to improve their lives. Becoming a "significant other" to someone with mental illness allows the practitioner to make suggestions to which the consumer will be honestly open. Because they have usually been in the system so long, consumers may not be used to having the option of choosing their own goals on both a short- and long-term basis. A trusting relationship allows consumers to truly listen to advice when they are establishing their own goals or when things get difficult for them, because they know that the practitioner is sincerely interested in their well-being.

A very important factor in establishing trust is dependability. It is critical that practitioners be on time, ready to begin, and ready to devote full attention to the consumer. The first several sessions may need to be short because of the consumer's limited tolerance for the intensity of a counseling situation. Consumers may need help in organizing a plan to identify goals. Using the goal areas established by Dincin (1975), consumers can be helped to design a structure within which they can identify and attain their goals.

Enthusiasm and Hopefulness

Practitioners must demonstrate enthusiasm and hopefulness throughout the entire counseling relationship with people with severe mental illness. Hope has often been crushed by the stigma of mental illness (Garske & Stewart, 1999) and, as a result, consumers may see their lives as a failure. Deegan (1992) describes her own experience of learned helplessness and the resulting despair and feelings of powerlessness. Families may also share feelings of hopelessness and helplessness (Spaniol, Zipple, & Lockwood, 1992). Vinogradov and Yalom (1989) identify instillation of hope as a curative or therapeutic factor in group therapy. Dincin (1975) described staff as having "dynamic hopefulness," which can be borrowed by clients when they feel hopeless. Hopefulness is seen as the first step in the recovery process by Russinova (1999). It is critical that counselors maintain hopefulness and enthusiasm in the face of the many difficulties that they are helping consumers to overcome.

Separation and Transition

In continuing to work with consumers, practitioners must try to anticipate difficult times. People with mental illness are especially sensitive to stress, since stress may increase symptoms. They are likely to feel stress during any type of change in their lives. Given that change is an essential and indeed expected part of most rehabilitation programs, practitioners must try to make consumers aware that a new situation might increase stress and to help them come up with plans to deal with the stress. Stress reduction techniques or medication evaluation can allow consumers to survive temporary increases in stress. Practitioners must also work with consumers to manage changes in their lives in order to avoid too many changes occurring at the same time.

Although an ongoing relationship with the same counselor is the optimum, it may become necessary for many reasons, both programmatic and personal, to transition consumers to new counselors. Consumers react to transition in different ways, but time must be allowed for them to react and work through significant changes in relationships. It may be necessary to reassure consumers that the separation is not a result of something negative that they may have done. If the transition is to another practitioner in the same program, consumers should have the opportunity to participate in choosing the new counselor. If possible, there can be several meetings with the consumer that include the old and new counselor. Topics discussed during transition meetings would include the positive accomplishments of the consumer, recognition and legitimization of feelings about separation, and looking forward to continued growth with the new counselor. No one can ever replace the old counselor, but a new and productive, although different, relationship can be developed with the new counselor.

Vocational Counseling

Wanting to work is by far the most common reason that people with mental illness come into contact with a rehabilitation counselor, because getting up every day and going to work makes one a part of the "normal" world. On the other hand, receiving disability benefits or not working usually tends to reinforce the stigma already associated with mental illness. Although most consumers want to work and can do so, they should also have an option to choose a satisfying lifestyle that may not include work.

An important service that rehabilitation counselors can provide is helping consumers decide on the kinds of job that they want to pursue. It is important not to unintentionally limit job choices to the usual array of entry-level positions available in most programs (Garske & Stewart, 1999). A case could be made that the low employment rate of people with mental illness is due to dissatisfaction with the type of work perceived to be available to them. In an unpublished study by Demopoulos and Hilburger (1998), an inverse relationship was found between years of education and job satisfaction among people with mental illness in supported employment. In that study the vast majority of people were working in jobs that were classified as unskilled. It is also important to keep in mind that schizophrenia generally first surfaces during adolescence, thereby robbing individuals of the exploratory career-choosing experiences generally occurring during this time of life. It is clearly incumbent upon practitioners to match the consumer to the job in the most effective way possible.

The simplest place to start in the matching process is with an in-depth review of consumer work history. Although there may be little or no work experience evident, consumers may have had part-time or volunteer jobs or other activities that may provide clues regarding job-related preferences. By starting at the time of leaving school, a picture of life can emerge, as it unfolded, from the person's own perspective. The practitioner is looking for a particular kind of work or other activity that the person enjoyed and that can be used as a basis for career choice discussions.

If the discussion of experience proves not to be helpful, other directions may be pursued. Has the consumer ever thought about a particular kind of work? What would he or she pick out as a "dream job"? In what kind of setting would he or she like to work (e.g., office, factory, store, indoors, outdoors, alone, in a group, day shift, night shift)? Such exercises may provide valuable insights into preferences and values. Although it is possible to use traditional interest testing, results from people with mental illness sometimes produce flat profiles, showing neither interest nor lack of interest in any particular field. A different approach might be to use the Career Interest Survey from the *Complete Guide for Occupational Exploration* (Farr, 1993), which approaches career choice using work values, school subjects liked, leisure activities, and preferred work settings, and then links these preferences directly to particular interest areas and job groups and subgroups. This method would seem to provide a straightforward and simple approach to job choice, which could be done as part of a group or in between sessions.

Once a career direction is chosen, there are several paths in which a consumer may proceed, depending on resources available in one's community. Will the consumer require education or training to achieve a goal? Is there a supported education program in the area? Is there a "Projects with Industry" or other program providing direct placement? Is there a psychosocial or clubhouse program with a supported employment program or job club in the area? Is there an individual placement and support (IPS) program available? Are you able to set up an IPS program in your mental health or vocational center? (Bond, 1998, has reviewed the growing body of support for the IPS model.) The important issue is that the practitioner and consumer spend much time and effort developing a relationship, making it possible to provide the support necessary to anticipate and respond to difficult issues and maintain the consumer in the community. Part of follow-along services is making sure that supports are available and accessible after consumers begin working. If consumers know that they can call on their counselors if something comes up (no matter how insignificant), there is a good chance of interceding before a job is lost. Of course, people will lose jobs, and practitioners must then intercede as soon as possible, trying to understand the reasons for losing the job, and repeat as many steps as necessary to return consumers to work with a new chance of success.

Finally, there are some issues that must be addressed during the vocational development process. First, it is important that consumers realistically understand the effects of working on SSI/SSDI, Medicare/Medicaid, and other benefits. Concepts such as trial work period, substantial gainful employment, and spend downs may be difficult to understand and explain, but it is important to help consumers understand so that they will continue to be able to pay for medications or other necessities. Second, it is important to be aware of medication-related issues that apply to working. Asking a physician to rearrange the times that medications are taken may accommodate for sleepiness during the day. How does one take and explain medications if privacy is not available? How does one deal with or explain the need for water to counteract dry mouth? Some medications may affect one's ability to dissipate heat or may enhance sensitivity to sunlight. If a consumer is looking for a job working outdoors or in very warm conditions, he or she should discuss these issues with the prescribing physician. Consumers need to choose whether or not to disclose a mental illness to employers, and if they choose to disclose, what are the appropriate reasonable accommodations they may need and can request?

THE NEED FOR SKILLS TRAINING FOR PERSONS WITH MENTAL ILLNESS

Experts in psychosocial rehabilitation have consistently emphasized the importance of skills training as an essential component for recovery (Anthony & Nemec, 1984; Bellack, Mueser, Gingerich, & Agresta, 1997; Corrigan, Schade, & Liberman, 1992). While psychiatric medication provides relief from severe and acute symptoms, skills training helps individuals acquire new skills and practice these skills so they can better negotiate everyday tasks. Skills training helps persons with mental illness recover their social, occupational, and instrumental role to the fullest extent possible. The goal of skills training is achieved through learning procedures and environmental supports.

Skills training, which is in its third decade of development, is a structured application of learning techniques designed to help persons with mental illness build a repertoire of skills. Proponents of skills training assume that consumers are capable of acquiring the ability to respond appropriately in diverse situations. In order to use skill training, rehabilitation professionals must possess the necessary skills to effectively help consumers both acquire and use interpersonal, vocational, and instrumental skills. Rehabilitation professionals may have knowledge regarding the importance of skills training, but the effectiveness of this knowledge is thwarted unless they know how to teach new skills to consumers. Professionals ensure repeated practice and success, which help individuals acquire, utilize, and maintain skills (Corrigan et al., 1992). The benefits of skills training deserve attention before the actual procedures are discussed.

Skills Training and Recovery

Skills training is important for recovery. Skill acquisition helps consumers to function more independently in order to meet their own needs. When individuals are better able to adapt to community living, they are better able to recover from the effects of their illness (Deegan, 1988). Furthermore, skill acquisition can be protective when a person becomes overwhelmed by stress. When a consumer has few skills, the impact of life stressors is great. When life stressors overwhelm a consumer's ability to cope, symptoms may become exacerbated. When symptoms are exacerbated, the ability to use acquired skills is diminished, which in turn creates more stress; the final result is greater acuity in symptoms. Skills training is vital for recovery, but which skills should be taught?

ESSENTIAL SKILLS

Basic skills are those necessary to increase effectiveness in interpersonal and role functioning, which comprises many separate skills, all of which help in achieving relational and concrete goals. Examples of relational goals are having coffee with a friend at the local diner or setting a date to take nieces and nephews to a movie. Concrete goals might include obtaining a job, going grocery shopping, and refilling a prescription at the pharmacy. Skills are sets of verbal and nonverbal actions that enable consumers to achieve certain goals.

Social, Instrumental, and Coping Skills

There are three broad skill categories essential to psychiatric rehabilitation: social skills, instrumental skills, and coping skills (see Table 18.1 for examples). Social skills facilitate interpersonal situations and include verbal

TABLE 18.1   Examples of Skills Training Content Areas

Social Skills
–Initiating conversation
–Managing a conflict
–Refusing the request of phone salespeople
–Talking with the psychiatrist about the need for a new medication

Instrumental Skills
–Budgeting money
–Shopping for groceries
–Creating a resume
–Securing entitlements

Coping Skills
–Self-administrating medications
–Getting the proper amount of sleep each night
–Calling a friend when feeling depressed
–Visiting the clubhouse regularly to structure the day

and nonverbal actions that allow the accurate communication of emotions, requests, and needs. Examples of social skills include conversation, assertiveness, and dating skills. Instrumental skills enable a person to attain independence and material benefits. Examples include meal planning and shopping, cleaning house, and using public transportation. Coping skills help individuals manage symptoms of psychiatric illness as well as the stressors of everyday living. Coping skills are further divided into skills that *alleviate* distress and skills that help individuals *tolerate* distress.

Correct self-administration of psychiatric medications can alleviate symptoms, such as auditory hallucinations. Taking psychiatric medications is then a skill to *alleviate* the distress of symptoms. On the other hand, if self-administration of medications does not alleviate symptoms, consumers may learn to *tolerate* auditory hallucinations by, for example, wearing a walkman to distract themselves. Here the consumer uses a skill to *tolerate* persistent symptoms. A combination of medications may alleviate symptoms of insomnia and lack of appetite for a consumer with depression. Consumers who experience depression and are unable to take psychiatric medications may need to use coping skills (e.g., only using bedroom for sleep; waking up each day at the same time; and cooking favorite foods) to tolerate their symptoms.

Assessment of Goals and Skills

The people who know best about the skills that they want to learn are the consumers themselves. Consumers make the final decisions as to the skills that they are lacking, want to learn, and will use. There are several ways in which to engage consumers to inquire about their interests in learning specific skills. Ideally, consumers want to learn skills that they need to reach their short-term and long-term goals. For example, a consumer interested in working may first want to learn skills to determine her interests. She may learn to use conversational skills to ask people about their jobs or learn problem-solving skills to access library information on career interests. If a consumer wants to cope with his psychiatric symptoms without turning to illicit substances and alcohol, he needs to learn and use coping skills to alleviate his psychiatric symptoms and urges to use substances (McCracken, Holmes, & Corrigan, 1998). If a consumer desires to have his own apartment, he needs to know how to manage his money, grocery shop, prepare food, and clean the apartment (Hemphill, Peterson, & Werner, 1991). Asking consumers about their goals is the best way to find out what skills they want to learn.

Overcoming Cognitive Barriers to Consumer Goal Setting

Some consumers with significant cognitive impairment may be unable to answer direct questions regarding short-term and long-term goals (Spaulding, Reed, Poland, & Storzbach, 1996). One way that professionals can ascertain consumers' wishes is to ask about current life situations (e.g., housing, material needs, and relationships). Following is a conversation between a consumer and provider:

Provider:	"Jane, do you like where you live now?"
Consumer:	"It is okay, but I wish that I could go out to eat more."
Provider:	"Oh. How could you go out to eat more?"
Consumer:	"I could go out to eat more if I didn't waste my money buying everybody else cigarettes."
Provider:	"So you have a hard time saying 'No' to people who ask you for cigarettes?"
Consumer:	"You bet. I wind up giving most of my cigarettes away. And then when I go to the store to buy more, I always buy a key chain, and I have so many key chains."
Provider:	"Sounds like you want to learn to spend your money better and to not always give in when you are asked for a cigarette."
Consumer:	"Yeah. That is it."

The rehabilitation professional has learned about skills that the person wants to learn and that would benefit her. A treatment recommendation could then be made to attend groups to learn assertiveness and money management skills. If consumers struggle with motivation to make a commitment to a particular goal, motivational interviewing can be employed (Corrigan, McCracken, & Holmes, 2001). Although asking individuals about skills that they want to learn is the prototypical way to obtain information, there are additional ways to gather information (see Table 18.2 for the different options), such as natural observation, role play, and structured assessments (Bellack et al., 1997).

TABLE 18.2   Ways to Gather Information for Skills Training

Informal interview
Natural observation
Role play
Structured interview

Information from Role Plays and Structured Interviews

Providers can observe the consumer in natural interactions. This type of observation leaves the consumer free to interact without interference from rehabilitation professionals. Consequently, consumers may feel more relaxed and less self-conscious, yielding a more accurate picture of current functioning. For example, the counselor may observe consumers while talking with their psychiatrists regarding medication; on a field trip interacting with service personnel; negotiating conflicts with peers; and performing their work responsibilities at a clubhouse.

Second, providers can observe the consumers in role plays designed by professionals. Some examples of role plays may include refusing a solicitation to use drugs/alcohol; obtaining information to plan a recreational outing; and deciding whom to call when one relapses. These role plays should be designed to give the consumer an opportunity to actually perform a skill (e.g., allow the consumer to practice assertiveness to refuse a drink or to role-play calling the skating rink and requesting information on hours, cost, and equipment).

Third, providers can ask consumers to participate in structured assessments of their current functional capabilities and deficits. Functional assessments are used to determine the ability to function in different life domains, such as symptom management, conflict resolution, money management, grooming and hygiene, dating, and vocation. Most functional assessments begin with rehabilitation professionals asking consumers a series of questions about their current functioning. Sample questions might include: "Can you pay your own rent?"; "Do you self-administer your medications?"; "Do you go out with friends at least once a week?"; and "How do you cope with your symptoms?" Functional assessments are used to help paint an overall picture of the consumer's current functional status.

Cultural Bias in Skills Training

Questions asked in functional assessments or scenarios used in role plays can have a cultural bias. The questions and scenarios are typically rooted in the cultural values of the tool developers. Before addressing specific ways to teach skills training, it is important to recognize possible cultural bias. Most skills training researchers are white middle-class males in academia. Consequently, the socially "appropriate" behaviors that are taught in skills training groups may not necessarily be relevant to *all* groups of people.

Numerous variables need to be considered when one attempts to teach socially "appropriate" skills, such as age, gender, race, ethnicity, and religion. For example, managing a conflict in the heart of a large metropolis may be very different from doing it in a small town, where residents know each other. In an urban area, direct eye contact and assertive statements may be most effective, whereas in a rural area, a smile, handshake, and request may more effectively solve the problem. In some cultures conversations with a psychiatrist about changing medications would be disrespectful. For example, in Asian cultures deference to an authority figure is viewed as respectful rather than unassertive (Tsui & Schultz, 1985).

There are ways to assess cultural values to determine culture-specific skills. A study of "street-smarts" in European Americans and African Americans helps to illustrate this point (Holmes, Corrigan, Stephenson, & Nugent-Hirschbeck, 1997). European Americans were found to be "reactive" in dealing with police, tending to handle conflicts *after* they arose. In contrast, African Americans were more interested in avoiding the conflict before it occurred. Socially "appropriate" behaviors for these ethnic/racial groups varied a great deal.

Goal setting is very much tied to the dominant American culture. Some ethnic groups, such as Native Americans, Asians, and Latinos, have an orientation to the here-and-now (Sue & Sue, 2003) and are not inclined to think of goals several years down the road. Good treatment planning can only occur when rehabilitation professionals know their consumers well. A best practice for rehabilitation professionals is to survey consumer groups to ascertain the skills that are "appropriate." Sample questions to assess skills might include the following: "In your culture, how might you resolve a conflict?"; "What is a typical topic of conversation?"; "Do people generally ask doctors questions, or merely listen to them?"

SKILLS TRAINING PACKAGES

There are many prepacked skills training curricula focusing on such skills as recreation, medication management, conflict management, sleep management, job finding, and dating. Prepackaged materials are highly structured, making it easy for providers to learn to use them (Corrigan, MacKain & Liberman, 1994).

Skill Areas and Learning Activities

Skills trainers distinguish between learning activities and skill areas; trainers conduct learning activities, while consumers practice skills (Liberman & Corrigan, 1993). Skill areas are the specific, socially appropriate actions that a person learns in order to achieve a desired goal. For example, in teaching someone to start a conversation, the consumer may be taught five separate skills: body posture, voice volume, appropriate content, volley of questions and answers, and ending of the conversation. Furthermore, skills can be further divided into smaller parts (e.g., body posture may include how one stands or sits, along with physical gestures).

Steps to Skills Training

There are seven distinct learning activities in skills training, as shown in Table 18.3 (Liberman & Corrigan, 1993). The first is an *introduction* to the skill, where the consumer is told what the skills are and when they are used. For instance, an introduction to symptom management skills would include an overview of individual skills (e.g., identification of warning signs, knowing whom to call if symptoms become acute) and a rationale for why the skills are useful (e.g., so that consumers can manage their illnesses and stay out of the hospital). Providing a clear rationale for learning a particular skill helps to build motivation to acquire the skill. For skills training to be successful, a consumer needs to be clear on *how* to change and *why* to change (i.e., motivation for learning the skill; Miller & Rollnick, 2002).

The next learning activity is *modeling*. Models can be actors on a prerecorded videotape or live consumers and rehabilitation professionals. Models afford consumers the opportunity to view the skill being performed. For example, consumer actors may discuss coping strategies that they use to combat symptoms of psychosis, depression, mania, or anxiety. Video actors may discuss a variety of conversational topics or ways to use the newspaper to find an apartment for rent. Modeling allows for vicarious

TABLE 18.3 Learning Activities in Skills Training

Introduction
Modeling
Role play
Resource management
Outcome problems
In vivo exercises
Homework

Maintenance

learning; however, not all people are able to learn vicariously. For some people, learning is solidified only when they are asked to repeat the information to which they were exposed.

A way to maximize learning during modeling is to devise a series of questions about the skill that was performed. Questions for modeling the skill of symptom management might include: "What coping strategies were mentioned?"; "Was the importance of taking medication mentioned?"; "How does taking medicine help you cope?" Asking questions helps to focus consumer attention on the models; if consumers are unable to correctly answer the questions, group leaders may want to repeat the modeling, reduce the amount of information, or slow down the pace of the models. Further discussion of techniques to ameliorate cognitive impairments during skills training will be reviewed at the end of the chapter.

Role play is the third and possibly the most important learning activity in skill acquisition (Liberman, 1988). Role play affords an opportunity to actually practice what was learned. Ideally, consumers receive feedback from the rehabilitation professional and peers on their performance of the skills. It is imperative that consumers receive praise and encouragement for their performance, while also receiving specific, positive feedback (e.g., "Your smile before greeting John was a great opener to the conversation" or "You did a great job identifying two side effects about which to ask your psychiatrist"). Praise is crucial, because (1) it helps consumers feel successful in their attempts to perform; (2) it may result in an increased sense of self-efficacy, which should help consumers to perform the skill again; and (3) fellow group members, seeing a successful peer, may be willing to participate more fully in this critical learning activity.

Feedback helps consumers consolidate their learning, since consumers learn what they are doing correctly and gain increasing comfort with actually performing the skills. Detailed feedback, which highlights key but subtle skill components (e.g., a smile before saying "hello") calls attention to these small points, which, when performed, will go a long way toward helping to achieve a goal. Praise and positive feedback are necessary ingredients to help support a person's sense of self-efficacy. Consumers feel that they can change. Canned or "pat" phrases will not help bolster self-confidence. The rehabilitation professional's warmth and genuineness make praise most effective.

The next learning activity is *resource management*. In resource management, consumers learn what a resource is, how to identify a range of resources to meet a specific goal, and how to obtain resources. For example, a consumer who has trouble sleeping might learn that there are resources to aid in falling asleep, such as using a fan as "white noise" to block out other sounds, drinking warm milk before going to bed, and drawing the shades to block out light from the street (Holmes, 1998). The final activity in resource management is helping the consumer determine the means to obtain resources. In the previous example, a consumer could determine ways to obtain a fan (e.g., buy one at the store or borrow one from family).

Outcome problems is a learning activity focused on teaching consumers how to identify barriers to implementing the skills and, subsequently, how to problem solve to remove or circumvent the barriers. Problem solving is taught in a stepwise fashion (D'Zurilla, 1999): adopt an attitude that the problem can be solved; define the problem so that all persons involved agree on the definition of the problem; brainstorm solutions to the problem; consider pros and cons of individual solutions; select a solution and plan its implementation; implement the solution selected; and, finally, evaluate the implementation to determine if the solution was effective or if an alternate solution should be used (see Table 18.4).

An example of an outcome problem is a consumer who experiences sun sensitivity as a side effect of medication. He enjoys being outside, but does not want to get sunburned. Some means to solve the problem include using sunscreen, wearing a hat and long sleeves, or staying in the sun for only short periods of time. The pros and cons of each means to solve the problem are discussed, and the option that would be best for that particular person is chosen. Making a decision about the problem-solving action is important; however, continued practice of skills to achieve the desired goal is most critical. Consequently, the consumer needs to learn to generalize the performance of these skills.

The next two learning activities are designed to enhance generalization, or the consumer's ability to transfer skill performance to different locations and settings and with different persons. Teaching new skills can be relatively simple, while the generalization of the skills beyond the treatment setting is far more difficult (Corrigan & Basit, 1997). For instance, generalization has occurred when a consumer uses conflict management skills not only with peers in the treatment program but also at home, with a store clerk, and with her friends.

The sixth learning activity is *in vivo exercises*. In an in vivo exercise, a consumer performs the skill in the community with a rehabilitation professional present to serve as an aide should the consumer need assistance. For example, a professional may accompany a consumer who is learning to ride public transportation. The professional provides necessary instrumental support, encouragement, and praise for performing the skill

TABLE 18.4   Problem-Solving Steps

1. Adopt a problem-solving attitude.
   "I believe that I can find a solution to asking Sheila for a date when she might say 'no.' "
2. Define the problem.
   "I'm afraid to ask for fear that she'll say 'no.' "
3. Brainstorm solutions.
   "Call her on the phone."
   "Ask her in person."
   "Write her a letter."
   "Have my friend ask her for me."
4. Identify pros and cons of each solution.

Pros	Cons
"Ask her in person."	
She could "yes" right away.	She could say "no" right away.
She could see that I'm sincere.	She might think I'm not handsome enough.
We could plan the date right then.	She might tell me she has a boyfriend.

5. Select a solution.
   "Ask her in person because she could see that I'm sincere, and she might say 'yes' right away."
6. Implement the solution.
   "Plan to ask her tomorrow when I see her."
7. Evaluate the implementation.
   "I asked her and she said "yes," and we planned to go see a movie, so I did it, and it worked out."

and useful feedback. For the consumer learning to ride public transportation, the rehabilitation professional congratulates her on paying the correct fare but provides direction when she attempts to take the bus in the opposite direction from her destination.

The last learning activity is *homework assignments*. A homework assignment is given to have the consumer practice the skills in the community without the aid of a rehabilitation professional. Homework assignments are one of the best ways to help a person generalize a newly learned skill (McFall, 1982). A consumer may begin to perform the skill with significant others present for support and in places where he or she will be relatively successful, encountering few barriers. As consumers become more adroit at performing skills, they gradually attempt to achieve their goals in situations with more barriers. For example, individuals may elect to try out newly learned conversational skills with their neighbors and then try talking to strangers at the bowling alley. "Successful" completion of homework is one indication that a consumer has learned the skills being taught. Furthermore, maintenance of the skills also needs attention if performance is to be sustained.

One last step in skills training is to provide continued opportunities for consumers to use skills that they have learned. When people do not repeatedly perform skills, their ability to perform the skills decreases over time. Ongoing practice of skill performance helps to maintain learning, which further enhances generalization of skills (Edelstein, 1989). Maintenance occurs when skills that are learned in the treatment program are remembered and performed many months or years later (Corrigan & Basit, 1997).

OVERCOMING COGNITIVE BARRIERS
IN SKILLS TRAINING

Persons with mental illness generally tend to have some level of cognitive impairment when their symptoms are acute. Cognitive impairment adversely affects the learning and performance of new skills. Difficulties with memory, attention, and problem solving are some examples of cognitive deficits. In teaching skills training, the leader needs to structure the group and the learning activities in such a way as to improve the consumer learning and retention of information (Bellack et al., 1997).

Most interventions to ameliorate cognitive impairments require professionals to help reduce the number of cognitive tasks that the consumer needs to perform (Corrigan, 1996). Specific suggestions to address cognitive impairment include decreasing the need for consumers to take notes in group by providing handouts; providing charts with big letters in group rooms to serve as visual prompts; giving clear and simple directions, with minimal steps; and having consumers repeatedly practice skills that they are learning, since the more automatic a response becomes, the less taxing it is to execute. In addition, when instructions are given to consumers to assess their understanding of the skill, the counselor should ask them to demonstrate the skill instead of merely eliciting a verbal reply. Finally, role plays should be short and only on the topic relevant to the skill. If a role play lasts too long, consumers may lose their focus and start to veer off into unrelated topics or, worse yet, feel discouraged because they were unable to stay on task.

REFERENCES

Anthony, W. A. (Ed.). (1980). Rehabilitating the person with a psychiatric disability: The state of the art [Special Issue]. *Rehabilitation Counseling Bulletin, 24*(1).

Anthony, W. A. (1996). *Community support systems: Lessons for managed care.* Boston: Boston University, Center for Psychiatric Rehabilitation.

Anthony, W. A., & Nemec, P. B. (1984). Psychiatric rehabilitation. In A. S. Bellack (Ed.), *Schizophrenia: Treatment, management, and rehabilitation* (pp. 375–413). Orlando, FL: Grune & Stratton.

Bellack, A. S., Mueser, K. T., Gingerich, S., & Agresta, J. (1997). *Social skills training for schizophrenia: A step-by-step guide.* New York: Guilford.

Bond, G. R. (1998). Principles of the Individual Placement and Support model: Empirical support. *Psychiatric Rehabilitation Journal, 22,* 11–23.

Chan, F., Leahy, M., Saunders, J., Tarvydas, V., Ferrin, J. M., & Lee, G. (2003). Training needs of certified rehabilitation counselors for contemporary practice. *Rehabilitation Counseling Bulletin, 46,* 82–91.

Corrigan, P. W. (1996). Models of "normal" cognitive functioning. In P. W. Corrigan & S. C. Yudofsky (Eds.), *Cognitive rehabilitation for neuropsychiatric disorders* (pp. 3–52). Washington, DC: American Psychiatric Press.

Corrigan, P. W., & Basit, A. (1997). Generalization of social skills training for persons with severe mental illness. *Cognitive and Behavioral Practice, 4,* 197–206.

Corrigan, P. W., MacKain, S. J., & Liberman, R. P. (1994). Skills training modules: A strategy for dissemination and utilization of a rehabilitation innovation. In J. Rothman & E. Thomas (Eds.), *Intervention research* (pp. 317–352). Chicago: Haworth.

Corrigan, P. W., McCracken, S. G., & Holmes, E. P. (2001). Motivational interviews as goal assessment for persons with psychiatric disability. *Community Mental Health Journal, 37,* 113–122.

Corrigan, P. W., Rao, D., & Lam, C. (1999). Psychiatric rehabilitation. In F. Chan & M. Leahy (Eds.), *Health care and disability case management* (pp. 527–564). Lake Zurich, IL: Vocational Consultants Press.

Corrigan, P. W., Schade, M. L., & Liberman, R. P. (1992). Social skills training. In R. P. Liberman (Ed.), *Handbook of psychiatric rehabilitation* (pp. 95–126). Boston: Allyn & Bacon.

Deegan, P. E. (1988). Recovery: The lived experience of persons as they accept and overcome the challenge of the disability. *Journal of the California Alliance for the Mentally Ill, 11,* 11–19.

Deegan, P. E. (1992). The independent living movement and people with psychiatric disabilities: Taking back control over our own lives. *Psychosocial Rehabilitation Journal, 15*(3), 3–19.

Demopoulos, V. K., & Hilburger, J. (1998). *Job satisfaction of people with severe mental illness.* Unpublished manuscript.

Dincin, J. (1975). Psychiatric rehabilitation. *Schizophrenia Bulletin, 13,* 131–147.

D'Zurilla, T. J. (1999). *Problem solving therapy: A social competence approach to clinical intervention* (2nd ed.). New York: Springer.

Edelstein, B. A. (1989). Generalization: Terminological, methodological, and conceptual issues. *Behavior Therapy, 20,* 311–324.

Farkas, M. D., O'Brien, W. F., & Nemec, P. B. (1988). A graduate level curriculum in psychiatric rehabilitation: Filling a need. *Psychosocial Rehabilitation Journal, 12*(2), 53–66.

Farr, J. M. (1993). (Ed.). *The complete guide for occupational exploration.* Indianapolis: JIST.

Garske, G. G., & Stewart, J. R. (1999). Stigmatic and mythical thinking: Barriers to vocational rehabilitation services for persons with severe mental illness. *Journal of Rehabilitation, 65*(4), 4–8.

Hemphill, B. J., Peterson, C. Q., & Werner, P. C. (1991). *Rehabilitation in mental health: Goals and objectives for independent living.* Thorofare, NJ: Slack.

Holmes, E. P. (1998). *Sleep management: A psychoeducational module.* Tinley Park, IL: University of Chicago Center for Psychiatric Rehabilitation.

Holmes, E. P., Corrigan, P. W., Stephenson, J., & Nugent-Hirschbeck, J. (1997). Learning "street smarts" for an urban setting. *Psychiatric Rehabilitation Journal, 20*(3), 64–66.

Horowitz, R., Farrell, D., Forman, J., & Dincin, J. (1995). The rehabilitation relationship. In R. Lamb (Ed.-in-chief) & J. Dincin (Ed.), *A pragmatic approach to psychiatric rehabilitation: Lessons from Chicago's Thresholds program, New Directions for Mental Health Services* (no. 68, pp. 21–32). San Francisco: Jossey-Bass.

Ingraham, K., Rahimi, M., Tsang, H., Chan, F., & Oulvey, E. (2001). Work support groups in state vocational rehabilitation agency settings: A case study. *Psychiatric Rehabilitation Skills, 5,* 6–21.

Ivey, A. E., & Ivey, M. B. (2003). *Intentional interviewing and counseling: Facilitating client development in a multicultural society* (5th ed.). Pacific Grove, CA: Brooks/Cole.

Liberman, R. P. (1988). Social skills training. In R. P. Liberman (Ed.), *Psychiatric rehabilitation of chronic mental patients* (pp. 147–189). Washington, DC: American Psychiatric Press.

Liberman, R. P., & Corrigan, P. W. (1993). Designing new psychosocial treatments for schizophrenia. *Psychiatry, 56,* 238–249.

McCracken, S. G., Holmes, E. P., & Corrigan, P. W. (1998). Cognitive behavioral strategies for persons with mental illness and substance abuse problems. *Psychiatric Rehabilitation Skills, 2*(2), 206–232.

McFall, R. M. (1982). A review and reformulation of the concept of social skills. *Behavioral Assessment, 4,* 1–33.

Miller, W. R., & Rollnick, S. (2002). *Motivational interviewing: Preparing people for change.* New York: Guilford.

Russinova, Z. (1999). Providers' hope inspiring competence as a factor in optimizing psychiatric rehabilitation outcomes. *Journal of Rehabilitation, 65*(4), 50–57.

Spaniol, L., Zipple, A., & Lockwood, D. (1992). The role of the family in psychiatric rehabilitation. *Schizophrenia Bulletin, 18,* 341–348.

Spaulding, W. D., Reed, D., Poland, J., & Storzbach, D. M. (1996). Cognitive deficits in psychotic disorders. In P. W. Corrigan & S. C. Yudofsky (Eds.), *Cognitive rehabilitation of neuropsychiatric disorders* (pp. 129–166). Washington, DC: American Psychiatric Press.

Sue, D. W., & Sue, D. (2003). *Counseling the culturally diverse: Theory and practice* (4th ed.). New York: Wiley.

Tsui, P., & Schultz, G. L. (1985). Failure of rapport: When psychotherapeutic engagement fails in the treatment of Asian clients. *American Journal of Orthopsychiatry, 55,* 561–569.

Vinogradov, S., & Yalom, I. D. (1989). *A concise guide to group psychotherapy.* Washington, DC: American Psychiatric Press.

Chapter 19

Persons with Mental Retardation Who Present Significant Behavioral and Emotional Challenges: A Habilitative Mental Health Therapy Approach to Treatment

William I. Gardner, Elizabeth Watson, and Kimberly M. L. Nania

B ehavioral and emotional challenges of persons with mental retardation present barriers both to vocational adjustment and community living. A number of writers indicate that significant mental health difficulties occur with greater frequency among this group than in the general population (Borthwick-Duffy, 1994; Nezu, Nezu, & Gill-Weiss, 1992; Tuinier & Verhoeven, 1993). The increased prevalence is reflected in the occurrence of more serious psychiatric disorders as well as in less severe but nonetheless clinically significant behavioral and emotional difficulties. In fact, surveys of counselors (Wittman, Strohmer, & Prout, 1989) and psychologists (Jacobson & Ackerman, 1989) have documented that persons with mental retardation served by these professionals present a wide range of life problems and concerns in such areas as interpersonal relationships with peers and family members, sexuality, problem behaviors, self-esteem, and issues involving work and residential settings.

The majority of psychological concerns are manifested as overt *behavioral* difficulties. The excessive and disruptive nature of these difficulties creates problems not only for the individuals themselves but also for others in their social, work, and community environments. Examples include verbal and physical aggression, excessive disruptive activity levels, sexually inappropriate acts, impulsive agitated or disruptive episodes, ritualistic or compulsive routines, property damage or destruction, excessive negativism, and acts of self-injury. This behavioral presentation is illustrated as follows:

> Mr. Jerome Verhouf, a young man with mild cognitive and adaptive behavior impairments, engages in frequent behavioral outbursts involving threats and acts of violence. These impulsive aggressive episodes previously had resulted in short-term hospitalizations in a local psychiatric facility. Additionally, the outbursts toward both peers and staff had resulted in termination of a number of previous work placements. Mr. Verhouf currently is working in supported employment and is provided close supervision.

Other psychological difficulties encountered by rehabilitation professionals serving persons with mental retardation have a predominant *emotional* presentation, including excessive fears, specific phobias, dysphoric mood, excessive anger, excessive shyness, poor self-esteem and related avoidance of activities requiring close social contacts, specific and generalized anxiety, and general irritability (Matson & Sevin, 1994; Prout & Strohmer, 1998). While frequently not as socially disruptive or visible, when unrecognized and untreated these problems contribute significantly to personal and vocational inadequacy and detract from quality of life. Ms. Katherine Engeler illustrates psychological difficulties with major emotional components:

> Ms. Engeler, a young woman with moderate cognitive impairment, recently graduated from a special education program located in a small school district. Shortly thereafter she moved with her parents to a large city in an adjoining state and enrolled in supported employment. Although she never had used public transportation, she now was expected to ride city buses to her job. Throughout her high school program, Ms. Engeler had been one of a circle of peers who on a daily basis depended on one another for social support. In her new location, she found herself without a familiar group of peers. In fact, in her job she was one of only two persons with cognitive disabilities among a large group of employees. Additionally, her two sisters and their families, with whom she previously had spent the majority of her leisure time, were no longer available.

In this new setting and without a familiar social support system, Ms. Engeler gradually began to isolate herself from others. Although capable of independent travel, she began refusing to use public transportation unless accompanied by a familiar support person. Her social interactions gradually reduced to the extent that she seldom talked except in response to direct questions. She lost interest in her usual leisure activities, appeared sad most of the time, and began to experience sleep and appetite problems. When prompted to "get involved" by parents when at home or by staff when in her vocational program, she most typically would become tearful and withdraw from social interactions. With increasing frequency, in apparent attempts to escape from interactions, she reacted to unwanted prompts with tantrums involving verbal and physical aggression. After a period of unacceptable job performance and increased disruptive behavioral outbursts, she was terminated from her job.

As this case illustrates, even in persons whose major difficulties are of an emotional nature, it is not unusual for these psychological features to represent significant contributors to overt behavioral difficulties, such as aggression or excessive negativism. Mr. George Irish provides an additional example of this relationship:

Mr. Irish becomes noticeably anxious and irritable whenever his ritualistic routine is disrupted. When prompted by staff or peers to engage in behaviors inconsistent with his routine, he frequently becomes verbally and physically aggressive. In these instances, his state of negative emotional arousal increases the likelihood of agitated and disruptive behaviors, which in turn on most occasions serve to remove the staff prompts. On other occasions when not anxious or irritable, Mr. Irish is most pleasant and cooperative.

MAJOR FOCUS OF MENTAL HEALTH COUNSELING

Problem areas similar to those presented by Mr. Verhouf, Ms. Engeler, and Mr. Irish have received extensive attention in the behavior analysis and broader behavior intervention literatures (Gardner, 2000; Nezu & Nezu, 1994). In contrast, only a small segment of the growing mental health counseling literature and training available to rehabilitation professionals or other direct care service providers represents treatments designed to provide solutions to specific behavioral and emotional difficulties such as those presented by these three individuals (Butz, Bowling, & Bliss, 2000; Perkins, 1999; Prout & Strohmer, 1998). Rather, as illustrated by Fletcher (1993), Hurley (1996), Hurley and Hurley (1986, 1988), and Lindsay, Howells, and Pitcaithly (1992), the counseling focus has often involved such personal characteristics as feelings of inferiority, social rejection, attitudes toward the client's own disability, or other emotionally or cognitively based concerns. These features are viewed by counselors as critical barriers to successful vocational, social, and personal adaptation and thus become a primary focus of counseling. Furthermore, when provided, counseling most frequently is conducted in the counselor's "office," separated from the natural environmental situations in which behavioral and emotional difficulties occur.

Fletcher (1993) and Hurley (1996) provide illustrations of these counseling features, emphasizing the need to develop a counseling routine as a means of building a trusting relationship between counselor and consumer. Hurley suggested that when first meeting with the client, the counselor may outline the process: "First we will meet and hear about work problems; then I will see you every Wednesday. We will talk about work every week for 30 minutes. I will help you do better at work by talking with you and trying to help you to solve problems" (p. 31). Additional counseling principles offered by Hurley include the following: (a) simplify verbal communication, (b) simplify counseling techniques (simplicity of language, goals, and homework assignments), (c) use a directive style (clarity, simplicity, and directiveness), (d) make the counseling process structured and predictable (specify time and purpose of counseling, possible outcomes), (e) clearly explain the confidential nature of the counseling relationship, and (f) deal with transference issues by carefully defining the counselor role in clear, concrete terms.

Even when modified to accommodate personal features of clients with mental retardation, the central technique used in counseling remains the cognitive approaches developed for use with persons with typical verbal and related cognitive abilities (Butz et al., 2000; Fletcher, 2000; Hurley, 1996; Perkins, 1999). A major implicit assumption of this approach is that modifying cognitive content and activities through counseling will result in changes in the person's social and work behaviors and emotions in different social and work environments.

To elaborate, this counseling approach uses verbal interactions and cognitive processing as the major modality of delivering treatment and training, viz., "I will help you do better at work by talking with you" (Hurley, 1996, p. 31). Potential effectiveness is based on the initial core assumption that the person with mental retardation will acknowledge an understanding of a situation or will gain an understanding or develop insight into his or her problems. Once this understanding is gained, the related assumption is made that the person not only is able to, but indeed will in fact utilize, the cognitive information to guide his or her behavior under future in situ conditions. To reiterate, this counseling approach assumes a close relationship between what the person with problems of behavioral and emotional expression says or states an intention to do and what the person actually does under future conditions. Further, the effectiveness of intervention is based on the supposition that knowledge and insights gained in counseling will generalize to later situations that typically are *quite different in a number of features*.

A final critical assumption of counseling is that the person is and will have the emotional and motivational features *to ensure the use of* the newly acquired knowledge and skills under future *in situ* conditions. In sum, these interrelated assumptions of cognitive understanding, generalization, and emotion-motivation supports imply that the person will use the cognitive knowledge to direct adaptive ways of behaving, thinking, and feeling under future conditions of provocation. These conditions typically involve explosive negative emotional arousal such as anger, anxiety, aggravation, irritability, dysphoria, or hypomania.

The typical modality of counseling indeed may be appropriate (i.e., effective and efficient) for verbally and cognitively skillful persons who have those characteristics that are critical to its success. First, such persons are self-motivated to gain cognitive and emotional understanding of the causes of their psychological symptoms (e.g., verbal aggression, sexual aggression, anxiety, disruptive outbursts, periods of anger or depression). Second, cognitively and verbally skillful persons have a successful history of using cognitive information to guide emotional and behavioral responses in problem situations that require cognitive coping or problem solving actions. These requisites combine with the new insights and related cognitive labeling skills and emotional responsiveness gained in successful therapy. Following counseling, the self-motivated person is thus in a position to use these newly acquired cognitive strategies to self-select and self-direct the use of prosocial coping skills in future problem situations in natural settings outside of the counseling room. Further, these newly acquired alternatives will be selected under future conditions of internal arousal (e.g., anger, sexual arousal, anxiety) or external provocation (e.g., provocative barbs from peers, reprimand from authority figures) that differ in type and/or intensity from those present during counseling.

These central criteria for traditional counseling, however, are unlikely to characterize most consumers, even in the general population without mental retardation. Beutler (2000), in offering standards and guidelines for psychological therapies based on a comprehensive analysis of research and clinical practice, offers support for this observation. He concluded that therapeutic change is greatest for persons presenting externalized difficulties when "the initial focus of change efforts is to build new skills and alter disruptive symptoms" (p. 1005).

APPLICATIONS TO PERSONS
WITH MENTAL RETARDATION

Various writers have suggested that office-based counseling techniques and assumptions are highly suspect, or at a minimum, not highly effective or efficient as a method of behavior change when used with persons with mental retardation (Cole & Gardner, 1993; Gardner, 1971, 2000; Gardner & Stamm, 1971; Matson & Senatore, 1981). Research reviews have consistently failed to detect a sound empirical base for the general use of such procedures (Butz et al., 2000; Hurley, 1989; Nezu & Nezu, 1994; Prout, 1994).

As emphasized, traditional counseling for persons with mental retardation uses techniques that rely heavily on verbal interaction between counselor and client. Cognitive skills, including verbal and other specific skills relating to verbal control over classes of behavior, appear to be critical to treatment effectiveness. It is assumed that changes in cognitive and verbal skills (insights, statements of relationships between events in the person's environment and the person's behavior) will result in changes in how the person behaves in future work, residential, and social settings that the verbal content represents. As an example, counseling may result in changes in verbal behavior from "I do not like to work and will not cooperate with my supervisor" to "I like to work and will cooperate with my supervisor because I can get along better if I do so." It is assumed that these changes in verbal behaviors will in fact be used by the person with mental retardation under future work conditions and will result in change in work and work-related behaviors. To emphasize, it is assumed that the verbal behavior will gain control over and give direction to other overt (nonverbal) behaviors in other settings that *typically involve disruptive emotional arousal components.* This central assumption is a tenuous one, especially as cognitive impairments become more general and severe.

One significant psychological deficit of persons with mental retardation who present difficulties of emotional and behavioral expression is the lack of adequate verbal control of emotional and other nonverbal behaviors. Stimulus events other than the person's own verbal behavior provide the major controlling influences over these other classes of behavior, especially those involving disruptive emotions such as anger, anxiety, or irritability. To illustrate, disruptive behaviors in the vocational setting typically represent impulsive acts triggered by specific sources of perceived noxious provocation. Any verbal control that the person may exhibit under less emotionally aroused states are generally overridden by the affective arousal and associated impulsive acting out.

Additionally, in many instances, a reliable controlling relationship has not been established between verbal behaviors and other classes of behaviors represented by the verbal content, that is, between *what one says and what one does*. The person may be able to verbalize "insight" into his or her problem emotions or behaviors and be able to state in the counseling situation, "When John yells at me, I will not get angry because I might hit him and get suspended from work." However, the person may have difficulty translating these *verbal statements of intent* into the intended prosocial coping behaviors when confronted with conditions of emotionally charged provocation.

In sum, a counseling approach that seeks to develop insight or even an expanded system of verbal behaviors as its major focus of treatment does not ensure therapeutic change in other problem behaviors or emotions, especially when these behaviors or emotions are under the instigating influence of disruptive emotional arousal. As a result, any new cognitive understandings or insights acquired in counseling most frequently would not be effective in influencing other classes of behaviors under future conditions that differ in critical features from those present in the counselor's office setting.

Brodsky (1967) provided an illustration of the ineffectiveness of focusing on changing verbal behaviors. The study involving persons with mental retardation was designed to assess both changes in nonverbal behaviors as a function of changes in verbal behavior, as well as changes in verbal behaviors as a function of changing nonverbal behaviors. The persons studied had high rates of verbal behavior but low rates of social behavior. Using a reinforcement system to strengthen social interactions with peers in a treatment setting, it was observed that the social interactions in a natural social situation increased. Additionally, an increase in prosocial verbal behaviors was noted. In contrast, reinforcement of verbal statements depicting social interactions in the treatment setting resulted in no increase in overt social behaviors in the natural setting. Thus, changes in verbal behaviors did not result in changes in those overt behaviors that the verbal depictions represented.

One common result of the misapplication of a verbally based counseling approach is to conclude that a person who does not use the cognitive information to change problem behaviors is "being resistive." It is of course equally possible that the person may not have the skills or motivation to benefit from a predominantly cognitively based intervention. The counselor's own emotional and cognitive reactions to this failure may be detected by the client and result in the interpretation that "now the therapist and the staff both think I am bad" (Matson & Sevin, 1994).

HABILITATIVE MENTAL HEALTH COUNSELING AS AN ALTERNATIVE

A habilitative mental health counseling approach is offered as an alternative to the traditional cognitively based approach to counseling. This approach incorporates the cognitive and relationship features of traditional counseling into a broader scheme. As an alternative to a focus on deficits, pathologies, disturbances, abnormalities, or limitations, the habilitative focus is on enhancing personal triads of interrelated emotional, cognitive, and behavioral *competencies*. The professional does not seek merely to remove pathological behaviors (e.g., aggression), emotions (e.g., excessive anxiety, feelings of inferiority), or cognitions (e.g., faulty beliefs or self-statements reflecting negative view of self). Rather, treatment seeks to provide specific alternatives as competency replacements for aberrant behaviors, emotions, and cognitions. These competencies may include self-initiated coping strategies of anxiety reduction, prosocial alternatives to aggression, and cognitions that in turn result in self-initiated positive feelings. The Habilitative Mental Health Counseling approach is characterized initially by a more direct teaching approach designed to facilitate change in *interrelated triads of behaviors, emotions, and cognitions*. A natural result of this habilitative emphasis of promoting development of those personal competencies that result in positive experiences outside of the treatment sessions is the evolution of a more positive view of self and related feelings of self-worth or esteem.

The approach does not assume on an a priori basis that "talk therapy" with a primary focus on changing faulty cognitions and related insights, or on modifying disturbed emotions via the therapist-client relationship, should represent the central mode or focus of therapeutic change. Rather than attempting to change bothersome cognitions *or* behaviors *or* emotions, all are viewed as intimately intertwined and thus constitute an interrelated set of conditions that becomes the object of intervention. Thus, as depicted in Figure 19.1, *interdependent triads of behaviors, cognitions, and emotions* represent the focus of intervention. To accomplish treatment goals, talk therapy is combined with a range of action-based and skill teaching and

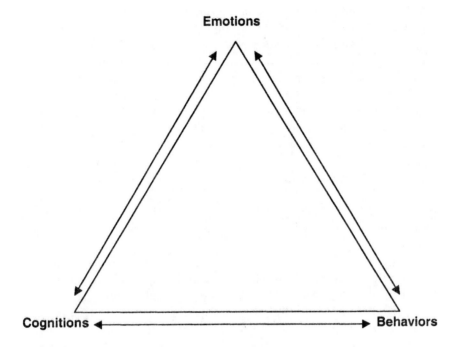

FIGURE 19.1.   Depicting the interdependent triads of behaviors, cognitions, and emotions.

rehearsal therapies. Those specific therapeutic procedures deemed most likely to accomplish the therapeutic objectives of addressing these triads that are selected for use. The professional may select from a wide range of social learning, relationship development, emotional enhancement, cognitive, and cognitive-behavioral strategies on the basis of empirical literature that documents efficacy with persons with mental retardation. Strategies may include anger management and related emotional retraining, panic control treatment, self-control training, social skills training, assertiveness training, interpersonal conflict resolution skills training, empathy training, social problem-solving strategies, cognitive retraining, contingency management, emotional desensitization, and biofeedback (Gardner, Graeber, & Cole, 1996; Nezu & Nezu, 1994).

To illustrate an application of the approach, a person's overt behaviors involving physical or verbal aggression in a work setting may represent reactions to comments from a feared peer. These behaviors may be influenced by or result in disruptive emotions such as anxiety or anger. These emotions in turn may be influenced by or produce provocative cognitions and related perceptions. Each may influence or be influenced by current environmental, biological, and related psychological conditions, such as psychological distress stemming from severe allergies or a perceptual set to interpret hostile intent in the actions of others. Thus, effective habilitative mental health intervention must be sensitive to these *reciprocal triadic interrelationships and seek to change this dynamic complex of personal features*. No assumption can be made that mere change in one member of this triad will automatically result in changes in other components that, in turn, will automatically generalize to future situations of instigation. It is evident that the specific combination of therapies provided to different individuals or groups will differ in the specific array of therapeutic procedures used.

As a second example, a person's verbal aggressions may reflect an attitude of "she's always trying to boss me" that results in anger following a directive from her work supervisor, Mrs. Waters. This triad of interrelated cognitions, emotions, and behaviors becomes the target of counseling. The initial focus of counseling may be to teach the person to control or reduce her anger under the specific conditions of instigation and to replace the emotional reaction with a more personally enhancing emotional experience. Specific counseling techniques may involve systematic desensitization through graduated exposure to the anger-inducing cues and related cognitively based procedures of teaching self-prompted relaxation responses or competing imagery. As a result, the likelihood of problem behaviors reflecting high anger arousal is reduced (Benson, 1992; Schloss, Smith, Santora, & Bryant, 1989). This may be followed by, or provided concomitantly with, conflict resolution and relationship-building experiences involving Mrs. Waters. Improved interactions would serve to produce positive emotional experiences and improved skills of coping. Such an increase in personal competencies and the positive results that ensue provide real-world experiences that contribute to the person's sense of adequacy, personal worth, and competency.

To continue, if a person with mental retardation engages in repetitive thoughts that a coworker holds a grudge against him and will retaliate when given the opportunity, these cognitions may create anticipatory anxiety. This stimulus complex (cognitions and related affective arousal) may contribute to impulsive aggressive acts when approached by the coworker. Modification of the ruminative thinking and reduction of the related emotional arousal paired with teaching alternative replacement communication and related interpersonal skills involving the coworker would remove critical instigating conditions for the aggressive acts (Gardner, Clees, & Cole, 1983). Use of these personal competencies will result in positive feedback from those involved in real-world day-by-day interactions. These positive experiences will in turn contribute to the person's positive image of himself or herself.

As a final example, if a person's exhibitionism is influenced by a faulty cognitive assumption and associated sexual arousal (e.g., "She wants me to do it. She enjoys it"), interventions used may consist of a number of interrelated components to address relevant cognitive-emotional-behavioral triads. These may involve changing the cognitions, replacing them with more realistic ones, teaching more socially and sexually appropriate interpersonal behaviors, and providing the motivation to use the prosocial alternatives under future conditions similar to those that resulted in the exhibitionism (Lindsay, Marshall, Neilson, Quinn, & Smith, 1998).

These case examples demonstrate that habilitative mental health counseling approaches for persons with mental retardation are selected to target specific adaptive emotional, cognitive, and behavioral triads. To emphasize, the objective is to reduce or eliminate the problem triads by replacing them with functional personal competencies. As noted, these functional alternative means of coping with specific environmental, intrapersonal, and biological conditions are selected on the basis of individually derived diagnostic formulations.

These examples also demonstrate that, whenever possible during habilitative mental health counseling, concrete rather than abstract cognitive representations of skill deficits are used to facilitate learning. These include such procedures as modeling, role playing, rehearsal of desired interrelated cognitive-behavioral-emotional triads, specific performance feedback, self-monitoring, self-evaluation, self-consequation, self-instruction, and gradual exposure to *in situ* conditions with prompted triad rehearsal (Gardner & Cole, 1989; Gardner, Graeber, & Cole, 1996). Situations in which problem behavioral and emotional expressions occur are progressively reconstructed during treatment to ensure functional utility for the person as these situations are faced in the future. Additionally, following success in specific situations of provocation, the person is taught more general problem-solving and coping skills involving affective, cognitive, and behavioral components for use in future similar situations (Gardner & Cole, 1989; Nezu & Nezu, 1995).

The reader will note the sequence: initially train a specific coping triad of skills with suitable motivational supports, then use these to teach more general problem-solving strategies, and finally provide training to teach skills of self-management to ensure self-directed used of these coping acts when confronted with problem situations.

The best therapeutic outcome of a habilitative mental health counseling approach, as with any therapeutic endeavor, is maximized when various "core conditions" are present. Beutler (2000) reported that "therapeutic change is greatest when the therapist is skillful and provides trust, acceptance, acknowledgment, collaboration, and respect" (p. 1005). Additionally, as illustrated, the habilitative mental health professional, with a major objective of increasing triads of cognitive-emotional-behavioral *competencies* relevant to success in vocational and interpersonal settings, is in an ideal position to contribute to the person's concept of independence, competency, empowerment, and self-esteem. As one additional example of this contribution, a person's impulsive anger-driven aggressive acts may have alienated him from valued vocational success and meaningful peer relationships. Habilitative mental health counseling that teaches not only anger management but also alternative interpersonal coping skills and a cognitive perspective of being responsible for one's own actions holds promise of more successful prosocial interactions that naturally result in feelings of competency and self-assurance. Additionally, these new relationship skills hold promise of resulting in more emotionally valuable social relationships with persons other than the mental health professional.

ADDITIONAL FEATURES OF THE HABILITATIVE MENTAL HEALTH COUNSELING APPROACH

A central assumption underlying the habilitative mental health counseling approach is that, to a major extent, current cognitive, behavioral, and emotional difficulties reflect the effects of past and present learning experiences that have been faulty or deficient (Gardner, 2000; Matson & Gardner, 1991; Matson & Sevin, 1994). Intervention is used to offset the effects of these experiences by changing *instigating, vulnerability*, and *maintaining* influences currently present within individuals and/or their physical, social, and vocational environments (Gardner, 1998; Griffiths, Gardner, & Nugent, 1998; O'Donohue & Krasner, 1995). The end goals are to increase a person's interrelated triads of behavioral, cognitive, and emotional competencies as replacements for the problem behavior-emotion-cognitive triads. Attainment of these objectives results in (a) reduction or elimination of current behavioral, cognitive, and emotional symptoms and, more importantly, (b) *reduction of the risk of their recurrence.*

To accomplish these objectives with a specific client, counselors or therapists select from an array of available habilitative mental health procedures that hold promise in effectively addressing current conditions influencing the presenting concerns. The selection process, described later, is guided by a set of diagnostic formulations derived from a study of the multiple specific personal and environmental contexts of the person's current presenting problems (Gardner, 1998, 2000; Gardner, Graeber, & Cole, 1996; Gardner & Sovner, 1994; Nezu & Nezu, 1995; Nezu, Nezu, & Gill-Weiss, 1992).

The specific cognitive, behavioral, and/or emotional coping features are identified during an individualized assessment of the person in the situations in which the behavioral and emotional challenges occur. The assessment identifies interrelated triads of emotional, behavioral, and cognitive components and the conditions that influence them. In the context of the habilitative mental health model, the functional utility of any intervention components and their objective(s) can be evaluated relative to the habilitation goals set for the person.

ROLES OF HABILITATIVE MENTAL HEALTH PROFESSIONALS

Habilitative mental health professionals assume a variety of roles in addressing the problems presented by persons with mental retardation. Since current problems reflect the effects of current experiences within physical and social environments as they interact with the person's psychological and physical features, one goal would be to change these experiences. If an adult is experiencing difficulties in relating to peers in her vocational setting as a result of her shy and passive demeanor, the peers and work supervisor, under the direction of the professional, may be used as cotherapeutic agents in encouraging a more confident and outgoing demeanor. If the client is experiencing major conflicts with parents or care providers in the place of residence, these persons may be enlisted to change the manner in which they relate to the client. As a result, the client and the relevant social environments change in a mutually beneficial manner.

In other instances, the habilitative mental health professional may work directly, either on a one-to-one or group basis, with the client or clients in a structured setting or relationship apart from the person's day-to-day world. This may involve facilitating changes, as illustrated earlier, in specific social, anger management, cognitive, conflict resolution, assertiveness, problem-solving, relaxation, self-management, visual imagery, or communication skills that the client may use at future times, which set the occasion for problem triads of emotions-behaviors-cognitions. Bensen (1992), Lindsay and Baty (1989), Lindsay et al. (1993), Lindsay et al. (1998), Nezu and Nezu (1994), and Nezu, Nezu, and Arean (1991) provide illustrations of this role in addressing problem triads involving anger, anxiety, cognitive distortions, depression, sexual aggression, and panic states. Systematic attention also is provided to ensure generalization from the intervention location and conditions to locations and conditions present in the person's real world (Griffiths, Feldman, & Tough, 1997).

HABILITATION VERSUS REHABILITATION

The central assumptions and objectives of the habilitative mental health approach differ from the typical rehabilitation model. (Re)habilitation assumes a preinjury or preillness level of competency that has been compromised by a physical or mental illness. The major goal of rehabilitation is restoration to the extent possible to a previous level of adaptive competency. The habilitative mental health counseling approach, in contrast, attempts to increase the person's level of competencies involving interdependent patterns of behaviors, emotions, and cognitions *beyond levels previously attained*. Persons with mental retardation who present mental health needs have most typically not attained desired levels of personal, social, and/ or vocational competencies. Critical areas of functional impairments are assumed to contribute significantly to current behavioral, cognitive, and emotional difficulties both within and outside of vocational settings. The habilitation mental health counseling goal thus becomes one of moving the person beyond previous areas and levels of functioning toward higher levels of interrelated emotional, cognitive, and behavioral competencies. Attainment of this objective offers realistic promise of providing the person with the personal coping resources to self-manage prosocial behavioral and emotional expressions and to develop an increasingly positive view of self.

Case Formulation Process

Since there is no single or simple psychological, environmental, or biomedical explanation for emotional, cognitive, or behavioral problems presented by a person with mental retardation, a diagnostic assessment is needed to determine the focus of counseling (Gardner, 2002). This assessment will lodge the referral symptoms into the various personal and environmental contexts in which they occur. Illustrations of referral concerns may include the following: "Gets into frequent arguments with peers and supervisor in the work setting," "Begins to tantrum when peers criticize her unkempt appearance," "Isolates herself from others and will not defend herself when more assertive peers take her belongings," and "Frequently states that she is mentally ill and cannot make decisions when asked to be accountable for her actions." These contexts included in the assessment process would involve:

1. the complete *antecedent stimulus complex* that serves to instigate occurrences or episodes of these actions;
2. the person's *vulnerabilities or risk* factors for engaging in these behaviors when confronted with the instigating stimulus complex; as well as
3. those *proximate consequences* that follow occurrences and contribute to their functionality and strength.

The case formulation process involves the following steps:

1. Describe what the person does (behaviors-emotions-cognitions) in what situations that create concerns. The description is based on information from both the person and from those in vocational and related settings who have indicated that problems exist.
2. Gather diagnostic information through assessment of these referral concerns in the three contexts of *instigating, vulnerability*, and *maintaining* conditions.
3. Form hypotheses about current medical, psychological, and social-environmental "causes" of the concerns (i.e., develop *diagnostic formulations relating to each set of instigating, vulnerability, and maintaining conditions*).
4. Describe specific treatment objectives relative to these "causes" and the ultimate outcomes of successfully addressing the causes.
5. Select a set of *intervention formulations* and specific interventions that address the conditions delineated in the diagnostic formulations.
6. Develop a staging plan for providing the various interventions (i.e., deciding on the interventions to be implemented initially and the sequence or timing of the remaining interventions).
7. Devise procedures for evaluating the effectiveness of interventions.
8. Modify diagnostic formulations and/or interventions based on evaluation results, and continuing this step until objectives are realized.

ASSESSMENT OF CONTEXTUAL INFLUENCES

Following delineation of problem areas, the next step in the case formulation process involves development of a set of interrelated diagnostic hunches about conditions that influence the occurrence, severity, variability in occurrence and severity, and persistent recurrence of the problem areas. This is accomplished by lodging the areas of concern within the contexts of *instigating, vulnerability, and maintaining influences.*

Contextual Analysis I: Instigating Influences

The initial contextual analysis seeks to identify those antecedent conditions that, individually or in combination, instigate specific behavioral-emotional-cognitive symptom triads. These include external physical and social environmental conditions, as well as covert psychological and biomedical features of the person. The antecedent conditions may serve a triggering or a contributing instigating role. *Triggering instigating conditions* refer to those antecedent stimulus states that are necessary conditions for the occurrence of specific target symptoms; that is, the symptom does not occur in the absence of these antecedents. *Contributing instigating conditions* refer to those antecedent conditions that, while in isolation are not sufficient to instigate occurrence of the target symptom, do, when present, increase the likelihood that the symptom will occur when triggering instigating conditions occur.

Behavioral-emotional-cognitive target symptom triads currently in a person's repertoire do not occur randomly or haphazardly. Rather, they occur in a discriminating manner at certain times, in specific places, and under certain instigating conditions. Examples of external instigating conditions may include the following physical and social events: (a) a work supervisor's reprimands for substandard work performance; (b) termination or reduction in frequency of staff attention directives from a specific staff person; (c) someone staring at the person; (d) taunts of a peer; and (e) physical and other stimulation from the social environment, such as high noise level, overcrowding, or agitated peer models.

Covert stimulus conditions may include (a) transitory or more enduring *affective states* such as anger, depression, anxiety, chronic sadness; (b) *cognitive influences* such as provocative covert ruminations and paranoid ideation; (c) *perceptual features* such as auditory and visual hallucinations; and (d) *psychological distress* resulting from biomedical states such as fatigue, seizure activity, drug effects, chronic pain, excessive arousal and irritability associated with neurological impairment, and premenstrual discomfort.

When assessing external and internal conditions that may serve to instigate target symptoms, it is highly unusual to identify any single physical or psychological condition that always precedes the symptoms. In most instances, a stimulus complex occasions the occurrence of the target symptoms. This complex frequently involves both triggering and contributing influences, representing both internal and external stimulus conditions. Additionally, instigating conditions vary in the degree of influence exerted over the occurrence of a specific target symptom. In illustration, an adult with moderate cognitive impairment who is highly prone to engage in behavioral outbursts under conditions of social provocation may behave appropriately on some occasions when in a state of positive emotional arousal, even when taunted by a peer. When aroused negatively (e.g., when angry or irritable in response to recurring verbal ruminations concerning an earlier reprimand from a supervisor), this person under the same external provocation is more likely to respond in a disruptive manner. This diagnostic information relative to the cognitive-emotional-behavioral triad would provide direction to the development of treatment formulations.

One component of the triad influences the occurrence, magnitude, and variability of other components. Also, a component of the triad may be more influential than other components. In illustration, in assessing the instigating conditions resulting in aggressive responding, it may be noted that the behavior involves female authority figures, but never males. Thus, the presence of a negative attitude toward female authority figures may be hypothesized as a significant instigating influence. It also may be noted that the severity of aggressive episodes increases when the person is in a state of negative emotional arousal relating to an earlier argument with a peer. The instigating stimulus complex would consist of the following:

corrective feedback from a female supervisor $\rightarrow$
cognitive attitude of negativism toward females + anger arousal $=$
aggressive responding.

Although the frequency of occurrence of the aggressive act may be under the major influence of the cognitive component of the triad, the severity level of an outburst may be influenced to a great extent by the affective state of anger. Treatment of any single component without attention to other components of the triad would lead to less than satisfactory results. Further, this current antecedent complex occurs in the context of risk or vulnerability features, discussed in the following section.

Contextual Analysis 2: Vulnerability Influences

Vulnerability influences refer to those features of the person and his or her physical and social environments that place the person at increased risk for occurrence or increased severity of target behavioral, emotional, or cognitive symptoms when the person is exposed to conditions of instigation. They may include personal features of a *psychological* nature (e.g., anger management, communication, or coping skills deficits) and *biomedical* nature (e.g., sensory, neurological, or biochemical impairments or dysfunctions). In addition, features of the *physical, social, and program environment* (e.g., limited opportunity for social stimulation, restrictions in the type and frequency of work tasks) may represent risk influences for a particular person.

Some vulnerability influences by their *presence and/or intensity* increase the likelihood of the occurrence of target symptoms. These conditions usually are viewed as pathological, excessive, or deviant biomedical, psychological, or social/environmental features (e.g., migraine headaches, trait of suspiciousness, chronic arthritis, bipolar mood disorder). To illustrate, pain associated with chronic arthritis on most occasions may be controlled by medication. When the medication loses it effectiveness or the person fails to take the prescribed medication, the pain may become psychologically distressing to the person. This current distress level in turn may contribute to the instigating stimulus complex for target symptoms when the person is exposed to other aversive sources of instigation such as a reprimand from a work supervisor.

It should be noted that vulnerability features typically remain *dormant* and only become involved in the instigating complex when they are active and result in aversive stimulus conditions such as anger, depressed mood, distress created by pain, or irritability produced by medications. A person with a diagnosed bipolar mood disorder provides a second illustration. When the disorder is active, a psychologically distressful dysphoric mood state is present. This distress in turn may represent an instigating stimulus event for other target symptoms such as verbal aggression and negative thoughts. When the disorder is inactive or when under effective medication treatment, a more positive mood state is present and is thus likely to influence prosocial cognitions and behaviors.

Other vulnerability features, by their *absence or low strength,* serve as risk factors and become significant under conditions of instigation that require the deficit skill. In illustration, a person may use aggressive acts as a means of coping with conditions of anger arousal. This person is at risk to continue using similar aggressive actions under future conditions of anger arousal if anger management skills or the motivation to use them are absent. Other skill deficits that place the person at risk for using problem behaviors, emotions, or cognitions as means of coping with stress include limited problem-solving skills, limited anxiety management skills, limited skills of assertiveness, limited skills of communicating one's needs or desires, and limited social skills. These and related motivational and personality features represent vulnerability conditions and become the major focus of habilitative mental health counseling.

Contextual Analysis 3: Maintaining Influences

The final set of influences evaluated refers to those psychosocial and bio-medical factors that may contribute to the functionality of the target symptoms. These symptoms may become functional in producing consequences that are valued by the person. In other instances, recurring patterns of symptoms may be strengthened by their effectiveness in removing or reducing aversive conditions. These reinforcing events may be located in the external environment or may represent internal conditions. To illustrate, agitated outbursts may be strengthened if followed by immediate staff attention or in other instances by the immediate removal of a supervisor directive. These same reactions may gain functionality if these produce a contingent reduction in physical pain or emotional distress. As a second example, a person's cognitive perspective that results in an interpretation of hostile intent in the neutral actions of a peer may be strengthened by the resulting aggressive response and the effects that are produced.

Interactive Effects of Influences

Most typically, a number of influences interact to produce the occurrence, severity, fluctuation, and persistent recurrence of emotional and behavioral concerns. As one illustration: Mr. Wouton's distress resulting from an earlier argument with his girlfriend during his coffee break produces a state of angry cognitive and emotional agitation. He has difficulty focusing on a task that requires him to complete one of several components used in an assembly line constructing automobile brakes. His emotional distress interferes with his work to the extent that the assembly sequence is disrupted. His supervisor prompts him to complete his work in a timely fashion. After the third prompt, Mr. Wouton becomes enraged, pushes the accumulated components onto the floor, and strikes out at the supervisor. The supervisor retreats and suggests that he should take a break and calm himself.

In assessing "why" the disruptive aggressive act occurred as a basis for designing a set of treatment experiences, several factors warrant attention:

Irritation → angry agitation →
(*contributing emotional state*) + persistent prompting from supervisor
(*triggering event*) +
limited skills in self-modulating his emotional state +
limited skills in communicating his emotional conflict
(*cognitive and emotional vulnerabilities*) =
aggressive responding →
removal of supervisor prompts and escape from the job demands
(*reinforcing consequences*)

DEVELOPING DIAGNOSTIC AND TREATMENT FORMULATIONS

Diagnostic hunches regarding triggering and contributing instigating conditions, vulnerability influences, and maintaining conditions form the basis for the formulation of diagnostically-based interventions addressing each of the presumed causes. Major therapeutic efforts are designed to address the vulnerability issues, with the objective of building psychological immunities through enhancing personal competencies. Therapeutic approaches are selected to teach prosocial coping alternatives and to provide personal motivation to use the newly acquired behavioral, cognitive, and emotional competencies as adaptive functional replacements for maladaptive symptoms. A skill enhancement focus to offset psychological vulnerabilities is especially pertinent for persons with restricted repertoires of coping behaviors. In this personal context, behavioral, emotional, and cognitive problems may represent highly effective and efficient functional coping reactions. If the problem areas are to be minimized or eliminated, they must be replaced by equally effective and efficient functionally equivalent prosocial coping skills.

SUMMARY

The habilitative mental health counseling approach is ideally suited for persons with mental retardation who, by definition, present impaired cognitive resources. As noted, the person is taught specific behavioral and related cognitive skills and is provided the emotional and motivational supports to use them to cope with situations relevant to that person in his or her daily life. The approach is more suitable than one assuming that cognitive representations learned during verbal exchanges or emotional attachments and changes developed in a one-hour-per-week counseling relationship will automatically be translated in future situations into similar triads of cognitions, emotions, and behaviors. Additionally, as noted earlier, the habilitative mental health counseling approach is consistent with standards of successful therapeutic practice offered by Beutler (2000).

REFERENCES

Benson, B. A. (1992). *Teaching anger management in persons with mental retardation.* Worthington, OH: IDS Publishing.

Beutler, L. E. (2000). David and Goliath: When empirical and clinical standards of practice meet. *American Psychologist, 55,* 997–1007.

Borthwick-Duffy, S. A. (1994). Prevalence of destructive behaviors. In T. Thompson & D. B. Gray (Eds.), *Destructive behavior in developmental disabilities: Diagnosis and treatment* (pp. 3–23). Thousand Oaks, CA: Sage.

Brodsky, G. (1967). The relation between verbal and non-verbal behavior change. *Behavior Research and Therapy, 5,* 183–191.

Butz, M. R., Bowling, J. B., & Bliss, C. A. (2000). Psychotherapy with the mentally retarded: A review of the literature and the implications. *Professional Psychology: Research and Practice, 31,* 42–47.

Cole, C. L., & Gardner, W. I. (1993). Psychotherapy with developmentally delayed children. In T. R. Kratochwell & R. J. Morris (Eds.), *Handbook of psychotherapy with children* (pp. 213–252). Boston: Allyn & Bacon.

Fletcher, R. (1993). Individual psychotherapy for persons with mental retardation. In R. Fletcher & A. Dosen (Eds.), *Mental health aspects of mental retardation: Progress in assessment and treatment* (pp. 327–349). New York: Lexington.

Fletcher, R. (Ed.). (2000). *Therapy approaches for persons with mental retardation.* Kingston, NY: NADD Press.

Gardner, W. I. (1971). *Behavior modification in mental retardation.* Chicago: Aldine-Atherton.

Gardner, W. I. (1998). Instigating the case formulation process. In D. M. Griffiths, W. I. Gardner, & J. A. Nugent (Eds.), *Behavioral supports: Individual centered interventions* (pp. 17–66). Kingston, NY: NADD Press.

Gardner, W. I. (2000). Behavioral therapies: Using diagnostic formulations to individualize treatment for persons with developmental disabilities and mental health concerns. In R. J. Fletcher (Ed.), *Therapy approaches for persons with mental retardation* (pp. 1–25). Kingston, NY: NADD Press.

Gardner, W. I. (2002). *Aggression and other disruptive behavioral challenges: Biomedical and psychosocial assessment and treatment.* Kingston, NY: NADD Press.

Gardner, W. I., Clees, T., & Cole, C. L. (1983). Self-management of disruptive verbal ruminations by a mentally retarded adult. *Applied Research in Mental Retardation, 4,* 41–58.

Gardner, W. I., & Cole, C. L. (1989). Self-management approaches. In E. Cipani (Ed.), *The treatment of severe behavior disorders: Behavior analysis approach* (pp. 19–36). Washington, DC: American Association on Mental Retardation.

Gardner, W. I., Graeber, J. L., & Cole, C. L. (1996) Behavior therapies: A multimodal diagnostic and intervention model. In J. W. Jacobson & J. A. Mulick (Eds.), *Manual of diagnosis and professional practice in mental retardation* (pp. 355–370). Washington, DC: American Psychological Association.

Gardner, W. I., & Sovner, R. (1994). *Self-injurious behaviors: Diagnosis and treatment.* Willow Street, PA: Vida Press.

Gardner, W. I., & Stamm, J. M. (1971). Counseling the mentally retarded: A behavioral approach. *Rehabilitation Counseling Bulletin, 15*, 46–57.

Griffiths, D. M., Feldman, M. A., & Tough, S. (1997). Programming generalization of social skills in adults with developmental disabilities. Effects of generalization and social validity. *Behavior Therapy, 28*, 253–269.

Griffiths, D. M., Gardner, W. I., & Nugent, J. A. (Eds.). (1998). *Behavioral supports: Individual centered interventions.* Kingston, NY: NADD Press.

Hurley, A. D. (1989). Individual psychotherapy with mentally retarded individuals: A review and call for research. *Research in Developmental Disabilities, 10*, 261–275.

Hurley, A. D. (1996). Vocational rehabilitation counseling approaches to support adults with mental retardation. *Habilitative Mental Healthcare Newsletter, 15*, 29–34.

Hurley, A. D., & Hurley, F. J. (1986). Counseling and psychotherapy with mentally retarded clients: I. The initial interview. *Psychiatric Aspects of Mental Retardation Review, 5*, 22–26.

Hurley, A. D., & Hurley, F. J. (1988). Counseling and psychotherapy with mentally retarded clients: II. Establishing a relationship. *Psychiatric Aspects of Mental Retardation Review, 6*, 15–20.

Jacobson, J. W., & Ackerman, J. J. (1989). Psychological services for persons with mental retardation and psychiatric impairments. *Mental Retardation, 27*, 33–36.

Lindsay, W. R., & Baty, F. J. (1989). Group relaxation training with adults who are mentally handicapped. *Behavioral Psychotherapy, 17*, 43–51.

Lindsay, W. R., Howells, L., & Pitcaithly, D. (1993). Cognitive therapy for depression with individuals with intellectual disabilities. *British Journal of Medical Psychology, 66*, 135–141.

Lindsay, W. R., Marshall, I., Neilson, C., Quinn, K., & Smith, A. H. W. (1998). The treatment of a learning disability convicted of exhibitionism. *Research in Developmental Disabilities, 19*, 295–316.

Matson, J. L., & Gardner, W. I. (1991). Behavioral learning theory and current applications to severe behavior problems in persons with mental retardation. *Clinical Psychology Review, 11*, 175–183.

Matson, J. L., & Senatore, V. (1981). A comparison of traditional psychotherapy and social skills training for improving interpersonal functioning of mentally retarded adults. *Behavior Therapy, 12*, 369–382.

Matson, J. L., & Sevin, J. A. (1994). Theories of dual diagnosis in mental retardation. *Journal of Consulting and Clinical Psychology, 62*, 6–16.

Nezu, C. M., & Nezu, A. M. (1994). Outpatient psychotherapy for adults with mental retardation and concomitant psychopathology: Research and clinical imperatives. *Journal of Consulting and Clinical Psychology, 62*, 34–42.

Nezu, C. M., & Nezu, A. M. (1995). Clinical decision making in everyday practice: The science in the art. *Cognitive and Behavioral Practice, 2,* 5–25.

Nezu, C. M., Nezu, A. M., & Arean, P. (1991). Assertiveness and problem-solving training for mildly mentally retarded persons with dual diagnoses. *Research in Developmental Disabilities, 12,* 371–386.

Nezu, C. M., Nezu, A. M., & Gill-Weiss, M. J. (1992). *Psychopathology in persons with mental retardation: Clinical guidelines for assessment and treatment.* Champaign, IL: Research Press.

O'Donohue, W. O., & Krasner, L. (Eds.). (1995). *Theories of behavior therapy: Exploring behavior change.* Washington, DC: American Psychological Association.

Perkins, D. M. (1999). Counseling and therapy: Revisited. *NADD Bulletin, 2,* 31–33.

Prout, H. T. (1994). Issues in counseling and psychotherapy. In D. C. Strohmer & H. T. Prout (Eds.), *Counseling and psychotherapy with persons with mental retardation and borderline intelligence* (pp. 1–21). Brandon, VT: Clinical Psychology Publishing.

Prout, H. T., & Strohmer, D. C. (1998). Issues in mental health counseling with persons with mental retardation. *Journal of Mental Health Counseling, 20,* 112–122.

Schloss, P. J., Smith, M., Santora, C., & Bryant, R. (1989). A respondent conditioning approach to reducing anger responses of a dually diagnosed man with mild mental retardation. *Behavior Therapy, 20,* 459–464.

Tuinier, S., & Verhoeven, W. M. A. (1993). Psychiatry and mental retardation: Towards a behavioural pharmacological concept. *Journal of Intellectual Disability Research, 37,* 16–24.

Whitman, J. J. P., Strohmer, D. C., & Prout, H. T. (1989). Problems presented by persons of mentally retarded and borderline intellectual functioning in counseling: An exploratory investigation. *Journal of Applied Rehabilitation Counseling, 20,* 8–13.

Chapter 20

Multicultural Rehabilitation Counseling: Challenges and Strategies

Elias Mpofu, Richard Beck, and Stephen G. Weinrach

T he reauthorization of the Rehabilitation Act and new legislative mandates have resulted in the need to make rehabilitation services more available to minorities (Rehabilitation Act Amendments, 1992), adding to the significance of diversity issues in rehabilitation counseling. The Rehabilitation Act Amendments (1992) stated:

> Patterns of inequitable treatment of minorities have been documented in all major junctures of the vocational rehabilitation process. As compared to White Americans, a larger percentage of African-American applicants to the vocational rehabilitation system is denied acceptance. Of applicants for service, a larger percentage of African-American cases is closed without being rehabilitated. Minorities are provided less training than their White counterparts. Consistently, less money is spent on minorities than their White counterparts. (p. 4364)

In spite of the relatively early awareness by rehabilitation professionals of the importance of cultural differences to service delivery (e.g., Ayers, 1967; Kunce & Cope, 1969) and the availability of legislation supportive of multicultural practices, there has been no corresponding urgency to integrate cultural sensitivity into service delivery or rehabilitation education curricula. For instance, the Code of Professional Ethics for Rehabilitation Counselors (2001), which consists of 10 canons and 72 rules, makes only one reference to multiculturalism:

Rehabilitation counselors will proceed with caution when attempting to evaluate and interpret the performance of people with disabilities, minority group members, or other persons who are not represented in the standardized norm groups. Rehabilitation counselors will recognize the effects of socioeconomic, ethnic, disability and cultural factors on test scores. (p. 29)

The Council on Rehabilitation Education (CORE) standards for rehabilitation counselor education programs have been criticized for giving insufficient attention to minority issues (Rubin, Davis, Noe, & Turner, 1996). A professional code of ethics and standards for curricula accreditation reflects the values of a profession, its current resources, and future prospects for responding to a diverse constituency. The apparent neglect of cultural diversity issues by the profession is clearly a cause for concern to counselors who expect their profession to provide comprehensive ethical and educational guidelines for practicing in a multicultural society.

Minority status serves to exclude individuals from mainstream culture through denial of economic opportunities, self-representation, and preferred lifestyles. The ways in which this marginalization translates into bias in rehabilitation service are discussed below. In addition, suggestions are presented on enhancing cultural sensitivity in rehabilitation settings.

PERSONS WITH DISABILITIES AS MINORITIES

Persons with disabilities constitute about 13.5% of the U.S. population and have been called a minority on the basis of their numerical inferiority (Storck & Thompson-Hoffman, 1991). However, numbers per se do not define minority status, because persons with numerical superiority can be minorities (e.g., females). Persons with disabilities are minorities because they, like racial, ethnic, and cultural minority groups in the U.S., meet the three criteria for minority status: economic deprivation, denial of communicative self-representation, and denial of access to a preferred way of life.

Persons with disabilities meet the criteria in many ways. For instance, persons with disabilities are overrepresented among people who are unemployed (Louis Harris & Associates, 1994; Yelin, 1991). Job and employment-related discrimination against persons with disabilities continues regardless of the passage of the Americans with Disabilities Act (Newman & Dinwoodie, 1996; Schall, 1998). Persons with disabilities have a two- to three-year lag in securing employment as compared to nondisabled persons (Levine & Nourse, 1998). They are also likely to be overrepresented in dead-end jobs because of their disability-related differences (Noble, 1998) and to have lower incomes as compared to nondisabled persons. Persons with disabilities have lower access to job networks tied to firms with job openings (Chima, 1998) and experience more work-related performance pressures (Harlan & Robert, 1998). The work contributions of persons with disabilities and their skill levels are undervalued (Yelin, 1991), even in programs in which they may be equal partners (Krogh, 1998).

Persons with disabilities were and are denied the right to communicative self-representation in that there is still a wide use of language that is disrespectful of persons with disabilities by the scientific community, general public, and the press (e.g., "the disabled," "the mentally handicapped"), in spite of the wishes of persons with disabilities to be referred to in preferred terms (e.g., "persons with disabilities") (Bailey, 1992). The term *disabled person* is considered disrespectful of persons with disabilities because placing a disability-related difference before the person may have the effect of overlooking the more numerous ways in which the individual with a disability is like many other nondisabled persons (Wright, 1991).

The person-first language (e.g., person with disabilities, person with retardation), which was first adopted by The Association for Persons with Severe Handicaps (TASH; Bailey, 1992), represents an attempt by a minority group to gain communicative self-representation from nondisabled persons. These efforts are a long way from achieving the intended purpose. For instance, Sandieson (1998) conducted a survey on the terms used to refer to persons with mental retardation by researchers in the area of mental retardation and developmental disabilities over the 10-year period from 1985 to 1995. Sixty-six terms were used to identify persons with mental retardation, 36 (56%) of which were unfriendly to those persons (e.g., intellectual deficiency, mentally handicapped, intellectual subnormality). Research on the terms currently used to refer to persons with disabilities by the general public and the press shows a higher use of terms unfriendly to persons with disabilities (Auslander & Gold, 1999; Wilgosh & Sandulac, 1997).

THEORETICAL AND EMPIRICAL BASES
FOR CULTURAL INFLUENCES

Counseling practices that are respectful of the diverse backgrounds of clients have been called diversity-sensitive counseling, multicultural counseling, or minority counseling (Weinrach & Thomas, 1998). Multiculturalism seeks to promote intercultural dialogue among majority cultures and minority cultures in the belief that such exchanges will result in the enrichment of both majority and minority counselors and clients. In practical terms, multicultural counseling seeks to recognize and utilize the unique worldviews of clients that are influenced by client background.

Regardless of the ample attention that has been given to multiculturalism in the rehabilitation and counseling literature, there is considerable inconsistency among rehabilitation (and other helping) professionals in the meanings of the client variables of *minority status, race, ethnicity, gender,* and *disability status,* as well as their relationships to one another. Lack of consistency or conceptual clarity on the key terms that are presumed to distinguish diversity-sensitive or multicultural counseling leaves open questions about what different professionals have in mind when they write about or practice counseling.

Sue and Sue (2003) enumerated the salient value systems of several cultural groups. The value of saving face in Far Eastern cultures is a prominent example, but other Asian culture-bound beliefs and values include behaviors that lead to restraint in showing strong feelings, loyalty and respect for one's family and elders, and a preference for clearly defined roles of dominance and deference. In Latino cultures, a distinction between "mental" and "physical" health states is not made. Moreover, Latinos engage in more body contact in greeting others, show a greater orientation toward the family than the more individualistic American culture, and display specific expectations of their members (e.g., the male parent is the breadwinner and decision maker).

SELECTED SOURCES OF MAJORITY BIAS IN REHABILITATION SERVICE DELIVERY

Use of Language That Mystifies Minority Clients

The language of counseling influences the utilization of health services by minorities (Green, 1999; Harry, 1992). The language that a client uses is an important indicator of his or her worldview and interpretation of health status. According to Green (1999), "To really know what and how people experience the things they do, to be truly empathic, we have to focus first on their language because language is our most direct window onto what they know and feel" (p. 125). For instance, a significant problem for psychiatric evaluators of Hispanic clients is language. Even with some fluency in Spanish, evaluators may diagnose Hispanic individuals differently than will professionals of the individual's own culture.

It is interesting to note that immigrant workers of Mexican origins have no words for *disability,* although they often experience chronic and severe health problems (Schaller, Parker, & Garcia, 1998). The fact that immigrant

Mexican workers may not be aware that chronic illness constitutes a disability suggests that they may be less likely to seek rehabilitation services. They are also more likely to prematurely terminate counseling as compared to majority clients. Similarly, many Native American languages have no terms for *disability, mental retardation,* and *handicap,* ostensibly because it is the social roles that a person performs in his or her community that define the person, rather than a disability per se. Perceptions of individuals by minorities in terms of social role functions contrast with that of rehabilitation professionals, who may focus more on medical categories and the associated clinical picture (etiology, diagnosis, prognosis).

The differences in perceptions reflect differences in underlying worldviews and can result in significant misunderstandings between counselors and minority clients with regard to the presenting condition and appropriate methods of rehabilitation. Minority clients may deny certain labels that are ordinarily used by rehabilitation counselors to describe certain disabilities, unless the condition is extreme (Harry, 1992).

Effects of Tokenism

Minority persons constitute the majority of persons with disabilities (Smart & Smart, 1997b), and at the same time they are less likely to utilize rehabilitation services, or are more likely to be denied services (Rehabilitation Act Amendments, 1992). The relatively few who access rehabilitation services may experience the tokenism effects of visibility, contrast, role encapsulation, and assimilation (Mpofu, Crystal, & Feist-Price, 2000). *Visibility* refers to those characteristics that mark individuals (e.g., racial minorities) so that they will tend to stand out in the groups in which they are involved. Such individuals tend to be watched more closely by the majority and may experience performance pressures. *Contrast* refers to those who are visibly different from the majority but whose similarities to the majority tend to minimize any perceived differences. *Role encapsulation* occurs when minority status members are treated by the majority in stereotypical ways. *Assimilation* effects of tokenism are the pressures that are exerted on minority persons by the majority to adopt the worldviews of the majority.

Possible tokenism effects of majority-oriented rehabilitation services may explain, in part, the lower utilization of rehabilitation services by racial minorities. For instance, rehabilitation clients who are racial minorities may be more visible among majority rehabilitation clients and counselors. As a result, they may experience greater scrutiny and different treatment than majority clients, which could lead to premature termination of rehabilitation service. Similarly, the underrepresentation of racial minority clients at rehabilitation service centers may add to the chances that minority clients will be seen as different from majority clients, even though they may be presenting with the same concerns. Consequently, minority clients may be at a higher risk of denial of services or unsuccessful case closure.

Visibility and contrast tokenism effects may also explain the reported higher frequency of "unable to locate" closures among racial minority as compared to racial majority rehabilitation clients (Mpofu et al., 2000). Racial minority clients may also avoid using rehabilitation services because they anticipate being treated in the stereotypical ways in which the majority treat them in the wider society. Racial or cultural minorities may also drop out of rehabilitation services because they experience cultural pressures from rehabilitation counselors to assimilate to the majority worldview on disability and treatment, or to abandon their perception of disability and preferred ways of coping (Harry, 1992; Schaller et al., 1998).

COUNSELING THEORIES AND TECHNIQUES

Rehabilitation counselors may incorrectly assume that mainstream counseling theories have universal applicability. Counselors may use terminology that makes it difficult for clients to participate meaningfully in the rehabilitation process (Schaller et al., 1998). Rehabilitation counselors may perceive their clients in the stereotypical ways in which minority persons are portrayed by the majority (Smart & Smart, 1997a). In addition, rehabilitation agencies and counselors may fail to project a service orientation that is consistent with the requirements of the user community (Schaller et al., 1998).

Most of the mainstream theories of counseling used by rehabilitation (and other) counselors are individualistic in orientation and assume that the core of the problems that the individual is experiencing is essentially of a personal and intrapsychic nature. Counselors operating from this premise may regard interventions aimed at changing the individuals' cognitions, behaviors, and emotions toward particular experiences (e.g., an acquired disability) as primary to the treatment efforts. Minority clients may have an interpersonal worldview and center their experience of a challenging event (e.g., an acquired disability) on the ways that it affects their cultural role expectations (e.g., for males and females, older, younger persons, first-borns) (Schaller et al., 1998). Thus, the experience of disability in racial minorities is more likely to be a family or community issue.

In turn, mainstream approaches to rehabilitation may be perceived by minority clients as treating persons like nonhistorical and nonsocial units. Such approaches may be viewed as pressuring minorities to adapt to the cultural values of the majority.

The use of counseling approaches that foster the notion that psychosocial adjustment will be resolved through insight and self-exploration may not be appropriate for all minorities. Insight-oriented theories assume a wide choice of self-representations and preferred ways of life, which may not be true of minorities due to their historical and ongoing experience of oppression and prejudice by the majority. For example, minority status persons may be relatively less troubled by how they see or feel about themselves than by society-wide restrictions on their economic participation, communicative self-representation, and preferred ways of life (Foucault, 1986).

Insight-oriented interventions also assume that the individual self is the center of a person's subjective well-being, a view that is inconsistent with that of racial or ethnic minorities, whose sense of self may be nested in relationships with the social and inanimate metaphysical environment (Landrine, 1992). Mainstream treatment approaches, with their goal of redefining the self as separate from the community and environment, would be inappropriate for those minority clients who have a relational sense of self.

Self-disclosure, an essential component of mainstream counseling approaches, is incongruent with the views of some minority groups that personal life stories are ultimately the stories of significant others (e.g., family) and should not be told to strangers, including counselors. Thus, expecting minority clients to self-disclose as a way of generating clinical material may be asking them to operate in an unfamiliar mode of self-representation and to violate the integrity of the life-stories of the collective of which the client's story is a part. For that reason, some minority clients have been observed to be very tentative in their initial commitment and participation with traditional counseling, and to take a longer time to establish a working relationship with a counselor (Chan, Lam, Wong, Leung, & Fang, 1988). Giving importance to personal relationship factors like empathy, genuineness, and warmth may be perceived by some minority clients as an attempt to substitute facilitative conditions for a true understanding of their situation as oppressed or disadvantaged persons (Green, 1999).

Minority clients may also bring to counseling a personal history of experiencing societal oppression and discrimination, which may predispose them to rejecting counseling services (Sue & Sue, 2003). For instance, mainstream counseling approaches that emphasize changing the individual may be perceived by some minority clients as attempts to blame them for sources of difficulty that are institutionally generated and are part of the oppression of minorities. The higher unemployment rate among persons with disabilities is a case in point. Failure to secure a job placement in rehabilitation service may be perceived by rehabilitation counselors as a problem of motivation or lack of skills, when the employment difficulties could be better explained by prejudice against persons with disabilities by employers (Yelin, 1991). The problems of securing jobs as part of the rehabilitation process are compounded for persons in multiple minority status (race, gender, and disability status).

CULTURE-SENSITIVE REHABILITATION INTERVENTION STRATEGIES

There are three issues to which rehabilitation counselors need to attend when working with clients from nonmajority cultures. First is a knowledge of the culture(s) with which the client identifies. Although there are many within-group differences in cultures (Weinrach & Thomas, 1998), the client's culture still provides hypotheses to investigate in the process of conceptualizing the client's perceptual world. Second is an awareness of the client's worldview. With an awareness of the counselor's own cultural beliefs and assumptions and their possible marginalizing effects on clients, counselors ought to listen and ask the client questions that educate them about their client's values and life meanings. Third, counselors need counseling skills that tend to accommodate client differences in terms of values, rate of conversation, style of nonverbal cues, and expectations. Only by reaching out to clients in terms of their worldview can counselors hope to provide culture-sensitive counseling.

Multicultural counseling has had a positive effect in making counselors more introspective about how their values and cultural blind-spots may have a negative impact on clients from cultural backgrounds that differ from their own. However, considerably less attention has been paid to translating multicultural counseling knowledge and awareness into improved services and practices (Green, 1999; Weinrach & Thomas, 1998).

Structuring Service Delivery

Clients want to feel that the person with whom they are sharing their life stories is genuinely interested in their worldview (Ivey & Ivey, 2003).

Authenticity with oneself and one's clients may be achieved by directly addressing a potential or real difference between the counselor and client at the beginning or during the course of counseling. For instance, a counselor and client may have different perceptions of the goals, resources, and procedures of rehabilitation service. In addition, counselors may differ from clients in terms of race, disability status, economic level, and gender. The counselor can minimize the chances of frustration arising from differences in expectations about counseling by negotiating with the client about the goals and procedures of counseling service.

Structuring service delivery for clients makes it possible for them to participate in their own rehabilitation by examining the fit between their needs and the resources and procedures of the particular rehabilitation agency. It also facilitates the referral of clients to compatible community resources. Visible differences (e.g., race, disability status, gender) can be addressed by (a) asking the client if he or she is comfortable working with a counselor who has an apparent difference (racial, disability, gender, or multiple differences) with the client; (b) openly acknowledging to the client the limitations that one may have in terms of experience in the client's world; (c) encouraging the client to inform the counselor if he or she may be overlooking a significant issue in the client's view of his or her situation; and (d) communicating a genuine willingness to learn from the client.

Confronting differences that may impact on the quality of service delivery in such a direct way communicates openness on the part of the counselor and invites the client to share ownership of the processes and outcomes of counseling (Ivey, Gluckstern, & Ivey, 1997). It may also help reduce any difference-related anxiety that counselor and client may have about unspoken and yet real differences in experience that have a bearing on client participation. Directly addressing the differences minimizes the chances of stereotyping and should assist in the forging of a working alliance at an early stage of rehabilitation service, when minority clients are most likely to drop out.

Assessing Client and Counselor Worldviews

The client's worldview may be a critical component of the information-gathering process during the intake interview. Counselors can also use semistructured or qualitative measures to assess client worldview. The qualitative measures would need to be checked for data convergence using multiple informant methods or observational techniques. A number of quantitative measures of worldview are also available to counselors (e.g., Ibrahim & Khan, 1987). Counselors can also assess their own worldviews and multicultural competencies (knowledge, awareness, skills) by using existing quantitative measures, such as the Multicultural Counseling Inventory (MCI; Sodowsky, Taffe, Gutkins, & Wise, 1994).

Employing the Language of Helping

In multilingual settings in which services are being provided to persons with a limited proficiency in English, the services of an interpreter or translator may help reduce some of the miscommunication arising from rehabilitation professionals and minority clients being unfamiliar with each other's languages (Phelan & Parkman, 1995). The interpreters may also help as culture brokers in cases where communication may be hindered by implicit differences in worldviews or culturally restricted use of terms.

Some basics in the use of translators apply: (a) facing toward and speaking directly to the client rather than to the translator; (b) keeping the translator fully involved throughout the interview; (c) repeating for confirmation with the client that he or she has been correctly understood; (d) requesting the client to correct any misunderstanding; (e) observing cultural protocols (age, kin, class, gender) about appropriate translators; (e) allowing extra time; and (f) keeping the agenda short and focused. The question of using family members as interpreters needs to be approached judiciously, since they are likely to be involved in the client's presenting situation and may be more helpful as information providers and allies in designing, implementing, and evaluating treatment, as opposed to being interpreters. Interpreters need to be trained in their role so that they convey the intended messages rather than personal versions.

Understanding minority clients' referent terms for disabling conditions is important for effective service delivery. Shweder (1985) discussed the cultural context of language in depictions of illness and pain that may be useful to rehabilitation professionals working with minority populations. He identified six areas of language participation and use that professionals may take into account: common illness states and their descriptions; individual interpretations; community-wide meanings; associated expressive styles; illness power; and social position. For instance, some racial minorities have been reported to present with physical symptoms for what may be emotional problems (Schaller et al., 1998).

Communication with minority clients may be facilitated by counselors compiling terms commonly used by minority clients to describe various disabling conditions and carefully equating them with corresponding terms used by the majority. The culturally grounded functional interpretations that minority clients give to particular conditions of illness may also help rehabilitation professionals identify treatment goals with which the clients and community can agree (e.g., social role perceptions of rehabilitation).

Minimizing the Effects of Tokenism

The effects of tokenism on minority clients may be minimized by involving family and significant others in all stages of rehabilitation. For instance, minority clients could be asked who they would like to be involved in their treatment planning. The nominated persons could then be invited to rehabilitation counseling sessions as often as the client chooses. Involvement of persons with a similar worldview serves several functions: (a) it enables the client to draw on the resources of persons historically involved in his or her situation; (b) it minimizes the tokenism effects of feeling isolated as a result of seeking rehabilitation services; and (c) it enhances the chances that salient issues to the client's rehabilitation will be addressed. Tokenism effects can also be minimized by locating rehabilitation services at centers that are accessible to minority clients and including other resources or services relevant to the client's needs (e.g., community centers). Carefully planned outreach programs may also be useful in increasing utilization of rehabilitation services by minority clients.

INCREASING DISABILITY CONSCIOUSNESS

The construct of disability consciousness has the potential to link group, community, and individual responses to minority statuses in persons with disabilities. Disability consciousness is a multidimensional construct and refers to collective consciousness by persons with disabilities regarding their minority status or disability identity, as well as disability-friendly environments and individual disability identity (Barnartt, 1996; Mpofu, 1999). Barnartt regarded disability consciousness as a collective awareness among persons with disabilities regarding their minority status, and the use of that consciousness as the basis for social movements that seek to advance the interests of persons with disabilities. In this regard, disability consciousness transcends gender, racial, and ethnic differences and may be a factor that rallies persons in the disability community together.

Collective disability consciousness may make it possible for persons with disabilities to form social movements through which they may achieve higher economic participation, gain control over self-definition, and achieve greater access to a way of life that validates their disability-related experiences. In other words, collective disability consciousness in persons with disabilities may be empowering at a group level and is similar to the Marxist notions of class consciousness. Disability consciousness may also be regarded as a sensitivity of the environment (e.g., community, work-places) to disability-related differences.

Environments that are supportive of disability-related differences (e.g., positive social attitudes, enabling structures, and resources) may make those differences less salient and enhance perceived similarities between persons with disabilities and those without. Persons with disabilities in such enabling environments may be less susceptible to economic depriva-tion, loss of control of self-referential terms, and limitations in choice of a preferred lifestyle. In other words, having a disability in a disability-enabling environment may not result in disability-related minority status effects, although other minority statuses (e.g., gender) may still apply.

Disability identity or consciousness may be positive or negative. Positive disability consciousness may result in proactive actions to restore the economic, self-identity, and cultural integrity of persons with disabilities. For instance, positive disability consciousness may be linked to higher levels of collective disability consciousness in persons with disabilities (Barnartt, 1996). Negative disability consciousness is exemplified by lower involvement in activities that would counter minority status effects in persons with disabilities or denial of their minority status in communities with high levels of prejudice against persons with disabilities.

TEACHING CLIENTS ABOUT INFORMED CHOICE

The language of service delivery is another area in which counselors can demonstrate sensitivity to the needs of minority clients. Minorities with disabilities have been found to be four times as likely as majority clients to be uninformed about disability legislation and their role in the Individu-alized Written Rehabilitation Plans (Smart & Smart, 1997a). Even more significant is the need for rehabilitation counselors to ensure that minority clients have the information that will enable them to make informed deci-sions. That involves understanding concerns from the client's perspective and sharing information with the client on resources that are likely to be useful in assisting the client to make effective choices, as well as helping the client evaluate the relative merits of each option with regard to the client's values, needs, and preferences. In that connection, some minority clients may expect the rehabilitation counselor to assume a leading role in rehabilitation service delivery because of cultural conditioning.

Only 10% of minorities have been found to be aware of the American with Disabilities Act, in contrast to 40% in the general population (Smart & Smart, 1997b). Thus, minority clients may not be informed of their rights and responsibilities under the act. Rehabilitation counselors may fail to mention the Americans with Disabilities Act and other related legislation to minority clients under the assumption that the clients were already aware of the legislation; failure to inform contributes to the mystification of clients regarding the rehabilitation process.

A significant component of rehabilitation legislation is informed choice in the provision of rehabilitation services to clients, which includes the collaborative preparation of an Individual Written Rehabilitation Plan (IWRP) by counselor and client. Minority clients may not be aware of the legal requirement of IWRPs as part of the rehabilitation process, or of their role in formulating, implementing, monitoring, and evaluating the IWRP. The active participation requirements of the IWRP may be incongruent with the worldviews and help-seeking behaviors of some minority clients (e.g., traditionalist Native Americans, Asian Americans), who may prefer to defer to the counselor in treatment decisions. Rehabilitation counselors who assume that minority clients know of their collaborative role in using IWRPs could create unintended difficulties for their clients. Such counselors may also experience higher minority client dropout rates, which could lead them to the erroneous conclusion that minority clients are unmotivated or uncooperative.

RECONCILING OPPOSING POINTS OF VIEW

The polemics accompanying the debate on multicultural counseling create the impression that there are no elements in mainstream counseling that could be useful to minority counseling or that the two approaches do not overlap at all. It is more realistic to perceive mainstream and minority counseling approaches on a continuum, with some aspects of mainstream counseling applicable to working with minority clients and vice versa.

A dichotomous view of counseling approaches (a) fails to recognize that clients in a multicultural society transverse realities in both the minority and mainstream contexts and may have their needs better met by being able to negotiate both contexts; (b) may have the effect of creating high levels of performance anxiety and guilt in majority counselors, which would compromise their ability to meet client needs; (c) creates the unjustified perception in majority counselors that the training they already have is totally irrelevant to serving minorities or cannot be the basis for personal growth and development in multicultural skills; (d) could create bad feelings in some majority counselors, who may misperceive diversity-sensitive counseling to be some preferential treatment for minorities; (e) encourages the incorrect belief that counselors from a minority background are necessarily better at working with minority clients than those from a majority background; and (f) leads to the stigmatization of minority counseling as being preoccupied with political, as opposed to counseling, agendas.

In addition, the professional literature that addresses the provision of counseling to specific minority groups tends to be very general, and counselors are thus left with little guidance as to how they can improve their practice with individual clients (Green, 1999). There are likely to be large within-group differences in clinically significant variables, so that overgeneralizations may have the unfortunate effect of perpetuating stereotypes and useless categorizations, narrowing the perspectives of practitioners (Weinrach & Thomas, 1998). The fact that persons of color vary widely among themselves in terms of acculturation to the majority culture also adds to the complexity of counseling racial minorities. Racial, ethnic, or cultural minorities at different levels of racial or ethnic identity development will vary in their identification with the majority culture and their responsiveness to mainstream methods of counseling.

Moreover, a meta-analysis of 66 studies on the association between racial, ethnic, or cultural minority status and counseling outcomes indicated that clients consistently rated counselor *competence* higher than *racial or ethnic similarity* (Coleman, Wampold, & Casali, 1995). The same meta-analytic study also reported that studies which reported preferences for counselors of a similar race or ethnicity were limited by apparent social desirability effects (e.g., choice limited to race, ethnicity, or culture only) and sampling bias (e.g., ethnic minority students at predominantly white universities). Majority and minority counselors were more alike than different in their worldviews (Mahalik, Worthington, & Crump, 1999). This similarity could be explained by counselor socialization during professional training or the personality characteristics of persons in the helping professions. To assume that mainstream methods of counseling and majority counselors are inherently unsuited to working with persons of color, on the basis of color alone, smacks of racism (Weinrach & Thomas, 1998) and may hurt the needs of persons of color who may prefer working with counselors from the majority.

CONCLUSIONS

It is important to address minority status issues in providing rehabilitation services. Persons of minority status share cultural syndromes that may be influenced by their historical and current oppression by the majority. They may experience denial of economic and sociocultural privileges in a manner that may make their worldviews and health-related experiences quite different from those of the majority.

Addressing diversity issues in rehabilitation service provision is an ethical imperative. What needs to be considered is the ways in which that can be achieved without stigmatizing the same clients that are supposed to benefit from services. Both multicultural and mainstream counseling approaches should be held accountable to meet client needs. The ethical objective to base treatment decisions on client strengths, preferences, and limitations is likely to be met when multicultural and mainstream counseling approaches are used in complementary ways. Ethnocentric biases in counseling represent serious ethical failures. Similarly, responding to individuals seeking rehabilitation services solely on the basis of visible characteristics (e.g., race, disability type) perpetuates stereotypes that are harmful to the client and significant others (e.g., family, employers). Client outcomes in rehabilitation are a product of an interaction between rehabilitation service capacity and client participation, and counseling outcomes improve as client participation increases.

REFERENCES

Auslander, G. K., & Gold, N. (1999). A comparison of newspaper reports in Canada and Israel. *Social Science and Medicine, 48,* 1395–1405.

Ayers, G. (1967). *Rehabilitating the culturally disadvantaged.* Mankato, MN: Mankato State College.

Bailey, (1992). Guidelines for authors. *Journal of Early Intervention, 15,* 118–119.

Barnartt, S. (1996). Disability culture or disability consciousness? *Journal of Disability Policy Studies, 7,* 1–19.

Chan, F., Lam, C., Wong, D., Leung, P., & Fang, X-S. (1988). Counseling Chinese Americans with disabilities. *Journal of Applied Rehabilitation Counseling, 19*(4), 21–24.

Chima, F. O. (1998). Workplace and disabilities: Opinions on work, interpersonal, and intrapersonal factors. *Journal of Applied Rehabilitation Counseling, 29,* 31–37.

Code of Professional Ethics for Rehabilitation Counselors. (1987). *Journal of Applied Rehabilitation Counseling, 18*(4), 26–31.

Coleman, H. L. K., Wampold, B. E., & Casali, S. L. (1995). Ethnic minorities' ratings of ethnically similar and European American counselors: A meta-analysis. *Journal of Counseling Psychology, 42,* 55–64.

Foucault, M. (1986). *The history of sexuality: Vol. 3. The care of the self.* New York: Vintage Books.

Green, J. W. (1999). *Cultural awareness in the human services: A multi-ethnic approach* (3rd ed.). Boston: Allyn & Bacon.

Harlan, S. L., & Robert, P. M. (1998). The social construction of disability in organizations. *Work and Organizations, 25,* 397–435.

Harry, B. (1992). Restructuring the participation of African-American parents in special education. *Exceptional Children, 59,* 123–131.

Ibrahim, F. A., & Kahn, H. (1987). Assessments of world-views. *Psychological Reports, 60,* 163–176.

Ivey, A. E., Gluckstern, N. B., & Ivey, M. B. (1997). *Basic influencing skills.* North Amherst, MA: Microtraining Associates.

Ivey, A. E., & Ivey, M. B. (2003). *Intentional interviewing and counseling: Facilitating client development in a multicultural society* (5th ed.). Pacific Groove, CA: Brooks/Cole.

Krogh, K. (1998). A conceptual framework of community partnerships: Perspectives of people with disabilities on power, beliefs and values. *Canadian Journal of Rehabilitation, 12,* 123–134.

Kunce, J., & Cope, C. (1969). (Eds.). *Rehabilitation and the culturally disadvantaged.* Columbia: University of Missouri-Columbia, Regional Rehabilitation Research Institute.

Landrine, H. (1992). Clinical implications of cultural differences: The referential versus the indexical self. *Clinical Psychology Review, 12,* 401–415.

Levine, P., & Nourse, S. W. (1998). What follow-up studies say about postschool life for young men and women with learning disabilities: A critical look at the literature. *Journal of Learning Disabilities, 31,* 212–233.

Louis Harris & Associates. (1994). *N.O.D./Harris survey of Americans with disabilities.* Washington, DC: National Organization on Disability.

Mahalik, J. R., Worthington, R. L., & Crump, S. (1999). Influence of racial/ethnic membership and Atherapist culture on therapists' world view. *Journal of Multicultural Counseling and Development, 27,* 2–17.

Mpofu, E. (1999). *Social acceptance of Zimbabwean adolescents with physical disabilities.* Unpublished doctoral dissertation, University of Wisconsin-Madison.

Mpofu, E., Crystal, R., & Feist-Price, S. (2000). Tokenism in rehabilitation clients: Strategies for quality enhancement in rehabilitation services. *Rehabilitation Education, 14,* 243–256.

Newman, J. F., & Dinwoodie, R. E. (1996). Impact of the Americans with Disabilities Act on private sector employers. *Journal of Rehabilitation Administration, 20,* 3–14.

Noble, J. H. (1998). Policy reform dilemmas in promoting employment of persons with severe mental illness. *Psychiatric Services, 49,* 775–781.

Phelan, M., & Parkman, S. (1995). Work with an interpreter. *British Medical Journal, 311,* 555–557.

Rehabilitation Act Amendments of 1992 (October 20, 1992). Public Law No. 102-569. *U.S. Statutes at Large, Vol. 106,* pp. 4344–4488.

Rubin, S. E., Davis, E. L., Noe, S. R., & Turner, T. N. (1996). Assessing the effects of continuing rehabilitation counseling education. *Rehabilitation Education, 10,* 115–126.

Sandieson, R. (1998). A survey on terminology that refers to people with mental retardation/developmental disabilities. *Education and Training in Mental Retardation and Developmental Disabilities, 33,* 290–295.

Schall, C. M. (1998). The Americans with Disabilities Act: Are we keeping our promise? An analysis of the effect of the ADA on the employment of persons with disabilities. *Journal of Vocational Rehabilitation, 10,* 191–203.

Schaller, J., Parker, R., & Garcia, S. B. (1998). Moving toward culturally competent rehabilitation counseling services: Issues and practices. *Journal of Applied Rehabilitation Counseling, 29,* 40–48.

Shweder, R. A. (1985). Menstrual pollution, soul loss, and comparative study of emotions. In A. Kleinman & B. Good (Eds.), *Culture and depression* (pp. 182–215). Berkeley: University of California Press.

Smart, J. F., & Smart, D. W. (1997a). Culturally sensitive informed choice in rehabilitation counseling. *Journal of Applied Rehabilitation Counseling, 28,* 32–37.

Smart, J. F., & Smart, D. W. (1997b). The racial/ethnic demography of disability. *Journal of Rehabilitation, 63*(4), 9–15.

Sodowsky, G. R., Taffe, R. C., Gutkins, T. B., & Wise, S. L. (1994). Development of the Multicultural Counseling Inventory: A self-report measure of multicultural competencies. *Journal of Counseling Psychology, 41,* 137–148.

Storck, I. F., & Thompson-Hoffman, S. (1991). Demographic characteristics of the disabled population. In S. Thompson-Hoffman & I. F. Storck (Eds.), *Disability in the United States: A portrait from national data* (pp. 15–33). New York: Springer.

Sue, D. W., & Sue, D. (2003). *Counseling the culturally diverse: Theory and practice* (4th ed.). New York: Wiley.

Weinrach, S. G., & Thomas, K. R. (1998). Diversity-sensitive counseling today: A postmodern clash of values. *Journal of Counseling and Development, 76,* 115–122.

Wilgosh, L., & Sandulac, C. (1997). Media attention to and treatment of disabilities information. *Developmental Disabilities Bulletin, 25,* 94–103.

Wright, B. A. (1991). Labeling: The need for person-environment individuation. In C. R. Snyder & D. R. Forsyth (Eds.), *Handbook of social and clinical psychology: The health perspective* (pp. 469–487). New York: Pergamon.

Yelin, E. H. (1991). *Disability and the displaced worker.* New Brunswick, NJ: Rutgers University Press.

Section V

Professional Issues

Chapter 21

Clinical Supervision in Rehabilitation Settings

James T. Herbert

A basic goal of rehabilitation administration and supervision is to ensure that client services are provided by competent personnel (Herbert, 1997). Toward this goal, supervision of clinical work becomes a necessary professional activity if rehabilitation personnel are to be effective service providers (Ross, 1979). In fact, without competent, ongoing clinical supervision, counselors can experience skill regression (Spooner & Stone, 1977; Wiley & Ray, 1986). Despite the importance of clinical supervision to rehabilitation practice, it is a topic that has been generally ignored in the literature (Herbert, 1995; Herbert, Ward, & Hemlick, 1995). Stebnicki (1998) found that only 1% of all clinical supervision dissertations published in the previous 10 years addressed rehabilitation counselor supervision. Consequently, as pointed out by Stebnicki, much of what is known about clinical supervision is borrowed from clinical, counseling, educational, and school psychology, counselor education, and social work.

In light of the limited consideration given to clinical supervision in the literature, this chapter provides a definition of clinical supervision applicable to various rehabilitation disciplines. An overview of clinical supervision practice related to the different supervision formats and methods used to develop professional competence is considered within the context of supervisee developmental levels. Although much of what is presented here is specifically directed toward rehabilitation counseling supervision, most issues raised are applicable across other allied rehabilitation professions.

CLINICAL SUPERVISION DEFINED

Working definitions of clinical supervision provided by various authors differ as a function of academic discipline and training (Bernard & Goodyear, 1998). For example, in nursing, Severinsson (1994) contends that clinical supervision occurs when one practitioner reviews another's ongoing clinical work and addresses the reaction to that evaluation. The American Occupational Therapy Association (1998) indicates that supervision "encourages creativity and innovation; and provides guidance, education, support, encouragement, and respect while working toward a goal" (p. 592). Kadushin (1992) identifies three administrative functions of clinical supervision in social work practice: administrative (adherence to policy and procedure); educational (dispelling ignorance and upgrading skills); and supportive (improving morale and job satisfaction). In recreation therapy, Gruver and Austin (1990) indicate that clinical supervision is designed to enhance client treatment by expanding therapist knowledge, improve client-therapist interactions, encourage professional autonomy, and develop professional identity. The American Speech-Language-Hearing Association (ASHA, 1985) indicates that clinical supervision requires self-analysis, self-evaluation, and problem solving.

Many aspects of supervision in other professional disciplines have been cited in earlier commentary regarding rehabilitation counseling supervision (e.g., Emener, 1978; James, 1973). Whether rehabilitation counselor supervision constitutes a unique practice different from other related professional disciplines is open to debate. Rich (1993) contended that clinical supervision involves a process by which supervisors (a) use clinical techniques to provide supervision, (b) focus on supervisee professional and personal development, and (c) direct the clinical work of front-line staff so that client services can be provided to meet organizational goals and professional standards. Stebnicki (1998) suggested that rehabilitation counselor supervision is different from other disciplines because of supervisee focus, requiring a variety of supervisory styles and approaches that (a) enhance supervisee processing skills as they relate to psychosocial interventions; (b) promote counseling self-efficacy and personal growth among supervisees; and (c) develop supervisee case conceptualization skills, particularly as they relate to disability issues. He contended that psychosocial aspects of chronic illness and disability represent the core of clinical supervision as supervisors assume educator, consultant, and counselor roles.

In attempting to find a working definition that accommodates various professional disciplines, Bernard and Goodyear (1998) suggested that supervision is an intervention provided by a more senior member of a profession to a more junior member or members of that same profession. This relationship is evaluative, extends over time, and has the simultaneous purposes of enhancing the professional functioning of the more junior person(s), monitoring the quality of professional services offered to the client(s) she, he, or they see(s), and serving as a gatekeeper of those who are to enter the particular profession. (p. 6)

Because of its evaluative nature, Bernard and Goodyear suggested that clinical supervision constitutes a different intervention than counseling, consultation, or education.

CLINICAL SUPERVISION PRACTICE

Across allied health disciplines, clinical supervision represents a critical component in professional development (ASHA, 1985; Butterworth & Faugier, 1992; Gruver & Austin, 1990; Herbert, 1995). During preprofessional training most allied health personnel require a supervised clinical internship. This experience serves as a self-regulating mechanism to ensure that beginning professionals demonstrate minimal competence in their practice. Once rehabilitation professionals complete formal training at the master's degree level, however, subsequent clinical supervision as part of postemployment responsibilities is not widely practiced or understood (Barretta-Herman, 1993; Titchen & Binnie, 1995), particularly for personnel not interested in or not requiring state licensure in order to practice. The emergence and continued growth of state licensure typically require supervised experience, and, at present, there may not be sufficient numbers of qualified state-licensed clinical supervisors with appropriate rehabilitation counseling experience (Stebnicki, 1998). In the case of licensure, the nature of the supervisory experience typically is subject to broad interpretation as to the activities that constitute appropriate supervision, including frequency, duration, and the credentials and training required of supervisors. Supervision may often focus on more administrative rather than clinical tasks and needs (e.g., Barretta-Herman, 1993; English, Oberle, & Byrne, 1979), and effectiveness can depend on such variables as supervision format, methods used to support clinical skill development, and supervisee developmental level.

Clinical Supervision Formats

Five basic formats may be identified for supervision. *Self-supervision* requires the person to examine and reflect on his or her own clinical skills and, if needs are perceived, to institute remedial work. Although this approach may be easiest to implement, potential problems and effective interventions to resolve them may not be identified without input from colleagues who are not directly involved in providing client services. *Individual or one-to-one supervision*, a common approach used in most professions, allows opportunities for one professional to critique the clinical work of another. This approach is used most often in academic settings to help professionals-in-training in emulating the behavior of more experienced supervisors (Mead, 1990). *Team supervision* occurs when professionals from several different disciplines are working together with particular clients (Butterworth & Faugier, 1992), an approach that is often used in medical and mental health settings (Stutts, 1991). *Group supervision* is similar to team supervision, except that supervisees are all in the same profession as opposed to different disciplines. Typically, each group member has opportunities to discuss particular clients and receive feedback from the others in the group regarding his or her clinical work, a format that is frequently used in professional education programs in academic settings. During early professional development, a more experienced clinician and knowledgeable supervisor provides feedback to less experienced professionals or professionals-in-training (cf., Herbert & Ward, 1989). The supervisor serves as a resource for new ideas, challenges repetitive therapeutic strategies, and provides meaningful input regarding client and helping professional dynamics (Powell, 1996). As professionals gain additional experience and competence, a different group format or *peer supervision* model may be implemented. This format is particularly helpful for professionals who maintain independent private practices and have limited opportunity to work with other professional colleagues. Used in this way, peer supervision allows for greater accountability by maintaining high standards of practice for professionals who do not have supervision available within their own practices (Schreiber & Frank, 1983). This format does not require any formal evaluation of the "supervisor" since each person participates voluntarily. Consequently, without the issue of performance evaluation, equal power is maintained among participants.

Assessment Methods to Support Clinical Skill Development

In order to assess the clinical competence of rehabilitation professionals, it is necessary to evaluate client-professional interactions. Depending on available technology and supervisee-supervisor preferences, there are four basic methods to document supervisee development.

Indirect Delayed

This method of assessment includes self-report and/or process-note descriptions of client-counselor interactions. Self-report requires the supervisee to conceptualize client problems, especially as they relate to the counselor-client relationship (Bernard & Goodyear, 1998). This method has also been referred to as the case presentation or case review method. Several examples, with varying content themes (e.g., Glickauf-Hughes & Campbell, 1991) and formats (e.g., Wilbur, Roberts-Wilbur, Hart, Morris, & Betz, 1994) have been described in the literature. The variations seem largely dependent on type of supervision provided (individual versus group), supervisory style, and supervisee developmental level. Process notes require supervisees to provide systematic written documentation of the client-counselor interaction and client progress. In comparison to other supervision formats such as audio or videotaping, Goldberg (1985) suggested that process notes allow the supervisor to better understand supervisee thoughts about the therapeutic process, feelings about clients, and interventions used to address client problems. Accordingly, this method may be more appropriate for rehabilitation professionals with greater clinical experience.

Indirect methods have been criticized as being less appropriate for counselors-in-training because they do not afford independent evaluations by the supervisor to clarify, support, or refute supervisee perceptions regarding client problems (Holloway, 1988). Self-report methods have also been criticized because they are unreliable or, at the very least, include biased interpretations of counseling content and process (e.g., Bernard & Goodyear, 1998; Borders & Leddick, 1987). Finally, Worthington (1987) noted that supervisors provide a different viewpoint, which is necessary if counselors are to change their perceptions and behavior. He contended that "counselors believe that they are actually counseling the way they say they are, but, as most supervisors know, the way in which a counselor talks about his or her counseling is not perfectly correlated with the way in which he or she counsels" (p. 203). For this reason, differences often exist between supervisor and supervisee perceptions regarding client problems and insight, motivation for change, and prognosis (Biggs, 1988). Still, indirect-delayed methods such as case review and verbal presentation are most used (Herbert & Ward, 1989; Stebnicki, Allen, & Janikowski, 1997) and most preferred (Herbert, Hemlick, & Ward, 1991) among beginning rehabilitation counseling students. Data with respect to rehabilitation counseling supervision preferences and the practices of experienced counselors in the public and proprietary rehabilitation sectors have, to date, been unexplored.

Direct Delayed

In contrast to indirect approaches, more direct methods of monitoring counselor-client interactions, such as audio or video recordings, have the advantage of documenting the actual interaction that transpires between client and counselor. By using recordings, the direct-delayed method allows supervisors to (a) make inferences about supervisee-client interactions that may change over the course of the counseling session, (b) examine how supervisees address presenting problems expressed by clients, (c) evaluate treatment interventions, and (d) evaluate supervisory interventions designed to improve supervisee competence. Most importantly, the direct-delayed method allows supervisors to conduct independent analyses of supervisee performance based on actual behavior.

Among the variety of formats in which to review tapes within counselor supervision, the Interpersonal Process Recall (IPR) method (Kagan, 1980) has historically been taught in many counselor education supervision programs (Borders & Leddick, 1988). This method requires the supervisee to examine intrapersonal as well as interpersonal dynamics between supervisee and client. In order to assist supervisees to recall underlying feelings or thoughts, the supervisor may ask questions such as, "Can you tell me what you felt at that point?" "Can you recall more of the details of your feelings . . . where did you feel these things, what parts of your body responded?" and, "What else do you think (the other [person]) thought about you at that point?" (Kagan, 1980, pp. 262–263). Using IPR, supervisors must consider when and what to review with supervisees. Bernard and Goodyear (1998) suggest that supervisors ask the following questions to facilitate determinations: "From what I can observe, does this interaction seem to be interrupting the flow of counseling? From what I know of the trainee, would focusing on this interaction aid in his or her development as a mental health professional?" (p. 101). They suggest that IPR supervisor leads promote affective exploration, provide opportunities to review unstated agendas and expectations, and encourage cognitive examination with respect to client dynamics and the counseling process. When a specific portion of an audio or videotape is reviewed, Bernard and Goodyear suggest that supervisees be prepared to explain (a) reason(s) for selecting a particular segment, (b) what transpired up to the point being reviewed, (c) what was being attempted by the supervisee, and (d) what help is being asked from the supervisor.

Although direct-delayed methods such as IPR allow supervisors to review client-counselor interactions and have proven to be effective supervision methods (Kagan, 1980), a potential disadvantage is that supervisory interventions are provided after the supervisee has met with a client. Should supervisee interactions with clients be inappropriate, unproductive, or potentially damaging, the supervisor can only help the supervisee to prepare for the next meeting. In some cases, because of what transpired in the previous meeting, clients may prematurely terminate counseling.

One final aspect of delayed supervision methods that has not been examined is the timing of supervision. Would it matter, for example, if the supervisor met with the supervisee several hours before counseling sessions as opposed to several days after? In most instances the timing of supervision is related more to convenience and personal preference rather than to supervisee skill development (Couchon & Bernard, 1984). A study conducted by Couchon and Bernard found that supervisees more frequently attempted to implement supervisor-approved counseling strategies if supervision was conducted within four hours of providing counseling services, as opposed to the day before providing services. It was further noted that supervision occurring more than two days before counseling sessions may be "too broad a treatment to have produced any definitive results" (p. 18). Finally, supervision sessions held the day before counseling tended to include more content-oriented information provided by supervisors. Given these results, Couchon and Bernard concluded that supervisees who conceptualize well but implement supervision ideas poorly would benefit more if supervision were held immediately before counseling. Conversely, supervisees who perform well but lack conceptual abilities may derive greater benefit if supervision occurs the day before supervisee-client interactions. Timing of supervision is therefore another consideration when considering delayed methods.

Direct Present

A more direct approach to supervision involves work with supervisees as they provide rehabilitation services. Although not practiced commonly in rehabilitation counseling, it is often used in related allied health disciplines such as nursing (Pertab, 1999) and physical therapy (Hayes, Huber, Rogers, & Sanders, 1999). Direct-present methods allow the supervisor to monitor supervisee progress as it happens and, if necessary, intervene to assist and support the supervisee. This "live" approach is one that both rehabilitation counseling practicum supervisors (Herbert & Ward, 1989) and their supervisees (Herbert, Hemlick, & Ward, 1991) prefer least, however. Possible reasons for not endorsing this approach more strongly may be attributable to supervisee anxiety associated with performance evaluation. According to Herbert et al., some rehabilitation counseling practicum supervisees perceived live supervision as bordering on unethical practice. Supervisees may also perceive supervisors as taking control of the counseling experience, resulting in feelings of disempowerment. This perception, if accurate, may be particularly important when supervisors are white males supervising rehabilitation counselors-in-training who are female or persons of color.

Two more specific types of direct-present supervision are cocounseling and live supervision. Cocounseling occurs when supervisors and supervisees collaborate in providing counseling services to clients (Reynolds & McWhirter, 1984). Consistent with social learning theory, this approach helps supervisees to learn by observing a more experienced counselor (supervisor). It also affords opportunities to learn by doing when a co-counselor is available for support. If used appropriately, this direct-active approach offers potential for supervisee growth by reducing anxiety, enhancing learning, and fostering accountability (Reynolds & McWhirter, 1984; Silverman & Quinn, 1974; Worthington, 1984). In contrast, live supervision occurs when the supervisor provides consultation to the supervisee with the client(s) present. The rationale for this live supervision is that it offers clients insight into presenting problems and a belief that clients have a right to "access to all information, including a discussion of interventions" (Bernard & Goodyear, 1998, p. 133).

Indirect Present

Indirect-present approaches, like direct-present approaches, allow supervisors access to supervisee-client interactions, but they do so with less intrusiveness. An example is the "bug-in-the-ear" technique that uses a wireless earphone worn by the supervisee. This arrangement allows the supervisor to communicate to the supervisee while counseling services are in progress. Bernard and Goodyear (1998) suggest that this technology (a) allows the supervisor to make adjustments without disrupting client-supervisee interaction, (b) increases positive counseling behavior through audible reinforcements, and (c) protects the therapeutic relationship, since clients are unaware of supervisee statements that are supervisor-generated versus those that are supervisee-generated. Bernard and Goodyear warned that the bug-in-the-ear may be ineffective if the supervisee relies too heavily on supervisor input or if the input becomes a distraction to the supervisee and client. It is the present author's opinion that supervisee developmental level should be a primary consideration in determining the appropriateness of this and other techniques.

Although not a method of supervision, the use of electronic online technology allows the clinical supervisor to provide supervision in any of the previously described formats. The use of electronic mail as an asynchronous form of communication offers an inexpensive and quick way to provide and receive input between supervisor and supervisee. In a recent pilot study, Stebnicki and Glover (2001) reported that e-mail combined with onsite face-to-face clinical supervision resulted in several benefits to supervisees and supervisors, including more timely feedback, increases in the supervisory alliance, and provision of greater access between participants. Such technology does not afford the opportunity to observe (either delayed or live) client-counselor interaction, and, as several authors have noted (Janoff & Schoenholtz-Read, 1999; Stebnicki & Glover, 2001), electronic transmission of textual messages should be used as an adjunct to the clinical supervision process.

A potentially more effective way to assess client-counselor interaction might be achieved through videoconferencing, through which counseling sessions are either videotaped and later transmitted or viewed as live client-counselor interactions by the supervisor and/or other supervisees. Although technology allows for communicating in real time, there are important ethical issues regarding confidentiality and informed consent. Implementing encryption software can reduce potential breaches of confidentiality, but human error in forwarding electronic documents occurs and, as a result, may represent a major breach in confidentiality (Kanz, 2001). Further, clients must be informed about the nature of supervision and understand that, while precautions will be taken when communicating supervisor-supervisee text messages, confidentiality cannot be guaranteed via electronic transmissions (Kanz, 2001). Despite these issues, it appears that the use of online supervision will have an increasing impact on how supervision is delivered in the future.

Supervisee Developmental Level

Goodyear and Bernard (1998) contend that supervisee developmental level moderates process and outcome in supervision. There are numerous developmental models that propose varying supervisor roles and behaviors to assist supervisees in successfully negotiating the transition from professionals-in-training to competent professionals. Although there is general support for the developmental process that supervisees experience, much of what is known about this process is limited to supervisees who complete practica and internships during graduate study. Based on available literature, beginning supervisees prefer greater encouragement, support, and structure than advanced supervisees, who express greater preference for examining personal concerns that affect client interactions (Stoltenberg, McNeill, & Crethar, 1994; Worthington, 1987). Earlier studies of counselor training found that entry-level supervisees prefer supervision that offers minimal direct confrontation within a structured, supportive framework (Stoltenberg & Delworth, 1987). Beginning counselors also want supervisors to provide direct and clear suggestions rather than using a Socratic method that focuses on client problems and counselor-client interactions (Stenack & Dye, 1982). Within rehabilitation counseling practica, Herbert and Ward (1990) found that supervisors perceived themselves as using a more collegial and relationship-oriented style, as opposed to a more didactic style with a specific content focus. Given results of other studies cited earlier, this style may not be particularly helpful for beginning rehabilitation counselors-in-training.

In contrast to beginning counselors, individuals with greater clinical experience and competence may prefer greater autonomy. In their review of supervision literature, Holloway and Neufeldt (1995) concluded that more experienced supervisees prefer supervisors who focus on personal growth issues, such as countertransference, self-awareness, and self-efficacy, and are more willing to examine counselor-client interactions that reflect less favorably on them as counselors. Although these preferences may hold for experienced rehabilitation counselors, there has been very limited empirical study to document supervision preferences, with only two published studies conducted with experienced rehabilitation counselors. A nationwide study by English et al. (1979) found that rehabilitation counselors wanted their supervisors to devote greater time to case consultation and less time to administrative tasks. Counselors indicated preference for a supervision model that demonstrates "democratic leadership." More recently, an investigation by Schultz, Ososkie, Fried, Nelson, and Bardos (2002) reported that public vocational rehabilitation counselors (VRCs) from two states experienced limited contact with their supervisors, with the majority having no more than 30 minutes of such contact each week. It was recommended that public VRC supervisors receive training in clinical supervision roles and functions.

In order to understand the developmental process of counselors-in-training, who later become experienced and competent professionals, Stoltenberg, McNeill, and Delworth (1998) proposed the Integrated Development Model (IDM). Although it is a generic model, the primary activities involved in clinical supervision are applicable to rehabilitation counseling practice and include assessment techniques (confidence when conducting psychological assessment), client conceptualization (ability to make correct diagnoses), individual differences (understanding cultural, ethnic, and racial influences), interpersonal assessment (conceptualizing client interpersonal dynamics), intervention skills competence (confidence and ability to perform therapeutic interventions), professional ethics (combining personal ethics with those found in professional ethical codes and standards of practice), theoretical orientation (understanding formal theories of psychotherapy and eclectic approaches), and treatment plans and goals (organizing one's efforts when working with clients). In the IDM model, supervisees can progress from Level 1 (counselors who typically have limited clinical experience) to Level 3i ("integrated" counselors who move smoothly across the eight dimensions). Within each level, there are three basic structures that influence the degree of growth across the eight dimensions: awareness, motivation, and autonomy. In examining the applicability of this model to rehabilitation counseling supervision, Maki and Delworth (1995) described these structures accordingly:

> In functional terms, these three structures provide the specific clinical indexes that supervisors must accurately assess to determine the needs of those who are supervised. First, through awareness, the supervisor can constructively consider the cognitive and affective focus of attention of those supervised. This structure is described on a continuum that indicates the extent to which the counselor's awareness is internally self-focused or externally focused on the client, or both. Second, motivation provides a structure that is descriptive of a counselor's level of clinical energy and is evaluative on a continuum ranging from high to low. Autonomy describes the extent to which counselors are cognitively and affectively independent from or dependent on their supervisors. This structure reflects a counselor's sense of self-efficacy. Collectively, these structures provide supervisors not only with a framework from which to assess the developmental level of those they supervise in specific aspects of practice but also with a basis for planning supervisory interventions. (p. 285)

The three overriding structures indicate the level of professional growth as supervisees evolve from counselors-in-training to proficient counselors. In short, they serve as benchmarks for clinical supervisors to use in determining supervisee growth and evaluating client progress. There is some empirical support for this developmental supervision model (McNeill, Stoltenberg, & Romans, 1992; Stoltenberg, Pierce, & McNeill, 1987; Tryon, 1996), it has been applied specifically to rehabilitation counseling practice (e.g., Murray, Portman, & Maki, 2003).

TRAINING AND DEVELOPING EFFECTIVE
CLINICAL SUPERVISORS

In order to become proficient clinical supervisors, formal coursework may be pursued as a part of preprofessional training, or training may be received as a part of employment experience (Herbert, 1997). If formal training in clinical supervision is pursued, one route would require a graduate degree in rehabilitation administration and supervision. Although there are 88 graduate programs in rehabilitation counseling, only 8 offer a specialization, certificate, master's, or postmaster's training in rehabilitation administration or related areas (e.g., executive leadership; National Council on Rehabilitation Education, 2002–2003). The extent to which graduate programs in rehabilitation counseling may also offer courses in rehabilitation administration and supervision is unknown. To have greater impact on the profession, an emphasis on developing clinical supervision skills as part of existing rehabilitation counseling programs may be advisable. Although developing clinical supervision competence from a supervisee perspective (via practica and internships) is one approach, counselors-in-training could likely benefit from further instruction and experience as part of the master's degree program (Herbert & Bieschke, 2000).

Preprofessional Training

Infusing or developing specific coursework designed to teach rehabilitation counselors-in-training to function as effective clinical supervisors may be challenged by some rehabilitation counselor educators (e.g., Patterson & Pankowski, 1988). Objections may be based on philosophical differences ("we train rehabilitation counselors, not rehabilitation counselor supervisors") or practical constraints ("our program is stretched to the limit; we cannot include additional coursework in this area"). While recognizing these objections, it is also important to realize that advancement from counselor to supervisor may occur for some counselors within only a few years (Riggar & Matkin, 1984). In other words, persons who provide supervision are often master's-level practitioners. It is typical, however, to find clinical training as rehabilitation counselor supervisors at the doctoral level of professional training (e.g., Allen, Stebnicki, & Torkelson-Lynch, 1995). In addition, existing Standards for Counseling Supervisors (Supervision Interest Network, Association for Counselor Education and Supervision, 1990) provide that "training for supervision generally occurs during advanced graduate study or continuing professional development. This is not to say, however, that supervisor training in the pre-service stage is without merit" (p. 32). Given the sheer numbers of master's-level versus doctoral-trained rehabilitation personnel, earlier exposure to clinical supervision seems both proactive and practical.

Even though practical constraints to developing coursework in clinical supervision theory and practice may be difficult to overcome, Bernard (1992) described a master's-level training intervention that rehabilitation educators might consider. Using advanced master's-level interns who serve as "peer supervisors" of students starting their practica, Bernard provided a 12-hour, weekend workshop to potential supervisors. This workshop included information regarding supervisor behavior, a model of clinical supervision (i.e., the Discrimination Model developed by Bernard, 1979), and an overview of ethical and legal concerns in supervision. Students also learn how to conduct supervisee evaluations. Once determined "ready" by faculty supervisors, each peer supervisor was assigned to one practicum student. Peer supervisors met weekly with their respective practicum students for individual conferences. In addition, peer supervisors were required to listen to one audiotape of a session between the practicum student and client beyond those heard by the practicum instructor. However, the peer supervisors had no evaluative responsibility or influence in performance evaluations of practicum students. As Bernard noted, "The role of the peer supervisor is to supplement, not replace, the supervision offered by the practicum instructor and the site supervisor" (p. 137).

After participating in the peer supervision experience, Bernard (1979) indicated that peer supervisors gained greater sensitivity to counseling dynamics and the supervision process. She believed that this model had an advantage over the approach that involves doctoral students who, under the direction of a faculty supervisor, are assigned clinical supervision duties with master's-level trainees. As Bernard noted, a disadvantage when using doctoral students is the differences in their career aspirations in relation to their supervisees. Given the diversity of career goals and, in many instances, differences in specialties within broader counseling practice between supervisor and supervisee (e.g., counseling psychology versus rehabilitation counseling), some discord may result. Bernard contended that this difference is not sufficiently addressed where doctoral students share supervision responsibilities. This issue may not pertain to other allied health professions, such as occupational and physical therapy, nursing, and social work, where clinical supervisors are more likely to be within the same academic discipline as their supervisees.

Training as Part of Employment Experience

Professional growth as a clinical supervisor requires ongoing learning. Simply having greater experience as a clinical supervisor does not mean that one functions more effectively than others with less supervisory experience (Ellis & Dell, 1986; Marikas, Russell, & Dell, 1985). Unfortunately, most counselor supervisors do not change supervisory styles and behaviors with increased experience (Worthington, 1987) and tend to remain in a stable pattern of using one style (Shanfield, Mohl, Matthews, & Hetherly, 1992). Eventually, ineffective supervisory patterns only further entrench ineffective styles that are "self-perpetuating, and resistant to change" (Watkins, 1997, p. 174). In order for growth to occur, clinical supervisors must engage in lifelong learning that includes continuing education, such as participation in professional conferences, seminars, and workshops about supervision. It also requires supervisors to review their work with other clinical supervisors to obtain independent evaluations as to the quality of their supervision. According to Watkins (1995), effective clinical supervisors are persons who critically and continually evaluate their supervision. These supervisors ask questions concerning what transpired during supervision, how it may have helped or hindered supervisee development, and whether supervision interventions were effective. Being mindful of how supervision affects the professional development of others sends an important message to supervisees. When supervisors do not engage in continuous efforts to develop and evaluate their clinical supervision, it perpetuates the myth that supervision does not require a great deal of commitment (Herbert, 1997). If supervision is not worthy of a continuing investment on the part of the supervisor, it seems likely that similar perceptions may develop on the part of supervisees.

FINAL COMMENT

Rehabilitation educators play a critical role in the professional development of competent professionals. Ensuring that future rehabilitation professionals possess the necessary clinical skills is initially dependent on the quality of practicum and internship experiences. This groundwork serves as the foundation for subsequent ongoing supervision throughout one's career. Opportunities to evaluate clinical competence through ongoing professional experiences must occur if one is to continue to grow professionally. Any doubts regarding the importance of maintaining clinical supervision throughout one's career can be answered by reflecting on the following questions:

1. "What kind of professional would I have become if my graduate training did not include clinical supervision?"

2. "Are my clinical skills at the point where I could not benefit from further clinical supervision?"

How one answers these questions determines whether clinical supervision becomes an important part of professional development. In sum, it is an indication of the professional commitment that each professional makes when working with persons with disabilities.

REFERENCES

Allen, H. A., Stebnicki, M. A., & Torkelson Lynch, R. (1995). Training clinical supervisors in rehabilitation: A conceptual model for training doctoral-level supervisors. *Rehabilitation Counseling Bulletin, 38*, 307–314.

American Occupational Therapy Association. (1998). Guide for supervision of occupational therapy personnel in the delivery of occupational therapy services. *American Journal of Occupational Therapy, 53*, 592–594.

American Speech-Language-Hearing Association (ASHA), Committee on Supervision in Speech-Language Pathology and Audiology. (1985). Clinical supervision in speech-language pathology and audiology. A position statement. *ASHA, 27*, 57–60.

Barretta-Herman, A. (1993). On the development of a model of supervision for licensed social work practitioners. *Clinical Supervisor, 11*, 55–64.

Bernard, J. M. (1979). Supervisory training: A discrimination model. *Counselor Education and Supervision, 19*, 60–68.

Bernard, J. M. (1992). Training master's level counseling students in the fundamentals of clinical supervision. *Clinical Supervisor, 10*, 133–143.

Bernard, J. M., & Goodyear, R. K. (1998). *Fundamentals of clinical supervision* (2nd ed.). Needham Heights, MA: Allyn & Bacon.

Biggs, D. A. (1988). The case presentation approach in clinical supervision. *Counselor Education and Supervision, 27*, 240–248.

Borders, L. D., & Leddick, G. R. (1987). *Handbook of counseling supervision*. Alexandria, VA: Association for Counselor Education and Supervision.

Borders, L. D., & Leddick, G. R. (1988). A nationwide survey of supervision training. *Counselor Education and Supervision, 27*, 271–283.

Butterworth, T., & Faugier, J. (1992). *Clinical supervision and mentorship in nursing.* London: Chapman &Hall.

Couchon, W. D., & Bernard, J. M. (1984). Effects of timing of supervision on supervisor and counselor performance. *Clinical Supervisor, 2*, 3–20.

Ellis, M. V., & Dell, D. M. (1986). Dimensionality of supervisor roles: Supervisors' perceptions of supervision. *Journal of Counseling Psychology, 33*, 282–291.

Emener, W. G. (1978). Clinical supervision in rehabilitation settings. *Journal of Rehabilitation Administration, 2*, 44–53.

English, W. R., Oberle, J. B., & Byrne, A. R. (1979). Rehabilitation counselor supervision: A national perspective. *Rehabilitation Counseling Bulletin, 22*, 7–123.

Glickauf-Hughes, C., & Campbell, L. F. (1991). Experiential supervision: Applied techniques for a case presentation approach. *Psychotherapy, 28,* 625–634.

Goldberg, D. A. (1985). Process notes, audio, and videotape: Modes of presentation in psychotherapy training. *Clinical Supervisor, 3,* 3–13.

Goodyear, R. G., & Bernard, J. M. (1998). Clinical supervision: Lessons from the literature. *Counselor Education and Supervision, 38,* 6–22.

Gruver, B. M., & Austin, D. R. (1990). The instructional status of clinical supervision in therapeutic recreation curricula. *Therapeutic Recreation Journal, 24,* 18–24.

Hayes, K. W., Huber, G., Rogers, J., & Sanders, B. (1999). Behaviors that cause clinical instructors to question the clinical competence of physical therapy students. *Physical Therapy, 79,* 653–667.

Herbert, J. T. (1995). Clinical supervision. In A. E. Del Orto & R. P. Marinelli (Eds.), *Encyclopedia of disability and rehabilitation* (pp. 178–190). New York: Macmillan.

Herbert, J. T. (1997). Quality of assurance: Administration and supervision. In D. R.Maki & T. F. Riggar (Eds.), *Rehabilitation counseling: Profession and practice* (pp. 246–258). New York: Springer.

Herbert, J. T., & Bieschke, K. L. (2000). A didactic course in clinical supervision. *Rehabilitation Education, 14,* 187–198.

Herbert, J. T., Hemlick, L., & Ward, T. J. (1991). Supervisee perception of rehabilitation counseling practica. *Rehabilitation Education, 5,* 121–129.

Herbert, J. T., & Ward, T. J. (1989). Rehabilitation counselor supervision: A national survey of graduate training practica. *Rehabilitation Education, 3,* 163–175.

Herbert, J. T., & Ward, T. J. (1990). Supervisory styles among rehabilitation counseling practica supervisors. *Rehabilitation Education, 4,* 203–212.

Herbert, J. T., Ward, T. J., & Hemlick, L. M. (1995). Confirmatory factor analysis of the Supervisory Style Inventory and Revised Supervision Questionnaire. *Rehabilitation Counseling Bulletin, 38,* 334–349.

Holloway, E. L. (1988). Instruction beyond the facilitative conditions: A response to Biggs. *Counselor Education and Supervision, 27,* 252–258.

Holloway, E. L., & Neufeldt, S. A. (1995). Supervision: Its contributions to treatment efficacy. *Journal of Consulting and Clinical Psychology, 63,* 207–213.

James, D. T. (1973). The supervisor as counselor-facilitator. *Journal of Rehabilitation, 39*(4), 18–20, 43.

Janoff, D. S., & Schoenholtz-Read, J. (1999). Group supervision meets technology: A model for computer-mediated group training at a distance. *International Journal of Group Psychotherapy, 49,* 25–272.

Kadushin, A. (1992). *Supervision in social work* (3rd ed.). New York: Columbia University Press.

Kagan, N. (1980). Influencing human interaction—Eighteen years with IPR. In A. K. Hess (Ed.), *Psychotherapy supervision: Theory, research and practice* (pp. 262–286). New York: Wiley.

Kanz, J. E. (2001). Clinical-supervision.com: Issues in the provision of online supervision. *Professional Psychology: Research and Practice, 32,* 415–420.

Maki, D. R., & Delworth, U. (1995). Clinical supervision: A definition and model for the rehabilitation counseling profession. *Rehabilitation Counseling Bulletin, 38,* 282–293.

Marikas, D. A., Russell, R. K., & Dell, D. M. (1985). Effects of supervisor experience level on planning and in-session supervisor verbal behavior. *Journal of Counseling Psychology, 32,* 410–416.

McNeil, B. W., Stoltenberg, C. D., & Romans, J. S. (1992). The Integrated Development Model of supervision: Scale development and validation procedures. *Professional Psychology: Research and Practice, 23,* 504–508.

Mead, D. E. (1990). *Effective supervision: A task-oriented model for the mental health professions.* New York: Brunner/Mazel.

Murray, G. C., Portman, T. A. A., & Maki, D. R. (2003). Clinical supervision: Developmental differences during preservice training. *Rehabilitation Education, 17,* 19–32.

National Council on Rehabilitation Education. (2002–2003). *Membership directory.* Logan, UT: Author.

Patterson, J. B., & Pankowski, J. (1988). Preparing the consumer of rehabilitation administration, management, and supervision: Preservice, inservice, and continuing education issues. *Journal of Rehabilitation Administration, 12,* 117–121.

Pertab, D. (1999). Clinical supervision in diploma in higher education (nursing) programmes. *Journal of Clinical Nursing, 8,* 112–113.

Powell, D. (1996). A peer consultation model for clinical supervision. *Clinical Supervisor, 14,* 163–169.

Reynolds, E., & McWhirter, J. J. (1984). Cotherapy from the trainee's standpoint: Suggestions for supervision. *Counselor Education and Supervision, 23,* 205–213.

Rich, P. (1993). The form, function, and content of clinical supervision: An integrated model. *Clinical Supervisor, 11,* 137–178.

Riggar, T. F., & Matkin, R. E. (1984). Rehabilitation counselors working as administrators: A pilot investigation. *Journal of Applied Rehabilitation Counseling, 15*(1), 9–13.

Ross, C. K. (1979). Supervision theory: A prescription for practice. *Journal of Rehabilitation Administration, 3,* 14–19.

Schreiber, P., & Frank, E. (1983). The use of a peer supervision group by social work clinicians. *Clinical Supervisor, 1,* 29–36.

Schultz, J. C., Ososkie, J. N., Fried, J. H., Nelson, R. E., & Bardos, A. N. (2002). Clinical supervision in public rehabilitation counseling settings. *Rehabilitation Counseling Bulletin, 45,* 213–222.

Severinsson, E. (1994). The concept of supervision in psychiatric care—Compared with mentorship and leadership. A review of the literature. *Joural of Nursing Management, 2,* 271–278.

Shanfield, S. B., Mohl, P. C., Matthews, K. L., & Hetherly, V. (1992). Quantitative assessment of the behavior of psychotherapy supervisors. *American Journal of Psychiatry, 146,* 1447–1450.

Silverman, M. S., & Quinn, P. F. (1974). Co-counseling supervision in practicum. *Counselor Education and Supervision, 14,* 256–260.

Spooner, S. E., & Stone, S. C. (1977). Maintenance of specific counseling skills over time. *Journal of Counseling Psychology, 24,* 66–71.

Stebnicki, M. A. (1998). Clinical supervision in rehabilitation counseling. *Rehabilitation Education, 12,* 137–159.

Stebnicki, M. A., Allen, H. A., & Janikowski, T. P. (1997). Development of an instrument to assess perceived helpfulness of clinical supervisory behaviors. *Rehabilitation Education, 11,* 307–322.

Stebnicki, M. A., & Glover, N. M. (2001). E-supervision as a complementary approach to traditional face-to-face clinical supervision in rehabilitation counseling: Problems and solutions. *Rehabilitation Education, 15*, 283–293.

Stenack, R. J., & Dye, H. A. (1982). Behavioral descriptions of practicum supervision roles. *Counselor Education and Supervision, 21*, 295–304.

Stoltenberg, C., & Delworth, U. (1987). *Supervising counselors and therapists*. San Francisco: Jossey-Bass.

Stoltenberg, C. D., McNeill, B. W., & Crethar, H. C. (1994). Changes in supervision as counselors and therapists gain experience: A review. *Professional Psychology: Research and Practice, 25*, 416–449.

Stoltenberg, C. D., McNeill, B., & Delworth, U. (1998). *IDM supervision: An integrated developmental model for supervising counselors and therapists*. San Francisco: Jossey-Bass.

Stoltenberg, C. D., Pierce, R. A., & McNeill, B. W. (1987). Effects of experience on counselors' needs. *Clinical Supervisor, 5*, 23–32.

Stutts, M. L. (1991). Supervision in comprehensive rehabilitation settings: The terrain and the traveler. *Clinical Supervisor, 9*, 33–57.

Supervision Interest Network, Association for Counselor Education and Supervision. (1990). Standards for counselor supervisors. *Journal of Counseling and Development, 69*, 30–32.

Titchen, A., & Binnie, A. (1995). The art of clinical supervision. *Journal of Clinical Nursing, 4*, 327–334.

Tryon, G. S. (1996). Supervisee development during the practicum year. *Counselor Education and Supervision, 35*, 287–294.

Watkins, C. E., Jr. (1995). Researching psychotherapy supervisor development: Four key considerations. *Clinical Supervisor, 13*, 111–118.

Watkins, C. E., Jr. (1997). The ineffective psychotherapy supervisor: Some reflections about bad behaviors, poor process, and offensive outcomes. *Clinical Supervisor, 16*, 163–180.

Wilbur, M. P., Roberts-Wilbur, J., Hart, G. M., Morris, J. R., & Betz, R. L. (1994). Structured group supervision (SGS): A pilot study. *Counselor Education and Supervision, 33*, 262–279.

Wiley, M. L., & Ray, P. B. (1986). Counseling supervision by developmental level. *Journal of Counseling Psychology, 33*, 439–445.

Worthington, E. L., Jr. (1984). Empirical investigation of supervision of counselors as they gain experience. *Journal of Counseling Psychology, 31*, 63–75.

Worthington, E. L., Jr. (1987). Changes in supervision as counselors and supervisors gain experience: A review. *Professional Psychology: Research and Practice, 18*, 189–208.

Chapter **22**

Risk Management for Rehabilitation Counseling and Related Professions

Linda R. Shaw

As the profession of rehabilitation counseling has evolved, rehabilitation counselors have taken on increasing responsibility and, consequently, have assumed increasing obligations to practice ethically, legally, and professionally. The importance of the roles of the rehabilitation counselor and the special nature of the rehabilitation counseling relationship has increasingly been acknowledged by legal bodies through the inclusion of rehabilitation counselors, as well as other counselors, in licensure and in other functions stipulated by statutory and regulatory bodies (Cottone & Tarvydas, 2003). Rehabilitation counselors, as well as other counselors, have fought long and hard to achieve legitimacy through licensure and through recognition by third-party payers as qualified service providers. Today, rehabilitation counselors in many places possess the legal right to make psychiatric diagnoses, perform evaluations of suicidal intent, initiate involuntary commitments to psychiatric facilities, and engage in a wide range of activities requiring specialized skills and the exercise of sound professional judgment (Backlar & Cutler, 2002). With that hard-won recognition, however, comes increased accountability and liability. Those same statutes and regulations that empower rehabilitation counselors to practice a broad scope of professional activities and to be recognized by third-party payers for the critical services that they provide also stipulate acceptable and nonacceptable behavior. Failure to perform in accordance with legal and professional standards may have serious consequences for all parties involved, including the possibility of punitive and damaging legal and professional consequences (Woody, 2000).

The need for counselors to address risk prevention transcends liability issues, however. When rehabilitation counselors manage risks in their service provision, they manage the risks not only to themselves, in terms of legal liability, but also to their clients. Good risk management practices decrease the risk of harm and promote the autonomy and well-being of the individuals served (Cullity, Jackson, & Shaw, 1990; Shaw & Jackson, 1994). The benefits of risk management transcend self-protection and extend to clients, specifically referred to in the Commission on Rehabilitation Counselor Certification (CRCC, 2001) Code of Professional Ethics for Rehabilitation Counselors as the rehabilitation counselor's primary obligation.

Over a decade ago Vallario and Emener (1991) asserted that rehabilitation counselors need to increase their familiarity with law and legal concepts, citing the potential for malpractice as a major reason. Additionally, numerous experts in both mental health and mental health law have emphasized the need for counselors to become aware of those practices that will mitigate against charges of unethical or illegal practice (Behnke, Winick, & Perez, 2000; Crawford, 1994; Otto, Ogloff, & Small, 1991; Picchioni & Bernstein, 1990; Woody, 1988). Although the focus of this chapter is primarily on risk management in rehabilitation counseling, much of the content is equally relevant to other rehabilitation and health professions.

THE LEGAL SYSTEM

While contact with the legal system may strike fear into the heart of many counselors, several investigations into the outcomes of such contacts should be reassuring. Otto and Schmidt (1991) maintain that there are few reported court decisions in which clients have claimed successfully that they were harmed by negligently provided psychotherapy. There is no doubt, however, that knowledge of the legal system and of laws applying to counselors may help mitigate against such claims and also may prove helpful should such claims be filed (Corey, Corey, & Callanan, 2003). Behnke et al. (2000) discuss laws within five categories: (1) constitutions; (2) statutes enacted by legislatures; (3) regulations promulgated by boards or agencies; (4) rules of court adopted by the judiciary; and (5) decisions made by the courts.

Constitutions establish laws affecting the practice of counseling at both the federal and state levels. At both levels, their respective constitutions establish the most important laws. The constitution is often referred to as "supreme" because it establishes the foundation for all other law and is the "touchstone" by which other laws are deemed legitimate or illegitimate.

Statutes enacted by legislatures are written and enacted into law by elected legislatures at both the federal and state levels. At the federal level the body that creates statutes is the United States Congress. At the state level, the elected state legislators create and enact statutes.

Regulations promulgated by boards and agencies are not technically laws, because they do not emanate from any legislative body. Rather, the legislature delegates boards or commissions to develop regulations or rules to interpret statutes and provide greater specificity and definition to them. Regulations do carry the weight of law, in that failure to comply is seen as a failure to comply with the laws in which they originated and which they serve to interpret.

Rules of court adopted by the judiciary govern the processes and activities of judges and attorneys in judicial proceedings, specifying how things should work. Failure to abide by the rules of court is harmful in that it could result in damage to, or even the dismissal of, legal cases. Understanding rules of court may be very helpful in understanding the legal process, including such concepts as admissibility of evidence, rules of discovery, and other "process" issues.

Decisions made by courts are not technically laws, but because they interpret statutes, regulations, or court rules, they are often collectively referred to as "case law." Such decisions often find their way to the legislature and become integrated into statute. Even when they do not become statutes, however, case law is legally binding.

Because all states differ in their legal structure, there is no absolutely uniform system to which all ascribe. Generally, however, all states have a system that is hierarchical or "tiered." The first level of courts, such as county or circuit courts, tries cases initially. The decision of the court may be accepted by both parties and will go no farther within the court system. Decisions made by the lower courts can also be appealed to an appellate court. Finally, the state's supreme court may agree to hear a small minority of cases coming out of the appellate court, with direct relevance to certain criteria established by the state. The federal system is similarly structured, with higher courts able to hear cases decided in the lower courts that have been appealed, with a very small number of cases eventually heard by the United States Supreme Court.

All laws may also be classified as either criminal or civil. Criminal law deals with violations of laws promulgated by the state. The state is responsible for charging and prosecuting the case, and a party found to be guilty suffers the punishments stipulated by the state. Such punishments may include loss of liberty, fines, and other penalties. Civil law involves an accusation by one party against another. The trial is an attempt to assign responsibility for harm that has accrued to the wronged party and to provide an appropriate remedy for that harm. Malpractice cases are generally heard in civil court proceedings, and penalties may include both compensatory damages (usually a sum of money that must be paid to compensate the individual for his or her losses) and punitive damages (money paid in order to punish the perpetrator of the harm).

Criminal and civil cases carry a different "standard of proof." Standard of proof is the degree of surety that must exist to prove guilt. In criminal cases, the burden of proof is very high because of the severity of the potential penalties. Because U.S. society places a high value on personal liberty, the standard is set very high in cases where a guilty verdict might result in loss of liberty. Consequently, for criminal cases, the state must prove that a defendant is guilty beyond a reasonable doubt. Note that the burden of proof, or the party responsible for proving guilt, is the state. While the accused party usually presents evidence in his or her defense, this is not necessary. Should the state fail to prove guilt beyond reasonable doubt, the defendant could, hypothetically, be found not guilty without presenting any evidence whatsoever. In civil cases, including malpractice, the standard of proof is much lower, referred to as "a preponderance of the evidence," meaning that there is more evidence that a party is guilty than not guilty. In civil cases, the burden of proof is on the plaintiff, the party that makes the accusation.

CODES OF PROFESSIONAL ETHICS

Codes of professional ethics are very relevant to a discussion of legal liability for several reasons. They are generally developed by private or professional organizations and reflect the collective opinion of the professionals that the code is intended to govern. They do not carry the weight of law per se, but may be critical in establishing the standard against which a professional who has been charged with negligence or malpractice is judged. For rehabilitation counselors, the Professional Code of Ethics for Rehabilitation Counselors (CRCC, 2001) stipulates the rules for ethical behavior for rehabilitation counselors. Other codes of ethics and standards of practice may also help provide greater specificity about some aspect of practice. For example, a rehabilitation counselor engaged in group work might find additional guidance from the Ethical Guidelines for Group Counselors promulgated by the Association for Specialists in Group Work (1989). Following is a list of sample codes and standards with relevance to rehabilitation counseling, other than the CRCC Professional Code and those of related professions that have been developed by various associations and groups (see *www.kspope.com/ethicscodes.html*).

American Academy of Forensic Psychology: Specialty Guidelines

American Academy of Psychiatry and Law: Ethical Guidelines for the Practice of Forensic Psychiatry

American Association for Marriage and Family Therapy: Code of Ethics

American Association of Christian Counselors: Code of Ethics

American Association of Pastoral Counselors: Code of Ethics

American Association of Sex Educators, Counselors and Therapists: Code of Ethics

American Board of Examiners in Clinical Social Work: Code of Ethics

American College Personnel Association: Statement of Ethical Principles and Standards

American Counseling Association: Code of Ethics and Standards of Practice

American Group Therapy Association: Guidelines for Ethics

American Medical Association: Principles of Medical Ethics

American Psychiatric Association: The Principles of Medical Ethics with Annotations Especially Applicable to Psychiatry

American Psychoanalytic Association: Principles and Standards of Ethics for Psychoanalysts

American Psychological Association: Ethical Principles of Psychologists and Code of Conduct

American Society of Clinical Hypnosis: Code of Ethics

Association for Addiction Professionals: Ethical Standards

Association for Assessment in Counseling: Multicultural Assessment Standards

Association for the Treatment of Sexual Abusers: Professional Code of Ethics

Association of Marital and Family Therapy: Code of Ethics for Marriage and Family Therapists Code of Ethics

California Association of Marriage and Family Therapists: Ethical Standards

Christian Association for Psychological Studies: Ethical Guidelines

Clinical Social Work Federation: Code of Ethics

Feminist Therapy Institute: Code of Ethics

International Society of Mental Health Online: Suggested Principles for the Online Provision of Mental Health Services

Joint Committee on Testing Practices: Code of Fair Testing Practices in Education

Mental Health Patient's Bill of Rights

National Academies of Practice

National Association of Alcoholism and Drug Abuse Counselors: Ethical Standards

National Association of School Counselors: Professional Conduct Manual—Principles for Professional Ethics

National Association of School Psychologists: Principles for Professional Ethics

National Association of Social Workers: Code of Ethics

National Board for Certified Counselors: Code of Ethics

National Career Development Association: Ethical Standards

National Council for Hypnotherapy: Code of Ethics and Conduct

Spiritual Directors International: Guidelines for Ethical Conduct

When states develop regulations, they often look to the respective professions for guidance about appropriate and inappropriate actions, within the context of the activities and responsibilities in the practice of the profession. Consequently, the boards that develop regulations often use and adapt much of a professions' codes of ethics. For licensed professional counselors, the American Counseling Association's Code of Ethics (1995) is most often a basis for licensing regulations.

Ideally, laws at all levels and all relevant codes of ethics would be perfectly in tune with one another, but this is not always the case. Cottone and Tarvydas (2003) stress that counselors may encounter situations where they must exercise their personal and professional judgment because legal and professional requirements are inconsistent. Counselors may at times have to choose between actions that are legal but not ethical (e.g., complying with a court order to produce information which a counselor believes will be harmful to a client), or are ethical but not legal (e.g., not complying with a mandatory spousal abuse reporting law out of concern for a client's safety). Such dilemmas are justifiably distressing to counselors and require careful deliberation and action. Recommended actions include the following (Behnke et al., 2000; Cottone & Tarvydas, 2003; Remley, 1996; Rivas-Vazquez, Blais, Rey, & Rivas-Vazquez, 2001):

1. Identify the laws, rules, or other forces affecting the counselor's possible actions
2. Seek legal advice regarding any legal requirements
3. Seek consultation from supervisors, regulators, professional boards, colleagues, and/or experts, as appropriate
4. Use appropriate models of ethical decision making to assist in approaching the dilemma in a structured, "clear-headed" manner
5. Document the process used to reach the decision

MALPRACTICE AND NEGLIGENCE

Black (1990) defines malpractice as

> failure of one rendering professional services to exercise that degree of skill and learning commonly applied under all the circumstances in the community by the average prudent reputable member of the profession with the result of injury, loss or damage to the recipient of those services or to those entitled to rely upon them. It is any professional misconduct, unreasonable lack of skill or fidelity in professional or fiduciary duties, evil practice, or illegal or immoral conduct. (p. 959)

Malpractice is a charge by one party toward another that an individual was harmed because of some action or inaction, in violation of the standards of practice established by the practitioners in the same profession. In order to prove malpractice, a preponderance of the evidence presented by the plaintiff must demonstrate that four conditions existed (Corey et al., 2003):

> *Duty.* For malpractice to occur, it is necessary to demonstrate that a professional relationship was established and that the therapist owed a duty of care to the client.
> *Breach of duty.* After the plaintiff proves that a professional relationship did exist, he or she must show that the duty was breached, or that the practitioner failed to provide the appropriate standard of care. The breach of duty may involve either actions taken by the therapist or the failure to take certain precautions.
> *Injury.* Plaintiffs must prove that they were harmed in some way, either physically or psychologically, and that actual injuries were sustained. Examples

of such injuries include wrongful death (suicide), loss (divorce), and pain and suffering.

   Causation. Plaintiffs must demonstrate that a professional's breach of duty was the direct cause of the injury that they suffered. The test in this case lies in proving that the harm would not have occurred if it were not for the practitioner's actions or failure to act. (p. 130)

In establishing the existence of a duty, two issues must be considered. What is the duty, and to whom is the duty owed? *Tarasoff* v. *Regents of University of California* (1976), one of the most famous cases in mental health law, directly impacted these two questions and will be addressed in some detail later in the chapter. Proving that breach of duty (sometimes referred to as dereliction of duty) occurred requires the plaintiff to show that the counselor's care was not reasonable. Reasonable care is generally defined as care that is within the standard of practice of an average member of the profession practicing within the specialty. Therefore, plaintiffs' attorneys often rely on professional codes and standards, literature from the field, and expert testimony to establish what the standard should have been for reasonable care and to establish that the defendant's care was not reasonable. It is important to remember that all four criteria must be met to establish malpractice. Therefore, even if the duty was clearly established and the defendant clearly breached that duty, malpractice cannot be established unless the breach of duty resulted in some type of injury to the plaintiff and the injury resulted directly from the breach of duty.

MALPRACTICE "MINEFIELDS"

Confidentiality and Privilege

Confidentiality is generally considered essential to the counselor-client relationship, since clients need assurance that sensitive and potentially embarrassing issues will remain with the counselor, with whom a trusting relationship has been developed (Woody, 2001). As Shaw and Tarvydas (2001) noted, unless explicitly informed otherwise, most clients assume that everything shared with counselors will remain strictly confidential. Consequently, it is very important that counselors be aware of limitations on confidentiality that are externally imposed by law or policy.

   Most clients will readily understand that some information must be shared with others in order to facilitate treatment. For example, counselors referring clients to physicians for evaluation will want to include any related medical information that they may already have procured, and most clients will readily agree to release the counselor to share such information. Permission should always be obtained in writing and should specify what information is to be released, to whom, and for what purpose. Additionally, the document should specify a time frame for which the permission is granted and provide a place for the client's signature. Many counselors and counseling agencies use preprinted "release of information" forms with blank spaces in which the above information can be specified.

There are a number of other situations in which information is commonly shared with others. In order to prevent misunderstandings and perceived violations of client trust, it is essential that the counselor review any possible situations where information or records might be shared with others and to secure the client's informed consent. Fairly routine situations where this commonly occurs include supervision, case audits by regulatory bodies, sharing of information among treatment team members, forwarding of reports to third-party payers, such as insurance companies or other funding agencies, and provision of information to parents or guardians when the client is a minor or has a legally appointed guardian (Campbell, 1994; Cobia & Boes, 2000; Cooper, 2000; Guest & Dooley, 1999; Harrison & Hunt, 1999; Plante, 1999; Sullivan, 2002; Tarvydas, 1995). Other possible departures from confidentiality are somewhat less routine, and it is essential that they be discussed and that clients be fully informed about the circumstances in which the counselor might need to violate client confidentiality so that clients can make fully informed decisions about what to share with the counselor. These less common and more perilous exceptions to confidentiality are discussed below.

Mandatory Reporting Laws

Generally speaking, mandatory reporting laws are designed to protect those members of society that are considered to be particularly vulnerable and unable to protect themselves. In these cases, counselors are not allowed the option of independent judgment. If counselors fail to report, they are in violation of state law. The types of information that must be reported vary from state to state, but most states, at a minimum, have mandatory laws that require the reporting of child abuse, elder abuse, and abuse of individuals with disabilities.

The conditions that must exist before reporting becomes mandatory also vary from state to state. For example, in some states a mere suspicion may be enough to trigger a mandatory report, while in others more definitive evidence may be needed. Definitions of abuse, negligence, and abandonment may also vary from state to state, as well as definitions of "child" or other protected classes of people (Renninger, 2002; Small, 2002). Often, counselors who must make mandatory reports are afforded protections against charges of malpractice due to violations of confidentiality; however, such protections may not prevent clients from feeling betrayed when the counselor has failed to warn them that there is some information that they are legally bound to report. Failure to fully inform clients about limitations of confidentiality deprives clients of the right to choose what they may or may not wish to disclose, with full knowledge of the consequences.

Duty to Protect

In all jurisdictions, the law allows counselors to violate confidentiality in situations where they believe that clients pose a serious risk to themselves or to others. In such situations, the state's obligation to protect others is seen as outweighing the importance of confidentiality. Several studies have established that most counselors will, over the course of their careers, confront the need to violate confidentiality to protect a client from harming him or herself (e.g., suicide) or another (e.g., homicide; Weinstein, Levine, Kogan, Harkavy-Friedman, & Miller, 2000). Counselors in such situations may need to take actions that the client will view as harmful, based upon uncertain evidence (Jobes & Berman, 1993). The difficulties in predicting dangerousness are well documented (Bednar, Bednar, Lambert, & Waite, 1991; Otto, 1992), and counselors often find that "threats" of suicide or of intentions to harm are never, in fact, carried out (Corey et al., 2003). When coupled with the devastating finality of the taking of a life, it is not surprising that suicide emerges as a common issue in many malpractice cases (Baerger, 2001; Szasz, 1986).

Although the law recognizes the difficulties in predicting violent behavior, it also holds counselors accountable for doing so in accordance with the standards established within their professions. Consequently, when a malpractice issue arises in connection with a duty to protect, the key legal issue in establishing negligence often becomes whether or not the counselor acted reasonably and prudently in a manner that rises to the standards established within the mental health professions. Courts will examine such evidence as whether the counselor utilized an accepted procedure for assessing the threat, consulted with others, and took reasonable steps to ensure safety (Fujimura, Weiss, & Cochran, 1985; King, 1999; Lewis, 2002; Picchioni & Bernstein, 1990; Pope, 1985; Rivas-Vazquez et al., 2001; Simon, 1999; VandeCreek & Knapp, 2000; Welfel, 1998). In other words, given the difficulty in predicting dangerousness with certainty, the courts are more likely to examine the process used by the counselor to ensure that he or she did at least as well as most counselors would have done in the same situation.

One of the limitations on confidentiality that is, perhaps, the most intimidating and anxiety-provoking is the counselor's responsibility to take steps to prevent harm from coming to the client or to another person or persons when the client has disclosed an intention to commit such an act. The counselor's duty in such a situation was highlighted and expanded following the outcome of a controversial malpractice case, *Tarasoff* v. *Regents of the University of California* (1976). In the Tarasoff case, Dr. Lawrence Moore, a psychologist at the University of California-Berkeley Student Health Center, was treating a graduate student named Prosenjit Poddar who had become obsessed with an undergraduate student, Tatianna Tarasoff. The two students had met each other at a social function for international students and had become friendly. The more serious Poddar became about the relationship, the more distant Tatianna became. Poddar had taped their calls and become consumed with furthering the relationship. Frustrated in his efforts, Poddar reported to Dr. Moore that he intended to kill a girl that he identified only as "Tatianna." Dr. Moore informed Poddar that he would have to report the incident if he persisted in his intention to harm the girl, at which point Poddar discontinued therapy. After consulting with others, Moore wrote a letter to the police department warning them of Poddar's intentions and recommending that Poddar be committed to a psychiatric hospital for observation. The police detained Poddar, but after questioning, they released him. A very short time thereafter, Poddar murdered Tarasoff.

Tarasoff's parents subsequently filed suit against several parties, including Dr. Moore and several colleagues with whom he had consulted, stating that they should have warned Tarasoff that her life was in danger. The defendants in the case argued that Tatianna was not a client and, therefore, the therapists owed her no duty. Consequently, they could not have breached that duty. Additionally, they argued that counselor-client confidentiality prevented the therapist from warning Tarasoff. The court decided otherwise, based on several points. First, they determined that a duty may exist when there is a "special relationship" between the parties. The court further decided that, when such a "special relationship" exists, the duty may be extended to a third party where that party is the foreseeable victim of harm perpetrated by the individual with whom the special relationship exists. The court then further defined that duty as "the duty to exercise reasonable care to protect the foreseeable victim of that danger" (p. 345).

Behnke et al. (2000) point out that the Tarasoff decision is frequently misinterpreted as a "duty to warn," when in fact it is a "duty to protect." The court also addressed the issue of the therapist's responsibility to explicitly identify the potential victim, noting that, while a therapist may not be required to "interrogate his patient to discover the victim's identity . . . there may be cases in which a moment's reflection will reveal the victim's identity" (p. 345). As Behnke et al. observe, this portion of the decision has resulted in many different interpretations regarding the degree to which the therapist must be certain of the identity of the potential victim before a duty to protect exists. Consequently, there is wide variation in state laws regarding this point. Regarding the defense that confidentiality prohibited the therapist from warning Tarasoff, the court clearly stipulated that the privilege of confidentiality is secondary to the therapist's responsibility to prevent foreseeable danger to others.

The negligence case against Dr. Moore was never decided, since the case was settled out of court (i.e., Ms. Tarasoff's family agreed to dismiss the lawsuit in exchange for a financial payment by the defendant). Regardless of the outcome of the civil case, however, the California Supreme Court had adopted the principles regarding duty and the limitations on confidentiality as a rule of law. The case reverberated throughout the mental health community, and, one by one, the states adopted "duty" laws, each of which differed somewhat in such issues as the definition of "forseeability," the stipulation of what actions are required for a therapist to be carrying out his or her "duty" appropriately, and the specificity of the required "threat."

Privileged Communication

The right of clients to have their communications with their therapists kept confidential is often referred to as privileged communication or testimonial privilege. In many states, this right is extended to client-counselor relationships, by statute, in recognition of the importance of confidentiality to the trust and freedom to disclose that must occur in therapeutic relationships. As discussed above, however, this privilege is not absolute. As mandatory reporting laws and the Tarasoff decision emphasize, the right to confidentiality must be balanced against the right to protect society, particularly individuals who are most vulnerable.

In such cases, the counselor may not be able to protect confidentiality, ethically or legally, and several factors must be considered. First, it is important to remember that the right to privileged communication is owned by the client, not the counselor. Clients may or may not choose to invoke this right. Should a client choose to waive the right to confidentiality, the counselor may not choose to maintain it. Second, because there are some situations where confidentiality cannot be maintained, counselors are obligated to fully inform clients of potential situations in which they may need to break confidentiality. As many researchers have noted, many counselors appear to be somewhat derelict in this responsibility because of concerns about inhibiting client disclosure or other concerns (Berlin, Malin, & Dean, 1991; Shaw & Tarvydas, 2001; Steinberg, Levine, & Doueck, 1997; Weinstein et al., 2000; Zellman, 1990).

Sexual Exploitation

When a counselor enters into a relationship with a client, it is assumed that the counselor's focus should be, at all times, the best interests of the client. This value is prominently featured in the counseling codes of ethics and professional literature (Hannold & Young, 2001) and is, in many ways, one of the most unique features of the counseling relationship, since the relationship is purposely one-sided. The counselor's needs must be purposely subverted to allow the relationship to focus on client needs. When the relationship between the counselor and client takes on other dimensions (e.g., friend, business partner, or romantic interest), the counselor's needs take on an increased importance in the relationship, often to the client's detriment.

Nowhere is this seen more graphically than when counselors develop sexual relationships with clients, which are almost universally viewed as detrimental to the client and to the counseling relationship (Bouthoutsos, Holroyd, Lerman, Forer, & Greenberg, 1983; Cottone & Tarvydas, 2003; Farnill, 2000; Pope, 1988; Somer, 1999; Somer & Saadon, 1999). Furthermore, they are among the most prevalent and most costly types of malpractice lawsuits brought against mental health professionals (ASPPB, 2001; Reaves, 1999). Such relationships are exploitive, almost by definition. In order to avoid the ethical and legal devastation of such relationships to both counselor and client, counselors must be extrasensitive to signs of sexual attraction, both in themselves and in their clients, and to carefully managing their own countertransference. Feelings of attraction toward a client are certainly natural and common (Bernsen, Tabachnick, & Pope, 1994; Nickell, Hecker, Ray, & Bercik, 1995; Pope, Tabachnick, & Keith-Spiegel, 1987; Stake & Oliver, 1991). They should, however, alert counselors to attend to their feelings about clients and to carefully self-monitor their own emotions and behavior. Some clients may be particularly vulnerable to therapist misconduct when they have a history of sexual or physical abuse, posttraumatic stress disorder, or promiscuous behavior (Pope, 1988).

Counselors are well advised to take precautionary measures, particularly with "high-risk" clients, both to set an atmosphere of therapeutic work rather than social or personal pleasure, and to establish a pattern of prudent behavior. Simple yet effective precautions might include not seeing clients after hours when they are likely to be alone, taping sessions (with client consent), and not meeting with clients outside of the usual and customary locations. Counselors should address transference issues as they arise, establishing clear boundaries for the relationship. The use of touch between counselor and client may be therapeutic but also may be misunderstood or misinterpreted, both by clients and by courts, should legal action arise. Counselors who make use of touch in their counseling interactions should do so cautiously and carefully. When uncertain about the nature of a counselor's feelings toward a client, a consultation is strongly advised.

It is also important to note that in some states, and in many codes of ethics, there is a presumption that the counseling relationship does not automatically end when the counselor and client have discontinued treatment or service. Many statutes and codes of ethics require mental health professionals to refrain from any sexual involvement with former clients for a specified period of time, which varies among statues and codes. Because client vulnerability to exploitation is not likely to automatically disappear upon termination, careful consideration prior to initiating such a relationship is recommended, even where legally permissible (Herlihy & Corey, 1997).

Other Liability Issues

Beyond violations of confidentiality and sexual exploitation, there are many other risk management issues for counselors. Other issues that frequently give rise to charges of illegal and unethical behavior include inappropriate financial exploitation, failure to report the unethical behavior of others, legal risks associated with supervision and administration, and failure to provide appropriate care, among others (APA, 2001; Bernstein & Hartsell, 2000; Bednar et al., 1991; Campbell, 1994; Smith, 1996; Otto & Schmidt, 1991; Vallario & Emener, 1991; Woody, 2000). While this chapter cannot address all of the issues relevant to each of these topics in detail, there are some general precautions that will help to prevent and to defend against charges of malpractice that apply to all of these areas of potential liability.

PROTECTIONS AGAINST MALPRACTICE

There is substantial literature within the mental health disciplines to suggest methods and practices that can prevent and defend against charges of malpractice. The following suggestions are compiled from recommendations from multiple sources (APA, 2001; Behnke et al., 2000; Bernstein & Hartsell, 2000; Bednar et al., 1991; Campbell, 1994; Doverspike, 1999; Montgomery, 1999; Otto & Schmidt, 1991; Smith, 1996; Vallario & Emener, 1991; Woody, 2000).

Abide by the Law of No Surprises

Behnke et al. (2000) use this term to describe the importance of thoroughly informing a client *in advance* about all of the potential information necessary for fully informed consent, as well as any other information that the client may need to thoroughly understand the counseling experience. Rehabilitation professionals should engage in a thorough process of written and verbal professional disclosure. Shaw and Tarvydas (2001) assert that the disclosure should consist of "all of the pertinent facts and considerations relevant to decisions that need to be made during the provision of services" (p. 40). These include, at a minimum:

1. Information about the procedures and duration of counseling
2. Limitations on confidentiality
3. Client's right to make complaints and/or discontinue services
4. Logistics of counseling (making and canceling appointments, etc.)
5. What to do in an emergency
6. Policies and procedures regarding fees (pp. 40–41)

Other items may be included in disclosure and it is important to tailor the professional disclosure process to the setting and clients for which it is intended.

Know Your Legal and Ethical Responsibilities

Rehabilitation counselors should become thoroughly familiar with the codes of ethics that apply to their profession and practice. Additionally, they must become thoroughly familiar with legally mandated responsibilities and structure their policies, procedures, and practices in such a manner as to comply with legal requirements. When in doubt, or at any point when a counselor may feel unsure or uncomfortable about potential liability, he or she should not hesitate to consult a lawyer experienced in mental health law for clarification of legal obligations. Counselors concerned with charges of malpractice or unethical behavior should remember that attorneys hired to represent the agencies that employ them may or may not have their personal best interests at heart. At times, the counselor's best interests may conflict with those of the employing organization. Additionally, the CRCC Ethics Committee will address questions of a general nature, submitted in writing, and will issue advisory opinions about any aspect of ethical behavior on the part of rehabilitation counselors.

Consult

Consultations are invaluable in helping counselors sort through the complexities of ethical and legal quagmires that can occur in counseling. Often, counselors are too intimately involved to see a situation with clarity, and they may lack information essential to developing the best response to ethical and legal challenges. Consultation allows counselors to "reality-test" and to obtain perspectives different from their own. Consultations also serve as a critical element in managing the risks associated with ethical decisions. Since the legal standard is based on the degree to which the profession views an action or care as "reasonable," it is critical for counselors to consult with members of that profession about their beliefs regarding the "reasonableness" of any action. Consultations demonstrate that counselors understood the seriousness of a given situation, afforded the matter due care and consideration, and reached out to the professional community to help make the best decision possible. Consultation is also a valuable hedge against charges of exploitation, since few counselors who are purposely exploiting their clients would voluntarily bring this to the attention of others within their profession. Supervision, which consists of obtaining guidance from a boss or supervisor, has a similar effect, with the added element of shared liability, since the supervisor is accountable for the work that he or she supervises.

Document

As mentioned earlier, when defending against charges of malpractice, the process is often considered just as important as the actions taken. Documentation can demonstrate that a careful process of deliberation was followed (Barnett, 1999). Counselors should document the facts surrounding the issue in question, the actions taken to determine the best course of action, including supervision, consultation, and fact-finding, and the results and follow-up activities associated with the incident. Notes should be clear, detailed yet succinct, and dated and signed. The notes should be objective, consisting of direct quotes and statements of fact to the greatest possible extent. Opinions, diagnoses, and hypotheses should be avoided. Cross-outs, erasures, and back-dating are viewed as suspect and should always be avoided (Barnett, 1999; Mitchell, 2001). The dangers of insufficient or poor documentation are summed up in the phrase "If it isn't documented, it didn't happen." Often, lawsuits occur months or even years after an incident occurred. The court is much more likely to put greater stock in a case note made at the time of the incident than in a counselor's vague recollections years later, after an accusation has been levied. Remley and Herlihy (2001) offer an excellent set of guidelines for self-protective documentation that emphasizes the appropriate timing, content, and disposition of case notes.

Insure Against Malpractice

Regardless of how careful or knowledgeable counselors may be, any counselor can have legal or ethical complaints filed against her or him at any time. Sometimes malpractice charges result from misinformation or misunderstanding and are relatively quickly resolved, but they may also result in a lengthy and expensive legal process. Even when the counselor has acted appropriately in every way, a suit can still be filed and the counselor may have to expend considerable time and money, not to mention anxiety, to address the charges. Counselors should carefully consider whether they have the resources to help them through this process. Malpractice insurance is considered essential, by most practicing counselors, to ensure adequate self-protection. The amount and cost of malpractice insurance will vary, depending on the type of practice, the volume of clients seen, and the extent to which a counselor is already covered by some type of corporate liability insurance. Most professional associations provide linkages and discounts to insurers who can issue malpractice insurance to practitioners.

CONCLUSION

As rehabilitation counselors have expanded their visibility, professional presence, and scope of practice, their liability risk has also increased.

Counselors should continually educate themselves regarding legal and ethical guidelines and responsibilities. Ethical and legal practice benefits everyone involved in the counseling relationship. Consequently, rehabilitation counselors should continually seek to enhance their understanding of this important aspect of practice.

REFERENCES

American Counseling Association. (1995). *Code of ethics and standards of practice.* Alexandria, VA: Author.

American Psychological Association. (2002). Report of the Ethics Committee. *American Psychologist, 57,* 646–653.

Association for Specialists in Group Work. (1989). *Ethical guidelines for group counselors.* Alexandria, VA: Author.

Association of State and Provincial Psychology Boards (ASPPB). (2001). *Ethics, law and avoiding liability in the practice of psychology.* Montgomery, AL: Author.

Backlar, P., & Cutler, D. L. (Eds.). (2002). Ethics in community mental health care: Commonplace concerns. In L. VandeCreek & T. L. Jackson (Eds.), *Innovations in clinical practice: A source book* (Vol. 17, pp. 237–254). New York: Kluwer/Plenum.

Baerger, D. R. (2001). Risk management with the suicidal patient: Lessons from case law. *Professional Psychology: Research and Practice, 32,* 359–366.

Barnett, J. E. (1999). Recordkeeping: Clinical, ethical, and risk management issues. In L. VandeCreek & T. L. Jackson (Eds.), *Innovations in clinical practice: A sourcebook* (Vol. 17, pp. 237–254). Sarasota, FL; Professional Resources Press.

Bednar, R. L., Bednar, S. C., Lambert, M. J., & Waite, D. R. (1991). *Psychotherapy with high-risk clients: Legal and professional standards.* Pacific Grove, CA: Brooks/Cole.

Behnke, S. H., Winick, B. J., & Perez, A. M. (2000). *The essentials of Florida mental health law.* New York: W. W. Norton.

Berlin, F. S., Malin, M., & Dean, S. (1991). Effects of statutes requiring psychiatrists to report suspected sexual abuse of children. *American Journal of Psychiatry, 148,* 449–453.

Bernsen, A., Tabachnick, B. G., & Pope, K. S. (1994). National survey of social workers' sexual attraction to their clients: Results, implications and comparison to psychologists. *Ethics and Behavior, 4,* 369–388.

Bernstein, B. E., & Hartsell, T. L., Jr. (2000). *The portable ethicist for mental health professionals: An A-Z guide to responsible practice.* New York: Wiley.

Black, H. C. (1990). *Black's law dictionary* (6th ed.). St Paul, MN: West Publishing.

Bouhoutsos, J., Holroyd, J., Lerman, H., Forer, B., & Greenberg, M. (1983). Sexual intimacy between psychologists and patients. *Professional Psychology, 14,* 185–196.

Campbell, T. W. (1994). Psychotherapy and malpractice exposure. *American Journal of Forensic Psychology, 12,* 4–41.

Cobia, D. C., & Boes, S. R. (2000). Professional disclosure statements and formal plans for supervision: Two strategies for minimizing the risk of ethical conflicts in post-master's supervision. *Journal of Counseling and Development, 78,* 293–296.

Commission on Rehabilitation Counselor Certification (CRCC). (2001). Code of Professional Ethics for Rehabilitation Counselors. *Journal of Applied Rehabilitation Counseling, 32,* 38–61.

Cooper, C. C. (2000). Ethical issues with managed care: Challenges facing counseling psychology. *Counseling Psychologist, 28,* 179–236.

Corey, G., Corey, M. S., & Callanan, P. (2003). *Issues and ethics in the helping professions* (6th ed.). Pacific Grove, CA: Brooks/Cole.

Cottone, R. R., & Tarvydas, V. M. (2003). *Ethical and professional issues in counseling* (2nd ed.). Upper Saddle River, NJ: Merrill Prentice Hall.

Crawford, R. L. (1994). *Avoiding counselor malpractice.* Alexandria, VA: American Counseling Association.

Cullity, L. P., Jackson, J. D., & Shaw, L. R. (1990). Community skills training. In B. T. McMahon & L. R. Shaw (Eds.), *Work worth doing: Advances in brain injury rehabilitation.* Orlando, FL: PMD Press.

Doverspike, W. F. (1999). Ethical risk management: Protecting your practice. In L. VandeCreek & T. L. Jackson (Eds.), *Innovations in clinical practice: A source book* (Vol. 17, pp. 269–278). Sarasota, FL: Professional Resource Press.

Farnill, D. (2000). Sexual relationships with former patients: Prevalence, harm, and professional issues. *Australian Journal of Clinical and Experimental Hypnosis, 28,* 42–60.

Fujimura, L. E., Weiss, D. M., & Cochran, J. R. (1985). Suicide: Dynamics and implications for counseling. *Journal of Counseling and Development, 63,* 612–615.

Guest, G. L., Fr., & Dooley, K. (1999). Supervisor malpractice: Liability to the supervisee in clinical supervision. *Counselor Education and Supervision, 38,* 269–279.

Hannold, E., & Young, M. E. (2001). Consumer perspectives on the revised Code of Professional Ethics for Rehabilitation Counselors. *Journal of Applied Rehabilitation Counseling, 32,* 5–9.

Harrison, L., & Hunt, B. (1999). Adolescent involvement in the medical decision making process. *Journal of Applied Rehabilitation Counseling, 30,* 3–9.

Herlihy, B., & Corey, G. (1997). Codes of ethics as catalysts for improving practice. In *Ethics in therapy. The Heatheleigh guides series* (Vol. 10, pp. 37–56). New York: Hatherleigh.

Jobes, D. A., & Berman, A. L. (1993). Suicide and malpractice liability: Assessing and revising policies, procedures, and practice in outpatient settings. *Professional Psychology: Research and Practice, 24,* 91–99.

King, A. (1999). Toward a standard of care for treating suicidal outpatients: A survey of social workers' beliefs about appropriate treatment behaviors. *Suicide and Life-Threatening Behavior, 29,* 347–352.

Lewis, B. L. (2002). Second thoughts about documenting the psychological consultation. *Professional Psychology: Research and Practice, 33,* 224–225.

Mitchell, R. (2001). *Documentation in counseling records* (2nd ed.). Alexandria, VA: American Counseling Association.

Montgomery, L. M. (1999). Complaints, malpractice, and risk management: Professional issues and personal experiences. *Professional Psychology: Research and Practice, 30,* 402–410.

Nickell, N. J., Hecker, L. L., Ray, R. E., & Bercik, J. (1995). Marriage and family therapists' sexual attraction to clients: An exploratory study. *American Journal of Family Therapy, 23,* 315–327.

Otto, R. (1992). The prediction of dangerous behavior: A review and analysis of "second generation" research. *Forensic Reports, 5,* 103–133.

Otto, R. K., Ogloff, J. R., & Small, M. A. (1991). Confidentiality and informed consent in psychotherapy: Clinicians' knowledge and practices in Florida and Nebraska. *Forensic Reports, 4,* 379–389.

Otto, R. K., & Schmidt, W. C. (1991). Malpractice in verbal psychotherapy: Problems and potential solutions. *Forensic Reports, 4,* 309–336.

Picchioni, T., & Bernstein, B. (1990). Risk management for mental health counselors. *Texas Association for Counseling and Development Journal, 18,* 3–19.

Plante, T. G. (1999). Ten strategies for psychology trainees and practicing psychologists interested in avoiding ethical and legal perils. *Psychotherapy: Theory, Research, Practice, and Training, 36,* 398–403.

Pope, K. S. (1985). The suicidal client: Guidelines for assessment and treatment. *California State Psychologist, 20,* 3–7.

Pope, K. S. (1988). How clients are harmed by sexual contact with mental health professionals: The syndrome and its prevalence. *Journal of Counseling and Development, 67,* 222–226.

Pope, K. S., Tabachnick, B. G., & Keith-Spiegel, P. S. (1987). Ethics of practice: The beliefs and behaviors of psychologists as therapists. *American Psychologist, 42,* 993–1006.

Reaves, R. P. (1999). *Avoiding liability in mental health practice.* Montgomery, AL: Association of State and Provincial Psychology Boards.

Remley, T. P., Jr. (1996). Counseling records: Legal and ethical issues. In B. Herlihy & L. Golden (Eds.), *ACA ethical standards casebook* (4th ed., pp. 162–169). Alexandria, VA: American Counseling Association.

Remley, T. P., Jr., & Herlihy, B. (2001). *Ethical, legal, and professional issues in counseling.* Upper Saddle River, NJ: Prentice Hall.

Renninger, S. M. (2002). Psychologists' knowledge, opinions, and decision-making processes regarding child abuse and neglect reporting laws. *Professional Psychology: Research and Practice, 33,* 19–23.

Rivas-Vazquez, R., Blais, M. A., Gustavo, J., & Rivas-Vazquez, A. A. (2001). A brief reminder about documenting the psychological consultation. *Professional Psychology: Research and Practice, 32,* 194–199.

Shaw, L. R., & Jackson, J. D. (1994). The dilemma of empowerment in brain injury rehabilitation. In B. T. McMahon & R. W. Evans (Eds.), *The shortest distance: The pursuit of independence for persons with acquired brain injury.* Orlando, FL: PMD Press.

Shaw, L. R., & Tarvydas, V. M. (2001). The use of professional disclosure in rehabilitation counseling. *Rehabilitation Counseling Bulletin, 45,* 40–47.

Simon, R. I. (1999). The suicide prevention contract: Clinical, legal, and risk management. *Journal of the American Academy of Psychiatry and the Law, 27,* 445–450.

Small, M. A. (2002). Liability issues in child abuse and neglect reporting statutes. *Professional Psychology: Research and Practice, 33,* 13–18.

Smith, S. R. (1996). Malpractice liability of mental health professionals and institutions. In B. D. Sales & D. W. Shuman (Eds.), *Law, mental health, and mental disorder* (pp. 76–98). Pacific Grove, CA: Brooks/Cole.

Somer, E. (1999). Therapist-client sex: Clients' retrospective reports. *Professional Psychology: Research and Practice, 30,* 504–509.

Somer, E., & Saadon, M. (1999). Therapist-client sex: Clients' retrospective reports. *Professional Psychology: Research and Practice, 30,* 504–509.

Stake, J. E., & Oliver, J. (1991). Sexual contact and touching between therapist and client: A survey of psychologists' attitudes and behavior. *Professional Psychology: Research and Practice, 22,* 297–307.

Steinberg, K. L., Levine, M., & Doueck, H. J. (1997). Effects of legally mandated child abuse reports on the therapeutic relationship: A survey of psychotherapists. *American Journal of Orthopsychiatry, 38,* 112–122.

Sullivan, J. R. (2002). Factors contributing to breaking confidentiality with adolescent clients: A survey of pediatric psychologists. *Professional Psychology: Research and Practice, 33,* 396–401.

Szasz, T. (1986). The case against suice prevention. *American Psychologist, 41,* 806–812.

Tarasoff v. *Regents of University of California,* 529 P.2d 553, 118 Cal. Rptr. 129 (1974), *vacated,* 17 Cal. 3d 425, 551 P.2d 334, 131 Cal. Rptr. 14 (1976).

Tarvydas, V. M. (1995). Ethics and the practice of rehabilitation counselor supervision. *Rehabilitation Counseling Bulletin, 38,* 294–306.

Vallario, J. P., & Emener, W. G. (1991). Rehabilitation counseling and the law: Critical considerations of confidentiality and privilege, malpractice, and forensics. *Journal of Applied Rehabilitation Counseling, 22,* 7–14.

VandeCreek, L., & Knapp, S. (2000). Real-life vignettes involving the duty to protect. *Journal of Psychotherapy in Independent Practice, 1,* 83–88.

Weinstein, B., Levine, M., Kogan, N., Harkavy-Friedman, J., & Miller, J. M. (2000). Mental health professionals' experiences reporting suspected child abuse and maltreatment. *Child Abuse and Neglect, 24,* 1317–1328.

Welfel, E. R. (1998). *Ethics in counseling and psychotherapy: Standards, research, and emerging issues.* Pacific Grove, CA: Brooks/Cole.

Woody, R. H. (1988). *Fifty ways to avoid malpractice: A guidebook for mental health professionals.* Sarasota, FL: Professional Resource Exchange.

Woody, R. H. (2000). Professional ethics, regulatory licensing, and malpractice complaints. In F. W. Kaslow (Ed.), *Handbook of couple and family forensics: A sourcebook for mental health and legal professionals.* New York: Wiley.

Woody, R. H. (2001). *Psychological information: Protecting the right to privacy: A guidebook for mental health practitioners and their clients.* Madison, CT: Psychosocial Press.

Zellman, G. L. (1990). Child abuse reporting and failure to report among mandated reporters: Prevalence, incidence and reasons. *Journal of Interpersonal Violence, 5,* 3–22.

Chapter 23

Counseling and Rehabilitation Outcomes

Brian Bolton

T he preceding chapters have described a variety of counseling theories, techniques, and procedures that may be valuable in the provision of rehabilitation services to people with disabilities. This concluding chapter is concerned with the measurement of benefits that clients receive as a result of the counseling and rehabilitation services that are provided to them. The first section of the chapter reviews evidence of benefits to clients that derive from the counseling context of rehabilitation service delivery. The second section describes twenty-two instruments that may be useful in measuring rehabilitation outcomes. The third section discusses practical applications of the instruments in assessing benefits to rehabilitation clients.

IS REHABILITATION COUNSELING BENEFICIAL?

The basic premise of this book is that the various counseling theories and strategies described are potentially valuable when applied in rehabilitation settings. However, as all rehabilitation professionals know, counseling with people with disabilities almost always occurs in conjunction with the planning and implementation of a comprehensive program of needed services. These services typically include several of the following: diagnostic evaluation, medical restoration, personal adjustment training, independent living training, job readiness training, vocational training, and job placement. Personal counseling or psychotherapy may also be provided as another component of the service program, but the latter is *not* what counseling refers to in the rehabilitation service delivery process.

Counseling in rehabilitation generally refers to the therapeutic context in which the service planning and delivery process takes place. Rehabilitation counselors are trained to be coordinators of the service delivery sequence and also to function as therapeutic facilitators of client improvement. The underlying assumption is that counseling is the central, integrative activity that serves to unify the rehabilitation service delivery process. This assumption reflects a strong philosophical commitment that derives from decades of clinical practice in social work, counseling psychology, and other helping professions.

Because the counseling context cannot be isolated or separated from the service delivery sequence, it would be very difficult to assess the *unique* benefits that result from counseling, apart from or in addition to the impact of the various rehabilitation services that are provided to clients. Yet, it is legitimate for critics to ask if there is any empirical evidence to support the basic premise that counseling—meaning the therapeutically oriented interpersonal relationship that the rehabilitation counselor establishes with the client—contributes to the effectiveness of rehabilitation service delivery and thereby results in benefits to clients.

Although there is overwhelming evidence that people with disabilities do benefit from the provision of rehabilitation services (see Bolton, 1981; Bolton & Akridge, 1995), there are no randomized experimental studies of the value of the therapeutic context of rehabilitation service delivery reported in the literature. Moreover, as mentioned above, it would be virtually impossible to design and implement a randomized study that would address the issue. However, there does exist a variety of *indirect* evidence that suggests that the counseling context of rehabilitation service provision does result in benefits to clients. Three lines of research evidence are briefly summarized: (a) randomized studies of counseling and psychotherapy, (b) a national self-report survey of recipients of counseling and psychotherapy, and (c) nonexperimental studies of the rehabilitation counseling process.

Literally hundreds of experimental studies of the efficacy of counseling and psychotherapy have been reported in the research literature during the past 50 years. The initial meta-analysis of these investigations concluded that clients benefit considerably from the various types of psychotherapeutic and counseling interventions (Smith & Glass, 1977; Smith, Glass, & Miller, 1980). Specifically, the authors demonstrated an average effect size of two thirds of a standard deviation on the outcome measure of the treatment over the control group. Stated another way, the typical client receiving counseling was better off than 75% of the uncounseled control participants, or the typical counseled client moved from the 50th percentile to the 75th percentile with reference to the uncounseled participants.

In a subsequent analysis, the investigators grouped outcome measures into 10 categories (e.g., anxiety, self-esteem, social behavior, and vocational success) and calculated effect sizes for each type of outcome. The largest effects occurred for anxiety reduction and enhanced self-esteem (almost one standard deviation), while considerably less benefit was realized for adjustment indices (about one-half standard deviation) and for educational and vocational improvements (about one-third standard deviation). These results have implications for the evaluation of the benefits of counseling to rehabilitation clients, as discussed below.

The carefully controlled, randomized, experimental investigations of counseling and psychotherapy that were integrated into the meta-analytic conclusions above are called *efficacy* studies. Another type of investigation entails asking former counseling and psychotherapy clients to evaluate the benefits of their treatment—this is called an *effectiveness* study. Seligman (1995) summarized the results of a national mail survey of readers of the magazine *Consumer Reports*. Respondents who had received counseling and psychotherapeutic treatment from mental health professionals answered a series of questions about the benefits they believed they had received.

Two major conclusions from the *Consumer Reports* study were: (a) about 90% of the respondents who felt "very poor" or "fairly poor" at the beginning of treatment were feeling "very good," "good," or "so-so" when they responded to the survey, and (b) no particular treatment strategy was more effective than any other approach to counseling and psychotherapy for any specific type of client complaint or problem. However, the *Consumer Reports* study was widely criticized on methodological grounds (see VandenBos, 1996, for several relevant articles).

Four investigations have examined the relationships between counseling outcomes and rehabilitation counselors' therapeutic skills, counseling orientations, and academic training. Bozarth and Rubin (1975) summarized the results of a national study of rehabilitation counselors that found some relationships between counselors' interpersonal skills and interview behaviors and clients' psychological adjustment and vocational improvement. The relationships were relatively few in number and small in magnitude. Bolton's (1976) investigation of therapeutically oriented rehabilitation counselors produced some evidence suggesting that graduate training programs that emphasize counseling skills prepare more effective professionals. Emener (1980) examined the relationships between rehabilitation counselors' orientations, attitudes, and therapeutic styles, and client outcomes and found very few significant correlations. Finally, Szymanski and Parker (1989) determined that rehabilitation counselors with master's degrees in the discipline were more successful in placing clients with severe disabilities in competitive employment.

The four investigations of rehabilitation counselors' therapeutic skills provide modest support for the proposition that the counseling context of rehabilitation service delivery does result in incremental benefits to clients. To put this conclusion in perspective, it is important to stress that the research task is a difficult one. Because rehabilitation counseling entails the provision of extensive services to clients, all of which most certainly produce substantial benefits to clients, it is especially challenging to design research studies that can identify *additional* benefits associated with the therapeutic counseling skills that are used. There are also further complicating factors, such as the substantial variability among rehabilitation counselors' skill levels and their overall competence. Also, vocational rehabilitation programs emphasize behavioral outcomes, including successful employment and independent living, which are more difficult to achieve, as documented by the meta-analytic results cited above.

A remaining critical question is the following: Can the findings of the meta-analysis of traditional counseling and psychotherapy studies and the *Consumer Reports* survey be generalized to rehabilitation counseling? Or restated, is the counseling context of rehabilitation service provision different from other forms of counseling interventions? Put simply, is rehabilitation counseling different from other types of counseling? With respect to the nature of the therapeutic orientation and counseling strategies, the preceding chapters in this volume suggest that the answer to the latter question is "No"; that is, counseling is counseling. However, it is equally clear that counseling as practiced in the traditional dyadic psychotherapy relationship is a more intensive and focused interaction. In contrast, the counseling context of rehabilitation service delivery is a pervasive therapeutic activity that permeates all aspects of the multifaceted counselor-client relationship. So, while there are some differences between rehabilitation counseling and the traditional counseling or psychotherapeutic relationship represented in the meta-analytic results and the *Consumer Reports* survey findings, it is still reasonable to argue that the common activity—a therapeutic interpersonal relationship established by the counselor to benefit the client—is the same phenomenon in both situations.

Hence, it is appropriate to conclude that the findings of the meta-analysis and the *Consumer Reports* survey are generalizable to rehabilitation counseling. Finally, then, the answer to the question posed in the title of this section is "Yes"; that is, clients do benefit from the counseling context of rehabilitation service delivery. It is important to emphasize, however, that this conclusion refers to the *average* or *typical* rehabilitation client. So, while the typical client does benefit from rehabilitation counseling, there is substantial variability among clients in the benefits that they receive. In other words, some clients improve more than others and in different ways. Thus, it is essential to assess the *unique* benefits that each client derives from the provision of rehabilitation services. Accordingly, the purpose of this chapter is to provide an overview of the instrumentation that will facilitate this task.

MEASURING REHABILITATION OUTCOMES

The rehabilitation service delivery philosophy is focused on the achievement of behavioral or life outcomes; in other words, successful employment, independent living, and community participation are the ultimate goals of the rehabilitation service program. This does not mean that clients' self-perceived personal adjustment is unimportant or irrelevant in rehabilitation. However, self-reported personality change is typically not regarded as a primary objective. Yet, it is widely recognized that improved intrapsychic adjustment may very well facilitate the accomplishment of the desired behavioral outcomes listed above. Hence, it is accurate to say that all types of rehabilitation outcomes are important in the measurement of client benefits.

Dozens of assessment instruments have been developed by rehabilitation researchers during the past 30 years. These include various diagnostic tests and inventories, as well as instruments developed primarily to measure the benefits that clients realize as a result of receiving rehabilitation services. Obviously, many diagnostic instruments may be used to assess client improvements by administering tests or inventories on subsequent occasions and calculating the changes that have occurred. Both types of instruments—diagnostic tests and outcome measures—are included in this compilation. It should be emphasized that the main reason for assessing rehabilitation outcomes is to quantify benefits to clients as a basis for understanding the service delivery factors that contribute to or explain client success in rehabilitation. A subsidiary goal is simply to document that clients do benefit from the provision of rehabilitation services, including the counseling context. This topic is the focus of this chapter.

In this section, 22 instruments that may be used to measure rehabilitation outcomes are briefly described. The capsule overviews give the purpose of the instrument, the areas of client functioning that are assessed, information about administration and response format, and a summary of the reliability and validity evidence. The 22 instruments cover all relevant facets of rehabilitation outcome, including economic, vocational, personality, psychosocial, independent living, and employment components. The instruments are reviewed in alphabetical order. In the final section of the chapter, the uses and applications of the instruments with respect to the domains of functioning measured and the type of assessment process involved will be discussed.

Acceptance of Disability Scale

The Acceptance of Disability Scale (ADS: Linkowski, 1987) is a self-report questionnaire that measures the extent to which an individual with a physical disability has made a satisfactory adjustment to the disabling condition. The ADS is based on a theory of acceptance of loss that postulates the occurrence of four value changes in people with physical disabilities who have accepted their loss: enlargement of scope of values, subordination of physique, containment of disability effects, and transformation from comparative values to asset values. The ADS consists of 50 brief statements that refer to the respondent's values and attitudes with respect to physical or medical disability. The 50-item responses are summed into a total score on the assumption that all items measure a common underlying construct, acceptance of disability. The internal consistency reliability estimate for the ADS score is 0.93. A variety of evidence suggests that the ADS is a valid measure of the construct variously characterized as acceptance of loss, adjustment to disability, and acceptance of disability.

Becker Work Adjustment Profile

The Becker Work Adjustment Profile (BWAP; Becker, 1989) is an observer rating instrument designed for use with clients in vocational adjustment programs. The conceptual domain measured by the BWAP includes work skills, habits, attitudes, and personal traits that constitute "vocational competency." The BWAP consists of 63 items in four subscales: work habits/attitudes, interpersonal relations, cognitive skills, and work performance skills. A total score, called broad work adjustment, is also calculated. The primary purpose of the BWAP is to identify deficits in client work behavior that can be remediated in vocational training facilities. Use of the BWAP assumes that the evaluator has had ample opportunity to observe the client in a simulated or real work setting. Three types of reliability evidence are provided: internal consistency, rerating by the same evaluator, and interrater agreement between independent evaluators. The median coefficients are 0.87, 0.86, and 0.82, respectively. Measured intelligence is highly correlated with the cognitive skills subscale, and, although the correlations of IQ with other subscales are somewhat lower, it appears that the BWAP is, in part, measuring intelligence.

California Psychological Inventory

The California Psychological Inventory (CPI; Gough, 1987) is a self-report questionnaire that measures 20 features of the normal personality, such as achievement, dominance, empathy, flexibility, independence, responsibility, self-acceptance, sociability, tolerance, and well-being. The 20 basic scales were conceptualized as dimensions of interpersonal behavior that exist in all human societies; hence the label "folk concepts." The author's goal was to develop a clinical instrument that would enable the accurate description of individuals and prediction of their behavior. Consistent with this practical objective, the CPI scales were constructed using observer judgments and measurable performance as criteria. In addition to the 20 folk concept scales, 13 special purpose scales, such as managerial potential and creative temperament, may be scored. Standard profiles are calculated with reference to demographically representative norm groups for males and females. Respondents typically complete the 462 true-false items in about one hour. Retest reliabilities for the 20 basic scales average 0.82. The CPI has been validated as a predictor of academic achievement, creativity, occupational performance, personal and social problems, and various other outcome criteria.

Disability Factor Scales—General

The Disability Factor Scales—General (DFS-G; Siller, 1970) is a self-report instrument that measures seven replicated components of attitudes toward people with physical disabilities: interaction strain, rejection of intimacy, generalized rejection, authoritarian virtuousness, inferred emotional consequences, distressed identification, and imputed functional limitations. The DFS-G consists of 69 statements that express reactions, describe assumed attributes, or advocate policies toward nine types of disabling conditions (e.g., amputation, blindness, epilepsy, and paralysis). Respondents indicate their opinions about each statement using a 6-point Likert format ranging from Strongly Agree to Strongly Disagree. The DFS-G was developed for the purpose of investigating the implications of psychoanalytic theory for understanding the nature and origins of attitudinal reactions to people with disabling conditions. Internal consistency reliabilities for the seven DFS-G scales average 0.82. Three independent factor analyses have replicated the seven attitude scales, while other studies have provided support for the theoretical rationale and construct validity of the DFS-G. The DFS-G can be used as an indirect or disguised measure of self-esteem or disability acceptance with clients who have physical disabilities.

Employability Maturity Interview Computer Report

The Employability Maturity Interview Computer Report (EMI-CR; Neath & Bolton, 1997) is a computer-generated report that is based on a structured interview consisting of 10 questions that assess readiness for the vocational rehabilitation planning process. The EMI-CR is useful as a brief screening instrument to identify clients needing additional vocational exploration and employability services. Readiness for vocational planning is measured in three areas: general knowledge of self and work, choice identified, and alternatives identified. Scores on these three subscales are organized into a performance matrix which provides the basis for a detailed interpretation of responses. The EMI-CR requires 10 to 15 minutes to administer and another 5 minutes to score. Five normative groups are available for generating the performance matrix. Reliability of the EMI-CR is high, especially for a scoring procedure that requires subjective judgment. The construct validity of the instrument was supported by a series of predicted relationships with external criteria.

Functional Assessment Inventory

The Functional Assessment Inventory (FAI; Crewe & Athelstan, 1984) is a 42-item rating instrument designed for use by rehabilitation counselors. All FAI items are focused on vocationally relevant behaviors and capabilities and provide data essential in rehabilitation service planning. The FAI consists of 30 behaviorally anchored rating items that assess client vocational capabilities and deficiencies, 10 items that identify unusual assets, and 2 global items that quantify severity of disability and probability of vocational success. The FAI is scored on six factor scales—adaptive behavior, cognition, physical capacity, motor functioning, communication, and vocational qualifications—as well as a total functional limitations score.

Interrater agreement and internal consistency of the FAI items, subscales, and total score are generally high. Available evidence supports the validity of the FAI as a measure of vocational potential. A computer report called the Functional Capacities Computer Report (FCCR) generates factor score profiles using five homogeneous norm groups and a general norm group (Neath & Bolton, 1998). The Personal Capacities Questionnaire (PCQ) is a self-report version of the FAI that can be used in conjunction with the observer rating form or independently.

Handicap Problems Inventory

The Handicap Problems Inventory (HPI; Wright & Remmers, 1960) was developed to quantify the impact of disability, as perceived by the individual with a disability. The HPI is a checklist of 280 problems attributable to physical disability. By marking those problems that are caused or aggravated by the disabling condition, respondents reveal the significance that they attach to the impairment. The HPI items are categorized into four life areas or subscales: personal, family, social, and vocational. HPI norms are based on a sample of more than 1,000 people determined by thorough medical examination to have substantial and permanent physical disabilities. Reliability coefficients for the four subscales are uniformly high, averaging 0.93. A variety of evidence supports the validity of the HPI (e.g., respondents with secondary disabilities reported more problems and patients who were rated as improved reported fewer problems earlier in their hospitalization). The HPI can be used clinically as an inventory of disability-related problems that require attention as well as a counseling outcome measure.

Independent Living Behavior Checklist

The Independent Living Behavior Checklist (ILBC; Walls, Zane, & Thvedt, 1979) provides a list of 343 independent living skill objectives that are carefully specified in terms of conditions, behaviors, and standards (CBS) of performance. Most of the skills were selected from 53 previously constructed independent living checklists. All 343 items were rewritten into the CBS format and allocated to six categories: mobility skills, self care skills, home maintenance and safety skills, food skills, social and communication skills, and functional academic skills. In a defined situation, performance of the specified behavior is observed and judged as satisfactory or unsatisfactory according to the specified standard. Repeat observer agreement for the ILBC over a 2-week interval averaged 98%. The content validity of the ILBC is supported by the use of 53 previously developed scales as the primary source of the 343 skill objectives, as well as the high overlap of the ILBC with a comprehensive independent living training program.

Minnesota Satisfaction Questionnaire

The Minnesota Satisfaction Questionnaire (MSQ; Weiss, Dawis, England, & Lofquist, 1967) was designed to measure respondent satisfaction with 20 different aspects of the work environment, such as ability utilization, achievement, coworkers, independence, responsibility, variety, and work conditions. The long form MSQ consists of 100 items that are scored on 20 job reinforcer scales, and the short form consists of 20 items that are scored on intrinsic, extrinsic, and general satisfaction scales. For the long form, 25 occupational norm groups are available, while 7 are provided for the short form. For the long form, the median internal consistency reliability for the 20 scales is 0.86 and the median retest reliability is 0.83. The internal consistency and retest reliabilities for the short form MSQ general satisfaction scale are 0.90 and 0.89, respectively. Construct validity evidence for the MSQ derives from a variety of investigations of theoretical propositions concerning the antecedents and consequences of job satisfaction.

Minnesota Satisfactoriness Scales

The Minnesota Satisfactoriness Scales (MSS; Gibson, Weiss, Dawis, & Lofquist, 1970) is an observer rating instrument that summarizes an employee's level of job performance as judged by the employer. The MSS consists of 28 items that can be completed by the employee's supervisor in about 5 minutes. Scores are calculated on four subscales: performance (addressing how well employees handle their work tasks); conformance (referring to employee cooperation with supervisors and coworkers); personal adjustment (concerning employee mental health and personal behavior on the job); and dependability (reflecting employee disciplinary problems and work habits). Raw scores for each of the subscales and a total score, general satisfactoriness, may be converted to percentiles using normative tables for four occupational groups and a workers-in-general group that is representative of the entire U.S. labor force. Internal consistency reliabilities for the five scales average 0.88, while retest stability coefficients over a 2-year interval average 0.52. Research indicates that the MSS is a valid measure of job satisfactoriness for rehabilitation clients.

Minnesota Survey of Employment Experiences

The Minnesota Survey of Employment Experiences (MSEE; Tinsley, Warn-ken, Weiss, Dawis, & Lofquist, 1969) is a follow-up questionnaire designed to be completed without professional assistance by former clients, making it possible to conduct inexpensive follow-up mail surveys to former clients. Twenty-two questions are presented on four pages that are carefully format-ted to minimize confusion and errors. Four types of information are ob-tained: work experiences prior to rehabilitation service, work experience from case closure to follow-up contact, details about current employment situation, and related vocational information, such as influence of disability and job search problems. The last page of the MSEE contains the short form of the Minnesota Satisfaction Questionnaire described above. The MSEE has been modified for use in a variety of follow-up studies of former rehabilitation clients. All indications are that it is a practical, efficient, data-collecting device.

Personal Independence Profile

The Personal Independence Profile (PIP; Nosek, Fuhrer, & Howland, 1992) is a self-report instrument that measures psychological and environmental aspects of independence that are not assessed by other instruments. The PIP was developed to operationalize a model of independence that emphasizes controlling one's life, having options, making decisions, performing daily activities, and participating in the life of the community. The four PIP subscales are: perceived control over one's life (10 questions about quality of life), psychological self-reliance (34 items addressing independence feel-ings and behaviors), physical functioning (25 items that assess indepen-dence in performing activities of daily living), and environmental resources (16 questions about housing, employment, and transportation). The reli-abilities for the first three subscales average .86. Intercorrelations among the first three subscales average .14, suggesting that the subscales measure separate components of independence. Preliminary evidence supports the validity of the first three subscales.

Personal Opinions Questionnaire

The Personal Opinions Questionnaire (POQ; Bolton & Brookings, 1998) is a self-report instrument that measures four components of intrapersonal empowerment for people with disabilities. Intrapersonal empowerment is a personality variable that encompasses intrapsychic processes such as perceived control, self-efficacy, and sense of community. It is apparent that intrapersonal empowerment is an internalized orientation consisting of behavioral predispositions that constitute a foundation for action. The POQ consists of 64 true-false items that are scored on four subscales: personal competence (sets challenging goals and works to achieve them), group orientation (works together with other people), self-determination (stands up for one's rights), and positive identity as a person with a disability (accepts one's disability realistically). The median internal consistency reliability coefficient for the four subscales is .85. The average subscale intercorrelation of .46 indicates that the four subscales measure independent features of empowerment, yet it justifies a total empowerment score. Preliminary validity evidence supports the content interpretation of the POQ subscales.

Preliminary Diagnostic Questionnaire

The Preliminary Diagnostic Questionnaire (PDQ; Moriarty, 1981) was designed to measure the functional skills of people with disabilities in the context of employability. The eight subtests are administered in a structured interview format using a self-contained consumable 12-page booklet. The PDQ assesses four broad areas of functioning: cognitive (measured by Work Information, Preliminary Estimate of Learning, Psychomotor Skills, and Reading Retention subtests); motivation or disposition to work (measured by Work Importance and Internality subtests); physical (measured by the Personal Independence subtest), and emotional (measured by the Emotional Functioning subtest). The normative sample consists of almost 3,000 rehabilitation clients from 30 state agencies. Internal consistency reliabilities for the eight subtests average .81, while retest reliabilities for six of the subscales with an interval of 30 days average 0.78. A variety of evidence supports the validity of the PDQ as a measure of the employment potential of rehabilitation clients.

Psychiatric Diagnostic Interview—Revised

The Psychiatric Diagnostic Interview—Revised (PDI-R; Othmer, Penick, Powell, Read, & Othmer, 1989) is a structured interview that evaluates 17 basic syndromes, such as organic brain syndrome, alcoholism, mania, antisocial personality, phobic disorder, and mental retardation, and four derived syndromes, including polydrug abuse, schizoaffective disorder, manic-depressive disorder, and bulimarexia. The purpose of the PDI-R is to determine whether an examinee is experiencing or has ever experienced a major psychiatric disorder. The administrative format of the PDI-R parallels the strategy used by skilled clinicians, beginning with very general questions and moving to increasingly specific questions, but only if earlier questions suggest the presence of a disorder. Because the PDI-R is a criterion-referenced instrument, there are no norms. However, base rates for the syndromes and diagnoses are given for various groups. A variety of studies support the reliability of the PDI-R. Research indicates substantial diagnostic agreement between the PDI-R and psychiatrists using conventional examination procedures.

Rehabilitation Gain Scale

The Rehabilitation Gain Scale (RGS; Reagles, Wright, & Butler, 1970) is a self-report instrument consisting of 20 items that reflect vocational functioning (e.g., earnings, hours worked each week, work status, primary income source, whether the respondent was having trouble finding a job, the respondent's expressed chances of getting a desired job, and the respondent's prediction of future employment) and personal and social adjustment (e.g., the respondent's assessments of physical and mental health, the amount of public assistance received, and the extent of the respondent's participation in various social activities and community organizations). The instrument is completed prior to and following the provision of rehabilitation services. Weights are applied to the pretest-posttest questionnaire responses, resulting in three composite scores: status prior to rehabilitation, status following rehabilitation, and rehabilitation gain score. The median reliability for the three scores is 0.75. Analyses of the relationships with rehabilitation service variables support the utility of the RGS.

Rehabilitation Indicators

The Rehabilitation Indicators (RIs; Brown, Diller, Fordyce, Jacobs, & Gordon, 1980) constitute a comprehensive assessment system for describing rehabilitation client activities of daily living and independent living skills. RIs focus on observable elements of client behavior, using lay terminology to characterize a broad range of content (e.g., vocational, educational, self-care, communication, mobility, household, recreation, and transportation) at varying levels of detail from specific to general. RIs were developed for the purpose of describing client life roles (48 indicators representing 6 role categories), daily living activities (106 items organized into 15 activity categories), and behavioral competencies (700 skills that represent 78 skill areas) in ways that are especially helpful in the provision and evaluation of rehabilitation services. The user selects only those items that are relevant to the purpose for which the RIs are being used. Depending on the mode of administration (interview, observation, or self-report), the RIs can be administered in almost any setting, ranging from the examiner's office to the client's home. The reliability and validity data supporting the RIs are fairly extensive and generally good.

Service Outcome Measurement Form

The Service Outcome Measurement Form (SOMF; Westerheide, Lenhart, & Miller, 1975) is a counselor rating instrument that was developed to reflect the employment orientation of the vocational rehabilitation process. The SOMF consists of 23 items that are scored on five subscales: difficulty, economic/vocational status, physical functioning, adjustment to disability, and social competency. A sixth subscale, education, requires only information about years of schooling. The rating items emphasize client capabilities in relationship to their employment potential. Clients may be evaluated at acceptance for services and again at case closure, with acceptance ratings indicating difficulty, closure ratings indicating outcome, and difference scores reflecting benefits due to rehabilitation service. Interrater reliabilities for the SOMF subscales (except education) average .81. The SOMF can be completed by rehabilitation counselors using routinely available case information in less than 10 minutes.

Sixteen Personality Factor Questionnaire—Form E

The Sixteen Personality Factor Questionnaire—Form E (16PF-E; Institute for Personality and Ability Testing, 1985) is a special-purpose personality inventory that was designed for use with persons with limited educational and varied cultural backgrounds. As its name indicates, the 16PF-E measures 16 primary characteristics of the normal personality sphere, such as outgoing, assertive, conscientious, imaginative, apprehensive, self-sufficient, and controlled. In addition, five second-order dimensions are also scored: extroverted, adjusted, tough-minded, independent, and disciplined. Each of the 16 primary scales is represented by 8 items. The five secondary scales are scored according to formulas derived from a factor analysis of more than 10,000 respondents. Norms are available for a heterogeneous sample of almost 1,000 rehabilitation clients. The norms are incorporated into a computer-generated report, the Vocational Personality Report (Bolton, 1987), which provides scores on the five second-order personality scales, two psychopathology dimensions, three vocational interest scales, and Holland's six occupational types. Retest reliabilities over a 1-week interval average .66 for the 16 primary scales and .77 for the five secondary scales.

Vocational Behavior Checklist

The Vocational Behavior Checklist (VBC; Walls, Zane, & Werner, 1978) consists of 339 vocationally relevant skill objectives that are stated in the uniform CBS format of conditions, behaviors, and standards of performance. The 339 skills were extracted from 21 previously developed vocational assessment instruments, organized into seven content areas: prevocational skills, job seeking skills, interview skills, job related skills, work performance skills, on-the-job social skills, and union-financial security skills. Client skill mastery may be quantified in a skill objective profile, which translates vocational achievement into a percentage of the critical behaviors mastered in each of the seven areas. Repeat rater agreement of the VBC over a 2-week interval averages 97% for the seven skill areas, while interrater agreement averages 95%. The content validity of the VBC derives from the source of the items, which was 21 independently constructed checklists. Criterion-related validity is supported by the 97% overlap of the VBC with the critical behaviors identified by employers as essential for job success.

Work Adjustment Rating Form

The Work Adjustment Rating Form (WARF; Bitter & Bolanovich, 1970) was constructed to measure the work readiness of rehabilitation clients. It was designed primarily for use by counselors who work with clients with mental retardation in sheltered workshops to assess potential for training and adjustment progress. The WARF contains 8 subscales, each having 5 items, for a total of 40 items. The 5 items for each subscale describe five different levels of performance from low to high and require a simple yes-no judgment by the rater. The subscales are: amount of supervision required, realism of job goals, teamwork, acceptance of rules/authority, work tolerance, perseverance in work, extent client seeks assistance, and importance attached to job training. Interrater reliabilities average .82. The WARF was predictive of employment 2 years after clients left a workshop program.

Work Personality Profile

The Work Personality Profile (WPP; Bolton & Roessler, 1986) is an observer rating instrument designed for use in conjunction with situational assessments of rehabilitation client work performance. The WPP consists of 58 items that specify behaviors critical to job maintenance. The WPP is usually completed by vocational evaluators, but it may be used by employers to identify work problems on the job. The 58 items are scored on 11 work performance scales (e.g., acceptance of work role, work tolerance, amount of supervision required, and ability to socialize with coworkers) and on five second-order factor scales (task performance, social skills, work motivation, conformance, and personal presentation). Internal consistency reliabilities average .84 for the primary scales and .89 for the factor scales. Retest reliabilities for the same raters average .80. However, interrater agreement is generally much lower, with an average coefficient of .52, which is not unusual for ratings of observed work behavior and suggests that independent evaluations by two or more raters be averaged into composite scale scores, a realistic procedure considering the simplicity and brevity of the WPP.

USING REHABILITATION OUTCOME INSTRUMENTS

To establish a framework for discussion of the uses of the 22 instruments in assessing rehabilitation outcomes, it will be helpful to reiterate the general definition of counseling that was given earlier in the chapter. In rehabilitation service delivery, counseling refers to a therapeutically oriented interpersonal relationship established by the rehabilitation professional that has the ultimate goal of improving the client's vocational and psychosocial functioning. Readers who desire a historical perspective on the role of counseling in rehabilitation are referred to Bolton and Jaques (1978). In addition, a brief overview of counseling process and techniques is provided by Sellick and Bolton (1989).

The purpose of this section is to offer practical information that rehabilitation counselors may find useful in evaluating the impact of their efforts on clients' outcomes. Each of the 22 instruments is classified according to the four basic measurement issues in Table 23.1. First, every instrument assesses one or more of three classes of variables: economic (E), vocational (V), or psychosocial (P). Second, most of the instruments generate assessment information from just one of three relevant perspectives: agency (A), client (C), or employer (E). The agency and employer perspectives are represented by observer rating instruments, while the client perspective

TABLE 23.1 Classification of Instruments According to Measurement Issues

Instruments	Variables[a]			Perspectives[b]			Dimensions[c]			Periods[d]		
	E	V	P	A	C	E	P	S	T	P	C	F
ADS			X		X				X	X	X	X
BWAP		X		X		X	X		X	X		X
CPI			X		X		X			X	X	X
DFS-G			X		X		X			X	X	
EMI-CR		X			X		X			X	X	
FAI		X	X	X	X		X		X	X	X	
HPI			X		X		X			X	X	X
ILBC			X	X			X			X	X	
MSQ		X			X		X	X	X			X
MSS	X	X				X	X		X			X
MSEE	X	X			X							X
PIP			X		X		X			X	X	
POQ			X		X		X		X	X	X	
PDQ		X	X		X		X			X	X	
PDI-R			X		X		X	X		X	X	
RGS	X	X	X		X				X	X	X	X
RIs		X	X	X	X		X			X	X	
SOMF	X	X	X	X			X		X	X	X	
16PF-E			X		X		X	X		X	X	X
VBC		X			X		X			X	X	
WARF		X			X		X			X		X
WPP		X			X		X	X	X	X		X

[a]Three classes of variables are coded: economic (E), vocational (V), and psychosocial (P).
[b]Three perspectives are coded: agency (A), client (C), and employer (E).
[c]Three levels of dimensions are coded: primary scales (P), second-order factors (S), and total score (T).
[d]Three time periods for assessment are coded: pretest before service initiation (P), case closure (C), and follow-up (F).

involves either self-report or structured interview formats. Third, each instrument provides score information at one or more of three levels: primary scales (P), second-order factors (S), and total score (T). Finally, each instrument may be used at one or more time periods: pretest before service initiation (P), case closure (C), and follow-up (F). It should be apparent that almost all of the 22 instruments could be used for follow-up assessment, but for many of the instruments this simply would not be feasible due to administrative costs.

Several general conclusions can be derived from the systematic overview of the 22 instruments presented in Table 23.1. First, the vast majority of instruments focus on the measurement of vocational and psychosocial variables, although four do assess economic variables. Second, about two thirds of the instruments assess traits or behaviors from the client's perspective, either by self-report or structured interview. Third, almost all of the instruments generate scores at the level of primary trait dimensions or behavioral scales. Fourth, with the exception of a few work behavior instruments, which presume that clients are either employed at follow-up or engaged in some other type of vocational activity, the instruments can be used at any point in the service delivery sequence. The overall conclusion that can be reached from the data in Table 23.1 is that there exists a broad range of instruments for assessing the benefits that clients may receive from the provision of rehabilitation services.

For the purpose of discussing counselor uses of the 22 instruments to measure client benefits, the presentation will be organized according to the content domain assessed. There are two large classes of instruments, each subdivided into three narrower areas. The vocational class includes vocational instruments, work behavior scales, and employment measures. The psychosocial class includes psychosocial adjustment scales, comprehensive personality instruments, and independent living measures. Within these categories, mode of administration is an important consideration (i.e., observer rating, self-report, and structured interview).

In the category of vocational assessment, six instruments are available for assessing rehabilitation outcomes: EMI-CR, FAI, PDQ, RGS, SOMF, and VBC. Two of these instruments address vocational issues alone. The EMI-CR measures readiness for vocational planning using a structured interview approach, whereas the VBC constitutes a library of several hundred behavioral tasks that are administered by a trained evaluator. In contrast, the RGS is a relatively brief self-report questionnaire that includes indicators of psychosocial adjustment, as well as economic and vocational items. The FAI is a comprehensive observer rating instrument that covers six areas of employability-related capabilities. The SOMF also provides a broad-based assessment, with a simpler response format for raters. Although the PDQ emphasizes employment-relevant capabilities, it generates eight traditional trait scores derived from a structured interview administration format.

Three instruments measure client work behavior in training or employment situations, as observed by evaluators or supervisors, using a standard set of items: BWAP, WARF, and WPP. Use of these instruments requires a minimum observation period of 2 weeks. The three scales all provide comprehensive coverage of client work performance, with slightly different response formats. Three additional instruments measure various features of client employment outcomes: MSQ, MSS, and MSEE. The MSQ is a self-report measure of job satisfaction, the MSS is an observer rating assessment of job performance, and the MSEE is a self-report summary of employment experiences. All three instruments have utility in assessing client vocational adjustment.

In the category of psychosocial adjustment, four self-report instruments measure different aspects of personal functioning: ADS, DFS-G, HPI, and POQ. The ADS and POQ are relatively brief and more focused instruments, whereas the DFS-G and HPI are somewhat longer and cover a broader range of psychosocial issues. Also, as noted previously, the DFS-G is an indirect measure of client adjustment to disability. It is important to emphasize that any of these self-report instruments can be used in conjunction with the FAI or SOMF to provide two perspectives on client level of psychosocial adjustment.

Three instruments provide more comprehensive assessments of clients' overall personality functioning: CPI, PDI-R, and 16PF-E. The CPI and 16PF-E are multiscale measures of the normal personality sphere from the perspective of the respondent, whereas the PDI-R assesses the domain of severe maladjustment or behavior pathology in terms of traditional clinical syndromes. The primary limitation of these three instruments with respect to the measurement of clients' benefits in rehabilitation is that they require considerable time to complete.

The final category consists of three instruments that measure independent living skills and attitudes: ILBC, PIP, and RIs. The ILBC and RIs are comprehensive libraries of tasks that objectively assess every conceivable aspect of functional independence skills. In contrast, the PIP is a self-report instrument that measures the respondent's psychological independence and perceptions of environmental barriers and resources. Any thorough assessment of independence should include selected tasks and scales from the ILBC, RIs, and PIP. Also, the PDQ contains a brief measure of independent living skills that may be useful, and the HPI is relevant to the assessment of functional independence.

This chapter concludes with brief discussions of three issues. First, the rehabilitation professional should begin by asking a fundamental question about outcome assessment: Which client benefits are more important? Clearly, the selection of instruments will be dictated by the answer to this question. And it should be equally obvious that the answer will reflect the counselor's values and the rehabilitation agency's service philosophy.

Therefore, the selection of instruments for measuring client outcomes must be preceded by an examination of rehabilitation values and philosophy, which will lead to the formulation of a rationale for choosing instruments.

Second, because the primary concern of this chapter is the assessment of benefits to clients, meaning the evaluation of progress or improvement as a result of rehabilitation service provision, it will usually be necessary to administer instruments on a pretest-posttest basis. In other words, an instrument would be administered at the time of application for services and again at completion of the service sequence. The score difference from pretest to posttest indicates the direction and magnitude of change. Although the measurement of change is a complicated psychometric issue, two points are important. In general, favorable change is more likely for clients who have lower scores at initiation of services, because they have more room for improvement. Also, it is not necessary to convert raw scores to derived scores to measure change—just calculate the raw difference score to estimate the client's improvement. However, normative translations are helpful in locating clients with respect to reference groups.

Third, counselors should take advantage of the flexibility inherent in the available instrumentation to develop short batteries of appropriate measures that reflect the philosophical goals of their rehabilitation programs. Because most of the instruments reviewed measure client outcomes at the level of primary scales, counselors can choose combinations of scales from different instruments that represent constructs of special interest. The opportunity to assemble "tailored" outcome assessment packages is further extended by those instruments that constitute complete libraries of performance tasks or items. In summary, the extensive range and variability of available instruments should enable counselors to measure virtually any type of rehabilitation outcome.

REFERENCES

Becker, R. L. (1989). *Becker Work Adjustment Profile: Evaluator's manual*. Columbus, OH: Elbern.

Bitter, J. A., & Bolanovich, D. J. (1970). WARF: A scale for measuring job-readiness behaviors. *American Journal of Mental Deficiency, 74*, 616–621.

Bolton, B. (1976). Case performance characteristics associated with three counseling styles. *Rehabilitation Counseling Bulletin, 19*, 464–468.

Bolton, B. (1981). Follow-up studies in vocational rehabilitation. *Annual Review of Rehabilitation, 2*, 58–82.

Bolton, B. (1987). *Manual for the Vocational Personality Report*. Fayetteville: University of Arkansas, Arkansas Rehabilitation Research & Training Center.

Bolton, B., & Akridge, R. A. (1995). A meta-analysis of skills training programs for rehabilitation clients. *Rehabilitation Counseling Bulletin, 38,* 262–273.

Bolton, B., & Brookings, J. (1998). Development of a measure of intrapersonal empowerment. *Rehabilitation Psychology, 43,* 131–142.

Bolton, B., & Jaques, M. E. (Eds.). (1978). *Rehabilitation counseling: Theory and practice.* Baltimore, MD: University Park Press.

Bolton, B., & Roessler, R. (1986). *Manual for the Work Personality Profile.* Fayetteville: University of Arkansas, Arkansas Rehabilitation Research & Training Center.

Bozarth, J. D., & Rubin, S. E. (1975). Empirical observations of rehabilitation counselor performance and outcome. *Rehabilitation Counseling Bulletin, 18,* 294–298.

Brown, M., Diller, L., Fordyce, W., Jacobs, D., & Gordon, W. (1980). Rehabilitation indicators: Their nature and uses for assessment. In B. Bolton & D. Cook (Eds.), *Rehabilitation client assessment* (pp. 102–117). Baltimore: University Park Press.

Crewe, N. M., & Athelstan, G. T. (1984). *Functional Assessment Inventory manual.* Menomonie, WI: University of Wisconsin-Stout.

Emener, W. G. (1980). Relationships among rehabilitation counselor characteristics and rehabilitation client outcomes. *Rehabilitation Counseling Bulletin, 23,* 183–192.

Gibson, D. L., Weiss, D. J., Dawis, R. V., & Lofquist, L. H. (1970). *Manual for the Minnesota Satisfactoriness Scales* (Minnesota Studies in Vocational Rehabilitation: 27). Minneapolis: University of Minnesota.

Gough, H. G. (1987). *California Psychological Inventory administrator's guide.* Palo Alto, CA: Consulting Psychologists Press.

Institute for Personality and Ability Testing. (1985). *Manual for Form E of the 16PF.* Champaign, IL: Author.

Linkowski, D. C. (1987). *The Acceptance of Disability Scale.* Washington, DC: George Washington University.

Moriarty, J. B. (1981). *Preliminary Diagnostic Questionnaire.* Morgantown: West Virginia University, West Virginia Rehabilitation Research & Training Center.

Neath, J., & Bolton, B. (1997). *Manual for the Employability Maturity Interview Computer Report.* Fayetteville: University of Arkansas, Arkansas Rehabilitation Research & Training Center.

Neath, J., & Bolton, B. (1998). *Manual for the Functional Capacities Computer Report.* Fayetteville: University of Arkansas, Arkansas Rehabilitation Research & Training Center.

Nosek, M. A., Fuhrer, M. J., & Howland, C. A. (1992). Independence among people with disabilities: II. Personal Independence Profile. *Rehabilitation Counseling Bulletin, 36,* 21–36.

Othmer, E., Penick, E., Powell, B., Read, M., & Othmer, S. (1989). *Manual for the Psychiatric Diagnostic Interview, Revised (PDI-R).* Los Angeles, CA: Western Psychological Services.

Reagles, K. W., Wright, G. N., & Butler, A. J. (1970). A scale of rehabilitation gain for clients of an expanded vocational rehabilitation program. *Wisconsin Studies in Vocational Rehabilitation,* No. 13. Madison: University of Wisconsin, Regional Rehabilitation Research Institute.

Seligman, M. E. P. (1995). The effectiveness of psychotherapy: The Consumer Reports study. *American Psychologist, 50,* 965–974.

Sellick, K., & Bolton, B. (1989). Counseling. In N. King & A. Remenyi (Eds.), *Psychology for the health sciences* (pp. 171–183). Melbourne, Australia: Thomas Nelson.

Siller, J. (1970). Generality of attitudes toward the physically disabled. *Proceedings of the 78th Annual Convention of the American Psychological Association, 5,* 697–698.

Smith, M. L., & Glass, G. (1977). Meta-analysis of psychotherapy outcome studies. *American Psychologist, 32,* 752–760.

Smith, M. L., Glass, G., & Miller, T. (1980). *The benefits of psychotherapy.* Baltimore, MD: Johns Hopkins University Press.

Szymanski, E. M., & Parker, R. M. (1989). Competitive closure rates of vocational rehabilitation clients with severe disabilities as a function of counselor education and experience. *Rehabilitation Counseling Bulletin, 32,* 292–299.

Tinsley, H. E. A., Warnken, R. G., Weiss, D. L., Dawis, R. V., & Lofquist, L. H. (1969). *A follow-up survey of former clients of the Minnesota Division of Vocational Rehabilitation* (Minnesota Studies in Vocational Rehabilitation: 26). Minneapolis: University of Minnesota.

VandenBos, G. R. (Ed.) (1996). Outcome assessment of psychotherapy (Special issue). *American Psychologist, 51*(10).

Walls, R. T., Zane, T., & Thvedt, J. E. (1979). *The Independent Living Behavior Checklist.* Morgantown: West Virginia University, West Virginia Rehabilitation Research & Training Center.

Walls, R. T., Zane, T., & Werner, T. J. (1978). *The Vocational Behavior Checklist.* Morgantown: West Virginia University, West Virginia Rehabilitation Research & Training Center.

Weiss, D. J., Dawis, R. V., England, G. W., & Lofquist, L. H. (1967). *Manual for the Minnesota Satisfaction Questionnaire* (Minnesota Studies in Vocational Rehabilitation: 22) Minneapolis: University of Minnesota.

Westerheide, W. J., Lenhart, L., & Miller, M. C. (1975). Field test of a Service Outcome Measurement Form: Client change. *Monograph No. 3.* Oklahoma City: Department of Rehabilitation Services.

Wright, G. N., & Remmers, H. H. (1960). *Manual for the Handicap Problems Inventory.* Lafayette, IN: Purdue Research Foundation.

Index

467